UNDER THE EDITORSHIP OF

HEROLD C. HUNT

CHARLES WILLIAM ELIOT
PROFESSOR OF EDUCATION
HARVARD UNIVERSITY

PHILOSOPHY

AND THE

AMERICAN SCHOOL

*&An Introduction to the
Philosophy of Education*

VAN CLEVE MORRIS

Rutgers University

HOUGHTON MIFFLIN COMPANY · BOSTON

THE RIVERSIDE PRESS
CAMBRIDGE, MASSACHUSETTS
PRINTED IN THE U.S.A.

﷼ EDITOR'S INTRODUCTION

In *Philosophy and the American School* Van Cleve Morris brings to the much discussed but fundamentally neglected area of educational philosophy a remarkable and individual insight grounded in solid scholarship. What is even more important, this book is consistently focused on the application of the principles of philosophy in actual, day-to-day practice; hence it serves to guide both the classroom teacher and the school administrator in formulating a workable and truly personal educational philosophy.

Dr. Morris first considers basic philosophical questions, then undertakes a detailed description and analysis of the principal schools of philosophic thought, supplementing the various source materials and references with his own keen interpretation and comment. Then, asking how these ideas may be used to understand and evaluate what is going on in American education today, he deals with the specific problems of teaching, supervision, and administration, examining innovations and new practices as well as long-established procedures and showing how different practices relate to the major philosophies.

A classroom teacher as well as a philosopher, Dr. Morris has studied in his field of specialization in several of the nation's most distinguished colleges and universities. While he has for a number of years been recognized as an able, stimulating, and challenging teacher and a popular lecturer, this book is certain to mark Dr. Morris as an equally brilliant writer. The student preparing for a professional career in education, the experienced teacher, the school principal, the supervisor or director of personnel, and the school superintendent — all will find this book helpful, as will the layman who seeks an understanding of the relationship between philosophic principles and the practice of education. Annotated bibliographies and questions for discussion follow each chapter, and original figures and charts effectively highlight the text; the closing chapter, expressive of the author's emphasis on the individual, outlines a procedure for building a personal philosophy of education. Pioneering in its approach, unique in its organization and treatment, *Philosophy and the American School* throws light on a field too long characterized by uncertainty, doubt, and confusion. As a teaching text it is a major and distinctive contribution to the literature of education.

HEROLD C. HUNT

ᘒ PREFACE

Books on educational philosophy are generally of three types. First, there are the "system" books, which take up one "ism" at a time, developing each system's basic views on how the universe is arranged and then showing how these views, taken together, yield a particular theory of education. Then, second, there are the "topic" books, which build the argument around philosophical and educational issues — e.g., human nature, morals, mind, culture, social change — showing how each issue is relevant to the educational task and how the several philosophies deal with it in their educational theories. Finally, there are the "partisan" books, in which an author, after a career of study and reflection, attempts to elaborate his own position as he locates himself somewhere along the philosophic spectrum.

At the risk of impiety, I have decided to break with this tradition and attempt to introduce the newcomer to educational philosophy by another route. This route, to use a shorthand title, might be designated the "philosophy-to-policy-to-practice" approach:

Philosophy. All philosophy deals essentially with three major questions: What is real? What is true? What is good? Sooner or later all philosophical discussion winds up under one of these three categories. In the technical language of the philosopher, these categories are called *ontology, epistemology,* and *axiology,* respectively. Before anyone can think intelligently about educational philosophy, he must first acquire a working knowledge of these three questions — what they involve, how the discipline of philosophy deals with them, and how they relate to educational theory. Accordingly, after a brief introductory Part I, I have devoted the first major portion of this book to these three questions. Part II takes up the question, What is real?; Part III the question, What is true?; and Part IV the question, What is good?

Each of these parts is composed of a triad of chapters. The first chapter in the triad attempts to show what the title question involves, what its philosophical dimensions are. The second chapter in the triad examines how the question is dealt with by five major philosophic schools of thought: Idealism, Realism, Neo-Thomism, Experimentalism, and, a recent arrival on the philosophic scene, Existentialism. The final chapter in each triad explains how these five ways of dealing with the question relate to educational theory.

The first four parts of the book carry us to Chapter Ten and represent perhaps two-thirds of the entire argument. Since all else depends on understanding here, they constitute the main thesis of the volume.

Policy. Most people, however, do not encounter educational philosophy in such technical form. They encounter it in public statements, editorials, magazine articles, and books. And these pronunciamentos are more in the nature of statements of policy than they are of tight philosophical briefs. Nevertheless, no matter how free of philosophical disputation they seem to be, these policy statements are essentially arguments which derive from the five philosophical positions we have analyzed in Parts II, III, and IV.

Hence, the purpose of Part V is to gather up all of the philosophical and theoretical concepts of the five philosophies and present them as organized policy statements for the management of American education. Chapter Eleven presents the policy positions of the traditional philosophies of Idealism, Realism, and Neo-Thomism; Chapter Twelve argues the position of contemporary Experimentalism; and Chapter Thirteen considers the still open question of Existentialism in American educational policy.

Practice. For the layman reading this book, philosophical theory and public policy may be as far as one needs to go. But those of us in the professional business of educating the young want to know how philosophy and policy come alive in the classroom. We want to know why teachers teach and administrators administer the way they do. And, make no mistake, no matter how much teachers and administrators may affect innocence about things philosophical, their behavior patterns in the school are outgrowths of the philosophical and policy positions they individually hold, whether they realize it or not.

Therefore, the purpose of Part VI is to bring the argument down to the concrete circumstances where boys and girls are educated and to show how philosophical theory and stated policy operate in educational practice. Chapter Fourteen examines the classroom teacher; Chapter Fifteen considers the educational administrator.

Chapter Sixteen closes the argument by showing how this book may best be used by the serious student wishing to take further steps in the organization and declaration of his own philosophy of education.

In writing this book I have tried to keep in mind that philosophy, defined literally, is "love of wisdom"; not wisdom itself, please note, but *love of* wisdom. As such, philosophy is one of man's oldest pursuits. It is also one of his most precarious. For philosophy is what men turn to when they are not sure of themselves, when they are confused and in doubt. Philosophy's attraction as a human enterprise, therefore, always teeters on the balance of whether or not it can successfully bring men from perplexity to certainty in what they are about.

There can be little question that in America today one of the areas of greatest confusion and uncertainty is education; in a troubled time we are drummed by competing voices on the proper schooling of our young. In these circumstances, we turn hopefully to philosophy in order to think about education more clearly. But, being a precarious undertaking, philosophy provides no assurances that it can successfully carry us to educational truth. I do not pretend therefore to hold out to any reader the prospect of a settled and certain philosophy of education upon completing this book. I offer the reader only an awareness of what is involved in the philosophic enterprise as it relates to policy and practice in our schools.

In this undertaking I have relied on the assistance of many individuals:

Dr. Rubin Gotesky, Professor of Philosophy at Northern Illinois University, to whom I turned for advice on the philosophical chapters and for a general critique of the entire manuscript.

Dr. Hobert Burns, Associate Professor of Education at Syracuse University, whom I consulted on the chapters on educational applications and who also criticized the entire manuscript.

Mrs. Jacqueline Berke, Instructor in English at Drew University, who read the entire manuscript and tried to teach me how to write.

My wife, Eloise, who wielded the blue pencil with an agonizing thoroughness and became, on that very account, my severest and therefore my most valuable critic.

I salute them all and thank them sincerely for the long hours of intellectual hard labor.

I should say also that Dr. Lucius Garvin, Chairman of the Department of Philosophy at the University of Maryland and consultant in philosophy to Houghton Mifflin Company, was of enormous help in maintaining philosophic accuracy in the account here presented. His criticisms were penetrating and sound throughout.

Still others were involved: Professor Robert Brackenbury of the University of Southern California and Professor James Wheeler of Rutgers University both read and commented on the manuscript; Assistant Professor Henry Vittum of Rutgers helped with proof; and Mrs. Rose Boehm, typist extraordinary, prepared the manuscript. To them all I extend my thanks.

Of course, in the tradition of prefaces, I must disallow in advance any suggestion that the above individuals are to be held responsible for whatever ways in which this book may not measure up. I say this now because all of the individuals are my friends and I want to keep them so. Furthermore, I wrote the book, and it is mine to answer for.

V. C. M.

Highland Park, New Jersey
January, 1961

ও CONTENTS

Part I

THE TASK OF EDUCATIONAL PHILOSOPHY

Part II

ONTOLOGY: WHAT IS REAL?

Part III

EPISTEMOLOGY: WHAT IS TRUE?

CONTENTS

xiii

CONTENTS

Part IV

AXIOLOGY: WHAT IS GOOD?

CONTENTS

Part V

FIVE PHILOSOPHIES IN AMERICAN EDUCATION

Existentialist Educational Policy

The social policy of the school · Responsibility for choice · The affirmative side of freedom · Self-transcendence · Involvement and care

Part VI

PHILOSOPHY IN ACTION

CONTENTS

ॐ FIGURES AND CHARTS

The Task of
Educational Philosophy

ᘐᕡ CHAPTER ONE

Educational Theory

THEORY AND PRACTICE

Why study theory?

Mortimer Adler, modern apostle of classical humanism, once posed an interesting educational question.[1] There are, says Adler, two categories into which all human endeavor can be placed: the *operative arts* and the *cooperative arts*. The operative arts are those activities in which a human being *operates on* nature to bring about some desired effect which nature itself cannot achieve. A cobbler operates upon rawhide and composes a pair of shoes. A sawyer reduces trees to lumber, and a carpenter takes the lumber and builds a dwelling. General Motors extracts iron ore from the Mesabi Range and fashions a Chevrolet. In every instance — shoes, dwelling, Chevrolet — the product would not have come into existence without the direct and active intervention of human intelligence.

The cooperative arts, on the other hand, are those in which man simply *cooperates with* nature, assisting it and facilitating its customary procedures by watchful attention and timely prodding. The practice of medicine is perhaps the best example of this. A doctor does not actually create health; he merely assists the natural physiological processes to restore health to the organism. Organisms tend toward health; a doctor

[1] See Mortimer J. Adler, "In Defense of the Philosophy of Education," Chapter V in *Philosophies of Education,* Forty-first Yearbook of the National Society for the Study of Education, ed. N. B. Henry, Part I (Chicago: the Society, 1942), p. 211.

3

rides this tendency, superintends it, and thus manages to hasten recovery of the patient. Or consider the farmer. He does not grow an ear of corn. He simply cooperates with nature in growing the ear of corn. By knowledge of botanical processes, the farmer oversees the procedures by which a kernel of corn, given the proper environing culture, naturally "becomes" an ear of corn.

In the one instance, then, nature lies quiescent and passive waiting for human intelligence to act upon it; in the other, nature is in motion already — striving, reaching, aspiring to a new fulfillment.

Now the question Adler poses is simply this: What is education — operative or cooperative? Taking education either in its generalized meaning of the total development of a human self or in the concrete setting of the classroom, i.e., Jack Jones in fifth grade or you yourself in this course in educational philosophy you may be taking, what is going on in the learner? Is it the gradual unfolding of a pre-existent set of possibilities which finally convene in adulthood to make a mature individual? Or is it the gradual acquisition of information, facts, understandings, attitudes, feelings, and skills supplied by adults which the individual takes on in the course of growing up?[2]

Here is a theoretical question that makes a vital difference in practice. If you are among the cooperative artists, you have the feeling you are doing the business of the universe, a deputy in the service of cosmic forces. In practical terms, this means that you as teacher do not consider yourself the actual creator of anything but merely a helper. You are assisting a pre-existent nature — the human nature found in every human being — to realize itself. Since this nature is common to all, your teaching methods are generally the same for all. And since this nature is given and fixed, your methods do not have to be altered or experimented with; rather, there is a standard and relatively stable methodology by which nature is to be cooperated with. Finally, since the curriculum of the school is built upon the natural, "built-in" tendencies of all learners, it does not have to be tailored to individual needs or modernized or tinkered with in any serious way from year to year.

If you stand with the operative artists, on the other hand, there is the feeling of *producing* something, something that nature by itself cannot

2 This conundrum has its analogue in an interesting etymological dispute, to wit: whether the word *education* stems from the Latin *educere* (to lead from, to draw out) or *educare* (to nurture, to rear, to raise). The distinction here is not quite so sharp as in the case above, but in general the "cooperative arts" camp has held the former Latin verb as the appropriate one; education, in its primal meaning, is the evocation and development of naturally prior possibilities already resident in the individual. As it turns out, however, etymological scholarship is on the side of the latter verb. Quintilian in his *Institutes of Oratory*, the classic Latin work on education, used the latter verb; and it is this sense of "nurturing" or "rearing" the young that stands as the progenitor of our contemporary word *education*.

produce. In this light, you introduce into the human organism certain features which were not there to begin with. You are as teacher, then, really a creator of human traits of character and personality. Since you draw these traits from a surrounding culture, there is a constant need to check to see if you are interpreting the culture rightly or to make sure that, in a changing culture, you are not still teaching things which are no longer relevant.[3] You have to keep studying the curriculum constantly, revising, eliminating, adding. And as the curriculum changes so must there be changes in teaching methodology. Furthermore, each individual's needs will be a little different from those of his fellows, or the desired traits to be created in him will be different, and so he will require different "operative" procedures in the classroom.

Whether you are about to become or already are a teacher, whether you are parent, administrator, board member, or merely interested bystander, your views on educational problems will reflect your stand on the above question. A matter of curriculum is perhaps as good an illustration as any. Let us say that in a school faculty or a board of education the question comes up as to whether to drop Latin from the curriculum. To the "cooperative arts" people, Latin is the kind of study that all youngsters should have; the discipline it provides "cooperates" with nature in sharpening the inner powers of the mind; studying it trains the mind to reason. Latin must stay! To the "operative arts" people it does no such thing; scientific studies have shown that it does not. Furthermore, facility in Latin is no longer relevant for growing up in America. To be sure, it is possible to "operate" on the child to produce ability in Latin usage, but that would be, for most youngsters, a waste of time. They no longer need this skill in today's world. Latin must go!

Now if you are one of those people who must help make such a decision, your vote will depend on where you stand on the operative-cooperative question. And since this is a question of theory, not practice, you are under an obligation to understand what theory is and how it serves to direct practice.[4]

How theory serves practice

Throughout history a distinction has been drawn between so-called "men of action" and "men of thought." Presumably the same distinction can be drawn between "societies of action" and "societies of thought." America certainly belongs in the former category. We pride ourselves on

[3] For an amusing satirical account of how this can happen, see H. Benjamin, *Saber-Tooth Curriculum* (New York: McGraw-Hill Book Co., 1939).
[4] For other examples of theory controlling practice, see V. C. Morris, "Movable Furniture and a Theory of Man," *Educational Theory*, VII, No. 3 (July, 1957), 187–193.

being "men of action"; we "get things done." We build great cities, big bridges, long highways, enormous navies, globe-girdling air forces, space-ships to other worlds. We produce refrigerators, automobiles, breakfast food, and cigarettes in wild, wild profusion. We *do* things. And we scoff a bit at "societies of thought" — China, Tibet, ancient Greece — where men find reward in thoughtful reflection. We are even a bit dubious of Western Europe for its loving attention to the intellectual tra-dition. And, finally, we visit this doubt and suspicion upon our own intellectuals — the celebrated "eggheads" — whom we condescendingly tolerate as necessary "freaks" of society.[5]

No wonder that, of the two, practice rides higher than theory in most of what we do in America. If there is a discrepancy between theory and practice, it is usually theory that is wrong. We say, "That's all right in theory but it won't work in practice," or "That looks good on paper but it isn't practical," meaning thereby that the practical is the more trust-worthy of the two and should serve as the yardstick for measuring theory.

It is true, of course, that practice does just this: It checks and verifies theory. When the social psychologist develops, say, a "socio-cultural theory of personality," wherein "personality" is the product of a young-ster's constant contact and interaction with his community, his family, his entire social environment, then the teacher can check the value of this theory by putting it to work in group procedures in the classroom to see how boys and girls grow in personality in direct contact with their peers. Or when the Progressive educator develops a theoretical idea like the "child-centered concept," for instance, the teacher can try it out in the classroom to see if it works. What he finds will condition his view of the concept.

But theory fulfills this same function with regard to practice: It "checks" and judges practice. When we find ourselves, in the heat of annoyance, using corporal punishment or piercing ridicule on children in school, we ask ourselves if this is right in light of our beliefs about the dignity of the human person. In this instance, our *theory* of human worth in a democratic order is the test of the legitimacy of our *practice* of imposing harsh or cruel punishment on children. Or when we find ourselves segregating the races in our schools and communities, we measure this practice against the theory of social justice we believe in. And what we discover when we make these tests against *theory* will con-dition our judgment of the *practice* we have called in question.

Always, whether we realize it or not, we are in the process of testing our beliefs through our behavior and our behavior through our beliefs. It is

---

[5] Max Lerner, student of the American civilization, and Adlai Stevenson, presidential aspirant of the 1950's, have both proposed a ringing Manifesto for Intellectuals to be-gin: "Eggheads of the world, unite! You have nothing to lose but your yokes!"

not so much that a particular practice specifies a particular theory, or that a theory, on paper, specifies a particular practice. It is, rather, that theory and practice *criticize* one another; they *check* and *warrant* one another. And since it is through a continuous course of criticism that we find our way to a higher order of activity — in running governments, in practicing medicine, in teaching the young — it is imperative to address ourselves, sooner or later, to the matter of fundamental theory.

Theory and philosophy

Every important human activity can be shown to have a basis in theory, a centralizing idea of what it is all about, what it is trying to do, and how it operates in human experience. Physicists have their atomic theory. They can't actually see atoms or tell what they are made of. But they can make guesses (which is an informal term for "hypotheses") and if these guesses help to explain or "rationalize" (i.e., make rational or understandable) a large number of phenomena which they *can* observe, then physicists say they have a tenable tentative theory of atoms. Or musicians have their contrapuntal theory. If sound is controlled by certain rules of composition, it will produce certain effects upon the eardrum. When this "eardrum effect" is seen to be associated with a set of ideas as to how music is built, then the musician says he has a theory of counterpoint.

So likewise in education there is a claim to theory, to the possibility of setting down general ideas which will explain and rationalize the various phenomena occurring in the educational enterprise. And, generally speaking, the larger the range of phenomena accounted for, the better the theory. We might say, for instance, that one theory of learning is that of *conditioning,* i.e., habituating the youngster to certain responses when given certain stimuli. When a youngster learns the multiplication tables he is doing just this — artificially building automatic reactions to problems posed either orally or on paper. This, then, is certainly one theory of learning.

But can "conditioning" be considered a general theory of *all* kinds of learning? Does it successfully explain what goes on when a child learns the duties of citizenship in civics class, or the appreciation of great music in music class, or the difference between right and wrong wherever? Is learning citizenship, aesthetic response, and moral judgment a matter of habit-conditioning? If yes, then we can arrange the educational situation accordingly; if not, we must state precisely how large a sphere of learning the "habit-formation" theory covers, and go in search of other theories to cover the remaining areas of education. We may, for instance, identify other theories that help us to understand other kinds of learning:

7

learning as "disciplining the mind," learning as "the absorption of factual knowledge," learning as "problem-solving," learning as "the development of the intuitive powers," learning as "the conformity to the Will of God." We continue in search of theories until we feel we have exhausted all the areas of human learning.

The trouble with extended theory-building, however, is that some theories may be found to be incompatible with others. So we attempt to organize the theories themselves into a meta- (super-) theory, which, in turn, seeks to harmonize, integrate, rationalize, and explain all the different conceptions we have built up to this point. It is this activity we call philosophy.

The educational philosopher seeks the single formula by which all human learning can be understood and managed. In this, he is principally engaged in the process of unification, in the endeavor to comprehend all that goes on in the educative process under a master set of consistent ideas, so that if problems come up for which ready answers are not available he can look to his theory for guides to practical action.

It is in this sense that a good theory is, as they say, the most practical thing a man can have. A teacher who teaches by impulse, like an aviator who flies "by the seat of his pants," may conceivably teach well, but when unexpected situations arise his actions are likely to be flustered and thin. With a well-thought-out theory or philosophy of education an individual knows what he is doing and why. And it is when our practical conduct becomes more and more rational, i.e., increasingly subject to critical theory, that we say it becomes more and more professional in character. The truly professional teacher is the individual who tempers and redirects native impulse with the rational theory of his craft. It is this which the study of philosophy can help to supply.

THE PHILOSOPHICAL DIMENSIONS OF EDUCATION

Education is a complicated business, especially in modern civilizations. One way of simplifying it is to separate its basic elements and to let those elements define the area of discourse in our study of it.

One of the things educational philosophers are interested in, for instance, is the client himself, the *individual human being* who shows up for instruction. Just what kind of creature is he? What, after all, is a man? What can a man become? What are his possibilities as a human being? What, in short, is the nature of human nature, on which all education eventually works?

The philosopher is also interested in *society,* in "man-in-groups."

What is a society? How does it work? What is the individual's relationship to it? Does the school stand in some special way between the individual and his society?

The philosopher is also interested in the *cosmos*. What kind of universe do we live in? What possibilities does it provide? What prospects does it hold out for man? What, in short, is the meaning of life? And can this meaning find expression in our school program?

These are the kinds of problems that philosophers study. A closer look at them may be helpful in getting your mind "in gear" philosophically and suggesting what this book is all about.

Education and human nature

Every educator wants to know what a human being is and what he might be. The anthropologists have told us that man is a curious biped who *makes* things — tools, instruments, machines. He is *homo faber*. This being the case, it is held that man's education should be organized around this "making," *technological* tendency. We know also, however, that man can talk; he can live in a world of his own, a world of symbols. He is *homo symbolicum*. Therefore his education should also be organized around his *symbol-using* tendency.

But the educator needs to know more than this, for *making* and *talking* can be used for very different ends. Taken together the technological and symbolic traits constitute man's ability to build "culture."[6] Over the course of time, men have built many different cultures, each with its own peculiar set of beliefs and practices. Hence when we go in search of a common element of human nature on which to build an educational program we are beset by a multitude of possibilities.

Some of these possibilities are to be found within our own culture here in the United States. For instance, some people claim that man is by nature acquisitive and aggressive. People who talk like this are usually staunch defenders of capitalism as an economic system and believe that the school should encourage individual effort and the competitive spirit, with each child pitted against the others to motivate learning. Other people contend that capitalism brings out the beast in us, that man is by nature loving, helpful, and cooperative. These people usually think that the school should teach cooperative effort and mutual assistance, with the youngsters associated together in a common enterprise.

Which of these groups is right about schoolroom procedure will depend, of course, on which is right about the nature of man. Is man basically competitive and aggressive, as the capitalists say? Or is he

[6] Culture may be defined as all of the man-made parts of our environment — tools, institutions, ideas.

basically cooperative and generous, as the Judeo-Christian ethic has claimed? It would be extremely helpful to get a definitive answer to this.

The social psychologists generally hold that man is really both competitive and cooperative, and that whichever trait the surrounding culture encourages will be the more prominent. Hence, man's basic nature is to adopt the patterns of life about him. There are a multitude of these patterns, as we have noted, but what is constant appears to be man's ability to learn any pattern of culture that is set before him. The plasticity of the psycho-social organism called man is such that a child of Chinese parents raised from birth in an American home would become as thoroughly American in character as his American foster brother; and an American child raised in China would become as thoroughly Chinese as any of his Chinese playmates.

What this signifies is that the general features of human character are social in origin; they arise out of the environment in which the child is found. It is theoretically possible, therefore, to modify and change certain aspects of human character through the control of an individual's experience. And since education is a specialized form of controlled experience, it is important for educators to remember that what the child experiences in the school he will learn. We are beginning to appreciate the fact that children who go to dingy, dirty schools, for instance, will grow up with different tastes in architecture, art, and interior design from those of children who go to bright, colorful, attractive schools; or that youngsters who are taught by teachers who make reading assignments a routine chore develop attitudes toward books different from the attitudes of those students for whom reading is made to seem an adventure into unknown and interesting places.

But, if man is the product of his culture, certainly he is more than a passive recipient of it. He is, if only potentially, an active contributor to it. Since cultures have been built, there must have been a creative element somewhere in the human material. It is this so-called creative tendency — of the original thinker, the poetic dreamer, the scientific inventor — that we have come to think the school should foster and nurture. We know that these abilities exist in some individuals. But are they, like other traits, themselves the product of social experience in a culture, or are they spontaneous and unique in each individual? In either case, can they actually be artificially excited and released in a deliberate program of education? Can a teacher teach creativity to a youngster?

These and other open questions concerning the possibilities of human raw material obviously play a central role in developing a philosophy of education, for the powers we assign to the human material necessarily set limits to what we consider a man's role to be, in society and cosmos.

Education and society

THE SCHOOL AS REPRODUCTIVE AGENT. Every American, of all the millions now living, will someday die. We know this. If it were not for continuous regeneration of this group through sexual reproduction, we should certainly some day pass into extinction as a society. But we also know that each of these individuals will take with him to the grave the complex aggregate of behavior patterns and beliefs that we speak of as "the American way of life." And every new individual who is procreated and introduced into our number must be taught this "way," so to speak, "from scratch." He is not equipped with it at birth. And if the society did not provide some method of social and psychological procreation we might conceivably survive as a physical group but we should certainly perish as an integrated society, with beliefs, values, and ways of living.

In uncomplicated, nonliterate societies this social procreation of new individuals and generations occurs in the normal course of growing up and in apprenticing the young to the ways and thoughts of their elders. But as civilization advances, the gap between young and old tends to widen; the growing-up, life-apprenticeship process is not efficient enough to equip the young with all they must know and understand in order to reach full adult maturity. At this point in their historical evolution, societies recognize the need for a formal and deliberate agency to take over this work, to concentrate and intensify the growing-up process, and to regulate it according to the developing necessities of any given social system.[7]

It is out of this social need for continuity that we get schools. Seen in this light, schools are not just places of convenience for the benefit of individuals — to expand their knowledge, to sate their intellectual curiosities, to prepare them for better, higher-paying jobs, or to give them an enriched form of social life. On the contrary, the schools' *first* function is to sustain and perpetuate a cherished pattern of living and to guarantee more surely that the society of which they are the instruments shall continue to prosper.

Viewed in this way, education is certainly the most important single function of a society. Not even the function of government outranks it; for while government may maintain order and tranquillity and fight off external enemies for short-run survival, there will eventually remain nothing to be governed if the society does not see to it that each new generation is inducted into its lifeways. So we can begin to see that education is not only a social institution of primary magnitude, but quite

[7] Cf. John Dewey, *Democracy and Education* (New York: The Macmillan Co., 1916), Chapter I.

obviously the vital core function, on which all else ultimately depends. It is imperative, therefore, for educators and educational philosophers to develop a theory of society, to understand what a society is trying to be and do, and then to translate that social-self-image into a working educational program.

THE SCHOOL AND SOCIAL CHANGE. What makes this philosophic task so difficult is that modern societies — ours in particular — do not stand still long enough for the philosophic surveyor to get a good plot. By the time it takes a generation of scholars and thinkers to arrive at the working ethos of the American way, to write their books and articles explaining this ethos, to render their findings to the encyclopedists and applicators who themselves write books and manuals, who in turn convey their work to the textbook writers and teachers of teachers, who then transmit these ideas to teachers and they to boys and girls — by the time all this has transpired, the fast-changing American ethos has found a thousand new interpretations, sufficient to make it appear almost a different way of life.

Perhaps the best example of this is the glacial tardiness of modern schools in teaching twentieth-century concepts in economics. The free-enterprise rugged individualism of the nineteenth century glorified individual initiative, risk-taking, small-entrepreneurship, and working for one's self. For the most part, this doctrine became the "religious manifesto" of the Capitalist Dream. As an economic theory it produced men of imagination and energy and it blossomed into the ungainly giant that we lump together in the term "American industry." But by the 1920's and 1930's it became apparent that free-enterprising behemoths unchained were perhaps a greater menace to our way of life than social and economic controls. Moreover, we began to see that perhaps new giants — the industrial trade unions — were necessary to help check the predatory impulses of the more ravenous. The years since the early Thirties and the Great Depression have been years of thoroughgoing reconstruction of the public mind concerning big business and the laboring man.

But the question is simply this: What has the public school been doing all this time — responding to this change in public sentiment or remaining detached from it? Any observer would have to report that the latter is more nearly the case. The schools have not discussed this turnabout in public understanding; explanations of its meaning and significance are soft-pedaled in the typical social studies curriculum in our schools. In fact, though the labor movement is over fifty years old, it is still a controversial issue, and therefore often omitted and ignored in civics classes. The world passes us by, and as social practices and beliefs are modified to fit new circumstances, boys and girls go on learning much that is neither true nor false but merely irrelevant to the world they can expect to live in.

This may serve to introduce a basic problem of the social philosopher of education: What role should the school play in a period such as the one in which we live — one of social and cultural transition? There are at least four distinct positions that the philosopher can take on this question.

(1) He can lay down the premise that social change is completely irrelevant to the educational process. This view, usually taken by that group we shall come to know as the Neo-Thomists, holds that, though the school is maintained by society, it is not necessarily a *social* institution in the literal sense. Its "social" function, if you want to call it that, is to *transcend* society, i.e., to deal in the absolute principles and changeless values on which all societies depend, whether they undergo change or not. Thus, in this view, a school betrays its true function if it turns away from eternal truth in favor of a shifting subject matter which has to be reshaped every September into a "modern, up-to-date" curriculum. For this reason, educators should, as the Neo-Thomist sees it, disregard social change and fix their attention on those First Principles or Eternal Verities which by definition never change and which every child must learn in order to grow up properly.

(2) The advocate of the second position does not disregard social change as an irrelevancy but considers it a phenomenon that the school should try to obstruct or, at least, reduce to manageable form for youngsters in school. From this outlook, which we shall see later as being compatible with the social thinking of Idealists and Realists, the school is viewed as a conservationist agency, compiling and preserving knowledge, reducing it to study-able form for youngsters, adding to and correcting it year by year as new things are discovered, but not troubling youngsters with the turbulent and changing character of this knowledge as it is put to use in modern life. Man has accumulated a great deal of important information about his world in the course of human time; he writes it down in books and encyclopedias, and teachers help young people learn it in school as preparation for intelligent living. The learning process, in this view, would be unwholesomely disturbed and disrupted if children were overly exposed to the changing character of their world even before they acquired the accumulated knowledge of those who have come before them. Thus, the school's job is to conserve knowledge, be its curator and caretaker, and dispense it to the young with the emphasis always on its reliable and enduring character. The school should not participate in social change; it should instead stand aside and equip the young with firm and stable knowledge with which they themselves can figure out what is going on in the outside world.

(3) These two positions strike the Experimentalist as both timid and unwise. Social change, says he, is but an everyday phenomenon which reveals the changing character of the universe itself. The universe isn't finished yet — it is "becoming." And societies reflect this becoming-ness, revising and altering their beliefs and outlooks as they move along through social history. If the school is to serve society it must acquaint young people with change as a prime ingredient of the lives they are to lead; this is the way, claims the Experimentalist, that the school truly serves society. We shall see later that the Experimentalist also holds that acquiring knowledge for its own sake is not what schools are for. Rather, schools exist to help boys and girls learn how to think, how to use their intelligence in solving problems. This world is full of problems, and our continual solving of them — under differing conditions and circumstances and with differing goals in mind — inevitably produces changes in it. Knowledge is to be acquired to be *used*, not just to be possessed in one's head. So, according to the Experimentalist, the school should take an active role in social change; in fact, the school should try to simulate the wider society by rendering itself a miniature replica of a problem-filled world. By learning how to solve problems, boys and girls not only acquire knowledge but learn how to cope with a changing world.

(4) The logical extension of this view would be one which is associated with a special branch of Experimentalism called Reconstructionism. As the name implies, this school of thought holds that schools should take the lead in reconstructing our social order. Social change, in this view, is not just an earthly symptom of a "becoming" universe; it is the very vehicle of human progress and fulfillment. Furthermore, social change is getting out of hand, and if things are not managed properly we shall all be atomic cinders before we can do anything about it. In addition, according to the Reconstructionists, we now know that man has the equipment — intellectual, technological, moral — to take charge of change, to gain control of its dynamic processes and turn it to his own account. If it were not for this, say these individuals, we should all be at the mercy of the forces which seem, in our time, to be carrying us, as on a huge ocean wave, to ultimate destruction on the rocks of our own stupidity. Out of a sense of urgency, then, if not for the more noble motive of achieving full use of our human powers, the Reconstructionist advises that we turn the school into the central headquarters for deliberate social planning and directed social change.

These four views, then, specify different functions for the school to perform in and for its environing social system. Since we shall consider these positions in greater detail later on, and since they help us to distinguish between educational ideologies, it may be useful to indicate graphically how they are related. Figure 1 (page 16) represents a time line from past to present to future. When we consider social history as a movement of human groups, through the time dimension, from past to future, we are forced to recognize that no single instant can be called The Present. Instead, we must consider the present to be the general region of the recent past, the present instant, and the immediately emergent future. Now if we can think of Western social life, particularly in a highly dynamic America, as moving along this time line, we may then consider the different roles the school might play as a social institution.

As we have already indicated, the Neo-Thomist holds that social change and historical movements are quite irrelevant to the work of the school. They are not genuinely real aspects of reality, but only surface characteristics of our temporal existence. Therefore, the school should be removed from and set above the chaotic conditions of men and focused upon eternal qualities as the proper intellectual and moral environment for the young.

Idealism and Realism, while differing in content, nevertheless join forces in their views on this question. Since they are essentially *conservationist* theories, their idea of the school is of a repository of the Western tradition, where knowledge can be accumulated, organized, and systematically disseminated to the young. Because the process of organization takes some time, there is an inevitable lag between a new discovery and its incorporation into the books and encyclopedias. Therefore, we place the Idealist-Realist school at the "trailing edge" of the present, where it can best operate to integrate new knowledge into the curriculum and delay the assimilation of uncertain new ideas until such time as they have won wide acceptance.

The Experimentalist camp would consider the "growing" or "forward" edge of the present to be a more advantageous and exciting place for learning to go on. It is in the solving of real and genuine problems of life today, in the criticism and evaluation of contemporary knowledge, that youngsters truly grow. For this reason, the school must get into the thick of social life, not insulating youngsters from the dynamics of progress by exposing them only to the settled and agreed upon, but having them share, in increasingly sophisticated degrees, in the total life of the community.

The Reconstructionist, carrying this view to its logical limit, would have the school adopt an admittedly Utopian doctrine, by which the dream we have of the future would be actively described and worked for in the school program. The Utopian future, then, would serve as the rallying focus for the Reconstructionist's curriculum, and his school would energetically nurture in the young a sense of social direction.

We shall find it necessary to expand upon and qualify these over-

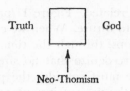

Neo-Thomism

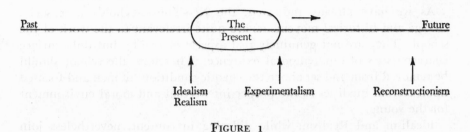

FIGURE 1

Historical Time Line

simple descriptions when we examine each individual position later on, in Chapters Eleven and Twelve. For instance, Neo-Thomism does look to the human, temporal past as a key to locating the eternal and absolute; we shall want to explore this idea. Another educational philosophy, Existentialism, which we shall also consider, has not yet developed much in the way of social theories. For this reason it will be difficult to assign any position on this question to this new philosophy. Enough has been said, though, to suggest *the type* of question that educational philosophers raise when they consider the school as a social institution, but the above will give you an idea of the kind of theoretical distinctions that can be drawn between different philosophies.

Education and the cosmos

THE MEANING OF LIFE. The most troublesome and yet most abiding question in philosophy is the question concerning the over-all meaning of life. What are we doing here? What is the purpose of man? What is a human life for? If there is a design in nature or a developing purpose in the universe it is not unreasonable to suspect that the human race is playing out some role in it.

Cosmologists have recently excited anew our interest in this question. They are the individuals who study the physical universe — earth, planets, stars, galaxies, matter, energy, and celestial motion. With their

16

telescopes, spectroscopes, and complex mathematics, they are telling us that there is every likelihood that star systems like our own inhabit the heavens in the order of several millions.[8] Biochemists and physiologists, with their increasing understanding of life processes, tell us that when the chemical ingredients for living tissue are present the likelihood is great that life forms will emerge and start evolving.[9] From all this work we are left with the distinct and apparently reliable impression that intelligences other than our own quite probably inhabit the outer reaches and that we are perhaps not so special in this universe.

When we consider these reports and these conclusions we are set to wondering just what this planet we inhabit is all about, what its place is in the total cosmos, and what we as its passengers are supposed to be doing here.[10] Theology, of course, views these ultimate questions as its special province, but philosophy also seeks to find answers to them. And educational philosophers are or should be especially interested in them for the simple reason that if some reliable answers can be given as to the end and purpose of man we shall be well on our way to understanding the kind of education he should have. If it is felt that there is a given design and structure to the cosmos one might conclude that our principal function is to discover this design and find our place in it. This conclusion would seem to call for an education to assist our adjustment to a given reality. Others might decide otherwise: that this cosmos is not yet finished and our role is to make it over — to the degree of which we are capable — into something closer to what it ought to be. This outlook would seem to call for an education that would awaken our creative and productive energies. A sizable amount of educational dispute in our time can be traced to the many aspects of this "cosmological" question.

MAN OR GOD. Closely related to these considerations, of course, is the companion question of whether education is principally man-centered or God-centered. If it is man-centered, then education should encourage the open and curious mind to inquire into and challenge any idea it chooses, trusting that "truth will out" in the end. If education, on the other hand, is essentially God-centered, then there will be certain subject

---

[8] For an exciting adventure into these probabilities, see Fred Hoyle, *The Nature of the Universe* (New York: Harper and Bros., 1950).

[9] See Harlow Shapley, *Of Stars and Men* (Boston: Beacon Press, 1958), and also J. H. Rush, *The Dawn of Life* (New York: Hanover House, 1958).

[10] C. S. Lewis, for instance, raises the question of what would happen were we, in our forthcoming space travels, to run into an "unfallen race," a race of creatures who never suffered as have we the misfortunes of a wayward Adam, who, through a momentary lapse of judgment, got us off on the wrong foot with God. Suppose these creatures are, unlike us, completely in step with God and have no understanding whatsoever of what good and evil are all about. Aside from the trauma such a discovery would surely set in motion, what effect might this have on our moral training of the young?

matters which the child must learn of necessity and which lie beyond the reach of question and individual judgment. Since they are authored by God, not man, they do not have to be investigated or discussed, only learned in and for themselves.

You can readily see that here is a region where a great deal of educational dispute originates. For knowledge and truth are the "stock in trade" of the school. Where knowledge and truth come from, then, God or man, bears directly on how this basic "commodity" is retailed in the school.

THE ULTIMATE MORAL NATURE OF EDUCATION. Finally it is necessary to connect what has been said with the essentially moral quality of all education. When we use the word *moral* in this context we do not have in mind the usual problems of moral conduct — stealing, lying, adultery, etc. — but the wider, all-inclusive meaning of all moral judgment, i.e., the making of decisions which represent what we want from life and what we want young people to become. Education, ultimately and fundamentally, is the process of deliberately attempting to make of the young something which if left to themselves they would not become. This basic definition of education will hold whether one classifies himself with the "operative arts" or the "cooperative arts." (See pages 3–5.)

If this is true, then it is clear that every deliberate system of education must make some fundamental decisions concerning both the type of society it prefers and means to bring about, and the consequent type of individual it values and means to produce. As John Childs has said:

> A school system is organized whenever a human group begins to become conscious of its own experience, and desires to select from the totality of its beliefs and practices certain things which it is concerned to preserve and foster by reproducing them in the lives of its young.[11]

> · · · · ·

> . . . A manifestation of preference for certain patterns of living as opposed to others is therefore inherent in every program of deliberate education.[12]

> · · · · ·

> . . . As we introduce the young to the various aspects of human experience — familial, economic, scientific, technological, political, religious, artistic — we inevitably encourage attitudes and habits of response in and to these affairs. In order to encourage, we must also discourage; in order to foster, we must also hinder; in order to emphasize the significant, we must identify the non-significant; and, finally, in order to select and focus attention on certain subject-matters of life, we have to reject and ignore other subject-matters.[13]

[11] John L. Childs, *Education and Morals* (New York: Appleton-Century-Crofts, Inc., 1950), p. 6.   [12] *Ibid.*, p. 7.   [13] *Ibid.*, p. 19.

The preferences and values that educators must perforce exhibit likewise reveal the kind of cosmos they think we live in or the kind of cosmos they think we *want* to live in. Professor Childs would prefer the "human order" as the final universe he would want to talk about. Moral judgments, he says, find their final validations in the social experience of men. To say, as Professor Childs does, that education is a moral undertaking is simply to say that deliberate education involves choices that make a difference in the individual and social lives of human beings.

Other theorists prefer to think the moral character of education extends beyond the human into the transhuman or supernatural. Here, they say, is the origin of all morality, all rightness and wrongness. Hence, education is a moral undertaking in the sense that it attempts to divine the absolute goods of the supernatural and translate them into ideal images of individual and society.

In either case, education can be seen to be far more of a value-judgment enterprise than most of us think. For as we go to school and learn we are actually also being inducted into a system of moral and ethical decisions that have, for the most part, already been made. We grow up in America to value monogamous marriage, private enterprise, and social "togetherness." These are, in a sense, all types of prepared moral judgments, ready and waiting for us as we grow up to adulthood.

Every educator is therefore concerned not alone with facts and ideas and concepts. He is, whether he knows it or not, concerned also with goods and preferences and desires and "shoulds," which eventually reveal the kind of universe he feels *ought to be*. It is this universe which he endeavors to realize through his education of the young.

THE PHILOSOPHIC TASK

The subject matter of philosophy

When the philosopher begins his work his occupational trait is to start asking questions. Questions, as a matter of fact, constitute the raw materials of his trade; philosophy is the study of questions, rather than the study of answers. The preceding section has indicated the general dimensions of education — individual, social, cosmic — within which the philosopher asks his questions.

What the philosopher is primarily concerned with, however, is asking the *right* questions. By *right* we mean relevant and meaningful; the philosopher's job is to ask the kinds of questions that are relevant to the subject under study, the kinds of questions we really want to get answered rather than merely muse over, the kinds of questions whose answers make a real difference in how we live and work. As this book intends to show, asking the right questions is not so easy as it may look.

One of the ways to study educational philosophy is to take up one philosophical question at a time, first examining the many points of view that different schools take on it and then indicating the type of educational practice that would seem to be called for. Another way is to examine the schools of thought, one at a time, to see how they answer all the theoretical questions that confront educators and what kind of educational practice they each suggest as a consequence of their individual systems of theoretical approach.

Eventually, every student of education should become familiar with these "schools," and it is the purpose of Part V of this book to help you to organize your thinking in this way. But before we do this, it will be necessary to take up the fundamental questions of philosophy itself and to show how they become educational problems, for the consideration of educators.

The three basic questions of philosophy

All philosophy asks three basic questions. The first of these is simply: What is real? This seems straightforward enough; it may sound, to the newcomer to philosophy, even a little too naïve and simple a question for grown men and women to spend their time on. But, as we shall see, it is a very prickly problem, and it concerns education most directly because of the necessity for the school to base its program upon fact and reality rather than upon fancy and illusion. A curriculum that announces the existence of gremlins and affirms the authenticity of giants in the earth is more than erroneous; it is downright pernicious. We shall wish to see, therefore, how the real, as against the fictional or illusory, is to be understood. In more homely language, we shall want to know what the world is made of. This branch of philosophy is formally known as *ontology*, the study of what is real. Viewed from the standpoint of what *exists* and what does not, ontology assumes the companion label of *metaphysics*,[14] or the study of existence or being. In essence, metaphysics is the study of the tiny infinitive *to be*. We shall take up these questions in Part II, which follows, considering first the problem itself, then examining different answers to the problem, and finally considering the influence these various answers have upon the educational process.

The second problem of philosophy can simply be stated with the question: What is true? It has direct kinship with the first problem, in that we want to know, first of all, how certain we can be of the statements we make about reality. Certainly we must have confidence in this knowl-

---

[14] *Meta* from the Greek, meaning "beyond" the physics, or simply the "appendix" or last section of Aristotle's book on physics for which he could find no better name.

edge before we go on to develop other knowledge. In reverse fashion, our knowledge actually depends on what reality makes possible; the real world, that is, must include the *ability to know* if we are to undertake the knowing process at all. All of these considerations come under the heading of *epistemology*, the study of knowledge or how we know things. We shall consider this in Part III, looking first at the problem itself, then at a number of views of it, and finally at its relevance for education.

The third and final problem of philosophy consists of asking: What is good? In formal discourse, this is customarily divided into two divisions, i.e., the question of *ethics* (What is right conduct?) and the question of *aesthetics* (What is beautiful?). In both instances, we are dealing not so much with reality or with truth but with *value*. These matters are known under the larger term *axiology*, the study of value. We shall take this up in Part IV, with the customary trio of topics: the question, the several answers, and the educational implications.

Philosophic systems and their uses

In Part V, as we have said, we shall try to collect these many points of view and arrange them into systematic schools of thought, so that you can see the direct relationships that exist between different parts of a theoretical system. Much that is said here will necessarily be a repetition of what has gone before, but the relationships themselves, rather than the individual concepts, will attract our major attention.

In Part VI we shall have a chance to examine the ways in which the use of this book and the study of educational philosophy itself can flow into practical action. Throughout the book there will be ample evidence of how theory makes a difference in practice. But Part VI will help you to organize your theoretical thinking in a practical setting, indicating how you can increasingly enable intelligent theory to guide your day-to-day conduct in life or at school or, preferably, both.

Each chapter is followed by a short bibliography. These entries indicate only a sampling of the references you might conceivably consult, but they are among the first you should go to if you are curious to expand your understanding of any given area. One way to quicken your curiosity and expand your understanding, both at the same time, is to engage in some "do-it-yourself" philosophizing. There is perhaps no more effective channel to keener perception in philosophy than the individual's serious confrontation of theoretical questions which he recognizes as relevant to his own life and work. You are encouraged therefore to indulge in this activity whenever the occasion prompts. Preferably you should not rely on the questions provided at the close of each chapter, but they are offered here to help you get started.

QUESTIONS

1. How would you define the relationship between theory and practice? Take, for instance, a field other than education — politics, agriculture, the game of bridge, architecture, interior design, football — and try to explain the function of both theory and practice in these activities. Is the relationship the same as in education?

2. In what ways do you think education is an "operative art"? A "cooperative art"? Which of the two is it primarily, do you think?

3. Social change can be measured in three dimensions: the technological (e.g, invention of the automobile, radio, television, rocketry to outer space), the social (e.g., social inventions, such as the labor union, Suburbia, "the organization man," etc.), and the moral (e.g., changing attitudes toward sex, divorce, God). What should the school's policy be with respect to these different sectors of change — to stand above them, to ignore them, to report them, to help to produce them?

FURTHER READING

Adler, Mortimer J. "In Defense of the Philosophy of Education," Chapter V in *Philosophies of Education,* Forty-first Yearbook of the National Society for the Study of Education, ed. N. B. Henry, Part I. Chicago: the Society, 1942.
The "operative-cooperative" question is fully developed in this essay by a leading Neo-Thomist. The answer he gives provides a conceptual setting for the understanding of the Neo-Thomist's theory of education.

Brameld, T. *Philosophies of Education in Cultural Perspective.* New York: Dryden Press, 1955.
The social and cultural setting of education is definitively portrayed in this book. Especially in Chapters 1 and 2 you will find the purpose — indeed, the urgency — for the study of educational philosophy in our time. Brameld, as the leading spokesman for Reconstructionism, has developed this outlook more fully and more forcefully in a companion volume, *Toward a Reconstructed Philosophy of Education* (New York: Dryden Press, 1955).

Brubacher, John. *Modern Philosophies of Education,* Second Edition. New York: McGraw-Hill Book Co., 1950.
In Chapter I the author discusses the occasion for philosophy, philosophy and common sense, and the linkage between theory and practice in the field of education.

Childs, John L. *Education and Morals.* New York: Appleton-Century-Crofts, Inc., 1950.
In his preface, Childs writes that "devotion to the ideals of democracy in no

way bars us from making a deliberate effort to nurture the young" in particular and specified ways. Selecting these ways is the basically moral task of the educator, and a study of philosophy is the prelude to the effective discharge of this task. Chapters I and II examine this theme in powerful and convincing language.

Dewey, John. *Democracy and Education.* New York: The Macmillan Co., 1916. Perhaps the most frequently quoted statement of Dewey's, at least by educational theorists, is his famous dictum: ". . . philosophy may be defined as the general theory of education." Certainly no other author has shown so vital a connection between these two branches of human endeavor. You will find this dictum and the compelling elaboration of it in Chapter XXIV.

Perry, R. B. "Education and the Science of Education," in Scheffler, I., *Philosophy and Education* (Boston: Allyn and Bacon, Inc., 1958).
This lead essay in a book of readings sets the stage for an understanding of the contemporary call for an educational science. By "science" the author means "working formula" or theory by which we may order the school's content, revive its necessarily moral role in civilized life, shape its work to a democratic end, and produce a truly liberal man.

Ontology:
What Is Real?

CHAPTER TWO

Ontology:

The Question of Reality

WHAT IS?

The problem

If philosophy is essentially a set of problems, the very first we must tackle is the problem of reality: What is the world "made of"? To many a reader, this will sound like the most fatuous of questions. Why should we waste our time arguing about the nature and character of a world which is so obviously clear to us day by day? It is just this kind of nonsense, some say, which brings philosophy into so much disrepute in the modern world, where men who disregard such ridiculous "ivory-towered" questions go blissfully and ignorantly ahead into their world and make it do what they want it to do.

The fatuity of our question, if any, is exceeded only by the fatuity of the above hypothetical response. The fact is that modern men have succeeded in their bold technological exploits by taking seriously the important question of the nature of the world, not by ignoring it. Perhaps the classic examples of this are the atom bomb and its successor, the thermonuclear bomb, which stand as a kind of symbol of our mighty supremacy over nature. These amazing devices became possible only when we changed our ontology, i.e., changed our theories of what the world, at its most fundamental and basic level, consists of.

After the early Greeks had spent a great deal of time and energy speculating on the relative merits of earth, air, fire, and water as the prime ingredients of reality, Democritus came up with the suggestion that perhaps the world is not made of any "natural essence"[1] but of tiny pieces — building blocks of the universe — which could be arranged in an almost unlimited variety of combinations. These tiny pieces came to be referred to as *atoms,* a word from the Greek which means indivisible. Hence, the tiniest piece of matter, the piece which finally resisted any attempt to split or cut it, would eventually be discovered to be the ultimate unit of physical reality.

Atomic physics, then, originated with the Greeks, in the sense that the search for the basic building blocks of the universe began with their original setting of the problem. This search has continued down to our own time, and much research in physics has sought to locate the final "piece of matter." It was presumed by many nineteenth- and early-twentieth-century physicists that the atom would probably be spherical in shape, and that matter, ultimately, would be discovered to be made up of an infinity of tiny particles resembling marbles or billiard balls in shape.

The twentieth century yielded information that the atom is actually constructed of still smaller particles — electrons, which revolve around a nucleus or "sun" much as the planets revolve about their sun. More recently, it was learned that the nucleus of the atom is composed of still tinier pieces of matter — neutrons and protons — and these of still tinier ones.

But physicists soon began to ask themselves where all this research was leading. Was it possible, they began to wonder, to plumb the depths of matter to locate the truly fundamental particle of matter, the absolutely indivisible unit of reality? They had, of course, by this time gone far beyond the reach of their own eyesight or even of the most powerful microscopes. Instead, they had to content themselves with theoretical models of atomic particles, which they used to describe the *behavior* of atoms. At this point they began to realize that, in truth, it is the behavior of matter, as well as its structure, that represents what they were really interested in. Furthermore, as research delved further down into the family of particles it became more evident that some nuclear force would

[1] The Pythagoreans believed that all four of these were aspects of reality, bound together and unified under the fifth essence or "quintessence," of which the heavenly bodies were composed. This quintessence, sometimes designated as "ether," represented the *undergirding quality* of all the lesser essences — an idea that is very close to Aristotle's notion of Pure Form (see Chapter Three).

seem to be required to hold the particles in place and to account for their motions and behaviors. Soon the motions and behaviors themselves attracted as much attention as the particles. In fact, the particles came more and more to be understood as points or poles of energy, as well as tiny pieces of something. This led to the rise of modern physics, which considers matter as "constructed" of what the physicist sometimes calls "congealed energy" as well as little "marbles." Energy and matter, in short, are merely two forms of the same thing.

With this fundamental revision of thinking, there obviously came a thoroughgoing revolution in the meaning of physics, a new alignment of procedures and experimental design. In fact, there were whole new problems which would never have even occurred to Democritean atomic physicists, with their exclusively "marble" theory of matter. One of these problems, of course, was that concerning the possibilities of releasing some of the energy trapped in the atom. The experimental results of this are by now familiar to us all. But these results would never have been possible, never even dreamed of, if we had not first arrived at a thoroughly unorthodox, novel, and radically different view of the nature of matter itself.

The point is that we must attend to the problem of reality precisely because our conception of reality controls the very questions we ask of our world. And without questions, we obviously cannot have the answers out of which we may eventually build our bodies of knowledge and subject-matter disciplines. Put another way, the curriculum of the school — its scope and content — derives directly from what man has come to know and value in this universe of his. What he has come to know — the sum total of his knowledge — is the product of curiosities he develops about his world and inquiries he makes of it in the course of his experience. These curiosities, these inquiries, quite obviously are controlled by what men think their world is like and what questions and inquiries are relevant to it. Hence our ultimate preoccupation in educational theory with the most primary of all philosophic problems: ontology, or the study of ultimate reality.

Ontology's close companion, as we have said in Chapter One, is the discipline of metaphysics. The two terms are almost equivalent in meaning. There is only a subtle difference: Whereas ontology is concerned with the nature of *reality*, metaphysics is the study of the nature of *existence* (or what it means for anything *to be*). Since that which is real is presumed to exist and that which exists is necessarily real, we need not quibble over the fine distinctions between the two concepts. At least for the present treatment, the two will operationally refer to the same area of concern.

The study of ontology: differing views

It should be said at this point that serious preoccupation with ontology is scorned by a sizable segment of the community of educational philosophers. These individuals consider ontology an area of inquiry which yields little or no fruit for the simple reason that questions asked here can never be answered, at least not with any finality or assurance. Hence, they insist, other questions that yield more readily to human intelligence should receive our attention.

To some individuals, for instance, reality must be considered a kind of "given" quality or "ground" of the human situation. We are unable to discuss the nature and character of this ground because we can never truly know it; there is nothing against which we can see it. It is, as they say, a "surd," i.e., basically irrational or a-rational, possibly even transrational, or beyond the reach of human mentality, and hence not subject to intelligent study.

You should not get the idea, however, that this view, which we shall see as associated for the most part with the Experimentalists and a group known as the Analysts, is taken with a kind of high-handed disregard of ontological considerations. On the contrary, it is taken only after the ontological and metaphysical problem has been explored and found to be unyielding to inquiry.

For this reason, no student of educational theory can safely take this position until he has examined the ontological field itself. Furthermore, educational philosophers are not unanimous on this point by any means. Many of them believe that the ontological question is a genuine problem, that it deserves our study, and that we must go ahead and make the most of what is admittedly a very difficult task. Reality, from this standpoint, cannot be dismissed as unfathomable; on the contrary, the meaning of reality, the very meaning of existence — that of the cosmos at large or that of our own selves — constantly clamors for explanation. To make a steady intellectual attack on this question — even if it has not yet appeared to yield any very substantial results — is certainly better than to give up in the face of difficulty.

The infinitive "to be"

It comes as something of an unsettling discovery to realize that the most impenetrable verb in our language is perhaps the shortest and certainly one of our most common — the infinitive *to be*. We say very casually, "I am an American," or "The apple is a fruit." We thus simply use the verb *to be* to identify something as belonging to a class of things.

But when it is not used to identify a thing as belonging to a kind, the verb *to be* takes on an altogether different meaning. Consider, for instance, the statement, "I am," or "I exist." We sometimes affirm our own existence by referring to the fact that we were born; our existence is measured from the moment of a physical event. But this doesn't help too much; what exactly does it mean to say "I am"? Does it mean that I am present in the world in a three-dimensional kind of way, i.e., that I am taking up space? Or is the spatial quality of my being relatively unimportant and the presence of my psychic, inner "self" the genuine meaning of my existence? If this, then can we say we exist as selves at the moment of conception, or the moment of birth, or at any other moment? When, indeed, does selfhood first take up residence in us? Is it gradual and evolutionary, or is it sudden and instantaneous? In either case, the meaning of our own existence is not clear.

The case of the apple's existence presents other difficulties, even though it lies outside of us and is presumably free of any complications of selfhood. For when we say, "The apple is," do we mean that it is present in the world in a spatial way, occupying cubic territory in the cosmos? If this, how does one ascertain the occupation of such territory? The answer, quite simply, is through our senses. But, then, if there are no sensations of the apple, does it exist?

Finally there is the question whether things which do not yield to our senses — the idea of loyalty, say, or the notion of time, or a thing like "democracy" — do or do not exist. If we hold that they exist, then quite obviously the use of perception as a criterion — the judgment of the senses — is not enough to affirm the existence of anything.

Perhaps, as some say, things that are said to exist actually exist in different ways; there are different classifications, as it were, of existence. Apples may exist in one way; feelings, like hunger, for instance, may exist in another; ideas, like love or Communism, exist in another, and perhaps human selves in yet another.

Reality and appearance

We can take a closer look at this problem of the varieties of *to be* if we consider briefly some specific varieties of ontological *procedure*. The first of these is used in distinguishing what is genuinely real and existential from that which only appears to be real and existential. (As noted above, we are considering the two terms, *real* and *existential*, as more or less interchangeable.) Our senses tell us that the stick is straight before we thrust it into the water; but when it is in the water our senses tell us it is bent. We retrieve it, and the first report is repeated. By such direct con-

frontation of competing perceptual reports we can make our selection of
which is more "really" real, assigning the other to the limbo of "appearance" only.

But what are we to do with differing perceptual reports which do not
directly confront one another? For instance, the floor on which I stand,
to me, seems a rather straightforward kind of existent — it is a flat surface
of a particular color which supports my weight. To a chemist, however,
it is no such thing. Rather, it is a body of hydrocarbons associated in a
particular way and subject to certain kinds of environmental behavior,
such as heat and cold, wet and dry, oxidation, etc. To a physicist it is
still different: It is described in terms of atoms, electrons, and other
forms of physical energy, which make my floor actually a jumping hot-
bed of atomic motion. That I can stand on such a thing is rather a
wonder to me.

But the point is that the floor presents its existence in a variety of ways,
and, what is more, all of these dimensions of existence seem plausible and
acceptable, in varying degrees, to the chemist, to the physicist, and to
me. Which, though, is most real? Which of these three "appearances"
of the floor (there are many others) most closely approximates reality?
Quite obviously, we are not prepared to say; the experience of the three
of us points to different existential qualities. The floor, indeed, may be
said to be existing in different modes.

We move from this rather simplified example of competitive perceptual reports to a slightly more sophisticated problem, in which the perceptual reports are the same but are interpreted differently by different
individuals. We are all familiar with the difficulty of securing the same
description of an event — an accident or a catastrophe, let us say — from
half a dozen independent observers. No chemists or physicists here, just
idle onlookers. Why can't they "see" the same thing? But, more important, in the variety of reports, which one describes what really happened?
How is one who was not a witness — a judge, say — to decide which
report is the most accurate duplicate of the real quality of the event?

Quite obviously, this failing in the human perceptual system is a very
real limitation in the field of jurisprudence. But it is also troublesome in
education. In the field of history, for instance, it is commonplace to say
that different historians see the past differently. One would think that
the past is the past, and that is that. Why then can't we all get together
and write one final, objective, and true history of the entire world? We
could then chop this up into smaller segments — chapters, topics, assignments — and hand it out to all the children of the world for their study
in school. Unfortunately, history doesn't seem to work this way. History
in and of itself may occur in a brute kind of way, but we never know
about this. All we ever know about history is what the historians —

either formal scholars or informal storytellers — tell us about it. It must always be filtered through a human mind, and every human mind has its peculiar opacities and translucencies concerning the meaning of human events.

What is more, suppose all witnesses to a catastrophe or all historians of a specific event in the past happened to agree on the explicit description of the catastrophe or the meaning and significance of the event. Would this be a warrant for us to say that the real quality of the happening had finally been revealed? If we say "Yes," then what we really mean is that reality can be ascertained through an "opinion poll" technique. If all the returns agree, then we have a picture of the actual existent — thing or event. But suppose one of a hundred reporters disagreed with the ninety-nine others. Does this invalidate the testimony of the ninety-nine? What about 51 per cent versus 49 per cent?

These questions, simple and rudimentary as they are, illustrate the extreme difficulty of locating ultimate reality except through the clouded medium of appearance. How one considers this matter makes a difference in educational work precisely because the teacher's assurance must reside in the thing that he is teaching; he must feel confident that it is a representation of the real world that he and his students inhabit. If he ignores the implicit warning of such ontological considerations, he may consider his subject matter certain knowledge and feel he can afford to be dogmatic in his teaching and to insist that his charges learn it without too much question. But if, on the other hand, he recognizes the unreliability of human perception and observation, he may be more inclined to remain open on the matter, permitting discussion and the weighing of evidence, if appropriate, in the learning situation.

Existents and symbols

Another procedural difficulty in the field of ontology concerns the manner or mode of existence exercised by physical things which we perceive through our senses as compared to that exercised by the symbols we invent to stand for these things and the ideas and concepts concerning things which we "manufacture" in our minds and think about. Take this book you are now reading. Our senses tell us that it is in existence here in our hands. But consider the peculiar little series of marks we put on paper — B O O K — and the noise we make with our mouths from these marks to designate the thing we hold in our hand.

Certainly these marks on paper exist in a perceptual sense; we can see them there. And the noise we make exists because we hear it. But what we see and hear is not what is important. What is important is that something has been introduced into our experience which is *not* the book itself or merely a visual image or a sound but something which stands for the book and makes possible our "having" the book in our experience even when the perceptual book is removed. We have had opened up to us, as it were, a new kind of reality, a reality which transcends the perceptual, five-sense world which is our customary habitat.

This "world of symbols" happens to be the most important "reality" that a human being occupies because symbols have the marvelous capacity to represent *all other kinds of reality* which man's experience provides. Symbols can stand for things we perceive with our senses; they can stand for feelings inside ourselves; they can stand for ideas we think about in our heads; they can stand for fictional existents (ghosts, gremlins) and the most nebulous qualities of our experience. In short, they can open up to us the full range of our existing as no other vehicle can.

It is the power to symbolize, incidentally, which is now considered to be the essential distinguishing feature that separates man from the rest of nature. For a long time, it had been thought that man stood above nature — most specifically the animal kingdom, of which he otherwise was a part — by virtue of his unique possession of reason. Thus the Greeks spoke of man as a "rational animal," thinking that this definition clarified the matter. It has turned out, however, that if the word "rational" means "intelligent," then animals share, if in a lower degree, the ability to exercise intelligence and reason upon problems in their own experience. So we have been forced to give up this unique distinction, even though we are admittedly far superior to animals in what is termed "intelligent behavior." We have turned once again to the problem of locating a distinction of *kind* rather than mere *degree* that separates us from animals; and the most recent hypothesis is that the use of symbols constitutes such a distinction.

If this hypothesis turns out to be correct[2] then we can say that the world of symbols is the exclusive property of man. But this does not answer our metaphysical question: Do symbols exist? And, if so, do they exist in the same way in which that for which they stand exists?

2 The issue is complicated because of the similarity, in the formal study of semantics, between *symbols* and *signs*. Signs — noises, gestures, visual images, calling for some specific behavior — fall within the powers of many animals. In this sense, animals can comunicate with one another by means of a "sign" language. Symbols — noises, gestures, visual images which merely represent other sectors of experience — appear to be beyond the powers even of the highest primates. There is some doubt about this, however, and in the case of some very complicated and sophisticated experimental "problem-solving" situations (see R. Linton, *The Study of Man* [New York: D. Appleton-Century Co., 1936], pp. 65–66, or D. O. Hebb, *A Textbook of Psychology* [Philadelphia: Saunders, 1958], pp. 133–134), chimpanzees appear to be attaching symbolic significance to poker chips which they collect for later use in a food-dispensing machine. For a thorough discussion of the problem of symbolism, see Suzanne K. Langer, *Philosophy in a New Key* (Cambridge: Harvard University Press, 1942).

This may appear to be getting quite far afield in the study of educational theory. But actually we are dealing with a very vital question in education — the role of symbols in the educational program. As we have seen, symbols and their manipulation are the medium through which human beings, most particularly youngsters in school, come into an acquaintance with their world. But historically there have been numerous instances in which the medium of symbols began to take on an educational value of its own and the understanding to which symbolic manipulation should eventually lead was considered secondary. The most familiar example of this is the obsession of educators down through the ages with the study of language. Language is but a catalogue of symbols through which ideas and information are passed between human beings. But the study of language, not as means but as end in itself, is an old story in man's efforts to educate himself. So rigid did this attitude become that in England and colonial America of the seventeenth and eighteenth centuries the very name for secondary education was *Latin grammar school*. The study of grammar was undertaken and made a central and almost exclusive part of a youngster's life for the avowed reason that the mastery of symbols in and for themselves was the mark of the truly educated person. To this day the single most important measure of the educated individual is the degree of his mastery of his own tongue. Content with this point of view, modern American educators allot more time to the study of English than to any other subject.

In the field of mathematics the situation is often repeated. Symbols — numbers — are properly tools for the understanding of mathematical ideas. But so much is made of mastering these symbols that they are eventually taken to be educational ends in their own right. And boys and girls continue in their study of mathematics — into logarithms, quadratic equations, and calculus — far beyond the point where mathematics represents the *medium* through which they are to come to understand their world. They continue beyond this point because mathematics is thought to be valuable in its own right, whether useful or not, simply because it is symbolic in character.

To return to our problem, we can say that educators who permit this to happen reveal their metaphysical classification of *symbols,* i.e., they elevate symbols to a higher existential rank than the things for which they stand. Other educators, more favorable to *things* — concrete experiences of perception of the environment — reveal their metaphysical leanings by their espousal of direct, unmediated experience for the young. Demonstrations in the classroom, object lessons concerning a physical thing brought into the school, or field trips outside the school to learn of places firsthand are all specific examples of this tendency. But the point is that whatever one believes about the relative ontological status of symbols and their referents will show up in his educational theory and practice. What appears to be a remote and esoteric consideration is actually a significant determinant of how we operate schools.

Thing and process

Another procedural problem in ontology concerns the relative emphasis we place upon the "thing" nature of reality as against its dynamic, "process" character. We made reference above to the fact that twentieth-century physicists came to see the atom as a constellation of *behaviors* rather than a structural *thing*. This was partially due to the "dead end" results of their "thing"-oriented inquiries. But it was also due to a whole new emphasis in physics which looked upon knowledge of the *behavior* of matter as of vastly greater significance to man than knowledge of how matter is built. Of course, in order to ask behavioral questions of atoms one must have some theory of their structure; but, increasingly, structure has come to be considered principally a means to the more vital end of comprehending the dynamic *processes* going on in the subatom. The very transfer of physicists' concern from matter to energy reveals keener interest in the dynamic as against the structurally static.

This points up a much wider philosophic problem — namely, whether the rest of us should make similar shifts in our outlook. In the study of biology, for instance, the emphasis before Darwin in the nineteenth century was upon structure — the physiologist and the anatomist were seeking to comprehend the structure of living tissue. Words like *protoplasm* and *cell* and *organ* all suggested the structural approach. But Darwin introduced the concept of evolutionary process, and today biologists are not so much interested in how living tissue is built as they are in how it behaves. According to this approach *function* rises to a new prominence, and words like *digestion, maturation,* and *metabolism* become the verbal counters in biological inquiry. The study of medicine, that special branch of physiology dealing with functional disorders, concerns itself almost entirely with the *processes* going on in the human body.

What has been happening in the physical sciences has also, in a lesser way, turned up in the social sciences. The shift in emphasis is perhaps not so clear-cut but it is nonetheless evident. Our social sciences used to consist only of history (the study of statically arranged sequences in human events), political science (the study of the structure of political institutions), and economics (the study of the structure of wealth-generating systems). But social scientists have gradually adopted a whole new family of disciplines — sociology, social psychology, anthropology — which turn from *structure* to examine *conduct* in human affairs. So thoroughly has this transition taken place that these are now spoken of as the *behavioral* sciences. Even the science of psychology, originally the off-shoot of physiology and neurology, now concerns itself principally with human *behavior*.

Now the significance of all these changes in emphasis is simply that we may be altering our ontological outlooks, i.e., our concept of reality, in favor of a changing, "becoming," evolving cosmos as against a stationary, static cosmos of pure being. Aristotle, of course, could see change taking place in his experience — nature is full of it — and certain features of his metaphysics appear to reflect a dynamic, world-in-motion point of view. But when he is all done explaining, it is clear that Aristotle believed change to be only a superficial characteristic of an underlying reality of things or "essences" which does not change. (The study of process, in our modern understanding of the term, would not have occurred to him, because essences, by definition, were static existents which "stood existentially still" in the Greek cosmos.) Indeed, it is still the popular theological view of reality that the universe was created in an instant and that, though it exhibits change and motion, it is basically in a state of indestructible "being." Except for Anaximander and Heraclitus in the sixth and fifth centuries B.C., men never very seriously considered the ontology of constant process until just recently — within the last hundred years or so, in which the scientific revolution has reached a climax. And since the dialectic between the static and dynamic theories of reality contributes so much to our understanding of the educational process, we shall wish, in Chapter Three, to study these competing views carefully.

Not the least of the educational referents of this discussion is the question whether youngsters in school should be introduced to a static world, where facts and formulas describe how things really are and always will be for all eternity, or, instead, to a changing, dynamic world, where facts and formulas are modified from one age to another and where only the *methods* and *procedures* of solving problems are necessary. The issue is considerably more complicated than this, but this will indicate its ontological significance and its educational relevance.

Purpose and purposelessness

One final element in the study of ontology centers on the problem of purpose. Purpose, of course, is familiar enough in our day-to-day lives. We all have purposes, either short-range and immediate, like buying groceries, or long-range and strategic, like raising a family or building a career. Purpose is so much with us, as a matter of fact, that we often are inclined to wonder whether nature itself or the cosmos at large is endowed with purpose. Nature seems to present to us the raw materials out of which we could possibly infer some purpose; i.e., it is characterized by change. Without observable change in condition or status, there is no question of purpose. It is difficult to conceive that a stone possesses purpose.

But whenever change is present, there is always the question as to whether movement from one condition to another condition is prompted by some underlying or inherent purpose in the process itself. For instance, does a caterpillar purposefully set about becoming a moth? We usually do not use the word *purpose* in this way. But how about this: Does *nature* set about purposefully to change caterpillar into moth?

On a somewhat more sophisticated level, we can ask whether nature, by its constant system of replenishing itself through reproduction, actually is expressing the underlying purpose of life. Nature, in this light, may be said to be sustaining itself through its "purposeful" movement toward more and more life. The only trouble with this hypothesis is that death is quite as much a part of nature as is life, and it would be difficult to demonstrate one tendency as more purposeful than the other.

At a still more sophisticated level, the matter of transhuman purpose is most often met in the field of philosophy and religion. The cosmos itself evidences qualities of change. Do these changes actually represent symptoms of a developing purpose in the universe? Is there a cosmic will — the Will of God, perhaps — which is unfolding before our eyes? If so, how do we establish the truth and accuracy of such a cosmic will? Are we once again driven to a kind of opinion-polling technique to find out what purpose is being expressed? This is legitimate to ask because many different religions have developed many different and even contradictory ideas of the presumably unitary "Will of God." Some hold that God will soon bring human life to a close, either because he did not mean for us to be permanent residents here and he has other plans or because he has become disenchanted with our conduct since Adam. Others hold that God supports us, benignly forgetting all of our sins if we are satisfactorily penitent. Still others say that God supports and "elects" a few of us, but damns the rest of us. Still others say that God's Will was simply to create the world and set it in motion; his influence, by his own choice, has been removed from it.

The point is that we are confounded not only by the problem of whether there is purpose in the cosmos but also by what such a purpose might be, presuming there is one. Boiled down to its simplest elements, this issue can be compressed within the question: Is the universe friendly to man? Is it, as it were, "on our side"? Here we enter perhaps the most difficult realm of ontology, the subjective, anthropocentric judgment of the "attitude" of the cosmos toward the human race. Most religions, almost by definition, resolve this problem in the affirmative: The cosmos in some mysterious way looks after our ultimate wants. Certainly, this is one of the universal appeals of religion — its capacity to provide a home for the human spirit, a final anchorage for our bewildered navigation toward ultimate meaning in life.

But this tendency is also found in philosophy. Almost every recorded philosophy down through the ages, with the possible exception of Schopenhauer's "will-is-evil" idea, Nietzsche's "God-is-dead" outlook, and the more recent "God-is-irrelevant" doctrine of the atheistic wing of Existentialism, has ended up with an ontology which is either friendly to human aspiration or, at the very least, sufficiently neutral to provide the ground for aspiration. No theory of the cosmos has ever come around to the view that the universe is actually working against us. No view of this kind would be popular; there is too much built-in optimism in the human soul.

We must be cautious, therefore, in evaluating various ontologies, for philosophers in general, like human beings individually, are tempted to let "the wish become father to the thought." And educators particularly must guard against this, for they must not deceive the child into thinking that the world into which he is being inducted is more hospitable to his needs and requirements than it actually is. How hospitable it actually is, of course, is an open question; different philosophies have taken different views. And consequently they lead to different programs of education. Some philosophies hold that the universe contains within itself the moral road signs which, if heeded, will lead us to the Good Life. School programs built on this premise mean to instruct boys and girls in what these signs say and how one is to follow them. Other philosophies, on the other hand, say either that there are no road signs at all or that what signs there are have been put there by the human community itself, to be changed and altered as the situation requires. The school program based on this point of view would lay a much heavier responsibility upon boys and girls not only to develop their own interpretation of the signs that are in place but also to locate the intersections in human experience where new or different signs are needed. The most urgent example of this is in the field of sexual behavior, where the established codes of conduct seem less and less relevant to modern life. Because this is so sensitive an area of human concern, and because we have not put up the new signposts, teachers in the schools prefer to remain silent on the whole matter, leaving the child to find his own way. Whether this is or is not an ethical moral posture for the educator to assume will depend finally upon the ontology we choose to believe in.

39

WHAT ISN'T?

But now that we have examined the dimensions of the question, "What is?," we are compelled to turn briefly to its opposite: "What isn't?" We have already intimated the scope of this problem by indirection, but we must confront it directly to assign its relevance to the educative process.

What was said earlier about the impenetrability of the infinitive *to be* can now be seen as the problem of distinguishing the real, existential world from what is illusory or fictional or simply nonexistent. Put another way, it is the problem of drawing a boundary line between what is real and what is not. If, as was pointed out, there is possibly a different mode for different existents — for physical things, for symbols, for ideas, for human selves — then we should wish to establish the specific standards to distinguish these existents from other candidates in the same category or mode which do not truly exist. If this book, a physical thing, exists, then how about the candidacy of a gremlin for existential status? If we conclude that a gremlin is really only an idea in our minds of a contrary little elf who commands an army of "bugs" which inhabit untried machinery, then what do we do with the idea of "careless workmanship" or "improper design," either of which seems to us a more plausible explanation for our technological setbacks? For these are but ideas also, and as symbolic referents they can claim no more existential status than the referent of the symbol "gremlin."

Clearly, the test in this case is our empirical judgment of what went wrong. As soon as we can lay it to our own errors, then we dismiss "gremlin" as a satisfactory explanation, and hence dismiss "gremlin" from the realm of true existence. But where empirical testing does not pertain, as it does not and cannot in the field of religion, for instance, what are we to do with such transempirical (i.e., beyond-experience) ideas as Satan or "heavenly angel" or Holy Ghost? Some educational theorists would even place the idea of "selfhood" in this trans- or at least nonempirical category. But the educational question is simply whether boys and girls can be introduced to such concepts as if they stood for actual, bona fide constituents of genuine reality. The secular school, it is true, has chosen to remove whatever might be classified as *mysterious* from its subject matter; mystery, except as a game or for motivational purposes, has no place in the public school program. But there are many educators who insist that mystery is a part of life and therefore ought not and must not be quarantined, like a disease, at a distance from the maturing and developing child.

On a much more prosaic level, we may point to the field of mathematics. Mathematics is, of course, a contrived system of symbols which refer to nothing in our experience; there are no twos and threes in nature. But we accept the reality of mathematical symbols without question and we make quite a business of teaching them to the young. Mathematics even invents purely imaginary numbers such as $\sqrt{-3}$, and makes good use of them in the development of mathematical skill.

In all of these ways, the world of unreality constantly makes overtures in our direction, asking to be let in to the scholastic world of the child. And yet there are as well the overtures of the mystics, the astrologers, the religious fanatics, and the crackpots. Educators certainly should have an ontological yardstick to use to determine which shall pass.

At its most sophisticated level, the problem of "What isn't?" terminates in the logical predicament of what to do with "nothingness." Consider this book, the shoes you have on, your own person. Now consider that all of these lose their existence, they pass out of being. Finally, extend this to every existent in the cosmos, whether it be physical, symbolic, or whatever. What do we have? We have complete nothingness. But the fact that we can assign a symbol — *nothing* — to this circumstance (a symbol, moreover, that seems to have meaning), and the fact that we can conceptualize this "state of affairs" or this "thing" called *nothing* and work it into our language and experience, might seem to qualify "nothingness" for existential status. Even if nothingness does not exist physically, it certainly stands as fully in our minds as any other similar symbolic quality, e.g., everything, cosmos, eternity. And if it gains entry as symbol, we are obligated to pay as much attention to it as to any other.

We come, then, to the ridiculous paradox of being required to say that "*Nothing* is a something," or, in the technical language of philosophers, "Non-being must be considered a special instance or mode of Being." We cannot easily indicate the relevance of this technical philosophical problem to education; it is pointed to here only to reveal how troublesome our world can really become if we take seriously our desire to comprehend it intelligently.

WHAT MIGHT BE?

Lying ontologically somewhere between what *is* and what *is not* is the logical no man's land of *possibility*. To sense the proportions of this problem, we need only point to two concepts. If we refer to a "square circle," we are obviously not talking about what *might* be; we are talking in contradictions and therefore of what simply *cannot* be. There is no possibility of a square circle coming into existence. But if we speak of a gold mountain on the outskirts of Albuquerque, we are quite obviously speaking of what is ontologically possible. There doesn't happen to be

41

a solid-gold hillock anywhere in the vicinity of Albuquerque, nor is there one anywhere in the world, to anyone's knowledge; but, though it is geologically out of the question, from a purely logical and ontological standpoint we must insist that a gold mountain occupies the realm of the possible.

Now what are we to do with "possibility" in human affairs? To be more philosophically practical, what should we do with the possibility of genuine world government, with the possibility of a world order of Christian love, with the possibility of fatal overpopulation of the earth? Do these represent actual existents in our experience — are they somehow in place in the order of things, so that we can speak of them intelligibly? Or are they really only the logically extreme extensions of particular attributes of our social experience? Are they like the idea of "infinity" in mathematics and logic, which is logically *possible* (i.e., not contradictory) but, by definition, practically out of reach? If so, do these, like "infinity," lie within or outside of the existential world?

It matters educationally how one goes at a question of this sort, for we are permitted to dismiss from scholastic concern whatever does not enjoy existential status. Placing world government, for instance, outside the realm of the possible into the realm of the impossible (non-being) is to say that we need not — in fact, *must* not — point to it and draw attention to it as an authentic if only potential aspect of the future lives of our boys and girls in the schools. This would be, in this view, outright deceit if we were to practice it. On the other hand, if world government is considered capable of existence even if only potentially, we are licensed to proceed with our examination of it, especially if its possibility is of transcendent concern to the affairs of men. We must, of course, make it clear to boys and girls that it is only possibility, nothing more; whether men choose to work for it is another matter. But at least it is *able to be worked for,* in this view, which is quite different from the contrary view, which postulates that it (world government) is an impossibility and *cannot be intelligently worked for* in the political occupations of men.

This brings us finally to the crucial linkage between this matter of possibility and education. To refer again to the section on Purpose, we may now say that purposes are empty if they do not refer to what is actually *possible* in the ontological frame of the cosmos. In this sense, all purposes — human or natural or divine — must somehow be contingent upon what is deemed possible. And if what is possible is constantly hedged in either by a kind of overriding skepticism of human powers or by a view of the universe as a place where the lines of human action are already laid down and specified (as in the Catholic religion or Marxist ideology, to cite a couple of examples), then it is clear that the educative process must be more dogmatic and doctrinaire, more unyielding in out-look, and more rigidly specific in terms of subject matter.

If, on the other hand, the range of possibilities in the cosmos is considered as practically without limit, and if, moreover, these possibilities are taken to be the occasion for authentic human purposing, then the school program will point them out to youngsters, will excite their interest in testing to see which possibilities should be aspired to, and will attempt to show the young how these finally can be reached. A school program of this sort will obviously exhibit greater flexibility in what it thinks important in the experience of the child and will place greater stress upon the curious and inquisitive tendencies of the young.

CONCLUSION

So we come finally to the technical questions of ontology: What truly occupies the realm of the real? What really exists? These questions are beset, as we have seen, by several procedural hazards. But they are also confounded by the difficulty of assigning strict criteria by which we can separate that which is real and genuinely existential from that which definitely is not, and, in turn, each of these from that which is existentially possible.

As the child is gradually inducted into the world of men, it is inevitable that his mind will increasingly take up the ontological question. His first ontological problem occurs perhaps with the issue of Santa Claus. As adults, we are piqued and amused by the intellectual awakenings that begin to stir in the five- or six-year-old mind. We forget, though, that ontological problems of greater complexity continue to arise in the child's mind throughout his developing years. And even after we reach adult-hood we are wrong if we think there is no more to ask of our metaphysics. For if we mean to take life seriously — not glumly or morbidly, but earnestly and seriously — and if we mean to teach the young as competently as we can, we must continue the ontological quest into those higher questions of God and the human spirit. Not only will examination of these questions help us to recognize the ontological stirrings in the life of the young, but it will, as this chapter has attempted to show, control and govern the quality and character of the educative process itself.

QUESTIONS

1. How would you define the infinitive *to be*?

2. How many different kinds of beings can you name? We have mentioned physical things, symbols, ideas, human selves. Are there any others? In what ways, if any, do all these *exist* differently?

3. Of all the things that make up reality, are there any that are more important than the others? That is, is there a kind of rank-order of existents (beings)? How would you go about defending your list?

4. What difference in ontological outlook would you expect from teachers of different subjects? For instance, would teachers of the physical sciences, the social sciences, the languages, and the humanities necessarily have different views of what ultimate reality is exclusively or primarily made up of?

5. How would you handle the ontological problem of Santa Claus with a young child?

6. In preparation for Chapter Three, set down a brief statement of what you believe to be the character of ultimate reality.

FURTHER READING

Brubacher, John. *Modern Philosophies of Education,* Second Edition. New York: McGraw-Hill Book Co., 1950.
In Chapter II Brubacher discusses the "generic traits of existence" as they are seen by various philosophies: Is reality changing or changeless? Are reality and appearance two different things? Is the world evolving novelly or has everything been planned out in advance? Is there a boundary to time (or space)? What is eternity? An excellent opener for a study of ontology.

Dewey, John. *Experience and Nature.* Chicago: Open Court Publishing Co., 1926.
This is Dewey's magnum opus on what passes for metaphysics. Dewey was never too much concerned with metaphysical questions, because of their opacity when handled in open forum, where all questions, Dewey thought, should be threshed out. But in this book he attempts a "metaphysic of experience." (Special attention should be paid to Chapter II.)

Hook, Sidney. "The Quest for Being," *Journal of Philosophy,* L, No. 24 (November 19, 1953), 709–731.
In this article Professor Hook summarizes the many philosophical attempts to define "Being." Then, in rather technical language, he goes on to declare these attempts futile. He believes with Dewey that "Being" is simply one of those "infinity" words (like "everything," "the world," etc.) we use to stand for the ground of discourse. We can't really say anything about it; we merely assume it, usually unconsciously.

Hoyle, Fred. *The Nature of the Universe.* New York: Harper and Bros., 1950.
For a startlingly novel and refreshingly anti-Genesis theory of creation,
read cosmology according to Hoyle. The universe was not born in a thunder-
ous cataclysm aeons ago, says he; it is being "born" all the time, with the
"continuous creation" of atoms of hydrogen, the virgin element. If so, is
reality then at root merely "variations" on the hydrogen "theme"?

Phenix, Philip H. *Philosophy of Education.* New York: Henry Holt and Co.,
Inc., 1958.
In a book of essays (completely free of footnotes, by the way, in order not to
distract from the ideas themselves) Phenix devotes one essay (Chapter 28) to
"the ultimate nature of things," discussing substance and process, structure
and function, things and events, essence and existence, mind and matter,
nature and supernature. He follows this with a chapter on "cosmic process."

White, Morton G. *Toward Reunion in Philosophy.* Cambridge: Harvard University Press, 1956.
The plan of the present book was inspired, for the most part, by White's
discussion in this volume of the three major questions in philosophy: the
ontological, the epistemological, and the axiological. For an advanced consideration of these areas in so-called pure or academic philosophy (as contrasted with educational philosophy), this is the place to go. In Chapters I-VI
White asks and reviews the answers to the question: "What is?"

CHAPTER THREE

Comparative Ontologies

It is admittedly a long way, both logically and psychologically, from the concerns of ultimate reality to teaching young Joey Doakes in, say, eighth-grade social studies. But eventually, as we have seen in the previous chapter, the way we handle Joey and the material we wish him to know reveals our idea of what we think the world is like. The task of educational philosophy, among other things, is not so much to justify one ontology over another, nor, as a consequence, to justify one teaching practice over another, but quite modestly to try to build a connection in thinking between our ideas of basic reality and our day-to-day procedures in the classroom.

While the possibility of this linkage was examined in Chapter Two, it is now necessary to come more directly to the business of particular ontologies and their implied specifications as to the manner in which boys and girls learn and teachers teach. In order to do this systematically, we will take up in turn five ontologies: Idealism, Realism, Neo-Thomism, Experimentalism, and Existentialism, establishing the main concepts of each and pointing to their educational significance. The history of philosophic thinking is not, of course, quite so neat as we are to present it here. These systems (and the many others) were not established and then put in place as distinct and disparate theories of life. Instead, they grew and developed, like everything else, out of the conditions of the human situation at the time. As such, they represent what different men, living in different places and times, believed to be significant and important in their experience. Viewing these separate theories in this light, we must not expect them to be mutually exclusive in every respect — that is to say, distinct theories which are entirely different from one another. Rather, they are "magnetic poles" of emphasis, around which certain beliefs are collected and made systematically intelligible. This means that some of the theories which we separate for the convenience of study and analysis will often be seen to have a kinship with one another. Or, attacking problems in human experience from different sectors, they will arrive at conclusions which are quite similar, even though expressed in different language. Just to give a brief example, we can point to the idea of "soul" in theological writings as being intellectually close to the idea of "self," particularly as the "self" is defined by Idealists. And when both the theologian and the Idealist philosopher, in the development of their notions of "soul" and "self," construe the idea of "will" in the same way, we should not be too surprised.

With this forewarning not to take these five sections as idea-tight compartments, but as regions on the spectrum of ideas, we may begin to see how different ontologies come into being by the way in which they point to and emphasize different characteristics of human experience.

IDEALISM: A WORLD OF MIND

Plato's Cave

The quickest and most efficient way of coming to understand Idealist ontology is to go directly to the forefather of all Idealists — Plato. In *The Republic,* his major treatise on the ideal state, Plato has given us the famous Allegory of the Cave.[1] Imagine, he suggests, a group of people sitting in a dark cave chained down in such a way that they can look in only one direction, toward the expanse of wall on one side of the cave. Several yards behind them is an open fire providing light, and between the fire and where they are sitting is a raised runway along which figures move, casting their shadows upon the wall. The individuals, chained so that they face the wall, cannot see the fire or the figures, but only the shadows. Now, if we imagine them confined to this position for their entire lives, we must expect them to consider the shadows as real, genuinely existent beings. Not knowing anything else, having no three-dimensional beings to use for comparison, these prisoners in the cave would come to believe that what they saw before them represented true reality.

Now imagine that they are unchained and can turn around to see the fire and the figures which have occasioned the shadows. Certainly, says Plato, they would readjust their conception of reality, altering it to fit the new perceptual data that their eyes are now able to collect. Moving

1 Plato, *The Republic,* Book VII (Steph. 514–518).

about the cave, they begin to get a sense of the three-dimensional character of their environment; and they conclude by thinking that they had been fooled all along, and that now they truly know what reality is.

But then imagine that they are led from the cave into the blinding brilliance of a noonday sun outside. Wouldn't they, asks Plato, be struck dumb by the complete impossibility of it? Wouldn't they turn away in complete bewilderment, not wishing to see the real truth of their world? Wouldn't they gradually retreat to their cave, preferring its more manageable environment to the fantastically incredible world of space and sunlight?

Well, then, suggests the allegory, here we humans are in our own cave — the world as we see it with our five senses. It looks real enough — rocks and trees and birds and men. But it is actually only a world of images, three-dimensional "shadows" of another, more genuinely real world — a world of *pure ideas* — standing "behind" this world we see and hear and touch. And this realm of pure ideas or "pure mind" is so absolute in its perfection, so superlatively complete in every way, as to possess an intensity beyond the reach of the human mind. Like the sun that blinds our eyes, the "Absolute Mind" completely overwhelms our feeble intellects; and we turn away from it, as we turn our eyes from the sun, bedazzled and "injured" by our attempt to perceive it. And so, preferring a more manageable and comfortable existence, even if less genuinely real, we retreat to our "cave," the world of sense perception, permitting our intellects only occasional and fleeting glimpses of ultimate reality.[2]

Figure 2 (opposite) may help you to visualize this "two-world" concept of Plato's. Everything we see in our experience — trees, chairs, books, circles, men — is only a limited and imperfect expression of an underlying idea. Every tree we see is different, but there is an *Idea* of tree-ness which they all share. Chairs we can see and sit in; but what is *really* real is not this chair or that, but the *Idea* of "chair," the idea which actually supports and sustains all the individual objects we call chairs; for without this idea no chair could come into being for us to use. Likewise, men can draw circles, but only imperfect ones; a perfect circle is only an idea in our minds which we try to copy. It is the Idea of circularity which is truly and genuinely real, for it is eternal and unchanging.

An analogy can be drawn with identical trinkets in a toy store — let us say, a shelfful of cast models of the Empire State Building. Each of these toy models is slightly different, showing imperfections of one kind or another. But they all came from the same mold. And it is the mold

---

[2] Like the yogi who finds supreme happiness in worshiping his deity by staring at the sun, man can find his highest being by "staring" at eternal and universal ideas, i.e., by pointing his mind toward the Absolute. Thus, to Plato, the highest form of human existence was the life of pure contemplation.

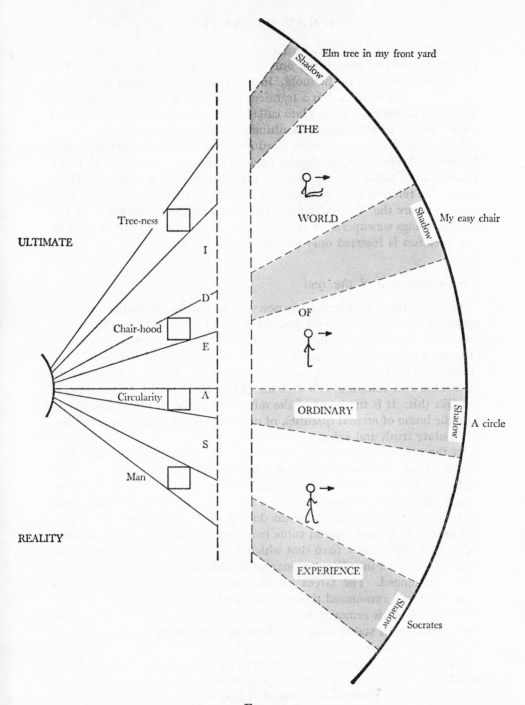

ULTIMATE

Tree-ness

Chair-hood

Circularity

Man

REALITY

I

D

E

A

S

Elm tree in my front yard

Shadow

THE

Shadow

My easy chair

WORLD

OF

ORDINARY

Shadow

A circle

EXPERIENCE

Shadow

Socrates

FIGURE 2

Plato's Two Worlds

which gave them form and meaning. Thus, the mold is the authentic reality; the several models are only limited expressions of the "idea" of the model contained in the mold. In like fashion, everything we see and perceive in this world is but a transient and fleeting replica or "shadow" of eternal qualities — what Plato called "Ideas" — and it is the world of these "Ideas" which constitutes ultimate and absolute reality.

It is from Plato's conception of ultimate Ideas that we get the word *Idealism*. Technically, it should read *Idea-ism,* an ontology of ideas. Plato was not talking about ideals in the sense of valued ends or goals to reach. He referred only to ideas and to the fact that ideas in their ultimate form are the "figures" behind us which cast their "shadows" (in the form of things we experience in our world) on the walls of our cave. The *l* in *Idealism* is inserted only for the sake of euphony.

The apparent and the real

There is, then, in Idealism, a necessity to divide all reality into two major divisions: the apparent and the real. The "apparent" realm is the day-to-day experience we have as mortals. This is the region of change, of coming and going, of being born, growing, aging, and dying; it is the realm of imperfection, irregularity, and disorder; finally, it is the world of trouble and suffering, evil and sin. The "real" world, fortunately, is not like this. It is the home of the mind, the realm of ideas; it is therefore the home of eternal qualities, of permanence, of regularity, of order, of absolute truth and value.

Of the two, quite obviously, the idea-l is of higher rank; not only is it distinct from the world we know directly, but it stands existentially higher. This is because perfection reigns there. Perfect things are those things which do not change; they don't have to. What conceivably could they change to? Since eternal ideas do not change, they represent a perfect order. This fundamental value judgment — that that which is of the mind is of higher rank than that which is of the world of things — is so deeply embedded into Western man's thinking processes that it is almost never challenged. The Greek philosophers more than 2000 years ago formalized and announced this doctrine, and we have believed ever since that that which is removed from this world and eternal is somehow of higher existential status than the world we experience, i.e., the world of change, of growth, of problems and purposes.

We see this bias most tenaciously held to, incidentally, in the field of education. To this day, in most high schools, the subject matter of ideas — literature, for example — is considered by most people to be of higher rank and greater importance than the subject matter of physical things — auto mechanics, for example. Throughout the curriculum there is a kind of established hierarchy of subjects. Toward the top of this hierarchy are the subjects whose content is constituted of ideas and concepts. ✓ These subject matters are, generally speaking, given and settled: mathematics, the languages, and history. In the middle of the list are the sciences, which, though they search for certainty and permanent truth, never seem to reach it because all science by definition is inextricably embedded in the physical world of indeterminacy and change. Finally, at the bottom, are the technical and manual subjects — home economics, wood shop, arts and crafts, and driver training — which are relatively less concerned with the theoretical and conceptual, stressing primarily tactics and techniques.

At the college level the Idealist bias is even more obvious. The liberal arts are thought to be those studies which provide substance for reflection and the liberation of the mind. Necessarily such studies are found among the subjects which are theoretical, abstract, and symbolic in character and which rely upon a great deal of book learning. Anything which is seen to be occupationally useful or applicable to preparation for a profession or a calling is immediately relegated to non-liberal-arts status — as, "pre-med," "pre-law," or "professional training." Thus, whatever is too closely related to the world of action, of change, of making a livelihood, is held of lower rank than that which is relatively abstract (in the best sense of that term) and more remote and insulated from ordinary affairs.

The world as Idea

The Idealists, then, begin their systematic thinking with this fundamental view that ultimate reality is of the nature of mind. There are different varieties of Idealism, and the ontology of Idea is expressed in different ways. But it is enough at this point to establish the root position from which these varying interpretations have historically developed.

Hegel, for instance, went beyond Plato and added the *dynamic* interpretation of Idealism. All reality, said Hegel, is the surging and moving contest between opposites: night and day, cold and hot, up and down, life and death. This "contest of opposites" represents the so-called dialectic of nature — a dialectic re-enacted in human nature also. Ordinary human thought is possible only by virtue of contending ideas competing for attention in our consciousness: love and hate, justice and injustice, individual and society, order and chaos. Indeed, thought Hegel, each of Plato's Ideas has its own antithesis. Hence, Plato's Ideal realm is not just an eternal residence for static ideas, but a moving, flowing stream of conscious intelligence at work in the world. It is, as it were, an Absolute Mind thinking out his world.

Technically, Hegel used the thesis-antithesis-synthesis triad to explain what he meant by this. Every *thesis* (e.g., man is an end in himself) can be set against its *antithesis* (e.g., man cannot be merely an end to himself — he must also live for others). This confrontation of opposites produces a resolution of the issue or *synthesis* (e.g., man fulfills his true end by serving others). The synthesis then becomes a new thesis, to be counterposed with a new antithesis, which, in turn, yields a new synthesis, ad infinitum. (See Figure 3, below.)

This, said Hegel, is the way in which history, for example, can be understood. Concrete events in the past are only particular expressions of much larger and longer-range movements and trends. The American Revolution resulted from a collision of the "thesis" of old-world monarchic authoritarianism and the "antithesis" of colonial libertarianism. The issue was joined and the "synthesis" of the American republic was the result. But almost immediately this synthesis became a new thesis, with Hamilton's Federalists representing a new "antithesis." The

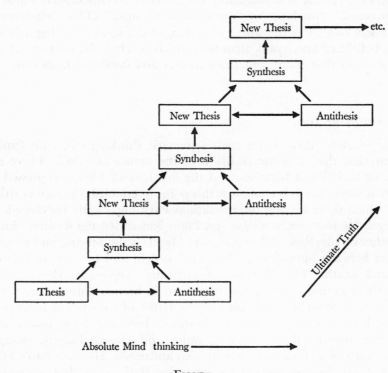

FIGURE 3

Hegel's Dialectic

synthesis eventually came to be the system lying somewhere between Hamiltonianism and Jeffersonianism.

But then this became a new thesis, to be contested by Jacksonianism later in the century. The dialectic continued, to find a new expression in the Civil War; this war subsequently produced a new set of circumstances, which themselves were seen to be in need of change and reform. On and on it goes, but through it all there is, thought Hegel, a Cosmic Idea trying to express itself in the historic events of men and societies; this Cosmic Idea is Ultimate Reality — or, at least, a segment of it — seeking expression in the world of physical reality and constant change. It is, as it were, an idea that is being thought by this Absolute Mind, which led Hegel to say that "History is God thinking." God thinks out his plans and purposes through the instrumentality of human history. He tries things out, waits for the results, weighs the pros and cons (the dialectic) and then tries new combinations (syntheses) to see if they will work even better.

Throughout the process, Ultimate Reality can be glimpsed from time to time by the limited intellectual perceptions of men; sages and prophets, scholars and poets, artists and theologians — all make a business of this attempt to peer into the Absolute. It is as if all men were straining to have the experience reported by Handel after composing *The Messiah* in the concentrated space of twenty-four days in 1741: "I did think I did see all Heaven before me, and the Great God Himself."

REALISM: A WORLD OF THINGS

If Plato is the "Father of Idealism," we can point to his pupil Aristotle as the "Father of Realism." The name *Realism* may strike some kind of ironic note to you; is Realism, you may ask, the only "realistic" philosophy? Does it somehow have a corner on reality, an authentic insight into what is truly real? The answer must, generally speaking, be no. We give the name *Realism* to those theories which find in the world of physical things, and our perceptions and experiences of those things, the basis for an understanding of what is truly real. Realists do not, as Plato did, feel the necessity to flee to some realm of non-sensory qualities to find out what is genuinely real. With this in mind, then, we can begin to understand more in detail what the Realist ontology is.

Aristotle's barehanded interpretation

Aristotle stands at the base of this intellectual structure by virtue both of the supreme simplicity of his approach to the ontological problem and of his extravagant genius in providing an answer to it — an answer, incidentally, which has served to shape the Western mind for over 2000 years and which, in many respects, is still dominant today. Working without microscope or telescope, ignorant of atomic or nuclear physics and concepts of heredity and biological evolution, Aristotle stood bare-handed before an awesome cosmos and asked himself the simple question: What do I see? His answer was the same as any man's would be: I see earth beneath my feet; I see objects — trees, birds, men, houses, a multitude of things — before my eyes; and I see sun and moon and stars high in the heavens.

Now what, to ask the first question, do all of these things have in common? What, that is, can we say of all of them taken together? First, they all seem to be made of something, some stuff which serves as a raw material. We shall call this Matter. Everything, without exception, can be said to be composed of Matter.

But we notice more. We notice that these things can be distinguished one from another; the Matter of which they are made is arranged in different ways, taking on one form in a stone, another in a blade of grass, another in man, still another in sun and moon. Each thing in its own way is different from the next thing; and this difference is occasioned by the particular form or design that the basic stuff, Matter, has assumed in each thing. We shall call this the Principle of Form.

The Form-Matter Hypothesis

Taking these perceptions, Aristotle then exhibited the magnificence of his genius by putting them together into what he called the Form-Matter Hypothesis. We can notice, he said, that looking downward we see the nearest thing to Prime Matter, the earth beneath our feet. This Matter is inchoate, apparently in its virgin state, just there in a brute kind of way and possessing only the minimum of Form. But as we lift our eyes, moving physically upward, we begin to see more and more of the distinguishing element in things; we see plants of different sorts, animals of different kinds; we see men. We notice also that men stand vertically erect and that, as Plato pointed out, as we move physically upward in man from genitals and viscera, the locus of purely animal functions, to heart and breast, the locus of the higher virtues of courage and valor, to head, the locus of the highest virtues of reason and thought, we can see a gradual reduction of the principle of Matter (Body) and a gradual increase in the principle of Form (Mind). Finally, as we leave Man and cast our eyes upward into the heavens, we see even less Matter, only points of light moving in regularly patterned and mathematically precise ways, which to Aristotle represented a more nearly pure expression of the principle of Form.

What we can actually see and perceive in our own experience Aristotle then put into a logical system. Matter, standing at the base of all things, became for him the Principle of Potentiality: Matter can become any thing; it can be shaped and organized into any kind of being; and without it no *thing* is possible. However, Matter cannot alone achieve thinghood; by itself, it is nothing; to become anything it requires the stamp of Form. That is, Matter has to assume the shape and form of some particular thing before it can actualize its potentiality. Hence, to Aristotle, Form was the Principle of Actuality. Each Principle — Matter and Form — must be considered logically separate; they are two different concepts. But they are never found separately in our experience; necessarily, they are always found associated in the things which constitute the cosmos.

We can visualize this Aristotelian system by means of a pyramidal arrangement of ideas. (See Figure 4, page 56.) At the base of the ontological pyramid is Matter, representing pure possibility; alone it is nothing, but it serves as the ingredient of potentiality, from which all things are made. As we rise in the pyramid, we see Matter assuming more and more Form (more varieties of distinguishable entities, more complex organizations of Matter in living organisms, and more evidence of immaterial qualities, such as sensation, thought, and, eventually, pure contemplation). As we rise in this system, the operations of order, pattern, regularity, and perfection — in short, the attributes of Mind and Reason — become increasingly noticeable, until ultimately there emerges Pure Mind, Absolute Reason, or, as Aristotle called it, Pure Form. As men, we can never hope to know or understand this apex of the pyramid; but we can, by logical extension, comprehend its role: It is the Principle of Reason, "knowing and ruling all the categories of nature. [Here is] the great First Cause, the Prime Mover, the Absolute Knower, independent of the world, but acting upon it and endowing it with movement, development, order, and reason."[3] It is as if an enormous ontological magnet — the magnet of Actuality — were drawing all lesser potentialities toward it.

Plato and Aristotle

By this stroke of genius, therefore, Aristotle put back together a world which Plato had rent asunder. There are not two separate realities, one

[3] Edward H. Reisner, "Philosophy and Science in the Western World: A Historical Overview," Chapter I in *Philosophies of Education,* Forty-first Yearbook of the National Society for the Study of Education, ed. N. B. Henry, Part I (Chicago: the Society, 1942), p. 12.

of ideas and another of sense, with one higher than the other, as Plato said; there is only one reality, a hierarchy of things stretching in both directions between the ground of potentiality and the pinnacle of actuality. We ourselves stand somewhere in the middle of the ontological spectrum, sharing through our bodies in the materiality of things but participating through our minds — at a very modest level, to be sure — in the rationality of Pure Form. Though we cannot ever directly know Pure Form, because of its infinite distance from us along the dimension of reality, we must logically recognize that it is truly there, governing all things and endowing the cosmos with rational meaning.

Through the master stroke of the Form-Matter Hypothesis Aristotle helped to redirect the attention of Greek metaphysics to the world we actually live in. What to Plato was an illusory world of shadows (which he dismissed in favor of a real world of Ideas) became for Aristotle the real world itself: hence, the simple designation of *Realism* for the view

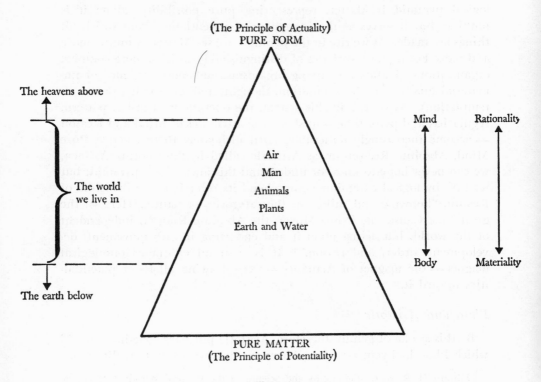

FIGURE 4

Aristotle's Form-Matter Hypothesis

that the world we experience is not some dim copy of reality but indeed the real thing.

At this point it is necessary to make clear something that will be increasingly bothersome in the chapters ahead: Sometimes philosophers' theories get worked over by succeeding generations of thinkers and are thus extended and improved. This is the case with Neo-Thomism, which has perpetuated Aristotelian metaphysics and extended it to a more sophisticated level of analysis. We shall take up this ontology of Neo-Thomism in the next section. At other times, however, a theorist's ideas are taken only as points of departure; and succeeding generations carry them so far along the road of intellectual development as to turn the original ideas into whole new theories, even while expressing their indebtedness to those ideas, which theirs no longer resemble. In a manner of speaking, this is what has happened to Realism. Over the last 2000 years Realism has come to take on quite a different meaning in men's minds. It is to this modern version we now turn.

Scientific Realism

What Aristotle fundamentally did for metaphysics, as noted above, was to direct attention to the world we actually experience, turning away from the tendency to concoct other worlds presumably more real than the one we wake up to every day. With the actual, three-dimensional world confronting us, what can we say about it in an ontological way? Without complicating the issue with the Form-Matter theory, we can return to the simple, primitive approach that Aristotle used. Using this method we can say, first of all, that the world is made up of (among other things) matter. This matter is constantly undergoing changes — physical, chemical, biological. It is more turbulent in structure than Aristotle thought — the molecules, electrons, neutrinos, and other particles of which it is composed are themselves in motion; but it is matter nonetheless. So the scientific realist has chosen to describe the physical world as "matter in motion."

Now, this motion of matter is what concerns the scientist; he tries in experimental situations to observe the many changes in the position and state of matter, so as to make certain generalizations. When he gets hold of a generalization which encompasses a fairly wide range of observed phenomena he calls it a "law." And if repeated experiments and the passage of years continue to confirm his findings, the original generalization is taken to be a "Law of Nature" (Newton's Law of Gravitation, for instance).

The Realist is of the view that the physical world we live in is the basic reality, and that its component elements all move and behave according to fixed natural laws. We do not know all these laws, but we discover them year by year through the instrumentality of science. It is for this reason that the Realist likens his cosmos to an enormous machine. A good analogue is the internal-combustion engine in an automobile. When it is running, physical and chemical changes are taking place constantly inside it. Levers, wheels, gears, electrical impulses, explosions, and the rushing of various gases here and there all combine to present what would be to an uninformed spectator a most delirious and bewildering confusion. But if our visitor chose to stay awhile and chart and plot the movements and changes he witnessed, he would soon begin to make some sense out of them. If he were particularly diligent, he could begin to generalize on what he saw and even arrive at certain "laws" apparently controlling the movements of the engine.

What is man, then, says the Realist, but a tiny spectator of an enormous machine, the cosmos? He stands before it as a flea before a UNIVAC electronic computer, but with one advantage: intelligence. Gradually, piece by piece, he can come to a wider and fuller understanding of his world. And this is made possible by the fact that this world, like any machine, is not a haphazard, fortuitous collection of atoms and molecules, but a structure built according to plan and endowed (as is the automobile engine) with predetermined and necessary movements. The task of the scientist, then, is literally *dis-covery*, taking the "cover" from a cosmos already in operation and quite independent of human understanding of it.

Man is the spectator of a running machine. When his observations become purposeful and controlled, then in that measure he becomes scientific.[4] When regularities are observed in this machine — in living organisms, in chemical changes, in physical phenomena — and when the scientist can set them down in unequivocal language, then we say science has made another discovery.

In the extended interpretations of this ontology it is asserted further that the objective machine of reality controls affairs even beyond the physical sciences. In human affairs, as in atomic affairs, there is a Rule of Law which is built directly into nature. When John Locke spoke of "the natural rights of man" he was talking about human rights that are embedded within the very texture of reality. And when Jefferson asserted that rights are "inalienable" he simply meant that alienating them is not unlike defying a law of nature. When Adam Smith spoke of "economic law" he was referring to the laws which he discovered operating in

4 This conception of what it means to be scientific is quite at variance with the view held by the Experimentalists, whose ontological position — both an outgrowth of and a departure from Realist ontology — we shall examine later in the chapter.

human nature but lying beyond the reach of human control, except through direct interference. What he did, of course, was to lay down an economic theory which would have us submit to these necessities of nature, thereby maximizing the welfare of all. Finally, in the field of ethics, some theistic variants of Realism hold to a *moral* law which operates in nature. Fundamentalist Protestant theology may be said to contain a good deal of this element. These laws of conduct and judgment — the Decalogue, for instance — control our lives absolutely. They can no more be violated than the law of gravity.

You will begin to notice the frequency with which the words "nature" and "natural" intrude into discussions of Realism. All varieties of naturalism — all the theories holding that nature is at the center of things — are blood kin of Realism, for they all posit a reality which can be witnessed, at least in part, through our own human experience, and they all hold to a fixed, orderly, and regular cosmic process which is the ground for human knowing.

This, then, is the Realist ontology: a world of things in motion, an enormous mechanism endowed with pattern, order, and harmonious movement.

NEO–THOMISM:
A WORLD OF BEING

Neo-Thomism is named for St. Thomas Aquinas, the famed "Angelic Doctor" of the thirteenth-century Schoolmen. It is *Neo* in the sense that St. Thomas' view of the cosmos has been updated to the twentieth century, made compatible with science, and yet been held consistent and true to the original insights formulated by this master metaphysician 700 years ago. In order to understand the "Neo" variety, however, we must obviously understand St. Thomas first. And in order to do this we must retreat still further, to the origins of his thought in Aristotle.

Aristotle revisited

In the preceding section we saw that Aristotle's metaphysics, because it directed attention to this world of things, gave rise to views which are generally subsumed under the heading of Realism. We want now to single out another feature of Aristotelian thought — the logical union of *potentiality* and *actuality* — and to show how St. Thomas advanced this to a higher level of interpretation.

You will recall that for Aristotle Matter was the Principle of Potentiality: capable of becoming nothing by itself, yet persisting as the basic stuff out of which all things are made. Form, the actualizing force, when joined with Matter brought material substance into the status of a recognizable "thing." Hence, Form was considered the Principle of Actuality. Now, when a thing is produced from the union of Form and Matter, we witness another logical phenomenon: This thing can be differentiated and distinguished from all other things; that is to say, it assumes a quality and character all its own. It gathers to itself an absolute identity. This identity Aristotle called *essence*. So, when Aristotle asked himself what do all things have in common, when he inquired what could be said of all things he saw in his world, he could respond very simply that they all represented one or another coming together of Form and Matter, i.e., they all were possessed of an essence. The essence of any thing is its basic "what-ness" (what the technical philosopher sometimes calls *quiddity*, from the Latin *quid — what*). And it is this root "what-ness" of things that Aristotle was in search of in his metaphysics.

One of the simplest illustrations of this concept lies in the question: What is man? The answer: Man is a rational animal. Within the predicate of this sentence, according to Greek philosophy, is the fundamental "what-ness" of a human being. Aristotle's "essence," it may be noted, was an improvement on Plato's "idea" precisely because it included the familiar ingredients of our own experience; it brought reality much more "within reach," so to speak. That is, whereas Plato divided all things into two worlds — the one ideal, and therefore real, the other sensory, shadow-like, and therefore unreal — Aristotle connected everything together and showed that Ideas (Forms) joined with sensory "shadows" (Matter) in a logical way: not two worlds, one of them out of reach, but one world, distributed along a logical continuum and eventually knowable by reason.

St. Augustine and the Christian message

Something like 1500 years elapsed from Aristotle's primary insights to St. Thomas' adaptation of them into a more refined metaphysics. During much of this time Aristotle's thought was unknown to most of Europe; his works had been lost and forgotten and his ideas had passed from currency. Moreover, in the meantime Jesus had come to the world. Whatever people might have remembered of Aristotle's complicated thinking would very likely have been forgotten under the compelling appeal of the simple but spectacular Christian message.

St. Augustine, for example, writing as early as the fifth century, had probably never heard of Aristotle. The first in a long line of systematic Christian theologians, Augustine attempted to organize Jesus' message into an ordered religious philosophy. The world that he saw was quite a different place from Aristotle's; it was a cosmos of compassion and love as well as truth and reason. Speaking metaphysically, the matter-of-fact, objective, and mathematically neat cosmic designs of Plato and Aristotle gave way to a world with a person — the Godhead — in it to make it all credible. There was no warmth, no "personality" to Plato's and Aristotle's world. It was just there, exacting of men a compliance of necessity rather than duty. To Augustine, however, who was perhaps fortunate in *not* having had this metaphysical tradition to build upon, the world was a place of warmth and love; a place where men are not merely "rational animals" but spiritual creatures — creations of a divinely inspired act, possessed of a direct linkage to the Absolute.

Down through the centuries, St. Augustine's vision seemed adequate enough as the intellectual rationale for Christianity. But in the tenth century some long-lost manuscripts of Aristotle were found. Avicenna in the tenth century and Averroës in the twelfth century (two Arabian physicians and philosophers) rediscovered Aristotle for the world. As they worked along, translating and interpreting these writings, it soon became evident that Aristotle's God-less metaphysics was incompatible with — indeed, downright hostile to — the Christian Church. But the more men came to understand Aristotle, the more the logic and beauty of his thinking took hold of the Western mind. Finally it became obvious that a rapprochement between the two must be found. This task eventually fell to St. Thomas Aquinas.

With St. Thomas to higher ground

It was possible, thought St. Thomas, to have a world of both mathematical symmetry and God's love at the same time. Though he began by accepting the major outlines of Aristotelian metaphysics, he was primarily fascinated by the notion of Potentiality and Actuality. He proposed to show how this concept could be advanced to a new and higher level of intellectual analysis.

In its simplest terms, the problem once again reverted to the question posed by Aristotle: What is it that we can say of everything in the world? What do all things hold in common? We have seen that Aristotle's answer was that every *thing* has its own peculiar "what-ness" or essence. But, said St. Thomas, this is not the most fundamental answer one can give. I am, he said, not so much interested in *what* things are as I am in the fact *that* they are! How is it that things even exist? The problem of "essence" is really a secondary problem; our inquiry into *what* things are will have to wait upon our understanding of what it means for things *to exist.* The root ingredient of all things is existence — the act of *be-ing.*[5]

With this master leap St. Thomas, in a manner of speaking, mounted Aristotle's intellectual shoulders. Caught within the curiosities of "essence," Aristotle never reached the more primary question of "existence." But he provided the logical structure for St. Thomas' work on it, i.e., the companion Principles of Potentiality and Actuality (see Figure 5, opposite).

Essence, to St. Thomas, was the Principle of Potentiality. Essences, by themselves, are nothing; they require the act of existing before they actualize themselves. There can be, let us say, the essence of man—"rational animal." But without the act of existence this essence remains in the limbo of possibility only. Like Matter in Aristotelian thinking, the essence of man would continue to be just essence, nothing more. But when joined with Existence, the Principle of Actuality, the essence of man completes itself. Real men, complete with existence and essence, come into being.

In like manner, Existence, the Principle of Actuality, depends upon Essence; that is, Existence must have some "stuff" to endow with being. Like Form in Aristotle's system, it requires an object on which to lay its powers; and this object is Essence. Existence, like Aristotelian Form, is pure principle; and as principle it is ontologically of higher rank than Essence. Just as Form outranks Matter as the higher principle in Aristotle's thought, so does Existence outrank Essence as the higher principle in Aquinas'.

Now, if we press further with the Aristotelian analogue, we can see, says St. Thomas, a hierarchy not only of Matter and Form but the ultimate hierarchy of Essence and Existence. There are, as it were, different categories of existence, in which essences exercise the act of "to be" in different degrees. Just as Aristotle held that some Matter possessed more Form than other Matter, so Aquinas tells us that some essences possess more existence than other essences. This is because all beings are contingent: They depend for their existence on something else; they are not responsible for their own being. But they are dependent in varying degrees. Though some essences in receiving the act of "to be" actually receive more *being* than other essences, they are all, said Aquinas, limited expressions of the Principle of Existence. But the limitations themselves are distributed in an uneven and hierarchical fashion. Thus, a stone,

[5] In his famous little essay *On Being and Essence*, St. Thomas says, ". . . every essence or quiddity can be understood without anything being known of its existing. I can know what a man or a phoenix is and still be ignorant whether it exists in reality. From this it is clear that the act of existing is other than essence or quiddity, unless, perhaps, there is a being whose quiddity is its very act of existing." (St. Thomas Aquinas, *On Being and Essence* [Toronto: The Pontifical Institute of Medieval Studies, 1949], p. 46.) As we shall see in a few pages, it turns out that there indeed is such a being.

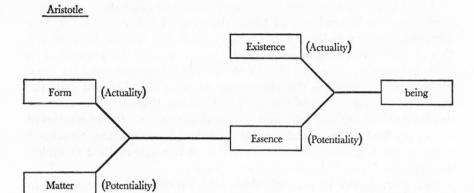

FIGURE 5

St. Thomas' Adaptation of
Aristotle's Potentiality and Actuality Principles

for instance, is the most contingent of all beings; it represents an essence existing, but it claims the least responsibility for its own being. On up the scale to plants, animals, and men, we see an increasing participation in the act of existing, an increasing share in the responsibility for one's own being. It is as if the limitations on existing are gradually removed, and a higher and higher expression of being is attained.

Even men, though, are not completely responsible for their own being, not free of limitation. Higher in rank still are the angels, who are, among other things, relieved of the limitations imposed by corporeal existence. Finally, at the top of the hierarchy is Pure Being, the Being in whom the principle of Existence reaches its absolute expression. Here, Essence and Existence are no longer divided; they are one. For it is the *essence* of this Being *to exist*. At last, the ultimate source of all existence is reached. We can designate this pinnacle with the name "Being" (using the capital *B*). It is not a principle, or a concept, or an idea, or a notion. It is above all these, for it is an immediate apprehension of the human intellect relying upon nothing in our sensory experience for intelligibility.

So, asks St. Thomas, where are we? We are at God. We have arrived at the Godhead via the intellectual route. For God and Being are one and the same. What our faith has already given us, our reason now confirms. For God is the source and origin of all being, the ultimate union of "what-ness" and "is-ness," whose very essence is simply *to be*. When Moses called up to God and asked his name, the reply was: "I am who am."

The Neo-Thomist

Since St. Thomas, of course, the world has witnessed the arrival of a whole new intellectual way of life — the Way of Science. To the Neo-Thomist, however, Science is but a new and rather spectacular exploitation of a relatively limited sector of the logical system, the sector dealing with Aristotelian essences. One of the primary approaches to the comprehension of essence is the observation of what the Thomist calls the attributes and properties of things. The function of science is to organize its observations methodically and systematically so that the properties of things can lead us to an understanding of their inner essence. So science is not so much a new world of the mind as it is a new method of understanding the inner "what-ness" of our universe.

Moreover, science increasingly deals with process and movement — in biology, physics, cosmology. This movement, this dynamic quality of the cosmos, is but a confirmation of the "becoming-ness" of the Potentiality-Actuality Principle. Things move and change and "become" in our experience, not only upward from Matter to Form but also upward from lower to higher expressions of being. Science is dealing with the cosmos at the Aristotelian level of essence. By the limitations of its own methods, science simply cannot reach into the genuinely metaphysical problems of being. Science really has nothing to say about these matters, and never will.

Teleology

The single most important concept in Neo-Thomist ontology for education is, of course, the Potentiality-Actuality Principle. An idea such as this is called teleological. By *teleology* the philosopher refers to any belief which holds that the universe as a whole or man within it is moving toward some prescribed culmination or destiny. The most primitive types of teleology hold either that the world is coming to an end or that it is evolving toward an ultimate union with God; the latter type is characteristic of most systematic religions, especially in regard to human destiny. The underlying idea of every teleology is that the *end* is implicit in the *process,* that the end point of the process is either known or knowable before it is reached, and, therefore, that the process itself can be understood only in terms of its end point.

Thomism posits a process whose destined fulfillment is Absolute Being; hence we speak of Thomism as a teleological doctrine. Plato's Idealism was a static doctrine of two worlds not proceeding to any end but merely existing; hence teleology could not be ascribed to Plato. Hegel's Idealism, however (see pages 51–53), represents a dialectical movement to an ever higher order of synthesis. It is presumed in Hegel that there is an absolute synthesis toward which all dialectic propends. Metaphorically, we might speak of such a synthesis as the state in which God, having thought out all his ideas through history, now sits back in sweet and final repose. In this light, Hegelian Idealism may be called teleological.

In the case of Realism, Realistic mechanism (see pages 57–59) may or may not be teleological. If the "machine" is "going somewhere," if its motions and changes are oriented toward a predestined outcome, then it is teleologic. If, however, the "machine" is just running, without terminal orientation, then it is not teleologic. It is this latter brand of Realism which serves as the "jumping-off place" for Experimentalist ontology, which we shall take up in the next section.

The main virtue of teleologic ontologies in educational thinking is their claim to greater certainty as to what men are tending to become, and hence as to how we can be helped to learn and grow in the fulfillment of this necessary destiny. Or, put another way, if we know the end of man then we know the end of the child. And if we know the end of the child it is a much simpler matter deciding upon what he should be taught and how to go about doing it. In the absence of such ultimate knowledge, say the teleologists, education — or any other significant human activity — is chaotic and aimless.

The "cooperative arts" theory of education (see pages 3–5) is a good example of a teleological theory of education. The end of man is given in his rational nature; his "end" is the attainment of Reason. As we shall see in later chapters, this theory leads quite appropriately to both a curricular program of studies providing mental discipline and a methodology of teaching emphasizing the exercise of the child's rational faculties. Or, man's fulfillment might be held to be ultimate union with God. Under the aegis of this doctrine, a school curriculum should contain studies, exercises, and rituals designed to assist man toward this union. Both of these positions grow directly out of the *a priori*[6] definition of the end of man, and both of these views, it may be noted, are firmly rooted in Aristotelian and Thomistic thinking.

The primary difficulty with teleologies, however, is the problem of agreeing upon the foreordained end. We must be absolutely certain that we have selected the true end; otherwise we risk working at cross-purposes with the specific fulfillment of man which the cosmos truly intends. But

6 The term *a priori* is an important one in philosophy and will occur frequently in this book. It refers literally to that which is prior, that which is antecedent, that which is already given. Thus, an *a priori* definition of the end of man is a definition which was prior to and therefore independent of man's actual coming into the world. Teleologies generally hold to *a priori* principles; that is, they hold that the end of a process is already given before the process itself takes place.

whether the human intellect is capable of fathoming the ultimate questions of the cosmos is still, to put it mildly, an open question. The fact that there are today so many competing views of "the true end of man" — just as there are multiple and competing theologies — would seem to call for the greatest diligence in considering the whole matter. More fundamentally troublesome is the fact that every "closed-end," teleological system has the ultimate effect of compromising man's freedom — his freedom to control his own evolution along paths of his own choosing. Generally speaking, the "open-end," nonteleologic outlook of science leaves man this privilege; teleologies, almost by definition, tend to hedge it in. But these problems we must leave until later.

We turn now to two "open-end" ontologies: Experimentalism and Existentialism.

EXPERIMENTALISM:
A WORLD OF EXPERIENCE

Experimentalism, as a formal and systematic philosophy, is less than 100 years old — a youngster as philosophies go. Following upon so illustrious a history of philosophic thinking, it has found itself concerned primarily with the negative side of fundamental thought, i.e., with denying and standing opposed to earlier views. While the twentieth century has seen Experimentalism move to somewhat more positive ground, it is imperative that we first understand what this philosophy rejects before we see what it affirms.

One of the ways to do this is to return to Plato's Cave. Like it or not, says the Experimentalist, the cave is all we have. The world we live in — the world of sensation, of change, of growth and death, of joy and misfortune, of trouble and misery, of problems and their solutions — is the only world we can intelligently manage in human discourse. The difficulty with all other worlds, says the Experimentalist, is that there are so many of them: The Platonist has his realm of Ideas, the Aristotelian has his Pure Form, the theologian has his Heaven, the mystic has his "inner sanctum of the soul," and the crackpot or lunatic has his own, very special idea of the Ultimate. Which of these interpretations of the "other," presumably more real or higher world are we to accept?

Other worlds may be fine for idle dreaming; they may serve as the stuff of vision and imagination; they may even help us see what we want to do and be in this life, what we want to make of our temporal circumstances here on this earth. But they are so unreliable and so variable in content as to be almost completely unmanageable in human thought. What is more, these "other worlds" are contaminated by a strange bias: They are always seen to be not only separate and removed from the world we actually live in but also *better than* this world. But, in the strictest interpretation of metaphysics, there is no necessary reason why this world we live our days in should be thought inferior to true reality. Perhaps, says the Experimentalist, true reality is something like what we have right here in front of us — oak trees and doorknobs, mothers-in-law and ice cream, sunsets and war, love and hurricanes. The whole thing, just as we experience it, is the way it *really* is.

We saw in the previous section that Realism in its nonteleological frame (i.e., having no culminating end point) may be considered the general region in which Experimentalist ontology has developed. It is important at this point to see that the world just as we find it, the world of mechanical regularity and also of unmechanical unpredictability, is the world that the Experimentalist starts with. John Childs, a leading contemporary Experimentalist, has put the issue this way:

> . . . the divisions between the natural and the supernatural, the real and the ideal, reality and appearance, subject and object, mind and body, thought and activity, all seem to many to be obviously natural dualisms. Our moral bias also makes it "natural" to believe that in the last analysis the good is the permanent and real, while the evil is transient and illusory. Thus it comes also to be a matter of mere "common sense" to perceive that confusion, ambiguity, uncertainty, and indeterminateness have their exclusive locus in man, and that nature is without any such irregularities, for nature is an orderly, fixed, and rational system. In other words, it becomes "natural" for us to think that things actually are not what they are experienced to be. Experience is good enough for managing everyday affairs, but if we desire to get a description of things as they really are, we must resort to something other than the common things of ordinary experience.
>
> At this point the experimentalist enters his objection. He asserts unqualifiedly that experience is all that we have or can ever hope to have. It is "the ultimate universe of discourse." In more homely language, "it is anything that anybody can talk about." As such it has the first word and the last word. Experience "sets our problems," and it "tests our solutions." Hence, if human experience cannot give us an adequate account of realities, then man has no possibility of gaining such an account.[7]

Naïve Realism

The position Childs takes in this passage is a variant of what is called

---

7 John L. Childs, *Education and the Philosophy of Experimentalism* (New York: The Century Co., 1931), pp. 50–51 (in Chapter III, "Has Experimentalism a Metaphysics?"). By permission of Appleton-Century-Crofts, Inc.

Naïve Realism.[8] Naïveté can be damaging in social situations, but in ontology it can be the greatest of virtues. In this context, it simply refers to an artless, guileless, and uncomplicated straightforwardness in telling the truth about what one sees in his world. What troubles the Experimentalist so much is the tendency among other philosophers — most particularly, Platonists, Aristotelians, and Thomists — to elaborate and sophisticate their primary conceptions with a superstructure of metaphysical presumption. In each of these positions, what is directly experienced in ordinary affairs has been extracted, extended, elaborated, and finally worked up into a systematic blueprint for all reality, a reality which nobody ever meets. When the Experimentalist refers to experience as the ultimate ground of human discourse, he means simply that experience — ordinary human experience, day by day — is where all thinking begins, and we must return constantly to ordinary experience to see if what we say of our world is actually true. We may invent ideas in our heads — whole ontologies, as we have seen — which go beyond the primary data of our experience; but we do so, says the Experimentalist, at the great peril of concocting false doctrines — doctrines which, precisely because they are imagined or intellectually "spun out" rather than directly experienced, cannot be checked for accuracy by other people.

For all its trouble and cussedness, this reality we wake up to every morning has one spectacular advantage over all other realities: It is open to the public — that is, whatever one may claim he sees here can be looked for by another; it can be, in the idiom of the warehouseman, "checked out." And if it fails to "check out" over repeated trials, then we can afford to forget it. If repeated trials confirm it, then we seek to work it into our previous knowledge. But the nobility of this ontology is its *public* character. There is no exclusiveness, no "country club" of saints and prophets who will explain to the rest of us how our world is built and what kinds of things it makes possible.

Experience

With the initial overview in mind, we must now begin to refine the meaning of this ontology. The key word is, of course, *experience*. But we must be cautious not to place too narrow an interpretation on it. It is not restricted, as the above might suggest, to sense experience only. It includes all that men do, and think, and feel. It includes quiet reflection as well as active doing, "feeling" as well as knowing, speculating as well as seeing and touching. What it does *not* include is a transformation of these quite ordinary experiences into the transempirical (beyond-experi-

8 For the purposes of this analysis Naïve Realism shall be defined as the view that reality is simply what we experience it to be.

ence) components of reality, which are intellectually out of reach and supposedly of higher ontological rank than the experiences themselves.

Figure 6 (see page 70), an adaptation of the Platonic Cave idea in Figure 2 (see page 49), will help to visualize the Experimentalist ontological position. We will take our world as we find it, heartache and happiness together. Call it a "cave" if you will; it becomes whatever you make it. The world-as-cave is for the faint of heart, those who think this world is not enough, who believe that they deserve better than this and expect to find it "outside" somewhere. The Experimentalist is much more positive of mind; he finds this world quite enough for the fulfillment of human purposes. Besides, what lies beyond is unknowable. We need assert neither that such a transempirical realm *does* exist nor that it *does not;* we are unable to say anything about it because we can never know it; and we cannot know it because we cannot experience it.

What we most definitely *do* experience is this world; and it is in this world, the Experimentalist maintains, that Reality is to be found. As we have noted, the Realist's world — the objective entity, the "mobile thing," the machine "out there" waiting to be found out about by human spectators — is very close to Experimentalist thinking. But even this, insists the Experimentalist, is saying too much, going too far beyond our primary data. For, says the Experimentalist, the designation we give to this "mobile thing," what we say it is, is itself the product of our experience of "it." "It" (the real world), therefore, cannot be certainly known. "It" must always be understood through the medium of human experience. What we say is true of the real world is only what our experience indicates is plausible to say about it.

So, therefore, not only is the transempirical realm out of reach and unknowable, but the real world of the Realist is out of reach — just barely, but, nevertheless, quite necessarily out of reach — and ultimately unknowable. We are forced, says the Experimentalist, to tear away the rind of all outer realities — the realities that come to us through traditional system-building and those that point to a physical reality we can directly perceive — and retreat to the virgin stuff of reality: *human experience in its raw form.*

This is never very easy to do. To most of us the world of the Realist is so clearly out there; we can see it; and it seems to persist and exist without our aid. Common sense dictates that the real world must exist in its own right. But the Experimentalist is adamant. The real world, when all is said and done, he says, is what human beings say it is; and they have nothing to go on except this thing called experience.

The "real" world, we are reminded, used to be flat; it also used to be at the center of the universe; before Darwin it was a closed cycle of organic forms. Today the "real" world is quite a different place: It is round, now but a minor planet in a speck of the universe, and evolving in all kinds of ways. If the real world is so existentially "out there," why do we have so much difficulty in locating it? But, you may say, we find out new things about it all the time; we can make mistakes about reality, but we correct them with closer inquiry. To which the Experimentalist returns to his ultimate position: It is our *inquiry,* he says, rather than the "real" world, which is the author of genuine and authentic reality. And

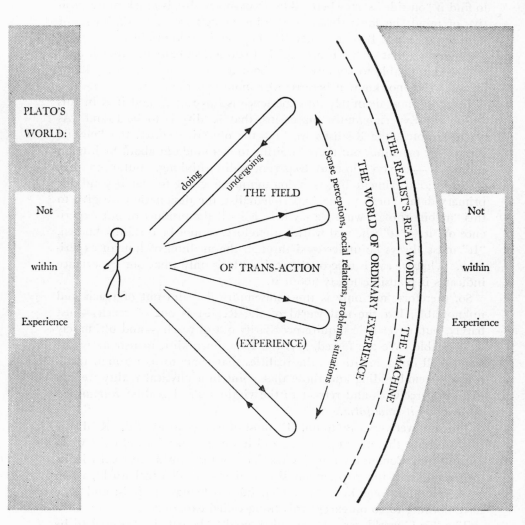

FIGURE 6

The Experimentalist Ontology

inquiry is but a name for systemized and regulated experience. In short, our *conception* of reality, resulting from careful inquiry, is as close to reality as we can ever hope to get. Let us call *it* reality and be done.

Transaction

The technical name the Experimentalist gives to this process of inquiry is *transaction,* a word first applied to philosophy by John Dewey (see Figure 6, opposite). Controlled experience, said Dewey, is in the nature of a "trans-action," a two-way movement of phenomena between ourselves and this reality we can never know directly. We do things to the world, we act upon it, and then it responds, it acts upon us. We dam a stream and nature "answers back" with water power; we bring together two masses of uranium and nature replies with an explosion; we educate a child and nature responds with certain changes in behavior. In Dewey's language, we *do* things to the world; and then we undergo the consequences. Gradually, man comes to associate his doing with the consequences; this is what we call "intelligence." As we civilize ourselves — as we come to see more and more sophisticated connections between our doing and our undergoing (the consequences provided by the response of our reality) — we grow in intelligence. The development of this power to see connections between what we do and what we undergo is, to the Experimentalist, what education is all about. It is to these concerns that we shall turn in Chapter Four.

We may summarize Experimentalist ontology by saying that if we must have an ontology, let us name it Experience. Experimentalists, however, do not as a rule concern themselves with ontology; they are, as theorists, much more interested in the problems of knowing and conduct, the branches of theory which we shall cover later in the chapters on epistemology and axiology. Experimentalism declines engagement in metaphysical conversation on the grounds of the private and therefore highly variable character of metaphysical conceptions. As we have noted before, an Experimentalist would be inclined to the view that one man's metaphysics is as good as another's. Furthermore, he contends, Reality is not something one can talk about. Either it is a kind of "given" (Dewey called it a "taken") assumption we all make about our world but do not discuss or it is, as the Experimentalist sometimes says, a "surd" — analogous to an "irrational number" in mathematics ($\sqrt{3}$ or pi), which is rationally *approachable* but not rationally *soluble*. Reality never, as it were, "comes out even." Its final closure, i.e., our final understanding of it, always seems to elude the human intellect.

Therefore, says the Experimentalist, let us turn our minds and energies to more dependable ground; let us turn to the next best thing, the ground of experience. For it is in experience that human lives are actually lived; and it is by experience that we determine both what "reality" requires of us and what this "reality" makes possible. Since we can never really know "it," let us turn to the study of how to *manage* "it."

Process

This points to one final reason why Experimentalists are not overly fascinated with ontological discussions. Their ontology, unlike the traditional ontologies, is an ontology of *process* rather than of a substantive "something." Idealists, Realists, and Thomists all, for the most part, view reality as a *thing* — either material or immaterial. *Reality,* according to these outlooks, is a name we give to a substantive. It is a *noun.* But to an Experimentalist, reality is a process: Experience. And as process Experience is better likened to an activity, a moving, flowing event, than to a substantive thing. Reality is more like a *verb.*

It is very difficult to discuss reality-as-verb with language that has, for more than 2000 years, been shaped to the notion of reality-as-noun. The very structure of our sentences — subjects and predicates — directs our thought. We state a subject, a substantive of some kind, and then we attach a predicate, a description or action of the subject. But when we utter the subject — the substantive — we are actually *assuming* the existential status of it, nothing more. And our predicates are merely appendages of these existentially tenuous assumptions called subjects.

To traditional philosophies, reality is all subject;[9] to Experimentalism it is all predicate. Western languages, for the most part, give greater emphasis to and are controlled by subjects. If we could invent a language oriented more to predicates, we could, say the Experimentalists, then begin to engage in intelligent discourse on the subject of ontology. Until then we shall speak with nouns that have the quality of verbs to them, e.g., *doing, undergoing, action, transaction,* and, the most important of all to educators, *problem-solving.* These kinds of nouns are about as close as we can get to reality, our language being what it is.

Taken all together, they describe what we call experience, the dynamic, "trans-actional" ebb and flow of human living. This ebb and flow of doing and undergoing has no particular pattern or rhythm to it; and a great deal of it is unreflective, i.e., it passes us by without our thinking about it. As Dewey put it, experience is simply "had." But we can introduce pattern and rhythm into experience by becoming reflective, by taking special pains to *do* under controlled conditions and then to

[9] The Thomists would argue this, saying that in their "being" (substantive) and "to be" (verb) they have found the ultimate union of subject and predicate.

undergo with our eyes open, so we can report what happens. This is what we call "science." It is also what we call "inquiry." In its most general form, it is what we call reflective thinking. And it is reflective thinking which the Experimentalist means to develop in human beings in the school.

The principal feature of this ontology, as we have said, is its "open-end" quality — reality can change! And so it does, down through the ages, because man's experience changes. It is also noteworthy as an ontology because it is oriented to man. The ancient Greek dictum, "Man is the measure of all things," is here reaffirmed in an almost literal sense. As an ontology it is important to educators because of its lack of interest, as we have seen, in the "substantive world," which allegedly contains objective truth that can be mined out, refined into encyclopedias and books, and then retailed portion by portion to the minds of the young. Instead, Experimentalism posits a world of process, where there are no pre-established truths, where inquiry (truth-*seeking*) and thinking (intelligence in *action*) and problem-solving are emphasized. Teaching and learning under this aegis will obviously take on a different flavor and quality. We shall see how in Chapter Four.

EXISTENTIALISM:
A WORLD OF EXISTING

If Experimentalism is philosophically adolescent, Existentialism is downright infantile, since it is, for the most part, a twentieth-century product. Its intellectual ancestry is usually traced to Sören Kierkegaard, a complicated and troubled Danish philosopher who lived and wrote in the first half of the 1800's. But elaboration and interpretation of his views has come only recently. None of his works was translated into English until this century, and most of the theoretical work in this philosophical camp has been done by European writers who are still living.

The relative recency of Existentialism as a philosophic outlook may be expected to limit its usefulness as the base for an educational theory. For the most part, Existentialists have addressed themselves principally to metaphysical questions, not yet having taken up examination of the areas of more direct concern to educational thinkers. Furthermore, Existentialism's primary concern with the individual has led to a neglect of that whole band of modern questions we designate as *social* — politics, institutional life, and social order. Since education, in our time, has come to be so thoroughly social in outlook and practice, Existentialism has not had much to say about it. Therefore, while we may be permitted a glimpse of its basic metaphysics, we are on our own when it comes to developing its implications for educational doctrine.

Essence and existence

There are many places to begin understanding Existentialist ontology; but perhaps the best place would be a matter we have already touched on in another connection — Aristotelian essence and Thomistic existence. We can, say the Existentialists, develop all kinds of interesting theories concerning essence and existence in the universe at large. But when we come to Man we are stumped. Traditional philosophies have always assumed the priority in time of the essence of man over his existence. That is, we look upon God, for instance, as a super-artificer — a maker and creator of things. When he made man, he had the *idea of man* in mind before actually creating him. Just as a carpenter holds the *idea* of a table in his mind before he fabricates the table from wood, so has our Creator worked from a prior design (essence) in bringing us into being (existence). Even without the metaphor of the master artificer, most philosophies hold to the notion that Man is a *something;* he can be defined. He is a something understandable in terms of a basic idea. In Platonic terms, the customary position is that even if there were no men on earth there would still be the Idea of Man.

Existentialism begins by turning this priority upside down: In Man, existence precedes essence. We first are; then we attempt to define ourselves. Man is the great contingency; his essence is not given. His very specialness lies in his "ungivenness." In the colorful and figurative language of the Existentialists, we have been "thrown into existence"; not knowing whence we came, we wake up to discover ourselves here. And once we discover ourselves in existence, we commence the long slow journey to find our essence. As we travel, as we perform this and that activity, make this and that choice, prefer this, reject that, we are actually engaged in the process of defining ourselves, of providing the essence for which we search.

This idea is not altogether farfetched. Every child, as he grows up, eventually reaches the point in life — usually around the age of puberty — when he recognizes for the first time that he is a person, a distinct personality in the world. Around this age he enjoys a rather spectacular insight: he clasps himself and declares, "It's me. I'm a person. I'm here!" For a while, he revels in his new finding. But then he gradually awakens to what it really means: He is, for the first time in his life, responsible for himself. Usually the youngster will recoil at the magnitude of this responsibility. After a severe remonstrance from his parents, perhaps, he will try to divest himself of himself by saying, "I didn't ask to be born!"

This remark, for all its poignant insolence, is perhaps the most absurd and irrational statement a human being can utter. It is the crowning achievement in human irrelevancy. For the magnificent irony is that, whether the youngster asked to be born or not, here he is! Here he is, in place in the world, existing, and therefore responsible once and for all for his thought and conduct. There is, as it were, no retreat; even if one chooses total retreat — taking his own life — he has, by this act, chosen, and thus "cast his vote" on the essence of man. Once we pass that moment in life — what might be called the Existential Moment — we wake up to discover ourselves, quite without any say in the matter, here in the world, committed to existence and confronted by the absolute necessity of choice.

From existence to choice

Now if the biological rule of "Ontogeny recapitulates phylogeny"[10] applies also to psychological phenomena we can say that what we experience individually is but a reproduction of what the race has experienced. Man, according to this view, has gradually awakened to his racial existence. He has found himself here in the world faced with the task of finding out who he is. The jungle primitive, like the child, does not know who he is; he doesn't even know *that* he is. He wanders about his environment, cleverer than other organisms, to be sure, but essentially innocent of his basic "*is*-ness."

Greek civilization might be likened to the Existential Moment in human history. Men awoke to Truth; they awoke to Value; in short, they awoke to themselves, to the idea that human life matters, that some ways of living it may be judged better than others, and that man has no one to turn to, save himself, to find this better way. We rightly speak of the Greeks as the first society to become deliberately self-conscious; they stand at the headwaters of Western civilization because they were the first to recognize the necessity of choice among competing alternatives in thought and conduct.

But no sooner had this awakening occurred — to continue with our allegory — than men began crying, "I didn't ask to be born!" Plato and Aristotle tried to remove man's responsibility for choice and relocate it in a logical system of rational necessity. The Christians relocated it in a God watching over and taking charge of all. St. Thomas relocated it in Being. Then the Realistic Naturalists said, "Follow nature; let nature be responsible." Today the Experimentalists say, "Look to the scientific

[10] Translation: The growth sequence of the individual organism retraces the developmental sequence of the species. Man, starting as animal on all fours, stands up on hind legs, develops speech, makes tools, builds cultures, learns writing, acquires history, reasons; baby first crawls on all fours, stands, walks, speaks, manipulates and constructs, learns to write, acquires a sense of time, begins to reason.

method"; and since this last method is a public procedure of thought and criticism, we are advised also to "look to the community," especially when involved in a social or moral problem.

The Existentialist balks at all this. In every instance, he says, man has been separated from his basic humanity, i.e., his circumstance of ultimate choice; he has been relieved of responsibility for himself. But the fact is that he is still confronted by choice. After all, he must decide which agency — Reason, God, Being, Nature, or Science — should be called on to relieve him. And this is an ultimate choice, for which he must take responsibility.

Thus, says the Existentialist, the ultimate and final Reality resides within the self of the individual human person. At the very core of the human being there operates the power of choice. And it is this power of choice, operating within the necessary medium of responsibility, which sets us off as men, which decides not only what is true but what criteria shall be used to determine truth, and what standards shall be used in choosing between competing criteria, and what judgments shall be employed in deciding on the standards, ad infinitum. Human choice is the ultimate court of judgment both in morals and in practical judgment; it rules between competing practical judgments, as it rules between competing choices of moral action. But it also rules on what moralities shall be used in making judgments, and what meta-moralities shall be used in deciding which morality is best, ad infinitum. Ultimately, when all the sham of Reason and Nature and Science have been stripped away, there stand you and I, our choosing selves naked before a cosmos of alternatives, trying to plot our human way through it and thus to give substance and essence to the Idea of Man.

In this admittedly rhetorical way, Existentialism reclaims the final responsibility for man to decide for himself who and what he is, and, by extension, what his reality is. If Experimentalism has given modern expression to the idea that "Man is the measure of all things," then Existentialism can be said to have carried this dictum to its final and absolute fulfillment. Indeed, Existentialism means to elevate this principle to a central position in its metaphysical superstructure, changing it from a somewhat wistful and provocative observation into an absolute moral imperative.

Self in a world of choice

To an Existentialist, then, *Reality* is even more elusive a concept than it is with the Experimentalists. The Existentialist might be willing to go along with the Experimentalist in asserting the primacy of experience. But experience is always individual experience; and it is always individual selves reporting on what they see and find. More technically, the doing-and-undergoing nexus is all very neat and pretty. But doing is always authored by an individual human person; and undergoing is always "had" by an individual human person. And whatever can be made in the way of a connection between doing and undergoing is, by necessity, the private operation of each separate individual. Science can point out plausible connections, but unless men individually accept those connections science turns into merely another "debating society."

Hence, Reality in Existentialist language is "self-operating-in-cosmos-of-choice" or simply "self-choosing." There is a sly double-entendre here. For not only is the self choosing, but it is choosing *itself;* that is, it is choosing its own definition, with every choice casting a ballot as to what a human being is, what he is for in this world, and what a human life is intended to be in this existence. It is through the lives we live, say the Existentialists, that we fashion the *essence* of man. Our existence is given; we wake up to it. Our essence is what is in question; it becomes our project. And having such a noble project is the exclusive privilege of man. No other creature can manufacture his own essence. It is difficult work, to be sure, and down through the ages man has tried to escape the heaviness of the awesome responsibility. But it is ours whether we choose to accept it or not. This is the towering irony of the human predicament.

The "open end"

We may now note that Existentialism, like Experimentalism, is characterized by what we have called "open-endedness." In fact, the quality of contingency, the element of nothing given beforehand, nothing prescribed, nothing necessary, is even more pronounced here. For in Experimentalism we always had Science to retreat to, or, in the case of a troublesome public question, the community. No such shelters can be found in Existentialism. The sky is open. But generally speaking these two philosophies stand opposed to the first three principally on this count: that they posit to reality no absolute or necessary qualities standing outside of and independent of human knowing. In these two philosophies reality is, in one way or another, man-made. As contradictory as this may be to your sense of common sense (to be purposefully redundant), it is this "reality-is-man-made" orientation which has given us so many new ideas in the modern world, not only in education but also in science, politics, and even religion.

Whether new ideas — in ontology or anywhere else — are really better than old ones is perhaps, as the Existentialist would certainly say, for each man to decide. But biding this troublesome issue for a time, we must now see how the five ontologies make their impact felt in differing educational theories. To this we turn in Chapter Four.

QUESTIONS

1. In attempting to organize in your mind what this chapter is all about, try now to give a general definition of the word *ontology*. Then look it up in the unabridged dictionary to see how close you have come. Would each of the five positions described conform to your definition? What changes, if any, would they individually require? Is it possible to get a commonly acceptable definition for this word?

2. Most traditional ontologies hold that that which does not change is more "real" than that which does. Give some examples of this. What views do you hold on this question?

3. Some of the antonyms for "real" are "unreal," "apparent," "illusory," "ersatz," "phony," "artificial." Which of these is (or are) best suited for discussion in ontology? Why?

4. Descartes in the seventeenth century "solved" the ontological puzzle, to his own satisfaction at least, by doubting the reality and existence of everything — except one thing: his own doubting. So his famous "Cogito, ergo sum" (I think, therefore I am) became for him the absolute starting point for all ontological thinking. What would each of our five positions have to say about this? Would Descartes fit into any of them?

FURTHER READING

Idealism

Du Noüy, Lecomte. *Human Destiny.* New York: Longmans, Green and Co., Inc., 1947. (Also New York: New American Library, Signet Books, 1947.)
In this compelling and highly readable volume, Du Noüy first dismisses the mechanistic ontology of the Realists by showing that some intelligence outside the realm of chance is at work in the world. Then he develops the idea that man, having reached the summit in *physiological* evolution, will now participate more actively in this macro-intelligence by embarking on a "Second Chapter of Genesis," i.e., *psychological* evolution, which will eventually culminate in our union with God. This theory of human destiny he labels "Telefinalism."

Plato. *The Republic.* Translated by Benjamin Jowett. New York: Random House, Modern Library Edition.
In Book VII you will find the full dialogue on the Allegory of the Cave — Plato at his most persuasive.

Realism

Montague, William P. *The Ways of Things*. New York: Prentice-Hall, Inc., 1940.
In two early chapters (Part I, Chapters IV and V) on the metaphysics of macrocosm and microcosm Montague works over, in semitechnical fashion, the ontological outlooks of Dualism, Positivism, Idealism, and Materialism. Then in a later essay (Part II, Chapter VII) he gives us a sketch of modern Einsteinian physics and its philosophic import.

Wild, John. *Introduction to Realistic Philosophy*. New York: Harper and Bros., 1948.
In Chapters 13–16 Wild explains the Realist's "Evolving World" by drawing attention to Change and describing how Change gets "caused," the substantive Cosmos that is doing the changing, and, finally, the First Cause.

Neo-Thomism

Maritain, Jacques. *Existence and the Existent*. Translated by L. Galantière and G. B. Phelan. New York: Belgrave Press, 1948.
Maritain explains the difference between the original (St. Thomas') existentialism and the newer and, to him, corrupted brand of Existentialism. Then he goes on to elaborate on what he calls the "Intuition of Being" and the various existents it encompasses.

————. *A Preface to Metaphysics*. New York: Sheed and Ward, 1948.
Seven lectures by the greatest twentieth-century Thomist on the central concept in Thomistic philosophy, i.e., Being — what it is, how we can think about it, and why the "First Principles" the Neo-Thomist talks about are necessarily attached to it.

Experimentalism

Dewey, John. *Experience and Nature*. Chicago: Open Court Publishing Co., 1926.
In Chapter I the most famous (to some, notorious) Experimentalist lays down the ground rules for ontological thinking. Then, especially in Chapters II, VIII, and X, he develops what for want of a better term we can call an Experimentalist metaphysics.

Hook, Sidney. *The Metaphysics of Pragmatism*. Chicago: Open Court Publishing Co., 1927.
The year after Dewey published *Experience and Nature* his student Sidney Hook attempted (and largely succeeded in) a more precise and thorough statement of the Experimentalist position.

Morris, V. C. "An Experimentalist on Being," *The Modern Schoolman*, XXXV, No. 2 (January, 1958), 125–133.
The present author attempts to state what an Experimentalist, if driven into a corner, would say about Being. Using Thomistic and Aristotelian language, this essay points to a "procedural" or "event-ual" (rather than "substantive") definition of being.

Existentialism

Harper, Ralph. *Existentialism: A Theory of Man.* Cambridge: Harvard University Press, 1948.
An exposition of the Existentialist position, with special emphasis on the Number One ontological fact: the *existence* of man.

Sartre, Jean Paul. *Existentialism.* Translated by B. Frechtman. New York: Philosophical Library, 1947.
To borrow from the translator, M. Sartre is "both a man of the library and a man of the streets and writes as such." Originally delivered as a lecture in 1945, this little volume explains in plain, straightforward language what Existentialism — at least the atheistic variety — is all about.

CHAPTER FOUR

Comparative Ontology and

the Educative Process

THE PROBLEM OF APPLICATION

Discussions in philosophy such as the preceding are necessarily over-simplifications of the complex and sometimes chaotic jumble of ideas that have been thought by men down through time. What we have tried to do in Chapter Three is to single out for special study and analysis those ideas which relate to the fundamental views of the world and the nature of ultimate reality as they have been formulated in five major philosophic outlooks. You are reminded again that these views are not so neatly disparate as we have been forced to make them appear here; our object is simply to separate ideas for the purpose of analysis and understanding.

The present chapter attempts another kind of analysis, that of showing how the various ontologies lead to different conceptions of the educative process. Later on, in Parts V and VI, it will be necessary to put these ideas back together again, not only for theoretical tidiness but to see how philosophies and educational theories finally come to operate in concrete educational practice in the day-to-day work of the school. When you reach these later chapters, you may wish to return to the present chapter (and also to Chapters Seven and Ten) to test and qualify what is said here.

It should be said that a sizable number of thinkers in the field of educational philosophy object to the pretension of showing logical linkages between fundamental outlooks and patterns for teaching and learning. The claim is made that, in the strictest terms of modern logic, it is not possible to proceed from a statement of basic point of view ("Ultimate reality is such and such . . .") to a statement of educational prescription ("Such an ontology leads to a curriculum of such and such . . ."). More generally, it is not possible to say that if the world *is* "built" in such-and-such a way then the education of man *should be* arranged in such-and-such a fashion. We cannot proceed from a statement of description (an "is" statement) to a statement of prescription (an "ought" or "should" statement).[1]

There is a counterview, however, which holds that when linkages are drawn between philosophy and educational doctrine no hard and fast logical products are intended. We are, when we do this, merely attempting to draw the most reasonable inferences we can from philosophic positions. We start with philosophies and then extend them into their practical, "situational" *implications,* seeking to show what they point to, what they *mean operationally.*[2] If what we wind up with is a collection of indistinguishable doctrines — if they mean operationally the same thing — then we would conclude that the philosophies themselves are indistinguishable. But if we wind up with doctrines which are *distinguishable,* we can point to this or that educational idea or practice as being associated with a given philosophic outlook. According to this position, if we are unable to refer to larger philosophical views in order to draw distinctions between educational doctrines and to use these distinctions in understanding and controlling educational practice, then we have to conclude that all philosophy is irrelevant to the guidance and control of practice, not only in the field of education but also in politics, social life, religion, and every other sector of human experience.

While some people believe this, it is not the view taken here. The whole thesis of this book is that differences in philosophical outlook have something to do with the way teachers teach boys and girls in the

---

[1] For a fuller treatment of this important point, see Edward H. Reisner, "Philosophy and Science in the Western World: A Historical Overview," p. 32, and Mortimer J. Adler, "In Defense of the Philosophy of Education," pp. 230–235, *Philosophies of Education,* Forty-first Yearbook of the National Society for the Study of Education, ed. N. B. Henry (Chicago: the Society, 1942); also Sidney Hook, "The Scope of Philosophy of Education," *Harvard Educational Review,* XXVI, No. 2 (Spring, 1956), 145–148.

[2] For a fuller development of this view see Joe R. Burnett, "Some Observations on the Logical Implications of Philosophic Theory for Educational Theory and Practice," *Proceedings of the Fourteenth Annual Meeting of the Philosophy of Education Society* (Lawrence, Kansas: University of Kansas Press, 1958), pp. 51–57. Also C. I. Stevenson, "The Scientist's Role and the Aims of Education," *Harvard Educational Review,* XXIV, No. 4 (1954), 231–38.

classroom. We know, as a matter of fact, that teaching and learning are carried on in different ways in different schools in the United States. These differences in practice are due not merely to temperamental variations in teachers' personalities nor merely to environmental variations in regional outlooks. At bottom, they are ideological differences. They spring from the differences people hold toward questions concerning man and universe. If there is no hard and fast *logical* connection, there most certainly is a psychological connection between philosophy and practice.[3] Empirically, there *is* a connection between what a teacher believes and how he acts, whether there *should* be or not. What a teacher says will tell you something of what to expect if you walk into his classroom and watch him teach. Conversely, how he teaches will tell you something of what to expect in his conversation over the coffee cups in the teachers' room. It is these connections that this book is all about.

THE WORLD
THE LEARNER LIVES IN

When the child goes to school he enters into an environment which is, for better or worse, different from what he experiences elsewhere. He is, first of all, placed in a situation of close association with others of his own age — more of them, really, than he would come to know outside of the school. Also, his life begins to take on a quality of formality and regimentation which is not characteristic at home. And, generally speaking, he deals from morning to afternoon with subject matters which are not typical of his out-of-school hours. In all of these ways, the environment of the school is an artificial one; that is, it is deliberately distinct from and (it is hoped) an improvement on the aimless and willy-nilly experience of the "natural" child growing up on his own. In this sense, the school is an intentionally contrived living situation where growth can be more effectively and efficiently provoked and directed.

Perhaps the most significant factor in the youngster's new world is the existence of a small group of adults — his teachers — who have taken on the task of managing his life. It is these individuals who establish the circumstances to which he is expected to adjust and who create this environment in which the difficult and delicate process called learning is intended to take place. It goes without saying that the tone and struc-

---

[3] For a convincing demonstration of this point, see Hobert Burns, "The Logic of the 'Educational Implication,' " *Proceedings of the Sixteenth Annual Meeting of the Philosophy of Education Society* (Lawrence, Kansas: University of Kansas Press, 1960), pp. 49–55.

ture of this world is necessarily conditioned by the life outlooks of the adults. In most of us, teachers as well as others, these outlooks may not be linguistically expressible on short notice. Trying to write a term paper on one's "philosophy of life" or preparing, say, a professional credo in less than 200 words for the inside cover of a P.T.A. pamphlet is a rather difficult undertaking.

But these outlooks reside within us nevertheless. They exist perhaps at the subconscious level in our nervous systems. Most people, for instance, can tap this store of belief on occasion for a philosophic attitude on a particular situation that arises in their life. In a very real way, then, this kind of subconscious philosophy moves within all of us, and it eventually serves to establish the "psychological climate" which we attempt to manufacture for the young to live in during their hours in school.

Since these outlooks which control the quality of the school's environment find their base in the ontologies we carry around with us, it is necessary and fitting that we examine briefly how the different ontologies view the educative process in its most general setting.

The learner and ideas

The Idealist is, of course, principally oriented to ideas. What the world itself was to Plato or Hegel, the school attempts to recreate in miniature, so to speak, for the child: Though there must be desks and blackboards and recess periods and lunch hours and bells that ring to move us from this place to that, the essence of a school is its *ideational* quality, i.e., its function as a vehicle for the things of the mind. An Idealist school, then, attempts to create for the young an environment of "mind"; it will, as we saw in Chapter Two, show special interest in the principal medium through which Mind operates: symbols. For it is through symbols — not only in language, but in mathematics and the arts also — that the mind of man transacts its business.

The learner and things

The Idealist's kind of school is a little too vague and intangible for a Realist. He wants things he can feel and see and measure. His world is a *thing*, as we have seen in Chapter Three, and he wishes to introduce the child to this enormous and complicated thing in as systematic and direct a way as he can. Ideas, as ideas, will come in their time; we must first start to expose the youngster to physical reality — the regular, orderly, and systematic natural reality which he inhabits. The school should attempt to recreate this kind of world in the experience of the child, and in so doing become, through its own procedures, as systematic and orderly and fully regulated as administrators and teachers can make it. Copying "Nature," the school will provide a time for everything, a place for everything. Its procedures will be systematic and prescribed, and the routine of the learner will simulate a smooth-running, "clock-work" sequence of learning activities. Orderliness in thinking grows out of orderliness in living.

The learner and being

The Neo-Thomist understands all of this and goes along with most of both Idealist and Realist views. But he sees no reason to select either "mind" or "thing" as the primary attribute of the cosmos; the world is both. What ties them together is the important thing. And what is it? Recalling the Potentiality-Actuality Principle (Chapter Three), we can say that this unifying force is *Being*, which is, as noted earlier, identical with *God*.

The Neo-Thomist now explains that this Absolute Pinnacle (Being and/or God) is accessible through two routes. Quite obviously, one of these routes is Faith, dramatized historically by Mosaic Revelation (see page 63) and practiced in the Roman Catholic religion. But we now see that we can reach this same eminence by a second route: Reason. The human mind can not only entertain "ideas" and perceive "things" but it can work its way to Absolute Truth, and in the attainment of Absolute Truth it can "see" pure Being. Reason now confirms and backs up what Faith has revealed.

Herein lies a distinction we must now make: Neo-Thomism is today made up of two divisions or "wings" — the Ecclesiastical Wing and the Lay Wing. The Ecclesiastical Wing, which in contemporary educational thinking is represented principally by the Roman Catholic Church and its educational spokesmen, finds its chief source of educational ideas in a somewhat literal use of St. Thomas' philosophic and religious writings; it is therefore the least "Neo" of the modern Thomists. This Wing is, of course, committed to both Reason *and* Faith, but its prescription for the "psychological climate" of the school is more nearly associated with the latter. Boys and girls should grow and learn within the warming environment of God's love.

The Lay Wing, on the other hand, has developed a much more purely rationalistic point of view, seizing upon the simple grandeur of Aristotelian logic and on St. Thomas' exhibition of the power of this logic in his rational demonstrations of the existence of God (see pages 61–63). The rallying point for Lay Neo-Thomists is Truth, spelled with a capital *T* and signifying a body of Absolute or Eternal Verities existing at the pinnacle of this world of "mind" and "thing." We do not have to introduce any theistic element into this Absolute, say the Lay representatives: It stands on Reason alone, without the assistance of Faith.

This realm of the Absolute is accessible to the human mind by special training and effort. The young should be provided an environment in their schools which will show them the existence of this realm of Truth, while making it clear that it is accessible only after careful and arduous training of the mind. The mental processes must be sharpened before Absolute Truth comes within reach. The climate of the school should be such as to awaken the young to the love of Truth, *in and for itself,* and to quicken and motivate the young to set to the rigorous task of attaining it.

In summary, what both wings of Neo-Thomism would provide for the child is an environment of ultimate certainty. In the case of the Ecclesiastical Wing, it is a certainty of the existence of God and the absolute assurance of his love. In the case of the Lay Wing, it is a certainty of Truth, a final culmination of our limited exercise of the faculty of Reason in an Ultimate Truth which stands steady for ever and ever — man's ultimate mooring to the cosmos.

The learner and experience

The Experimentalist has not been too tactful, in decades past, in the skepticism, scorn, and even contempt he has shown for the Neo-Thomist position. Of course, since we in America have affirmed the principle of the separation of church and state and made our schools nonsectarian and secular (concerned with things of *this* world only), religious and theistic educational doctrines are considered somewhat out of bounds for use in the public schools. Experimentalism, therefore, which has turned secularism into a primary item of belief (see pages 67–70), would not be expected to have much in common with the Ecclesiastical Wing of Neo-Thomism.

But the Lay Wing thereof is another matter. For the Lay Neo-Thomists insist that, while God may not belong in the public school, Truth most certainly does; and their program is offered as supremely suited to the public schools. Consequently Experimentalism has confronted an earnest and persuasive opponent in recent years in the public debate over what the philosophy of American education should be. The controversy has raged over the spirit and climate of the school, over what truth is, and, figuratively, over the question whether the word *truth* should or should not be spelled with a capital *T*.

The capital *T*, it turns out, makes quite a bit of difference. The Experimentalist, you will recall, rejects all transempirical (beyond-experience) features of so-called reality. Reality is what our experience in this world says it is; hence, our experience itself can be taken for ultimate reality, since it is the source of all our problems and the ground for all our thinking and knowing. If we are to spell *truth* with a capital *T*, say the Experimentalists, we are turning it into a transempirical component of reality. No one has even genuinely experienced Absolute Truth. Truth, upper or lower case, must earn its way in the "market place" of human experience: If a statement is a candidate for becoming an Absolute Truth, it must first be returned to concrete day-to-day affairs to see if it works — to see if it is true. And when we make this test we merely affirm the criterial priority of our concrete experience over whatever our minds may tell us is true. Hence, says the Experimentalist, the environment of the school should be of ongoing experience, a living circumstance, in which ideas and truths are tested in action. Young people should be constantly reminded that truth is not something that is attained and clutched for its own sake; truth is sought and reached because it can be *used* in our lives. "Knowledge for Use" (as we shall see in the section on epistemology) is the educational aim of the Experimentalist. As such, it indicates the kind of environment he means to create in the school.

The learner and choice

The Existentialist, bewildered by all of this elaborate system-building and the consequent argument over whose system is best, asks us to return, quite simply and guilelessly, to the individual human being. Here, he maintains, is where it all gets settled eventually, right within the "choosing mechanism" of every person. And since it is never possible to force a choice on anyone, not even if the choice is offered as "scientifically true," there is a certain futility to all this argument over what kind of environment to create and sustain in the school. The environment of the child should be one of complete and absolute freedom, a freedom where his selfhood can operate without hindrance. We should not impose upon him any environment whatsoever — neither Mind, nor Things, nor God, nor Truth, nor Experience lived with and among other human beings. In every case, says the Existentialist, the prearranged environment tends, just by its presence, to favor certain choices over others; and to "rig" the choices, even in the slightest degree, is to intrude upon the autonomy of the human self.

The individual himself will have to decide what role ideas and things and God and Absolute Truth will play in his cosmos. Even the function of other people — the milieu of social experience the Experimentalist talks about — must be decided upon by the individual. Democratic group decision may be an improvement on dogmatic, authoritarian decision, but it is still inferior to an even more basic level of action — individual decision. Indeed, says the Existentialist, Experimentalism has fooled us with its apparent hospitality to individuality; for it eventually winds up putting all of us in the social collective. There is no tyranny so insidious, we are reminded, as the tyranny of "other people" — what we have lately come to refer to as social conformity.

The environment of the school, then, should be as completely unspecified as it is possible to make it. The educator's task is to place at the disposal of the young as many different "climates" as he can conceive of: the autocratic and the democratic, the religious and the atheistic, the doctrinaire and the open-ended, the teacher-dominated and the pupil-dominated, the ordered and the anarchic. From these "climates" the youngster's own selfhood will create its own climate: It will select out of this endless continuum of possible human experiences what it considers relevant to its fulfillment as a unique and ultimate human self. When we choose for the child, says the Existentialist, by giving prior design and tone to his environment in the school, by that much we diminish him as a human being.

THE CURRICULUM
OF THE LEARNER

Now that the youngster is in school, what should he learn? What, in short, should the content of his experience in school consist of? The problem of curriculum is complicated by a confusion in educational circles as to the meaning of the word itself. Stemming from the Latin, *curriculum* literally means a "race course," or a course of studies through which one "runs" to reach the end, an end presumably of full knowledge, keen insight, and mature citizenship. Generally speaking, we still use the word in this sense, even though there are a multitude of curriculums or courses of study which individuals can, as we say, pursue.

The confusion lies, rather, within the nature and quality of the "studies" which make up the course. On the one hand, they can be considered as substantive *bodies of information,* organized in advance and set out before the learner to be learned, like English literature or plane geometry. On the other hand, they can be considered as *experiences that the learner is to have,* dynamic, ongoing events deliberately contrived to take place in the life of the student, like experimentation in the laboratory or field trips to the courthouse or a project in raising pigs. In Chapter Two we took note of the shift from "thing" to "process" thinking. In Chapter Three we expanded on this idea by noting the distinction between the "substantive" ("subject") ontological tendencies in Idealism, Realism, and Neo-Thomism[4] and the "predicate," "action" ("verblike") ontological tendencies in the more modern philosophies of Experimentalism and Existentialism. We can now make these running distinctions even more explicit by pointing to associate variations in conceptions of the curriculum.

Generally speaking, we can say that the "substantive" ontologies will lean in the direction of substantive subject matters, those subject matters which are best characterized by the word *content,* while the "verbal" ontologies will lean in the direction of "verbal," "process" subject matters, those subject matters best characterized by the word *experiences.* (Indeed, we might logically rename the latter "verb matters" or "predicate matters" if we were to celebrate the shift in emphasis which these curricular patterns often express.)

The subject matter of symbol and idea

From our study of ontology we could expect to find an Idealist curriculum principally interested in and concerned with subject matters of the mind, that is, those studies whose content consists of *ideas.* We are forewarned, of course, that in a sense all of man's education — indeed, all of his experience — is mental or ideational in character. But we speak here principally of those branches of knowledge which are concerned with the development and exploration of ideas in and for themselves. Perhaps the most appropriate example of this is the field of literature. Literature is, by definition, concerned with "letters," with symbols. It is through these "letters" that we convey human feeling and insight; and in their most advanced form, in the works of the literary giants, "feeling and insight" are sufficiently removed from the immediate, day-to-day world to enable them to endure as valid from one age to another. A Lucretius or Cervantes or Shakespeare is just as provocative today as he ever was; and this is due principally to the fact that he is dealing with permanent and enduring ideas of the human condition and not with this or that passing expression of it.

A subject matter with which the Idealist is even more closely associated is history. Through history, it is thought, the individual can begin to discern the total meaning of life — not so much by the study of so many battles or presidential administrations as by trying to catch the underlying currents of human affairs, trying to sense the *meaning* of history

---

4 As noted earlier, some features of Neo-Thomist ontology would require a qualification of this placement of it among the "substantive" ontologies. Nevertheless, Neo-Thomism represents a "closed-system" ontology, along with Idealism and Realism. In this sense, at least, it is "substantive" in quality.

through the careful connection of one event with another, one movement with another, one epoch with another. Here, it is thought, may lie the most fruitful territory for finding man's true role in the cosmos. Every historian who proceeds beyond the mere data of his subject will inevitably come upon the larger question of "what it all means." *What,* a Hegelian might ask, is trying to express itself through the ongoing ebb and flow of human affairs? If we could somehow fathom the dynamic essence of the past, the master formula of historical movement, we would be in a position to understand more completely the "idea" of the cosmos, i.e., what it ultimately means.

Although they are not all classifiable as Idealists, many historical scholars and philosophers have attempted just this sort of grand distillation of human events. Plato himself, in *The Republic,* sought to condense all the meaning of man's political life into the concept of Justice. Out of this analysis he sought to build the ideal political state. Much later Tolstoi, in *The Kingdom of God is Within You,* saw in history a grand rhythm from the animal or pagan epoch to the human or social epoch to the finally emergent universal and divine epoch, into which we are now very gradually passing. Lecomte du Noüy, in his *Human Destiny,* has spun out a fascinatingly elaborate idea that the evolutionary force of the cosmos, having spent itself in the inorganic (cosmological) and organic (Darwinian, biological) sectors of the cosmos, will now come to a halt in those areas and shift to the psychological. The earth has finished evolving and man, as an animal, has arrived at the limit of his physiological development. But psychologically man is just beginning to evolve. His intelligence is now sufficient to control his biological evolution: Through nutrition and genetics, he can theoretically guide the biological development of the species along any course he may select; or he may, with nuclear energy, bring it to a halt. But these are only small beginnings, for his true fulfillment as man lies not in his physiology but in his psychology. And, says Du Noüy, man will now embark upon his final adventure to find final union with God.

Hegel, as we have seen, maintains that the central feature of history is dialectic, the continuing rhythm of the contest between opposites. Marx, building upon this theory in *Das Kapital,* explains that in human terms this struggle is fundamentally an economic one, between those who do and those who do not control the means of production. In agrarian epochs this struggle is kept relatively quiescent, but in industrial, technological periods it reaches proportions beyond the control of the ruling classes. There follow economic upheaval and revolution and (through some mysterious political alchemy Marx never convincingly demonstrates) the struggle, the dialectic, is brought to a halt in the supreme synthesis of a classless society. Aside from the utter illogic of the view that a fundamentally dialectical human world can culminate in its exact opposite, a fundamentally *un*dialectical human society, Marxism still fascinates us as a supreme example of a "theory of history" attempting to reveal the inner meaning of human existence.

From all of these (and many other) examples[5] we can testify to the continuing interest man has exhibited in the questions of the basic "lesson of history": Where have we come from? And: Where are we headed? These, to the Idealist, are the central questions in life; and so they should become the central focus of the curriculum of the school. Though the educator will not be unmindful of science and geography and all the rest, these subjects should play a secondary role to those subject matters which awaken us to the basic *ideas* of the cosmos. At the college level, we call such subjects *the humanities:* literature, art, philosophy, religion, intellectual history. The Idealists have no monopoly on this segment of the curriculum, as we shall see; but that is not the point. The important thing is to see that Idealist ontology signifies an abiding interest in the study of the things of the mind.

The subject matter of the physical world

To a Realist the humanities seem vague and indefinite. In their worst form they border on mysticism, a kind of transcendental set of generalities which, because they are so general, cannot even be "right" or "wrong" — merely "interesting." We can never come directly to grips with them; and so, the Realist is likely to say, perhaps we had better leave them to the theologians and philosophers to reflect on. For educational purposes they are too indefinite.

In their best form, the basic ideas of the cosmos are represented by the laws of nature. If this is what we are talking about, says the Realist, then perhaps we can get somewhere. But the laws of nature are not learned in literature and history. They are learned by the direct study of nature, which we have come to associate with the subject matters of science: biology, zoology, botany, geology, chemistry, physics, astronomy, and their many subdivisions. These subject matters are definite and specific; one doesn't have to guess about things or speculate on the meaning of the material. It is either right or wrong.

Mathematics, as the language of quantity, is the symbol system we use

5 We should point also to more recent contributions: Toynbee's thesis of the "life (and death) cycles" of civilizations, which in his earlier work seemed "open-ended" and humanly controllable but more recently are seen by him to be directed by some kind of cosmic force; George S. Counts' thesis of "cultural transition," from nomadic to agrarian to technological to collective social life; and David Riesman's thesis of the "characterological shift," from tradition-directed to inner-directed to other-directed to autonomous man.

in studying the physical world of nature. So it will be necessary for the child to master mathematics in order to grow into a mature understanding of his world. Mathematics, moreover, is the very epitome of order and precision, two of the basic features of the "world-as-machine" ontology. Mathematics may be abstract; but it certainly is not vague. *Vague* and *abstract* are *not* synonyms. What mathematics does is to render symbolic the absolute precision and regularity of the cosmos we live in. As symbology it should be attractive to Idealists as well, but as the medium of discourse for work in the sciences it is an essential in the Realist curriculum.

Generally speaking, then, we can point to mathematics and the natural sciences as the central feature of the Realist educational program. Mathematics will serve as the symbolic tool for this program in somewhat the same way that language is the symbolic tool for study in an Idealist curriculum. Whereas the Idealist will stress reading, writing, and spelling (the "Language Arts") as the "basic tool subjects," the Realist will be inclined to stress arithmetic, algebra, geometry, and trigonometry (what we might designate as the "Measurement Arts") as his tool subjects. At the risk of oversimplifying things, we might also note that the Idealist is primarily interested in *qualities* in the universe and in *qualitative* or *normative* subject matter, whereas the Realist is primarily interested in *quantities* in the universe and in *quantitative* and *mensural* subject matter.

Insofar as the subject matters beyond the natural sciences can be rendered quantitative, the Realist will embrace these also. Perhaps the most generalized dictum of the Realist position was made by the famous psychologist E. L. Thorndike when he said, "Whatever exists exists in some amount." He was talking, at the time, about mental factors of intelligence; and in defense of his efforts to measure intelligence he insisted that if a thing called intelligence exists at all it must exist in a quantitative sense; that is, it must exist in such a way that a person can measure it. Out of this prior assumption he proceeded, along with others, to develop quantitative measuring instruments — intelligence tests — to assess the relative presence or absence of what had always been thought too indefinite to measure. The quantitative interpretation of *mind* has now been carried so far that it is thought possible to express intelligence by means of a number: the intelligence quotient, literally a quotient, computed from a fraction whose numerator is the *mental age* (in months) and whose denominator is the *chronological age* (in months) of the individual. In order to get rid of the untidy decimal places, we multiply the result by 100.

Well, one may say, if *mind* can be treated in so purely and precisely a mathematical way as this, then presumably everything else can also. For what is more immaterial than mind? If immaterial mind can be measured, then we can go ahead and measure other things as well. This is the true significance of Thorndike's dictum.

To this end the social sciences have been pushing forward in the measurement of other immaterial factors, most notably that "thing" we call *behavior*. In the field of psychology, for instance, we attempt to isolate "units" of behavior just as the physicist isolates units of energy or heat. Having started out with the study of rats in a maze, the psychologist moves on to more complicated forms of observable reactions to specific stimuli: the behavior of a child deprived of love at home, the reactions of an adolescent to group pressures, the "attitude structure" of an adult as revealed by his responses on a questionnaire. For all of these cases, units of behavior have been isolated for measurement and analysis; when properly observed and noted they can be plotted on a scale.

Another example is the field of economics; we can measure not only the familiar dollars and cents or the productive output of a factory but also a society's whole "economic behavior," i.e., of buying, selling, bargaining, etc. The impact of an advertisement on our spending habits, for instance, can be ultimately reduced to units of economic behavior, which then can be manipulated, analyzed, and studied for the extraction of regularities of human conduct.[6] Just as we study atoms and molecules to see what they do under specifiable conditions, so can we study human beings as "social molecules" in motion in society. And we can, it is thought, derive from these studies certain "laws of behavior" (the law of supply and demand in economics, for example), which, if found regular and consistent, can assume the status of *natural* law. Those behaviors, for instance, which we designate by the term "human nature" are presumably regulated by laws outside ourselves; these laws control human beings everywhere.

Taken to its extreme limit, this Realist tendency would make of the social sciences the study of mechanical forces, represented by environmental stimuli, which come to bear upon the human being and *make* him do what he does. A determinism in human conduct, much like the cause-and-effect determinism which Newtonian physics has held operates in the physical world, is the major postulate. Not all Realists, of course,

---

[6] One of the most interesting developments along these lines — both exciting and frightening — is the recent union of Sigmund Freud and Adam Smith: subliminal advertising. In these experiments, "imperceptible" images are flashed rapidly on a movie or TV screen — *"Eat,"* for instance, after which theater popcorn sales are said to increase, or *"Chilly,"* after which a rustling of putting on of coats is observed. One wiseacre, sensing the Victorian possibilities of this, suggests that we continue to flash on outdoor movie screens, *"Abjure Fleshly Wants,"* for the better control of the morals of young lovers in their parked automobiles.

take such an extreme position. Only the Behaviorists, as we shall see later, have carried Newtonian naturalism to its ultimate limit. But the spirit, at least, of Realism is revealed by this search for regularity and predictability in human as well as nonhuman affairs. And, returning to our curricular problem, insofar as the social sciences point to and magnify this aspect of their subject matter, they will find a welcome place in the Realist educational program.

Whether *all* things that exist exist in some amount is still an open question, however. In the humanities (the special interest of the Idealist) we can point to love and friendship and freedom and beauty — all "things," we may say, which exist in our lives. But do they exist *in some amount?* Can they be reduced to measurable units and segments which we can plot on a curve? Most of us would be inclined to say "No"; to measure such things is to spoil them. Once you "touch" them you destroy them. Partly because of their immunity and resistance to measurement, the Realist finds it difficult to work such subject matters into his educational thinking. As a *person* he may feel these qualities, but as an *educator* he is inclined to the view that they are too vague and indefinite to be taught.

The subject matter of the spirit and the intellect

The Neo-Thomist's orientation concerning the content of the school program is both more specific and more logically sophisticated than that of the Idealist or the Realist. It is more specific, even if bifurcated, in that both the Ecclesiastical and the Lay divisions of this philosophy have clear ideas of what educational content can best reveal to the young the type of world they must come to know.

The Ecclesiastical Neo-Thomist can be expected to include a good deal of religious and liturgical material in the school program. The Holy Scriptures, the Catechism, and the explanatory materials on Christian doctrine and dogma necessarily play a large and significant role in the curricular organization of Catholic parochial schools, where Ecclesiastical Neo-Thomism is most fully realized. In the literature courses, for example, wherever theistic works can be studied with profit they will take precedence over purely secular works. Indeed, in these schools some secular works are not only passed over but actively avoided. The *Index,* a list of books felt to be potentially corruptive of young Catholic minds, specifies those works which youngsters *must not,* at risk of ecclesiastical penalty, ever come in contact with, except with the express permission of the priest.[7] If the young are to be introduced to the true world of the

7 For instance, Edward Gibbon's *The History of the Decline and Fall of the Roman Empire,* Victor Hugo's *Les Misérables,* Blaise Pascal's *Pensées,* Jean Jacques Rousseau's

divine spirit they must be shielded from statements which blaspheme that world. Hence the Ecclesiastical Neo-Thomist makes no apologies, even in the open, no-censorship society of America, for placing the most rigorous of censorship on what kinds of things boys and girls are to learn in their schools.

No such censorship operates in the Lay Wing of Neo-Thomism. In fact, a militancy of freedom, a freedom to think and speak and write on any subject, is more in keeping with the Neo-Thomist outside the theological restrictions of the Catholic Church. One of the best spokesmen for Lay Neo-Thomism, Robert M. Hutchins, has consistently championed the absolute necessity in a democratic community for scholastic and academic freedom for both teacher and student. But despite this emphasis on freedom, it is mandatory that we provide the student with subject-matter content which will make him equal to the task which academic freedom places upon him. In short, we must train his mind to think; for without a trained and sharpened intellect no amount of freedom will produce an intelligent and educated person.

The Lay Neo-Thomist, then, is more inclined to lean in the direction of the disciplinary subject matters, those subject matters which attempt to reveal the Absolute Truths of the cosmos and also toughen the mind to the arduous task of reaching such truths. Traditionally effective in this office have been the various branches of mathematics. Mathematics may be, as the Realist insists, the "language" of the sciences. But it is much more than that; it is the nearest approach man has made to Pure Reason, uncontaminated by the irregularities and indeterminacies of ordinary day-to-day affairs. Mathematics is, indeed, so disconnected from ordinary experience as to be *trans*natural, somehow removed from and ruling over the physical world. There are, we are reminded, no twos or sevens in nature; there are no binomial theorems or equilateral triangles lying around in a natural state for us to pick up and examine for closer study. Not at all. These things are purely rational dimensions of the cosmos which force themselves into our consciousness because they are *in* and *of* the world of Absolutes; our minds "think" them because they *must,* just as our eyes *must* see light, our ears *must* perceive sound, our bodies *must* feel temperature. There is an inevitability of rational structure which the mind cannot permanently deny; it is the rational structure with which the very cosmos itself is endowed. Mathematics happens to be the closest human approximation to this structure; it gives us the "counters" and the rational procedures for moving systematically toward Absolute Truth.

Émile and *Du Contrat Social,* all of George Sand's love stories, and all the works of Jean Paul Sartre, André Gide, Anatole France, Giovanni Gentile, David Hume, and Émile Zola.

We shall have occasion to examine the disciplinary function of such studies as mathematics when we come to the epistemological question in Part III, which follows; but it should be enough to say here that if ultimate reality is represented best by the idea of Absolute Truth, we must provide youngsters with the mental equipment to reach it. Subject matter, then, has two jobs: to explain the world to the student (the ontological function) and to train the intellect to understand the world (the psychological or, more generally, the epistemological function). Fortunately, according to Neo-Thomism, studies like algebra and geometry discharge both of these functions; they not only epitomize Absolute Truth (the central ontological principle of Neo-Thomism) but also assist the mind in developing the powers to grasp it.

Of somewhat lesser precision but of coordinate importance are foreign languages. Languages are not so absolutely systematic as mathematics; their syntactical rules are subject to exception dependent on usage. But, generally speaking, languages in their design and structure reflect the immanent order that inhabits the human mind. Like mathematics, language arises without any perceptual counterpart in nature; i.e., nature does not contain symbols. Symbols must be created; and, once created, they must be organized and codified into syntactical systems and grammars — a task which the human mind has performed without any prompting or insistence from nature; languages simply arise. And the reason for this, according to Neo-Thomist theorizing, is the rational necessity for the mind to lay its powers of organization upon its raw materials, symbols.

Languages do, of course, differ. Their grammars are not all organized in the same way, nor are they all equally systematic. Latin and Greek, for instance, which are perhaps the most rigorously systematic, stand at the top of the list of linguistic studies in Neo-Thomist educational thinking. The modern languages of English, French, and German are less grammatically precise (especially English), and so they are of secondary importance in Neo-Thomist curriculums.[8]

Other subject matters will of course be studied in Neo-Thomist programs, but their value will be distributed along a curricular scale according to the degree in which order and system inhabit their content. The

[8] Some philologists hold that it was, in fact, the inflexibility of Latin and Greek which caused their demise, making them now "dead" languages. The modern languages, most notably English, while less orderly and more linguistically chaotic, are, by that very factor, less rule-ridden and more flexible in providing symbolic expression for the variegated and expanding types of experiences human beings have. In English — especially the American variety — the coining of new words and the taking of liberties with grammatical form are going on constantly. Latin, it is now believed, could never serve adequately as the vehicle for modern technological and organizational life; it is too linguistically "tight." It has become defunct because of the very virtue for which the Neo-Thomist wishes to sustain it in the program of the school.

natural sciences reveal some of this; the social sciences somewhat less. The humanities possess perhaps the least of all; but for very special reasons, which we shall examine in the section on epistemology, the humanities are specially treated in such a way as to find their way back into Neo-Thomist study programs. Reference is made to the Great Books program, which is discussed in Chapter Eleven (see pages 349–351).

The subject matter of social experience

It is now necessary to pass over to a newer philosophy, which looks upon the curriculum of the school in quite a different light. In the first place, as we have noted, Experimentalism holds to an ontology of process, a world which is not "sitting still out there" in a state of "being" waiting to be found out about, but rather a world in a dynamic process of becoming. It is what William James called "the universe with the lid off."

In order for boys and girls to reach an awareness of this kind of cosmos, the Experimentalist holds, it is necessary to provide a similar tone and quality to their studies in the school; that is to say, the curriculum should consist not of a given set of facts or ideas or bodies of knowledge set out in advance to be mastered, but rather of a series of experiences in which the evolutionary and "becoming" quality of our world is represented in the microcosm of the classroom. No truths about the world we live in, says the Experimentalist, not even the most rigorously achieved scientific truths, are ever absolutely and forever true; they are always subject to change. And this is because the final ontological reference point is human experience, which is a moving, flowing event. We are therefore required to engage in a perpetual revising and correcting of our knowledge as we continue to make sense out of our experience. For this reason, knowledge cannot be set out in so many compartments for the student to master; such an arrangement would give the student the impression that the world the curriculum tells him about is static and fixed. But the world is not like that, says the Experimentalist, and the curriculum in its office as intermediary and liaison agent between reality and the learner must therefore assume the same "contours" as the reality it represents, i.e., the "contours" of "becoming," of dynamic movement, of process.[9]

Once we have this principle in mind it is possible to proceed into the more specific curricular preferences of the Experimentalist position. Obviously, if we must begin with schools as they are we must begin with

[9] We must point again to the semantic difficulty of developing Experimentalist ontological concepts with pre-Experimentalist linguistic forms: the word "contour" refers to a physical and material characteristic rather than, as we would wish, a characteristic of quality or process. We use it here for its metaphorical value; if you are alert to the semantic problem it should cause no difficulty.

the familiar subject-matter curriculums most schools still maintain. The less militant among Experimentalists might be satisfied simply to emphasize those subject matters which are most "procedural" in character and de-emphasize those subject matters which are most "substantive" in character. In this case the social studies might be singled out as most representative of the type of thing the Experimentalist has in mind. The social studies are the closest to the unsettled and indeterminate features of the cosmos; this is because they have to do with human beings and with the institutional structures human beings invent to organize their life. With the possible exception of the arts, the social studies are the least systematic, settled, and "given" among the subjects taught in today's schools. Because they are the closest approximation in contemporary curricular practice of the "open-endedness" of the Experimentalist ontological persuasion, they should be elevated to a position of primary importance in the life of the young.

The impact of Experimentalism in twentieth-century America has certainly borne this out. Most of the major changes in curricular structure in our schools have taken place in the social studies division of the schools' work. New courses in Citizenship, Social Living, and Problems of American Democracy have been established to take over from systematic, chronological History the task of educating the young in their social heritage. The study of the past — especially the distant past — says the Experimentalist, inclines the child too much to the "substantive" features of human life. The past is just "there," in a brute kind of way, irretrievable and existentially static. All one can do with history is to learn it; nothing can be done *about* it. But the prime reason we study history, the Experimentalist reminds us, is to comprehend and manage the present. We must, then, start our social learning in the present and work into historical materials when and as (but only when and as) they will assist us in understanding the present. This is what history is for. Too often, says the Experimentalist, we insist that the child learn history for the same reason Mallory gave for climbing Mount Everest: simply because "it is there." This motivation may seem plausible enough for the adventurous spirit of a Himalayan mountain climber, but it is not much of an educational principle. Knowledge, as we shall see in Experimentalist epistemology, is to be gained to help us live better; there is too little time for the luxury of scholastic endeavor solely because knowledge exists.

Our "Minimum" Experimentalist, in rounding out his curriculum, might simply say that the more substantive subject matters should be expected to hold a lesser position in the hierarchy of studies. Latin, for instance, will probably have to go. For some students it might be valuable, but its static quality — its "deadness" and consequent lack of utility in customary social life — makes it too expensive a "frill" for most schools to maintain. The sciences will, of course, be emphasized, not so much for the scientific knowledge already accumulated but for an understanding of the way in which scientists work, how they inquire into their subject, and what traits of mind they exhibit as scientists — i.e., *scientific process* or *method*. This, to the Experimentalist, is the necessary emphasis in chemistry, or biology, or physics: not so much a valence table to be committed to memory, but *how* chemists contrived the valence table, how new elements are being added to it all the time, and how chemists decide where in the table each new element should go.

We must consider also a much more authentic strain of Experimentalist theory: the problem-solving curriculum. The more resolute of Experimentalists, since they consider fundamentally wrongheaded the "subject-matter-set-out-to-be-learned" approach to learning, would favor scrapping the whole traditional curriculum. If we are really serious about inducting the young into a "cosmos of process," then working with the old order and compromising with a basically static substantive curriculum will only weaken our efforts and blunt the force of our argument. We must rid ourselves, they say, of the fundamental notion that learning goes on in compartments, that learning is essentially the mastery of preordered materials, organized and systematized into study-able form and set, like so much pastry, before the learner.

Learning is essentially growing. And growing, in Experimentalist language, means the increase of intelligence in the management of life; and this in turn means the expansion of reflective thinking and the consequent application of thought to action in the wide reach of affairs we honor with the name "human." If we are to produce growth effectively we must turn the whole learning process, as traditionally conceived, upside down! That is, we must start with the affairs of life, wherever we may meet them, and let those affairs dictate what should be learned and known in order to manage them properly. Hence the entire curriculum will be inverted from *subject matter,* which is intended to be applied later to life situations, to the *life situations* themselves, which provoke the kinds of learning in or between subject-matter areas that intelligent living calls for. The most convenient and available paradigm for this is, once again, the social studies course called "Problems of American Democracy." In this type of learning situation we begin, without shame or apology, with real-life problems: crime, divorce, juvenile delinquency, segregation, etc. Teacher and pupil combine their forces in studying and understanding and proposing solutions for these problems. In the process they have need of information — the police functions of government, court procedure, the psychological basis for aberrant behavior, the responsibilities of freedom. On and on one could go, says the Experi-

mentalist, delineating the outward extensions of knowledge and skill —
reading, writing, computing, comparing, judging — which the thorough
study of real-life problems will call into play in the school.

We shall examine this procedure more carefully in the section on
epistemology, for it should be apparent by now that the Experimentalist
curriculum is primarily an epistemological (How do we know?) problem,
rather than an ontological (What is real?) problem. The complete reconstruction of fundamental principle — from substance to process —
has served to alter fundamentally what is meant by the phrase "the curriculum of the school." At the very least, to use familiar language, the
Experimentalist may describe his curriculum as a series of problems to
be solved rather than a set of subjects to be learned. But even his series
of problems is not specified in advance; it will grow out of the interests
and needs of the young. That is, the problems will grow directly out of
ultimate reality — the *experience* of human beings.

In the Experimentalist school, therefore, we are likely to find the so-
called project method in full flower. Boys and girls studying botany so as
to understand the best type of grass to plant in the schoolyard, adolescents
investigating nuclear physics in order to comprehend the true meaning
of a Civil Defense evacuation drill, college students putting out a literary
magazine as a part of their course in literary criticism: These are the
situations out of which genuine growth emerges. These types of experiences — properly motivated, joined to the real concerns of the young,
and carried to full and meaningful termination — are the prime ingredients of the Experimentalist curriculum.

The subject matter of choice

As we have noted earlier (see page 73), Existentialism, as a still developing philosophy, has not yet taken up what we might classify as the
mundane, nonmetaphysical problems of organized social life — politics,
social organization, institutional education. The problem of a curriculum, therefore, which is a specific and tactical branch of institutional
education, has not yet come under discussion in Existentialist literature.
It may be too early, in fact, to venture anything definitive in the way
of a curricular program for this body of theory. What we must be content
with is a presumed (and therefore potentially presumptuous) extension
of Existentialist ontological doctrine into the more proximate area of
learning experiences in the school, hoping of course that as little violence
as possible is done to what one or another Existentialist may conceive to
be the authentic message of this challenging point of view.

Essentially, we may approach the task in somewhat the same way as was
done with Experimentalism; that is to say, given the prevailing subject-

centered curriculum of the school, with which everyone is directly familiar, what might an Existentialist point to in such a curriculum as its most important features, as far as his ontological outlook is concerned? We should recall, at this point, that the Existentialist has found unconvincing the ontological views that either the physical world of things or the Platonic world of transcendental ideas represents ultimate reality. And although St. Thomas, on account of his metaphysical establishment of the absolute ultimacy of "Being," can, in a manner of speaking, be considered the first existentialist, still the modern Existentialist finds Neo-Thomism wanting because it assigns absolute existence to an external God or Cosmos rather than to the inner self of man, where existence actually originates. Existence "originates" in the inner self of man because it is here that the primal cognition of the idea first occurs. Both the microcosmic individual and the macrocosmic human race utter the expression "I am" before they have anything to say about the existence of nature, other people, God, Truth, or the cosmos at large. Therefore, man first *is;* then he undertakes the task of determining *what* he is. But beyond this — and this is our present point — man is the *first thing that is.*

Now carrying forward these purely metaphysical notions, the Existentialist must necessarily proclaim, with an understandable firmness, the ultimate primacy of the individual self. He must also, therefore, turn away from the Experimentalist's notion of experience as the ground of reality. For experience itself is secondary; it necessarily has to *follow,* not precede, the initial cognition that "I am." Here I find myself, "thrown" into existence, an existence of indeterminate qualities. I may, if I choose, decide that this existence is an existence of "experience," as the Experimentalist says, but I must *choose* this. It just isn't there, forced on me.[10] I choose it; I create it. Therefore, I first *am;* then I specify the nature of my "am-ness": the experiential ground of existing.

What this means in more prosaic language is that the final court to which all questions must be brought — even the most transcendental and metaphysical questions — is the human self. Experience, as the Experimentalist uses the term, is merely a convenience we employ to denote the region in which we choose to exist. It is only a thin "surface" area, where human selves congregate and communicate with one another; but beneath the surface they exist ultimately as autonomous human selves.

From all of this we may tentatively suggest that the Existentialist considers the Experimentalist school too superficial, too involved with group process, too concerned with sharing and communication. In fact,

---

10 The Experimentalist might be inclined to say that it *is* forced on you. No matter what you choose you are still "experiencing." Hence, experience is the ultimate ground.

in its more extravagant form, the Experimentalist school has become so enraptured of "group dynamics" and "sharing" and "communication" that it has lost the individual. Johnny becomes so enmeshed in the "group," and the teacher and the class become so interested in "togetherness" in and for itself, that Johnny — with his own private self, unique and absolute — is forgotten as the unit which makes it all possible. For it is within Johnny's own selfhood, not in the group, that things are seen to be true or untrue, right or wrong, relevant or irrelevant. Before any group can function, there must be individual selves to make choices.

Therefore, to follow our line of argument, the individual self in its function as "choice-maker" must somehow be "set in the eye" of the entire educative process. To this end, we should be in search of those sectors of the school program where the individual comes into the greatest prominence; for wherever in the school program the individual private judgments of the child come most actively into play is the likely center of greatest Existentialist interest.

Among the most promising candidates for this preferential position are the arts: music, painting, poetry, creative writing. Probably the field of painting is the best case in point. Certainly here the individual is most at liberty, at least nowadays, to exert the power of ultimate choice, to expose to public view his private notions of what his world is all about, without intimidation or fear of rebuke. There is a kind of finality to a piece of art; there it is for all to see, uncompromisable, immodifiable, not subject to refinement — as is the case with an idea or concept — by further discussion. Perhaps the symbolism or "message" of a painting can be clarified with words; but this is only symptomatic of its failure *as* a painting. A painting is the inner life of a human being laid bare. Its value or authenticity does not depend upon group discussion or democratic process.[11] It is simply *there,* inserted once and for all into our lives. As such, it represents, along with the other art forms, the nearest approach to what is ultimately real in this world: the selfhood of a single human person.

Already in our school programs we are witnessing this approach in the field of art. Boys and girls, especially in the elementary schools, are given experiences in painting and clay-modeling and mobile construction which do not rely upon prearranged concepts or inherited forms that they are expected to follow. Rather, they are deliberately left as free as possible to explore the realm of color and shape and relationship and form to find there what they want to say about the world they live in. No judg-

---

11 Here again the Experimentalist would demur. As we shall see in the section on axiology, the Experimentalist holds that works of art are ultimately tested for their aesthetic quality in the same way that ideas and beliefs are tested, i.e., in the market place of public judgment.

ments are required on their work; their designs and creations simply stand as a public expression of private feeling.

There is more to this, incidentally, than mere Freudian catharsis. Nondirective art teaching may have this function, too, of course, but the Existentialist is not primarily interested in psychic regurgitation of old experiences for the sake of inner cleansing of the subconscious. He is, rather, interested in the guileless, uncomplicated, and "unsocialized" release of human feeling, old *or* new, and in the integration of these authentic feelings into our developing conception of man.

There is every likelihood that as Existentialism becomes more and more explicit about its educational views it will turn in the general direction of the arts as the most provocative vehicle for its ontological and metaphysical message.[12] One would expect that as the subjectivity of the learner finds increased elbowroom for action in this area, the Existentialist would then explore similar possibilities in, perhaps, the social sciences. Although the social sciences are, almost by definition, studies of group behavior, they must ultimately be seen as studies in human motivation; and since motivation is fundamentally not social but individual, it may be possible to evoke Existentialist tendencies in young people in their study of such topics as the disparities in male and female viewpoints on family life and marital affairs, divergent political parties and their appeal to the emotions, the differences in political ideology between East and West and the resulting conflict in cultures, the collisions between value systems such as materialism and intellectualism, and the strife born of competing religions in their attempt to commandeer the mind of man for the service of God. Certainly wherever these fields of inquiry call for moral judgment — and, of course, they often do — then Existentialist educational theory may have much to contribute to their curricular role in the life of the school.

THE REAL MAN

To sum up the discussion and to restate in more specific terms the linkage between ontologies and the work of the school, we have only to summarize what each of these curriculums aims to perform in the life of the growing person. We can do this best by drawing attention to what shall be spoken of here as "Paradigmatic Man," the image of the most genuinely *real* (in the ontological sense) man which can serve as the educational model in the school. Every philosophy, once its ontology is

12 For a more detailed examination of this position, see V. C. Morris and I. L. de Francesco, "Modern Art and the Modern School," *The Clearing House*, XXXII, No. 2 (October, 1957), 67-71.

elaborated and "in place," will necessarily seek to locate Man in some important and prominent position in its scheme of things. To this end, every philosophically oriented school program will seek to realize its purpose by working with every child for the development of the full and "compleat" man. It does not matter, at this stage, whether human material as we know it is capable of fulfilling all the aspirations that various philosophies have for it; this is for the educational tactician — the teacher in the classroom — to determine and report back. What we are concerned with here is simply the kind of person — the paradigmatic "Perfect Man" — each philosophy means to have emerge under the curricular influence of the school.

The Idealist, quite understandably, is likely to have in mind a "man of arts and letters," an individual facile in the intellectual heritage of his race. He is going to be interested, of course, in how well this person lives and moves in the practical world of time schedules and earning a living and getting things done, but these are and must be subordinate to the life of the mind which he will wish this person to consider his home. A life among books is both the *idea* life and the *ideal* life. The life of the mind is not only ontologically required by the character of ultimate reality but morally good in its own right as the best life to lead.

The Realist would be expected to have in mind a more precise and practically oriented person as the model to follow. Paradigmatically, such an individual might be summarized as "the master of the machine of nature," provided, of course, that we understand the word *machine* in its widest context. Generically we conjure up the image of the "man of action," an individual who studies the world for principles and regularities and laws, and then turns his understandings into programs for doing things. It is more likely that this person will be more regulated in his personal life than the other types; he will systematize his work and perhaps even his play, in order to harmonize with the essentially systematic character of the world about him. Efficiency and economy are both inherent attributes of Nature. The more we can imitate these characteristics in our own lives, the more fully human we shall become.

When we arrive at Neo-Thomism we are, as previously noted, faced with two patterns of personality development: the spiritual (Ecclesiastical Wing) and the rationalistic (Lay Wing). Quite obviously, the man of reverent spirit before the awesome God of Absolute Being will serve as the model for a Roman Catholic parochial school. As the highest expression of one's limited existence, a fully developed sense of duty — to family, to Church, to God — represents for this Wing the attributes of the model man. The Lay Neo-Thomist, less concerned with theological qualities and interested principally in the intellect, would set before us the model of the highly trained mind, sharpened to a keen edge of intuition of First Principles and Absolute Truth. We could expect this person to consider his first business to be the training of his intellect, the disciplining of his mental processes by the most rigorous logic. Only in this way can a human being rise to the fullest expression of his unique role as a rational creature.

Experimentalism withdraws from all these high-minded and traditional images of the perfect individual and asserts simply that the world of the twentieth century requires trained *intelligence*. *Intelligence*, to employ a term quite different from *intellect* (at least, as the latter is used by Neo-Thomists), is the name given to the bringing of thought *to bear upon action,* i.e., the function of mind in guiding conduct. In this light, then, our model man is a reflective do-er, a man whose humanity is measured by the intelligence of his behavior. In digested language, we can say he is the supreme "problem-solver," scientifically oriented to the continuing task of confronting and resolving the problematic situations with which this life is filled. Since problem-solving can best be carried on in concert with others, we may expect Experimentalist Man to be effective in group endeavor, socially attuned to the motivations and capacities of others, and able to lead or follow, as the dynamics of group process requires.

There is a kind of "infinity" to the Existentialist conception of self so final and absolute as to prejudice in advance any "definition" we might draw up of the Perfect Man. One of Existentialism's central tenets is that the Idea of Man is not yet finished. We help make this Idea with our lives, with our choices. The highest form of human existence would therefore be the repudiation of any so-called Paradigm. Man is not done finding himself; how, therefore, can we say what he ought to be? However, if we see an individual who is awake to his existence, who knows *that* he *is,* and who feels the heavy burden and enormous challenge of his "is-ness" in an earnest and serious concern with the life choices he must make day by day as his contribution to the "meaning of Man," then we may suspect the presence of an Existentialist in our midst.

QUESTIONS

1. How would each of the five ontologies react to the curriculum of the high school you attended? What changes would they each make, would you say, in order to bring it into line with their basic outlook?

2. The most widely known college-level curriculum is what is generally called "the liberal arts." Although this curriculum customarily covers much more than the arts, it reveals a number of ontological biases. Explain what these are.

3. What would each of the ontologies think of the following recent additions to the high school program: Driver Training, Distributive Education, Social Living, Space Physics, Logic, 100 Great Books?

4. Mention was made in this chapter of the shift from "substantive" to "process" thinking in philosophy and education. Can you cite any examples outside these fields which are symptomatic of the shift?

5. Attend the next meeting of the board of education in your city. Prepare a report indicating the ontologies of the members of the board based upon their remarks in board debate and their subsequent votes in taking action.

6. From what they say and write, what ontological preferences are revealed by (1) the editorial writer of your local newspaper, (2) the most vehement critic of public education you can think of, (3) the instructor of this course? How can you tell? Do you think every individual should be required to announce his ontological outlook before discussing education?

FURTHER READING

Idealism

Brameld, T. *Philosophies of Education in Cultural Perspective.* New York: Dryden Press, 1955.
Chapter 8 develops the educational theories of Idealism together with those of Realism. Strangely enough, as Brameld shows, these two contrasting ontologies make warm bedfellows in educational thought.

Horne, H. H. "An Idealistic Philosophy of Education," Chapter IV in *Philosophies of Education,* Forty-first Yearbook of the National Society for the Study of Education, ed. N. B. Henry, Part I. Chicago: the Society, 1942.
In the latter portions of this chapter, especially in the section on the curriculum, the ontological "dimension" of program-planning is explicitly developed. Horne winds up with the notion of "the Ideal-Centered School."

Realism

Brameld, T. *Philosophies of Education in Cultural Perspective.* New York: Dryden Press, 1955.
In Chapter 8 you will find a discussion of the Essentialist "pattern of educational beliefs," a splendid summary of what Realism and Idealism have to say about educational theory as regards concepts of learning, the design of the curriculum, and the role of the school in society.

Brubacher, John. *Modern Philosophies of Education,* Second Edition. New York: McGraw-Hill Book Co., 1950.
In Chapter II you will find a splendid review of the ontological problems — appearance and reality, change and the changeless, the novel and the prim-

ordial, the individual and the universal, time and eternity — and how these bear on educational theory.

Neo-Thomism

Adler, Mortimer J. "In Defense of the Philosophy of Education," Chapter V in *Philosophies of Education*, Forty-first Yearbook of the National Society for the Study of Education, ed. N. B. Henry, Part I. Chicago: the Society, 1942.
Adler here defends what he considers not *a* but *the* (i.e., *the only*) philosophy of education. In grand syllogistic fashion, he claims that since philosophy deals with truth and since by definition several different theories or philosophies cannot be true at the same time, therefore there can be only one true philosophy. And he tells us about it here, with thumping emphasis on the First Principles.

Maritain, Jacques. *Education at the Crossroads*. New Haven: Yale University Press, 1943.
The entire volume, built from the twentieth Terry Lecture Series at Yale, is a Neo-Thomist's testament on education. Part I, on Aims, is the most relevant to this chapter. Dealing with "seven misconceptions," the author poses the Christian Idea of Man and what it calls for in the way of education.

Redden, J. D., and Ryan, F. A. *A Catholic Philosophy of Education*, Revised Edition. Milwaukee: Bruce Publishing Co., 1956.
In Book I of this volume the modern Thomist position is stated and applied to various topics: science, the intellect, morals, aesthetics, physical education. Chapter XI, on philosophy and the curriculum, discusses the content of the Catholic educational program, but Chapter I provides a better view of the linkage between ontology and education.

Experimentalism

Brameld, T. *Philosophies of Education in Cultural Perspective*. New York: Dryden Press, 1955.
Chapter 5 surveys the Progressivist pattern of educational beliefs. In the sections on learning and the curriculum you will find a clear exposition of Experimentalist educational theory.

Dewey, John. *Democracy and Education*. New York: The Macmillan Co., 1916.
In Chapters XI, XIV, XVI, and XVII the real meaning of an "ontology of experience" is brought forth in educational terms. Here Dewey explains the "experience concept" as it relates to human thinking; then, after discussing the nature of subject matter, he proceeds to show the application of the concept in such fields as history, geography, and science.

Existentialism

Harper, Ralph. "Significance of Existence and Recognition for Education," Chapter VII in *Modern Philosophies and Education*, Fifty-fourth Yearbook of the National Society for the Study of Education, ed. N. B. Henry, Part I. Chicago: the Society, 1955.

In this powerful and illuminating chapter Harper points to the loss of recognition in modern "mass" man. The "ontology of the ultimate self" can here be seen in its educational setting, as the author discusses educational aims, the curriculum, the school and society, and the school and the individual. The chapter is followed by a short essay by Professor Robert Ulich of Harvard, a sympathetic critic of Existentialism.

Morris, V. C. "Existentialism and Education," *Educational Theory*, IV, No. 4 (October, 1954), 247–258.

In this article the present author develops the main Existentialist concepts, compares them with those of Experimentalism, and then signifies their meaning for educational practice. In the idiom of paradox so often found in philosophical thinking, Existentialism and Experimentalism are seen to share much in basic outlook; but when they arrive at the practical business of educating the young, they take quite contrary positions.

PART III

Epistemology:
What Is True?

Epistemology: The Question

of Truth and Knowledge

KNOWLEDGE AND
THE SCHOOL

We come now to our second major set of problems in the study of philosophy, those that cluster about the seminal question: What is true? If our first consideration, comprising Part II, had to do with the onto-logical question, "What is?," we must turn now to the more immediate concern of determining what precisely we can *say* about that which is; that is, we are required to pay attention to what we say about reality as well as what we assume reality to be. And as we pass into this second set of problems, we come much closer to the concrete work of the school, i.e., the work, basically, of saying things about (describing and explaining) the world to neophyte inhabitants of it.

This second set of problems represents all of the questions we have concerning *knowledge:* how knowing takes place, how we *know* that we know, how we decide between competing "candidates" for knowledge (what to do, for instance, with the Biblical versus the Darwinian version of Genesis), how we decide what knowledge is most worth having,[1] and,

[1] This is also an axiological (value) question, with referents in Part IV. Knowing is one thing; ordering our "knowings" in a hierarchy is another. At least we can say

111

finally, coming full circle, how we *know* our ontologies and how we become certain that our own ontology is the really correct one. Can there be, really, more than one ontology? We shall return to this question in the final section of the chapter. But here we are concerned with the problem of knowing — what is designated *epistemology.*

Knowledge as the school's "stock in trade"

One of the principal tasks of the school is to transmit to each generation the heritage of the race, to equip the young with as much as possible of what man has come to know about the world he lives in. To use a somewhat questionable simile, the school can be likened to a store whose stock in trade is knowledge; knowledge of all types lines its shelves, and its principal task is to retail this knowledge to each wave of customers, i.e., each succeeding generation. But as an epistemological retail establishment it has two fundamental problems. One concerns the authenticity and accuracy of the stock itself; can we have confidence that all of the items on the "shelf of knowledge" are really true? In order to be sure, we are forced to inquire into how these things were first found out. If we have confidence in such-and-such a method of finding something out, then we can return to the "store," tag the "merchandise" as authentic, and proceed to retail it as true.

Epistemology is a problem, and thus occupies the philosopher, because there are several alternative ways of knowing and some of them are held to be better than others. What is more, the way in which something is found out and, hence, *known* tells us something about how much trust we can put in it, or at least the manner in which we shall use the item of knowledge. Say, for instance, that we are told by a voodoo artist or palm reader that we are scheduled to encounter, in the unspecified future, a misfortune of some kind causing great hardship and inconvenience. We should certainly treat this bit of information quite differently from the information that, upon investigation of the garage mechanic, our automobile engine at some unspecified time in the future may be expected to break down due to a developing weakness in a crankshaft bearing.

In the latter instance we are confronted by empirical information resulting from data gathered by a trained observer. In the former instance we are confronted by mystical knowledge, which is — because it is occult — beyond the reach of our criticism or judgment. We tend to place more trust in one than in the other, and if we are professional educators we are inclined toward the inclusion of the latter type and the

---

here that axiological ordering of knowledge cannot get under way until some alternatives are available from which to choose. In the present instance, our understanding of knowledge-making must provide us with what knowledge is *possible* before we can engage in knowledge-judging to decide what knowledge is *worthiest.*

exclusion of the former type of knowledge in the school's curricular program.

How we know, then, has much to tell us about the authenticity and trustworthiness of our "stock" of curricular knowledge, and, to return to our retail establishment, our judgment of an item on the shelf rests only partially on seeing it on a page of a book or even hearing it firsthand from an authority; it rests ultimately on the manner in which the item of information was originally gathered in and added to the sum of human knowledge.

Our second concern in the epistemological retail establishment concerns the "customers": How do they come to know things? If we understood how knowing-in-general takes place, perhaps we could get a better idea of how boys' and girls' knowing in the classroom takes place. Especially would this be true if, more specifically, we could discover a similarity between the knowing process of the research scholar, standing at the frontier of knowledge and probing the unknown, and the knowing process of the youngster standing at his own "frontier" and being taken by his teacher in successive stages into wider and wider spheres of thought and action.

To raise this question at all is to intimate that different philosophic schools have different positions on it, some holding that the way discoverers learn new things is essentially different from the way youngsters learn things in school. Others hold, on the other hand, that there is a generic identity in procedure in the two cases and that the "level of sophistication" is the only factor that needs to be varied as we proceed up the educational ladder. We shall take up this whole question in Chapter Seven.

To summarize, then, epistemology takes as its range of discourse those problems relating to the nature of knowledge and the character of the procedures we use to attain it. Since this study bears directly on the dependability of knowledge and the propriety of various methods of reaching warrantable truth, it stands at the very base of the entire educative process. It is every philosopher's obligation — and that of every student of philosophy — to comprehend the epistemological dimension of philosophic thinking (the topic of the present chapter), to appreciate the variety of epistemologies presently available to him (Chapter Six), and to recognize their significance in controlling the educative process (Chapter Seven).

THE DIMENSIONS OF KNOWING

The intelligibility of the cosmos

In taking hold of the epistemological problem, we can find no better starting place than the ontological concerns which we have just left behind. And we can put the question without complication: Whatever reality is, can it be known? Or, to say it another way, with longer words, is intelligibility one of the attributes of the real world? This is, as we shall see later, somewhat of a circular question; but at this stage we are asking for a fundamental ground rule to be agreed on before the epistemological expedition can set out — namely, that knowing, in and of itself as an occurrence in the cosmos, is *possible*. Its possibility is contingent in part upon the psychology of human beings, most evidently revealed in the varieties of knowing to be discussed below. But the possibility of knowing is also contingent upon whether the cosmos will "cooperate," whether its very structure or character permits or supports this thing we call knowing.

To raise this question is to imply that the answer to it is, in a manner of speaking, "open." And to say that it is "open" is to suggest that a hornets' nest of troubles awaits us as we try to answer it. This unfortunately is precisely the predicament we find ourselves in. For if the answer is "No," we are stopped dead in our tracks; we are prevented from advancing to any knowledge whatsoever, except perhaps a set of fancies and fantasies we are able to concoct in our own minds. If, on the other hand, the answer is "Yes," then we are obligated to go on to specify the *kinds* of knowledge ultimate reality is prepared to yield. It should be obvious that the kinds of knowledge reality makes possible will depend upon our conceptions of reality; and this is to say that the kinds of knowledge available to us will vary from ontology to ontology.

Idealism, for instance, will accept the possibility of perceptual knowledge but will hold that reality is prepared to yield a more genuine knowledge — the knowledge of ideas, existing behind the sensory screen — if we but take the trouble to find it out. Realism will hold to a reality which has only sensory knowledge to offer; out of such knowledge we can expect to extract relations and associations *among* things but certainly not ideas *behind* things. The Neo-Thomist will not only accept the possibility of sensory knowledge but go on to show that the powers of the intellect are such that we can find our way to absolute truth (Lay Thomism) or that the spiritual powers of man are occasionally receptive to revealed knowledge from God (Ecclesiastical Thomism). The Experimentalist, holding the "transactional" ontology that he does, will center his attention on the possibility of empirical knowledge, based in sensory experience but reflectively fashioned into "working truths," which are tested in action. Finally, the Existentialist, not yet inclined to deal with epistemological matters in philosophically customary ways and basing his ontology in sheer existence, might be willing to say that all of these types of knowledge *have occurred* historically, though none of them has any ontological base other than ultimate human choice; even to decide among competing epistemologies is itself a choice.

"Truth" or "truth"

For better or worse, we can say here that almost all philosophies (certainly those presented in this book) hold to some kind of position which makes knowledge ontologically (not necessarily psychologically)[2] possible and which serves to justify the generalized statement, "The cosmos is fundamentally intelligible," even though — we are warned — the precise definition of *cosmos* and *intelligible* in this statement may require elaborate qualification. Forsaking for the moment, however, the more technical points of philosophy, we now have at least a working base on which to build, i.e., the ontological *possibility* of knowledge. We are now in a position to ask some things *about* the knowledge that our "reality" makes available.

Is this knowledge, for instance, presented to us in such a way that we are *obligated* to believe it? That is to say, are there some items of knowledge which are not only seen by men to be true but which are always and eternally true, in every century and for all time, and universally true, in all societies and in all places? Is there, to use our customary linguistic shorthand, such a thing as *absolute* truth, absolutely true without qualification of any kind? If this kind of knowledge is contained in the universe, then it would certainly be to our advantage to find it out, for it would obviously be of great help in finding our way in a troubled world. And, of course, it would be ideal material to place in the curriculum of the school, for it would not have to be tampered with or modified every five years in a "curriculum revision" project.

The great difficulty with this type of truth (often spelled with a capital *T: Truth*) is that men are, generally speaking, not agreed on what it is. There might be considerable agreement that the statement "The internal angles of a triangle equal 180 degrees" is an absolute truth.[3] But in the social sphere when, let us say, the political status of men is up for consideration, there is precious little agreement among men or societies on what truths control political arrangements. When Jefferson said in the Declaration ". . . all men are created equal" (or, to render it in more

---

2 We must continue to make this distinction, because to say that such-and-such type of knowledge is ontologically available to us is not to say that human beings, as knowing creatures, are capable of knowing such knowledge. As the Existentialist Karl Jaspers once put it epigrammatically, "It is thinkable that there should be something unthinkable." In most philosophies, however, there is assumed to be some equivalence between the knowledge the universe makes possible and that which the human mind can take hold of — another instance, incidentally, of the propensity to egocentrism of the human race in constructing a reality "in its own image," so to speak, i.e., a cosmos built along lines which are compatible with human powers and purposes. Metaphysically speaking, there is no defensible warrant for this.

3 Even this, believe it or not, is open to challenge. In non-Euclidean geometry it does not hold. And even in Euclidean geometry it is held to be on the order of a "tautology," a statement whose predicate merely contains one of the definitions of the subject, and which, therefore, says no more than "A = A," hence, nothing.

secular terms, "all men are equal") he sought to elevate this principle to an absolute status by claiming that it was "self-evident." But its presumed self-evidence is somewhat gratuitous. Indeed, as any careful chronicler could demonstrate, the history of mankind has been one long, episodic exhibit of the "self-evidence" of its opposite. And even among contemporary societies there prevails a disturbing lack of unanimity on this question. When Jefferson composed this phrase he was referring, of course, not to physical or intellectual equality but to equality before the law. But since laws are made by men rather than by some cosmic legislature, we are forced to reduce and rephrase Jefferson thus: All men are equal before man-made institutions. Even this might require considerable going over before being acceptable to world sentiment. But the point of all this is merely to demonstrate that what claims to be absolute may quickly be seen, according to some philosophies, to require a libraryful of adequately grounded reservations and qualifications. And only one reservation is required to repeal the absoluteness of a statement.

In the moral sphere, which is treated in more detail in Part IV, the question of absolutes is still more precarious. If, let us say, questions of sexual behavior are up for discussion, there is even less agreement among men on how life should properly be lived. And the irony of it all is that the sexual sphere is one of those areas of social thought in which every society thinks itself to have found something closely approximating absolute truth. A more confounding irony is that it is in the social and moral regions of living — not the geometrical and mathematical — that we are most in need of absolutes, i.e., sure moorings to the cosmos; but it is precisely in these areas that absolutes are so difficult to come by.

For these (and many other, more complicated) reasons, the notion of "Absolute Truth," for all its attractive qualities in educational concerns, has lost some of its sheen in modern secular thought. We are driven back, say the secularists, upon the finite limitations of human knowing and are required to settle for "truth" with a lower-case *t* — that is, truths which are *thought* to be eternal and absolute but which are always open to substantial qualification or to change and repeal.

Vicarious and direct knowing

Moving gradually away from our ontological base of epistemological operations, we must now ask a series of questions concerning the *human* "dimensions" of knowing. The first of these has to do with a distinction that is made in epistemology between "knowing by acquaintance" and "knowing by description." Knowing by acquaintance consists in having a direct and immediate awareness of some feature of our environment — what we had for breakfast, the personality quirks of our friends and associates, the meaning of free enterprise in American economics. But we are not limited to direct knowledge. We can as well know *about* things which we never directly experience but which are described to us — what the "boss" had for breakfast, the personality quirks of the President of the United States, and the meaning of "freedom" in the Soviet Union. Now, although this distinction may border on the innocuously obvious, it has important ramifications in understanding the knowing process and, ultimately, in managing the learning process.

Our problem comes to immediate focus in the consideration of epistemological circumstances of the "how-to-do-something" variety. Suppose a man wants to teach his wife how to drive an automobile. He begins by the "descriptive" approach of having her read a book on the subject. Then he proceeds to explain it to her, perhaps embellishing the discourse with appropriate gestures. Then he proceeds to demonstrate by getting into the vehicle and letting her watch him drive, all the while providing a running verbal commentary on what he is doing and why. Suppose this reading and listening and watching is kept up for a period of, say, six months, to the point that the wife is completely knowledgeable about driving a car. Question: Does she or does she not know how to drive a car?

The usual course to follow in answering this question is to let her try it and *see* if she knows. But whether or not she is successful in the trial, the epistemological question remains: Did she know before she tried it? The reason this is a troublesome issue is precisely that in most knowing situations and in most learning situations we are required to operate in what is here spoken of as the "vicarious" region of action — reading books, listening to people, observing processes under way. Especially in education is this vicariousness of experience carried to its extended limit, for a school is deliberately removed from life. It is thought that an ordered presentation of learning material through the written and audible symbol, together with some limited "spectator" experience, will produce genuine knowing and hence genuine learning.

To change our example, and thereby to point to the significance of this issue: Can a child learn democratic behavior by reading books and doing scrapbook projects in civics class? We are not teaching someone to operate a machine; we are teaching a youngster what democracy means, what a democratic way of life — social, political, personal — is all about, what feelings and attitudes we hope he will acquire toward democratic patterns of living. In a general way we are teaching him *how* to live democratically. Can we, to ask our question again, manage to do this through the manipulation of symbols in his experience (words and numbers, both written and oral)?

Upon confronting *this* question we are seldom badgered by a similar impatience to "let him try it." How is he to try it? Practically speaking, he cannot "try it" until he grows up. So we give him a paper-and-pencil test, reduce his answers to a score, and record a number or letter on a report card to designate how much he now *knows*. The society at large, however, is only incidentally interested in paper-and-pencil knowledge; it is looking for attitudes, feelings, behavior patterns. And it expects that these are developed in some meaningful way in the civics classroom — which deals almost exclusively in "knowledge by description."

The whole set of relationships between thought and action are thus brought into play in epistemology and in education. And the position and function of these two ingredients of human experience will noticeably alter as we move from one epistemology to another.

Subjective and objective knowledge

Closely related to the preceding problem is that of the nature of the knowing process. Again we can get right at the difficulty by asking the question: Is knowledge something that comes to us from the "outside" — is it inserted into our minds and nervous systems somewhat the way iron ore is dumped into a ship? Or do we, as knowers, contribute something in this engagement of ourselves with the world in such a way as to be partially responsible for the knowledge that ends up in our beings and eventually flows into our behavior? Or do we, to consider a third alternative, actually exist as "pure" *subjects,* and thereby become the manufacturers of truth rather than either the recipients of it or the participants, along with the real world, in its identification and use? That is, do we introduce *into* reality whatever meaning and truth and knowledge we then say it already contains?

From our previous study of ontology, it should be evident if not obvious that different philosophies will take a different stand on this matter. For if reality is essentially "out there" waiting to be found out about, then we may consider knowledge as a commodity that enters from the outside and is then worked into our mental equipment, our personalities, and our day-to-day conduct. If our ontology is of a "transactional" sort, we shall incline toward the second position, namely, that we *know* things by receiving impressions from reality, which we then turn into guesses or hypotheses of what is true, which we then verify by acting them out "on" reality to see how they work. If, finally, our ontology is a kind of "in-here" subjectivism, we shall lean in the direction of the third alternative — an epistemology of ultimate human authorship of the truths and values which are said to exist in this universe but which exist only on sufferance of our saying that they do.

While the educational implications of this question are to be more thoroughly examined in Chapter Seven, it would not ruin our story at this point to note that the first of the above positions tends to be held by mathematicians, physical and natural scientists, and historians. In these areas, a body of factual content can be identified as quite independent of what human beings think of it. The second position, on the other hand, tends to be more compatible with the thinking in the social and behavioral sciences, in which a body of empirical and conceptualized knowledge constantly requires rechecking and reinterpretation. The human knower is trying to *know himself,* albeit in groups; and in knowing himself, the individual must be both subject *and* object. The third position above, the "man-creates-truth" view, is more likely to be held in the humanities — the arts, literature, and those subjects dealing with moral questions and ethical interpretations — where individual human judgment (although not necessarily *behavior*) is permitted the greatest latitude of expression.

That is why, to add to our aside here, the Realist (and, with some qualification, the Idealist) will do the bulk of his educational thinking in the sciences and objective history; why the Experimentalist feels more at home when he is dealing with social studies and the human sciences; and why the Existentialist remains relatively silent on physics and sociology and dwells instead upon those humanistic matters relating to feeling and commitment, especially those having to do with moral decision.[4]

The a priori and the a posteriori

We must now sum up by pointing to a final and perhaps decisive epistemological consideration, i.e., the logical and chronological locus of genuine knowledge. To come right to the point, is true knowledge *prior* to or *posterior* to human experience? Can a truth be said to be in hand before it is introduced into human concerns or must it wait upon its involvement in life's affairs to attain whatever sort of "truth-fulness" we say that it enjoys? This may be recognized as a generalized and somewhat more sophisticated restatement of the difficulties encountered in the previous sections.

When we speak of *a priori* knowledge we designate that which is known and knowable in and of itself. The ratio existing between the diameter and the circumference of a circle — *pi* — may be said to be

---

[4] Do not be misled into thinking that the several philosophies, in holding to a given view on the "subjective-objective" question, would restrict their curriculum to any one of the three divisions mentioned. Instead, they each attempt to show how their epistemological view can be applied to *all* studies in the school. Since a given curricular area yields more readily to their epistemological position, it is used primarily to *exemplify* how things should be managed elsewhere in the school's work.

prior to our knowledge of it. This relationship is inherent in the characteristics of circles; it is a truth antecedent to any human attempt to know it. Therefore, once this relationship is seen as inherent to circles we are not obligated to test it out in our experience every time we confront a circle.

But the relation existing between one circle and another circle is not given. That one circle is above, or larger than, or in a different plane from a second circle requires human experience for verification. Whatever knowledge we attain, therefore, is *a posteriori*, i.e., it is posterior to the onset of human awareness of it.

Traditional philosophies have always regarded *a priori* knowledge as superior to *a posteriori* knowledge. For one thing, being prior, it is thought to represent the real world; it has an ontological status; it is woven into the very texture of reality. If reality is fixed and permanent, these philosophies hold, then *a priori* truths are fixed and permanent. They are eternal, outside of time, and hence absolute. (See the earlier section on absolute versus relative truth.) For this same reason, *a priori* knowledge enjoys another advantage: It is free of contamination by human knowers, with all their emotions, opinions, and interpretations. One cannot have opinions about *a priori* knowledge. It is simply true.

A posteriori knowledge, on the other hand, resting as it does in human experience, is subject to all the ills and frailties of the knowing mechanism of man. Such truths must suffer the same infirmities suffered by men, with their clouded perception and limited abilities of comprehension. Such knowledge, therefore, is always in some measure unreliable, impermanent, corrigible.

For this reason, the traditional philosophies have given *a priori* knowledge — especially as it is found in mathematics and geometry — the "inside track" in education, leaving *a posteriori* knowledge — in general, we can call all scientific knowledge *a posteriori* — a subordinate position in the curriculum. Neo-Thomism, as we shall see in the next chapter, is particularly partial to this view.

The newer philosophies, most especially Experimentalism, tend to invert this, claiming that all knowledge, sooner or later, must be tested in experience. There is a suggestion that *a priori* knowledge actually does not exist, that as soon as knowledge is *had* by some human knower it has entered the zone of experience and is therefore *a posteriori*. The mathematical computation of *pi* (3.1416), for instance, did not come into our knowledge until some human being somewhere became curious about that relationship, worked it out, checked and rechecked it, and finally accepted it as true. The fact that the relationship is true of all circles was itself established in experience.

In every case, then, the quest for knowledge originates in men's curiosity about their world, and whatever is claimed to be knowledge must first have satisfied some human knowers somewhere as being relative to and contingent upon their experience.

In a further elaboration of this point, the Logical Positivists and Analysts have shown that *a priori* knowledge is tautological; that is, propositions of this kind simply restate what is already assumed. To say that the relation *pi* is an inherent characteristic of all circles is simply to say that this is one of the things we mean by the term *circle*. We have said nothing new, really. We have merely elaborated upon the *meaning* of the object in our experience. It is much like saying that roundness is a characteristic of all circles.

We shall consider the Analyst's thesis in more detail in a brief section at the close of Chapter Six.

Although there are other, more complex "dimensions" to the epistemological problem, these will suffice to indicate the type of considerations in the understanding of the knowing process which have direct relevance to the educational task. We must now turn to the different ways of knowing which are pointed to by various epistemologists and which provide the foundation for the various educational theories.

THE VARIETIES
OF KNOWING

Sense data

Every philosophy must come to terms at the outset of its epistemology with the most immediate of all types of knowledge, the knowledge to which we have access through our five senses. There is no convincing way to gainsay the authenticity of such knowledge, at least as it seems to be experienced by individual human beings. When I walk outdoors and see snow falling, feel the dry chill of a wintry day, hear the rumble of the train in the distance, smell the exhaust of nearby industries, and taste the chocolate bar I'm munching, I am knowing things, and no one can say me nay. There are, to be sure, many refinements that can and should be made on this kind of knowledge; the "seeing" of the outdoor thermometer sharpens my knowledge of the "feeling" of cold. And many psychological studies in sensory perception — in the field of optics, in the determination of space relations, in auditory acuity — have revealed that our sensory apparatus is far less reliable a knowing instrument than we may think it is. Even so common a thing as reporting an event, whether over the backyard fence or in a newspaper dispatch or before a court of law, is fraught with unnumbered hazards of error in relating what actually happened. The persistence of unsubstantiated rumor, letters of correction to the editor, and widely divergent testimony on the witness stand all suggest that human knowing via the senses is considerably less dependable than we individually think our own sensory knowing to be.

But the presence of sensory data cannot be denied. We cannot escape their impact on our beings. If we are alive and awake, we are engaging in sensory perception all the time, and our senses cannot be shut off, except temporarily in slumber. This inexorability of sensation suggests, at the outset, that our epistemology must somehow take account of the fact that we are existentially "plugged in" to nature, that we cannot entertain ideas or notions which consistently seem to contradict the sensory truths we feel ourselves capable of apprehending directly, and, therefore, that sensation, as undependable as it may be, must somehow stand at the center of whatever knowing theory we choose to concoct.

As a matter of philosophical fact, the primacy of sensory knowledge is recognized in most, if not all, philosophical positions, at least in the sense that it is the *starting place* for all knowing. But the trouble with sensory knowledge is precisely what we have already alluded to, i.e., its lack of dependability. Furthermore, it does not account for all or even a very large share of what we seem to feel is the range of human knowing. It is only a partial and limited type of knowledge, which we share with the rest of the animal kingdom.[5]

Sensory knowledge is therefore insufficient on at least two counts: undependability and incompleteness. These two deficiencies provoke us into further inquiry, for epistemologies are in the business not merely of recording types of knowing but of exhausting, without remainder, *all* the channels of epistemological activity men are capable of and of evaluating and criticizing those channels for their comparative effectiveness in coming to genuine truth. Consequently we must proceed to other possibilities.

Common sense

The first extension we can make in this undertaking is in the direction of the other sentient creatures who possess with us, it appears, the same sensory equipment. The great advantage of human beings over all other animals is their ability to reduce their sensory experience to symbols, i.e., to noises, gestures, and designs made on surfaces. This makes it possible not only to share sensations — which animals cannot do — but, what is

[5] Indeed, while the totality of our sensory apparatus is perhaps of higher competence than that of any other single organism, there are many animals which can outstrip us in any one of the five senses — eagles in sight, dogs in hearing and smell, etc.

more important, to check the accuracy and authenticity of our sensations with others — which animals cannot do either.

Immediately this can be seen as a very great epistemological convenience, for it helps to discard what is untrue or at least *less* true and fasten upon that which is more true and hence more dependable in organizing and managing our lives. If I cannot detect the odor of toxic ozone in a closed room, but ten others *do* detect it, I am likely to readjust my understanding of the situation in their favor and get out of there; but even in considerably less urgent circumstances I am still inclined to discount my own sensations if there is a sufficient weight of reports from others that I am either missing something or perceiving the "wrong" thing. So extensive is this tendency that it has become something of a socially recognized epistemological axiom: "Fifty million Frenchmen can't be wrong!" And in modern scientific sociology and anthropology this willingness to yield to the "common sense," the generally held sense perceptions, of the community is taken as a basic concept in understanding political and moral behavior.[6]

The primary difficulty with this "common-sense" way to true knowledge is that it rests ultimately upon individual sensations. It is therefore theoretically subject to the same kind of error that any individual is subject to in his perceptions. A majority vote of a group's individual sensations is not, after all, a genuine guarantee that real truth has been achieved, especially if the sensations are fleeting and incomplete. The ten people *could* be wrong about the ozone; their sensation might be due merely to a super-exotic perfume on one of the ladies. And fifty million Frenchmen *can* be wrong, just as wrong as seventy million Nazi Fascists or 100 million Soviet Communists, or even 175 million Americans.

What we must do, therefore, in the epistemological enterprise, is to search further for more creditable and dependable ways of knowing, against which to check both individual sensations and common sensations. The most widely applicable of these meta-methods in our time is science, which attempts to control sensory experiences in such a way that the sensory reports will be confined to a limited set of circumstances, reduced to objective measures, and codifiable within a rigorous system of specific (even if tentative) conclusions. But before we take up this epistemological tack we must examine other possibilities.

[6] One of the most grotesque psychological experiments along these lines was conducted at the Laboratory of Social Relations at Harvard University and reported in Solomon E. Asch, "Opinions and Social Pressure," *Scientific American* (November, 1955), 3. In this study all the subjects but one were instructed to give erroneous reports of their perceptions of various geometric shapes — relative lengths of lines, relative sizes of cubes or circles, etc. Then the experimenters measured how long it took for the lone individual to repudiate his own senses (!) and agree to go along with the group's judgment. The fact that almost every test subject eventually did yield tells us a great deal about modern man.

Logic

To the classical logician the difficulty with sensory knowledge is that it stops short of true knowledge. We forget, he says, that the intellect is already "in place" before sense data are received; and the intellect has the capacity to extend the process of knowing by utilizing sensory information in a purely non-sensory and wholly mental progression to a new kind of truth. This capacity is customarily exemplified by the use of the syllogism, a series of statements which proceeds from the base of experience to the intellectual apprehension of truths which sensory experience cannot yield.

Consider the familiar syllogism:

> All men are mortal.
> Socrates is a man.
> ∴ Socrates is mortal.

In order to assert the first statement (the major premise) we need only generalize from our sensory data concerning the mortality of individual men. Certainly not one single sensory datum has yet been collected to disprove it. So we assert it as true that "All men are mortal." The second statement (the minor premise) is based completely on sense data. We experience the entity of Socrates and assign the word *man* to him. Now, by purely intellectual means we proceed to the third statement, "Socrates is mortal." This truth, so long as Socrates lives, is not to be verified through sensation. It is a truth which is *based* in sensation but not verified there. Hence it is an item of knowledge to be added to what we have already gathered in through our senses.

It is the position of those who hold to the possibility of logical knowledge that this same procedure can be applied to many other areas of knowing. Whenever we can assert certain things about our world and can arrange these assertions in specifically definable ways, we can then proceed to genuinely new knowledge. This knowledge can then be systematized and, just like sensory knowledge, arranged in different subject matters and included in the content of the educative process. The most obvious example of this is seen in the field of mathematics, most notably geometry, where certain truths are not immediately known but, rather, *derived* from proof. (For a refutation of this position, see the section on the Analytic Movement at the close of Chapter Six.)

Self-evidence and intuition

Closely related to the logical position is the view that the human intellect is capable not only of *building up* truths from the raw materials of experience but of *apprehending* certain truths directly and immediately, with no recourse whatsoever to experience. It is capable, say the proponents of this position, of taking hold of certain ideas and recognizing them, on a purely intellectual basis, as true. These truths are true in and of themselves, and come by their truth in a state of supreme independence of ordinary human experience.

Perhaps the most common examples of this type of truth can be found in geometry and mathematics. When we assert that "Two things equal to the same thing are equal to each other," we are not reporting observations from previous experience nor are we setting up a hypothesis to be tested later in some experiment. We are, rather, asserting a statement whose truth lies wholly in a mental apprehension of the intellect. It is simply true, and the intellect needs no assistance whatsoever — either from the senses or from mathematical demonstration — to assert it.

We speak of such truths as "self-evident," i.e., containing their own verification. We shall wish to take a much closer look at this kind of knowing in Chapter Six, especially in the examination of Thomistic epistemology; but the above example is sufficient at this point to suggest the general nature of immediately apprehensible intellectual knowledge.

The point at which the intellect makes this final leap to new truth is spoken of in Aristotelian epistemology as *intuition*. Among moderns the word *intuition* has a faintly mystical, somewhat magical quality. In popular parlance we speak of "woman's intuition," by which we mean to suggest a knowing power beyond all reasonable description. But in formal epistemology intuition must be taken more seriously, since it refers to a kind of knowing whereby the rational faculty of man takes hold of an idea and sees it to be true necessarily.

Nowhere is this injunction to seriousness more binding than in religious and theological thought, where "intuitions" are being had and reported all the time. Probably every human being, at one time or another, has had the feeling that he has seen something that no one else has ever seen; account must somehow be taken of that "inner fire" of conscience, of the artist's awakening to a new feeling he wants to express, of an idea seen excitedly for the first time. Finally, there are those mystical intuitions which claim to have revealed God himself touching us directly.

But the major difficulty with knowledge of this variety, especially the last named, is that it originates and must live out its entire existence in a circumstance of supreme privacy. There is, as it were, no way to get at these truths save through individual subjective experience, one individual at a time. These feelings and insights are exceedingly difficult to communicate to other people; they lose much of their integrity "in translation," so to speak, striking us as delusory, or fanciful, or, at the very most, merely interesting ruminations of the "inner man." They do not, according to many epistemologies, contribute much to the hard and rigorous business of human knowing.

The problem they present is perhaps most vividly illustrated when we are forced to deal with the "crackpot" or religious fanatic, an individual who, it is presumed, has as many qualifications for and as much right to the having of intuitions as the reasonable man. In the intermediate zone we might place the "prophet." Where, indeed, are we to draw the line between the fanatic's intuitions and those of the benign but erroneous prophet, or between the erroneous prophet and the true prophet, the individual we speak of as the "statesman" or the "man of vision"?

There is no sure way, of course, except to wait and see how things turn out. And when we do this we are relegating intuitions to the "humiliating" criterion of empirical testing. It is to this method of knowing that we now turn.

Science

Science is a term which conjures up in the modern mind a host of associations having to do with laboratories, jet airplanes, and rockets to the moon. It designates, in one of its meanings, a tremendous body of knowledge which we have put to use in our lives to control disease, to fashion machines, and to produce a lavish profusion of consumer products all the way from "Scarlet Rage" lipstick to I.B.M. "THINK"-ing machines. But in the epistemological sense science is considered not so much a body of knowledge as a *method of knowing*. It is the *method* of science which is of such profound importance to modern man, rather than the knowledge it produces or the technology which that knowledge makes possible. And the *method* of science lies principally in the testing of ideas in what is metaphorically referred to as the "crucible of experience."

Given sensory experience, men seem capable of seeing relationships and associations and connections between the various sectors of their sensory world. They then attempt to identify and assert those relations as items of knowledge about their world. A primitive huntsman may come to the view that wild game is more plentiful in the open valley than in the jungle thicket, but only on cloudy days. Or the physiologist may have a hunch that cigarette smokers fail victim to cancer more often than nonsmokers. But in either case we are dealing only with hunch or guess or, in the scientific lexicon, *hypothesis*. We do not yet really *know*. Even intuition is admissible at this point, as long as we treat it as simply a *candidate* for truth rather than a matter of settled fact.

What must follow is a rigorous testing of the hunch or intuition to see if it is really true. And we do this by organizing a more refined and controlled interval of "experience," customarily spoken of as an "experiment," in which the relevant conditions of the problem are systematically ordered and taken account of in the experimental procedure. If the huntsman pretended to a scientific approach to the validation of his notion, he would have to begin counting the animals in both valley and thicket on both cloudy and sunny days. His tabulations would soon lead him, if he were thorough and persistent enough, to a more accurate and dependable generalization concerning the availability of his food supply. And the physiologist likewise, entering upon a fantastically more complex problem, is essentially under the same obligation — to begin counting the cigarettes smoked, the cancer cases showing up in the hospital, and the cancer cells detectable in the diseased bodies. Only through this procedure can he arrive at anything that he would accept as physiological knowledge. The handling of intuition is perhaps more involved, but if the intuition is such as to yield to empirical treatment, which, as noted above, is not always the case, then the same procedure would be expected. If a so-called parapsychologist holds that human beings have a "sixth" or "extrasensory" sense which enables them to control an external event such as coin-flipping, it is theoretically possible to design an experiment in which the truth of this hypothesis may be tested.

We may summarize all of this by saying that scientific epistemology insists on staying outside the interior workings of an assumed intellect, sticking to the region of open and public observation, but being rigorous and systematic in the collection and organization of data. There is no pretention, as we shall see in more detail in Chapter Six, that this procedure will lead to absolute truth. Whatever is found out, and therefore *known,* is to be held only temporarily and tentatively, until such time as the conclusions must be modified or overturned. Since all scientific truth is at the mercy of observed phenomena and of the procedure by which those phenomena are reported and tabulated, any change in the phenomena or the reports must eventuate in altered conclusions.

Choice

Perhaps not an epistemological method at all, but only a strategic feature of all knowing, is the matter of ultimate choice. We must include choice here primarily in anticipation of the epistemological considerations associated most directly with Existentialism.

The fittest approach may be to go back to the nonreferability of all human reports in the knowing process. At the base of all these procedures described in the previous sections is an individual "I" making certain assertions about experience. In the case of sense experience, I am the one who avers that the industrial exhaust "stinks." In the case of common sense, I am the one who asserts what the common sense of the community happens to be on a political question. In logic, I am the one who accepts the credibility of the statement "All men are mortal" and the credibility of a linkage between this and a similar pronouncement concerning Socrates; I have to "string along," as it were, step by logical step, in order for the logician to make any headway. And to "string along" I must make ultimate, if only minuscule, choices along the way in order for the knowing process to terminate in anything.

In the case of self-evidence and intuition, the situation is perhaps most concretely illustrated. For I am most certainly the active agent in asserting what is and what is not genuinely self-evident; and in the case of intuitions I am quite obviously the ultimate author of them. No one else can have intuitions for me.

But even in the case of the scientific method, which presumably transcends and "covers" all subjectivism, we are beset by the same problem. The scientist is, after all, dependent upon what human beings report concerning phenomena. To refine and order the circumstances in which phenomena are permitted to occur does not in any way change the situation with respect to the reporting of them; the reports must still be made by a human person relating his personal assessment, even if rigorous and disciplined, of the phenomenal situation as he sees it. This epistemological caveat may appear somewhat labored when applied to the physical sciences — in counting the animals in a valley or the tar content of cigarettes. Can there really be significant dispute in such reporting? But the caveat assumes crucial importance in the social sciences and the humanistic studies, where human assessment of a situation is open to considerably greater variation; for instance, the Platonic "justice" of capital punishment is still, to put it mildly, an open question.

To speak, then, of the "nonreferability" of human choices is simply to make clear that at some point in every epistemological enterprise decisions have to be made which cannot be referred any further; the epistemological "buck" cannot be "passed." I must take a stand — on how many animals I see or on whether the gas chamber is or is not morally right. And no particular stand is absolutely *required* of me, for if certain stands *were* required, in an absolute sense, then there would be no epistemological problem at all. We should all just yield to what *had* to be said about this or that sensory experience, this or that logical progression, this or that phenomenal situation.

Nothing *has* to be said about *anything*, really. Epistemology, and indeed philosophy itself, has assumed the importance it has because of the "open-endedness" of human knowing and, therefore, the unspecified character of the content of our knowledge.

EPISTEMOLOGY AND ONTOLOGY

It is at this point that we may now address ourselves to the inherently circular character of all epistemological ventures. While this may be a somewhat unhappy note on which to close this discussion, we are obligated to make ourselves aware of it if we wish to be honest in the philosophical enterprise.

Our predicament can be gotten at directly by noting that *nonreferability* is characteristic not only of procedural decisions in our epistemology but of the very base of the procedure itself, i.e., the ontology we start out with. I am not absolutely required to accept *any* ontology. I am free to choose. I am at liberty to select from a goodly number of theories the ontology I wish to have as my epistemological foundation. The only thing I can do is to draw attention to certain features of my world which seem to me to be more *real* than others. And I pursue the examination of these features so as to back up my ontological choice.

Temperament, whether we like it or not, has a great deal to do with this. If I am a bookish sort of fellow, happiest when manipulating ideas, I am likely to lean in the direction of a mentalistic or "idea-filled" ontology. If I enjoy working with machinery I am likely to favor a mechanistic ontology. Of course, my ontology may have some feedback effect on my temperament; but, as the Idealist Herman Horne once put it, ". . . we probably live our way into a system of thinking rather than think our way into a pattern of living."

At any rate, when it comes to selecting an ontology I am very much on my own. The only systematic thing I can do — if I do not want to trust my temperament — is to look more closely at those features of my world which I claim are most real to see *why* it is I claim that they *are* most real. How do I know that they *are* real? How do I know that ideas are more real than things, or things more real than ideas, or "experience" more real than either?

When I ask this question, I am really asking how do I *know*. And so I am back in my old difficulty, epistemology!

To generalize this, we may say that an epistemology makes sense only if it appears compatible with a basic ontology. For the many reasons discussed in this chapter, any method of knowing must somehow be supported and made possible by a previously held ontology. But, in like manner, an ontology cannot be set in place without making some statements about reality. Since these statements signify some knowledge we have of reality, they immediately reveal a previously held epistemology. Thus, ultimately, our ontology is contingent upon our epistemology.

So we are, as it were, "trapped." Once engaged in the philosophical enterprise, we become committed to this or that circle of theory. But this is not so hopeless as it sounds. For one of the functions of philosophy, as stressed in Chapter One, is to unify all of our disparate thoughts into a master formula, by which not only education but all the activities of life can be intelligently carried on. Each epistemology, then, may be expected to attempt to reach out and pull into its circle *all* the items of experience which men are said to have, to "colonize" all beachheads and frontiers of human existence, and to "imperialize" all human thought and action under its own intellectual hegemony. As you may already suspect, this is not an easy task. How it is attempted we shall now examine in Chapter Six.

QUESTIONS

1. Take each of the following statements and analyze the epistemological problem it poses:
   "I just know we're going to have a war with Russia."
   "Know thyself."
   "You can be *sure* if it's Westinghouse."
   "Know, think, do! God will follow you!"
   "He's all right, once you get to know him."

2. A distinction is often made between "knowing what" and "knowing how." Which of the several varieties of knowing would be most closely associated with these two terms?

3. Some educators say we have had enough of "know-what" and "know-how." What we need is a little "know-*why*." What epistemological difficulties are likely to be encountered in knowing "why"?

4. Take a thorough look at the *Encyclopædia Britannica* and the *Encyclopedia of the Social Sciences*. These two encyclopedias (literally, from the Greek, "circle of knowledge") contain what we may designate as knowledge. Is the type of knowledge contained in the two different in any way? How?

5. A proposal was once made to the United Nations Educational, Scientific, and Cultural Organization (UNESCO) to sponsor and finance an international group of historians to write an authoritative, once-for-all world history, which could then be translated into every language and used in all the schools of the world. If you were selected to manage this project, what epistemological problems would you anticipate?

FURTHER READING

Brennan, Joseph G. *The Meaning of Philosophy*. New York: Harper and Bros., 1953.
In a survey of "the problems of philosophy," Brennan devotes Part II to "Problems of Knowledge" and in successive chapters considers truth and certainty, our knowledge of the world outside us, and methods of knowledge. These three chapters, thorough and at the same time eminently readable, explain the problematic character of knowledge and knowing.

Hocking, William Ernest. *Types of Philosophy*. New York: Charles Scribner's Sons, 1929.
In Chapter VIII Hocking confronts the question of what we human beings are fitted to know and what limits there are, if any, to reason. He discusses naïve rationalism, sophistry, skepticism, scientific rationalism, and agnosticism. The remainder of Part II is a comparison of pragmatic and intuitive knowing.

Mead, Hunter. *Types and Problems of Philosophy,* Revised Edition. New York: Henry Holt and Co., Inc., 1953.
In this textbook in philosophy, Chapter 7 considers "Truth: Pilate's Problem and Ours," including various theories of truth. Thereupon Chapter 8 takes up the sources of knowledge: authority, mysticism, reason, and experience.

Montague, William P. *The Ways of Things*. New York: Prentice-Hall, Inc., 1940.
After a brief preamble on formal logic, Montague devotes Chapter II of Part One to the general problem of knowing and to six varieties of approach to the problem: authoritarianism, intuition, rationalism, empiricism, prag- matism, and skepticism.

Phenix, Philip. *Philosophy of Education*. New York: Henry Holt and Co., Inc., 1958.
In Chapter 17, on "Knowledge," Phenix considers: contrasting aspects of knowledge, knowledge as subjective and objective, the sources of knowledge, and, finally, the organization of knowledge into "knowable" categories.

Ryle, Gilbert. "Knowing How and Knowing That," a selection from the author's *The Concept of Mind* (London: Hutchinson University Library, 1949), in I. Scheffler (ed.). *Philosophy and Education*. Boston: Allyn and Bacon, 1958.
In drawing the distinction between the "how" and the "what," Ryle pene- trates to the core of the modern epistemological problem: the role of scientific, operational knowledge in a residual intellectualist tradition that insists there be some absolute truths which the mind grasps before it starts to "think."

Comparative Epistemologies

As it was noted in Chapter Five, knowing has become a "problem" because there are several ways of engaging in it. And these several ways of knowing compete for attention among thoughtful men and attempt to establish themselves as the most dependable or the most fully authenticated procedure to follow if one claims to be really interested in getting at genuinely true knowledge. Since most of us — especially educators — *are* interested in true knowledge, we must pay careful attention to the competition in epistemology and to the relative claims for this or that epistemological procedure. We are under this obligation not only from the standpoint of authenticating our own day-by-day knowledge but, perhaps more important, from the standpoint of authenticating the procedures we follow in the educative function in managing the knowing process of boys and girls. This, after all, is where our epistemology is put to work, where it is tested in the real affairs of life, and where it does or does not "pay off."

As we proceed through these various epistemological theories, therefore, you should attempt in your study to anticipate the discussion in Chapter Seven — namely, how each theory is to be applied to the educational situation, the kinds of learning each makes possible, and those sectors of the school's curriculum to which each is most relevant. As in the discussion of ontology, we are not concerned here with engaging in polemics or in arguing a case for this or that way of knowing. We are involved, rather, in an exposure to and, it is hoped, an understanding of the various epistemological alternatives open to us in the work of educating the young.

IDEALISM:
TRUTH AS IDEA

The Absolute Mind

Since the Idealist's ontology is composed principally of mental "stuff," of ideas existing in a purely mental realm, we may suspect at the outset that an epistemology to match would be one which holds knowing to be principally an enterprise in mentally grasping ideas and concepts. This turns out to be the case. To return briefly to the ontological discussion in Chapter Three (see Figure 2, page 49), we may say that men are but prisoners in a three-dimensional "cave," a world of physical dimension and physical sensation. But the genuinely real world lies somewhere beyond all this. Knowing, then, is not merely "sensing" something; knowing is, rather, taking hold of the *idea* of something and retaining it in the mind.

For example, I may have sense experience of many trees during the course of a day: the already cited elm tree in my front yard, the maple trees lining the avenue, the pear tree on the campus. But I truly know these objects in my experience only when I understand what they all have in common — what it is, in short, that makes them trees rather than something else. To put it more explicitly, I genuinely *know* them when I know the *idea* of "tree," the Idea which stands "behind" all trees and which they individually, but imperfectly, express.

Now if we were to collect all such Platonic Ideas — Tree-ness, Chair-hood, Circularity, Man, Sparrow-ness, Doorknob-hood, Love, Democracy, Frog-hood, and all the rest — if, that is, we were to conceive of the absolute sum total of *all* Ideas, we would have in hand what might be designated the Platonic conception of absolute and ultimate reality. But ideas, by themselves, are only fictions; they require a mind to think them. And so, in later developments in Idealism, it has been held that there exists an Absolute Mind, which is constantly thinking these thoughts and ideas; indeed, to Hegel, it was the thinking of these ideas by the Universal Mind which explained their existential status: "History is God thinking."

The concept of the Absolute Mind is not so mystical as it may seem on the surface. In our own experience we know that some minds are "larger" than others; that is, some individuals can know more, have a wider grasp of the affairs of the world, see more deeply into life's problems, than others. In Platonic terms, they are able to penetrate the sensory screen to the Idea World beyond much better than their less gifted fellows. Now, if we were merely to extend this ideational power to its logical limit, we should be able to imagine a Mind which exists wholly and completely beyond the sensory screen, which has no thoughts save those which are resident in the Universal and Idea-l realm, and which, by these same tokens, is completely free of the error and passion which becloud human knowing.

Microcosm and macrocosm

Epistemology in the Idealist setting, therefore, is primarily a description of how the human mind, with all its limitations, can be brought into communication with the Absolute Mind. In order to understand the circumstances in which this problem is met, Idealists customarily bring to mind the bipolar concept of microcosm and macrocosm. The simplest analogue is the microcosm of the physicist's atom and the macrocosm of the astronomer's solar system. As we noted in Chapter Two, atomic particles are thought to revolve about their nucleus somewhat in the fashion that the planets orbit about the sun. Consequently we speak of the atom as a microcosm — that is, a miniature replica — of the solar system.

Now, analogically, we may say somewhat the same thing of the human mind and the Absolute Mind. All of the qualities of the Absolute Mind are present in our own; the qualities are simply found in more limited form. Therefore, our limited human minds are theoretically capable of communicating with and sharing in the Absolute Mind; they are made of the same "stuff," so to speak. Our minds, to return to the first metaphor, *participate* in the cosmic activity of thought in somewhat the same fashion that an atom participates in the solar system. There is a fantastically wide gap separating the two, to be sure; but this gap is not one of kind but of degree. The human mind and the Absolute Mind are fundamentally *en rapport,* even at the great "psychological" distance by which they are separated, by virtue of the fact that they are constructed of the same type of "material."

At the outset, then, Idealist epistemology posits a fundamental compatibility between a knowable reality and a capable knower. With these two "polar" points the epistemological problem is narrowed to the task of showing how they are brought into communication. Before we pass directly to this matter, however, it may be helpful to examine another aspect of the microcosm-macrocosm nexus: the dimension of selfhood.

The Absolute Self

What has already been said of the Absolute Mind may now be translated into similar designations concerning an entity which is at once more precise and more nebulous than the concept "mind" — the human *self*. When Descartes began his philosophizing he decided to start with the field of ontology, and he began by doubting the existence of everything. Everything that had, previous to his time, been placed in some kind of existential category he systematically chose to doubt the reality of. He went down the list: things, ideas, Ideas, spirit, God, everything. Everything is to be doubted! Except one thing: my doubting. I cannot doubt my doubting; simply by doubting it I affirm it. I am therefore forced to begin, ontologically speaking, with my own doubts, my own thoughts. There is no escape. "Cogito, ergo sum": I think, therefore I am. What proceeds from this Descartes built into a philosophic system. But at the root of it all stands this entity, the "I" in the "Cogito," which somehow is required to serve as the point of origin for all thinking, all ontologizing, and hence all knowing.

For want of a better term we may designate this entity as the *self*. The concept of the "self" has been a subject of ardent philosophic discourse through the ages, and largely because it is almost impossible to define. As a symbol-concept it is almost as unyielding to definition as the Thomist term *Being* or the metaphysical infinitive *to be*. We come perhaps as close as anything to it with our common, everyday word *person*. To think of a *person* as providing the vehicle for what we call *personality* takes us even closer to the idea of the "self." And the *person* is what the Idealist sometimes calls the "self-conscious center of experience."

Beyond these few notations, however, it is difficult to set down precisely what selfhood consists in. We are blocked, as it were, from making any high-styled analysis of it.[1] But there is, nevertheless, a kind of nagging necessity to affirm the reality of the self, if not for other human beings then at least for our own individual being. I must somehow affirm the identity of my own existence; I can somehow point to something in myself which seems, to me at least, to be something more than the accretions of past experience; for, as the Existentialists are at great pains to point out (see pages 73–76), I am ultimately capable of *renouncing* my prior experience and adopting new and unconditioned forms of behavior. My selfhood is not locked into some determined system; indeed, the whole idea of "self" (as in *self-control, self-discipline,* etc.) contains the root notion of some kind of autonomy.[2]

The Idealist, then, must make a primary affirmation of his own self-

[1] Contemporary social psychology has, to be sure, attempted to prove that selfhood is but the empirical product of social experience, being built up over the years from the results of countless conditionings. See W. H. Kilpatrick, *Selfhood and Civilization* (New York: Teachers College Bureau of Publications, 1941). But this whole proof begs the question of the origin of that "center" of thought and will which performs the assimilation and integration of the conditionings.

[2] Some individuals dismiss all this as "mere subjectivism." An Idealist might respond: If this be subjectivism, make the most of it! Subjectivism is precisely what we're talking about. Subjectivism is a real quality, existentially present in the real world.

hood and of selfhood as a real quality in the world. Now, let us suppose there is a concentric progression of selfhood similar to the logical extension of "mind" discussed above. In Figure 7 we graphically represent the possibility of enlarging our concept of self. At the center is the ordinary human being, conscious of himself, of other things in his reality, and of other selves. As he grows and matures he expands the reach of his selfhood, claiming larger and larger territory in knowing, understanding, feeling. He has more and more experiences, learns more and more, assumes deeper and more sensitive responses to the world about him. We say he has matured. But even among the so-called mature, there are some whose "selfhoods" may be said to encompass more than others; they are more knowledgeable about the world, they understand more, they feel more keenly the beauties and tragedies of life, they reach out more readily and absorb the experiences of other people. Certainly an Albert Schweitzer or an Eleanor Roosevelt possesses a "larger self" than I do. In this sense, then, we may be permitted the license of saying that some human beings are "larger selves" than others, and, to generalize further, that selfhood as an existential quality is capable of expansion and enlargement.

If we are willing to grant this bit of logical metaphorizing we can proceed ultimately to the logical possibility of a self whose reach is ultimate, whose knowledge is complete, whose empathic powers know no bounds: the Absolute Self. Theologically, this is recognizable as the Omnipotent Person — God. God, in most theologies, has the qualities of a *person* which are elevated to their unlimited and absolute level.[3] But to introduce theology at this point would only deflect us from the genuine Idealist position, for God is not absolutely necessary to Idealist ontology or epistemology. All we need affirm at this point is the Absolute Self, which, like the Absolute Mind, serves as the ultimate ground in which we human beings participate.

This may seem a somewhat mystical approach to epistemology, and in a sense it is. For in Idealist epistemology we are concerned not only with providing linkages of communication between mind and Absolute Mind but also — and this is a somewhat more sophisticated notion —

---

[3] John Locke, while not an Idealist in the Platonic sense, expressed it very well. In a section on the "Idea of God" in his famous *Essay Concerning Human Understanding*, he says: ". . . having, from what we experiment in ourselves, got the ideas of existence and duration, of knowledge and power, of pleasure and happiness, and of several other qualities and powers which it is better to have than to be without; when we would frame an idea the most suitable we can to the Supreme Being, we enlarge every one of these with our idea of infinity; and so, putting them together, make our complex idea of God. For that the mind has such a power of enlarging some of its ideas, received from sensation and reflection, has been already showed." (Chicago: Gateway Editions, Inc., 1956, p. 111. The *Essay* was first published in 1690, and the selection quoted is drawn from Book II, Chapter XXIII.)

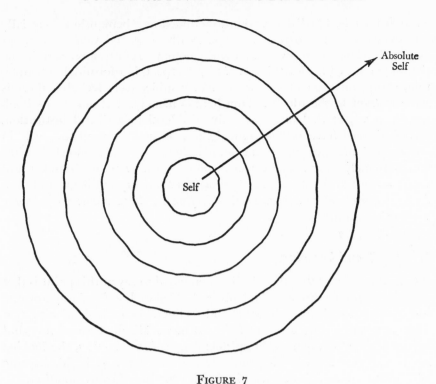

FIGURE 7

The Microcosmic-Macrocosmic Self

providing a medium of contact between the microcosmic *self* and the macrocosmic *Absolute Self*.

The emergent self

The Idealist epistemology may now be seen to involve something more than merely bringing a limited mind into contact with an absolute one: It involves as well the provocation and nurture of an emerging personality in the human being. This, it goes without saying, includes not only intellectual activities but moral and aesthetic and emotional aspects of growth as well. And here is where Idealist epistemology becomes most vague and mystical. That is to say, we are dealing with a quality — selfhood — which we have already indicated is largely beyond definition and analysis, and yet we say that this quality of selfhood can somehow be made to grow and expand under the special ministrations of the school.

It is a temptation at this point (and many educational theorists yield to it) to dismiss the Idealist attention to selfhood as a benign but essentially misdirected exercise in poetic license: Selfhood is too vague a concept and its development too vague an epistemology to get us anywhere in the shaping of our educational ideas. This, to repeat, is a formidable temptation, except for the fact that we somehow subjectively feel that there is some warrant to the Idealist claim here — namely, that our own schooling, especially at the college or university level in a liberal institution, say, did indeed have an "enlarging" effect on us. We somehow feel "in our bones" that we are fuller human beings — more knowledgeable, more intensely aware of the world, more sensitive to its beauties and values — for having been immersed for four years in the liberal tradition. As ill-defined and nebulous as this feeling is, there seems to be some authenticity to it.

Mind, self, and knowing

One of the things that the Idealist is prepared to say at this point is that an individual may discover the Universal Mind and Self — in microcosm, to be sure — in his own thoughts and feelings. I can look within, as it were, and find a tiny replica of the Ultimate Mind. One of the vital keynotes, therefore, of Idealist epistemology is *introspection,* the looking inside ourselves for what is genuinely real and true. It is this keynote which Plato sounded so beautifully in his doctrine of contemplation.

> True knowledge comes only from the spiritual world of eternal and changeless ideas, and this knowledge is innate in the immortal soul, which has dwelt in the spiritual world before being incased in the mortal body. Knowledge is thus acquired, not by sense experience, but by a process of reminiscence, by which the intellect remembers what it knew before its association with an imperfect body. To remember perfectly, the intellect must rigorously close the windows of the body to the external world and open only the windows of the intellect, so that it may look upon and contemplate eternal truth. Intellectual discipline of the strictest kind, achieved by means of mathematics and philosophy, is the only true road to knowledge.[4]

It is, therefore, as if we were compelled to shut our eyes and ears to the sensations of this world and to see, almost literally "in our mind's eye," the truths of an ideational and spiritual reality. It was this idea which led Plato to the view that learning is essentially a process of "remembering," of "recognition" — literally *re-cognition,* or cognizing again. Our senses give us only the surface of things; we must deliberately turn from

[4] R. F. Butts, *A Cultural History of Western Education,* Second Edition (New York: McGraw-Hill Book Co., 1955), p. 49.

them in order to *know again* what the mind, because it participates in the Absolute, already knows.

To speak thus is to suggest that we can never know the world directly, that is, by looking at it. We must have a theory of knowledge which explains how it is that we achieve true knowledge through some more dependable means than mere sensation. While the Realist, as we shall see in the next section, is willing to settle for sensation, the Idealist requires a more elaborate if somewhat less precise theory. He calls it the "Consistency Theory of Knowledge."

Immanuel Kant, in his systematic works, spoke of percepts (the data we receive through the senses) and concepts (the ideas which arise in our minds). Is there a linkage between these? asked Kant. Most certainly, he said. For concepts depend upon percepts for the raw data of thought; and percepts must terminate in concepts, else they are merely physical impulses impinging upon bodily tissue. As Kant has put it: "Concept without percept is empty. Percept without concept is blind." We may say simply that the mind requires the "fuel" which the senses can deliver it in the way of sense perceptions. The mind needs to have something to work on; and the five senses are its "tentacle receptors" in the knowable world. Without these tentacles, the mind would be isolated, an empty vacuum with nothing to do, no sense data to assimilate and organize, no impressions to test or evaluate — indeed, no thoughts to think whatsoever.

There is, then, a very vital role for sense perception to play in Idealist epistemology. But note one important feature of this epistemology: *It presupposes the existence of the mind itself.* We shall see that in other epistemologies the mind is thought to depend for its very existence upon sense data, or, a more generalized term for the same thing, "experience." But in Idealism the mind is held to be pre-existent to all sensing and all experiencing. It is, therefore, the ultimate explainer of what happens to it, and hence the ultimate explainer of the world.[5]

As ultimate explainer of the world and itself, therefore, the mind enjoys an ontological autonomy which puts it at the very center of all

---

[5] It is in this vein that the Idealist often succeeds in dismissing the Realist's view that physical matter, rather than Idea, is the fundamental "stuff" of reality — most particularly, the view that the mind must be seen as a physicochemical organ functioning according to physical laws: ". . . the very notion of the mind as a function of the brain or of the living organism is itself one of the conceptions held of mind. The mind that can formulate such a conception to describe and explain itself is more than the conception it formulates." (H. H. Horne in *Philosophies of Education*, Forty-first Yearbook of the National Society for the Study of Education, p. 145.)

The counterview, of course, would insist that even the mind's view of *itself* is a physicochemical reaction made possible by "chemicals in motion" in the brain. Obviously, physiologists and psychologists could keep up this intellectual "Ping-pong" ad infinitum.

epistemological activity. And this is precisely the point of entry for what we have termed "consistency." The mind's task is to receive data from many different sources, to assimilate them, to arrange them in some systematic order, to associate them with other sense data received earlier or in other circumstances, and, finally, to locate consistencies among them. When this point is reached — depending on the degree of consistency among empirical reports — the mind can be said to have attained truth.

I can, for instance, in examining a piece of unknown mineral material feel its hardness, see its color, heft it, smell it, hear the sound a geologist's hammer makes on it, maybe even taste it. If all of these reports seem to hang together and to confirm my previous experience, I say I have in my hand a piece of coal. Or, in a less material setting, I may read Locke and Jefferson and Rousseau, and then study the French Revolution and the American Revolution, and then read Adam Smith, and then study the Civil War and World War I and World War II. I may then have it dawn on me that there was a big idea trying to be expressed in all of these events and writings. I say I have my hands (my mind) on the Idea of Freedom. This idea is revealed to our perceptions in this phrase, in that book, in this battle, in that war, in this public utterance, in that Declaration. And finally we take hold of the idea, and it is ours, not in tiny pieces, like our perceptions, but whole and complete in our minds.

The mind therefore is in its epistemological office the organizer and systematizer of sense data. The sensory environment may provide the basic data for thought, the so-called stimulants to conceptualization, but it is the mind that does the knowing. And it performs this function through seeing relationships, finding connections between one impression and another, and finally arriving at a defensible conception of truth. Our minds proceed by getting successive "plots" on our position, by taking this and that "reading" of the situation, this and that "sighting" of landmarks; then, by a process of organization and comparison, an assessment is made of "where" we are, i.e., what our existence is all about. It is as if, to use a nautical metaphor, we were "triangulating" our way through the sensory (and therefore ontologically inferior) world heading for the ultimate harbor of the Absolute Mind.

REALISM:
TRUTH AS OBSERVABLE FACT

Natural Law

As we have intimated before, every philosophy must present to thinking men a view of life and thought which can be seen to accord with common sense. Philosophical doctrine which repeatedly repudiates what we call common sense has never proved to be long-lived. That is not to say, however, that common sense cannot be improved upon, only that it must be accounted for and adjusted to in the day-by-day operations of philosophy.

It is to the fundamentals of common sense that Realism would have us turn for the foundation blocks of our epistemology — a common sense uncomplicated by mystical, otherworldly realms of Ideas or transcendent Persons or Selves. In Plato's terms, the Realist is content to live in the so-called cave. He finds there his reality, and so there it is that he engages in his epistemological activity, the activity of knowing. But let us, says the Realist, be done with the metaphor of the "cave" forthwith! The mere metaphor is compromising. Here the world is, in all its ontological existentiality. It is not some kind of shadow of a presumably more real world, as the Idealist would say. No, the world we see *is* the real world. Epistemologically, we come at it without mystery; we come at it with our senses. And since this world is knowable — because it provides the occasion for sense perceptions — we engage in epistemological activity with some assurance that we are getting at the real thing, and not some illusion.

Reality is not an Absolute Mind thinking thoughts or an Infinite Self of which we are microcosms. Reality just *is,* without regard to human plans or purposes. It is, one might say, epistemologically neutral; to render it anthropomorphically, we might say that reality is "out there waiting to be known"; ontologically it is simply "there" and awaits the onset of epistemological activity toward it. If anything can be called a common-sense view of the ontology-epistemology relationship, certainly this can.

We know further, says the Realist, that this reality — which we can just as well now speak of as "Nature" — contains certain regularities: Water runs downhill, the sun comes up regularly in a certain sector of the sky, seeds placed in the earth will sprout and grow. If we look more carefully we can see that water runs downhill, for example, according to a regular pattern, a pattern which never varies given a certain set of circumstances. There is, as it were, a law of downhill-running-water. And there is an associate set of laws of sun-rising-in-the-East and corn-kernels-tossed-on-the-ground. In these and myriad other ways, the real world which we encounter every day contains regularities and patterns of structure and motion which represent its epistemological fascination for us. It exists, yes; it exists in a wonderful way — according to a vast plan — and it moves and evolves according to an even vaster plan, the plan of Natural Law. It is this Plan of Nature which is the object of our epistemological enterprise.

The "Spectator Theory"

The Realist, unlike the Idealist, is not concerned with where the Plan came from, or Who (in the sense of an Absolute Mind) conceived it. He is concerned with simply *what* the Plan is. His epistemology focuses upon the straightforward though arduous task of looking at the world and describing what it is and how it works. This epistemology (refer to Chapter Five, pages 121–123) can be rendered in philosophical shorthand thus: Man knows by being a *spectator of a world-as-machine*. In this sentence, the word *spectator* refers not just to eyesight but to all the five senses; the word *machine* metaphorically signifies that the object of our knowing is a physical thing in motion, controlled by built-in laws which it can be made to reveal.

To the Realist, then, the epistemological problem boils down to what we might call "organized spectating," i.e., taking pains to "spectate" carefully and rigorously, checking our results, and, if our observations are systematic enough, coming up with generalizations, principles, and laws which tell us how our world is built and how it works. This may be readily recognized as the common-sense understanding of the word *science;* and it is in this uncomplicated meaning of science that the Realist locates the basis of his epistemology.[6] This meaning of science, incidentally, extends beyond the physical sciences into social and political affairs. As pointed out in the discussion of Realist ontology in Chapter Three, there may be said to be a "natural law" of human affairs embedded within the very texture of Nature, as the classical economists were so fond of saying. And while moral and ethical matters are further afield, there is a sense in which Realists can speak of a moral law at work in the cosmos; there is, so to speak, a moral, good-and-bad dimension to the texture of Nature as well as an epistemological, true-and-false dimension. We shall examine this last point more thoroughly in the sections dealing with Realism in Part IV on Axiology.

It may be noted, at this point, that Realist epistemology shares some of the tendencies and interests of Idealism. The concept of Natural Law, for instance, is conceptually very proximate to Universal Mind. But these two ideas are different and distinct, and it is not just a profitless splitting of hairs to take note of the difference at this point: Idealism's ultimate and primary principle is Mind — Mind-in-Ultimate — which by its

[6] It should be noted at this point that the word *science* has become something of an epistemological troublemaker because it has taken on two rather distinct meanings: first, *a body of knowledge,* and, second, *a method of knowing.* By and large, the Realist is more interested in the knowledge than the method, whereas the Experimentalist, as we shall see later in this chapter, has become so interested in the method as to turn it into a systematic logic in its own right, a logic so imperial, says he, as to be epistemologically applicable to *all* knowing.

transcendent operations makes Nature, and therefore Natural Law, possible. Nature, in short, is the expression of a *prior* Mind. Realism's ultimate and primary principle, on the other hand, is Nature — a Nature-in-Ultimate — which by its existential motions and energies makes individual brains and nervous systems possible and therefore makes individual minds, and therefore Absolute Mind, possible. Mind, in short, is the expression of a *prior* Nature.

Perhaps an even more subtle point of contact relates directly to the so-called spectator epistemology. This theory of knowing, so evidently applicable to Realism, is likewise characteristic of Idealism — that is, if we are willing to allow the metaphor a bit more poetic leeway. That is to say, Idealism can be called a spectator theory in the sense that the inner mind does the "spectating." Our everyday phrase, "to see with the mind's eye," is an accurate if homely expression of how the Idealist views the spectator qualities of the knowing process.

This is not an idle point to make, for it is crucial to understand that both Idealism and Realism are *objective* doctrines, at least insofar as they are treated in this book.[7] When we say *objective* we refer to the "out-there-ness" of the ontologies of both schools of thought. Idealism's "out-there-ness" is the Universal Mind, with which the individual, microcosmic mind has contact; Realism's "out-there-ness" is the real physical world. The point is that both ontologies are objective; and, therefore, both epistemologies view the knowing process principally as a bridge between the individual human being engaging in the knowing process (the subject) and the "out-there" world to be known (the object).

To restate the significance of this Principle of Objectivity,[8] we can say with the Realist that Nature seems to exhibit certain patterns of structure and regularities of performance which are occasionally refined into Law; that these Laws can be known and utilized to guide our conduct and to control what would otherwise be a pesky and arbitrary environment; but that in the "controlling" we are actually adjusting to and cooperating with an antecedent Nature, whose ways must be known and followed in order for them to be turned to human account. When General Motors initiates its engineering activity upon Mesabi iron ore with the general aim of producing a Chevrolet, it must work upon the ore in ways consistent with what the ore can do; it cannot treat the ore as if it were something else. Hence, environmental "control" is only a sophisticated, an-

---

[7] There is a position spoken of as "subjective" or "personalistic" Idealism; this, however, is not discussed herein. When Idealism is referred to it is in the Hegelian sense of the term, i.e., an Idealism holding to a Universal Mind at work in the world.

[8] Also developed as the Principle of Independence (the world is existentially independent of the knower) in F. S. Breed, "Education and the Realistic Outlook," in *Philosophies of Education*, Forty-first Yearbook of the National Society for the Study of Education, ed. N. B. Henry, Part I (Chicago: the Society, 1942), pp. 104–105.

thropocentric euphemism for human adjustment to a prior and necessary natural state. We "operate" *on* nature by "cooperating" *with* it.[9]

Pure Theory

The Realist, then, is epistemologically concerned primarily with the business of discovering — literally *dis-covering*, removing the cover from — a pre-existent and existentially independent reality and thereby gaining knowledge of it. Another way of looking at this is to attend to what the Realist considers the highest kind of knowledge, Pure Theory. Here, again, we are not dealing with any esoteric or mysterious epistemological activity but, rather, with a commonplace of everyday life, namely, the theoretical knowledge that rationalizes practical understanding of life's daily affairs, from nuclear physics to child care. This theory is the epistemological "distillate" of countless observations of the real world; as such, it is "continuous" with the real world, both *in* and *of* it — not dispatched, as in the case of Idealism, to some other region of reality. The wave theory of light or the Freudian theory of neurosis is ultimately built up, says the Realist, out of concrete observations of what goes on in the sense world.

And we would not be wrong if we were to take this last statement quite literally. Knowing, to the Realist, is founded ultimately in sense perception. It is the gathering up of those perceptions, organizing them and rendering them systematic, that comprises the epistemological process. Here, once again, the value of common sense is recognized. For not only are our ontology and epistemology consistent with the common sense of the "man in the street," but epistemological *use* is made of common sense, i.e., literally the *common sensations* of men in arriving at a genuine and dependable knowledge of their world. The Idealist's notion of "Consistency," says the Realist, is all well and good; but the seeing of consistencies is primarily a private activity of the individual mind, rather than a public process of several minds acting in concert to validate their beliefs. Common sense is just what it says it is: a commonly held sensation of the way things are. As such, common sense is the first leg of the journey to "pure knowledge."

The second leg, of course, is the criticism of common sense, the exten-

---

9 With this comment in hand, we may now refer again to the "operative-cooperative" problem discussed in Chapter One. If the "operative" position can be rendered, as above, as merely adjustment to a prior natural state in the child, we are then prepared to ask the more difficult question: Does the "operative" notion of "natural *state*" coincide with the "cooperative" notion of "natural *tendency*"? That is, is a child more like Mesabi iron ore, which has the *capacity* but not the *tendency* to become a Chevrolet; or is the child more like the kernel of corn, which has both the *capacity* AND the *tendency* to become an ear of corn?

sion of our common sensations into more rigorous and controlled "spectating" circumstances, and the sophistication of our common sensations into more generalized and more refined truths. Finally, if our investigations succeed, we are in a position to state generalized laws and principles which represent the way nature ultimately behaves, the kind of knowledge the Realist designates as Pure Theory.

This refining process goes on all the time in the physical sciences. For example, we make a distinction between "pure" research and "applied" research in physics. Studies having to do with the structure of the sun or with the so-called parity principle of matter may be thought of as "pure" problems,[10] whereas studies of space-vehicle navigation, which depend upon but essentially *apply* the findings of the "pure" scientist, are spoken of as "applied" problems.

Pure Theory is sometimes thought of as the highest form of knowledge; scholars seek it not to *use* it but simply to *know* it. Knowing is its own reward. If a use can be found for such knowledge, so much the better, but ultimate use is not the justification for finding it out. *Knowing* it is the primary motivation. Of course, it is important to point out that so-called pure knowledge still depends on the observations of a human being; in studying the sun we are still required to peer through telescopes, analyze photographs, measure temperatures on spectrographs, read dials and meters. We have not, in any absolute way, transcended the world of physical action, the Realist reminds us.

Here we must pause to remind ourselves of a subtle but important distinction in Realist theory. The *object* of our knowing, i.e., the real world existing "out there," does not depend for its existence on any epistemological activity we engage in toward it. But the *content* of our knowledge-claims does depend for its existence on our epistemological activity. The structure of the sun is as it is; we are not going to change it in any way by knowing it. But our knowledge of the structure of the sun is subject to error, because it is ultimately contingent upon our ways of knowing. Pure Theory is the name we give to knowledge when it comes into conformity with and correspondence to the existential world as it really is.

The Correspondence Theory

We may now examine the central proposition in Realist epistemology: the Theory of Correspondence. We are not, to review, concerned with

10 The use of the word *pure* in this context reveals an interesting bias of modern man which runs all the way back to the Greeks. An idea or theory for which there is no immediate use or application is considered valuable in its own right, whereas an idea or theory having to do with some practical matter is "contaminated" by association with everyday circumstance — hence, of an inferior epistemological rank! A Platonism

the problem of bringing the finite mind into communication with an Infinite Mind, as the Idealist epistemologist would say, but, rather, with the essentially simple, straightforward, and uncomplicated problem of seeing to it that our statements about the world we live in do in fact correspond to the way things really are; this, as guileless as it may sound, is all there is to Realist epistemology.

It turns out, of course, that this is a bigger order than it may appear to the uninitiated epistemologist, and even Realists are not inclined to make light of the problem. Their position is that the epistemological enterprise, while difficult, is not in any way mysterious or mystical; it is open and public, because it is carried on in an open reality, a reality which, to be sure, does not give up its secrets easily but which nevertheless is not hostile to giving them up. This reality gives up its truth when we "come and get it." And we say we really possess "it" when our ideas correspond to the way things truly are.

There are three modes by which this "purchase" of truth may be understood in Realist terms. The first of these is the simple and omnipresent sense mode, i.e., knowing things by direct sensing of them in our waking moments. So simple and immediate is this procedure that many Realists consider it unnecessary to contrive an epistemological theory to account for it.[11] Human beings are, after all, animals. They share with animals a nervous system and sensory network which possess the power (1) to gather in stimuli from the physical environment, (2) to organize those stimuli into what may be called a kind of immediate knowledge, and (3) to allow those stimuli to terminate in overt behavior — what is spoken of in the psychologist's lexicon as "response." Response to stimuli is but the overt sign of an inner knowledge held somehow in suspension in the nervous system and employed in the direction of conduct. In teaching the multiplication tables or typewriting, we rely almost exclusively on this kind of immediate (i.e., unmediated) mode of knowing.

The second mode is the scientific. As noted above, we know things in varying degrees, less or more thoroughly. Science, to the Realist, is a procedure for looking more deeply into the nature of things and how they work by rigorously regulating the perceptive process and systematizing the reporting of what is observed. When we study geography, for instance, we do not merely step outside and look around at the local topography; rather, we are moved (sometimes literally, in this subject matter) to dig beneath the surface of things, to explore more adventurously the nooks and crannies of geographic reality. Similarly, when we study his-

of two worlds — one practical and inferior, the other ideal and superior — may be said to account for this peculiar wrinkle in Western thought.

11 J. S. Brubacher, *Modern Philosophies of Education* (New York: McGraw-Hill Book Co., 1950), p. 77.

tory we are not content just to read the newspapers of the period under view; rather, we are drawn to a more systematic comparison of the events of that period with what preceded and what came after it, in order to discern, if possible, any linkages which would make our knowledge more sophisticated and mature. It is in this sense of wider and deeper *investigation* that the Realist understands the word *science,* and it is this mode which activates the greatest part of Realist knowing.

The third mode of arriving at truth, more complicated and recondite than the other two, is not often emphasized in contemporary Realism but is nevertheless native to it. It may be labeled the "epistemology of essences." Reference was made in Chapter Three (see page 57) to the fact that Aristotelianism has historically culminated in two somewhat divergent ontologies: modern scientific Realism (here under discussion) and Neo-Thomism. Though they are divergent, these world-views share enough to make it possible for them to come to terms with each other on epistemological matters. The matter of "essences" happens to be a common interest of both these doctrines.

To get right to the point, the Correspondence Theory comes to full application when we can say that the *idea* in our minds corresponds perfectly with the *thing* being known. And the *idea of the thing* is what is called "essence," the underlying, constituent, and central element which makes the thing what it is and not something else. Knowing, in the most mature mode, is to have a complete understanding of *what* things are. This interest in "what-ness," this central concern with the *quiddity* of the world, is seen as thoroughly consistent and harmonious with the ontology of the Realist, who considers reality to be a substantive something or collection of "somethings." It is this *quiddity* of the world which is the ultimate epistemological goal of Realist knowing.

The Realist, however, does not customarily concern himself with this type of knowing, leaving its elaboration to the similar but essentially more complicated epistemology of the Lay and Ecclesiastical Thomists, to which we now turn.

NEO-THOMISM:
TRUTH AS REASON AND INTUITION

Ontological underpinnings

As is true of any epistemology, that of the Neo-Thomist may best be approached by understanding first the ontological ground in which the knowing process is carried on. If we know what kind of a reality we are dealing with, we are in a much better position to describe the procedure by which we can come to true knowledge of it. So, to refer to Chapter

Three briefly, we may remind ourselves that, like the Realist, the Neo-Thomist is dealing with only one world (rather than the Idealist's two) and that what we see and perceive is genuinely existent. However, according to the Neo-Thomist, this world we see is characterized by *logical* as well as existential features, most notably Matter and Form, which stand as logical constructs in Aristotelian thought. Matter is the principle of potentiality and Form the principle of actuality.

As St. Thomas reworked Aristotelian logic, he demoted Essence (i.e., the union of Matter-and-Form) to the principle of potentiality and placed a new, and *ultimate,* logical construct — Existence — in the position of the principle of actuality. When essence and existence come together, there results a "being." This is the final thing one can say about anything: that it *is*.

In both Aristotelian and Thomistic thought, we must remember, the potentiality-actuality nexus is uppermost, leading finally in Aristotle's system to Pure Form and in St. Thomas' system to Being or God. Also, whatever epistemology may be derived from this plan must recognize that reality is *logically* put together; that is, reality is necessarily, not capriciously or fortuitously, just the way it happens to be. Therefore, our epistemological activity is directed toward a fixed ontological object. To put it in plainer language, what it is we are trying to know is existentially permanent and unchanging and logically ordered and regulated. Reality is there, logically precise and necessary, and our epistemological attack on it will in no way upset its logical order. This Neo-Thomist reality is exceedingly difficult to understand, to be sure, but once it is understood, in this or that degree, we may say that we have put our minds upon genuine truth.

So certain of this is the Neo-Thomist that he speaks of truth with a capital *T:* Truth. In the end, he says, what we are after and what we can actually attain is a kind of knowledge which is permanent and absolute because it is a logical apprehension of a reality which is permanent and absolute. Moreover, since reality itself is a *logical system* as well as a collection of either ideas (Idealism) or things (Realism), and since our minds are capable of logical thought, we are as it were already in epistemological touch with reality; we are "tuned in," one might say, to the wave length of ultimate reality. And as we gather in the signals, we become increasingly knowledgeable about our world. With these preliminaries out of the way, then, how does Neo-Thomist epistemology work out?

The intellect

Fortunately, the epistemological enterprise may be begun without too much difficulty, for, according to the Neo-Thomist, the human mind naturally tends to know. As Mortimer Adler puts it, "The human mind naturally tends to learn, to acquire knowledge, just as the earth naturally tends to support vegetation."[12] In dealing with a more complex point about the axiological or "value" dimension of knowing ("To know is good"), Adler confirms the above view:

> In the case of the intellect itself, which, as a power of knowing, naturally tends toward the possession of truth as its perfection, the habit of knowledge is good by reason of conformity to the natural tendency of the cognitive power, and the habit of error is bad by reason of violation of that tendency. If the intellect were indifferently a power of knowing and not-knowing, possession of truth and possession of error would be indifferently good as actualizations of the cognitive power.[13, 14]

So the epistemological expedition can set out without any special prodding. Man already leans toward knowledge; we are disposed here only to show how his leaning is translated into forward epistemological motion.

Self-evidence and intuition

To say, as was said earlier, that the mind is naturally oriented to reality by virtue of its logical structure is to say that the mind — or, more precisely, the intellect — can take hold of certain truths in and by itself. It can, in the language of the Neo-Thomist, *intuit* truth. To understand this concept of intuition, it is necessary to point to two kinds of truth characteristic of Aristotelian thought: synthetic or "evident" truth and analytic or "self-evident" truth. Synthetic truth is the garden-variety type of knowledge with which science deals. If I say that the distance between New York and Chicago is so many miles, I am uttering a synthetic truth, synthetic in the sense that the predicate of a proposition is not contained in the subject. Evidence is required. But if I say that two things equal to the same thing are equal to each other, I am uttering an analytic truth — the kind of statement whose predicate is analyzed out of

12 "In Defense of the Philosophy of Education," *Philosophies of Education*, Forty-first Yearbook of the National Society for the Study of Education, ed N. B. Henry, Part I (Chicago: the Society, 1942), p. 211.

13 *Ibid.*, p. 243.

14 A logical demurrer may be entered here in the following form: If we posit a *natural tendency*, then we must rule out *free choice*; if the mind naturally tends to know then it "cannot help it" if it knows. How, then, can knowing be called a good when it is, in a sense, "forced" on the mind? How can anything be good which is the product of a necessary and "built-in" characteristic? In modern ethical theory, especially in Experimentalism and Existentialism, good is the result of free and undetermined choice. We shall take up these matters in more detail in Part IV.

the subject and which therefore does not have to be tested out in action. There is no need for me to draw two lines each equal to a third and then measure them to see if they are equal. My intellect tells me this is true; I intuit it as true.

At the base of both kinds of truth, the Neo-Thomist will readily admit, lies sense experience; both synthetic and analytic knowing originate and have their impetus in the ground of ordinary perceiving. Certainly sense data are needed in the New York-Chicago statement. And in the second statement one must have a background of experience in order to understand the terms — *two, thing, equal,* etc. But here the similarity between synthetic and analytic truth ends; for in the latter category experience is not necessary to establish the truth of the statement. Its truth is an immediate apprehension of the intellect.

Self-evidence, then, is the key to a whole range of truth which is not accessible through science. And to the Neo-Thomist this kind of truth is far superior to scientific truth precisely because it stands above the changeable weather of day-to-day experience and the resultant storms of controversy in the empirical world. Scientific knowledge, says the Neo-Thomist, is only a kind of "edging toward" or "sidling up to" truth. Analytical, self-evident truth is the real article; it is epistemologically pure because, once taken hold of, it is ours forever!

Self-evidence and intuitive knowing can lead us, as we have seen in the example, to many relatively "low-order" truths, such as the mathematical proposition about equality. But this kind of knowing can also be used to carry us into the highest regions of metaphysics and into that exclusive "country club" of truths which the Neo-Thomist calls the "First Principles." A prime example of this kind of truth is the statement: *All things have a cause.* Based ultimately in experience but essentially transcending the empirical world, this principle can be asserted as true without any recourse to experiment or testing. Furthermore, this First Principle is particularly pertinent to our discussion because it opens up some illuminating territory in the psychology of knowing.

To expand on this point, we may say that Aristotle considered this the central principle in his search for the essence or "what-ness" of things. He found in causation the clearest road to true essential knowledge and finally came to the view that *to know anything is to know its causes.* In Aristotle's thinking there are four distinct types of causes:

The Material Cause = Matter
The Formal Cause = Form
The Efficient Cause = Maker
The Final Cause = Purpose

As it turns out, we actually proceed psychologically in somewhat this order in coming to know things. We first "sense" what a thing is made of, the basic stuff of which it is constructed. We then attend to its design and form, the total plan by which the material substance is arranged. Then we come to know it still better if we understand how it came into being, what caused it to be (our modern use of the word *cause* is confined largely to this third sense). Finally, we know it fully when we comprehend the purpose or function which the thing is to serve.

Thus, in the case of a house, the lumber is the material cause, the blueprint design is the formal cause, the carpenter is the efficient cause, and the Basic Idea of the house, i.e., its role as a dwelling place, is considered the final cause. The final cause, of course, serves as the gathering point for all the other causes; it is the occasion for all the other causes to be introduced into the logical situation. It is therefore the most important. Also, we are epistemologically satisfied when — but not until — we have reached the fourth and final cause; we say we really know something when we know its purpose.

To illustrate this, let us say that I place a piston ring before a young college girl. (In using this example, there is no intention of proclaiming any educational value in this exercise; it's just an apt case.) She has never seen one before, doesn't know anything about it, and hasn't the vaguest idea of its *raison d'être* in the world of things. But she begins by sensing its properties — shiny, hard, heavy, etc. She comes to the material cause, steel. She then notices its design: circular, sharp corners, grooves, etc., leading to the formal cause, a sharp-edged, grooved ring. She is then told that it was manufactured by a group of metalworkers in an automobile-parts factory. This helps a good deal in narrowing the possibilities. But she is essentially still outside the full knowledge of the item because she has not yet determined what it is *for*, what its final cause is.

At this point, the Aristotelian and Neo-Thomist epistemologist claims that the next step is a purely intuitive step. Sense perception must precede it, to be sure, and we must have the first three causes clearly in hand before proceeding. But the fourth step is exclusively a "leap of the intellect" into the realm of intuitive insight. To discover what the piston ring is *for*, what purpose it fulfills, what function it performs, is to be visited by an immediate apprehension of its ultimate essence, by an intuition.

It is in this sense that intuition is the summit and climax of all knowing, partly because it comes last, partly because it comes instantaneously, but principally because it has the effect of producing epistemological satisfaction in the knower, a kind of closure to the undertaking which represents complete knowledge. It is as if our minds had finally and ultimately fastened upon truth and, in so doing, come into touch with ultimate reality.

Of course, comprehending the final cause of piston rings is one thing and comprehending the final cause of other existent beings is quite another. The supreme test case is to apply this epistemology to Man. What is the essence of Man? Materially he is constructed of blood and bones. Formally he can be spoken of, in Platonic language, as a "featherless biped." But we are, admittedly, a long, long way from taking hold of his essence from these meager data. Ecclesiastical Thomists incline, in their epistemologies, to hold the third or efficient cause to be of vital importance. If you want to know what a thing is, ask its maker. And so, in the case of Man, the Almighty is appealed to in order to ascertain the fourth or final cause. What is Man *for*? we ask. And the Roman Catholic Church supplies the answer: to reclaim the Life of Grace lost by us through the Fall of Adam, which means to find our way back to the source of our being, namely, Being or God. This, to the Roman Catholic, is what we are *for*.

To a Lay Neo-Thomist, however, "straight" Aristotelianism, without St. Thomas' theological overtones, is sufficient. According to this doctrine, to understand the essence of Man does not require any theological commitments, Christian or otherwise. All it requires is a steady gaze at the question of the Final Cause of Man until intuition is ours. And we have not long to wait if we are willing to return to Aristotelian thinking on this question. For in Aristotle's system Man's Final Cause was clear: "The specifically human function, the reason why [Man] exists, what he is 'for,' is the development of his rationality, both in practical and intellectual affairs."[15]

Intuition and revelation

We must now make explicit what has been implicit in the above discussion, namely, that, while Lay and Ecclesiastical Neo-Thomists share intimately in their Aristotelian heritage and in the logic of Aristotle's thought, they contemporaneously divide in epistemological questions by virtue of their slight ontological divergencies. As noted both in Chapter Three and in the above analysis, the Lay Neo-Thomist is willing to adopt pretty much intact the Aristotelian frame of things insofar as philosophical matters are concerned. It is not mandatory that there be a God, a spiritual headwaters of human reality to which we must defer. There is only a logic to reality which we must yield to. However, a Lay Neo-Thomist could defensibly accept St. Thomas' philosophical system as long as he stayed on the side of (capital-*B*) Being, a purely philosophical concept, without drifting over the line into the theological concept of God; for

---

[15] R. Brumbaugh and N. Lawrence, Jr., "Aristotle's Philosophy of Education," *Educational Theory*, IX, No. 1 (January, 1959), 8.

in making the shift the Lay Thomist would be adding more to his understanding than unaided reason will provide. That is to say, one can proceed logically from Matter to Form to Essence to Existence to existing beings to Pure Being. By sheer intellectual force this progression can be run. But it is an extra-rational lurch to make the final step of saying that Being is the same as God. One *need not* worship Being; one *must* worship God. The two ideas are quite different.

For these and other, more sophisticated reasons, the Lay Neo-Thomist confines his epistemology to synthetic or scientific knowing capped by the highest form of knowing, analytic or intuitive knowing. If he is rationally rigorous, he will not try to claim too much or go beyond the limits set by these two methods.

The Ecclesiastical Neo-Thomist, on the other hand, because he holds to a theistic ontology, finds a still higher dimension to his epistemological activity: revelation. God reveals himself to us through the intellect. Admittedly, intuition and revelation are closely related concepts; semantically they are practically touching each other. But technically they are distinct. For intuition is, metaphorically, a "reaching out" to seize upon a truth already resident in an independent reality, whereas revelation is a "receiving in" of truths from an outside source. Intuition, therefore, is active, while revelation is passive; indeed, the former is usually expressed in the active voice (I *had* an intuition; I *intuited* something) while the latter is expressed in the passive voice (It *was revealed* to me; I *was made to see* something).

Notwithstanding this distinction, the Ecclesiastical Neo-Thomist holds that revelation is one way of knowing; it is a way of knowing, moreover, which has been authenticated down through history and which therefore claims as much right to epistemological attention as any other. Furthermore, since the author of such knowledge is God himself, this is the highest and supreme category of epistemological activity known to Man. Therefore, if there is conflict between revealed and intuitive knowledge, or between revealed and scientific knowledge, revelation shall carry the day. We are, then, in Ecclesiastical Neo-Thomism, dealing not only with three varieties of knowing: scientific, intuitive, and revelatory. We are dealing also with a *hierarchy* of knowing, by which the varieties are ordered. When there is tension in the hierarchical ranks the higher form must prevail.

This hierarchy of knowing is misconstrued by many commentators on Thomism to mean that revelation and faith actually supplant and take the place of other kinds of knowing. Especially in philosophical matters, it is said, Neo-Thomists begin with spiritual commitments which they then attempt to justify in reason. This is not accurate. What the Neo-Thomist insists on is the *complementary* nature of various kinds of knowing, i.e., that faith confirms and backs up what we have already achieved by reason, or, conversely, that reason properly applied will lead us independently to truths already revealed to us. Moses, it will be recalled, learned the "Name" of God ("I am Who Am") through revelation. But a couple of milleniums later, St. Thomas arrived at the concept of "Being" through rational procedures exclusively. St. Thomas thus demonstrated *rationally* what Moses had received through *revelation* from God.[16]

The Roman Catholic insistence on separate and autonomous epistemological realms has its practical application in political and social affairs. In these matters it is held that separate realms are inhabited by church and state and that each is sovereign in its own sphere. The difficulty with this view, as developed in greater detail in Chapter Eleven, is the segregation of religious principles from ordinary day-to-day affairs. If religious matters are to be sealed off in their own compartment, then they can have little to say about how we are to live out our lives. If, on the other hand, religious principles are applied to everyday concerns, they must expect to encounter competing secular and scientific ideas, with which they will occasionally collide head on. In collision, what then? Which principles — the ecclesiastical or the secular — shall prevail?

This is by way of suggesting that the Ecclesiastical Neo-Thomist epistemology is quite obviously destined to run into a good deal of trouble in a scientific and secular America unless carefully boxed in and confined to Roman Catholic churches and schools and insulated from the wider affairs of civil society. The mood of modern America is increasingly inclined toward the scientific and empirical; and when some religious or philosophical group claims that its spiritual or metaphysical or merely intuitive visions contradict what the scientist can see in plain daylight to be the truth of the matter, the American temper is likely to give the final nod of approval to the scientist.

This temper is the result of a new intellectual outlook, which has swept across the Western world within just the last couple of centuries and which has taken the modern (especially the American) mind by storm. Serving as both the storm troopers and the occupation forces for

16 The presumed autonomous independence of rational truth and revelatory truth is, in more sophisticated circles, still argued. Even Catholic philosophers have been known to yield some ground here. For instance, Étienne Gilson, one of the leading Ecclesiastical Neo-Thomists, says, in his *The Spirit of Medieval Philosophy* (New York: Charles Scribner's Sons, 1936): ". . . it is a fact that between ourselves and the Greeks the Christian revelation has intervened, and has profoundly modified the conditions under which reason has to work. Once you are in possession of that revelation how can you possibly philosophize as though you had never heard of it? The errors of Plato and Aristotle are precisely the errors into which pure reason falls, and every philosophy which sets out to be self-sufficing will fall into them again . . ." (Page 5.)

this intellectual revolution have been the Experimentalists, to whose epistemology we now turn.

EXPERIMENTALISM:
TRUTH AS WHAT WORKS

Historical perspectives

By all measures, the philosophical colossus of our age is the scientific philosophy of Experimentalism, variously called Pragmatism or Instrumentalism. As a philosophy it is relatively young, stretching back less than 100 years. It is, however, the systematic expression of a movement that began much earlier. Customarily Galileo is considered the father of the scientific tradition. Although it is difficult to locate the origin of so nebulous a thing as an intellectual movement, there does seem to have been an epoch in time when men's minds took a new turn. This epoch, the latter sixteenth and early seventeenth centuries, serves in retrospect somewhat as a "Great Divide" or intellectual watershed in the historic course of human thought: on the other side, the reliance on logical, self-evident, and *a priori* truth; on this side, the reliance on experience and overt phenomena. Through the words of a brilliant commentator on the history of science, Herbert Dingle, we may begin to assess the magnitude of this shift in intellectual orientation. In an article on "Cosmology and Science," Dingle writes:

> To appreciate what kind of thinking created the cosmology of the Greek pioneers, beginning, as it inevitably had to in early times, from the natural assumption that the earth was the center of the universe, we must understand a fundamental characteristic of Greek thought — which is at variance with the scientific outlook. They presupposed certain *principles,* which were assumed to be inviolable and were accepted without question. If appearances seemed to contradict them, then the appearances were deceptive . . . For example, they asserted that the only activity possible to heavenly bodies was perfectly uniform and circular movement, and that apart from such eternal circulations no change of any kind could take place in the heavens. . . . since the planets appeared not to move in circles at uniform speed, the apparently erratic movements of each planet must be the resultant of a set of circular movements.
>
> The aim of Greek cosmology was to arrive at the complex system of interlocking spheres in motion that made up the universe . . . Geometers of genius such as the Greeks produced were able to represent the observed movements of the planets with an accuracy equal to that of their imperfect observations at any given time, but as time went on the discrepancies between the geometrical requirements and the observed positions

of planets increased, and so more spheres were introduced to annul them. This went on throughout the Middle Ages, until by the sixteenth century more than eighty spheres were necessary to account for the observed movements, and even that number did it very imperfectly.

. . . by the sixteenth century the cosmic machinery of spheres had become so unwieldy that Copernicus, a man dominated by the mathematician's passion for simple generalization, ventured to make what seemed to him the very slight change of transferring the center of the universe from the earth to the sun. By this device he was able to reduce the number of cosmic spheres by more than half.

He made no other change, nor did he realize that any other was necessary. He clung as firmly as the most orthodox medieval philosopher to the machinery of spheres and to the Aristotelian principles of perfect celestial substances and uniform circular motions. . . . By the time of Galileo, some three quarters of a century later, it had become clear that there was no need for any spheres at all, and the simple change that we would now describe as no more than choosing a different origin of coordinates had generated a conflict of world-views such as the world had never before seen.[17]

This, then, was the Aristotelian epistemology at work: starting with presupposed and "self-evident" principles and then attempting to make the observations of natural phenomena conform to them. In contrast to this procedure was the method of science:

The Galilean-Newtonian philosophy, on the contrary, brought knowledge in apparently boundless measure but was logically [from the Aristotelian standpoint] outrageous. From a few phenomena, or experiments, it proposed to derive principles to be applied universally. Some bodies attract one another; this is a body; therefore it attracts every other body in the universe. No more patently invalid syllogism could be imagined; it was an error in Aristotelian logic of which even the youngest scholastic child could hardly have been capable. But it worked. And not only so, but similar generalizations later in other fields were found to work, and they go on working. We have never known heat to flow by itself from a colder to a hotter body, and we take it that it never has nor ever will anywhere in space. The brightness of a lamp in our laboratory falls off as the square of the distance as we walk away from it; hence we infer what the brightness of a distant galaxy must be. That is science. Its assertions about the universe are unlimited generalizations from a few momentary observations at a point in space.

From a purely logical point of view scientific cosmology would appear to have no justification, to be a gigantic impertinence. It is saved from this by a frank recognition by scientists of what it is and what its limitations are. The work of three centuries has shown that the scientific approach

17 *Scientific American*, CXCV, No. 3 (September, 1956), 224–230.

is on unassailable ground when it declares itself to be the best prescription yet devised for obtaining knowledge of the relations between phenomena. Whether or not its generalizations have any right to be regarded as the *truth*, they lead to further knowledge — which, so far as we can see, would be quite unobtainable otherwise. But they do this only on the condition that we abandon them the moment we see that they cease to hold. They originate in phenomena and they are at the mercy of phenomena.

The Aristotelian general principles, on the other hand, were conceived *a priori*, independently of phenomena, and phenomena were distorted at liberty so as to exemplify them. The problem was to "save the phenomena." The basic principles themselves could not be threatened; it was the phenomena that stood in need of salvation.[18]

Ontological background

We noted in Chapter Three that the Experimentalist's reality is the moving, changing, "process-in-flux" event spoken of as experience. Experience is the ultimate ground for human existence; it is both the originator and the supreme court of whatever we do or say. To put it bluntly once again, whatever reality is is what we say it is, and what we say it is is founded in ordinary experience. Experience is as close as we can get to the "name" of reality; as exasperatingly nonsubstantive as this may be, it is the best we can do.

Knowing, then, must take on a quite different notation in this philosophy, for we are immediately confronted by the necessity to settle for something much less than fixed and permanent truth as the end point of our epistemological labors. Since our reality is itself characterized by flux and movement and change, certainly our knowledge cannot be otherwise. We must therefore initially retrain ourselves to recognize that whatever knowledge is possible is that kind of knowledge which is temporary and tentative in character. If our conception of truth (knowledge) is ultimately "at the mercy of phenomena" as we experience them, as Dingle has said, then we must be willing to alter our truth and our knowledge as new and variable phenomena come into view.

Furthermore, in Experimentalist epistemology we must rid ourselves of the subjective-objective dualism so characteristic of the three positions already discussed. Both Idealism and Realism (and, with minor qualification, Neo-Thomism) are what we have called essentially "objective" doctrines, holding to an epistemology which considers the knower as one agent and the reality-to-be-known as the alter-agent in the entire knowing process. In these doctrines epistemology is the explanation of how the two substantive agents are brought together. This, to an Experimentalist, is all wrong; it presupposes, in the first place, an ontological dualism

18 *Ibid.*, 230–234.

between the knower and his world. This presupposition is both un-warranted in ontological thought and obstructive to the epistemological enterprise. What it does is to *create* an epistemological problem where none exists.

Man is, after all, part of the world which he is knowing. Furthermore, he is integrally *one* with it in a state of constant interaction. To extricate him from Nature and to assign him the role of spectator (ideational spectator in Idealism; perceptual spectator in Realism; logical spectator in Neo-Thomism) is to do irreconcilable violence to his true condition. He is both *in* and *of* his cosmos. He never can look at it — ideationally, perceptually, or logically — as an outsider. He is inevitably, inexorably, irreconcilably "plugged in" to his world.

When the Experimentalist suggests Experience as his name for reality, he is not merely thinking up a new category; rather, he is pointing to an already existential but hitherto unrecognized and unappreciated feature of the epistemological situation, namely, the *dynamic relationship be-tween* the knower and his world. What Experimentalism does is to render truly existential what the other philosophies consider only superficially phenomenal, namely, the interactive relationship itself. Granted, this is not a substantive existent in the classical sense; it is a process-existent, what we may now refer to, recalling Chapter Three, as a "verb-al" or "event-ual" existent. There is no reason why events and processes cannot be as truly existential as substantive entities.[19]

So, therefore, the Experimentalist's *Experience* is the name for an interactive relationship, the relationship of *transaction*, of *doing-and-undergoing*, which is moved to the center of the stage and given the lead role in Experimentalist epistemology. Unlike previous views, the new interest will be ᴇ interaction, in relation, in the nature of the "con-nectedness" *between* things, rather than in some underlying "idea" or "essence" or "logical substance" which metaphysically inheres in things.

The nature of truth

Following up on these ontological considerations, we may now investi-gate more carefully the knowledge-problem before us. In such an on-tology, what kind of truth is possible? As we have indicated, all knowledge to an Experimentalist must be considered temporary and conditional. Indeed, the word *truth* is an equivocal term which is hazardous to use in Experimentalist theory. So heavily laden is this word with the traditional

---

[19] In the more technical discussions of ontology, the Experimentalists attempt to demonstrate that even existential *things* are really *events occurring* rather than *sub-stantives existing*. Indeed, the very word *exist* means, in Experimentalist ontology, *to occur*. See V. C. Morris, "An Experimentalist on Being," *The Modern Schoolman*, XXXV, No. 2 (January, 1958), 125–133.

meaning of permanent and unchanging statements of fact about an existential reality that it often tends to jar rather than facilitate understanding of the Experimentalist position. To overcome this hazard, the qualifying adjective *tentative* is customarily placed before the word *truth* to designate more precisely what Experimentalists really mean in this context.

This point is labored at some length here because it is a crucial feature
of Experimentalist epistemology. The analogue of the scientist in the
laboratory is perhaps illustrative of this point. Let us say that a scientist
in his investigation comes upon a discovery of some kind. In the histri-
onics of science he is supposed to exclaim, "Eureka!" (I have found it!).
But no scientist, if he ever does say such a thing, really means that he has
fastened upon a permanent and immutable truth. The scientist simply
means that he has found a new way to understand the phenomena before
him. This discovery, like every other, is subject to change or repeal tomorrow morning if the phenomena then seem to require it. Taken literally, the statement "I have found it" is not a scientific statement but more
in the nature of a theological one. A Realist scientist, thinking he had
peered into the ultimate nature of the physical world, might possibly be
caught saying such a thing; but an Experimentalist scientist never. All
he says is that he has come upon an idea which will serve as truth until
something better comes along.

Knowing as process

With this caveat in hand, we may now proceed to another epistemological implication from Experimentalist ontology. Reference was made
above to the "transactional" character of experience. In the enterprise
called knowing, what we are actually engaged in is a kind of dialectic
with the cosmos. As we experience, various ideas occur to us as to the way
things are. We may speak of these as hunches, guesses, hypotheses, intuitions,[20] or insights; basically, all these terms designate the same genera of
assertion. At this point, they have no epistemological status except that
they have occurred to us; they are, as it were, only "candidates" for truth.

At this point we begin to redirect our behavior and to act *as if* such and
such were true. That is, we enter the *do-ing* phase of knowing; we *act on*
the cosmos. Then we receive the reaction of the cosmos; we *undergo* the
consequences of our doing. In simpler language, we see how things turn
out. In the turning-out of things, we have a chance to see how well our

[20] Here is a vital and illuminating distinction to see in connection with intuition.
In Neo-Thomism (and, to a lesser extent, in Idealism) intuitions are the *end point* of
knowing; once had, they represent the termination of epistemological activity. In
Experimentalism, however, they are the *starting point* for knowing; once had, they become hypotheses for inquiry — they invite investigation, i.e., they provoke epistemological activity.

original hunch or hypothesis stands up. If things turn out the way we expect, we say our hunch was correct, i.e., true. If things turn out some other way, we discard that hunch and try another. If the consequences provide phenomena which we have not expected or imagined, we return to our original hunch and integrate these findings into another, more sophisticated hunch.

Then, taking this new hunch, we again act upon the cosmos to see if we have come any closer to true knowledge; and we continue the doing-undergoing procedure until we arrive at a view of things which seems to satisfy the requirements of the conditions under which we are working. If the conditions change, then the consequences we undergo will change, and our original hypotheses will have to be reworked, thus directing us to engage in new *do-ings* and, hence, new *undergoings*. Furthermore, every new experience, every new set of consequences, has the effect of suggesting to us new hunches, new guesses, new intuitions of the way the world works, and we are led on into an endless array of hypotheses, which we then attempt to test out in action.

This endless progression, this open-ended series of doing-undergoing-doing-undergoing, etc. is the process by which the Experimentalist engages in epistemological activity. It is what he calls "reflective thinking." This is not to be confused with "reflection" in the classical sense of sitting quietly in one's study and contemplating the universe. It is, rather, literally re-flective, a "bending back again" of thought, from experienced consequences to tentative hunch. In more generalized terms, it is a reorganization of our hypotheses resulting from the experiencing of the consequences of our acts, a criticism of what we *think* by virtue of *acting on* what we think and seeing what happens. In its most generalized expression it is what Dewey called "the reconstruction of experience." This single phrase sums up the entire sense and meaning of scientific Experimentalist epistemology.

We may see then that knowing is an activity which never reaches a terminus; we never know something once and for all. Knowing is always open-ended. To know some *thing* is to hold it only temporarily, until new phenomena upset it. Meanwhile, we hold it as know*ledge* — the suffix *-ledge* signifying the substantive aggregate of our knowing activity — but we hold it only "on trial," never ceasing to re-test it, to question it, to inquire into it again to see if it is still relevant to the circumstances before us.

The scientific method

What we have been describing above in quite ordinary and pedestrian terms turns out to be the very same procedure as that used by the sophisticated scientist in the research laboratory. Contrary to popular belief, there is nothing fundamentally mysterious about how scientists work. Their procedures, which are essentially the procedures of the common man trying to reach intelligent decisions, can be abstracted and set down into five fairly distinct steps:

(1) First, there occurs what Dewey called "an indeterminate situation," a situation in which there is some rupture, great or small, to the smooth on-flowing of life's affairs. To the ordinary citizen it may be only a feeling or disposition, a tension which has been set up in his routine. To a research scientist it may be an idle puzzlement, an inchoate curiosity or a gap somewhere in his scientific knowledge that he wants to close.

(2) There then occurs a refinement of the difficulty into more particular problematic form; steps are taken by the individual to diagnose the situation, to see more precisely what the problem is. To the ordinary citizen this may turn out to be only a matter of how to get to work while his car is in the repair shop. To the scientist it may be the more sophisticated problem of locating the cause of polio.

(3) At this stage the individual sets out in search of every conceivable potential solution to the problem. He permits his imagination to run free; any guess, any hunch, any intuition is admissible. Indeed, the doctrine of "freedom of thought" has its epistemological as well as its political root at precisely this point. For no hypothesis can be tested unless it is *thought of;* no possible solution can be introduced into a problem situation until it is objectified and admitted as a candidate for the final answer. Hence the scientist defends his freedom with a passion, for freedom of thought — the freedom to consider anything, no matter how unorthodox — is absolutely essential to the scientific procedure. Riding his son's bicycle to work may strike the ordinary citizen as preposterous, but it is one possibility to be examined. That a tiny living organism is the culprit in polio may seem unlikely, but it must be considered as a possibility.

(4) The fourth stage consists in projecting these possible solutions in the mind so as to consider the consequences each would be likely to lead to; we think through what would happen if we adopted one or another plan of action. Dewey called this the stage of reasoning, reasoning in the sense of associating ideas — hypotheses and conjectured consequences — in a purposeful, meaningful way. (This is to be contrasted with the kind of reasoning characteristic of the older philosophies, especially Neo-Thomism, in which reason is exercised on abstract syllogisms having little to do with practical affairs.) If Step 3 could be called the "inventory of possible solutions" (what Dewey called "guiding ideas"), then this Step 4 can be called the "inventory of conjectured consequences." Riding the bicycle to work will wrinkle the clothing, be somewhat tiring, and strike the

neighbors as undignified, but it will be cheap. To suggest a living organism as the cause of polio infection will involve "catching" and identifying a moving object somewhere in the body; but if a vaccine can be administered which will either kill or neutralize the organism, then a decrease in infection will follow.

(5) Finally, the fifth stage is that of testing. We consult experience directly to see if the conjectured consequences do in fact occur. The citizen tries walking, taking the bus, riding with a neighbor, riding the bicycle. He tests out each solution individually; that is, he acts on each proposal *as if* it were the answer; he literally acts it out, so as to experience the consequences to which it leads. With the consequences for all alternatives in hand, he is then in a position to evaluate and judge. Likewise, the scientist tests out each of his hunches. He designs experiments, prepares medicines, controls some groups of organisms, and arranges the variables systematically among other organisms, and he does all these things so as to witness the consequences that flow from each of his separate acts in the laboratory; that is, he *acts on* each hypothesis developed in Step 3 to get at the consequences, to see what happens.

The issue of consequences is especially labored at this point, and for very good reason: Here, within the texture of *consequences,* lies the heart of Experimentalist epistemology. It is the consequences of acts that contain the raw material for making epistemological decisions. The citizen decides on the bicycle, possibly because riding in the open air turns out to be more pleasant than he had anticipated. The scientist chooses the virus hypothesis and develops a vaccine to control the polio virus in the body.

We may now present the Experimentalist epistemological system schematically. Figure 8 shows the five steps:
  (1) An indeterminate situation, a feeling of tension, a "felt difficulty";
  (2) The diagnosis and definition of the difficulty or specification of the problem (P);
  (3) An inventory of possible solutions (1, 2, 3, 4, 5);
  (4) The conjecturing of consequences (C);
  (5) The test for consequences (T).

It is the Experimentalist's view that all knowing takes this form, whether the knowing is in science or art or engineering or sociology, or whatever. In some subject matters, it is true, the procedure may be somewhat obscured. In the social sciences, for instance, we are not permitted to test out each suggestion in direct experience; we are required to project our imaginations to assess what the consequences will probably be. In the matter of a national health policy, for instance, we are not permitted to

STEPS

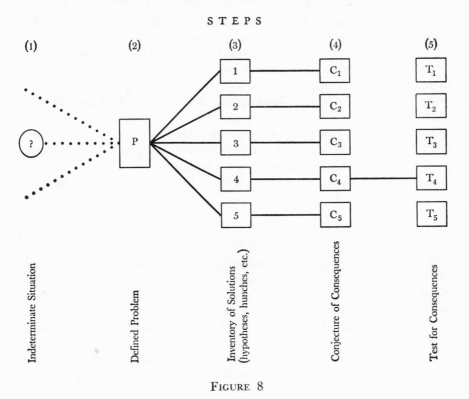

FIGURE 8

Schema of the Scientific Method

test out first voluntary health insurance plans, compulsory health insurance plans, complete socialization of the medical profession, and whatever other notions may be submitted. Rather, we are required to stop at Step 4 to make an educated guess as to what the consequences are likely to be. And, to be sure, the status quo is always one of the choices in social questions, and its consequences must stand before the bar of judgment like any other. But the point is that even in social questions the scientific procedure, in its most generalized form here described, is the procedure most commonly used. In social problems we do not trust to luck or appeal to a benign deity or consult an astrologer. We try, instead, to reduce the whole circumstance to intelligent and systematic control, by defining the problem, testing out various solutions (either directly or imaginatively), and seeing which solution yields the most socially profitable consequences.

This procedure, so celebrated in Experimentalist literature, is also called "The Complete Act of Thought," a name that designates the manner in which reason is introduced into human experience. Except for Dewey's original use of the term, however, Experimentalists rarely employ the word *reason* because of its substantive overtones in classical thought. Reason or rationality is not some kind of mental entity contained in the brain, as the Greeks held. Better to speak of *intelligence,* which is a label for the *activity* of reason in life's affairs. *Intelligence* is a dynamic term, signifying not a substantive entity of mental "stuff" but an activity, a process, a form of behavior. To possess intelligence, then, in Experimentalist terms, is not to possess some *thing* but *to be able to do* something, namely, to handle life's affairs in the scientific manner just prescribed.

Truth as what works

We may now generalize by noting that the ultimate test of truth is whether the hunch or hypothesis which is tried out and acted upon really "works." Does it, that is, explain the situation, rationalize the disparate phenomena that have been observed, solve the problem? *In the degree that it performs this duty* it is said to be true. Hence, truths in Experimentalism are always true *in degrees,* always true contingently or relatively. That is, they may seem to work better in some circumstances than in others; the "wave" theory of light works in one instance, but the "particle" theory is invoked to understand another.

Whether a hunch does indeed solve a problem or rationalize an indeterminate situation may be assessed, in part, by whether the conclusion leads on somewhere. Is more thought, more doing, more undergoing, signaled and prompted by the conclusion? If not, perhaps it has not resolved the indeterminacy. If so, and if new inquiries are forthwith suggested, then *to that degree* it may be said to be a solution.

The test of workability, then, is quite as open-ended as the test of that for which workability is itself the test: truth. We are led on and on, epistemologically, in a flowing and ongoing knowing event, tentatively stopping and holding to certain things as true, but true only insofar as they help us to manage the world. To manage the world is the generalized empirical problem facing mankind; knowledge and truth are but the instrumentalities for carrying on this work.

As we shall see in Chapter Nine, the principle of "workability" is, according to the Experimentalists, applicable also to aesthetic and moral questions. What has originated and been found spectacularly successful in the physical sciences, and is now being increasingly applied to the social sciences, may one day, say the Experimentalists, take over in the moral and ethical sphere as well. When this occurs, our values will cease being valuable merely by heredity and tradition. Our values will become subject to the same procedure as our truths, i.e., criticism and test. What this may mean for modern man we shall see in later chapters.

In summary of Experimentalist epistemology, we may say that the entire knowing process is an open-ended, ongoing, and restless activity of human beings. By this time you may begin to appreciate why such an epistemology is exasperating to many people. It has no "anchor to wind-ward," no absolutes to tie to, no quiet harbor of truth where testing can be permanently halted. There is no resting place where a man can say, once and for all, "I know this for sure." The element of contingency and relativity so pervasive in this doctrine is simply emotionally un-acceptable to a great many individuals; they cannot stand the strain of "open-endedness" in the sphere of thought and belief. And their re-jection of this philosophy is in a sense understandable, for Experimen-talism *is* a "tough-minded" outlook. One has to have a thick intellectual and moral skin to manage it. But Experimentalism, like any other phil-osophic point of view, is interested not necessarily in what is comfortable but in the actual situation in which men live: To retreat to more secure doctrines is, as William James put it, "a failure of nerve."

The great advantage of Experimentalism is that it is a *public* episte-mology; it is a method of knowing which is out in the open, available to all. The Experimentalist does not deny private experience; all he says is that it does not produce knowledge. The sort of experience which is common to all men, testable, and warranted is the only kind of experience that is capable of yielding what we call knowledge.

For this reason "community" plays an important role in Experi-mentalist epistemology. Indeed, many Experimentalists speak of the "uncoerced community of persuasion" as the central criterion of truth. Science, you will note, is of this general character; it is an open, public knowing procedure, to which many people, in communication with one another, contribute. And there must exist some common "persuasion" among them before anything can be labeled as knowledge.

EXISTENTIALISM:
TRUTH AS EXISTENTIAL CHOICE

Existential requirements

As with the other sections, the best way to undertake the examination of Existentialist epistemology is to take another look at the ontology of this position discussed in Chapter Three. At the very least, this procedure enables us to see better what is going to be required of us in the way of knowledge, if it does not actually ascertain what kinds of knowledge will be possible.

As the earlier discussion has shown, the central metaphysical principle in Existentialism is the priority of existence over essence. Man arrives on the scene devoid of "what-ness." His essence is not given. Man is, so to speak, an open question. Men, then, are committed to something which they have not asked for, i.e., existence. They are "locked in," as it were, to a condition from which they can never escape. In the making of choices they reveal *what* they think Man is. Hence, even in suicide, in attempting to "resign from existence," one has made a choice. Or, more commonly, in burying oneself in one's society — in letting society guide the choices — one has made his choice. There is no escape from this unutterable freedom.[21]

Now when we use the word *choice* it is to be understood in its largest and fullest meaning. Making a choice is not confined to deciding to *do* something. It also includes deciding to *believe* something, to accept something as true. Hence, we are confronted at the outset with the epistemological significance of the Existentialist ontology, namely, the existential freedom of man in choosing his own truth. Each man is his own supreme court of epistemological judgment, and he is, therefore, in an ultimate sense, absolutely on his own when it comes to deciding between candidates for truth.

This is sometimes interpreted, incorrectly, to mean that Existentialist Man is driven by passion and impulse through all of existence, that he is the complete expression of hedonism in modern life in believing only what he *wants* to believe, or that he doesn't really *care* what is true. All of these criticisms are very wide of the mark in describing the epistemological "posture" of Existentialism. For, on the contrary, the Existentialist cares very much to know the truth. He is especially interested in the truth about himself, about what he is. But since what he *is* depends on his choices of truth lying outside himself, he is equally earnest about these also. To know that $E = mc^2$, to know that *Hamlet* is a great work of Western letters, to know that biological forms are evolutionary, is to say something about what one is. Especially in religion: When a man says he knows there is a personal God he is really saying something about himself, about what he thinks he is. His choices make him and thereby reveal him.

Concerning wanting to believe anything, we are all guilty. What we individually believe to be the truth is what we *want* to believe. How else could it be? I believe the world is round; it does not appear that way but I have it on good authority that it is. So I believe it. But I don't *have to*

21 See Eric Fromm, *Escape from Freedom* (New York: Farrar and Rinehart, Inc., 1941).

believe it if I choose not to. Nobody is insisting that I do; no one is forcing this belief on me. I actively choose it as one of my beliefs. If this be impulse, then we are all impulsive. This, however, is not the usual sense in which we use the word *impulsive*.

All this suggests that the Existentialist has little to offer in the way of a method of knowing, a systematic epistemology. Rather, he is concerned with pointing out that in all knowing — sense perception, logical demonstration, scientific proof, intuition, revelation — it is the individual self which must make the ultimate decision as to what is, as a matter of fact, true. As we live out our lives, believing our histories, our literary insights, our multiple gods, our sense perceptions, we make the grand mistake of thinking that these truths are in some way forced on us, either by an external and objective reality (Realism and Idealism) or by a necessary and insistent logic (Lay Neo-Thomism) or by an Absolute Being who can have it no other way (Ecclesiastical Neo-Thomism). Even the Experimentalists have led us down the primrose path to self-delusion; for there is nothing in science which makes ultimate epistemological demands on me. If a scientific truth doesn't seem to make sense to me, I can call it false, and who can contradict me?

The Existentialist, however, does not spend all his time in such carping dialectic. What he is interested in is simply reminding us that there is an element of *personal appropriation* in all knowing. When all the data are in, each individual on his own must make a personal choice to believe something. Indeed, he must make his own personal appropriation of an epistemology. Nothing could illustrate this better than to point to the present chapter on comparative epistemologies and to recognize that, as individuals, we must make our personal selection from among these (and other) epistemological theories on the basis of which of them seems to be the most acceptable explanation of how knowing takes place. Each individual involved in this chapter, both author and reader, must make a personal commitment to some theory of knowledge. Each individual is, then, not only the final court of truth but the final court of how truth is arrived at — the ultimate point of origin for every epistemological program.

The modes of knowing

Having said all of these things, we are now in a position to approach more technically the problem of Existentialist knowing. If the prime metaphysical concept in Existentialism is the priority of existence over essence, the prime epistemological concept is the division of knowing into two *modes,* for which, unfortunately, no handy labels are available. Let us simply call them Mode One and Mode Two.

Preliminary to this analysis is Sartre's distinction between two modes of being: "being-in-itself" and "being-for-itself." I see a tree outside my window: I am, that is, perceptually conscious of a tree. The tree possesses "being-in-itself." Like other objects, it just *is*. My perceptual knowledge of it (Mode One) is of a brute fact of existence. However, I am conscious not only of the tree but of my consciousness of the tree, i.e., I am cognitively aware of my cognition. Ultimately this means that I am conscious of my own being as well as that of the tree, but not in the same way, not perceptually. Rather, I have epistemological access to my own being through quite a different route, an internal, subjective awareness, which we are calling Mode Two. I feel myself in existence, as an existential center of knowing; but *how* I know this is quite at variance with the "how-I-know" that the tree is a similar sort of existential center of other qualities. In an immediate kind of way, I feel my own being, a self-conscious, self-returning being — "being-for-itself" — which the tree does not share with me.

To put this in plain language, we can say that in Mode One I am conscious of an existential world (somewhat in the manner of the Realist; see pages 142–144), and that in Mode Two I am also conscious of my consciousness of this world. I somehow know my own existentiality.

Now, this may seem a trifle in a treatment of so recondite a subject as epistemology; but its far-reaching significance can be recognized if we extend it beyond the regions of simple sense perception into the realm of science. For science is the "Mode One" of knowing in its most elaborate and sophisticated form; science seeks to know the existential reality we humans inhabit.

As an epistemology, science initially took as its subject matter the physical world about us. As everyone knows, it has enjoyed spectacular success as a method of "Mode One" knowing. Gradually it took up and developed more and more subject matters[22] — astronomy, physics, chemistry, biology — until, about 1900, it stumbled on Man. Here, astonishingly, was some open territory that strangely had been overlooked. What has happened since is history — an explosive proliferation of human sciences, beginning with the *social* sciences of economics, political science, and sociology, which were later augmented and in some cases overshadowed by the so-called *behavioral* sciences, i.e., psychology, social psychology, cultural anthropology, etc.

The important point to note, however, is that in this application of "Mode One" or scientific knowing to the study of Man there has been a gathering presumption that Man can be ultimately understood in the same manner that we have come to understand atoms, frogs, and machines, i.e., through the scientific method. In short, the feeling has grown

[22] In this discussion it would be more apt to call them "object matters."

that Man, the last unknown, is about to yield his secret to himself. This has not happened, of course, and the Existentialist claims that it never can happen, because there is an absolute chasm separating "being-in-itself" from "being-for-itself," and, therefore, a similar chasm separating "Mode One" from "Mode Two" knowing.

Psychology is an apt illustration in the above list because it began, as its name implies, as the study of the "psyche." It originated, if you will, as an attempt to employ "Mode One" knowing to get at and to understand the "Mode Two" knowing of the self. In short, it was an attempt to see whether science could unlock the doors of the selfhood's center, of the "Mode Two" consciousness of consciousness. The fact that psychology has given up on this and has turned instead to the study of *overt behavior* is a clue that science simply cannot penetrate the human self. Mode Two is scientifically out of reach.

At this point two things must be said. First, the above analysis is not meant to imply that psychology is a fraudulent discipline. On the contrary, the application of "Mode One" knowing to human behavior, an unheard-of thing only a short century ago, is a "technological," methodological invention of the very first magnitude. All we are saying here is that, so far as Existentialist, "Mode Two" knowing is concerned, psychology has not made a dent in it. The second thing to say is that this last sentence must be somewhat qualified by the partial successes of depth psychology and psychiatry. To be sure, insofar as these are scientific — in the objective, hypothesis-forming, data-gathering, problem-solving sense of the term — it may safely be said that they have added very little to the understanding of the "being-for-itself" of the human person; but insofar as they have sought to awaken the patient's selfhood, insofar as they have quickened his consciousness of his consciousness, in that degree we can say that they have served the Existentialist cause. Too often, however, psychiatry has been the vehicle merely for dredging up from the bottom of a person's life the "objective," empirical "cause" of the emotional turbulence on the surface of his living. Laudable as this is as therapy, it has nothing to do with the awakening of the self's inner powers of choice, as the Existentialist sees it. In fact, what this type of psychotherapy does is just the reverse, i.e., it relieves the patient from making choices. He leaves the doctor's office no larger in selfhood but only muttering, "So *that's* why I'm so neurotic! I'm really not responsible for my neurosis, after all; I couldn't help being this way." This attitude, it may plainly be seen, is the ultimate contradiction of the meaning of "Mode Two" knowing: It is the denial of consciousness of consciousness.

In summing up the so-called human sciences, therefore, we are forced to observe that Mode Two has remained largely untouched; it is a much deeper and more complicated dimension of human experience than science is apparently equipped to handle. What is more, there is a kind of moral paradox in even trying to understand it: Man would destroy himself if he did! To explain this, Sartre reminds us that man is trying to know everything, he hungers after complete and absolute knowledge. Now that he is within reach of complete knowledge of his environment he has turned upon himself. But he has turned upon himself, necessarily, as an *object* of knowing, as a "being-in-itself." To study man this way is perhaps necessary and fruitful, but if we were ever to come to know him completely this way we would have driven out his "being-for-itself," i.e., his selfhood. There would be nothing left to do; we would have passed from a state of "being-for-itself" into the state of "being-in-itself"; we would just exist, like trees, as objects, but not as subjects.

It is because of this, say the Existentialists, that we really don't want to know ourselves completely. We never wish to discover that we are nothing but objects. We wish to retain our subjective base. But nevertheless we go on trying, because we have to know more and more. So we are, in Sartre's terms, *"une passion inutile,"* "a futile passion."

Mode Two and the scientific method

The prime epistemological task of the Existentialist, as may be surmised from the above, is to comprehend and understand what is here labeled "Mode Two" knowing. This turns out to be a sizable project, because this mode of knowing almost defies description and definition. About as close as we can come to it in nontechnical language is *awareness,* a kind of total feeling-tone which is simply *had* by the individual. As George Kneller puts it:

> The existentialist epistemology (if such it may be termed!) assumes that the individual is responsible for his own knowledge. Existentialist knowledge is "intuitive." It is "human." It originates in, and is composed of, what exists in the individual's consciousness and feelings as a result of his experiences and the projects he adopts in the course of his life.[23]

Furthermore, when we say, as Kneller does, that the individual is "responsible" for his own knowledge, we mean that he ultimately *must* be, because he is the only individual who has this knowledge. He is responsible for it because it is privately *his* knowledge and that of nobody else.

Kneller continues by saying that ". . . the validity of knowledge is determined by its value to the individual."[24] What this means may be

[23] *Existentialism and Education* (New York: Philosophical Library, 1959), p. 59.
[24] *Loc. cit.*

vividly illustrated by comparing this kind of private knowledge with the open, public procedure of the scientific method of the Experimentalist. If we attend closely to the analysis of the Experimentalist's method (see pages 160–164) and the schema of it presented in Figure 8 (page 163) we notice that his "Mode Two" knowing can be found implicitly residing in Step 5, which, incidentally, is also the crucial step in Experimentalist epistemology.

It is easy enough for the Experimentalist to explain that alternative hypotheses should be judged by whether they do or do not work, i.e., by an appeal to the consequences to which they lead when acted upon. But he never explains how it is that alternative *consequences* are sorted out by those undergoing them; he more or less assumes that when all of the alternative hypotheses are acted out, and the consequences are thus set in motion and "undergone," the rest of the epistemological action will take care of itself, i.e., the individual will make up his mind on the hypothesis that works. This is all very true, but how, asks the Existentialist, does the individual choose among the *consequences?* In terms of Step 5 in Figure 8, how do we decide between Consequence of Hypothesis 1 (T_1) and Consequence of Hypothesis 2 (T_2)? How (in this illustration) did Consequence 4 (T_4) happen to be chosen as best? What are the conditions required for saying something "works"? What is the measure of "workability" as it is understood in Experimentalist terms?

At this point the Experimentalist is likely to invoke a kind of sophisticated epistemological democracy of majority rule: the "uncoerced community of persuasion." But, says the Existentialist, there can be no community of persuasion until there is individual persuasion. Each individual must cast his vote on certain consequences before there can be any community decision on those consequences, let alone a community decision on the hypotheses. Each individual must be heard from *as an individual* before the community can get into epistemological action. Hence, no knowing can occur until there is first "feeling"; or, more accurately, no "Mode One" knowing can occur until there is "Mode Two" knowing (awareness, "feeling," etc.).

Another way of looking at this is to recognize that scientific knowledge is ultimately contingent upon the scientific method. In discussing Karl Jaspers, Kneller states:

> . . . scientific knowledge is universally valid, once established as true; and agreement may be expected from all who possess the necessary qualifications for understanding the truth of a given scientific proposition. But the meaning of any such truth is necessarily limited, since it is relative to the methods and assumptions that have been used to obtain it.[25]

25 *Ibid.*, pp. 59–60.

In all fairness to the Experimentalists, it must be pointed out that they are quite willing to settle for this limitation on scientific knowledge; all they say is that experience is all we have to go on, and that, therefore, scientific knowledge, as incomplete and contingent as it is, is the best we can do. And, in light of what it has accomplished, it is no mean achievement. Any quixotic adventure into "Mode Two" knowing, they say, is just a retreat into mysticism or rational humanism, or, at the very best, into "poetry."

Nevertheless the Existentialist insists on the validity, indeed the primacy, of "Mode Two" knowing. Each one of us recognizes this knowing within himself. Although we cannot report on it concerning other people, we certainly cannot deny its existential presence within our own being. If this be poetry, let it stand. For there is a kind of knowing in poetry, after all. Poetry is not sterile of epistemological content. Quite the contrary, poetry is the vehicle of feeling and awareness; it is the vehicle for the expression of "being-for-itself." So, likewise, are the drama, the novel, the arts generally, and philosophy — particularly the last, because here we can begin to generalize our awareness, to engage in "meta-awareness" by becoming self-conscious of our self-consciousness.

*　　*　　*

We have, then, in a manner of speaking, come full circle. Beginning with the Self in Idealism, we posited an Absolute Mind of which the individual, microcosmic mind partakes. Knowing, in this tradition, is the increasing identification of the microcosmic with the macrocosmic mind. In Realism, however, the act of knowing is a far simpler operation. Working within a physical reality, the individual simply witnesses, perceptually and organically, a regulated, machine-like Nature, which he then *knows* by reducing its structure and motion to facts and formulas. The Neo-Thomist attempts to combine the Idealist and Realist outlooks by laying a *logical* form upon all Being and by assigning the knowing process to the enterprise of introducing this logic into the human mind — which, fortunately, is already disposed, because of its inherent structure, to receive it. Experimentalists, of course, dismiss all of the above as archaic and old-fashioned mumbo jumbo. All knowledge, they say, is contingent on experience; and it is in social and collectivized experiencing that we can come to some highly effective working truths. Finally, the Existentialist brings us once again to the self of man, insisting that all knowing, all intuiting, all experiencing, are certified within the private awareness of the human person.

Thus, from the "Imitation of the Absolute Mind" of Idealism to the "Spectation of Nature" of Realism to the "Logical Apprehension of Being" of the Neo-Thomist to the "Scientific Doing and Undergoing in

Experience" of the Experimentalist to the "Individual Feeling and Choosing" of the Existentialist, we have come to see what a variety of ways there are for men to know.

THE ANALYTIC MOVEMENT

Before passing on to Chapter Seven to see how these theories affect the educative process, we must take account of a major demurrer in modern philosophy which challenges much of what we have discussed in this lengthy chapter on epistemology. This demurrer comes from those who represent a new movement in philosophy — variously called Logical Positivism, Scientific Empiricism, or, sometimes, Linguistic Analysis.

Stated very briefly, the Positivists defer questions of *truth* in favor of questions of *meaning*. In epistemology one cannot ask whether a proposition about the world is true or not true until he knows what it means. If a proposition has no meaning it is foolish to ask whether or not it is true. This interest in meaning is characteristic of the related discipline of *semantics*, which may be defined as the study of the meaning of meaning. But whereas semantics deals primarily with the meaning carried by single words, Positivism has chosen to investigate the meaning carried by sentences. Hence, because it deals with whole propositions rather than single word-symbols, Positivism is essentially an exercise in logic or an exercise in the analysis of the language we use to utter our ideas.

Although the term *Linguistic Analysis* may appear rather imposing, the argument is relatively simple, and it runs somewhat as follows:

All philosophy is carried in language; a philosophical idea, to be thought of, communicated, and believed in, must first of all be rendered in linguistic form. Philosophical language, although perhaps more sophisticated, is essentially the same as ordinary language, i.e., it is constructed of sentences. A sentence is a group of words divided into a subject and a predicate. The subject presents some substantive (a thing, a process, an event, an idea), and the predicate tells us something about the substantive (what it is like, what it does, how it behaves).

Our first problem arises at this point. Suppose that for a given subject, say, an apple, we were to compose *all* the possible predicates that could be attached to it — all the adjectives ("An apple is red, round, juicy, edible, succulent. . .") and all the predicates ("An apple grows on trees, contains seeds, taken daily keeps the doctor away . . ."). Other philosophies have troubled themselves over the questions: Is the existence of the subject (apple) independent of all the possible predicates we could attach to it? Or, on the other hand, is our subject nothing more than all of its possible predicates?

As we have seen earlier in this chapter, Aristotelian and Neo-Thomist logic lays great stress on the inner essence or "what-ness" of things. For this reason, these philosophies hold that the subject of a sentence is always more than all the possible predicates one could attach to it. There is an *essence* to which all predicates are attached. The Experimentalists, on the other hand, dispute this claim to essences and assert instead that processes and behaviors in our experience are to be emphasized. Hence, Experimentalists contend that subjects are known through their predicates and are nothing more than their predicates. In the shorthand of some Experimentalists: "A thing *is* what it *does.*"

The difficulty with the Experimentalist position, the Positivist explains, is that it must be couched in language forms which originated in an Aristotelian tradition and which are no longer adequate to the accurate expression of ideas.

> It happens to be the case that we cannot, in our language, refer to the sensible properties of a thing without introducing a word or phrase which appears to stand for the thing itself as opposed to anything which may be said about it.[26]

The Experimentalist difficulty, then, is not an intellectual fault, says the Positivist, but a fault of language itself. At any rate, what the Experimentalist has already hinted at Positivism now affirms forthrightly, namely, that *predicates* are the key to the philosophical problem, for they give us the basic data about the world. Subjects are nothing but "condensed" predicates, linguistic conventions we use to stand for a host of predicates that relate to one another, rather than to some "inner essence." In this office, subjects are merely convenient handles by which to manipulate and order our predicates. It is to predicates, therefore, and to the linguistic relationship they bear to their subjects that the Positivist turns his analysis.

This subject-predicate relationship is found in every sentence, but it becomes of crucial importance in those sentences which purport to tell us something about our world. For the sake of precise terminology, such sentences are called *propositions*. There are two generic types of propositions: analytic and synthetic. An analytic proposition is one whose predicate is analyzed out of the subject. A synthetic proposition is one whose predicate is attached to the subject on the basis of empirical evidence.

We met these two terms earlier in this chapter, in the section on Neo-

26 A. J. Ayer, *Language, Truth, and Logic*, Revised Edition (London: Victor Gollancz, Ltd., 1950), p. 42.

Thomist epistemology.[27] To the Neo-Thomist, an analytic proposition is absolutely true because it is intuited by the intellect to be true, everywhere and always. But to the Positivist, an analytic proposition is absolutely true because it is a tautology; that is, the predicate is contained in the *meaning* of the subject. Thus, the proposition "Two things equal to the same thing are equal to each other" is held by the Neo-Thomist to be absolutely true because the intellect apprehends it intuitively; but the same proposition is held by the Positivist to be absolutely true because the predicate "equal to each other," is contained in the meaning of the subject, "two things equal to the same thing." Hence, the proposition is true by definition or, as the Positivist sometimes says, "by legislation."

Consider a simpler series of examples. The statement "A equals A" is absolutely true. But it tells us nothing about the world; it is a tautology. Now consider the proposition "Two plus two equals four." This also is absolutely true. And it appears to be saying something. It turns out, however, on closer analysis, that the predicate can be found in the meaning of the subject. "Four" is one of the *meanings* of "two plus two." Hence, another tautology. The Positivist claims that every analytic proposition is of this character. The predicate of such a proposition tells us nothing we didn't already know; all it does is elaborate on the *meaning* of the subject.

You should not get the impression from this discussion that tautologies are completely useless. They serve, in fact, a very helpful function, namely, of recording "our determination to use symbols in a certain fashion," as A. J. Ayer has put it. They have meaning but they cannot produce knowledge.

As for synthetic propositions, all philosophies are agreed that they are not absolutely true; their predicates depend upon empirical evidence, e.g., "The distance from New York to Chicago is so many miles," or "The Federal government is organized into three branches." What the Positivist claims is that these are the only propositions that are capable of producing knowledge.

There are a good many propositions which are not analytic tautologies and which bear a superficial grammatical resemblance to synthetic statements, e.g., "The world is all mind," or "God is love," or, one which Ayer quotes from Bradley's *Appearance and Reality*, ". . . the Absolute enters into, but is itself incapable of, evolution and progress." The trouble with these examples, and other propositions like them, says the Positivist, is that there is no evidence one could conceivably gather to determine their truth or falsity. They are therefore without any meaning.

27 These two classes correspond roughly to *a priori* and *a posteriori* knowledge, discussed in Chapter Five.

In order to have meaning a proposition must be such either that it is true by definition (as in the case of analytic tautologies) or that some possible sense experience would be relevant to the determination of its truth or falsity.

> If a putative proposition fails to satisfy this principle, and is not a tautology, then I hold that it is metaphysical, and that being metaphysical, it is neither true nor false but literally senseless.[28]

This line of argument eventually leads to the Positivist's main thesis, to wit: The meaning of a proposition is to be found in its method of verification. If it has no method of verification, it has no meaning.

If we adopt this principle, then we are forced to conclude that the great bulk of philosophical literature is nonsense. In terms of the present chapter, Idealism, Realism, Neo-Thomism, *and* Existentialism all rest upon what the Positivist would call pseudo-propositions, i.e., propositions which grammatically resemble synthetic propositions but which have no method of verification. When an Idealist says that "Reality is mind"; when a Realist says that "Nature contains moral law"; when a Neo-Thomist says that "The intellect naturally tends to know"; or when an Existentialist says that "Existence precedes essence," they are all talking nonsense. Even the Experimentalist, while trying to avoid it and talk in a meaningful way, sometimes slips into nonsense with such phrases as "Reality is experience" or "Experience is the ultimate ground of knowing."

With this in mind, says the Positivist, and recognizing the linguistic nature of our problem, we may conclude that all philosophical disputes are quite fruitless. They are fruitless because they originate in language, in how we form our sentences and in how our sentences acquire meaning. Since many sentences in philosophy cannot pass the Positivist's test for meaning, it is little wonder that there is so much disagreement about matters of truth. And disagreement will continue as long as philosophers persist in using sentences of this sort. When all is said and done, says Ayer, the task of philosophy is not to build grand systems of the mind but merely "to elicit the consequences of our linguistic usage."

* * *

Having said all these things, we must step lightly back to our philosophical workbench and continue the argument. If most of this be nonsense, keep in mind that it is the kind of nonsense that many well-meaning people have considered worth their while.

We now therefore proceed to Chapter Seven, where we shall examine

[28] Ayer, *op. cit.*, p. 31.

how our several epistemologies make themselves felt in the conduct of the educative process.

QUESTIONS

1. "For ye shall know the truth and the truth shall make ye free." What is the epistemological significance of this epigram? What epistemology is suggested? In what way does truth set one "free"?

2. Some of the antonyms for *truth* are *lie, error, falsehood, misconception, mere opinion.* Which of these is (are) appropriate for use in epistemological discussions? Why?

3. Pick out an expository tract (a selection from an encyclopedia) or an emotive selection (the Declaration of Independence or the Gettysburg Address) and examine the kinds of statements made therein. What epistemologies apply to these statements? That is, how would their authors defend their validity?

4. Compare the concepts of *hypothesis* and *intuition*. In what way might it be said that they are the same thing?

5. A "closed-universe" ontology usually suggests a "closed epistemology," that is, a sum total of knowledge in the cosmos which man may, theoretically at least, ultimately comprehend. What would each of our five epistemological positions have to say about this?

FURTHER READING

Comparative Epistemologies

Montague, William P. *The Ways of Knowing.* London: George Allen and Unwin, Ltd., 1925.
For the serious student of epistemology, this is a classic, standard work. In it, Montague takes up six methods of *logic:* authoritarianism, mysticism, rationalism and empiricism, pragmatism, and skepticism. Then he examines the three generic methods of *epistemology:* objectivism, dualism, and subjectivism. Finally, he attempts a reconciliation of these three in a unified epistemology, closing with an imaginary quadrilogue among an Objectivist, a Subjectivist, a Dualist, and — as reconciler — a Realist.

Idealism

Butler, J. Donald. *Four Philosophies and Their Practice in Education and Religion,* Revised Edition. New York: Harper and Bros., 1957.

In one of the best syntheses of Idealist thought, Butler has in Chapter VIII drawn together the metaphysics, epistemology, logic, and axiology of Idealism. The first three of these sections are particularly relevant to the epistemological development in the present chapter.

Greene, Theodore M. "A Liberal Christian Idealist Philosophy of Education," Chapter IV in *Modern Philosophies and Education,* Fifty-fourth Yearbook of the National Society for the Study of Education, ed. N. B. Henry, Part I. Chicago: the Society 1955.
A leading contemporary Idealist here brings his insight to bear on the educative process. In the early part of the essay he sets down "My Basic Philosophical Presuppositions," the third and fourth of these being directed to epistemological and ontological matters. Here is the Idealist Platform clearly and concisely stated. The remainder of the chapter "fleshes out" these fundamental propositions.

Realism

Montague, William P. "A Realistic Theory of Truth and Error," in Holt, E. B., *et al. The New Realism.* New York: The Macmillan Co., 1912.
In an authoritative and somewhat technical essay, Montague sets forth the systematic outlines of Realist epistemology. He says, "Physical objects send forth waves of energy in various directions and of various kinds . . . These energies impinge upon the organism, and the sensory end-organs and the nerve fibers then transmit to the brain the kinds of energy to which they are severally adjusted or attuned." (Page 286.) From this he shows how knowing is accomplished.

————. *The Ways of Things.* New York: Prentice-Hall, Inc., 1940.
In this later (and somewhat less technical) book, Montague develops in Chapter 5 of Part Two a systematic treatment of Realism's theory of knowing. Then he shows its relation to Idealism and Pragmatism. A lively and informative essay.

Neo-Thomism

Adler, Mortimer J. "In Defense of the Philosophy of Education," Chapter V in *Philosophies of Education,* Forty-first Yearbook of the National Society for the Study of Education, ed. N. B. Henry, Part I. Chicago: the Society, 1942.
This chapter in the widely read Forty-first Yearbook is essentially not an essay on education but a systematic exegesis of Lay Neo-Thomist logic couched in the language of education. After a brief introduction, Adler takes up the problems of education having philosophic dimensions and then shows how the First Principles may be utilized to resolve these problems. Adler's style — and, indeed, the singular "Philosophy" in his title — bears out his fundamental belief: There is but one Truth; and if you will but pay attention and think hard you will see it. Then we can stop writing yearbooks on philosophies of education.

Maritain, Jacques. *The Range of Reason.* New York: Charles Scribner's Sons, 1952.
In this technical and authoritative volume, the leading Catholic philosopher of the twentieth century develops the Ecclesiastical Thomist's epistemological thesis. Chapter I, "On Human Knowledge," and Chapter III, "On Knowledge through Connaturality," are the most directly relevant to the treatment in the present chapter.

Experimentalism

Childs, John L. *American Pragmatism and Education.* New York: Henry Holt and Co., Inc., 1956.
One of the most cogent of Dewey's interpreters, Childs here develops, in Chapter 2, on "Experimental Method and the Nurture of the Young," a working idea of how epistemological activity is undertaken in an Experimentalist frame. Beginning with the fundamental ideas of Charles Peirce, he describes the characteristics of experimental inquiry, then considers some alternative methods of certain knowing, and, finally, develops a systematic "Pragmatic Theory of Experimental Inquiry." Here, in clear and concise language, is the Experimentalist position on epistemological method.

Dewey, John. *How We Think,* Revised Edition. Boston: D. C. Heath and Company, 1933.
The classic work on Experimentalist knowing theory. The word *know* was never comfortable to Dewey; rather, he thought, we must search for "knowing in action," i.e., thinking. Chapter One examines the question "What is Thinking?"; Chapter Seven analyzes the reflective thought process, the so-called Complete Act of Thought, or, in terms of the present chapter, the scientific method in its most generalized setting.

Existentialism

Kneller, George F. *Existentialism and Education.* New York: Philosophical Library, 1958.
In the second section of Chapter V, Kneller examines the topic of "The Knower and the Known." Drawing from Kierkegaard, Jaspers, Marcel, and Niebuhr, he directs our attention to the *un*reasonable, emotional-response, subjectivity-centered base of all knowing — a doctrine necessarily harmonious with the absolute primacy of existence in Man.

Ulich, Robert. *The Human Career.* New York: Harper and Bros., 1955.
Writing in the "twilight zone" between Idealism and Existentialism, Ulich opens up some remarkable new insights. In Chapter 2, Section II, "Our Mental Equipment," he deals with instincts, feelings or emotions, intelligence, and reason. Within reason can be found contemplation, intuition, and faith. Then, in Chapter 4, he undertakes an analysis of thinking as "theoretical self-transcendence," in which he examines the three levels of man's relation to reality (i.e., knowing), namely, natural reaction, system, and meaning; finally, he concludes with a section on the "meaning of thinking."

Comparative Epistemology

and the Educative Process

EPISTEMOLOGY AND EDUCATION

Knowing theories and the nature of learning

If philosophy has anything to do with education, we should expect to find this relationship at the very juncture where we now find ourselves: the juncture between a theory of knowing and a theory of teaching. Our present situation can be contrasted with that in which we found ourselves at the beginning of Chapter Four. On account of the technical and abstract nature of metaphysical problems, it could perhaps be argued that the study of *ontology* should be left to the philosophers, that it is too far removed from the professional concerns of teachers. But this could never be said of epistemology — our present concern — for epistemology is an active and fertile breeding ground for some very important educational ideas. This is so for a variety of reasons.

First, whatever the world is ontologically, it must somehow be "gotten at" by an ordinary human being, by the individual who has neither the sophistication nor the specialized terminology of the trained philosopher, if it is to have any human use to him. That is, while ontology is essentially a study of the cosmos, epistemology is the study of how human beings take hold of their cosmos. Epistemology, as it were, introduces the human element for the first time; and since education is, if nothing else, a supremely *human* undertaking, the attention of the educator is likely to be much more readily aroused by studies in knowing than by studies in reality.

In the second place, as we saw in Chapter Five, epistemology is not only a necessary check on the credibility of our knowledge — a kind of "intellectual Pure Food and Drug Act" — but a body of fundamental theory which underlies the nature of the mind and how it works. Just as anatomy and physiology are the basic sciences underlying the study of medicine or pharmacy, so in somewhat like fashion is epistemology the basic subject matter underlying the study of psychology and learning theory.[1] That is, we must have some grasp of the generalized epistemological setting in which man finds himself before we can study in greater detail how he goes about knowing and behaving intelligently. Or, to put it another way, we must understand man's epistemological circumstance before we can even begin to ask the right questions for psychology and learning theory to investigate.

Third, and certainly most pertinent, is the matter of sheer relevance: Theories of knowing are, in a sense, direct pointers to theories of learning. And since learning theory is at the very heart of the educative enterprise, we should not be astonished to find the various epistemologies having very relevant things to say about what goes on in the classroom.

THE METHODS OF LEARNING

Absorbing ideas

Children go to school, ultimately, for one fundamental reason: to be inducted systematically, efficiently, and deliberately into a way of life. Whatever else education is — and it may be more — it is certainly this. To a nonliterate society, maintaining a place where something like a quarter of their number did nothing all day long but learn things would be an outlandish luxury: but to a modern, technological society this sort of thing makes the greatest of sense. The patterns of behaving, thinking, and feeling necessary to men in these societies are simply too vast in number and too complex in nature to be assimilated by the normal procedures of enculturation. Some place is required where induction into the patterns of conduct can be carried on without interference and interruption.

---

[1] The analogy is admittedly weak, as most analogies are, in that the former set of terms refers to empirical and scientific subject matters, while the latter set does not. If we are alert to the qualifications required by this difference, we can still find some warrant in the comparison.

SYMBOLS. What is more, modern man is much less dependent than nonliterate man upon direct experience for his learning; he has learned to abstract his experience into a vast array of symbols, which he then manipulates and refashions into "reproductions" of experience for others to have "vicariously." Indeed, it is this power to symbolize experience which makes education — as we understand it today — possible; it is The Symbol which makes it possible for boys and girls to spend the whole day inside a school building learning about the world outside.

So remarkable is the symbol in the eyes of man that it has sometimes been declared the first existent: "In the beginning was the Word" — a bit of Scripture, incidentally, which fits rather well the Idealist ontology discussed in previous chapters. Robert Frost, the famed American poet, has celebrated this view in some of his lectures; his own philosophy of education, he says, can be reduced to what he thinks is the shortest poem on record:

A B C

1   2   3

This — word and number — is all there really is, says Frost, to learning; and he believes this couplet, itself a symbol of symbols, should appear on the coat of arms and above the entry gate of every school and university in the country.

At the very base of every program of education, then, is the task of equipping the child with symbols, almost literally the tools of learning. Although the quaint and lilting "Readin', 'Ritin', an' 'Rithmetic" may no longer be in vogue as a condensed summary of the elementary curriculum, these three subjects still remain the first business of every elementary school.

SYMBOLS AND MIND. We cannot therefore escape the fact that, whatever else education is, it is and must be first of all a symbolic activity. And it turns out, epistemologically speaking, that symbols take on a higher rank than mere tools of learning. For they are the instruments of the mind itself; they are the medium through which mind operates. And in this office they become the vehicle by which the mind comes into union with ultimate reality, the reality of Ideas. Ideas, as the Idealist sees them, are the real existents behind the sensory screen; they are thus barred from our perceptions. But fortunately, because we are human, we have access to this reality through mind, i.e., through symbolic forms. For ideas have no existential expression except through symbols; we are absolutely dependent upon symbols to reach this reality.

For this reason, it is imperative, says the Idealist, to make symbols the very medium of the child's educational life, i.e., the medium of the pedagogical "environment." Learning is primarily a continuous activity in symbols — principally reading books and listening to the teacher, but also writing and reciting. It is a graded and systematic introduction to the life of words; for words, the Idealist maintains, are the keys to truth and reality.

IDEALIST SCHOOL PRACTICE. What this means in concrete terms may now be suggested by the generalization that Idealist educators tend to consider the library the hub of all educational activity. The classroom is, in a sense, a kind of operating arm of the library; it is the place where the symbols are explained, vitalized, brought to the life of the learner in a vibrant and meaningful way. But the classroom is also an environment of symbols, in the form of the teacher's lectures and questions and, of course, the students' responses.

It is because of this centrality of classroom and library that the Idealist is lukewarm about other, out-of-school learning experiences: field trips, use of community resources, or home projects. If there is a choice between a field trip and a day in the library, the Idealist will tend to favor the latter. Especially at the college level this preference will be unequivocal. College students, it is held, are not so dependent upon direct experience for their learning; they can learn through books. So, time taken from books, while perhaps valuable, actually costs too much in deductions from the student's symbolic experience.

Colleges and universities are sometimes accused of being "ivory towers," enclaves of thought removed from the realities of life and therefore of questionable value in an "activist," materialist society. Idealists would make no apology for this whatsoever; they would insist that ivory towers are precisely what colleges and universities most certainly should be! Ordinary life is too ridden with action, they say, too saturated moment by moment with problems and requirements to *do* something. Man will never find truth *there;* indeed, he will never find reality there. For to say that the realities of life are "down in the street" is merely to express a Realist sentiment. Reality is truly "up in the tower"; every society must maintain places of retreat where the mind can think and know. This is what colleges and universities are for.

Imitating the Absolute Mind and Absolute Self

We are now in a position to examine another educational outgrowth of Idealist theory: the task of bringing the learner into a more vital and fuller identification with the Absolute Mind and Absolute Self. Granted, specifications for how this is to be done may be vague and imprecise;

nevertheless there is a way in which we can see the learning process in distinctive Idealist terms.

LEARNER AND MIND. To refer to our systematic treatment of Idealism in the previous chapter, we may say that the individual human mind exists as a microcosm of the Ultimate or Absolute Mind. Learning, then, in Idealist thinking is the process of the learner coming into a gradually larger and larger expression of mental awareness; and since this can be done most efficaciously through reading and study, the learner shall, as we have seen, spend most of his time with books and teachers. The learner's ultimate aim, however, is not just a grinding mastery of factual content, but a broad and general understanding of the world in which he lives, i.e., an understanding that to some degree approximates the omnipotent understanding of the Absolute Mind. The learner is, in a manner of speaking, attempting to expand both quantitatively and qualitatively, to imitate the fullness of the Absolute and Universal Mind, insofar as his mental capacity permits.

LEARNER AND SELF. This means, among other things, that the Idealist student will be expected to respond *to* his world as well as to learn *about* it — which is to say that the student will be involved as well in an expansion of his microcosmic selfhood in imitation of the macrocosmic Absolute Self. Besides Mind, that is, he is attempting also to approximate the fullness of the Universal *Person*.

This idea is very much in line with modern democratic educational practice, for one of the ways to expand one's *self* is to attach oneself to other "selves," i.e., to have friends, to know people, to respond to them and to be responded to. Another way is to identify with a self "larger" than one's own, e.g., to join a club, to adopt a religion, to take an active part in one's community or national life through self-conscious (and nation-conscious) citizenship. The "Group," then — whether it be the neighborhood gang or the family, or the Republican Party, or the First Methodist Church or the American People, or World Judaism, or simply Mankind — is the "instrumentality" for enlarging the sense of self.

And since the classroom is potentially a "medium of enlargement" of this genre, the Idealist will encourage the beings in it to respond to one another and develop a sense of group *esprit*. For the classroom is, in Idealist language, a "community of selves." Youngsters grow in selfhood in proportion to the contact they have with other selves. And a large part of learning, we have lately discovered, is this intangible "communion of selves"[2] in the classroom, the interchange of feeling and re-

---

[2] The Experimentalists do not wax quite so poetic about this phenomenon. They call it "peer-group relationships."

sponse that individual human beings have to their world. The teacher also, as we shall see later in the chapter, is a special case, a self individually "larger" than any of the students. And thus it is his or her job not only to facilitate the "communion-of-selves" process but to serve in an exemplary capacity with respect to the growth of selfhood on the part of the students.

One of the ways to make this point even more concretely recognizable is to refer to what is sometimes called the "psychological climate" of the school. A school, it has often been pointed out, is not essentially a pile of bricks; it is primarily an intimate, institutionalized association of human beings. In Idealist thinking, it is "Mark Hopkins on one end of a log and a pupil on the other"[3] — meaning that learning requires the active involvement of the selfhood and personality of the participants if it is to be successful. Therefore the "tone," the "psychic climate" of the classroom and the entire school, is a vital concern of the Idealist educator; if rapport is not established between teacher and student, if there is no feeling of mutual respect and warmth between adult and youngster, then by so much is genuine learning prevented from taking place.

At the college level this "climate" is perhaps more actively cultivated. Colleges sometimes make a deliberate and overt attempt to create an "image" of the quality of their campus environment, and will seek to "stamp" that image upon their students prior to graduation. This "fourth dimension" of what we might call institutional "ethos" is very much a matter of educational concern among Idealists, for it is through this nebulous but nevertheless very real quality of an educational institution that young people really learn.

Absorbing facts and information

Just living in a stimulating human environment, however, is not all there is to learning. One must take hold of some bodies of knowledge; one must assimilate facts and master information about his world; one must, in short, confront his world with the realization that there are definite things about it that can be known and that he is in school to know them.

To return to an earlier point, symbols are indeed the medium of our epistemological work, but — and here the Realist may be heard speaking

---

[3] A popular corruption of a remark made by President James A. Garfield on the occasion of a Williams College alumni dinner at Delmonico's in New York on December 28, 1871: "A pine bench, with Mark Hopkins at one end of it and me at the other, is a good enough college for me." (Stevenson, *The Home Book of Quotations.*) Mark Hopkins, serving at the time as the fourth president of Williams, was disdainful of all educational apparatus, even books, and was widely known for his emphasis at Williams on the personal and uncluttered relationship between teacher and student.

— it is not the symbol itself we are interested in but, rather, the objective existent for which the symbol stands. To become enamored of symbols for their own sake is to lose sight, says the Realist, of the real purpose of symbols, i.e., to stand for a real world which we can perceive day by day and which, with the help of these symbols, we can turn to our own account. Granted, then, that we need symbols but only as instruments to get at a physical reality which is existentially present in our lives every day.

REALIST PEDAGOGY. We are reminded here that the Realist bases his epistemology in sense perception. Nothing can be known save through being worked up from the raw material of sensation. And if this is the case the child's learning in school should be organized as much as possible around the "sensate" (as opposed to the purely intellectual or ideational) activities of learning. The Realist, therefore, though he will certainly insist on a good deal of reading and study, i.e., work with symbols, is likely to favor direct experience with what the symbols stand for. This means that demonstrations in the classroom, either by the teacher or by a fellow student, will become a vital pedagogical tool. Comenius, the seventeenth-century Moravian bishop and educator, became famous for his books, *Orbis Pictus* and *Didactica Magna,* in which he astonished the educational world by suggesting that visual aids — pictures — be used in instructing boys and girls in the schools! A century or so later Pestalozzi went Comenius one better. Why have just pictures? he asked in his quaintly titled *How Gertrude Teaches Her Children.* Let's have the real thing! Thus was the so-called object lesson installed in educational theory: literally, a lesson built around a physical object either brought into the classroom or observed outside the school by the class. Comenius and Pestalozzi thus stand at the head of a long line of educational Realists, who want to place the learner in direct sensory contact with his world.

It goes without saying that the Realist will tend to favor field trips as pedagogically sound and desirable. If, to cite the Chinese proverb, "A picture is worth a thousand words," then perhaps direct and immediate contact with what the picture depicts might be conservatively estimated to be worth a million. This is probably saying too much; but Realist sentiment is consistent with the direction, if not the full extent, of this line of thinking. Certainly a day at the United Nations or in the Senate gallery in Washington could never be duplicated by any number of words in a civics textbook.

We have already, in Chapter Four, taken note of the fact that the Realist educator would incline in the direction of the sciences as the primary materials in his curriculum. Quite obviously the tactical (i.e., pedagogical) application of the Correspondence Theory (see pages 145–147) of knowing comes to bear most directly in this kind of learning material. Both the demonstration and the field trip, as described above, are concrete examples of how the Correspondence Theory may be activated in the school's work.

But beyond these purely tactical, sensate learning procedures the Realist will employ the Correspondence Theory, in a semidirect way, through the medium of so-called audio-visual aids. Pictures, filmstrips, tape recordings, motion pictures, and television presentations are all means of simulating the real world in nonsymbolic but still vicarious forms. Hence, to the Realist these channels of contact with the real world represent a happy compromise between removing the student from the school environment for a trip outside it and holding him in the library or classroom to read or hear, only in words, about the world outside. It is this middle position which audio-visual aids occupy in the pedagogical spectrum that makes them so important to Realist teaching.

REALISM AND SYMBOLS.   If we are eventually driven back to symbols in our pedagogy — and we frequently are, of course — then let us, says the Realist, emphasize the existential situation these symbols may reveal. In history, for instance, we should not permit symbols to assume more stature than they really deserve; they are merely the vehicles for telling us what happened, the sequence in which things happened, and the causes and effects of historical events. When the Realist includes history in his curriculum, as he is in most cases obligated to do, it will be as a systematic study of existential fact; what happened is what happened! History "stands there" as so much existential "past." And we may learn history — albeit through symbols — in somewhat the same way we learn mathematics or chemistry, i.e., by learning the factual content of it.

This is not so severe as it may sound, for the Realist reminds us that one of the prime purposes of studying history should be to get a sense of historical time, and we study history because the chronological unfolding of events can be reduced to a series of facts all linked together in a temporal series. It is among the powers of the human mind, says the Realist, to absorb and assimilate these serial facts and to discern from them the regularities of a natural social order, a historical unfolding of events which reveals the laws and regularities of human nature.

REALISM AND IDEALISM.   At this point we are not so far distant from the Idealist doctrine of the transcendent *meaning* of history — the thoughts of a Universal Mind as they are being thought out through the vehicle of human history. But there is, nevertheless, a difference in emphasis, for the Realist is more inclined to consider history as the *chronicle* of human doings, which reveals a regular and lawful cosmos, whereas the Idealist is more inclined to view history as the *interpretation* of human doings, which reveals an Ultimate Mind at work. In the one case the child is introduced to a mechanistic and "cause-effect" social tradition; in the other, to an intelligent, personalized, "friendly" cosmic design.

Although this may be embellishing what actually goes on in history classrooms, it is nevertheless indicative of the subtle motivations behind certain types of assignments as they are given. If the student is asked to prepare an outline of the causes and effects of the Civil War, he is likely to get a different historical sense of this event from the "sense" he would be likely to get if he were asked to write an essay on what the Civil War was all about. Generally the former of these assignments is harmonious with Realist thinking, while the latter is harmonious with Idealist thinking.

REALISM AND S-R LEARNING. Realists, as this analysis suggests, are more interested in the precise and definitive types of subject matters and in the precise and definitive methods by which such subject matters may be conveyed to the learner. The development of various skills is particularly consistent with Realist practice. Learning to typewrite, play volleyball, drive an automobile, compose compound and complex sentences, or solve quadratic equations — all are examples of educational situations of which the Realist feels himself capable of taking direct hold. Drill, practice, habit formation, and conditioning are all apt methods for these situations. Indeed, perhaps the concept of "conditioning," in its largest and most inclusive sense, best represents Realist pedagogy.

The "conditioning" theory goes back to the Russian physiologist Pavlov (1849–1936), who startled the scientific world by artificially creating a new kind of dog: a dog which would salivate at the sound of a bell! In this now famous experiment, Pavlov simultaneously offered food to the dog and rang a bell. After repeated trials he stopped offering the food — and discovered the astonishing phenomenon of salivary action "outliving" its natural stimulus. By substituting an artificial for a natural stimulus and getting the same response, he thus revealed a new "frontier" of behavior control.

What Pavlov did for physiology the psychologists picked up, early in the twentieth century, and turned into a full-blown theory, which in its clinical setting came to be known as "Stimulus-Response" — or simply S-R — psychology. In its wider application it assumed the institutionalized label of Behaviorism. This school of thought, which turned into something resembling a missionary movement led by John B. Watson, held that human personality and character are totally the product of experience. Theoretically, if the totality of the experiential environment of the child were artificially specified and controlled, then the behavioral and characterological outcome in the child could be predicted. Every thought or movement has a cause; or, in psychological terms, every response has a causal stimulus. If we can specify the stimuli we can predict — hence, specify — the responses; it was as simple as that. If one were given charge of a child at birth, Watson claimed, it would be theoretically possible to turn him into any adult form — gangster, musician, financial wizard, scientist, writer, gambler — by ordering his experiences.

No one, of course, has been able to test this hypothesis in a rigorously controlled experiment, although there is some limited evidence in its favor. As hypothesis, of course, it still stands; but since the 1930's interest in it has moderated somewhat, partly as a result of later advances (e.g., Gestalt theories) in psychology. However, recent research, which we shall examine in Chapter Eleven, seems to give some new support to Behaviorist concepts. The implications of these new findings for educational theory are both profound and exciting.

But the point here is that Watson was operating within the Realist frame in considering the human being a kind of mechanistic responder and reactor to an equally mechanistic world. If, somehow, man could intervene, i.e., *intelligently interfere,* with the stimulus-response "history" of human beings, he might be able to produce future generations more nearly to his desire.

It does not matter, for the moment, whether this hypothesis is true or not; merely to ask the question, merely to pose the hypothesis, reveals a Realist tendency. For the hypothesis is posed because it seems important; the question is raised because the answer to it appears potentially profitable. An Idealist would not be likely even to raise the question, because S-R behavior is to him a relatively superficial level of human motivation and action. It would be interesting to know about, of course, but not strategically important. But to the Realist, his ontology and epistemology being what they are, this question, for all its complexity, is considered the central issue in learning theory.

One of the more spectacular practical accomplishments coming out of this curiosity in mechanistic psychology is the "teaching machine," most interestingly developed by Professor B. F. Skinner of Harvard. Skinner, a psychologist in the Pavlovian tradition, has come up with a mechanical device which may be used to lead an individual systematically through a prescribed body of subject matter and instruct him in it. Into a box with a window in its top is fed a roll of paper on which is printed a patterned "program" of carefully prepared *leading* questions. Through the window the learner reads one question at a time, attempts an answer, and is immediately informed whether his answer is correct or incorrect. Proceeding to subsequent questions, he sees *why* his previous answers were right or wrong. By completing an entire "program," he carries on the learning experience and assimilates the material.[4]

The research behind this development occasioned, among other things, Skinner's discovery that it is possible to teach extremely complicated physical-movement patterns to animals by the mere expedient of precise and planned reinforcement procedures. It is reported that Skinner can set a pigeon in the middle of a bare floor and in five minutes "teach" it to walk a figure eight just by making signals with a hand clicker and tossing food pellets to it at precisely the right times and places. Reinforcements designed for human use are equally effective, Skinner maintains, in teaching human subject matters.

Here again, whether Skinner is right or wrong is not the central issue; the important thing is the fact that he is interested in the question. For, whatever man is, Skinner believes him to be *primarily* a "machine" of some kind. And man *is* that, undeniably. Man *is* at least partly a machine. But whether he is this primarily or exclusively is more a philosophic than a scientific judgment. And because this judgment finds expression in psychological experiments like the above, we say it has an affinity with Realist tendencies in epistemology and pedagogical theory.

The Receptacle Theory of learning

We may now draw together our discussion of both the Idealist and Realist doctrines concerning the relationship between epistemology and learning theory by showing how these two otherwise quite different points of view do share a common platform in educational thinking. You will recall from Chapter Three (see pages 47–59) the argument that both Idealism and Realism may be considered *objective* ontologies, at least as they are discussed in this book. We saw in Chapter Six that, insofar as they remain objective ontologies, the "Spectator Theory" of epistemology may be said to apply to both, almost literally in the case of Realism, somewhat figuratively in the case of Idealism (e.g., "seeing" with the "mind's eye").

If they share in some measure the "Spectator Theory," then both of these doctrines will consider education as the gradual introduction to the young of knowledge of an external world — in the case of Idealism, a knowledge of mind and idea; in the case of Realism, a knowledge of fact and habituated response. In both cases the learner may be likened to a receptacle into which adults "pour" knowledge. Indeed, we often speak of the "capacity" of the learner, revealing by the very use of this term an inclination to view the learner as a receptacle. Our schoolrooms

4 For a description of the machine, see George R. Price, "The Teaching Machine," *Think*, XXV, No. 3 (March, 1959), 10–14.

are built in accord with this principle, with the teacher facing the learners, as in an auditorium. Indeed, the schoolroom is literally an "auditorium," where pupils sit and listen and *receive* knowledge.[5]

Or, to use another metaphor, some educators have likened the mind to a kind of giant psychological warehouse which is capable, by means of the learning process, of receiving and holding in "cold storage" a multitude of facts, theories, formulas, concepts, feelings, attitudes, habits, skills, etc. Then, when the occasion calls for one or another of these articles of learning, the mind delivers it to the stage of action, that is, to the "foreground" of our conscious behavioral lives. The most spectacular example of this is, of course, the expert and specialized quiz contestants who have appeared on television. In their on-camera agonies they seemed almost literally to be reaching back into the dark and dingy recesses of their minds for bits of information the quiz master was ready to give them a small fortune for.[6] But all of us, in varying degrees, are capable of this process, and it is part, at least, of how we learn.

Now if we were to view this metaphorical theory of learning — the Receptacle or "Cold-Storage Warehouse" Theory — in the most generous light, we should be close to a generalized pedagogical doctrine harmonious and consistent with the so-called Spectator Theory and, hence, with Realist and Idealist epistemological views. Where subject matter is descriptive of the world — either a physical or an ideational world — and where its function is to explain the world to the learner, then we have Idealist and Realist tendencies at work. Wherever subject matter is prepared in advance, wherever it is set out before the learner to be learned, and wherever the quantitative assimilation of such subject matter through paper-and-pencil tests and examinations is thought to be the basis for measuring the effect of an educational experience, we may suspect that we are in the presence of either an Idealist or a Realist in education.

Training the mind

Teaching the mind ideas and facts and habit patterns represents, certainly, a large part of education. But to some, this is but the "anteroom" of more basic things going on inside. Perhaps the most traditionally

[5] Some particularly bitter critics like to refer to this as the "Two-Gallon Jug" Theory of education.

[6] The fact that some of these individuals were pretty sorry specimens of what we consider the "educated man" to be is a reminder of one of the criticisms of Idealism and Realism made by the Experimentalists, namely, the tendency for these traditional positions to advocate knowledge for its own sake, without any interest in whether it has genuine human utility, except in contrived "quiz" situations. (Disclosures of corruption among some of these contestants raises an entirely different problem, of course.)

popular and persistent of all pedagogies is that of "training the mind." And it is this so-called entity called "mind" or "intellect" which is the ultimate object of all these "lesser" educational measures. What the intellect does "inside," so to speak, is the primary question of education.

THE RATIONAL FACULTY. To a Neo-Thomist the Idealist's "imitation of the Absolute Mind" is too vague a pedagogical theory, and the Realist's "learning of factual knowledge" is relatively superficial. What we must do, says the Neo-Thomist, is to drive to the very core of human nature — the faculty of Reason — and devise educational measures for developing it. Once this is done, then the intellect will be able to take care of itself, including the management of its own continued learning.

In the previous chapter Neo-Thomist epistemology was described principally in terms of *logic*. Knowing, according to this outlook, is primarily an exercise in logical activity; and this is true because the ontological base of Neo-Thomism is itself a logical one. That is, Aristotelian and Thomistic metaphysics represents a reality of logical form.

If logic is the ground of our reality and the medium of action in the knowing process, obviously we must look to the training of the instrument of logic — the intellect — in the education of man. At the base, therefore, of Neo-Thomist educational doctrine stands a theory of mind or intellect, which has come to be known as Faculty Psychology, or the psychology of the mental faculties.

Down through the centuries there has been an abiding temptation on the part of man to compare his mental activity with his physical activity, i.e., to find some analogue between his mind and his body. It is easy enough to see that the body is made up of a variety of parts — organs, limbs, etc. — which operate in a kind of federated system; that is, they each perform a distinct function, but they all exist together in a living union of organism. We know that it is possible by exercise to train each of these physical components; each part has a particular potential which can be cultivated by calisthenics and drill. We can increase the power of muscles through lifting, we can increase the endurance of the lungs through running, we can improve and refine the coordination between eye and limb through repeated drill and practice. Engaging in this kind of thing may be dull and monotonous — indeed, downright unpleasant — but it works; any athlete knows it.

Now, then, if this is true of the body, might it not also be true of the mind? We know the mind has certain powers, which may be said to originate in and be the function of certain mental "parts," or faculties. Customarily and traditionally these faculties are three in number: Reason, Memory, and Will. Although there are subdivisions and elaborations of these three faculties, they represent the central powers of the intellect. Of the three, of course, Reason is the dominant faculty; the rational faculty is the core and center of logical activity. But the other two are necessary adjuncts. And when all three are tuned and sharpened to their highest performance, they collectively make possible the highest kind of mental activity: the apprehension of self-evident and absolute truth, or Intuition.

NEO-THOMIST PEDAGOGY. The primacy of the intuitive power is obvious: Intuition leads to ultimate truth. And so Neo-Thomist pedagogy centers its theory on procedures for developing this highest faculty of man. If perfect health may be said to represent not only freedom from disease but also the perfection of all the bodily processes, we know that we can reach this highest bodily state by careful nutrition and physical training. So likewise with the intellect; we must "feed" it the proper materials and engage it in specially designed mental "calisthenics."

In the case of Reason this is done most effectively with what is known as "formal discipline." The term *formal* is not meant to connote a rigid or ritualistic procedure; rather, the term is used in its literal Aristotelian meaning, i.e., discipline in the *forms* of thought. Hence, Neo-Thomists are interested in the subject matters which are the most characterized by given forms — that is, the most "form-al" of subject matters. These are, at the top of the list, mathematics, which according to classical thinking is uncontaminated by irregularity or exception and completely endowed with logical forms and necessities, and language, which is somewhat less regularized but still endowed with formal structure. Languages are never planned in advance, never thought up anew and then put to use. Rather, they simply emerge in the course of human history. The fact that grammars develop signifies to the Thomist that the mind *naturally* tends toward logical structure; the intellect by its own nature evolves in the direction of logical organization. Language is the expression of this logic; and philology, if one were to study it seriously, would be revealed as the epitomized history of the intrinsic and necessary logic upon which the human mind is built.

Training in formal discipline, then, in mathematics, in the languages, in the Latin Trivium of Grammar, Rhetoric, and Logic, is the way to the development of the rational powers.

In the case of Memory (another of the prime faculties) the pedagogy is already suggested. Practice and drill in memorizing things — "Thanatopsis," or the Gettysburg Address, or the Binomial Theorem, or any other "memorable" artifact — will serve to exercise the memory. Here again the *form* rather than the *content* of the learning experience is of uppermost importance. While the Gettysburg Address is perhaps better than an equal amount of nonsense syllables by virtue of its idealistic, affective content, nevertheless in strict Faculty Theory the nonsense syllables would do as well in training the memory. Except for his other interests, it does not matter to the earnest athlete developing his biceps whether he lifts a bar bell or a lovely girl, each weighing 120 pounds. So also is the rational faculty ultimately indifferent; the strategic question is that of the "discipline of form."

In the case of the faculty of Will (our third mental component) Neo-Thomist pedagogy leans in the direction of situations in which the learner is required to exercise will power by forcing himself through tasks which he finds somewhat distasteful. Physical calisthenics are, after all, something less than pure pleasure to most of us. There is no reason to expect that mental calisthenics will be much different. But just as the athlete of truly top-rate caliber forces himself in his training so that he may later force himself to win the race, so does the incipient intellect force itself through mental exercises in order to be able later to force itself to the full application of its mental powers to the problems of life. Thus the Will is the constant ally of the Reason, and it must be trained alongside. The learner must expect to be forced through exercises he finds unpleasant. His will is tested and thereby strengthened by his sticking to the task until it is done.

The Victorian exhortations to perseverance and "stick-to-it-ive-ness" have been common companions of school children for a good many decades; and even before the nineteenth century, when these virtues flowered, there was open talk of "breaking the will" of the child (in colonial Calvinism, for instance) and resetting it along more socially acceptable lines. In any event, the Will is seen as a developable faculty in the human person. It is supposedly the base of "character." Insofar as education makes attempts at so-called "character-building," it will have to take some kind of stand on the Will. And the Neo-Thomist position, being the most unequivocal of all, is consequently the simplest: The Will is a faculty of man which is capable of development through controlled didactic measures.

REALISM, IDEALISM, AND THE FACULTY THEORY. Realists, generally speaking, do not often have much to say about the Will, just as they do not look at the mind from the standpoint of faculties. The Idealists, however, while disinclined to the Faculty Theory, are nevertheless emotionally drawn to the idea of Will because of their subjective, internalized notion of the Self. Thus an Idealist, while close to a Realist on the "Spectator" and "Receptacle" Theories, is in close touch with Neo-Thomists in their emphasis upon discipline, mental training, and the development of will in the human selfhood.

LAY AND ECCLESIASTICAL NEO-THOMISM. In the field of pedagogical theory there is never much "open territory" between the Lay and the Ecclesiastical Wings of Neo-Thomism. Both, generally speaking, hold to a disciplinary approach to teaching; both place the rigorous subject matters of mathematics and languages high on their curricular list; and both give top priority to training the intellect.[7] But whereas the Lay representatives of this position are in search of Truth in their educational program, the Ecclesiastics are in search of God, and this variance in ends will necessarily influence the educational means. For instance, because Latin is the language of the Roman Church, it is of greatest prominence in the language study in Catholic schools; a Lay Neo-Thomist, while approving Latin, might prefer Greek or perhaps would settle for a modern language — a little more chaotic in grammar, but suitable to the purpose.

Or, again, since the Ecclesiastics have for centuries employed the Catechism in their doctrinal rites, the catechetical method is widely employed in their schools. In this procedure the learner commits to memory specific and standard answers to a list of specific and standard questions. When he is asked a question in the classroom his "recitation" consists in giving the precise standardized answer. Here again the "form-al" principle is exemplified; by shaping the child's mind to the "form" of doctrine, the Church organizes the mind's powers in orientation to the Church's conception of Truth.[8] The Lay Neo-Thomists, on the other hand, are not particularly partial to the catechetical method; rather, they are concerned with having the learner see and understand logical connections — between, say, grammatical forms in language study or propositions in geometry.

Finally — and one would normally expect this — the Ecclesiastical Neo-Thomists, with a primary ontological and epistemological interest in Being and God, will include in their educational program a considerable amount of out-and-out religious material. There will be not only doctrinal lessons and ceremonial rites but also prayer and devotions. Prayer, in a manner of speaking, is a direct approach to intuition; it is, as it were, a deliberate invitation to be visited by spiritual truth. As such it holds a pedagogical place in Ecclesiastical Neo-Thomist schools. Lay

[7] In this connection it is interesting to note that some Ecclesiastical Neo-Thomists complain that their Lay compatriots have turned intellectual training into not just one of the ends of education but the *only* end of education, ignoring physical education, the creative arts, and the social development of the learner. Indeed, Catholic parochial schools remain dedicated to the so-called "whole" child even though placing the intellectual and spiritual in a primary position, whereas Lay Thomist theory would leave nonintellectual sectors of development to nonschool agencies, i.e., home, church, community. (See Chapter Eleven.)

[8] If this be indoctrination, Ecclesiastical Neo-Thomists make no apologies for it. What is wrong, they say, with indoctrinating the child with what is absolutely true? This is hard to answer, unless one chooses — as many do — to argue the last two words.

Neo-Thomists, on the other hand, do not choose to make such an open bid for intuition. Intuition becomes possible on the base of intellect. Therefore, intellectual training must precede intuition; that is, if the circumstances are favorable, intellectual development will culminate in intuitive powers. Of course, insofar as the Aristotelian or Platonic kind of "contemplation" approximates devotional prayer, one might say that Lay Theory would go along. But generally speaking the Lay Neo-Thomist will settle for rigorous and disciplined training of the Reason, leaving meditation, prayer, and contemplation to the individual.

REALIST AND IDEALIST REACTIONS. The relationship of Neo-Thomism to Realism and Idealism is certainly not difficult to see. Realists, being materialistically and naturalistically inclined, will put no great stock in any of the Neo-Thomist interests — language, catechism, or prayer. To be sure, there is an ancestral linkage between Realism and Neo-Thomism (especially the Lay variety) in their common appreciation of the orderliness and regularity of the cosmos. Insofar as Latin exhibits a similar orderliness — albeit in symbolic subject matter — a Realist might choose it also; he probably would not choose it for its supposed disciplinary value, however, because his theory of mind development is more one of external environmental conditioning than of internal exercise of incipient faculties. As for the catechetical method, the Realist might be ambivalent. He likes precise and definite answers to things; but prepared, "canned," unscientific answers, no. Skinner's "teaching machine" might be considered as a variant of this, somewhat of an "automated catechism," but the program fed into the machine can, after all, be altered to suit the situation. This sort of flexibility obviously would not be possible in Neo-Thomism. Certainly, being the Naturalist that he is, the Realist would have little use for prayer or meditation or contemplation in his pedagogy.

The Idealist, to review the list again, would value language study. But not Latin. It is dead. Linguistically, perhaps, it is useful in learning other, modern languages, including English, but as symbolic vehicle for the Living Mind — microcosmic or Universal — it is deficient. If we must have Latin, let it be through literature — Cicero, Vergil, *et al.* — but not too much grinding on grammar. The catechetical method, as a kind of mental conditioning, is somewhat alien to Idealist tendencies; it is something of a repudiation of the self to impose something on it from the outside in so uncompromising a manner. Of course, the "Spectator Theory" is sympathetic with this general "impositionist" approach, but the Idealist would prefer a more personalized procedure. Understanding is what he is after, more than "answer-chopping" in catechetical "question-and-response" periods.

It is in connection with the meditational part of learning that the

Idealist has the greatest contact with Neo-Thomism. For the process of coming into identification with the Absolute Mind and Self is a meditative and prayerful kind of activity. Idealists in America are often associated with religious bodies, particularly the Protestant churches, and they are eager to infuse into school life — even on a secular basis — some quality which will remind the child of his cosmic origins. Prayer as such is not possible in the secular school in America; but identification with a school's spirit or with a college's "ethos" is perhaps one way to get a sense of one's heritage; from this base, the study of all of Western civilization can become a bridge to an understanding of the wider, cosmic bearings from which one springs. Further, the Idealist shares with the Neo-Thomist an abiding interest in the so-called humanities (as against the physical or social sciences), for the humanities are the special province of Mind and Intellect.

These are admittedly tenuous points of contact, but they seem authentic nonetheless. At any rate, the Idealist and the Neo-Thomist do enjoy a certain amount of intellectual companionship.

Solving problems

At this point in our analysis there must be a discrete break in mood; for it should become increasingly clear, if it has not already, that Experimentalism is the "Great Break with Tradition" in philosophic thinking. Its ontology is a repudiation of the whole long chronicle of "out-there-ness" and the resultant dualism between man and reality; its epistemology is a repudiation of "spectator-itis" and "logic-chopping"; and so its pedagogy too represents a clean separation from antecedent conceptions of the learning process.

Drawing directly upon their unified ontology of experience and their epistemology of "testing for consequences" (the scientific method), the Experimentalists have found the locus of learning in *problems*. "Problematic situations" is perhaps a better term, as we saw in Chapter Six, for it connotes a much wider sphere of application. And this is precisely what is intended, for we are now in a position to see, says the Experimentalist, that all situations — all experience — have an educative potential; that is, they have the potential power to *teach*, to initiate growth in us, to quicken our awareness of our world and to lead us on to more mature use of our world for human ends. To put it simply and bluntly, *all experience educates*.

But, as simple as this may sound, it is only part of our conceptual base of understanding; for, while all experience educates, it doesn't all educate equally well. Some experience has more educative potential than other experience. That is, some circumstances call forth more concern, some situations elicit more activity — to wit, those circumstances and situations which are *problematic* in character. And it is in this type of experience that true and genuine learning takes place.

There is only one general qualification we must lay upon this principle, says the Experimentalist, and that is that the problematic character of the situation must be recognized by the learner himself: He must see the situation as *his* situation, the problem as *his* problem. He can, of course, be placed in other people's situations and handed other people's problems — in school, for instance, the teacher can prepare problems for him — but to that degree his growth becomes artificial, linked to motivations and promptings that are generically external to his own being.

At the very base, then, of Experimentalist pedagogical theory is the identification by the learner of his interests, the sectors of the world seen from where he stands to be most problematic. If this identification can be made honestly, if the teacher can elicit some genuine curiosities in the learner, then learning is truly under way.

LEARNER-CENTERED LEARNING. What this means, in more concrete terms, is that the educative process must begin with the learner's identification of his own curiosities and concerns. What should eventuate in the classroom is the evolutionary expansion of a question in the child's own mind: Why do leaves fall off the trees in the fall? Why doesn't the moon ever go away? Why do people join labor unions? How is the Cost-of-Living Index computed? Why not make Puerto Rico a state? Somehow, the learner must be awakened to his own scholastic needs. To any teacher who has tried teaching in this fashion this will be recognized as one of the most difficult of all pedagogical enterprises; but the Experimentalist maintains that, while difficult, it is absolutely central to the educative process.

This has come to be known as the "learner-centered" or "child-centered" concept in teaching. It has, of course, been the object of much ridicule among educational critics. One is immediately reminded of the famous cartoon of a small boy confronting his first-grade teacher on a given morning with the wistful lament: "Do we *have* to do what we *want* to do today?" But such ridicule misses the essential point, says the Experimentalist, for it turns the principle into a license for mere entertainment, fun, and play in the classroom, when the real meaning of the principle is quite the opposite, namely, to awaken the *interest* of the learner, as a prior condition of motivation, to get him to learn what we as a society want him to learn.

LEARNING WHILE USING KNOWLEDGE. Presuming that this initial task has been accomplished, the procedure of learning then follows the general plan outlined in Chapter Six in the discussion of the scientific method and the "Complete Act of Thought." That is, the learner is encouraged and helped to specify and narrow his curiosity to a workable and study-able "project"; to investigate and research the object of his curiosity to locate possible answers to the question or possible resolutions of what we may generally call "an indeterminate situation"; to test his findings for adequacy by way of explaining or resolving the "problem"; and, finally, to set down his conclusions.

In this sequence of activities the learner will obviously require a great deal in the way of information; he will require skill in organizing and reporting this information; and he will require a degree of intelligence in making sense of what he has found out to other people. Thus, he needs to learn *content*: factual information, background history, current knowledge concerning the problem. He needs to learn *how to communicate:* reading skills, writing skills, speaking skills. He needs to learn *how to analyze a situation:* the application of intelligence to the understanding of a situation.

There are many other things he must learn, of course, but the point is that he learns content — so dear to the hearts of traditional methodologists — in the process of using that content to solve a problem or answer a question. The knowledge thus accumulated is learned not in some limbo of contrived necessity — a teacher's assignment, for instance — but within the very context of situations in the learner's own life. The learner *uses* his knowledge — and *by using learns it.*

THE LOGICAL VERSUS THE PSYCHOLOGICAL. John Dewey in several of his writings abstracted and clarified this principle of learning-through-use by pointing to the distinction between the "logical" and the "psychological" methods of teaching. The logical method is characterized by the presentation in systematic, organized, logical form of a body of material which has been especially arranged for learners — "intellectually predigested," one might say. In commenting on this well-known procedure, Dewey says:

> There is a strong temptation to assume that presenting subject matter in its perfected form provides a royal road to learning. What more natural than to suppose that the immature can be saved time and energy, and be protected from needless error by commencing where competent inquirers have left off? The outcome is written large in the history of education.[9]

This may be, Dewey contends, the *logical* way of doing things, but pedagogically it is not the most effective way. For learning does not proceed in so neat and convenient a way as this. Learning originates in a life

[9] *Democracy and Education* (New York: The Macmillan Co., 1916), p. 257.

situation, not in a book. It originates in some circumstance where what is already known is recognized by the learner as inadequate; it begins, ultimately, in a state of *dissatisfaction* with one's own condition. From this seemingly unpromising, sometimes confused, perhaps chaotic condition, the learner advances by inquiry to a larger and wider grasp of the situation with which he began. All learning, says Dewey — whatever the subject matter and whoever the individual learner — proceeds basically in this way.

We may, of course, tell the learner exactly what to learn by presenting it to him in books and lectures and requiring him to master it; that is to say, we can have learners "go through the motions" of learning. But in contriving what appear to be learning situations, we are often disappointed; for what appears to have been learned is quickly forgotten and dismissed by the learner from his own life. What really stays with the learner is the learning that he has engaged in as the result of genuine interest. Of this, Dewey says:

> The apparent loss of time involved is more than made up for by the superior understanding and vital interest secured. What the pupil learns he at least understands. Moreover, by following, in connection with problems selected from the material of ordinary acquaintance, the methods by which scientific men have reached their perfected knowledge, he gains independent power to deal with material within his range, and avoids the mental confusion and intellectual distaste attendant upon studying matter whose meaning is only symbolic.[10]

A good example of this dichotomy of procedures is geography. The logical method of teaching this material would be to begin with the earth as a planet, noting its revolutions and its circulations about the sun. From these general facts an understanding could be gained of the seasons and of certain geographical characteristics of the globe entire. Then the water areas would be distinguished from the land areas, the northern from the southern hemisphere, and the eastern from the western hemisphere. The major topographical characteristics of the continents would then be examined, whereupon an American school would probably select North America for special study. After this continent had been examined, the study would arrive at the United States, its land and mineral resources, its flora and fauna, its major waterways, its crops, its weather. Then, depending on the location of the school, a particular region would be studied, and the home state would be geographically analyzed, with possibly a day or two devoted to the home town itself. Certainly this is the way most geography texts are written, and it would

10 *Ibid.*, p. 258.

seem to be a not unlikely description of how such material would be presented.

It so happens, however, that the learner naturally grows in geographical understanding in quite the other direction, starting with as immediate a surrounding as the schoolyard itself. To employ the psychological procedure would be to move from this base of direct understanding to the progressively wider spheres of neighborhood, community, state, region, nation, continent, and globe. This gradual expansion to larger geographical entities is ideally made, says the Experimentalist, by awakening in the child certain curiosities as the material unfolds — why his schoolhouse is built of brick, why his mother pays so much for oranges, why industries move away or come to town, why American foreign policy is tied to oil, etc. But such curiosities should be aroused *before* the presentation of the material, not after; for this is the way the experience of the learner customarily unfolds. And it is only when genuine curiosity precedes learning that the learning will be permanent.

Another instance is that of history. Customarily history is taught logically, i.e., *chrono*logically. We begin American history with the Vikings and Columbus, proceeding down the years to the present. When we do this, says the Experimentalist, we start at the point which is the most remote — both in time and in interest — from the learner. We start, that is, with the material in which it is most difficult to evoke the interest of the learner. Thus from the outset we deplete the fund of motivation on which we may draw, trusting instead that applications to the learner's present knowledge can be made as we take up one historical situation after another. The Experimentalist reminds us that history courses taught this way and history books written this way (and almost all of them are) have had a sorry record of appeal to school children down through the decades, making history one of the least interesting — and therefore least enjoyed — subject matters.

To the Experimentalist, this unhappiness is traceable to Realist and Idealist and, in some small measure, Neo-Thomist influences. For history taught by the logical procedure is the same as history taught from the basis of the "Spectator Theory," that is, by setting out a specified and codified body of subject matter to be mastered by the student. The student acquires learning by mastering this content, and if he balks or wonders why, he is told that the content is to be mastered for its own sake.

To reverse this, to quicken (instead of deaden) concern with the vitality of the past, is to turn the pedagogical procedure entirely around, so that we once again — as with geography — *begin with the experience of the learner*. For it is here, not in the remote past, that we are most likely to find problematic situations, curiosities, and interests on which the learning of history can be built. As Dewey has put it:

... past events cannot be separated from the living present and retain meaning. The true starting point of history is always some present situation with its problems.[11]

Acting on this advice, the Experimentalist educator would attempt to arouse in the learner an interest in some present problem having historical antecedents necessary to its understanding: the cold war, the exploration of space, unemployment, racial segregation. Consider the last named, for example. Here the teacher could capitalize upon the interest lying within the learner's own experience so as to work backward through American history to see what historical materials are relevant to the study of this problem: the 1954 Supreme Court decision, the Plessey-versus-Ferguson "separate-but-equal" doctrine of 1897, the Reconstruction Period, the Fourteenth Amendment, the Civil War, the Emancipation Proclamation, the Missouri Compromise, slavery, the Declaration of Independence (and perhaps even Aristotle's views on the political legitimacy of a slave class in Greek society).

It is evident that a teacher proceeding in this way might not "touch all the bases" that the logical, forward-working teacher would touch, but only those which would be relevant and illuminating to the problem under view. The difference lies in (1) the point of origin for study, *the present,* and (2) the criterion for the selection of materials to be studied, namely, *relevance.*

To learn best, according to Experimentalist thinking, is to engage in problem-solving and inquiry and to initiate such activity from the ground of a genuine life interest. In making the recommendation to *start where the child is* (to employ a standard professional cliché), the Experimentalist, it may now be noted, is doing no more than making a special application of his general theory of knowing — the scientific method. For inquiry and problem-solving are pre-eminently what scientists do when they are trying to find things out. They employ, in short, what we are here calling the "psychological" method, i.e., starting with their own understanding, singling out a specific curiosity, and then investigating their "problem" to find the answer. It is only *after* they have found them out that they organize their new findings into what may be called "logical" form, in the books they write and the lectures they deliver to their classes in the university.[12]

---

11 *Ibid.,* p. 251.

12 The book you hold in your hands, incidentally, is an open and shameless violation of the "psychological" principle, i.e., to begin where the learners are. Take a look at the Table of Contents. You will recognize the material as having been organized from the most intellectually remote (ontological theory) to the more immediately practical (classroom practice). This is true not only within each of the

The way the teacher looks at subject matter is quite different from the way the student looks at it, for the teacher already knows the material and has it logically organized both in his mind and in the textbooks he has selected for use. But the learner does not learn it in the same way; he must advance upon it from the base of his own interests and curiosities, considering the knowledge of the teacher and the textbook as resource material for the investigation of his topic. The "project" method, then, as against the lecture, "tell-it-to-them" method, is a favorite Experimentalist procedure; for the *project* method is the learner's version of the research scholar's *scientific* method. Although the magnitude and level of sophistication of the two are, of course, quite different, they are basically cut from the same epistemological cloth.

Basically, argues the Experimentalist, children in the first grade learn the same way research scientists do — by the problem-solving procedure. All learning follows this pattern, and hence the pedagogy of the school should be shaped to it.

IDEALISM, REALISM, AND NEO-THOMISM DISSENT. It goes without saying that spokesmen for the other methodologies bridle somewhat at this supposedly universal dictum of the Experimentalists. To place all learning in a problem-solving context is to deny a well-known feature of human education, i.e., that it is both possible and feasible to introduce knowledge into an individual with no problem whatsoever being present. Certainly the Realist's conditioning does not depend on problems; and the Idealist's absorption in the Universal Self does not depend on problems; and the Neo-Thomist's mental discipline does not depend on problems. In fact, as the advocates of these positions would contend, one must be taught some things about one's world before problems can even be entertained, let alone solved. Problems grow out of knowledge; not the other way around. If we are going to teach boys and girls to live intelligently, if we mean to teach them "how to think," as the old saying goes, then we must first give them something to think about and not expect them to wallow about in problems until something strikes their little curiosities.

Much of the current controversy over education, as you may already have surmised, centers on this focal topic of "substantive content" versus "problem-solving" in learning theory. This is not so much a matter of which of the two theories is correct, since each side recognizes that both factors are involved in the educative process; it is more a question of which factor is primary, which represents the initiating point of genuine growth on the part of the young.

---

substantive Parts II, III, and IV, but of the book as a whole. If this disturbs you, better turn immediately to Chapter Sixteen and read the book in reverse.

Finding the self

Finally we pass into the comparatively uncharted territory of the Existentialist. As it has been pointed out, the Existentialist has not had much to say about education, most particularly about the practical and technical questions of pedagogical method. But we can, nonetheless, begin to see the outline features and the general mood of an Existentialist approach to the training of the young.

THE EXISTENTIAL MOMENT. One of the central doctrines of Existentialist thought, as you will recall from Chapter Three (see pages 74–76), is that of the central primacy of human existence. It is when we wake up to discover that our existence is the ineluctable fact of the human condition that we begin to see the meaning of the companion doctrine that moral choice is inescapable. Because man is "thrown into existence," because he "turns up on the scene" and finds himself here, he is inescapably "locked in" a circumstance of choice. He has to choose; even to choose not to choose is a choice; even suicide is a choice.

It may be said that in macrocosmic terms mankind has begun to awaken to this moral predicament; but we also know that in microcosmic terms each individual must awaken to it in his own life. What has happened to the race is seen to take place in each individual. About the age of puberty there is a more or less abrupt awakening to the fact of one's own existence. We somehow become existentially awake; we discover ourselves for the first time. Prior to this moment — which we might here designate The Existential Moment — the child has been aware of the existence only of things beyond his own skin; but once seized by this new idea of *self* he can never retreat to his infantile, childlike state of existential innocence. He has passed The Existential Moment.

This "moment," which generally occurs while the youngster is in the later elementary- and junior high school grades, is not an easy time, since it includes the first, agonizing recognition of being responsible for what one does and how one behaves. Frequently, as we noted in Chapter Three, children will try to postpone or forestall the full impact of The Moment by disavowing responsibility for their having come into existence. But the child soon realizes that he cannot live out the rest of his life upon this thesis, refusing responsibility for what he does and is. He must, once he passes this "moment," take on the heavy moral burden of his every thought and move.

THE EDUCATION OF CHOICE. Educationally, of course, this means that the individual must become awake not only to his own existential condition and the responsibility it entails but awake to the alternatives before him from which his choices shall be made. To choose in ignorance of

any alternative is to choose unfreely; therefore the individual must be given — in the classroom and outside — every conceivable latitude to find for himself all the possibilities open to him. This means that any subject matter is "fair game" for the school, and that boys and girls must be perfectly free to follow their own inclinations in learning. To hem them in with required assignments, to codify and channel their growth along narrow lines, to suppress their individual reactions to life and learning on the grounds of some preconceived notion of propriety, is to insulate them from the truly *real* world of choice. And since *choice* in the Existential setting is fundamentally *moral* choice, the learner must be given opportunities for genuine moral choice in the learning process.

If one were to put it in Neo-Thomist terms, the learner should exercise his "choice-making" power; or, better, he should be awakened to his possession of that power and the necessity for him to use it. To an Existentialist, modern education is noticeably "antiseptic" in this regard; boys and girls are rarely asked to make choices, moral or otherwise. Experimentalist pedagogy comes the closest, perhaps, in specifying that youngsters should be led to solve problems by selecting from among alternative solutions; but here the "community of consensus," not the individual self, is the true "engine" of choice. And the traditional philosophies are even worse, since they set the child in a context — in Mind (Idealism), or in Nature (Realism), or in Being (Neo-Thomism) — in which his basic choices are for the most part already made for him.

THE EMOTIONS. We must extricate the learner from this predicament, says the Existentialist; and one of the most promising places to look for the key is in the emotions. Here the choice-making function of the individual is most active, and, therefore, here we can most efficaciously gain access to the self and incite it to existential action. Indeed, Robert Ulich, an expositor of Existentialist tendencies, says that the school of tomorrow must find the thesis for its general education in the emotions.[13] This is said with the understanding that in the special subject matters of the emotions — the arts, most particularly — the most fertile ground for human growth will be found.

In Chapter Five, in a section devoted to subjective and objective knowledge, it was pointed out (see pages 118–119) that an "in-here" ontology — which is how Existentialism has been characterized — calls for an "in-here" kind of knowing. And this would mean, pedagogically speaking, that the learner should be given more scope for "in-here" subjective knowing. He should be given assignments in reacting to the world — in creative writing, in drama, in responding to literature. He should be more

---

[13] *Crisis and Hope in American Education* (Boston: The Beacon Press, 1951), Chapter III.

often asked to respond to the other "selves" around him — not in a *social* way, but in a subjectivist, individualist way. There is today, says the Existentialist, too much "Group Think" in schools; not enough "Individual Think." The learner should be quickened to respond affectively and emotionally to his world, to the people in it, to the things it makes possible, and to the things, among those it makes possible, which are genuinely worth doing.

In short, the learner must become *involved* in the world, involved in the value questions of life:

— We subsidize farmers from the national treasury to grow more wheat than we can possibly use, then spend more money to store it in a cave in Kansas. Meanwhile millions go underfed in the world. How about this? Isn't something dreadfully wrong here?

— We squander our lavish wealth on liquor, filter tips, and sleekly chromed chariots from Detroit. Do these represent what we really "believe in"?

— We send CARE "Midwife Kits" to, of all places, India. Considering India's population problem and her lack of interest in reducing infant mortality, should we continue to send the kits?

— We try to find our way in an "open" cosmos, where the little questions of home and work get solved but the big questions of life and destiny go unanswered. In such a cosmos as this can there be a God? In such a cosmos, is God really necessary? If he really were to exist, what difference would it make?

This conversational cadenza is inserted simply to show that there is an emotive content to Existentialism which suffuses the entire educative process. And this content, originating in the individual-as-subject, belongs to no one but the subject himself. For the subject, ultimately alone and friendless in the moral universe, must find his own way. Boys and girls may live superficially in a *social* setting in the school, just as their elders do in the wider adult society. But existentially they must remain alone, and to shield them from this lonely moral existence is to shield them from what is truly human in them.

THE TEACHING METHOD. This whole pedagogical model which we have been discussing is the complete obverse of the "Spectator Theory." Existentialism has been described as "philosophizing from the standpoint of the actor instead of, as has been customary, from that of the spectator."[14] As such, it turns "inside out" the whole enterprise of educating the young; learning begins with the self, not with knowledge.

14 E. L. Allen, *Existentialism From Within* (London: Routledge & Kegan Paul, 1953), p. 10. Quoted in George F. Kneller, *Existentialism and Education* (New York: Philosophical Library, 1958), p. 147.

The learner must be set in the very "eye" of the entire proceedings. The moral self must become the ultimate object of pedagogic attention.

Kneller suggests that perhaps the most available access route to the moral self is through a revival of the famed Socratic method. "In methodology, there is no question that the existentialist favor [sic] the Socratic approach."[15] This method, says Kneller, implies that the teacher — and Socrates used it this way — has no knowledge to begin with: He is interested in eliciting knowledge from the learner. The only kind of knowledge that can be elicited from the learner without prior study and inquiry is moral knowledge, i.e., the subjective response of the individual to his world. It is this kind of knowledge, says the Existentialist, which we must revive in our schools. For this kind of knowledge will tell us again what man is trying to become. We have forgotten who we are, and therefore what we might make of ourselves, because we have forgotten what it means to exist. We have forgotten it because we have forgotten what Socrates was all about. But Socrates is no distant saint; he is a living tradition — and, most fortunately, a *pedagogical* tradition of methodology by which we can revive the existential sense of the young.

THE TEACHER

What has been said in the several sections above concerning the nature of the learning process has provided ample occasion for glancing references to the role of the teacher and the methods he uses as an initiator and guide to learning. There are, however, a few special notes that can be added concerning his particular role; for the role itself — in the literal sense of *role* in theatrical talk — does take on different characterological nuances from philosophy to philosophy.

The teacher as paradigmatic self

The Idealist is looking for those qualities in the teacher which will provide for the learners a "working model" of selfhood. Since the teacher is older and more mature, he stands somewhat as a "liaison agent" or "middleman" between the microcosmic self and the Absolute Self; and he should also represent the same sort of middle position with respect to Mind. He is more knowledgeable than his charges; by continued study and growth in his field he should attempt to approximate the Absolute Mind more and more closely. And by so presenting himself to his students he should draw them toward him, constantly seeking from them fuller microcosmic expressions of selfhood and mind.

15 Kneller, *op. cit.*, p. 133.

This signifies that the personality of the teacher is crucial in Idealist theory. It is on constant display, and it should be, for through identification with this personality students should grow in the qualities of personality. The lecture method is not especially singled out by Idealists, but it is obvious that this method provides the greatest "exposure time" for the selfhood of the teacher. Wherever and however the selfhood of the teacher — through his enthusiasm, his feeling for his subject, his warmth as a person — can be brought to bear on the learner, there will the teacher be fulfilling his proper role in the school.

The teacher as demonstrator

The Realist is looking for different qualities. He wants his teacher to be a precise and business-like explainer of the world. This teacher might be likened, to use another comparison, to a guide in a national park, i.e., he is essentially a "show-er," a teller, an expositor and demonstrator of how the world works. He of course employs the lecture and the recitation to dispense and to measure, respectively, the information he is concerned with.

He is dealing, ultimately, with a pre-existent reality of which both he and his students are spectators. The task is to cause the learner to know this reality, to produce in him an adjustment to its requirements, and thus to prepare him to build further upon the established knowledge of it. The teacher, thus, is a kind of "liaison agent" between the learner and Nature. His function is to know Nature in all of its many faces and to introduce this Nature systematically to his students.

Generally speaking, the personality of the teacher is not crucial in this activity. Indeed, the Realist would prefer that the selfhood (the personality) of the teacher be muted and screened from the learners in order that the *content* of education assume the "front-and-center" position. The personality of the teacher tends to divert the attention of the child from what he is to learn; hence it is best to make the teacher as neutral as possible, at least insofar as his personality is concerned. Stand aside, then, O Teacher, and let the factual knowledge of the cosmos come across the desk, straight and true.

The teacher as mental disciplinarian

The concept of mental discipline and the entire Faculty Psychology Theory have been empirically weakened over the course of the last half century by continuing studies in the possibility of "transfer of training." To discipline the mind to learn so-called intellectual habits, which are then transferable to various subject matters, is now seen to be something less than the relatively direct and systematic procedure it was once thought to be. Psychologists who study learning are generally of the view that the mind is not made up of so many faculties which can be exercised, like muscles, in isolation one from another and then transferred to other tasks unconnected with the context of learning. Transfer does take place, we are told, but only in the degree to which the learning situation and the transfer situation are similar.

The Faculty Theory of mind dies hard, however, notwithstanding mounting scientific evidence[16] against it, and there are many educators who persist in the belief that certain studies and certain disciplinary teaching procedures train and harden the mental faculties for life activities after the young leave school. The teacher, in this frame of thinking, should assume the role of a rigorous though benign "taskmaster of the intellect." Or perhaps a better, if somewhat ungenerous, figure would be that of a "director of mental calisthenics." If intellectual training is principally a development of rational powers by exercise and practice in logical procedures, then the teacher should become the chief officiator of the proceedings: not so much a model of personal selfhood; not so much a neutral dispenser of factual information; but a benignly demanding developer of mental powers.

Obviously, such a teacher should himself be possessed of well-developed logical powers; he should have a good memory and a strong will and, above all, be capable of straight and clear reasoning. He must exhibit these qualities as a teacher, but, what is even more important, he must be the developer of these incipient powers in the youngsters in his classes. In Chapter One the "operative arts" were contrasted with the "cooperative arts." (See pages 3–5.) The teacher in Neo-Thomist thinking should be the cooperative artist par excellence — cooperating with the natural unfolding of prior powers with which the child is born. He is, to use still another metaphor, an "intellectual horticulturist," nurturing, feeding, and "fertilizing" the young intellect as it unfolds and develops its rational powers.

The teacher as research-project director

Someone has described Experimentalist educational theory as considering the teacher as "chairman of the board of directors" of a learning "industry." The figure is not inaccurate, for the teacher in "problem-solving" pedagogy, while still chief-in-charge, nevertheless solicits and

16 The article on "Transfer of Training" in the 1950 Edition of the *Encyclopedia of Educational Research* reviews the research on this question all the way back to 1890. Little in the way of affirmative evidence is reported. Transfer *does* take place, it is true, but only when (1) the learning and applying situations are similar, (2) the learner sees the similarity, and (3) the learner is given practice in making the transfer. Under these conditions almost any subject matter, from auto shop to zoology, can be disciplinary.

utilizes the energies and resources of the learners in a very active way. That is, the learner is not — as in the previous three conceptions — a passive recipient of learning; rather, he is, in Experimentalist thinking, an active participant in the business of learning — investigating, inquiring, reading, thinking, testing, etc. Furthermore, as we shall see in greater detail in Chapter Twelve, he is constantly enmeshed in the active participation of other students; he is engaged in an essentially *social* undertaking.

Hence the teacher must be a director of a social, corporate enterprise, maintaining harmony and morale, provoking from each member of the group his full powers of participation, and serving as manager of the learning project so that genuine growth takes place in the group and in each individual. An understanding on the part of the teacher of human motivation, of the psychic backgrounds to behavior, of the theory of emotional balance, and of all the other facets of human psychology begins to assume a new and decisive importance. The teacher must know his subject matter, but he must also know his *students*. To borrow a phrase from Dewey:

> When engaged in the direct act of teaching, the instructor needs to have subject matter at his fingers' ends; his attention should be upon the attitude and response of the pupil.[17]

And to have one's attention fastened on the "attitude and response" of the pupil is to attempt to see there a unique and individual personality reacting to, i.e., "transacting with," his world. And since this world is a world of experience, the teacher is in some ways engaged in transactional activity *with* the learner; he is learning along with the student. Indeed, in the carrying out of projects in which the teacher learns as much as the students, we have an ideal model for teaching skill in Experimentalist terms.

The teacher, then, is one with the process. He does not stand outside it as a "liaison agent" between the self and the Absolute Self or as a conveyer belt of factual information between the encyclopedia and the receptacle of the child's mind, or as a mental calisthenicist trying to train the mind like a muscle. Rather, he is a partner, a *senior* partner, in the investigation of topics, in the inquiry into unresolved questions, in the carrying out of meaningful student projects.

The teacher as provocateur of the self

There is a good deal of puzzlement over what might be said concerning an Existentialist teacher. At the very least the matter is ambiguous, be-

17 Dewey, *op. cit.*, p. 215.

cause of the overriding concern in Existentialism for individualism and the primacy of the choosing self. What use at all, one may ask, is a teacher in this context? The very presence of a second person immediately "socializes" the learner's condition and thereby compromises the possibility of his developing his own individualistic view of things.

This difficulty may account for the relative silence of Existentialism on so social an undertaking as education has turned out to be in the modern world; but it need not necessarily block us from surmising certain things that the teacher could and might do in the educational process.

The issue is joined in the concern for moral judgment in Existentialism. A second person — the teacher — can awaken the child to the moral dimension of his life without prescribing the moral decisions the child must make. The teacher should pose moral as well as intellectual questions in the classroom; he should raise questions of metaphysical import, so that the youngsters can occasionally confront the root issues of being human. Who am I? What am I *for* in the world? I have maybe seventy years to live; what am I going to do with it? These and a few other probes should open up the raw nerve of "metaphysical conscience," and the teacher should constantly keep this conscience agitated and alive as the child grows.

However this may be done, the teacher will certainly not assume the role of paradigmatic self, or conveyer-belt explainer, or mental disciplinarian, or corporate problem-solver. Rather, he will, via the Socratic model, jar and stir the maturing youngster into a recognition of his moral selfhood, so that there will never be any question as the years pass that the student will genuinely take charge of his own life and take responsibility for how he lives it day by day.

All of the other philosophies, says the Existentialist, tend to place the individual in some kind of ready-made system where he doesn't have to take responsibility for his life. The three traditional outlooks, as we have mentioned, provide external systems — ideational, natural, or logical — in which the moral content of a person's life may presumably be discovered and adopted. And in Experimentalism the social group represents an external gathering point for moral decision; though the social group never locates Absolute Truth and Right, it does serve as an external "system" to which the individual may refer his moral questions.

This is all wrong, says the Existentialist. We have socialized education so much in the modern school that the child has no "moral sense" left. We have, it is true, extricated him in the secular American school from the moralities of transcendentalism (Idealism), of naturalism (Realism), and of Aristotelian spiritualism (Neo-Thomism), but we have now become the prisoners of a new moral tyrant: the social group (Experimentalism).

The teacher's job, says the Existentialist, is to break this bond and to set the individual once again in the very center of moral commitment.

*   *   *

The task of this chapter has been to show the operating relationship between epistemological theory and pedagogical procedure. The business of knowing is essentially the business of coming into some kind of human touch with reality. This business is complicated, of course, by the fact that our conceptions of reality are many and various, as Part II has attempted to show. But it is complicated further by the "internal" difficulties of epistemology as they relate to the nature of man — his perceptual apparatus, his psychology, his powers of symbolization and ideation, and his "feedback" application of those powers upon the reality in which he finds himself and which he is trying to know.

It has been the secondary task of this chapter to show that the difficulties in epistemology are visited in turn upon pedagogical theory; they create confusion and disagreement on how youngsters actually learn. Which suggests — to borrow a phrase from modern technology — that "the state of the art" of epistemology, or of philosophy as a whole, is not sufficient to support a unified conception of the learning process. This sentence probably breaks some kind of record for understatement, but it is offered here as one more reminder that as far as educational theory and practice are concerned we are obligated in our utterances to maintain a humble, though not humiliating, posture.

Eventually, though, there wells up within each of us a desire to single out *one* of the many pedagogical theories as the most suitable one to "believe in." Even though it is conceivable that there is more than one "true" epistemology, nevertheless there must be some that are more adequate, i.e., more "true," than others. And there seems to be a normal and natural tendency in us to seek out the more adequate theories for use in our own lives and work.

When we launch upon this undertaking, we are brought face to face with the whole universe of value judgment. To choose among pedagogies, to choose among epistemologies, even to choose among ontologies, is to enter upon a judgment of worth and value. To make choices among these high-minded and relatively sophisticated regions of philosophical theory may require more study than this book or your course can provide. But we certainly ought to study the question of choosing, even if at a lower level of discourse.

For, whatever else man may be, he is certainly a "valuer": He prefers some things to others, whether they be apples in a basket, women in a room, behavior patterns in a social system, or Gods in a cosmos. And to find out how he makes such value decisions we must examine the whole complex of factors which are involved in his judgments.

It is to this region of value — axiology — we now turn in Part IV.

QUESTIONS

1. One of the "battle cries" of the twentieth century in education has been the "education of the whole child." From the standpoint of the various pedagogies discussed in this chapter, would you say they would be equally proficient in fulfilling this requirement in the work of the school? Explain.

2. One of the logical extensions of Realist "conditioning" theory is the belief that any educable dimension of the human person is subject to conditioning and habituation. This includes not only motor skills, such as typewriting, but also intellectual behavior, like learning the multiplication table; social behavior, like cooperation or respecting others; and even moral conduct, like telling the truth or paying the proper amount of income tax. The conditioning theory holds that we can turn any behavior — verbal or physical — into habituated response. What do you think of this as an educational theory? What would you think the other four philosophies would say about it?

3. One of the standard clichés of the modern educational age is that "the learner learns to do by doing." Precisely what function does *doing* have in the five pedagogies? Is *doing* necessary to *learning*? What represents genuine *doing*? What doesn't?

4. Perhaps at the other end of the epistemological scale from *doing* is *intuition*. What function does intuition play in the several epistemologies and pedagogies discussed in this chapter? If Roman Catholic schools "invite" spiritual intuition through prayer, would there be any virtue in seeing if public schools could "invite" secular intuition through a meditation period sometime during the school day?

5. Visit a classroom in your community for a day. After careful observation, set down in essay form your estimate of which epistemologies and pedagogies were most in evidence as you observed. Then, referring to the discussion on the teacher in the present chapter, compare this analysis with your estimate of the role chosen by the teacher you observed.

6. At the end of every learning experience there is some necessity to measure the effect of the experience on the child, i.e., to give tests and assign grades. How would each of the pedagogies go about this? What would they be looking for? What would they wish to test?

FURTHER READING

Idealism

The Harvard Committee. *General Education in a Free Society*. Cambridge: Harvard University Press, 1948.
Although this famous "Harvard Report" was not written as a philosophical testament, it nevertheless reveals strong Idealist sentiments. And because it deals with educational realities rather than philosophical speculations as such (and, one might add, because it is a beautiful piece of writing), you should find it helpful in seeing how Idealists think about education in America. Chapter II, on the "Theory of General Education," and Chapter IV, on "Areas of General Education," are the two most relevant sections for study.

Horne, H. H. *The Teacher as Artist*. Boston: Houghton Mifflin Co., 1917.
There comes a time in any theory of education at which theoretical and scientific prescriptions cease to have effect and the teacher is on his own. At this point, teaching passes from a science into the realm of art. In this warm little volume the famed Idealist Horne has celebrated this passage by showing that the "teacher as artist" is the teacher as creator of the psychic envelope in which the immature expands to new boundaries of selfhood. Mark Hopkins could hardly have put it better.

Realism

Breed, F. S. "Education and the Realistic Outlook," Chapter III in *Philosophies of Education*, Forty-first Yearbook of the National Society for the Study of Education, ed. N. B. Henry, Part I. Chicago: the Society, 1942.
The contributions to the Forty-first Yearbook were, for the most part, dialectical arguments against Experimentalism. This essay, both sharply polemic and generous in tone, explains clearly and without complication where the Realist stands, what he thinks is important in the educational program, and how he goes about the business of teaching. As a "straight-from-the-shoulder" statement of position, this article has few equals.

Wild, John. "Education and Human Society: A Realistic View," Chapter II in *Modern Philosophies and Education*, Fifty-fourth Yearbook of the National Society for the Study of Education, ed. N. B. Henry, Part I. Chicago: the Society, 1955.
Wild is not primarily an "educational" philosopher but a so-called "pure" philosopher, in the academic sense of the term. As one of several such individuals contributing to this Yearbook, he has put together an interesting and readable treatise on how an "academic" Realist looks at education. Here he presents his thesis that "the school is the home of Pure Theory," from which he develops the Realist's position on "The Educational Process and Curriculum," "The School and Society," "The School and the Individual," and "The School and Religion."

Neo-Thomism

Brumbaugh, R. S., and Lawrence, N. M., Jr. "Aristotle's Philosophy of Education," *Educational Theory*, IX, No. 1 (January, 1959), 1–15.
In a splendid summation of Aristotelian thought on education, drawn from a number of places in his works, these two Yale professors have provided a magnificent service for students of educational philosophy. Here is set down in clear and unmistakable language the Aristotelian logical system of causes, the procedure by which the human being knows, and the patterns of pedagogy implicit in Aristotle's thinking. An illuminating presentation of the basis of the Lay position in Neo-Thomism.

Hutchins, Robert M. *The Higher Learning in America*. New Haven: Yale University Press, 1948.
Throughout Hutchins' writings there runs a strong and strident tone of disgust and despair concerning the deterioration of education in the United States. In this most popular of his many works, he speaks with expressive sharpness about higher education, the topic, incidentally, on which he has had the most to say. Here the Lay Neo-Thomist (or, more accurately, the Neo-Aristotelian) is in full flight and at his polemic best. No student's education is complete until he has read something of Hutchins'.

Redden, J. D., and Ryan, F. A. *A Catholic Philosophy of Education*, Revised Edition. Milwaukee: Bruce Publishing Co., 1956.
In Chapter V these two Fordham professors develop the Ecclesiastical Neo-Thomist position concerning "The Intellect and Its Function" (the nature of knowledge, truth, belief, and certitude); then they proceed to a systematic account of educational theory by way of a section entitled "The Intellect: Its Education" (the act of learning and the acquisition, preservation, and modification of knowledge).

Experimentalism

Bode, B. H. *How We Learn*. Boston: D. C. Heath and Company, 1940.
In this interpretative "companion-piece" to Dewey's *How We Think,* one of Dewey's most articulate commentators examines a variety of concepts of "Mind." He considers first the Classical Tradition, the Formal Discipline Theory, the Mind-Substance Theory, and Behaviorism, and then, in Chapter XIV, presents "A Pragmatic Theory of Mind," which is followed by Chapter XV on "Education from a Pragmatic Point of View." While there is much psychological material in these chapters, the point of view is essentially philosophical; as such, it expresses the Experimentalist position in learning theory.

Dewey, John. *Democracy and Education*. New York: The Macmillan Co., 1916.
Certainly the most authentic source to which one can turn on Experimentalism is John Dewey. Some of his "commentators" may have explained him better than he explained himself; but in this famous book, in Chapters XIII and XIV, dealing with "The Nature of Method" and "The Nature of Subject Matter," Professor Dewey sets down in clear and concise language how the Experi-

mentalist scientific epistemology takes on pedagogical "life" in the classroom. Later on, in the chapters on geography, history, and science in the course of study, he spells out more precisely his pedagogical ideas, including the "logical-psychological" problem in the arrangement and presentation of subject matter.

Existentialism

Kneller, George F. *Existentialism and Education.* New York: Philosophical Library, 1958.
Kneller has, in a sense, blazed a new trail into the relatively unexplored regions of Existentialism. Drawing upon Kierkegaard, Heidegger, and some American commentators, he has put together, necessarily by the process of deduction, a fascinating and thorough review of Existentialist educational theory. In his long, 110-page Chapter V, on "Existentialism and Education," he has sections on "The Knower and the Known," "The Teacher and the Student," and "The Educational Process," which are the ones you should pay particular attention to.

Ulich, Robert. *The Human Career.* New York: Harper and Bros., 1955.
Ulich writes, as we have mentioned in an earlier annotation, in the "twilight zone" somewhere between Idealism and Existentialism. This book is largely a testament of his personal faith, and it must be read in its entirety for maximum effect. Nevertheless, Ulich speaks from the platform of education, and his Chapter 2, on "Man as the Self-Transcending Being," Chapter 4, on "Thinking as Theoretical Self-Transcendence," and Chapter 10, on "Education as Cultural Self-Transcendence," are the most directly relevant to the study of the present chapter.

PART IV

Axiology:
What Is Good?

Axiology:

The Question of Value

THE SCHOOL AND VALUES

We pass at last into our third and final set of philosophic problems, those which collect about the pole of what men have come to call "value." Man is not only a "knowing" organism; he is also a "valuing" organism — he likes some things more than others, i.e., he has preferences. Man's valuing, moreover, is perhaps an even more decisive characteristic of his behavior than his knowing. This is the view, for instance, of many people who believe that the *quality* of a person's life, i.e., what he cherishes, what he truly wants out of life, is a better measure of his humanness than the "quantity" of his life, i.e., how *much* he knows, how widely read he is or how knowledgeable or learned he may be. We all know people who are highly educated and conversant on a great many topics but whose life values leave them, in our eyes, short of attainment of the humane and cultivated life.

So likewise do we judge whole societies and cultures. The true measure of a society, or even of a whole civilization, is better looked for in what the society basically *wants*, rather than in how sophisticated its technology may be or how efficient its political institutions are.

This is a particularly poignant reminder in our own time, for many

Westerners, especially Americans, having witnessed the extraordinary and astonishing advances of science — into the atom, into medicine, into outer space — are beginning to wonder what exactly all of this splendid knowledge is for. They contend that the meaning of our civilization lies not so much in atomic energy but in *what we do with it,* not so much in the control of disease but in *the use to which we put* the fuller and longer lives we thereby purchase, not so much in the conquest of the moon as such but in *what human ends* the conquest of the moon makes possible. And the meaning of our civilization — rather than its gadgetry, its glitter, or even its many wonderful and marvelous accomplishments — strikes us as the central question we must ponder if we are to be worthy of inclusion in the history textbooks of future ages.

What a civilization ultimately "means" is in part determined by what it *wants* to "mean" in the big record book of history. And since those "wantings" and preferences — as well as knowledge itself — will most certainly die out if not perpetuated generation by generation, we get a sense of the importance of education in enabling a civilization to express itself down through the ages.

It is the thesis here in Part IV that this sense of the importance of education is not a delusion. Educators are not only in the business of transmitting knowledge and developing trained intelligence. They are also in the business of recommending to the young a value system, a look at life, an "environment of preferences," which it is their concern as adults to make live anew in the experience of the young.

Whether or not it is the educator's privilege or duty to go beyond the perpetuation of a value system to the criticizing of it, or, further, to the encouragement of his students' criticizing the society's values, is the kind of question which is answered differently by different schools of axiological thought. This will be taken up in Chapter Nine. But for the moment we are concerned with the theory of value, what the problem really amounts to and what considerations enter into its study.

Value defined

First of all, the word *value* is a difficult and elusive symbol. It is, as the philosopher Charles Morris says, "one of the Great Words, and, like other such words ('science,' 'religion,' 'art,' 'morality,' 'philosophy'), its meaning is multiple and complex."[1]

One of the most troublesome complexities, for instance, lies in the location of a person's values. How do you tell what a person values — from what he says or from what he does? Morris points out that one type of values, called "conceived" values, represents what people believe

[1] *Varieties of Human Value* (Chicago: The University of Chicago Press, 1956), p. 9

in and openly profess but do not necessarily act on. The cigarette smoker may believe that he really ought to quit, but he doesn't "act accordingly." But his conceived, symbolic preference — and who can deny it him? — is for a state of nonsmoking. His continued smoking, however, reveals another kind of value, a behavioral or, as Morris labels it, an "operative" value. Our overt behavior, in this sense, is a clue to our values. The old epigram, "Your actions speak so loudly I cannot hear what you say," is a popular case of applying this distinction.

Put in a slightly different way, in the field of ethics, we can ask whether a person's intent — what he "means to do" — is a better measure of his values than his observable conduct and the practical effect of that conduct. We sometimes excuse a person for an act if he can establish that he "did not mean to do it." There is a legal graduation of penalty, for instance, which distinguishes among "premeditated," "unpremeditated," and "unintentional" murder. A Catholic priest in confession can excuse sinful acts if the suppliant can prove that his intentions were good. We sometimes say, in other connections, that such-and-such a person is mean, or greedy, or rude, but that "his heart is in the right place" or "he means well." What this suggests is that what he *does* is not so reliable a measure of his values as what he believes "down deep inside."

In the field of aesthetics we must ask whether a person's tastes are revealed better by what he says he likes in the way of art, music, poetry, literature, cuisine or by what he actually surrounds himself with day by day, i.e., the kinds of clothes he wears, the automobiles he buys, what he orders for lunch, the way he decorates the interior of his home, the records in his hi-fi cabinet, the magazines and books an unannounced guest might find on the coffee table.

At the outset, then, we are confronted with a basic difficulty, and it has serious educational implications, because when we get to the education of the young we must have in hand a reasonably well-based criterion for determining when a youngster has and when he has not come to accept a certain value judgment.

But, for all its importance, this may be said to be only a "tactical" difficulty compared to a still more serious and "strategic" matter, namely, not what we prefer or what we *say* we prefer, but what we *ought* to prefer. This is the familiar distinction between the preferred and the preferable, between the desired and the desirable. For all men, whatever their tastes, do desire and prefer things — either in their overt behavior or by symbolic profession — but the truly axiological question is whether their desires are really desirable, i.e., whether they ought to desire what they in fact do desire. Put in blunt and somewhat cryptic shorthand, we may ask: What *ought* men to ought?

Education: the development of preferences

This may be said to be the ultimate question in axiology, and it has a central place in educational theory by virtue of the peculiar function of the educator, the function of serving as the instrumentality of a social system which means to perpetuate itself through its young. For whether the educator is skillful or not in teaching values, whether he uses the "operative" or the "conceived" criterion for judging the growth of his students, his position requires him to defend the values which make up the subject matter of his teaching as representing those values that all men — and therefore his students — *ought* to value. Furthermore — and this is in a way more crucial — he must be able to defend the values which make up the subject matter of *his own life,* which is, after all, on display before the young every day and which the teacher, because of his position, implicitly recommends to his students to imitate. No matter how he tries, a teacher cannot "turn off" his moral self during his teaching hours. Whether he likes it or not, he is on constant view as the paradigmatic model of a mature adult.

This predicament is, in a sense, the microcosmic version of the larger problem facing the school, the problem of bearing ultimate responsibility for what may be generally called the "moral integrity" (*integrity* in its connotations both of *integratedness* and firm *commitment*) of the social system. We attempted to characterize the nature of this responsibility at the outset of the book. In Chapter One (see pages 18–19) we saw that one of the primary reasons for studying educational theory is what Childs has called "the moral nature" of the educational enterprise. (The term *moral* here is considered in its largest meaning of *making value judgments.*) When a society becomes "conscious of its own experience," says Childs, it reveals a concern for the management of that experience toward its own future. Hence, says Childs, "the organization of a system of schools signifies the deliberate attempt of a human group to control the pattern of its own evolution."[2]

The importance of value theory for education is most readily seen, then, in this "moral" characteristic of education; if, as Childs intimates, we are deliberately attempting to make the future "come out" the way we want it to — either for an individual or for a whole society — then we are engaging in an unmistakably value-oriented enterprise. And since the school is the "caretaker" of the future by virtue of its contact with the young, the heart of the moral enterprise of society in recreating its moral self resides in the school.

Educators, as a rule, do not wax overly self-conscious or reflective about

2 John L. Childs, *Education and Morals* (New York: Appleton-Century-Crofts, Inc., 1950), p. 6.

this phase of their work. But they are engaged in it constantly. When we teach boys and girls to take turns on the swings on the playground, when we encourage cooperation with their classmates in organized study projects, when we ask for quiet in the library so that others can study, when we punish cheating on examinations, when we challenge the quality of hillbilly music, when we pipe Toscanini by Muzak into the lunchroom, we are making individually minuscule but collectively significant selections of what we want boys and girls to prefer. And such preferences, from the ridiculous to the sublime in life, represent what kinds of citizens they will become in the days ahead.

Education and ultimate values

There is another and more sophisticated point of contact, however, between the study of axiology and the education of the young; it has to do with the values we exhibit and proclaim not just for our own future but for the future of all mankind. Childs' theory of "the moral nature" of education is principally a social or culturological concept; that is, it relates to the choices and decisions that societies and civilizations make for their own perpetuation. While not selfish in spirit, these choices are nevertheless to some extent parochial and limited in scope; while such choices — like freedom and democracy and private property — may possibly be recommended for adoption by men everywhere, they are still expressions of a given culture, of a particular society living in a given time and occupying a given geographical space. Professor Childs himself reminds us that, as far as he is concerned, all moral decisions must be understood in this socio-cultural context.

But there is another, wider sphere in which it may be said that men value; they value not just for this or that civilization, not just for "the free world" or "the Communist world," not just for "the West" or "the East." They value for Man, and when we spell it with a capital *M* we are designating here a level of valuing which refers to what we think we ultimately are as the only valuing inhabitants of this spinning planet. Experimentalism, from which Childs speaks, does not customarily have much to say about this mode of valuing, leaving such comment to the other four philosophies we have taken up. There is nevertheless a way in which we can employ a famous remark by a leading Experimentalist, John Dewey, to get a grip on the meaning of this kind of valuing.

To lead up to it, we are reminded that when we deal with valuing at this level — what we might speak of as the "metaphysical" rather than the "culturological" level — we are not asking the question, "What values for our time?" We are not asking, "What can we make of twentieth-century man?" We are asking, rather, "What can we make of Man?"

Seen in this light, the moral dimension of human preference is practically without limit, and in asking what we can make of Man we are, in a manner of speaking, asking what programs of reform and enlightenment can be wrought upon mankind to achieve the true "human spirit." And this, at bottom, is an educational question; it is to ask what kinds of educational programs can be invented to bring men to a higher expression of themselves.

And so, in the brilliance of his insight, John Dewey uttered one of his most famous and oft-quoted dicta: "If we are willing to conceive education as the process of forming fundamental dispositions, intellectual and emotional, toward nature and fellow men, philosophy may even be defined *as the general theory of education.*"[3]

At long last, then, after having traversed the fields of ontology and epistemology, we come in axiology to an ultimate reunion between philosophy, as the study of the universe and Man's place in it, and education, as the study of men and how they grow to fuller stature in their world. For philosophy and education are really two versions of the same activity. They both ask, "What can we make of man?" Philosophy asks it in macrocosm — "Man." Education asks it in microcosm — "men." So philosophy is indeed "the generalized theory of education." And conversely, education may be termed "the specialized practice of philosophy"; it is, one might say, the "testing laboratory" for our philosophies. For if some value, some program, some life choice is seen to be good for *Man,* it must somehow recommend itself ultimately as good for individual *men.* Philosophy, most especially the study of axiology, examines, analyzes, and suggests values; education "tries them out" on men.

The branches of value

Having said these things, we can now set down a few ground rules concerning the discussion of the kinds of problems that are met in the study of axiology. As we have already pointed out, the field of value theory called axiology is customarily divided into the two branches of ethics and aesthetics. Ethics is that sphere of concern which deals with conduct, with what men do; aesthetics is that sphere which deals with what men consider beautiful, with what they enjoy.

Terminologically, we have in the preceding discussion permitted ourselves the license of using the word *moral* to cover all valuing, including, by implication, aesthetics. In the passages which follow, however, we shall employ the term *moral* to refer principally to ethical considerations. This is likewise true of such words as *right, wrong, good, bad* — words

[3] *Democracy and Education* (New York: The Macmillan Co., 1916), p. 383. (Author's italics.)

which also may have a wider sphere of application. In aesthetics these words shall be avoided as much as possible. Instead, we shall have need of such terms as *lovely, beautiful, enjoyable,* etc.

This admittedly arbitrary distinction is made only to assist in the understanding of the value problem. It is conceivable, indeed rather common, to speak of "good" art or "good" music (although we never hear of a "good" sunset or a "good" flower garden) but this is merely a linguistic convention; certainly *good* in this context does not refer to moral "rightness." So we shall reserve *good* for ethical matters. Conversely, it is sometimes fitting, for the sake of emphasis or hyperbole, to speak of a "truly beautiful act," or a "really beautiful person" (referring to something other than an individual's physical features). But this is just the point; by noting such exceptions we can see the warrant for making the distinction in language because there is a different mode of value being explored in the two cases.

ETHICS: THE QUESTION OF CONDUCT

Morals

At the base of all ethical considerations lies the question of morals. The term itself stems from the Latin *mos, moris,* meaning custom or manner. Our pluralized *mores* is the more familiar term. But while *morals* and *mores* stem from the same root they differ in meaning in a rather decisive way. The former term refers to a reflectively considered custom or procedure, whereas the latter term denotes some kind of blind or unthinking habit we have fallen into. One might say that we begin with mores but that when mores become reflective and deliberately singled out as interests they become morals. Thus, when through cultural circumstance we fall into the practice of "togetherness" and "organization" in modern life, it may be designated a reflection of American mores. But when "togetherness" and "organization" are singled out for special comment, either pro or con, we may speak of them as having attained some kind of moral stature.

Also involved in the term *morals* is the concern for decisions in conduct. As pointed out previously, ethics and morals refer to the direction of conduct, to the guidance of the human act. The central question in all ethical situations is: What should I do?[4] The question may include

[4] Dewey has pointed out somewhere that the traditional moral systems, e.g., the Decalogue, center more on the negative "What *shouldn't* I do?" This "accentuation on the negative" in most inherited moral codes has had the unfortunate effect not only of deflecting men's interests from more positive concerns but also, more seriously, of discouraging people from considering moral problems in general for fear that the resolution of such problems would issue in yet another negative injunction. It was in

a prior question or two: What *may* I do? — i.e., What are the possibilities open? — or What *can* I do? — i.e., How many alternative courses of action am I capable of? But, aside from these special, circumstantial questions, the moral issue is resolved in deciding, either symbolically or actually, on some course of action.[5]

It is in this sense that we speak of honesty, adultery, murder, forgery, embezzlement, charity, loyalty, fairness, justice, or slavery as *moral* problems; they have to do, that is, with the conduct of men. There is a qualification to this definition, however, to be found in segments of religious doctrine; for instance, Christian moral theory holds that a man's *thoughts* are quite as morally culpable as his *deeds*. Thus, for example, "he who looks in lust upon a woman" has, in Jesus' sense of the term, committed adultery.

In secular life this interpretation generally does not hold: It is only the *conduct* of men that becomes subject to the moral criterion. Insofar as we codify our morals in our law, it may be said that the distinction between thought and deed is all the more definitive; for a man cannot be convicted for his thoughts or his opinions, but only for his overt acts and deeds. Of course, morality extends considerably beyond civil law, but generally speaking modern man thinks of morals in terms of conduct.

The good and the Good

To find morals in conduct, however, does not tell us much about them. Given the range of conduct in which men operate, and given the particular situations in which the proper course of action appears problematic — which is what we may call moral situations — how is one to go about the discovery or determination of that specific course of action considered right and good? At the base of disputes in moral theory is the issue of *absolutes*. Are there, to get right to the point, patterns of human conduct which are always right or always wrong, considered everywhere and throughout all time as morally good or bad, without regard to circumstance?

This question seems reasonable enough. And it seems worth our while to investigate, especially because it has potential educational significance.

---

this spirit that Alexander Woollcott uttered his famous lament: "Everything I like to do is either illegal, immoral, or fattening!"

5 The question "What *must* I do?" is sometimes suggested as another possibility here. To some moralists this is a forbidden question, because it removes the element of choice and, therefore, the element of "should-ness" or "ought-ness." An individual cannot, they say, really *choose* something which is forced on him. Other moralists, however, insist that morals are those patterns of action which men must follow if they would be men; in this sense they are "forced" on us as ways of acting. This problem will have fuller treatment in Chapter Nine.

For if there are absolute goods — what we here designate with the upper-case G in "Good" — then the educator's function, among other things, is to locate them and teach them in the school. The problem is almost identical to that of Absolute Truth discussed in Part III. And you should be able to detect by now that the issue of axiological absolutes is very much tied up, as is the issue of epistemological absolutes, with the ontological questions of a static, objective, existential reality as opposed to a dynamic, evolutionary, "becoming" reality. Many of these inter-locking considerations you should now be able to supply yourself out of your study of the previous sections of this book. But in any case we shall have to review them briefly at the outset of Chapter Nine.

The question of absolutes, on its surface, seems reasonable, we say, because there are many human behavior patterns which are quite gen-erally and universally held to be good — such things as charity and suc-cor to others, for instance — and other behaviors which are quite gener-ally condemned — injury and murder, for instance. Common sense would suggest that such things as these would surely classify as unqualifiedly "good" or "bad." But for a moral value to achieve the status of an abso-lute it must be shown to hold in *every* situation confrontable by men. If there is but one qualification or one instance to which it is relevant but inapplicable, then it cannot be an absolute principle. It is this rather stringent requirement which has disallowed so many candidates for ab-solute status; even the principle "Thou shalt not kill," perhaps one of the strongest candidates for absolute status, is seen by many moralists as a circumstantially qualifiable principle. What this means is that in the circumstance of defending oneself, for instance, one may justifiably take the view that "Thou shalt not kill" does not hold.

The problem is considerably more complex than this, of course, but this is the type of axiological problem that arises in considering "the good" and "the Good." Educationally speaking, there is a world of differ-ence between these views; for if, as we have intimated, there is no abso-lute company of *Goods*, but only a circumstantial company of *goods* — in specific situations or, at most, in certain classes or types of situations — then the training of the child in making moral judgments must take on a whole new texture and direction in the school.

Whatever else happens, the moral training of the young will become considerably more difficult under this view. Teaching prescribed (liter-ally "pre-scribed," written down beforehand) moral rules to youngsters, notwithstanding the difficulty of getting rules to flow into behavior, is far simpler than teaching youngsters how to develop their moral dispositions as they go along from one new situation to another. But the relative difficulty or simplicity of a procedure is not in itself a measure of its soundness, so we must take into consideration other problems as well.

Means and ends

One of these other problems is the old stand-by of means and ends. It is most commonly phrased by the question: "Does the end justify the means?" Is the theft of a loaf of bread to feed a hungry child a defensible act? Is a man morally justified in exploiting other people in order to make a fortune which he then gives to these people? Are modern governments morally justified in contaminating the atmosphere with their bombs and thereby taking a few thousand lives in the name of saving us from an all-out war which would take several million lives?

Are the Marxists morally justified in contending that a "dictatorship of the proletariat" is the only suitable means to achieve the end of a Utopian "classless society," or is it more morally sound to insist that democratic ends can be achieved *only* by democratic means? This question has a rather ironic application to education, incidentally, by way of considering the teacher's "political" function in the classroom. If democracy is so precious a value in our land, is the teacher ever justified in indoctrinating democratic principles in his students? Is he, in short, permitted to use undemocratic measures to implant democratic dispositions in his students?

To many educational theorists this question makes no sense because, aside from moral considerations, a youngster learns his attitudes by the *way* he is taught rather than by *what* he is taught. But aside from this pedagogical concern, which is after all a determinable matter of fact, what can one say about the moral prerogative of a teacher in "stacking the cards" of the classroom procedure and the classroom discussion so that the child will come to favor American ideals and disavow Fascist, Communist, or Socialist ideals? By violating his values in his procedure the teacher would be compromising his moral position; but by utilizing illicit values in directing his procedure he might be able to show that wholly licit and noble results were attained. Is he morally right or wrong?

This is the kind of moral conundrum which most people try desperately to avoid, partly because competing values are here seen to be in conflict, partly because one of the competitors (end) has traditionally been thought to outrank the other (means) in importance (thus complicating an already complex problem), but mostly because there is no real answer to the puzzle. We moderns are less sure than the Ancients that ends outrank means; generally speaking, it could be argued that we therefore do not support the view that "the end justifies the means." But there are few Americans who did not embrace this principle when they realized in 1941 that the defeat of Nazi Germany was about to require the slaughter of millions of people and in August of 1945 that the final defeat of Japan was worth the price of almost 100,000 human beings exterminated in a microsecond at Hiroshima.

When things are going right we feel we can afford to strike a pose of insouciance about this whole matter of means and ends. But when the chips are down we reveal by our behavior where our genuine sentiments lie — which is, by the way, to express a bias in favor of "operative" as against "conceived" values as being the more authentic (see pages 220–221).

Morality and ethical relativity

Another problem, of somewhat more recent vintage in moral theory, has to do with the variability of values — both operative and conceived — throughout the world and down through history. Men have long been aware, of course, that they believed in and acted upon different principles. What they have not generally known until the invention of scientific, "inter-cultural" anthropology is that these differences of belief and practice do not seem to be judicable by any higher standard.

When men disagree on matters of law, there are courts to which they can go. But when men disagree as to the Rule of Law in the affairs of men, that is, when they disagree on whether to be lawful or not, then there is no arbiter of reference except open force. If baseball players disagree on the rulings of the umpire, they can protest. But if they disagree on the rules from which the umpire draws his rulings, then there can be no game whatsoever.

As scientific and cultural anthropologists have roamed the earth within the last fifty to seventy-five years, their summary findings have seemed to indicate that the values that men live by are so different and ultimately so arbitrary that the only sensible conclusion is that, depending on circumstance and history, men simply believe in different values, and that is that. What is more, each culture defends its ways as vigorously and aggressively as any other, usually proclaiming some divine sanction for this or that practice, which sometimes may seem to others to be the crudest and most uncivilized of habits. No amount of argument seems to have any effect; men go on believing in the same things and acting on their beliefs, sure and certain that they alone have the truth. And this trait is just as evident among Western civilized men as it is among the Trobrianders or the Navajo Indians.[6]

One of the liveliest and most succinct discussions of this point is found in W. T. Stace's *The Concept of Morals*. Although Stace will have none of ethical relativity himself, he states its central idea thus:

[6] For a typical treatment of this problem, see Ruth Benedict, *Patterns of Culture* (Boston: Houghton Mifflin Co., 1934).

. . . the whole notion of *progress* is a sheer delusion. Progress means an advance from lower to higher, from worse to better. But on the basis of ethical relativity it has no meaning to say that the standards of this age are better (or worse) than those of a previous age. For there is no common standard by which both can be measured. Thus it is nonsense to say that the morality of the New Testament is higher than that of the Old. And Jesus Christ, if he imagined that he was introducing into the world a higher ethical standard than existed before his time, was merely deluded.

. . . on this view Jesus Christ can only have been led to the quite absurd belief that his ethical precepts were better than those of Moses by his personal vanity. If only he had read Westermarck and Dewey he would have understood that, so long as people continued to believe in the doctrine of an eye for an eye and a tooth for a tooth, that doctrine was morally *right*; and that there could not be any point whatever in trying to make them believe in his new-fangled theory of loving one's enemies. True, the new morality would *become* right as soon as people came to believe in it, for it would then be the accepted standard. And what people think right is right. But then, if only Jesus Christ and persons with similar ideas had kept these ideas to themselves, people might have gone on believing that the old morality was right. And in that case it would have been right, and would have remained so till this day. And that would have saved a lot of useless trouble. For the change which Jesus Christ actually brought about was merely a change from one set of moral ideas to another.[7]

In this admittedly broad language, Stace thus puts the thesis of the ethical relativist, albeit somewhat sarcastically. But this relativism is not merely nihilistic in spirit, for out of it have come numerous attempts to catalogue human values and to reduce them by combination to a few major value-complexes. This work, the province of the social psychologists, has gone on apace as the anthropologists have brought in their data. Charles W. Morris in his book *Paths of Life* developed the thesis that there are three distinguishable types of value systems: (1) the Dionysian, in which the primary principle is self-indulgence, (2) the Promethean, in which the controlling value is to manipulate the world, and (3) the Buddhistic, in which the moving idea is the regulation of the self. By a kind of terminological shorthand, Morris felt that these three positions could be described respectively as ones of (1) dependence, (2) dominance, and (3) detachment. Moreover, there seemed to be some congruity, he thought, between these "paths of life" and the three temperament categories identified and studied by the psychologist W. H. Sheldon, namely, viscerotonia, somatotonia, and cerebrotonia.[8]

7 *The Concept of Morals* (New York: The Macmillan Co., 1937), pp. 48–49.
8 Charles W. Morris, *Paths of Life* (New York: Braziller, 1956), p. 28.

In addition to these attempts at value classification are many other arrangements. Karen Horney, for instance, in her book *Our Inner Conflicts* seeks to classify all temperaments within a triad of "tendencies": "toward," "against," and "away from" people. All value judgments, she thinks, collect about one or another of these "poles of choice." David Riesman in his astute and provocative *The Lonely Crowd* suggests still another set of character categories, with a certain historical twist: "tradition-directed," "inner-directed," and "other-directed." We are today in America, says Riesman, moving into the last of these three stages in almost every area of life.

There are, of course, many provocative insights in all of these attempts at cataloguing and "polarizing" human values. What they all seem to say is that, while value constellations may be reduceable to three or some other convenient number of categories, there persists a plurality of value positions men can take and, more important, that there appears to be no method by which we can adjudicate among value positions to find which is best or axiologically of highest rank.

If we are dealing with genuinely primary values, and these studies are of that sort, then we must recognize that when we reach this level of discourse we are traveling in unmarked territory; there are no ultimate reference points on which we may train our "moral sextants" to find out where we are and where we ought to be headed. As an educational case in point, it would not appear morally sound for a teacher to rebuke a child for being too "Buddhistic," i.e., too contemplative and withdrawn. Likewise, a teacher should not reward a child for being gregarious and outgoing in his manifestations of cooperation, helpfulness, and getting along well with others. For who is to stand in judgment and say that the Buddhistic, "away-from-others" individual is not to be preferred to the Promethean or Dionysian, "toward-others" creature so prevalent in America today? The American people, to be sure, eschew "Buddhistic" tendencies; but there is no final method by which we can say we are morally right in doing so.

On the other hand, a teacher is not a genuine guide to the young unless he assists his students in developing a sense of values. This means that choices must be made somehow, somewhere. And the classroom is the place where the teacher has some jurisdiction over the quality of such choices. Hence it is in the classroom that the teacher must somehow make a selection among competing life patterns and proceed to recommend a given pattern for adoption by his students. The fact that, beyond social convention, there is no Supreme Court of moral judgment is the very crux of the moral predicament in which the educator finds himself.

Morality and religion

Of course, many say that there *is* a Supreme Court of morals: God. If we follow his way, our moral teaching will be anchored to something sure and right. In this view there is an Author of morals, to whose judgments we may refer.

It is common knowledge, of course, that one of the predominant concerns of organized religions has been this area of ethics. Perhaps more than any other single area of human life, that of ethics and right conduct has been taken over — almost monopolized — by organized religions as their special province of discourse and prescription. What theologians have seemed to say, thus, is that there is some inevitable and necessary connection between religious commitment and right conduct. So long as this connection is held to exist, then moral training cannot be effective outside the context of religion.

You may recognize that this theological position on morals bears close relationship to the absolutistic position on morals spoken of in the section above on "The good and the Good." If there is a God to prescribe our morals for us, certainly his prescriptions must be perfect, hence definable as *The* Good.[9] In this line of thought, then, the educator's task is to locate God's Good and teach the young to follow it.

With the rise of the scientific and objective study of human behavior and value, described briefly in the preceding section, there has developed an attendant skepticism of the notion of Absolute Good. If men value so many different things, and if competing conceptions of how life should be lived appear to be injudicable and hence impossible of collection under a single rubric of value, then how can we say that there is a single Good to which all other goods eventually refer? Especially is this question asked when theologians themselves differ on the nature of this Good, and when competing religions throughout the world prescribe variant programs for living the Good Life. Under these circumstances, the determination of the Good, let alone its successful propagation among men, is put in question.

At this stage the question may be raised whether this marriage between morals and religion is really necessary. Is there an ineluctable bond between a man's views on conduct and his views on the supernatural? Increasingly, the position has been taken that there is not. While the two deal with generally the same subject matter, and while they have historically been found together, there is no necessary connection, this position

---

[9] It is important to note that the reverse connection does not necessarily follow; that is, the concept of "God" implies capital-G "Good," but the concept of an Absolute Good in the universe does not require a God to author or dispense it. Good could exist just as another existential feature of the cosmos, along with Mind, Cause, and Essence.

holds, between the moral question, "What should I do?" and the religious question, "Who is God?"

Hence, the question of right and wrong has been at least partially removed from religious jurisdictions, and secular methods have come to be applied to moral questions. It is not an altogether recent development, either. An age-old maxim like "Honesty is the best policy," while stemming from a Puritan tradition, is nevertheless wholly secular; in fact, it is downright pragmatic: Honesty is recommended not because it is morally right but because it is "the best policy," i.e., it works out.

In summary, then, it is becoming increasingly apparent that some moral questions — perhaps all, says the Experimentalist — can be resolved or at least examined outside the reach of supernatural considerations. *Moral* and *spiritual* values, it is held, are not the same thing, and therefore need not be treated together in the school; there can perhaps be, as some say, a "division of labor," in which the secular school takes charge of the *moral* values and the various organized religions the *spiritual* values. The practice of "released time" (releasing children to their churches an hour each week for religious instruction) is, in effect, founded on this principle.

This whole question, as you can readily see, is at the center of a rather widespread controversy in American education; for there are many of the "inseparability-of-moral-and-spiritual-values" position who believe that the modern American school, so splendidly boastful of its secular character, has thrown out not only God but good as well. That is, even if morals can be taught without religion, the secular American school is simply not doing it. They remain to be convinced of the position that the two are not indissolubly linked. The secularists, on the other hand, remain firm in their view of the ultimately secular nature of moral judgments. We shall wish to examine both of these competing positions in Chapter Nine.

There are, admittedly, many other features of the "problem of conduct" which might be discussed here. What, for instance, is the role of the "will" in moral judgment? This, in turn, raises the issue of the will itself, whether it is genuinely free or whether all of our behavior is in some sense "caused." If human behavior is thought of as a "natural phenomenon" and if it is stipulated that "all natural phenomena are caused," then there seems no escape from the view that our moral judgments are quite as circumstantially dictated as water running downhill. On the other hand, we all have an inner sense of freedom of action; we think we can arbitrarily and "causelessly" make things happen. Hence, even if we are not existentially free, we live our lives *as if* we were. And, when you come right down to it, what is the practical difference between these two?

Other matters as well might concern us. The problem of morals is virtually endless in scope. But the function of this chapter is not so much to analyze questions as merely to raise them as a prelude to the systematic treatment of the value question in Chapter Nine. We must pass on, then, to a brief look at the question of aesthetics before taking up the separate axiological theories.

AESTHETICS: THE QUESTION OF ENJOYMENT

Taste

At the very outset it must be stated that the problem of aesthetics is here to be put in a slightly unorthodox way. The word *enjoyment,* rather than the more familiar and orthodox word *beauty,* has been designated as the theme for this discussion, because of its more universal connotations.

There is unfortunately a kind of snobbish cultism often surrounding discussions of aesthetics which tends to take art away from the ordinary citizen. But anyone who finds beauty in his life, who wants to increase its presence in his experience, eventually wants to develop some kind of judgment for what he likes (aesthetics) as well as for what he knows (epistemology) and for what he believes to be right conduct (ethics). That is to say, aesthetics is just as human and prosaically oriented an area of discourse as any other in philosophy. It treats of how ordinary human beings respond to their world. And since the word *enjoyment* seems to provide more ready access to this idea than the somewhat more specialized word *beauty,* we choose to use it here.

This is by way of introducing our topic by saying that, while ethics centers about the question "What should I *do*?," aesthetics centers about the question "What should I *like*?" In formal language, we usually speak of this as "taste." What tastes does a person exhibit by his aesthetic selections throughout every day — what does he appreciate and favor in what he sees, hears, touches, smells, and tastes? What, in short, does he *like* in life? This is, to begin with, the widest and most generalized meaning of aesthetics as it is to be discussed here.

The point here made should not signify that all things that men like — from peanut brittle to Gauguin — must be taken up and examined; it is only to say that all things that men like represent the ground for our discussion. And since some things *ought to be liked* more than others — just as in ethics some conduct *ought to be valued* over other conduct — we are confronted with the aesthetic problem of singling out those things that men *ought* to like from the welter of things that they indeed *do* like. If a man actually likes what he ought to like, we say he has taste.

The nature of aesthetic experience

Taste, however, is a term which refers to the behavior of the individual as he confronts alternative candidates for his enjoyment and appreciation. It is by what an individual *selects* from the world of beauty that we measure his taste. What he surrounds himself with, what he chooses to experience, what he actively seeks out to enjoy, is the measure by which we judge his taste. The question now before us is the nature and quality of these experiences of enjoyment which are selected and therefore become the attributes of taste. What are these experiences like? What features do they exhibit? What can we say of all of them, taken together?

In order to deal with these questions, we are here using the phrase "aesthetic experience" to refer to the "episode of enjoyment." Something takes place in aesthetics, something occurs in the individual when he says, "That is beautiful." It is the business of aesthetics to get some kind of idea of what that "something" is and to make it occur increasingly in the lives of men. And, obviously, the educator's function is to make it occur, at increasingly sophisticated levels of response, in the lives of the young.

To explain our concern with "aesthetic experience," it is necessary to note that the primary problem in aesthetics has to do with what may be referred to as the *artificial production of beauty,* i.e., music, painting, dance, sculpture, architecture, poetry, literature. These are the standard and customary "arts." We know, of course, that there is beauty in nature and that response to it is possibly as variable as is the response to man-made products of art. We shall wish to concern ourselves below with this natural mode of aesthetic experience. But for the moment our concern is with the artificial, i.e., man-made, stimulants to aesthetic response.

One of the things which all the arts have in common is their appeal to the senses. Of man's five senses, of course, sight and hearing predominate in the arts. But the question is legitimately raised whether the other three senses may be said to be capable of what is here designated as aesthetic experience. Is the enjoyment of a fine perfume an aesthetic experience? Is the tasting of exotic wine and delicate cuisine an aesthetic experience? And as far as the sense of touch — in some ways the bluntest of our senses — is concerned, is it possible to include a hot bath, or a massage, or a roller coaster ride, or the tactical sensation of a fine stroke at golf or tennis within the category of aesthetics?

And, more important, is the artificial production of these experiences an artistic activity? Is the perfume-maker an artist? Is the chef who prepares fine food for the gourmet engaged in aesthetic production? Is the masseur or the roller coaster engineer classifiable as an artist? None of these questions has an easy answer, for the line between a truly aesthetic experience and a merely sensory experience has never been accurately drawn.

The confusion becomes perhaps even more troublesome in the other branch of aesthetics, i.e., the nonartificial or natural realm of enjoyment. We are all familiar, of course, with the intense response we have to certain sensory experiences in nature — to a striking sunset, to a special bit of scenery, to the sound of a bird on wing, to the smell of flowers in the field, to the taste of wild blackberries, to the feel of warm sunshine or cool water. And again, concerning our sense of touch, where are we to place the ultimate in tactical sensations — sexual play and intercourse? Is sexual orgasm an aesthetic experience?

Of course, sex is so confounded with other, extra-aesthetic factors that it is a wonder we can even raise the question at all. Perhaps by its very intensity it has ruled itself out of aesthetic consideration. Man has feared the sexual drive so much he could not value it, he has been so terrified at its power that he has hardly been willing to admit that he enjoys it. Even to this day, the female of the human species, at least in American culture, is not permitted publicly to declare that she likes sex. But the fact of its sensual ultimacy in our lives cannot be denied; no other experience can come close to it. It was not with facetiousness that Hemingway had his characters declare that "the earth moved." Certainly no sunset has been capable of this.

What we mean to suggest here is that every axiological theory must somehow stake out the areas of discussion before proceeding with value analysis. Since aesthetics is the study of the "beauty dimension" of life, we must not arbitrarily restrict the *enjoyment* of beauty (here employed as the central principle) to the standard categories of traditional upper-class taste, unless of course we are willing to rationalize such a restriction with some axiological principle. That is to say, to use a few examples, that opera, symphonic music, ballet, poetry, painting, and sculpture are not the only things of beauty in the world. To consider them so is to render aesthetics a recondite, genteel subject matter accessible only to the "long-hairs," the bearded Bohemians, and the moneyed classes. It is also to remove art from the experienced world. As Ralph Barton Perry has so pithily put it:

> It is a common and not unjustified complaint that the esthetic interest which was once associated with every form of utility and with the common experience of common men, has through the obsession of its devotees lost its proper place in life, at a loss both to itself and to the life from which it has been abstracted. Celibacy, here as elsewhere, may purchase concentration at the cost of barrenness.[10]

[10] *Realms of Value* (Cambridge: Harvard University Press, 1954), p. 325.

On the contrary, we must affirm that aesthetics is just as much Everyman's subject matter as ethics or politics. Especially is this admonition aptly pointed at educators, for if they claim to be in the business of educating *all* American youth, then they must not turn away from aesthetics merely because historically we have allowed it to become the private plaything of aesthetes.

Art for art's sake

This brings us to a couple of seemingly incompatible dimensions of aesthetic experience, namely art (its production and enjoyment) for its own sake versus art as a means to other experiences. This may, at first sound, seem to be a rather needless puzzle to get into. And perhaps it is; but it nevertheless stands at the bottom of much educational controversy today, and an understanding of it may help our thinking.

In the section on epistemology we saw that some philosophies hold truth to be independent of men and their affairs and that men come to know it for its own sake, i.e., simply because they want to know. In contrast, other philosophies, most notably Experimentalism, hold that truth always comes to be known in a circumstance of *use;* that is, we learn things when we need to learn them and, in this sense, truth is never to be considered or sought after solely for its own sake but always in terms of its function or use in some affair of life.

In the aesthetic sphere there is the same sort of dispute. Some philosophies consider values to be existentially equivalent to knowledge and truth, namely, independent of men, an *a priori* feature of the cosmos, and embedded and woven into the very texture of reality. Men come to have values when they discern them in the world and adopt them; most particularly for our case here, men come to have certain appreciations and likings because those preferences are somehow authenticated and confirmed in the real world. The paintings on the ceiling of the Sistine Chapel seem timeless in their appeal because they evoke a universal sense of the cosmos in the beholder. Handel's *Messiah* is treasured because Handel testified that, as he was composing it, he saw "the Great God Himself," and his listeners seem to see him too.

From this point of view, art must be considered an end in itself; a career in art is to be pursued for the intrinsic enjoyment there may be in simply painting pictures or arranging sounds or making graceful movements. There is no motive to sell anything or to improve the beholder's morale or state of mind; in fact, in the purest sense, there is not even the motive to arouse him. There is only the motive to create beauty and communicate it, whether others agree or not. The art collector, the connoisseur, the critic — as consumers, rather than producers, of art — engage in their activities not for gain or prestige or fame but for the intrinsic joy of engaging in aesthetic experience for its own sake.

The art that is produced or consumed, according to this view, is not to be *used* for anything else, not to be the means to any end or object outside itself. This is what we mean when we speak of some arts as being *fine* arts. They stand alone, unattached to any other interest. To refer to an earlier comment concerning the catholicity of art, this view would hold that the chef, the dress designer, or the architect can never achieve membership in the fraternity of the fine arts because they work their art on a basically useful object. The *fine* arts are, in an absolute sense, unnecessary; that is, they are not indispensable to the survival of man. But food, clothing, and shelter most certainly are. And any art worked upon such materials is "contaminated" by the principle of *use;* hence, not *fine.*

In this tradition, then, the subject matter of aesthetics can be narrowed to consider just the fine arts. Of course, there are also aesthetic considerations in the so-called practical or applied arts. There is balance to be achieved in automobile design or in the façade of a skyscraper, there is a certain "poetry of motion" in athletes — baseball players, basketball players, pole vaulters — as they go about their games, there is a grace of line achieved by Parisian clothing designers. But in none of these cases is there a pure and solitary concern for the aesthetic in and for itself. Therefore, these arts, while important, are nevertheless secondary. Whatever aesthetic interests they provoke must be judged by criteria established in the primary or fine arts.

In terms of education the relevance of this view is obvious. A school orchestra will be held more valuable to the musical interests of the students than a school band because the latter is, in at least some measure, a means to a nonmusical end, i.e., the emotional arousal of fans at a football game. Courses in the fine arts — sketching or water-color painting, say — will be held in higher place than projects in landscaping the school grounds, because the latter is tied to the prudential and practical interests of the physical school plant. In these and many other ways, as we shall point out in Chapter Ten, the *"Ars gratia artis"* position bears upon educational policy.

Art for our sake

There is an alternate position, however, which may be intimated from the previous discussion. It considers art, in its most general connotation, to be an instrument for the elevation and improvement of human experience. To speak of art as an "instrument" is to some to demean art to a lower position, but this is claimed to be merely a vestigial residue of the classical position developed in the preceding section.

For if art is to be considered for its own sake alone, then there is a temptation to fence it off from the ordinary concerns of life. It is to imply that art is to be found only in art galleries and that artistic discussions cannot be legitimate in the things men do every day — in planning cities, in building houses, in designing and marketing a multitude of products all the way from paper clips to airliners. If aesthetic considerations are held irrelevant to these concerns, then we lose the whole sense and meaning of art in life, namely, the improvement of taste wherever it is capable of improvement.

Art, after all, like the Sabbath, was invented to serve man, and not the other way around. Therefore, if beauty is to enter our lives in increasing measure, say the "Instrumentalists," it must do so within the context of use. And to use art — to design graceful buildings, to shape our automobiles, to decorate our homes — is not to demean it but to ennoble it, for art becomes a human discipline when it can be made to enter into our lives in ever more meaningful ways. To hang a picture on a wall is to *use* it, in the best sense of the term. But if it does not create the desired mood, if it jangles when it should soothe, or if it soothes when it should jangle, depending on the context, then it must be replaced, no matter who the artist.

This general position, most closely associated with Experimentalism, will obviously call for a different approach to art in the school. It will value the learning of artistic concepts in the context of utility and function. It will concern itself with the aesthetic environment of the school itself, with its location, its architecture, its landscaping, its interiors, the colors on the walls, the design of the furniture — in short, it will seek to engage the total sensibilities of the learner. Even the good looks of the teacher will assume a new importance, for the looks of the teacher are not irrelevant to the learning morale of the child.

Aesthetics and the relativity of taste

We are confronted in aesthetics with the same difficulty encountered in morals, namely, the variability of what men like throughout all human societies. It is an implicit obligation of aestheticians and of educators in general to expose us to all the preferences men exhibit as a prelude to the study of what they *ought* to prefer. And, as they are practiced, the arts already are more international and "inter-cultural" than moral judgments or philosophic truths. This means, of course, that the universal subject matter of aesthetics is more readily accessible and more hospitably looked upon than other subject matters.

But this is not to say that the ultimate axiological question — what men *ought to like* — is any easier of resolution. For different cultures and civilizations are equally insistent that their aesthetic sensibilities are more noble and mature than those of their neighbors. What constitutes genuine nobility and maturity in aesthetic preferences is the kind of question, therefore, which various philosophies will wish to consider, and their ultimate purpose in this endeavor will naturally be to recommend a "principle of evaluation" by which all human preferences can be not only understood but also judged and measured. It is this theme which will dominate the discussion in Chapter Nine.

THE AXIOLOGICAL SITUATION

All of the attention we give to valuing in men would be merely an "academic" question (in the narrowest sense of the term) if it were not for the fact that we live in an age some writers have described as one of moral crisis. The old patterns of conduct and choice increasingly seem to be not only irrelevant to the requirements of our time but outright obstructive to human purposes. It is not just a popular cliché that we live in a time when men's beliefs are undergoing something on the order of a revolution. It is a fact.

It is in the political and ideological sphere that this revolution is most readily recognized. We seem to be passing, for instance, from an era of individualism, sometimes garnished with the adjective *rugged,* to an as yet undefined era of collective action. In America, particularly, the incentives to individual endeavor, to hard work, and to quality performance are gradually yielding to the incentives of group effort, organization, social adaptability, and human relations. We are passing, as some social analysts have explained, from the era of *production,* in which men have strained to work upon their physical world to reshape it more to their hearts' desire, to the era of *consumption,* in which men find that they have solved the "problem of production" and now turn their attention to the enjoyment of the world they have so mightily brought into being.

During the early years of World War II, as America girded for total military effort, the question was repeatedly asked: "Shall it be guns or butter?" To a nation in crisis this had the ring of a rather ominous question. But the historic irony of it was that, far from being ominous, it did not seem for us even to be relevant. For Americans, with their special brand of arrogant optimism, decided to have both. And they did! Having just emerged from a serious depression, we had no chance to realize that during those dark years we had developed a technological know-how which, for all practical purposes, had solved once and for all the problem of producing all the wealth, in both goods and services, which we required as a people. So fantastic was our production during the war years that we not only had both "guns" *and* "butter," but we supplied most of the free world with their requirements of both as well.

Indeed, we have succeeded so well at this in this country that we have not been able to "turn it off." Our technological skills and productive energies since World War II have been so great that we have been producing more in many fields — most notably agriculture — than we can consume. The problem now is how to get rid of the stuff! And "getting rid of the stuff" is essentially a human problem of social organization and politico-economics.

It goes without saying that the new importance of the social sciences in our public affairs, in our social criticism, and in our schools can be traced directly to this recent revolution in technology. Furthermore, as we have turned from the physical to the human world, we have had time to develop new sciences, the so-called sciences of human behavior: psychology, anthropology, social psychology, and psychiatry. "People" are now the problem. And the persistence of turmoil and strife in the world, the grinding, grueling pressure of hate and fear benignly described as a "cold war," should be enough to remind us that people shall remain the problem for some time to come.

But to say that people are the problem is to say that the values men live by is the central issue for our time. And this is the message of the axiologist: that, of all the branches of inquiry in philosophy, the inquiry into human values is the most urgent for modern man. If freedom seems so vulnerable a good in modern times, if human liberties can be so easily violated in an epoch of crisis, if plain human decency is something we must become self-conscious about and actively work for instead of merely assume and expect, then we can conclude nothing else but that something has gone wrong in the world of men.

There are, of course, many dimensions to this crisis, some more strategic than others. Even on the domestic front we recognize a kind of disintegration of values. *Disintegration* is used here not in its connotation of decay or degradation, but in its technical, etymological meaning of "disintegration," of a "coming apart," of a taking apart of our sense of life and a struggle to put it together anew in some humane way.

We are, to cite one illustration, passing to a new morality in the field of sexual conduct, certainly the most sensitive if not ultimately the most important sector of moral affairs. We are moving from a Victorian, puritanical prudishness, in which man's animality has been considered a kind of embarrassment to be endured and where sex has been considered mean and dirty and evil, to a new and as yet unspecified libertarianism, in which our animality is celebrated and glamorized in advertising and public life and in which sexual freedoms are increasingly considered positive signs of maturity in social behavior. The moral crisis, however, does not consist in a mere change of behavior; it consists, rather, in a widening gap between such behavior and the semi-Victorian values still insisted upon by otherwise modern adults. A reading of the exhaustive works of Kinsey[11] on sexual behavior can only confirm an already sensed truth that in this sphere we profess one thing and do another. To employ our earlier terminology, there is a frightening gap opening up between our "operative" (behavioral) values and our "conceived" (professed) values. Herein lies the true moral tragedy of our sexual predicament.

We are, to cite another example, passing from a morality of work to a morality of play. As Max Lerner has put it in his monumental *The American Civilization,* America is increasingly dedicating itself to "the morality of fun." This is only a specialized illustration of the previous observation that we are passing from an epoch of production to one of consumption. But when consumption becomes the central activity it brings with it a change in moral outlook. Adaptability to others holds precedence over self-direction. Gregariousness has now been lifted to a moral determinant. We are exhorted to "get along," to mix well, to join, to engage increasingly in the public and socialized dimension of life. Privacy is a new and somewhat suspect immorality. One is not supposed to prefer solitude in "the coffee-break culture." If Greta Garbo's "I vant to be alone" was a news item a generation ago, it is a fanaticism today.

On the other hand, there are symptoms of a growing disaffection with "socialization" and "adjustment" as the prime moral counters in modern life. The "organization man" is, it is true, a phenomenal invention of our time, and he does make for harmony and lubrication of the social machine; but at a price. The price is nothing less than the loss of his own soul. Business executives are shaped to the will of their corporations; teachers are hired and fired on how well they "relate," rather than on how effectively they teach; and all of us bend to convention, in neighborhood and nation, in search of a more serene existence. But somehow serenity is not enough; beneath it all each of us hankers to be heard from. What we seem to need is a new individualism, a new statement of the authentic self, in a world of *others.* Just what form this new autonomy will take is, of course, very much an open question; the only thing we are reasonably sure of is that it will *not* be merely a retread of the "rugged individualism" of the nineteenth century. The point is simply that we have not found a suitable moral position in "organization" life; we may soon be moving on to something else.

Or, to cite a final instance, we seem to be passing to a kind of "structurelessness" in aesthetic taste. Modern art has escaped from inherited form.

11 See Alfred C. Kinsey *et al., Sexual Behavior in the Human Female* (Philadelphia: W. B. Saunders, 1953) and *Sexual Behavior in the Human Male* (Philadelphia: W. B. Saunders, 1948).

There is an opening up of possibilities, a free, deliberately experimental scattering of drops and blobs on canvas. In modern music the older harmonies are eschewed and a new and unplotted region of discord and plain noise is being explored for tonal effect. In the field of poetry and writing, "nonsense" seems to have a beguiling kind of sense all its own; it can move, even if it cannot always explain. Finally, amidst this clatter of experiment, arises a primitivism in popular music which carries us back to the savage beat. Passion is heralded in ballads with wordless words. And love, which was always like this but, then again, never like this, triumphs anew.

Revolt from established patterns seems to many people impious. But impiety is the nominal price we pay for human invention and creativity. We may not yet be ready to comprehend, much less appreciate, what the new arts are attempting to say. But there is no gainsaying the excitement found there; if excitement is prelude to idea, then something seems to be on its way.

There is, to be sure, a constant temptation to consider the new always a little outrageous. Oldsters ask constantly, and not a little plaintively, "What is the younger generation coming to?" And the young, unmindful of coming to anything in particular, shrug at such anguish. But the point is that as we raise our young today there are new and uncodified preferences increasingly making themselves available to us. Moral choice and aesthetic taste now swim in an ocean of possibilities. And axiologically we are in search of a rudder. But rudders are for pointing, and, without stars or landmarks to steer by, to have a rudder is not much better than having none.

It is to the consideration of the stars or the landmarks, whichever you may prefer, but at any rate to the question of what men "ought to ought" and "ought to like," that we now turn.

QUESTIONS

1. Take the "Ways to Live" preference test on pages 15–19 of Charles W. Morris' *Varieties of Human Value* (see FURTHER READING below). Then write out a defense of your selection; that is, explain why you think your selections are preferable to the other alternatives.

2. In what other areas besides sex is there a noticeable difference between man's "operative" and "conceived" values? In these spheres, which is closer to what you think men *ought* to value — their behavior or their professed beliefs? Why?

3. One of the implicit themes of this chapter has been the distinction between

absolute and relative values. Another theme has been the distinction between art as end and art as means. What connection, if any, is there between these concepts? Explain.

4. Develop an essay on your views concerning moral and spiritual values, bearing in mind the following questions: Are moral and spiritual values necessary to each other, or can they be treated separately in value theory? Are aesthetic values related to or necessarily hooked up with moral values? With spiritual values?

5. Make a list of the things you like in the field of the arts. Then make a list of what you think you *ought* to like in the arts. Is there a difference in the two lists? If so, explain the discrepancies; that is, explain why you think you should like the things that did not appear in the first list.

6. In anticipation of Chapter Nine, pick out any two buildings on your campus or in your home town, one that you like to look at and one that you find ugly. How would you go about analyzing your aesthetic taste in architecture? From what you know of the five philosophies studied, what would they have to say about these buildings?

FURTHER READING

Bergson, Henri. *The Two Sources of Morality and Religion*. New York: Henry Holt and Co., 1935.
In this widely read work the author considers the emergence of morality in childhood behavior, then examines its relations with "static" and "dynamic" religions, closing with a discussion of mechanics and mysticism. The long first chapter, on "Moral Obligation," poses the problem of ethical value.

Edman, Irwin. *Arts and the Man*. New York: W. W. Norton and Company, Inc., 1939.
In this warm and friendly essay Edman isolates the role of art in experience and its function in civilization. Then, in separate sections, he considers the literary, the plastic, and the musical arts, concluding with a discussion of art and philosophy. An interesting and readable introduction to the field of aesthetics.

Everett, Walter G. *Moral Values*. New York: Henry Holt and Co., 1918.
Here is a comprehensive semihistorical introduction to moral theory. Everett first defines the scope of ethics and considers various theories — teleological, formal, hedonistic, perfectionist — by which values have been rationalized. He then takes up separately "happiness" and "perfection" as ultimate values and closes with a discussion of social values — duty, conscience, virtue, moral law, and religion.

Fromm, Erich. *Man For Himself*. New York: Rinehart and Company, Inc., 1947.
In this volume, which is subtitled "An Inquiry into the Psychology of Ethics,"

the author of *Escape From Freedom* examines the historical emergence of a so-called humanistic, i.e., man-centered, ethic, then considers man's equipment for handling such an ethic in terms of the temperaments and character traits man brings to "The Human Situation." Fromm concludes with a discussion of the problems of humanistic ethics and a short final chapter on "The Moral Problem Today." Read this last chapter first.

Morris, Charles W. *Varieties of Human Value.* Chicago: University of Chicago Press, 1956.
In this sequel to his previous *Paths of Life,* Morris considers the possibility of applying the scientific method to the study of values. Having isolated thirteen relatively distinct and discrete "ways to live," he analyzes the social, psychological, and biological determinants of value from questionnaires administered to hundreds of individuals throughout the world.

Parker, DeWitt H. *The Philosophy of Value.* Ann Arbor, Michigan: University of Michigan Press, 1957.
In this posthumously published book Parker considers rival theories of value and then the expression, analysis, organization, and evaluation of values. His first chapter, on "The Definition of Value," which poses the seemingly simple but actually complex problem of human preference, is a provocative opener for the study of axiology.

Perry, Ralph Barton. *Realms of Value.* Cambridge: Harvard University Press, 1954.
This is a monumental sequel to Perry's earlier volume, *General Theory of Value.* Having defined the term *value* as relating to the "interests" of men, he proceeds to work through the implications of this definition in social organization, cultural science, conscience, politics, law, economics, science, art, history, education, and religion. Chapter I, on the definition of value, Chapter VI, on moral theory, and Chapter XVIII, on aesthetics, are the most relevant for the present chapter.

Rader, Melvin M. (ed.). *A Modern Book of Esthetics,* Revised Edition. New York: Henry Holt and Co., 1952.
In this splendid anthology Rader has brought together some of the best statements of students of aesthetics. In his own editorial Introduction, which would be of most immediate help, he attempts a definition of art. Then he considers four alternative approaches to art which provide the context of the several selections, and finally takes up "meaning and truth" in the arts and "isolationist and contextualist theories" in aesthetics. The remainder of the book, a treasury of different expert views on aesthetic theory, may profitably be referred to in connection with Chapter Nine.

Comparative Axiologies

AXIOLOGY AND
PHILOSOPHICAL THEORY

Valuing and the theory of reality

At the outset of Part III on Epistemology, time was taken to explore the connections between ontological theory, discussed in Part II just preceding, and the theories of knowing about to be brought under discussion. The burden of this discourse was simply that to hold a theory of reality is, in itself, to say something about the knowing process, if no more than to set the limits of knowing or to prescribe the "ground" in which knowing is to be carried on. That is to say, an ontological position suggests, even if it does not insist upon, a particular approach to epistemological matters. And the kind or kinds of knowing that are considered worthy of examination are in a measure the "products" of — i.e., the kinds of knowing made possible by — a particular ontological theory. Later in this discussion in Chapter Five we brought the argument full circle by noting the fact that one's ontology, in turn, depends on one's epistemology; that is, what one says about reality is true only by virtue of a previously stipulated theory of how truth is found out and uttered. In these reciprocal ways there is an intimate logical and psychological relationship between ontological and epistemological theory.

The same relationship, generally speaking, prevails between ontology and value theory. The fundamental question in ethics, as we have said, is: What ought I to ought? Now, if our ontological position has already been set out and delineated, there is every reason to believe that this position will implicitly suggest some things as favored courses of action over others. For an immediate example, an Idealist is likely to consider the "life of the mind," the life lived in books and with ideas, to be a *higher,* a *better* kind of life to live than other kinds. An Experimentalist is likely to consider "sharing with others" *good* by virtue of the ontological and epistemological position he has chosen for himself. Therefore, we can say that what one says about the reality he considers himself to be inhabiting is suggestive of what he finds in it to merit and consider worthy.

In like manner, one's ontology makes some implicit prescriptions concerning aesthetics. If the central question is: What ought I to like?, then the character and quality of one's world — as set out in one's ontological position — provide the ground for what is to be enjoyed. In this office, an ontology "sets the tone," one might say, for the identification of beauty and the enjoyment of beauty. If, let us say, we hold with the Realist to a mechanistic ontology, in which the world is a giant machine, we are likely to appreciate and enjoy works of art which exhibit the principles of order, of balance, and of thought-out design, whereas if our ontology consists in an undefined, open-ended, essence-less condition of existing, as in Existentialism, it is probable that enjoyment will be had in arts of a more irregular, self-expressionistic character. In both ethics and aesthetics, then, there is a kinship between our estimate of ultimate reality and our judgment of what we find in it to value.

There is another consideration, also found analogically in our previous discussions of ontology and epistemology, which may occasion more trouble. This is the notion that the linkage between our reality and our values is one of necessity, rather than the more incidental relationship suggested in the previous paragraphs. As in epistemology, some philosophies hold that there is a moral dimension to the cosmos which has ultimate sanction over us; that is to say, there is a "capital-G" Good (like the "capital-T" Truth) which may be said to inhabit reality absolutely and which therefore prescribes certain values for men to hold everywhere and always. The business of the axiologist, according to these outlooks, is to determine in detail what this Good consists in and what it prescribes. Then the educator can get busy helping young people learn the prescriptions and adjust their behavior to them. Generally speaking, our first three philosophies tend in this direction; in one way or another, Idealism, Realism, and Neo-Thomism all hold to the possibility of locating, defining, and applying values which the cosmos contains irrespective of the wishes or purposes of men.

Our other two philosophies, however, take quite a different view of the matter. Values are man-made. Like truth, say the Experimentalist and the Existentialist, values are what men say they are — in Experimentalism through an examination of consequences, in Existentialism through choice. Our attention to ontology, they say, is justified primarily because our ontology, too, is man-made. Furthermore, in the matter of values, especially in ethics, we cannot look outside ourselves for moral prescriptions, because to do so is to eliminate the possibility of choice. And without choice between competing courses of action, in either "What should I do?" or "What should I like?," there can be no genuine *valuing*. As was mentioned in Footnote 5 of Chapter Eight (see page 226), I cannot simultaneously say that something is forced on me and that I freely choose to prefer (value) it. That would be a contradiction.

Thus, Experimentalism and Existentialism never consider legitimate the questions: What *must* I do? What *must* I like? Such questions remove the logical ground on which all axiology stands.

The question of whether values are cosmos-made or man-made is a troublesome one; it is raised here not for explication but, rather, to show that on this issue our five theories may be said to divide into two "camps." But there is a puzzling irony to the whole issue: Which side one takes in the argument is a matter of preference; the choice an individual makes at this juncture is itself a value judgment! It represents the way one *wants* to think about his world.

Which brings us to our final note on ontology and axiology, which is, briefly, that our ontologies depend ultimately upon our axiologies, for our ontologies are ultimately statements of what we prefer to think the cosmos is like. This may appear an inconsequential point; but not so. For every ontology — with the possible exception of Existentialism — arrives at a view of the cosmos which shows it hospitable to man. That is, almost every philosophy so far concocted by man has found itself, at the end of its investigations, possessed of a view of the cosmos which makes human life and human purposing possible and which, moreover, provides a certain measure of assistance in the human undertaking.

To put it in more homely language, we can say that every philosophy, except possibly Existentialism, holds that the cosmos is "on our side." Idealism posits a realm of ultimates which give us guidance; Realism posits a rational and ordered nature which provides direction; Neo-Thomism gives us Absolute Truth or God to "hold the lamp" and point the way. Even Experimentalism posits a hospitable reality, a reality which supports the scientific method: Problems do, after all, get solved. In this minimum sense, the cosmos is "on our side," in that it makes scientific hypothesizing something more than just idle fantasying and renders scientific experimentation a worthwhile pursuit. In short, it makes problem-solving possible.

Not only possible, but *probable* as well. Our latter-day creation of a "problem-solving" labor force — research scientists and investigators — is final proof that we believe deliberate problem-solving, intentionally undertaken and consciously institutionalized in research centers, will probably and very likely lead to solutions; and by this institutionalization of problem-solving we reveal a new trust in our environment, a trust that reality will yield to human intelligence.

And this trust, at bottom, is a value judgment! It is something we choose to believe — an "article of faith," if the Experimentalist will pardon the expression. And, therefore, the point is made that all ontologies (at least the traditional ones) finally boil down, when all the questions have been raised and dealt with, to a preferential "leaning" in this direction or that, to a *desired* view of the world which, given the meager data we have to go on, we want very much to be the ontological case if, as, or when all the data are eventually brought in.

The point of all this is simply that the idea of the cosmos being "on our side" may tell us more about ourselves than it does about the cosmos. There is really no certain warrant for believing it to be true: which is to say that we should all, therefore, be a little more cautious of what our ontologies proclaim — for oftentimes our axiologies are "showing." Not that there is necessarily anything wrong with our axiologies; but we should be awake to the possibility that, ontologically speaking, we may be permitting "the wish to be father to the thought," and, hence, subconsciously saying that our wishes and preferences are prior to and therefore more ontologically real, more existentially authentic, than the reality which we are presumably speaking of.

Valuing and knowing

We also, in Part III, have examined the particular function of epistemology as it relates to the ordinary business of living and the specialized business of educating. At that point we saw that the criticism of our knowledge, the checking and rechecking of what we think to be true, is the continuous task of epistemology. In this connection we likened the school to a retail establishment, in which we were pleased to authenticate the knowledge "on the shelf" before retailing it to the young. This metaphor, as was pointed out in another setting in Chapter Eight, applies also to value theory. For we are obviously concerned to test and judge the values "on the shelf" of the school before transmitting them to the young. The following five axiological theories are, of course, quite different; but they each provide a procedure by which we may check our values and test our preferences for adequacy.

There was with epistemology, and there is with axiology, however, a more practical consideration to attend to. We commented in Chapter

Five that a theory of knowing has direct assistance to give in the theory of education, because knowing is the principal activity in which a school child is engaged. Therefore, how human beings, in general, know is thought to have some bearing upon how boys and girls know. The same is true in the present instance of axiology. For if knowing is the principal activity of the youngster in school, then valuing is certainly the next most important thing he does. And if this is so, then a theory of value may be expected to bear directly upon an educational theory of valuing on the part of the child.

We cannot, at this point, show this intimate connection. That is the business of Chapter Ten. It is mentioned here only to remind you that as you study the five axiologies to follow you should be anticipating Chapter Ten by surmising how these axiologies would go about the value training — sometimes called the "character-building" — of the child.

*　　*　　*

Before we move on, a brief procedural note. When we discussed comparative epistemologies in Chapter Six, the method was to recall the ontological theory of each position and then develop its corresponding theory of knowing. We shall have occasion to repeat this procedure, but this time only very casually and, you may think, cryptically. Cryptic or not, the procedure is defended on the ground that by this time in this book you should be able to do some of your own "back thinking." Procedurally, it is not very difficult. All you are invited to do is to refer to the appropriate sections of Chapter Three, "Comparative Ontologies," as background to the understanding and comprehension of the axiologies to follow.

Possibly you will have occasion to refer to the appropriate sections of Chapter Six, "Comparative Epistemologies," as well. This is said in anticipation of your discovery of a similarity between epistemological procedures and axiological procedures. Because they are both procedures for the attainment and authentication of some object — in the one case, a truth, in the other, a preference — you should not be too surprised to find a certain consonance of method in the two spheres. This, as you are intended to see in the remainder of the chapter, turns out to be the case.

IDEALISM

The Idealist's reality is Absolute Mind inhabiting the cosmos. Epistemologically, the business of knowing is the approximation of this Mind through the absorption of ideas and the "enlargement" of the microcosmic mind in increasing imitation of the Absolute Mind through symbolic learning. This Absolute Mind of which we partake may also be thought of as an Absolute Self; it is on the order of a human being extended to the limits of his perfectibility in every conceivable direction, a human person — a personality — magnified to infinity and written across the reach of all existence.

Ethics: the imitation of the Absolute Self

If we may use the metaphor of the Infinite Person, we are immediately put in touch with the Idealist's notion of how the value question is handled. For if our individual selfhoods do somehow participate in an Ultimate Selfhood, and if we consider ourselves "morally oriented," i.e., capable of seeking and doing right, then by extension we can say that the Ultimate Selfhood, or Infinite Person, contains this same capability absolutely and with none of the doubts and uncertainties of ordinary men.[1] The Infinite Person contains the ethical directions we are looking for, in somewhat the same way that the Absolute Mind is thinking the ultimate ideas which constitute reality.

So, then, our axiological task is set out for us: We must go in search of the Infinite Person and the moral prescriptions contained therein. One of the ways to initiate this search is to proceed from individual persons to the study of *groups* of persons. That is, a group of human beings, each individually making moral decisions, but acting in concert for a larger end, will reveal a larger "personhood" and hence a larger and more dependable morality. It is as if we could find a larger "selfhood" inhabiting a community of selves.

Many moralists and political writers of the Enlightenment worked this theme by insisting that there was a kind of "Popular Will" or "Sense of the Community" which expressed itself in history. In colonial Puritanism the chief magistrate was permitted to be absolute in power precisely *because* he was popularly elected. The will of the body politic, expressed through the ballot (of the landed only, to be sure), produced a larger selfhood, a new existential entity, the State: God works his will not through a monarch but through the individual, and when aggregates of God-driven individuals express their individual wills they bring into being a larger, communal will, which then, in the person of the magistrate, assumes absolute power over them.

---

[1] We have already commented on the bias to rule out doubt and uncertainty as basically not a part of reality. Experimentalists have never been able to figure out why all of the meaner and uglier qualities of human beings do not have *their* infinity as well. Why, they ask, is infinity always toward Good and not toward Evil? Infinity is, after all, a mathematical notion that goes down as well as up. The only attempt at the "Infinity of Evil" is the Puritan's Satan, who to put it mildly does not figure very largely in modern thinking.

In more benign, more democratic circumstances, the same principle may be said to hold. When men live freely together, an Idealist might contend, they gradually gravitate to a "group mind" on how they want to live. When this pattern of living is written down we call it law; when it remains unwritten we call it custom. In either case it is the expression of the "larger selfhood" of the group, whether the group be a street gang, a garden club, a labor union, a national society, or a whole civilization. And this "larger selfhood" represents a "way station" on the long axiological journey from an individual self to the Infinite Person.

But this method is really not very satisfactory, for we know that the "Popular Will" or "group mind" often changes; and the Idealist is looking for something much more steady and reliable. What we want is a rule of conduct which applies everywhere and always, one which can always recommend itself no matter what situation comes up and which, furthermore, is not too vague to be applied to concrete affairs of everyday.

A strong candidate for such a status is the famous Golden Rule: "Do unto others as you would have them do unto you." Although the Rule is usually associated with Christian teachings, it is not a religious rule. On the contrary, it is wholly secular in spirit and content. And it appears to satisfy our conditions, that is, to apply in every circumstance; and, since it is "anchored" in the individual person who is hypothetically asking "What should I do?," there is no chance for corruption. More mystically, it could be said to be the kind of thing that the Infinite Person might say.

It turns out, however, that this Rule will not qualify. Precisely because it is "anchored" in the individual person, it produces an essentially selfish and egocentric value judgment. That is, I begin with my own selfhood. How do *I* want to be treated? What is the best for *me*? What is good for me, this Rule says, is good for everybody!

Obviously, this is not much of a moral principle. Immanuel Kant was particularly distressed by it. "It cannot be a universal law," he said, "for it does not contain the basis of duties toward oneself; nor of the duties out of love for others; nor, finally, of the bounden duties to others (for many a person would gladly agree that others should not help him, if only he could be relieved of doing good to them)."[2]

Furthermore, it is doubtful if the Rule really works. In the international politics of the cold war, for instance, we should very much like the Soviets to "do unto us" by ceasing and desisting in their efforts to extend their influence throughout the world. But if this were reversed to become our policy toward the Soviets, we should be expected to cease

[2] *The Fundamental Principles of the Metaphysic of Ethics,* trans. Otto Manthey-Zorn (New York: D. Appleton-Century Co., Inc., 1938), fn. p. 48. Quoted by permission of Appleton-Century-Crofts, Inc.

and desist in our efforts to extend freedom everywhere — certainly a questionable kind of surrender.

It is to Kant, as a matter of fact, that we may turn for the most authentic expression of the Idealist position. Kant insisted that in making moral choices we must separate ourselves absolutely from our individual selves and from the individual exercise of the will. Furthermore, we must remove ourselves from the empirical, that is, the day-to-day moral experiences we confront, to find what we are looking for; this because ". . . examination of moral values does not depend upon the actions that one sees, but upon their inner principles, which one does not see."[3]

The empirical realm, which we can see, calls for what he called "hypothetical imperatives," or rules which apply to this or that circumstance to achieve this or that result. But the "inner principles" of all moral actions will lead us eventually to a "categorical imperative," or an imperative that not only serves in every circumstance but, moreover, serves to validate and authenticate our several "hypothetical" imperatives.

In keeping with the "microcosm-macrocosm" model of Idealist ontology, Kant makes the following comment:

> Now as we look back upon all attempts that have been made in the past to discover the principle of morality, we can see why they had to fail. They saw man bound by his duties to laws, but it never occurred to anyone to see that man is subject *only to his own* and yet to universal legislation, and that he is obligated to act only in accordance with his own will which, however, in view of the end of nature is a universally legislating will.[4]

This individual will carries on its "universal legislating" in what Kant called a "realm of ends," by which he meant "the systematic union of different rational beings by means of common laws."[5] In this "realm of ends" were to be found the universal laws of conduct. And Kant's famed Categorical Imperative is, like most great ideas, really quite simple: *Act only on that maxim which will enable you at the same time to will that it be a universal law.*

So we come at last to an essentially straightforward ethic: Do unto others not as you would have them do unto you but as you would have all men do unto all other men in keeping with a universal law. It is our apprehension of the universal law, sometimes seen only darkly, that provides the assurance that we know the Good. In answer to critics of

[3] *Ibid.,* p. 22.
[4] *Ibid.,* pp. 50–51. (Author's italics.)
[5] *Ibid.,* p. 51.

this Platonic, other-world doctrine of morality, Kant concludes his treatise:

> . . . the idea of a pure world of reasoning as a totality of all intelligences, to which we ourselves as rational beings belong (although we are at the same time members of the world of senses also), still remains a useful and proper idea for the purposes of a rational faith. Even though knowledge ends at the border of this idea, this faith still is useful to awaken in us a lively interest in the moral law by means of the splendid ideal of a universal realm of *ends in themselves* (of rational beings), of which we can be members only if we conduct ourselves painstakingly according to the maxims of freedom as if they were laws of nature.[6]

Aesthetics: the reflection of the Ideal

We may now abstract from this moral theory a companion aesthetic theory. In short, it is the search for the "idea" of the work of art. What is the ultimate and universal quality which a work of art is expressing? Here is the locus of the aesthetic criterion.

At the outset of our discussion of Idealism a linguistic distinction was made between the words *idea* and *ideal*. This was done to insure a purely intellectual and unemotional approach to ontology and epistemology. In both these branches of discourse it is more proper to speak of this school of thought as "Idea-ism."

In axiology, however, we are permitted the use of the word *Idealism* in its more or less literal sense, for in aesthetics *idea* and *ideal* are convertible expressions. Or, in other words, the aesthetic universals, which correspond to the moral and epistemological universals, may be thought of as whatever is *ideal* in life, in the common, everyday use of that word.

We also employ the common expression "to idealize" something. A portrait painter will remove the *real* blemishes from a face to render it more proximate to the ideal face. The sculptor will attempt to "capture" the true, i.e., the idealized, person in shaping a bust or statue of a statesman.

Tchaikovsky romanticizes and idealizes the world of love, making it more pure and splendid than it really is. Anne Lindbergh in *A Gift from the Sea* idealizes a loneliness at the seashore to find in the coils of various sea shells the inner symbols for the meaning of life. The French nation proclaims with a monumental Statue its great love and admiration for the American idea of liberty; and poet Emma Lazarus has this great lady say: "Give me your tired, your poor,/Your huddled masses yearning to breathe free,/The wretched refuse of your teeming shore,/Send these, the

6 *Ibid.*, p. 83.

homeless, tempest-tost to me:/I lift my lamp beside the Golden Door."
A finer testament to an idea — an idea both true and good and beautiful
— could hardly be imagined.

Turning to other quarters, an Idealist would say that photography
cannot be considered a true art form, because its business is to depict
things the way they happen to be in our experience. But occasionally,
says the Idealist, photography can, let us say in the hands of a "Karsh of
Ottawa," arrest the inner man, can seize upon the true person in the
flick of the shutter to reveal to us the true Churchill or Baruch or Eisen-
hower within![7]

The function of the artist is not to represent, literally "re-present," the
world to our sensibilities, but to portray the world as the Infinite Person
sees it, that is, in its perfect form. A work of art is recommended for our
appreciation, and for the developing appreciation of the young as they
grow in taste, in the degree to which it cuts through the imperfections
and blemishes of the empirical world, through the crudity and ugliness
and baseness of ordinary experience, to reveal true loveliness transcendent.

REALISM

We may let a leading contemporary Realist summarize our prior discussion of Realist doctrine:

> Our "common sense" tells us, first, that we inhabit a world consisting of
> many things which are what they are, independent of any human opinions
> and desires; second, that by the use of reason we can know something about
> these things as they actually are; and third, that such knowledge is the
> safest guide to human action . . .
>
> These basic beliefs of mankind are also the three basic doctrines of
> realistic philosophy: (1) There is a world of real existence which men have
> not made or constructed; (2) this real existence can be known by the
> human mind; and (3) such knowledge is the only reliable guide to human
> conduct, individual and social.[8]

These three doctrines correspond, of course, to the trio of philosophical
questions raised in this book: What is real? What is true? What is
good? It is to the third of these questions we presently want the Realist's
answer.

[7] In *Portraits of Greatness* (New York: Thomas Nelson and Sons, 1959), containing
ninety-six of his most famous photographic portraits, Yousuf Karsh offers a most
articulate Idealist sentiment: "[I am striving to reveal] an inward power . . . the
mind and the soul behind the human face."

[8] John Wild, *Introduction to Realistic Philosophy* (New York: Harper and Bros.,
1948), p. 6.

Ethics: the law of nature

We are directed first of all to the natural world, which, being ultimately real and existential, is therefore the ground of value. To approach the problem of right and wrong by way of nature may strike you as none too promising. Nature, when one looks at it out his front window, does not seem to have much value in it; it is just existentially *there* to be looked at and known. The burden of the argument, then, is quite clearly on the shoulders of the "naturalist."

But there really is no burden, says he. As a matter of fact, the call to nature is very much a part of our moral tradition. We say, "Just be yourself; be *natural.*" By this we mean to suggest a *desired* and *preferred* pattern of action. To act *un*naturally is not to act well; an *un*natural person is usually considered someone to be avoided. He is phony, putting up a front. The phrase, "Doing what comes naturally," is not only an erotically suggestive title to a song, but a moral prescription covering the remainder of human affairs.

But we should not infer that to follow nature is pleasure-seeking hedonism. That was the mistake of the Puritans, who considered pleasure to be inherently evil. To follow nature is merely to abide by the conditions that nature sets — indeed, to conform to them. And conformity in this sense is the highest kind of virtue, for it is conformity to that which is existentially real and, therefore, existentially good.

Another way of getting at this notion is to speak of "natural law." We have used this phrase before, in Chapter Six, concerning the Realist's conception of truth. We may now speak of a nature-borne law of conduct, which controls us quite as insistently and absolutely as does natural and ultimate truth. Natural law in ethical theory is usually called "moral law," and by this term we mean a law of right and wrong which is embedded in the very structure of nature. Nature contains not just laws of gravity, and thermodynamics, and energy, and metabolism — that is, laws of the behavior of completely material, subhuman entities; it contains laws of *human* behavior as well.

In speaking of *group* behavior, we can cite economic and political laws, like the oft-cited Law of Supply and Demand or Lord Acton's famous law of political life: "Power corrupts; absolute power corrupts absolutely." Likewise in *individual* behavior, says the Realist, there is a moral law intrinsic to the real, natural world which men must obey if they choose to be men. Injunctions against taking human life, lying and cheating are the kinds of moral taboos which may go unwritten, even unspoken, in human societies; but they are nevertheless constantly operative in the lives of men, for they persist in time-space and exert their force on the conduct of men in as immanent a way as the law of gravity. Further-more, all men *know* these laws, whether they can utter them or not. They live "within" them, if not always "by" them.

We meet this kind of valuing explicitly in the Declaration of Inde-pendence, in which Jefferson wrote of men being "endowed . . . with certain inalienable rights . . ." — meaning that men live in a world which contains human rights just as really and existentially as it contains trees and muskrats and oceans. Human rights are "built in" to reality and cannot be alienated by some men against others. Hence, Jefferson went on, we have no alternative; we must fight! This is the way things are; we cannot be true to our own nature by tolerating this evil one moment longer. We are "victims," one might say, of a benign reality which *demands* that we fight! We can choose no other course. In this curious but powerful Enlightenment logic, Jefferson stirred the colonial heart to revolution.

In Chapter Six we devoted a full section to the Realist's notion of "pure theory." Pure theory is that kind of truth which is sought solely for its own sake. It has no necessary utility in the lives of men; it is simply to be known, in and for itself. Sometimes, of course, purely theoretical concepts come to have application in human affairs, but that is not why they are sought. They are hunted for simply because human beings like to know what their world is and how it works, i.e., they like to *know*.

Now, pure theory in epistemology is the analogue of natural or moral law in ethical discourse. Moral law is that law of behavior which is beyond human utility, which is unconnected with the interests or desires of men, and which consists merely in a statement of what the universe requires in the way of conduct. Moralists search for these laws for the same reason scholars search for truth, i.e., just to *know* them. These laws may have no immediate application, but because they are laws of the cosmos we desire to know and hold them, for their own sake. If they are seen to apply to this or that circumstance, so much the better; we make use of them. But the first and primary business of ethics is to know and commit oneself to natural and moral value.

On first glance it may appear that the Realist's "moral law" coincides with Kant's Categorical Imperative. It comes extremely close, of course, but as things turn out the Realist will have none of it. Perhaps the best spokesman for this view is John Wild, leading contemporary apostle of the Realist cause. In his *Introduction to Realistic Philosophy,* he dis-cusses "Subjective Alternatives to Natural Law," and in particular the famous Kantian dictum. Criticizing it first in terms of Kant's other doc-trines, he asks how it is possible for Kant to believe simultaneously (1)

that we *cannot* ever know anything as it really is in itself but only the
way it appears and behaves in our experience[9] and (2) that we *can* know
what is really good in itself, without qualification. If not one, why the
other? asks Wild.

This is admittedly an internal doctrinal dispute and one which Kant
unfortunately is not alive to answer. Of greater consequence is Wild's
distress at the barrenness of the Categorical Imperative; that is, it is so
splendidly theoretical that it neglects to tell us how to act. "How," he
says, "can any concrete, moral duties be deduced from a categorical
imperative which contains nothing but the empty form of logical universality?"[10]

Take the case of lying, an illustration used frequently by Kant. Employing the Categorical Imperative, Kant suggests that a man should not
lie because he cannot simultaneously "will the universal law" to lie, that
is, he cannot will that lying be a universally applied law of conduct. Wild
asks, Why not? There is nothing to stop me; there is no *formal* reason
preventing me from willing the universality of lying. What stops me
from universalizing such a thing is my concrete observations of natural
man behaving in natural circumstance.

> Men are, as a matter of fact, rational beings, capable of learning from
> experience. They will soon detect a liar and distrust him. Hence it is
> easy to see that universal lying would bring forth universal distrust and
> render rational communication, and hence human life, impossible.[11]

So, Herr Kant, says Wild, your "will to universal law" is itself grounded
in the plain and ordinary sensory perception had every day by ordinary
men. Your Imperative, therefore, is no more categorical, i.e., ultimate,
than the categoricity or ultimacy of my observations. And since the
ultimacy of my observations resides in nature, it is nature which contains what I am looking for.

In furtherance of this theme of concrete experience, Wild develops the
companion idea that we learn our values by "conditioning," by voluntarily adopting prescribed and partially automatic behavior. Rejecting
the clinical psychologists' mode of conditioning — what he lightly calls
the "white rat theory" of conditioning — Wild says he prefers the model
established by Aristotle, namely, the mode of conditioning conceived as
the *cultivation of the intellectual and moral virtues.*

As a case in point, the child is not born generous; but he is not born
stingy either. "Our original nature is neutral in this as in all other
specific moral respects."[12] But nature itself is not neutral. Nature calls

9 A central and primary feature of Kantian philosophy.
10 Wild, *op. cit.*, p. 50.   11 *Loc. cit.*   12 *Ibid.*, p. 72.

for a pattern of action toward other men which we can discern through social observation. The Law of Generosity (i.e., the proper balance between generosity and stinginess) is embedded in reality, and the conduct of man in his natural behavior will reveal it to us. Once it is revealed, it is our task to condition the young to follow it, not like blindly led white rats in a cage but as human beings who freely adopt this pattern of action as they grow to see *why* it is good. Rats never can know "why"; men can. This is the difference. Virtue is found in the *rational comprehension of natural necessity.*

As a final exhibit of the Realist's penchant for materialist, naturalist analogues for his moral theory, we may cite William P. Montague's argument on "The Geometry of the Good Life,"[13] which runs somewhat as follows: Good and bad are scattered through life in "amounts." Furthermore, individual goods and "bads" are distributed discontinuously, that is, in units and clumps which can be singled out for analysis and manipulation, just like geometric figures. The manipulation of clumps of good and bad is governed by "The Law of Increasing Returns." This law is the counterequivalent of the economic "Law of Diminishing Returns." In economics returns legally diminish (in a natural kind of way, of course) with increasing concentration of effort; but in human values the situation is reversed, namely, each increment of input (concentration of effort) will yield geometrically compounded profits. A philanthropy of a million dollars concentrated among, say, twenty people will evoke a yield of good — happiness, gladness, joy, etc. — far greater than a million dollars "pulverized" down to a dime for each of 10,000,000 persons.[14]

So, says Montague, individual goods should be concentrated to maximize their yield; but since the same law holds with evil — tragedy, misfortune, pain, etc. — such "bads" should not be concentrated, but, rather, spread out evenly among the population by means of insurance, mutual assistance plans, and welfare legislation. In this way we weaken the social and individual impact of evil and at the same time fortify and accentuate the impact of good. And all this becomes possible when we recognize the essentially *natural* base of morals and attend to the laws governing human conduct in valuational situations.

Aesthetics: the reflection of nature

As with Idealism, we may now abstract and extrapolate from the above ethical theory a companion notion of aesthetics. Such a notion must be

13 *The Ways of Things* (New York: Prentice-Hall, Inc., 1940), Chapter 23.
14 This illustration of Montague's is rather spurious, because it has nothing to do with the Law of Diminishing Returns; but it's interesting, anyway.

looked for, obviously, somewhere within the context of what the Realist understands by the word *nature*.

One of the things human beings like most about nature is its order — "a place for everything and everything in its place." The art in which this kind of order can most immediately be perceived is music. Music has consistently been esteemed as a carefully organized, regulated, and ordered art form. Indeed, in classical thought, music, logic, and geometry were all closely related members of the Seven Liberal Arts.[15] There is, moreover, a close similarity between the emotional reactions to a piece of music and to a difficult and involved mathematical problem successfully solved. We all have experienced this latter kind of rapture, which, according to Montague, is "not exactly sensuous yet very intense and bright."[16] With this analogue to work from, perhaps we might even say that music can be defined as mathematics rendered in sound. In this connection, Montague wonders, not altogether facetiously, whether the Binomial Theorem could be given a musical "incarnation," possibly comparable to the *Doxology*.[17]

Perhaps this is as far as we can carry the mathematical simile; but the point is that aesthetic quality is the kind of thing which nature already contains, and it contains it in somewhat the same way that it contains algebraic symmetry and geometric pattern. Art, therefore, should attempt to approximate the order and regularity of nature in its expressions in color, sound, and movement. It should represent, in the literal sense of "re-presenting," or presenting anew, the rationality of nature as that rationality is revealed in pattern, balance, line, and form.

The George Washington Bridge is not just a means of getting across the Hudson River; it is a work of art. Without aiming principally at doing so, the engineers produced structural loveliness, a truly beautiful thing to behold; and they did it by submitting to natural laws and to what nature fundamentally requires.

In painting, the artistic endeavor should be to render faithfully what one sees in the world, to re-create it *realistically*, so as to accentuate *pattern* and *order* and *design*, whether in a seascape, a still life or a portrait of a human face. Portraits are works of art when they reflect what truly is, rather than what ideally ought to be, for there is a real beauty in what truly is. For this reason photography definitely qualifies for aesthetic production, says the Realist; the camera can catch and hold

15 Grammar, Rhetoric, and Logic (the Trivium) and Arithmetic, Geometry, Astronomy, and Music (the Quadrivium), a curriculum fixed and codified by Martianus Capella in the late fourth century A.D.

16 Montague, *op. cit.*, p. 124.

17 *Ibid.*, p. 125. See also G. D. Birkhoff, *Aesthetic Measure* (Cambridge: Harvard University Press, 1933), for an elaborate and very serious theory on reducing art to mathematical formulas.

moments when nature is splendidly triumphant — as it always ultimately is — over the gross and chaotic clumsiness of man.

Taking all these ideas together, we may say that the central Realist theme is "the celebration of the orderliness and rationality of nature." It is this continuing celebration which the Realist calls Art.

NEO–THOMISM

In discussions of value it is really but a short step from Realism to Neo-Thomism. We have already seen, in Chapter Three, the common ancestry of both these views in Aristotle. In Chapter Six this congruity of approach turned up again in the theories of knowing. We should not be too surprised, then, to recognize a kind of affinity of temper between the two schools in the consideration of the problem of value. For what the Realist sees to be the *natural* requirements of the axiological situation the Neo-Thomist sees, similarly, to be the *logical* requirements of that situation.

Which is to say, by way of review, that the Neo-Thomist looks at the world as a *logical system,* to which the human intellect is "tuned" and oriented. In this logical system the monumental Principle of Potentiality-and-Actuality is seen to govern all being and change, whether it be applied (in Aristotelian terms) to Matter and Form or (in Thomistic terms) to Essence and Existence.

Out of this ontological model comes a second important principle, the Principle of the Hierarchy of Being, by which some things, i.e., existents or beings, exercise the act of "to be" in greater degree than others. In a manner of speaking, some things *are* or *exist* more than others.

In epistemology the Principle of Potentiality-and-Actuality reappears as the explanation for man's natural tendency *to know,* that is, the propensity of the intellect to actualize its inherent potentialities through the apprehension of ultimate truths. And the Principle of Hierarchy reappears as the ground for saying that there is a hierarchy of knowing: at the lowest level, scientific or synthetic knowing; at the next level, analytic or intuitive knowing; and at the third and highest level, mystical or revelatory knowing.

Now we must take these two ideas — Potentiality-Actuality and Hierarchy — to see how they apply to the value situation; for they clearly do apply, and, indeed, govern as supremely in ethics and aesthetics as in ontology, metaphysics, and epistemology.

Ethics: the rational act

The first thing we must say is that goodness follows from reason; the good act is that act which is controlled by the rational faculty of man. In keeping with classical Greek thinking, the Neo-Thomist believes that ignorance is the source and core of evil. If men do not *know* what is right, they cannot be expected to *do* what is right, except by accident or chance. On the other hand, if men *do* know what is right, they can be held responsible for what they do. They may not always follow the right, but this will be due only to the fact that they have not been habituated to it. With the assistance of habituation men may both *know* and *do* right.

All of this is built upon an essentially benign theory of human potentiality. In applying the first of our two ideas, the Potentiality-Actuality doctrine, the Neo-Thomist affirms that men *naturally tend toward the good*. Just as, in the case of knowledge, men *naturally tend to know* (see the discussion on the quotation from Adler in Chapter Six, page 149), so do men naturally tend toward goodness. To be sure, this does not mean that all men are good, no more than all acorns are destined to become oak trees. It means only that all men incline toward good, just as acorns incline toward becoming oak trees. They are, to use a homely expression, "given to" that sort of thing, and given to it by their very natures.

Therefore, the axiological enterprise, as the Neo-Thomist sees it, can be begun without any special prompting or stimulus because it is initiated and carried on under the general aegis of nature, that is, it is founded in a natural tendency. As in the case of knowing, man *cooperates* with nature in the achievement of moral values.

The simile is vastly imperfect, but the moral enterprise is something like paddling a canoe downstream. Forward direction is already a "given," i.e., a prior and assumed, condition of the paddling. Man's task is to watch where he is going, avoid shoals and hazards (both natural temptations and man-made diversions), and contribute to the forward motion of the canoe by paddling (training himself in good habits), so as to hasten and expedite the achievement of what would eventuate in any case but not so promptly or economically, namely, the terminus of the canoe trip, or, metaphorically, the desired moral end.

The pilot in charge of this expedition is the human will. The will is a companion instrument to the intellect, in Neo-Thomist thinking, and, although it must always be held subservient to the intellect (since the true essence of man is reason), it must, like the intellect, be trained and developed by special instruction. By "special instruction" is meant the habituation of the will to virtue, that is, to good habits. And since the formation of good habits is nothing more or less than the perfecting of the will's own powers — what we commonly call "will power" — we may say that the moral enterprise boils down, essentially, to the business of bringing to perfected actuality, through the agency of moral virtue (i.e., the forming of good habits), the incipient and potential capacities and tendencies of the human will.

The central problem here, of course, is to determine what constitutes a "good," as against a "bad," habit. But this is easily taken care of by noting our prior requirement that the will must be subservient to the reason. As Adler puts it:

> In the case of every human power, other than the intellect itself, the natural tendency of the power is toward that actualization of itself which conforms to reason. This follows from the subordination of all human powers, in their exercised act, to reason itself. Hence, in the case of every power there is a natural tendency which habit can violate or to which it can conform; and in conforming, the habit is good; in violating, it is bad.[18, 19]

Thus we have in hand a ready and workable criterion for conduct, both habituated and unhabituated, namely: Does it advance the power of reason or does it fulfill the requirements of reason in the life of man?

Now, it is a commonplace that most men do not always do right even when they know what they ought to do. But the test of a man's true character in Thomist thinking is not what he does but what he knows in his reason he ought to do. It is on this count that Ecclesiastical Thomists in the Roman Catholic Church are willing to cleanse an individual of sin at confession if the penitent honestly and sincerely demonstrates that his intentions were other than what his overt behavior turned out to be.

[18] Mortimer J. Adler, "In Defense of the Philosophy of Education," Chapter V in *Philosophies of Education,* Forty-first Yearbook of the National Society for the Study of Education, ed. N. B. Henry, Part I (Chicago: the Society, 1942), p. 243.

[19] There is a kind of nagging and bothersome circularity to statements like this, not alone from Adler but from other Aristotelian Thomists as well, and it is difficult to resist the temptation to remark on it.

Every human being, we are told, is equipped with a set of natural powers which tend to actualize themselves in conformity with reason. And reason is itself a natural power which is said to actualize itself in terms of itself. A habit is good to get into, then, if it helps to actualize either the power of reason or any of the other powers seeking fulfillment in terms of reason.

Now let us say that a human being is equipped with the power, i.e., the perfectible potentiality, of steadfastness and persistence; this is a reasonable and *reason*-able type of power. Now if we were to actualize the full potential of such a power by habituation, we would wind up with stubbornness and a closed mind. When does the tendency toward rational steadfastness veer off into irrational stubbornness?

Or take some other illustrations:

Will not boldness and courage, good traits both, turn eventually, if heightened and improved, into recklessness? And what is rational about recklessness?

Will not the noble habit of suspending judgment, brought to full being in a man, turn into ignoble indecisiveness?

Will not the habit of charity, begun at home but actualized abroad to its fullest and most complete limit, turn into a senseless, self-imposed penury?

That is, there are occasions in which our overt behavior slips loose from the moorings of reason and is led instead by undisciplined emotion — which is another way of saying that the will temporarily breaks away from its subservience to the reason and runs wild on its own. When reason reclaims will — when conscience feels the twinges of guilt — then it is time to confess.

If a man does not know any better, if he does not know his actions were wrong, he obviously cannot be held morally responsible for them. But if he *does* know better, that is, if he knows his actions were wrong, then he *can* be held responsible — unless it can be shown that he was not in rational control of himself at the moment he entered into those actions. In such fashion the Neo-Thomist explains the moral situation of the individual.

But all of this so far has served only to develop the inner psychology of morality. It is quite as important to attend to the ground of values itself, for it is in this ground — the ground of reason — that ultimate values are found. And the notion of ultimate values, values that are not contingent upon the whims or preferences of men, is as central to Neo-Thomism as it is to Idealism and Realism, if not more so. As it has been put by William McGucken, a spokesman for Ecclesiastical Neo-Thomism:

> There are certain human acts which are of their very nature good and deserving of praise, and therefore independent of all human law; other actions are of their very nature, that is, intrinsically, bad and deserving of blame.[20]

If it weren't for this objective moral "map" by which man can measure his way, man would be but "a weathercock, carried now in this direction, now in another, according as whim or the influence of his fellows or his environment is most prevalent."[21]

The general rule to follow, McGucken reminds us, is reason. But within reason there is a tripartite division of moral obligation. For man has duties (1) to himself, (2) to his fellow man, and (3) to his God.

> He must so live his life that the higher part of him, the spiritual, be not made subordinate to the organic. Consequently, drunkenness is in itself evil, because it is not in conformity with man's rational nature, rather it places the soul and its powers in a subordinate position to the animal appetites. Secondly, he has duties to his fellow man. Certain of these duties are

[20] "The Philosophy of Catholic Education," Chapter VI in *Philosophies of Education*, Forty-first Yearbook of the National Society for the Study of Education, ed. N. B. Henry, Part I (Chicago: the Society, 1942), p. 254.
[21] *Loc. cit.*

in conformity with his social nature, as a member of domestic society, the family; as a member of civil society; as a member of world society. Therefore, assisting one's neighbor, playing the good Samaritan, supporting one's children, and obeying parents are things good in themselves because in conformity with man's social nature. On the other hand, dishonesty, lying, stealing, and murder are intrinsically wrong because they run counter to man's social nature. Thirdly, man's contingent nature indicates clearly man's duties to God. Therefore blasphemy, irreverence toward God are things bad in themselves. Worship and service of God are good because in accord with the contingent nature of man. Suicide is an evil thing in itself because man, as a contingent being, has no dominion over his own life.[22]

We are now in a position to introduce our second strategic principle — the Principle of Hierarchy. For these three divisions of obligation, says McGucken, represent an ascending order of duty in moral choice.

> . . . there is a hierarchy of values. If there be a conflict between man's duties to God and to his neighbor, the inferior right must cede to the superior. First things come first. Charity is a good thing, but if giving away one's possessions means impoverishment of one's dependents, right order would show that this was not a good thing. Man's duties are first to his own household.[23]

We shall wish to comment on this moral theory in greater detail later, but for now it is enough to say that the Neo-Thomist answer to our question is clear. If the question is raised: "What should I do?" the answer should ring out loud and clear: "Let Reason reign." And it is fitting and proper to close on this note, for the exercise of reason, in and for itself, is considered by Neo-Thomists to be the highest good of all. Happiness as the ultimate moral condition of man can be reached, said Aristotle, not through the pursuit of instruments outside ourselves — money, power, fame. Genuine happiness, the highest good, can be ours only by actualizing our own inner nature; and, since reason is at the center of this nature, it is to the exercise of our own minds that we must repair to find the truly Good Life.

Aesthetics: creative intuition

It is not so easy, as in other instances, to abstract an aesthetic theory from the above moral theory. Such heavy stress on reason and the rational nature of man may appear to compromise the issue from the

22 *Ibid.*, pp. 254–255.
23 *Loc. cit.*

outset. We do not usually associate art with reason. Indeed, it is with the subservient faculties of will and emotion that we customarily connect the world of art. It is partly for this reason that Neo-Thomist aesthetics is considerably more difficult of lucid presentation than some of its other features.

Our first major concept is that of creativity. Aesthetics is concerned not with what is to be done, which is the sphere of ethics, but with what is to be made, or brought into being. We have already seen that man by nature tends toward knowledge and truth and also toward goodness. The surmise at this point would be that man naturally tends also toward the creation of beauty. This turns out to be the case:

> Creativity, or the power of engendering, does not belong only to material organisms, it is a mark and privilege of life in spiritual things also. . . . The intellect in us strives to engender. It is anxious to produce, not only the inner word, the concept, which remains inside us, but a work at once material and spiritual, like ourselves, and into which something of our soul overflows. Through a natural super-abundance the intellect tends to express and utter *outward,* it tends to sing, to manifest itself in a work.[24]

Now this creativity is manifested in two spheres — what we usually call the fine arts and the practical arts. The fine arts are those in which beauty is created for its own sake, "cleared," as Maritain remarks, "of all adventitious elements." This mode of art is, of course, the more noble, for "it is not extraneous to the intellect," as utilitarian art tends to be, but "one with the intellect." "For beauty, which is of no use, is radiant with intelligence and is as transcendental and infinite as the universe of the intellect."[25] Symphonies, paintings, and ballets, for instance, are superior to love songs, illustrations, and calisthenics because they are an attempt of the intellect to express itself outwardly into the sensory regions of experience, with no other recommendation than that they are pleasing to perceive.

But it is in the practical arts that most art originates. Here we are concerned with tools, ornaments, dwellings, clothing. Our creative tendencies are worked upon existent materials so as to combine utility with enjoyment. Here the work is partially extraneous to the intellect: hence inferior.

In either the fine or the practical arts, however, the intellect plays the ultimately decisive role, and true art is controlled by what the Neo-

24 Jacques Maritain, *Creative Intuition in Art and Poetry* (New York: Pantheon Books, Inc., 1953), pp. 54–55. Bollingen Series XXXV, 1, Bollingen Foundation, Inc.
25 *Loc. cit.*

Thomist calls "creative intuition," a somewhat mystical, probing lurch of the intellect beyond itself in the direction of Being. In this lurch it appears to be trying to escape from itself, i.e., art gives the appearance of trying to escape from reason, as in the case of modern art and poetry. But in actuality the intellect is attempting to lay hold of its preconscious self, what Maritain describes as "intuitive reason." When it succeeds in this, modern art may be said to have achieved true aesthetic dimension. When it fails and wobbles around in nonsense or buffoonery, then obviously it cannot qualify.

Because the intellect is the ultimate producer of art, we must look to it to understand the manner in which man consumes, i.e., appreciates and judges, art. We do this through the agency of intelligence, which serves as the headquarters for the three essential constituents of art and which, therefore, provides us a firm set of criteria in aesthetic judgment. Maritain expresses it this way:

> Now, that which knows, in the full sense of this word, is intelligence. Intelligence, then, is the proper perceiving power, the sense, as it were, of the beautiful. If beauty delights the intellect, it is because it essentially means a certain excellence in the proportion of things to the intellect. Hence the three essential characteristics or integral elements traditionally recognized in beauty: *integrity,* because the intellect is pleased in fullness of Being; *proportion or consonance,* because the intellect is pleased in order and unity; and *radiance or clarity,* because the intellect is pleased in light, or in that which, emanating from things, causes intelligence to see.[26]

EXPERIMENTALISM

Experimentalism, of all the philosophies considered in this book, has spent by far the most time and energy on the problem of value. The philosophies previously considered have concerned themselves principally with ontology and metaphysics, spinning out from those bases their associated doctrines in epistemology and ethics. For Experimentalism, however, it has been somewhat the other way around. As the philosophical historian Edward H. Reisner has written, the Experimentalist "has been indifferent to the problems of being, or metaphysics, and has confined his interests to the analysis and description of experience, particularly to the problems of knowing and conduct — to the conceptions of truth and goodness."[27]

---

26 *Ibid.,* p. 161.

27 "Philosophy and Science in the Western World: A Historical Overview," Chapter I in *Philosophies of Education,* Forty-first Yearbook of the National Society for the Study of Education, ed. N. B. Henry, Part I (Chicago: the Society, 1942), p. 30.

We have already seen, in Part III on Epistemology, how Experimentalism handles "truth." We now ask the Experimentalist to discuss how he goes about the business of "goodness."

In asking this, there may be some surprise at the Experimentalist's deep and loving interest in the question. How, one might ask, can so scientifically oriented a philosophy address itself systematically to value, the age-old "renegade" from science? Science can tell us what is true; but can it tell us anything about what is good? Science can give us knowledge, but can it tell us what we ought to do or what we ought to like? These are fair and appropriate questions, and answering them has become a central passion of Experimentalism because it is in the field of values — the prickliest and most troublesome of all areas — that a philosophy runs its ultimate test. If Experimentalism can set forth a scientific value theory and "make it stick," then Experimentalism as a whole must be accounted a mature philosophy.

As Experimentalists have attempted to do this they have found the task far from easy; for the application of a scientific methodology to ethical and aesthetic questions is admittedly somewhat novel and unorthodox, and, they contend, it takes time to explain and defend it in comprehensible and acceptable terms to the ordinary citizen, who has been conditioned by something like 2000 years of rationalistic, absolutistic system-building, and doctrinaire theological metaphysics.

Ethics: the public test

As was true in our discussions of comparative ontologies and epistemologies, we must recognize a sharp break in continuity between the traditional philosophies just covered and the newer members of the philosophical community. The first to venture a systematic break with the inherited ethical doctrines was Experimentalism; for it repudiates the whole thesis of the earlier points of view — the thesis that we must search for ultimate and changeless values in some reality outside of, i.e., beyond the control of, man. It makes no difference whether this objective realm of values is the nebulous "archive of moral universals" of Idealism, or the equally mystical "natural law" of Realism, or the immanent "reason," both beyond and within man, of Neo-Thomism. In adventuring into any of these regions to search for value, the Experimentalist contends, we misconstrue the whole point of our searching and wind up doing our exploring in the wrong place — that is, beyond the boundaries of experience, within which, after all, men do their valuing.

There is a kind of delusory aspect to all this adventuring, the Experimentalist continues, a hankering to concoct imaginary worlds where things are neater and nicer than here. It is a common temptation among men to become disgruntled at the way things go in this life, for so often we see our noble intentions come to nothing and a perverse destiny frustrate our hopes and cravings.

> Under such conditions, men take revenge, as it were, upon the alien and hostile environment by cultivating contempt for it, by giving it a bad name. They seek refuge and consolation within their own states of mind, their own imaginings and wishes, which they compliment by calling both more real and more ideal than the despised . . . world [they live in].[28]

This repair to other, morally nicer and neater worlds is nothing more, says the Experimentalist, than "a failure of nerve." We relinquish a certain amount of our human dignity when we cravenly slink off to put our lives and fortunes under the protection of an absolute. For once we do this we must give up thinking about our values. Absolutes are not inquirable. They cannot be questioned or looked into; they can only be obeyed.

But men are the constructers of their values, just as they are the constructers of their truth. The reason they can risk this construction on their own, without transcendental help, is simply that they test their value claims in experience and are modest, therefore, in what they say of their values, namely, that they are only tentative and temporary statements of what ought to be done. Furthermore, such statements are never to be considered universal; they always apply to this or that situation, insofar as the situation can be blocked out for ethical analysis.

To explain this, the Experimentalist reminds us that every ethical situation arises from a desire to improve some state of affairs; every value judgment stems from a prior longing of some kind or other to rearrange in more desirable fashion a specific sector of experience (the Experimentalist's reality).

Hence, the question "What should I do?" can never be thought of as having come down out of the blue somewhere, i.e., considered as an ultimate question. It must always be considered in some human context. If I ask "What should I do?" the only sensible answer is the familiar qualifying counter: "It all depends." It depends on what ends I have in view, on what circumstance I wish to have prevail in this corner of reality. What rearrangement of the situation would be an improvement on what I have at this moment? What results do I wish when I make up my mind and go ahead and do something? All these are antecedent questions to "What should I do?"

It should be apparent that the famous Experimentalist "Doctrine of

28 John Dewey, *Democracy and Education* (New York: The Macmillan Co., 1916), p. 405.

Consequences" finds splendid application at this point. For, just as in epistemology, the principle of "What works?" is also valid here. A good act, an ethical act, is measured by the results it yields. An ethical principle is measured by what happens when one acts on it: which is by way of saying that if a Kantian universal or a naturalistic moral law or a rationalistic dictum prescribes some course of action, men will *try it out* in their lives before really putting their stamp of approval on it. If such a prescription — absolute or otherwise — consistently leads to unwanted consequences, men will eventually get rid of it.

This has happened, too, in history. The "divine right" of kings was once considered an absolute truth, and absolute obedience to the king or magistrate was therefore an absolute good: It was what God expected of you. We finally got rid of this notion — not because God repealed it but because it did not yield the kind of life we wanted to live.

Divorce was once considered evil, the breaking of a divine covenant. We are changing our minds about this; our moral values are undergoing revision, and, again, not because some heavenly universal has been legislated out of existence but, rather, because men in their wisdom can see the concrete effects of alternative moral policies on the institution of marriage. And they gravitate to that policy which when acted upon leads to the most beneficent experiential results.

This attention to consequences is nothing more than the scientific method applied to ethical questions. As in epistemology, we are confronted with a situation which is indeterminate; that is, how it will come out depends on what actions we take. We "try out" various policies. And that policy which when acted upon yields desirable consequences we isolate and identify as an ethical principle, or a "good." We make no claims, in keeping with the scientific method, that we have found some "absolute." We simply say that, generally speaking, in situations like this the preferred course of action is such and such.

Now obviously we cannot engage in this procedure with quite the same neat control that a physical scientist enjoys in his laboratory. In the social sciences and in moral problems we must deal much more slowly and deliberately with our variables. Human beings cannot be manipulated like test tubes, and so our "testing for consequences" must be carried on over the long stretch of history, unmanaged, for the most part, by deliberate efforts at experimentation. But this does not disqualify the theory; for the same procedure is followed, if not formally and systematically then informally and merely "historically." For men *do* make up their minds on moral questions, in terms of the kind of life which ensues from their application in ordinary affairs. If history may be thought of as a kind of giant, humanistic "test tube," then values are quite as scientifically arrived at in human experience as is any biological or chemical truth in a laboratory.

To say that "what works is good"[29] bothers many people because it has the ring of a scandalous, licentious form of hedonism — a kind of "what-works-is-good-and-what-works-is-what-works-for-me" doctrine. While Experimentalists do not object to defending the scandalous, if by *scandalous* is meant a break with tradition, nonetheless they mean to set their theory into wider context to quiet such anxieties.

The wider context is simply the community. What "works" is not just what works for me but what works for all. It is what we might call the "pebble theory" of the act, that just as a pebble thrown into a pond produces wider and wider concentric circles of effect on the pond's surface, so likewise does a human act produce wider and wider effects as the products of this act flow into the community.

Hence, a thief may be excused for saying — according to this morality — that thievery is good because for him it produces desirable consequences, i.e., wealth. If it didn't yield such satisfactions he probably wouldn't thieve. But the thief's own private corner of experience is not the whole of the context of his act. His conduct has public consequences as well, quite beyond his own life. When those consequences are measured in the larger context, we say his conduct is bad.

The scope and intensity of public consequences are what help us to measure the morality or immorality of the act. But the point is that we do not have to go outside the public arena of consequences to find our ethical principles. Indeed, to do so is to create axiological problems where none exists. To insist, for instance, that there are some absolutes which govern in all circumstances for all men, no matter where or when, is immediately to put ourselves in the position of defending exceptions. There can be moments, after all (indeed there are), when a man must steal to feed a hungry child, when he must lie to protect another's safety, when he must take a life to save his own.

Thievery, lying, and murder cannot therefore ever be absolutely taboo. They each have their human context, which means they each have a variety of consequences to which they lead. And since not all such consequences are undesirable, we cannot say that this kind of conduct is absolutely undesirable. In the context of the act, i.e., in the totality of public effects, moral right may be found.

To turn to the positive side of the case for a brief illustration, we can say that a value like "equality" or "brotherhood" is held to be good by virtue of the quality of social consequences to which it leads. The notion that "all men are equal" is a *good* notion, a defensible political ethic to work from, not because it is self-evident, as Jefferson insisted. There

29 There is an interesting logical conundrum here: The traditional philosophies prefer the reverse order, "What is good works," or, epistemologically, "What is true works." To which the Experimentalist replies, "Well, yes, but how do we find out 'what is true (good)'?" Answer: We have to try it out and see!

is nothing self-evident about it at all. It is a *good* notion because *it works.* Life lived according to it is preferred by men to life lived according to other notions. The political and social consequences that flow from it are the kind of consequences we want.

But what, to ask the final question, *ought* we to *want*? To this the Experimentalist has no answer, for it is an ultimate question, and ultimate questions have no answers. Since values are to be found in the context of experience, men will have to find out what they *ought* to want in this selfsame, relativistic circumstance of ordinary experiencing. There simply is no absolute answer.

The only kind of sensible answer one can give is that men *ought* to want what they in fact *do* want when presented with all the alternatives and the knowledge of their consequences — which is no more than saying that a community of men, employing a kind of public sharing of preferences and values and being intelligent about the whole business, can come to a working notion of the kind of civilization they would like to build, that is to say, the values that they would like to work for and attain. But in the working for and attaining of these values, other values have a tendency to suggest themselves. Man's valuing becomes, then, a constant creation of and accommodation to the changing moral environment about him; as the consequences which flow from his principles change, his principles themselves change.

This public sharing of values, incidentally, comes close to qualifying as an "ultimate" in Experimentalist moral theory. The very "public-ity" of experience, i.e., its public and open character, tacitly requires an open and public procedure by which morality can be questioned, challenged, and constantly tested in the lives of men.

But the "ongoing-ness" of moral experience is perhaps an even stronger candidate for ultimacy in Experimentalist value theory. For the *process* of shaping values is more often emphasized than the *substantive values* that are shaped — which can be restated by saying that the Good Life to the Experimentalist is not some describable state of affairs, some Utopian content to human circumstance; it is, rather, the *process of valuing* itself. Or, to employ a bit of epigrammatic shorthand: The Good Life is *seeking* the Good Life! If anything could possibly qualify as an absolute Experimentalist value, this might.

Aesthetics: the public taste

If the application of a scientific temper to ethical considerations is difficult, we find the aesthetic application even more so. All right, then, you may say, we test our value judgments in a scientific, consequence-oriented way! How can this possibly apply to art, and music, and poetry, and the dance?

For our edification or bedevilment (however it may strike you) John Dewey wrote a long and difficult but monumental book on the subject.[30] For clues to an Experimentalist aesthetic we could hardly go to a better source.

In the first place, said Dewey, we must repudiate the substantive concept which we have traditionally assigned to a work of art, the notion that a painting or a symphony or a poem is a special type of entity to which we must assign certain existential qualities to account for the work's aesthetic effect on us.

Rather, said Dewey, the work of art is really the "working" of the work of art in our lives; that is to say, ". . . the work of art is what the product does with and in experience."[31] Here again we are face to face with the primacy of "consequences." The operating, experiential consequences of a so-called work of art are the measure of its aesthetic value.

In contrast to the earlier philosophies, which find aesthetic determinants in some objective standard beyond the world of men, Experimentalism insists that aesthetic judgment must ultimately rest on what men respond to in their world — what they feel, what they sense, in the presence of things which claim to be beautiful. Is Beethoven's *Ninth Symphony* beautiful? The answer does not lie in some transcendent realm of criticism, or in the verdict of the musicologist, or in some inherited criteria. The answer lies in how men feel when they hear it! It is as simple as this.

We must have our critics, of course, to help us discover our tastes. But in the long run the appreciating public tells the critics what to applaud and what to scorn. If the critics consistently repudiated our preferences we would soon cease reading them.

By way of further contrast, we may also say that the earlier doctrines have held that the function of art is to idealize or reproduce or rationalize the objective reality of which we are spectators, i.e., to celebrate the inherent qualities of what ultimately *is*. To an Experimentalist this is so much nonsense. The function of art is to communicate; ". . . the work of art tells something to those who enjoy it about the nature of their own experience of the world: . . . it presents the world in a new experience which they undergo."[32]

The purpose of the artist, then, is not to behold ultimate reality and depict it for us in form, color, or sound. It is, rather, for him to have new insights, new feelings, new experiences, and to see how skillful he can become in enabling the rest of us to experience them too.

Every art communicates because it expresses. It enables us to share vividly and deeply in meaning to which we had been dumb, or for which we had

[30] *Art as Experience* (New York: Minton-Balch and Co., 1934).
[31] *Ibid.*, p. 3.   [32] *Ibid.*, p. 83.

but the ear that permits what is said to pass through in transit to overt action. For communication is not announcing things, even if they are said with the emphasis of great sonority. Communication is the process of creating participation, of making common what had been isolated and singular; and part of the miracle it achieves is that, in being communicated, the conveyance of meaning gives body and definiteness to the experience of the one who utters as well as to that of those who listen.[33]

We see, then, that aesthetic taste, as well as moral judgment, is grounded in what we may call *public experience*. We are concerned first of all with the consequences of art objects, what they do in and with our experience, what they cause to be aroused in ourselves. But then we wish to share those arousals, to test and compare, to see if the artist has shared well his inner experiential feelings.

What, then, am I to like? The answer can be given in the kind of terms intelligible to the man in the street as well as the aesthete: If in the presence of a work I see new meanings in my life, if new dimensions of feeling come into my experience, and if by these novelties of meaning and feeling I make better emotional contact with my fellow man, then I am experiencing a work of true art.

EXISTENTIALISM

We come finally to the most recent and, in a sense, the least orthodox of all our axiologies. If Experimentalism has given over a lion's share of its time to value theory, we may safely say that Existentialism is almost obsessed with it. For Existentialism is principally a value theory, a philosophy according to which everything must pass through the funnel of choice. And since choice is fundamentally an exercise in valuing, the entirety of philosophical content in Existentialism may be described as axiological.

The only — and single — thing which escapes this classification is man's existence. We did not choose that; we had no domain over coming into being. We just "turned up" and discovered ourselves in being. This single and singular nonaxiological doctrine of *existence* is, of course, better located in metaphysics or ontology. And it should be plain to you by now that it is the central principle of Existentialism.

But everything that flows from it, as we have said, is axiological. For existence necessitates choice; we cannot get out of it. Indeed, to exist means to be in a condition of forced choice. The troublesome infinitive *to be* has finally been given a definition: *To be* means to be engaged in choosing. There is no escaping the making of choices; the two terms.

[33] *Ibid.*, p. 244. Quoted by permission of G. P. Putnam's Sons.

to be and *to be engaged in choosing,* are synonyms and mutually convertible.

Ethics: the anguish of freedom

What, then, can we say about the question: What should I do? Quite obviously, this question must now be looked at in a somewhat different light. For at the outset we must realize — as the other philosophies sometimes do not — that ethical situations absolutely require *doing something.* Even doing nothing is to do something! We cannot step back from an ethical problem and calmly decide whether we are going to enter it or not. We are already *in it.* Even by retreating from it, refusing to take part in it, refusing to choose a course of action out of it — even by these seemingly neutral behaviors we are actually asserting a positive choice.

The problem of ethics, therefore, is not just an entertaining indoor sport of moralists and philosophers; it is a serious and important activity we engage in every moment of our waking days. Every move we make, every word we utter, every feeling we show, is a small but significant "building block" of choice in our definition of Man. For it is by these tiny "building blocks" — these axiological "votes" we cast in the metaphysical "election" — that we construct over the years of our lives our definition of the essence of man. This is, of course, what the Existentialist considers to be the business of our lives: to define man. And since, by reason of our existence, we cannot get out of it, we might as well make the most of it.

To make the very most of it, we must first own up to a lavish egotism: We want to be God! We want to be like him, to imitate him. Epistemologically, we want to know everything, to be absolute in our knowledge of truth (see the discussion on the two "modes of knowing" in Chapter Six, pages 167–170). But axiologically, which is more important, we want to know and do the right, the *absolute* right; we want to value absolutely, i.e., with absolute certainty; we want our conduct to be *divine,* not in a facetious but in a thoroughly earnest sense of that word.

But we have already seen, in Chapter Six (see pages 167–170), that this program in the "imitation of God" can lead only to a very mixed blessing, namely, ultimate union with God. The blessing is mixed because we really do not want to reach it, for to come to absolute and perfect union with God is to pass from becoming to being; it is to pass out of the zone of choosing, for there is no more choosing in God. God, by definition, has no ethical problems, no indeterminate moral situations. So God makes no choices: He simply is.[34]

[34] If, as mentioned earlier, to be engaged in choosing is equivalent to existing, this

If we were to succeed, therefore, in this grand adventure — or any adventure in coming into perfect union with Absolute Good — we would lose our capacity to choose, and hence to choose ourselves, our own essence. Ethics, as a philosophical subject matter, would pass into use-lessness; there would be no more decisions to make. And without decisions man would pass from existence.

The Existentialist therefore repudiates all absolutes, for to tangle with even a "little" absolute is to compromise one's essential humanity, the freedom to choose. As we have pointed out earlier, to tangle with an absolute is to surrender moral autonomy; to embrace an absolute is to place oneself within its mandatory dominion. If one does this, then he forfeits his freedom to choose.

> [If] certain values exist prior to me, it is self-contradictory for me to want them and at the same [time] state that they are imposed on me.[35]

But if I find no absolutes to rely on, how am I to value? The Experimentalist, as we have seen, answers this by saying that I should test my values for their consequences, share the results, and, by conjoint activity with others, develop some working situational values as ethical guides. This is good advice, says the Existentialist, as far as it goes. The trouble with it is — as we pointed out in similar circumstances in discussing epistemology in Chapter Six — that it creates a new absolute, the social group, to take the place of the earlier, doctrinaire absolutes. And the dominion of the group can be even more pernicious than the dominion of some transcendental ultimate.

> To battle against princes and popes — and the nearer we come to our own times the truer this is — is easy compared with struggling against the

---

statement would appear confusing. A terminological difficulty is encountered here: We have no word for the "existing" of God, who does no choosing. We have to coin one arbitrarily.

You will recall that in Chapter Six a distinction was made between "being-in-itself" and "being-for-itself." In Existentialist lexicography, the former is usually rendered simply as *being*, and the latter is customarily rendered as *existing* or *existence*. The former describes the mode of being exhibited by God, a mode which is a being without choice because it is complete and final. The latter describes the condition of man, a condition of constant choosing because it is not complete and final. God, one Existentialist explains, entered the "zone of existence," i.e., the "for-itself," the "choosing realm," in the form of Jesus Christ. Whether this was itself a "choice" of God presents, of course, an extremely troublesome metaphysical problem to Christian Existentialists.

The problem is, in fact, so troublesome that the atheistic Existentialists seize upon it as the clincher for their atheism. Their argument is that God is the combination of the "in-itself" and the "for-itself," but because this combination is impossible there is no God.

35 Jean Paul Sartre, *Existentialism*, trans. B. Frechtman (New York: Philosophical Library, 1947), p. 53.

masses, the tyranny of equality, against the grin of shallowness, nonsense, baseness, and bestiality.[36]

Let us, says the Existentialist, go the whole way in ethical theory and simply say what we *must* say, namely, that our values consist of our own choices. In choosing we make our values *out of nothing*. No God, no pope, no society can tell me what I must value. They can try, of course, to insist on something, but there is never a case in which I *have* to value anything; I am never "locked in" to this or that value commitment; I am free.

If I simply *had* to do something, if there were no other choice than to cherish some one end or value in life, then I couldn't call myself a man. I would just be another lowly existent, a determined creature, like an insect, taking up space in the cosmos. There would be nothing distinctive about me. If I have any dignity at all, if I really believe myself to be a human being, then I must remain free of "entangling alliances" with everything outside myself which pretends to help me in my valuing enterprise. It doesn't matter what the external thing is — a God, a Nature, a doctrine, or even the "uncoerced community of persuasion" of a scientific morality. In all cases, I must be the final arbiter of what is good.

And this is precisely where the anguish comes in. For when I wake up to discover that I am on my own — not just on my own as one man among other men, as Experimentalism holds, but on my own in a complete and ultimate kind of way — I begin to see that this business of choosing is really baseless.

> My freedom is the unique foundation of values. And since I am the being by virtue of whom values exist, nothing — absolutely nothing — can justify me in adopting this or that value or scale of values. As the unique basis of the existence of values, I am totally unjustifiable. And my freedom is in anguish at finding that it is the baseless basis of values.[37]

I am therefore ultimately responsible for my own choices. The individual is the author of his own goods. He can make himself accountable to no other moral force or factor. I must take responsibility for what I believe and for what I do. If there is anything for which I am not responsible, then to that degree I am not fully existing.

With this logic, the Existentialist looks with abiding scorn on the

[36] Sören Kierkegaard, *The Journals*, ed. A. Dru (London: Oxford University Press, 1938), p. 502 (from page 1317 of the original *Journals* set down in 1854).

[37] H. J. Blackham, *Six Existentialist Thinkers* (London: Routledge & Kegan Paul, Ltd., 1952), pp. 155–156. Quoted by permission of the Macmillan Co.

Catholic confession. For a suppliant to say "I didn't mean to do it" is to say "I couldn't help it; I was being carried along by forces beyond my control; and so I am not responsible." What kind of morality is this? asks the Existentialist. This is no morality at all. Unfortunately, it has been taken over by secular man as well in explaining his excessive materialism, his conformity-ridden life, his aimlessness: "I can't help it; I am conditioned by my culture to be this way; I am a prisoner of circumstance!"

You can take this stand if you wish. But if you do you have voluntarily withdrawn from human status. You are an "insect"! You are driven along like a self-less organism, required by necessity to do the things you do and, therefore, to be what you are. If you are willing to accept this condition, this surrender, however partial, to "insect-like" determinism, you are of course under no obligation to accept the Existentialist message. It is your choice to make; you are still free. But if you choose to believe this way, i.e., that you are not in charge of your choices, then you cannot be held responsible for them. And if you cannot be held responsible for them, then you cannot qualify as a man.

This admittedly is pretty hard advice. But to the Existentialist there is no moral escape from this logic. It represents the "human predicament" in all its simple anguish, and we turn from it only at the prohibitive cost of relinquishing our aspiration to be men.

Men do turn from it from time to time, of course, as history so often shows. Systematic philosophies are a case in point. They start off in search of the universe, but their abiding concern is the nature of man. If the nature of man — his essence or definition — can somehow be fashioned out of a systematic construction of the nature of the cosmos, then philosophy has succeeded in its primary function. But the quest to define man, says the Existentialist, is completely wrongheaded. For in defining man we limit him; we specify what he is and therefore what he must be. He cannot pass beyond this definition because this is his essence. To box man in thus is to destroy him.

> Classical philosophy comes to an end in Hegel, because it has become folly to construct intellectual totalitarian systems in which everything is taken up, harmonized, rationalized, and justified. Such palaces are still marvelous, but nobody can live in them. The savour and reality of human existence, its perils and triumphs, its bitterness and sweetness, are outside in the street.[38]

Even the more modern views, such as Experimentalism, fall into this error. They studiously avoid the question of man's essence, it is true,

[38] *Ibid.*, p. 44.

but they persist in attempting to place men in some *context* — either the context of sociality and community[39] or the context of some ultimate Method which assumes the office of final criterion for all that shall pass as human.

In either case, what is sought after is a "ground" of some kind in which man is to be understood. But contexts are just as much penitentiaries as definitions; they specify the boundaries of our essence even if they do not specify the essence itself. Philosophic systems of all kinds, therefore, have the effect of satisfying our quest for essence; but when they do this they unwittingly provide an escape from the anguish of our ultimate freedom, thus reducing us as men.

Religion is another example of men's turning from their "awful freedom" to find comfort in the embrace of an authority to which they may submit their choices. Man is necessary to the cosmos, we are told; indeed, he is not only necessary but specifically singled out for special care and attention by an Ultimate Being. As a finite creature, endowed by the Higher Being with certain attributes and qualities, he is enjoined to yield to certain moral canons of thought and conduct — hence, to submit to some *a priori* essence.

Men forget, however, that to view man as either central or necessary to the cosmos is in the very beginning a prodigious "as if" that we place beneath our theological scaffolding before proceeding to build our systems. In the office of an "as if," such a notion has no ultimate justifiability or warrant as a statement of truth. It is completely unjustified. It is merely a hypothesis, and a rather subconsciously uncritical one at that. As such, it reflects a choice men make about themselves, not something that is embedded in reality or forced on them from on high.

It is in this context that we may understand the distinction between the "theistic" and "atheistic" wings of Existentialism. To the theistic wing, represented principally by Christian Existentialists, the "as if" itself is enough to build on. Man has a longing for an ultimate being, for God. This longing, in and of itself, is no verification of the existence of God, but at least it points to the possibility of God. So we accept it as an "as if" and let it work in our lives; we live our lives *as if* there was a God. The "as if" has the effect of reminding us of our responsibility without at the same time specifying what our choices should be. Working in this way, the "as if" levies its ethical pressure on us while leaving us free. To paraphrase the Spanish philosopher De Unamuno: "Let life be lived in such a way, with such dedication to goodness and the highest values, that if, after all, it is annihilation which finally awaits us, that will be an injustice."

39 See V. C. Morris, "Freedom and Choice in the Educative Process," *Educational Theory*, III, No. 4 (October, 1958), 231–238.

To the atheist Existentialist, however, it is hazardous to assign too much stature to the "as if" simply because of our temptations as men to distort it from what it is — an "as if" — into a substantive and credible truth, which it is not. Furthermore, to recommend it as providing "moral pressure" is simply another instance of the weakness of men; if men claim to be men, then they should not have to depend on "as if's" as reminders to do their duty. A sense of responsibility is not achieved by entertaining a fantasy; it is achieved by awakening to one's existential condition. Finally, the "as if" has the effect of deflecting man's concern from his choices — which are, after all, the real business of existing — to the secondary concern of the possibility of divine recognition. To be interested in recognition is to be interested in currying favor or, at best — remembering De Unamuno's remark — in wresting justice from the hands of a God.

But, says the atheistic Existentialist, this is not what we ought to be doing around here. We are not seeking favors. Nor are we seeking justice from an Ultimate Being. We are trying to be men, in the noblest sense of the term, and we can get about this business more directly if we do not worry too much about what is going to happen to us. Therefore, the being or nonbeing of God is an irrelevancy in moral theory. As Jean Paul Sartre has so splendidly put it for the atheist:

> Existentialism isn't so atheistic that it wears itself out showing that God doesn't exist. Rather, it declares that even if God did exist, that would change nothing . . . Not that we believe that God exists, but we think that the problem of His existence is not the issue.[40]

Aesthetics: the revolt from the public norm

A theory of aesthetics is almost directly derivative from the above ethical theory. When in Existentialist thinking we encounter the question What should I like?, the answer can be given only in terms of what each individual chooses for himself. Indeed, it is in the active selection of what we like, in our preferences, our appreciations, our day-by-day takings and rejectings. But this is not to say that what *is* preferred and rejected, day by day, is therefore what *ought* to be preferred and rejected. For there is no external criterion to which we can refer. When it comes to aesthetic choices we are ultimately on our own.

Once again, we have the beginnings — but only the beginnings — of the Existentialist position in Experimentalist aesthetics, discussed in the preceding section. Aesthetic quality is not what works of art contain; it is, rather, what works of art do to and for us. It is, in a manner of

[40] Sartre, *op. cit.*, p. 61.

speaking, the "having of feelings" within us. And the having of feelings constitutes the focus of our inquiry in aesthetic judgments.

Thus, what Dewey and the Experimentalists so splendidly set out to do was to expand the theme of "operationalism" in aesthetic judgment by making much of the response and private feelings of the "consumers" of art. But, according to Existentialism, they take away with their left hand what they have just offered with their right by saying that one's private aesthetic feelings must ultimately be authenticated and validated in the open territory of public experience. When this territory is systematically explored, says the Experimentalist, certain commonly held criteria can now and then be identified and thought of as the "public standard of taste." The Experimentalist goes on to say that, while this public standard is by no means absolute or unchanging — in art, music, architecture, etc. — it nevertheless assumes a stature superior to that of the private standard of any given individual, and, hence, recommends itself as something to which the individual aesthetic consumer may refer when he wishes to "check" his tastes.

The only trouble with this aesthetic doctrine is that it finds outside the individual's own feelings the standard by which his feelings are to be certified. And this is precisely our old difficulty, says the Existentialist. For there are no standards outside ourselves in the setting of taste. We are as unjustifiable in this sphere as we were seen to be in the field of ethics; we are a baseless base of taste. Existentially we are suspended in "mid-air," choosing our way to beauty and loveliness with never any assurance that we have selected rightly. This baselessness is admittedly exasperating and annoying, but it is the price we pay for aesthetic freedom. For if we were *not* baseless, but instead had a base for our aesthetic preferences, then we would *have* to choose some things over others; our choices would be given, hence unfree. Under those conditions we could not claim to be men.

It is no accident that Existentialism finds the field of aesthetics so congenial to its message, for aesthetics is perhaps the one domain of life in which the ordinary fellow is not easily forced into line. It is that sphere of experience in which neither the canons of inherited judgment nor the views of contemporary experts seem to have much effect on the individual. Toscanini used to insist that Beethoven's *Ninth* was "the greatest piece of music ever written." Considering the source, this judgment is the kind of thing one is likely to pay attention to. But actually it reduces simply to an interesting but otherwise insignificant statement of preference. Aesthetic pronouncements, even those of a great man, appear to have precious little lateral impact on others in the establishment of their own tastes.

The common citizen is, of course, famously conservative when it comes to painting or sculpture. But he is also just as splendidly independent of the judgments of others. The common cliché in superficial discussions of art, "I know what I like," illustrates the deceptive simplicity of our problem. For this cliché, as ingenuous as it may sound, is as good a description as any of our aesthetic situation as the Existentialist sees it. It simply says: I have a knowledge of beauty and loveliness, a knowledge which is utterly baseless, absolutely nonreferable to any final criteria, but authentic just the same. For better or worse, I shall have to find my aesthetic answers here, and thus contribute my share to the aesthetic essence of man.

QUESTIONS

1. Select a work of art — a Brahms symphony, a Frank Lloyd Wright house, a Grandma Moses primitive — and apply the five aesthetic theories to it. How would they evaluate the work?

2. Now that we have examined five ethical doctrines, what is your reaction to the problem of absolutes in morals? Are there any moral prescriptions which are common to all of these moralities? Does this make them absolute? Explain.

3. To what extent do you think intelligence and reason may be said to pertain to aesthetics? Is art in any way rational, as the Neo-Thomists say, or is it all emotional, nonrational, and glandular?

4. Would you say that the more intelligent an individual, the more sensitive he is in the field of aesthetics? Are intellectuals better judges of art than non-intellectuals?

5. Consider a contemporary moral issue — racial segregation, premarital sexual experience, divorce — and examine it from the standpoint of the five ethical systems. Do they all come to the same conclusions as to what is right?

6. Referring back to Question 6 for Chapter Eight (see page 244), how would you now re-evaluate your analysis of the two architectural examples you chose? Would all five of the aesthetic theories tend to confirm your judgments?

FURTHER READING

Idealism

Greene, Theodore M. *The Arts and the Art of Criticism*. Princeton, N.J.: Princeton University Press, 1940.

In Chapter XX, on "The Nature and Criteria of Criticism," Greene develops the thesis that style, as a historical concept, and perfection, truth, and greatness, as normative concepts, are the four ultimate criteria for the judgment and criticism of art. In succeeding chapters he analyzes these four concepts more fully.

Kant, Immanuel. *The Fundamental Principles of the Metaphysic of Ethics.* Translated by Otto Manthey-Zorn. New York: D. Appleton-Century Company, Inc., 1938.
This essay, which first appeared in 1785, was Kant's first attempt at a systematic moral theory. In some ways it still stands as the core thesis of Idealist ethics. Kant examines the transition from rational to philosophical knowledge of morality, from popular morals to metaphysics, and from the metaphysic of ethics to the critique of pure practical reason. It is a relatively short book and not so difficult as it sounds.

Realism

Montague, William P. *The Ways of Things.* New York: Prentice-Hall, Inc., 1940.
In an essay entitled "Beauty Is Not Enough," Montague argues for a broadening of aesthetic endeavors to include not only pleasurable sensations but *all* emotional response — the sad, the terrible, and even the horrible — so as to "set off" more singularly that which is to be called beautiful.

Wild, John. *Introduction to Realist Philosophy.* New York: Harper and Bros., 1948.
In Part I of this very readable book, Wild examines the Realist approach to ethics under the heading "The Perfection of Human Nature." In this discussion he considers the basic moral facts of life, how men make themselves happy or miserable, intellectual and moral virtue, and the rational guidance of appetite and action.

Neo-Thomism

Huxley, Aldous. *The Perennial Philosophy.* New York: Harper and Bros., 1945.
With a liberal anthological use of quotations from other writers, Huxley spells out the many-faceted design of philosophical thought in the tradition of Aristotle and St. Thomas. The short chapter on "Good and Evil" is particularly pertinent to the discussion of Neo-Thomist ethics in the present chapter. Here we see that, for the Perennial Philosophy, "good is the separate self's conformity to, and finally annihilation in, the divine Ground which gives it being; evil, the intensification of separateness, the refusal to know that the Ground exists."

Maritain, Jacques. *Creative Intuition in Art and Poetry,* The A. W. Mellon Lectures in the Fine Arts, National Gallery of Art, Washington, D.C. New York: Published for the Bollingen Foundation by Pantheon Books, 1953.
In this handsome volume, the leading contemporary Neo-Thomist considers art as a virtue of the practical intellect, the nature of the preconscious life of

the intellect, and the phenomenon of creative intuition in all artistic activity. Constantly stressing the part played by the intellect, Maritain develops what might be called a rationalist theory of aesthetics.

Experimentalism

Dewey, John. *Art as Experience.* New York: Minton-Balch and Co., 1934.
This lengthy and relatively difficult book is the most frequently cited source for Dewey's theory of aesthetics. The first chapter, on "The Live Creature," and the concluding chapter, on "Art and Civilization," are suitable preludes to the study of the entire volume, and will provide a glimpse of the Experimentalist approach to aesthetics.

———, and Tufts, James H. *Ethics,* Revised Edition. New York: Henry Holt and Co., Inc., 1936.
This book as a whole is a historical and systematic analysis of the entire problem of morals. Part II, "Theory of the Moral Life," considers the nature of moral theory, ends as they relate to good and wisdom, moral judgment and knowledge, and the moral self.

Existentialism

Sartre, Jean Paul. *What Is Literature?.* Translated by B. Frechtman. New York: Philosophical Library, 1949.
After suffering considerable abuse from literary critics, Sartre says, he decided to strike back by examining the title's question via the subordinate questions: What is writing? Why write? For whom does one write? Chapter I, on the first of these questions, stresses the "engagement" of the artist and the "in-the-situation" character of all truly creative endeavor.

Tillich, Paul. *The Courage To Be.* New Haven: Yale University Press, 1952.
In this powerful little volume, a leading Christian Existentialist poses the problems of "Being and Courage" and "Non-Being and Anxiety," and then proceeds to an analysis of the courage to be in group participation, the courage to be as oneself, and, finally, the courage to be in the transcendent divine encounter.

Comparative Axiology and

the Educative Process

AXIOLOGY AND EDUCATION

Education as a moral enterprise

Now that we have completed a tour through some of the major theories of ethical and aesthetic valuation, it is time to address ourselves to the more important question of what these axiological theories have to say about the management of the learning process. In Chapter One the argument was offered that education is at bottom a value enterprise. We are now in a position to see the meaning of this idea in a more sophisticated setting.

For instance, to some philosophies, most particularly Neo-Thomism, as well as most theistic systems of belief, the school is a value enterprise in the sense that it inducts the young into a scheme of belief and commitment which is ultimately certified in the cosmos by a super being or a transcendent, transempirical authority. The content of these values and preferences is of course found in social life, in our daily circumstances of ethical and aesthetic choosing, but the standards for such choices have their ultimate origin and locus somewhere beyond the historical traditions of the race. In schools of this persuasion, there is a certain surety of mood, a confidence that the values and tastes being recommended to children need not be questioned for adequacy but may be inculcated and indoctrinated in the young without argument.

To other philosophies, most notably Idealism, Realism, and Experimentalism, an educational system is a social device which civilized societies have invented to induct their young into the outlooks and preferences implicit in the living and working patterns of the community. In this context the educational enterprise is, in the best sense of the metaphor, a "tradition-transmitting mechanism," a social and cultural instrument for the perpetuation of a cherished heritage. In the case of Idealism and Realism, this cumulation of belief and tradition, by virtue of its slow assimilation and long tenure in the annals and archives of man, is an approximation of what is ultimately and finally true and good and is, therefore, necessarily includable in the experience of the young.

In the case of Experimentalism, however, one of the indigenous ingredients of this American tradition of ours — in contrast to other traditions — is a certain skepticism of tradition itself, a drifting away from the idea that the past is true and good merely because it *is* the past, which in turn inclines to a certain reluctance to look backward instead of forward in the planning and shaping of human experience. But this is itself a value which is lodged in the mind of the community, a value which to the Experimentalist is actually more genuinely "tradition-al," i.e., more authentic a reflection of our cultural spirit and national character, than some of the other things we have merely inherited from an increasingly irrelevant past. Hence, it most certainly belongs in the value structure of the school and deserves to be introduced into the working patterns of the young as they grow to maturity.

But it is still a value judgment, a position taken, a preference objectified — in short, a plank in the argument for a certain way of living and of life. And Experimentalism, which espouses this value, must be looked at as just as partisan a philosophy of life as any other and its schools as much dedicated to its point of view as other schools are to theirs.

When we examine the anatomy of commitment and partisanship itself we confront a peculiar paradox of all educational programs: They can sometimes argue too well for a set of values. "Nothing succeeds like success," we sometimes say; but in the case of the axiological and ideological base of modern education, it is perhaps the other way around: "Nothing fails like too much success." Take the case of twentieth-century nationalistic educational programs. A Fascist education succeeds beyond telling and brings a world to arms. A Communist education, seized by purpose and fired by ideological energy, succeeds to enslave a people and to intimidate the uncommitted in cold war. Or, to return to our more immediate references, Idealist, Realist, and Neo-Thomist schools glorify and venerate what is past and absolute and ill prepare today's youngster for the fast-moving, relativistic present. Experimentalism and its schools concentrate on current experience and lay themselves open to the criticism of "an obsession with Present-ism," with the thinness and superficiality that such an obsession implies.

All of this is reminiscent of a remark once made by Ralph Harper: "There is nothing worse than a good idea insisted on too much." Which brings us to a very troublesome feature of education — indeed, its fundamental dilemma — namely, the equivocal character of ends. Ralph Barton Perry explains it thus:

> To define in advance an end result and then to seek by all possible means to achieve it, is held to be too narrowing, too repressive, too authoritarian. But if, on the other hand, there is no end in view, educational activity is confused and incoherent. Its various parts and successive phases do not add up to anything. Without a definition of the end there is no test by which means can be selected, and no standard by which practice can be criticized and improved.[1]

Perry goes on to say, in an Experimentalist moment, that there is an escape from this dilemma if we not only proclaim ourselves *against* narrowness, rigidity, and authoritarianism of all sorts but also proclaim ourselves *for* their opposites — breadth, flexibility, and freedom. "These opposites," he says, "and other kindred ideas themselves define an end — an end that can be methodically and constantly pursued, and that must be methodically and consistently pursued if it is to be realized."[2]

What this ideology reduces to, obviously, is an affirmative commitment to openness, to unfettered inquiry, to freedom. It is, in short, the "commitment to noncommitment," a value judgment both logically outrageous and superlatively coherent. Is freedom, really, an idea which could ever conceivably be "insisted on too much"?

Maybe we have our hands here on something that may qualify as an ultimate value: freedom. But if it is to be ultimate, then it must indeed be ULTIMATE, supremely unqualified by and unreferable to any other principle. It is this message of absolute and unqualified freedom which is the axiological "bomb" that is exploding over the mass societies of the twentieth century in the form of Existentialism. Existence in our time has increasingly come to be seen as axiologically absurd, totally without moral content except for what we place in it by our choices. We have come to see ourselves as completely unjustified in these choices, finally and utterly baseless in taste and judgment. Not even the Experi-

[1] Ralph Barton Perry, *Realms of Value* (Cambridge: Harvard University Press, 1954), p. 426.
[2] *Ibid.*, p. 427.

mentalist's presumably ultimate method of science can ever certainly justify a moral choice; all it can do is render it objective, systematic, and public.

Therefore, what the Existentialist school does with tradition is even more subtle than in the case of Experimentalism. It must transmit the heritage so as to provide the child with a knowledge and awareness of all the ideological choices men have ever made; it must go further to include in this heritage the Experimentalist's value commitment to open inquiry, public sharing, scientific procedures, and freedom of thought, association, and expression. But, finally, it must return the child to himself; it must awaken the child to the final knowledge that he is alone, completely and beautifully alone, in the value enterprise.

Values and the school

What this extended analysis is intended to show is that the school is universally considered to be a place where a "value sense" is to be acquired by the young. To some, this "sense" has a foundation: in ultimate Mind, in objective Nature, in transcendent Being, or in social experience (as our first four theories would hold). To others, it has no foundation whatsoever, but is completely baseless (as our final theory would hold). But it is still correct to say that to all of these positions the school is at bottom an axiological institution.

The above distinction will begin to be felt almost immediately in our discussion, for it will necessitate a new division in our ranks, a division which will increasingly set Existentialism off from the others. But for the time being we may permit ourselves the further (although not altogether accurate) observation that the school is a value enterprise, not so much by virtue of the values that are taught didactically or by inference in the presentation of subject matter, but by virtue of the selection of subject matter to be presented, in the procedures employed by the principal and the teachers in dealing with the young, in the climate prevailing in the classrooms, in the art works hung on the walls and displayed in the lobby. Regardless of the way one views the axiological enterprise itself, in education, Professor Childs reminds us, "The moral factor appears whenever the school, or the individual teacher or supervisor, is *for* certain things and *against* other things."

> It appears, for example, in the affairs of the playground — in the kind of sports that are favored and opposed, and in the code of sportsmanship by which the young are taught to govern their behavior in the actual play of various games. It appears in the social life of the school — in all of the behaviors that are approved or disapproved as the young are taught the

288

manners — the conventional or minor morals — of their society. It appears in the school's definition of the delinquent and in its mode of dealing with him. It appears in the way children are taught to treat those of different racial, religious, occupational, economic or national backgrounds. It appears in the department of science: in the methods the young are expected to adopt in conducting their experiments, in their reports of what actually happened during the course of their experiments, as well as in the regard of the teachers of science for accuracy, for precision, and for conclusions that are based on objective data rather than on wishful thinking. It appears in the department of social studies: in the problems that are chosen to be discussed, in the manner in which they are discussed, in the historical documents and events that are emphasized, as well as in the leaders that are chosen to illustrate the important and the worthy and the unimportant and the unworthy in the affairs of man. It appears in the department of literature: in the novels, the poems, the dramas that are chosen for study, in what is considered good and what is considered bad in the various forms and styles of human conduct and expression. It appears in the organization and the government of the school: in the part that superintendent, supervisors, teachers, pupils are expected to play in the making and the maintenance of the regulations of the school. It appears in the methods of grading, promoting, and distributing honors among the children of the school. It appears in the celebration of national holidays: in the particular events that are celebrated as well as in the historical and contemporary personalities who are chosen to exemplify the qualities of citizenship and worthy community service. It appears in the program for the general assemblies of the schools: in the various leaders from the community who are brought in to speak to the children. It appears in the way teachers are treated: the amount of freedom and initiative they enjoy, in the extent to which teachers are permitted to take part in the life of their community, and the degree to which the young believe that they are studying under leaders who are more than docile, routine drillmasters in assigned subjects. It appears in the way the community organizes to conduct its schools: in the provision it makes in its schoolgrounds, buildings, and equipment, in the kind of people it chooses to serve on the school board, and in the relation of the members of the board to the administrative and teaching staff.[3]

We are, therefore, not dealing with anything trivial when we view the school in an axiological way; we are, on the contrary, dealing with the most strategic and crucial side of the school's work — indeed, with the very medium within which teaching and learning are carried on. In the pages to follow, therefore, we cannot confine ourselves simply to the "value" dimension of education as it is popularly thought of in what we sometimes call "character-building," or even in the more inclusive sense of

[3] *Education and Morals* (New York: Appleton-Century-Crofts, Inc., 1950), pp. 17–19.

the development of "moral and spiritual values." What we are dealing with is the *total* life of the young, what they are taught to cherish and desire, what they are taught to reject and avoid. These decisions inhere in practically everything the school does.

LEARNING TO LIVE
THE ETHICAL LIFE

How does an individual learn right conduct? Probably more than any other single question in learning theory, this continues to evade our understanding in the training of the young. And so long as theoretical understanding escapes us, our classroom practice will probably continue to be confused and incoherent. In a sense, this is what we find in the typical American school today; very little deliberate moral instruction, surprisingly enough, is actually being given there. In spite of what has been said in the previous section concerning the value choices implicit in the practical functioning of educational programs, very few of these choices are made deliberately by teachers and principals with the express idea of bringing about some preferential attitude on the part of the young. They are made, rather, in a subconscious, routine way as the daily patterns of teaching and learning regularize themselves.

Such choices fail of their full axiological impact on youngsters in the degree to which they pass from conscious attention into the habitual routine of the school. For example, when a high school principal, through the "magic" of his "Big Brother" public-address system, leads the entire school in the flag salute, the ostensible object of this exercise is to arouse healthy instincts of national feeling, that is, to educe certain attitudes which are thought to be good. But such an impersonalized procedure, especially if it becomes through repetition merely another ritual in the morning home-room period to satisfy a state law, will obviously lose its power to move youngsters to a value commitment. And so such practices become useless and empty in the moral training of boys and girls.

As the value practices of the school cease being intentional and deliberate and become increasingly more routine and automatic, there is a tendency for the school as a whole to take on the appearance of being morally neutral, perhaps even uninterested, in the entire question of ethical training. As a matter of fact, there is in contemporary educational circles a certain pseudosophisticated embarrassment concerning this whole matter. Morals, we have come to think, are old-fashioned things; there is a Victorian ring to the very word itself. For the modern, glass-front, ranch-style high school, the idea of deliberate thought being given to ethics and conduct seems inappropriate. Or perhaps, as some say, a secular public school necessarily must leave value training to some other agency, be it home, church, or neighborhood.

It is generally true that as we proceed up the educational ladder, from nursery to elementary to secondary to higher to graduate and professional education, we can recognize a gradual reduction of deliberate and intentional moral instruction. Whether this is as it should be is another question. In light of our growing commitment to the lifelong, "learning-has-no-age-limit" conception of education actualized in vast adult-education projects, it is noteworthy that training in belief and conduct in ethical matters is thought *not* to be lifelong but is confined to the standard years of public school instruction.

At any rate, the resultant absence of deliberate moral instruction at the college level is now pretty much a matter of fact. It must be said, of course, that perhaps colleges do teach their students values and ethical norms by the more indirect methods of association. Perhaps the academic life itself and the living of it have a kind of absorptive, "osmosis" effect with respect to desired ethical traits. Operating on this hunch, Dr. Philip E. Jacob of the University of Pennsylvania a few years ago attempted to measure the changes in the value orientations of college students from the freshman to the senior year.[4] To his dismay and the consternation of a large segment of the educational community, he found precious little change in outlook on the part of his subjects, even in those particular spheres — politics, social relations, and personal morality itself — which have traditionally been thought to be most responsive to the influence of the liberal college in America.

Why, one might ask, is deliberate education in ethical values and right conduct so ineffective? Part of the answer may lie in our ignorance of educational psychology or of pedagogy itself, i.e., how to teach values. It may be due also to the grosser fact that American education only reflects a larger trouble in the adult community itself — indeed, in the total culture. There is a moral confusion in contemporary America; we are not sure of our values. This is not necessarily to say that American civilization is beginning its "decline and fall" in the Roman tradition, as some moralists contend; it is only to say that there are many areas of uncertainty as to what we ourselves believe and what we therefore wish to teach our children.

Social life is always a going contest between the good and the bad, however one defines these two poles of the moral life. And certainly there is no shortage of the latter to point to as symptomatic of some deficiency among Americans in taking proper care of their public morality. Crime advances, juvenile delinquency spreads, hoodlums infiltrate our business and labor groups, dope addicts fill our hospitals, unwed and deserted

[4] *Changing Values in College* (New York: Harper and Bros., 1957).

mothers expand our relief rolls, divorce increases and homes are broken. And let us not forget the transgressions closer to home: Petty pilfering from offices and plants by workers has become a major industrial expense, banks annually lose six times as much from their own employees as from armed robbers, traffic tickets get "fixed" by individuals who otherwise appear keenly sensitive to what is right, and income tax evasion — piecemeal, retail, or wholesale — grows into a major indoor sport as common citizens fondle their guide manuals like a tout his Racing Form and corporation lawyers think up new loopholes to outwit and outflank the Internal Revenue Service.

What all this means is simply that both within and beyond the working sphere of the school in America there is plenty of work to be done in public ethics. What our five axiologies have to suggest in this concern has obvious and immediate reference to a major public problem in America today.

Ideas, examples, and conduct

To an Idealist the moral problem in education is by no means an easy one, but it can be thought about best by viewing the ethical conduct of men as growing out of a social tradition. "Social conventions are the wisdom of the past functioning in the present," says Herman Harrell Horne, a leading spokesman for the Idealist position. "For most persons," he says, "only bad characters come from the indulgence of appetite contrary to social usage."[5]

It then obviously becomes necessary to transmit the social conventions to the young in the school, and since this can best be accomplished through the medium of words and symbols it is recommended that in all those subject matters having to do with convention and social ideals particular stress be laid upon such values and didactically taught. It is evident that such subject matters as history and literature afford the best vehicles for this kind of instruction. In historical legends and documents there is a lavish abundance of this type of material. At the elementary-school level, for instance, the legend of George Washington and the cherry tree seems to have a hardy endurance. It does not matter too much whether it is true or not; it suffices as a paradigmatic example of the moral life which is being recommended to the young. As the youngster proceeds through school he will increasingly confront more substantial representations of our moral past: the *Areopagitica,* the Magna Charta, the defense of Peter Zenger, the Declaration of Independence, the speeches of Patrick Henry, Émile Zola's appeal for Captain Dreyfus, the Constitution of the United States, the Gettysburg Address, Woodrow

[5] *This New Education* (New York: Abingdon Press, 1931), p. 182.

Wilson's "make the world safe for democracy," the 1954 Supreme Court decision on racial segregation.

These are the containers of our moral tradition. They speak the conscience of the Western mind and the American ethic. As such they stand for an inherited sense of the right, and, closely studied and emotionally absorbed, they and other materials like them become the base upon which an Idealist morality can be built in the child.

In the field of literature it is also true that moral content is persistently present. The famous "Little Red Hen" is not just a trivial tale; it has a "hard" message, the virtue of self-reliance, to deliver to the child. "The Three Little Piggies" is more powerful a document than adults sometimes think; it brings home the moral principle that a sturdy house not only deflects the predatory tendencies of the wolf but is itself the mark of a sturdy character. Fairy tales, Aesop's Fables, stories like *Hansel and Gretel* — all contribute to the growing moral sense of the elementary-school child.

Later on, the student may be introduced to King Arthur and his Court, to the Arabian Nights, to *Beowulf,* the *Song of Roland,* perhaps to Homer's *Iliad.* Not only are these works examples of masterly writing, but they contain a message that we hope is not wasted on the adolescent. After school hours, the young boy is provided more moral incentives. Horatio Alger may be out of date as the exemplar of a middle-class Victorian ethic of striving and succeeding by hard work, and Tom Swift's gadgeteering now seems, in the age of rockets, somewhat puerile; but they have been replaced by other, more sophisticated heroes like Buck Rogers, Steve Canyon, and the space astronauts. All of these continue to represent the adventurous, "frontiersmanship" morality for which America has always stood.

The fictional hero has, in a scientific age, somewhat subsided in favor of the historic and contemporary hero: Benjamin Franklin, Abraham Lincoln, Henry Ford, Babe Ruth, Eleanor Roosevelt, Roy Campanella. Here, through biography or autobiography, the youngster is brought into the presence of the "larger self" which occupied our attention in Idealist axiology in Chapter Nine. These individuals, through persistence, hard work, excellence of performance, and sometimes raw courage, have shown us the way to a higher life. These are the heroic carriers of our moral tradition; they are human approximations of the Infinite Person. And, as such, they are recommended to the young for imitation.

Nature and conduct

To a Realist the Idealist approach might appear a trifle sentimental. Sentimentalism is a very real and genuine part of our lives, and it may indeed be celebrated in historical legend and the fictional or real hero. But this is not enough for shaping the conduct of the child to the moral dimension of a real world. If looked at carefully, the real world, the world of events and occurrences, the world of an observable Nature, can bring the child nearer to right conduct.

Perhaps the most trivial, but then again not so trivial, instance of this is a direct look at Nature to find there a moral content. We show to the child the habits of robins and sparrows, show them feeding their young and helping them learn to fly. We encourage animal pets in the home and promote small "zoos" of hamsters, turtles, and goldfish in the elementary classroom. Finally, we educate in biological reproduction by representing this delicate subject matter in the litter of kittens brought to the classroom with their mother by a member of the class. In all these ways, we are, whether we are aware of it or not, implicitly sensitizing the child to the wonderful manner in which Nature tends to support and sustain life; we are sensitizing the child to the morality of life itself. These are vastly oversimplified but nonetheless authentic instances of implanting in the small child's mind the notion that there is something sacred about life; with the small kernel of this idea as a beginning, he is then brought stage by stage to a higher ethical application of it to humankind. It is, in a sense, the proper starting point for so noble an ethical principle as Albert Schweitzer's "reverence for life," which he has adopted as his own ultimate value. And Schweitzer actually acts this value out in his role of physician and missionary in Lambaréné, French Equatorial Africa. One does not have to take the Idealist detour through fictional legend or human heroes to get the child to feel an intense and vivid love for life; it can be found directly by observing the procedures of Nature.[6]

Realists will admit that looking for morals in Nature does, of course, have its limits. As the child grows older he will become more sophisticated and skeptical about the presumed moralities of Nature, particularly if they are represented to him in the romanticized fashion of the animal world. However, he is not through with "natural morality" even when he studies biology, chemistry, and physics in high school. For these subjects, so widely thought to be value-free, still aim, as one of their underlying motifs, to portray the supreme *order* of nature to the adolescent. And what is order but a particular value which we wish to implant in the behavior patterns of the young?

It is perhaps a little too precious to intimate that the child's sense of

[6] We shall not inquire of the Realist at this point why Nature's exhibit of tenderness and concern for life is singled out and set axiologically above Nature's equivalent exhibit of violence and concern for death. If Nature is the model, should not a child be exposed to a spider eating a fly or, better yet, to a really wild and bloody dog-and-cat fight? There is certainly some moral content there.

orderly routine and self-discipline can be extracted from the economy and "single-mindedness" of a chemical reaction or an electrical circuit, but the over-all effect of systematic study of nature's ways, if pointed to specifically and related to life's affairs, may conceivably contribute to the child's ethical growth. Patience, as a case in point, was found during World War II to be a human value with its analogue in nature; William Knudsen, as the nation's production chief, responded to his critics concerning the delay in mass production of bombers by alluding to similar difficulties in biology: "Gentlemen, no matter what you may desire in the matter, it still takes nine months!"

We often say that nature has "her own rhythm," that "letting nature take its course" quite often results in problems' solving themselves. "Early to bed and early to rise," while of doubtful value in the production of health, wealth, and wisdom, still contains a residual flavor of virtue. This aphorism, coming down to us as it does from Franklin's agrarian-minded, "rule-of-thumb" way of life, sounds a little quaint in our time; but it nevertheless describes, albeit somewhat obliquely, how nature actually comports herself in the rhythmic dialectic between night and day, rest and activity. We are advised to discipline ourselves to the schedule of nature in the search for the good life. In contrast to Idealism, Realism tends to look for moral exemplars not so much in human persons as in natural processes.

Concerning pedagogy itself, Realism cannot be said to have any hard and fast prescriptions. The only tendencies that seem consistent with the above have to do with the possibility of conditioning the youngster to certain behavior patterns as a prelude to his later, more mature understanding of their dominion over him. Reference was made in Chapter Nine to the underlying thesis of Professor Wild's axiology: "the rational comprehension of natural necessity." Standing behind this psychological dictum is the belief that:

> . . . all men share certain essential tendencies which require that certain moral principles be obeyed by all men if they are to live authentic human lives. . . . The realist believes that men are free within limits to act as they choose in the light of what they understand. Thus, they may violate the moral law if they so decide.[7]

Hence, putting these ideas together when we come to the moral instruction of the young, we must set the limits to behavior by explaining to the child the moral laws involved and enforce certain behavior until

7 John Wild, "Education and Human Society: A Realistic View," Chapter II in *Modern Philosophies and Education,* Fifty-fourth Yearbook of the National Society for the Study of Education, ed. N. B. Henry, Part I (Chicago: the Society, 1955), p. 23.

the child can grow into a rational understanding of the laws on his own.

We must point out here that the Realist shares with the Idealist the willingness to appeal to the accumulated sense of the community as to what these moral laws may be. As Professor Harry Broudy puts it:

> Ask a representative body of citizens what they want in the way of moral education, and the answer will be somewhat as follows:
>
> We want our children to develop reliable tendencies to tell the truth, to respect the codes of right and wrong of the community, to be courageous, to be persevering in the face of obstacles, to withstand the temptations of disapproved pleasures, to be able to sacrifice present pleasures in favor of more remote ones, to have a sense of justice and fair play.
>
> Parents do not expect a guarantee that their child will do this or that at any given time in the future. What they are after are character traits, i.e., reliable tendencies or dispositions to react in certain ways in the presence of difficulties, duties, and conflicts.[8]

We are therefore dealing with tendencies and dispositions which comply with natural and moral law and which the community feels it has a right to insist on. It proceeds to insist on these tendencies by what Professor Broudy calls "moral training."

> We call it training because that is what it is. Through the constant approval and disapproval of others we form these dispositions. By living with others and feeling their pleasure and displeasure, we introject these moral attitudes so that we expect them from ourselves with the same force that others expect them from us.[9]

The Realist may possibly object to calling this procedure "conditioning" in the narrow Pavlovian or, as Wild says, "white rat" sense. But it is certainly drawn from the understanding that behavior in morals is conditionable and that it is legitimate to condition it *in advance of* the child's understanding of what he is doing and why, notwithstanding the importance of such understanding to the mature moral life. It is this feature of behavioral enforcement *prior to* (even if not independent of) genuine rational understanding that marks the Realist position.

The hierarchy of values and the rational act

There is much in the Neo-Thomist position on moral training which coincides with and supports what has been described in Realism. This

---

[8] *Building a Philosophy of Education* (Englewood Cliffs, N.J.: Prentice-Hall, Inc., 1954), p. 405.
[9] *Ibid.*, p. 406.

is true for the same generic reason given in earlier sections of the book where the affinity between these two schools has already been noted, namely, that modern Realism and contemporary Neo-Thomism have a common ancestry in Aristotle. What Neo-Thomism does, in a sense, is to clarify and intensify the Realist pedagogy and to supply it with a powerful ally, the training of the human will.

We may recall at this point the paramount concern in Neo-Thomist axiology (see Chapter Nine) for Reason as the ultimate criterion of the good act. It would appear to follow that the training of the Reason, the full development of its powers, is a major pedagogical objective throughout the moral instruction of the young. This should not be considered to compromise or pre-empt the conditioning of the young to certain behavior patterns by the approval-disapproval, i.e., enforcement, procedure advocated by the Realist. Indeed, the Neo-Thomist would be likely to be even more earnest and rigorous in this phase of teaching. What the Neo-Thomist insists on with perhaps greater vigor than the Realist is that this training of the Reason is a precondition of the rational comprehension of moral law and certainly of the understanding of any specific moral dictum.

Hence, the first pedagogical prescription of the Neo-Thomist would appear to be a thorough training of the Reason through the discipline of the subject matters discussed in Chapter Seven (see pages 191–194). It is through these subject matters that the rational faculties of the mind are brought to peak power and, consequently, to a potential understanding of the rightness or wrongness of certain acts. Insofar as the rational test can be applied to specific ethical precepts — for example, to continence, charity, honesty — so much will a teacher's instruction become more meaningful; but the essential condition is the preparedness of the youngster to see the distinction between right and wrong on purely rational grounds.

Coming, then, to more tactical (as against strategic) considerations in moral education, the Neo-Thomist addresses the teacher's attention to the will. Here is more precisely where the moral enterprise has its origin. Now, the will is quite like the intellect in that it exists in the child but only in a state of potentiality. It is present incipiently in the young but needs training and development in order to be of use to the individual in his moral life.

The will may be very weak, of course, but this is due primarily to the unfortunate events which followed its original endowment upon human nature. According to Ecclesiastical Neo-Thomists, after the so-called Fall of Man at the hands of Adam, Man's supernature was withdrawn, but his intellect and will were left standing, albeit in a weakened condition. Pope Pius XI, after tracing the Fall and Man's Redemption, says: "There

297

remain, therefore, in human nature the effects of original sin, the chief of which are weakness of will and disorderly inclinations."[10]

The second job of the teacher, then, after the strategic training of the Reason, is the more immediate matter of the training of the will. This may be done in a variety of ways, the most familiar and traditional method being that which accords with similar procedures with the intellect, namely, discipline. To discipline the will is to exercise it, to give it tasks which will strengthen those potentialities of will power which reside in every child in the classroom.

According to a strict rendering of this methodology it might be suggested that, just as he is given difficult subject matter in language or mathematics to train his Reason, the child in school should also be given difficult and distasteful tasks, which he would be enjoined to stick to until they were completed. In the enforced application of will power to see an unpleasant job through, the child would be given a chance to strengthen his will in preparation for more strenuous moral undertakings in the future.[11] We see, then, that the development of the will is also a strategic instead of a purely tactical affair, because we have not yet reached the particular method by which specific moral prescriptions are learned by the child.

We come to this final step in Ecclesiastical Neo-Thomism in the form of the *catechism*. The catechism is, of course, the method of instruction by which standard questions together with specific and unchanging answers are taught to the child by memory and rote, and are then tested in catechetical recitations. Once the answers to the questions have been learned, as we say, "by heart" (which itself has poetic overtones of the mystical nature of such knowledge), then the child may be said to have learned moral truth.

This procedure is defended on the supremely simple assertion that

---

[10] *Christian Education of Youth,* Encyclical Letter of His Holiness Pope Pius XI (Washington, D.C.: National Catholic Welfare Conference, 1936), p. 23.

[11] In an overzealous and somewhat ridiculous application of this principle, some educators, particularly in the latter nineteenth century, insisted that so important was the training of the will that unpleasantness should be made a regular feature of the educational program: If we develop character through the sharpening and toughening of our powers of self-discipline, then whatever is unpleasant to do in the school can be turned by the teacher into the vehicle of moral training. This eventually led to the view that if the child found some task unpleasant it must be good for him. Finally, this was turned into a general educational theory — what may be called the "Spinach Theory" of education — that placed educational experiences and materials in a descending order of difficulty and distastefulness. If the subject with its attendant assignments day by day proved difficult and/or distasteful (preferably both) it must be of high educational value and therefore should be placed at the head of the list of subjects. As we all know, mathematics and languages — particularly grammar — have consistently met such qualifications.

indoctrination of ultimate truth can by no stretch of the imagination be considered illegitimate. A Catholic layman says:

> The Church does not say that morality belongs purely, in the sense of exclusively, to her; but that it belongs wholly to her. She has never main-tained that outside her fold and apart from her teaching, man cannot arrive at any moral truth . . . She does, however, say, has said, and will ever say, that because of her institution by Jesus Christ, because of the Holy Ghost sent her in His name by the Father, she alone possesses what she has had immediately from God and can never lose, the whole of moral truth, *omnem veritatem,* in which all individual moral truths are included, as well as those which man may learn by the help of reason, as those which form part of revelation or which may be deduced from it.[12]

All moral truth, therefore, and *all particular* moral truths and pre-scriptions are now in hand and secured safely in the "safe-deposit boxes" of the Church's dogma. If these truths can be rendered in question-and-answer form and committed to the memory, it can then be said that the child has received his moral education.

In support of the training of reason and will and the subsequent in-struction in the Catechism, the Ecclesiastical Neo-Thomist customarily adds certain curricular instructions to educators that bear upon the ethical problem. A typical trouble spot is sex education, certainly in any school a very delicate topic but in a Neo-Thomist school almost a trau-matic matter. Says Pope Pius XI in another passage:

> Far too common is the error of those who with dangerous assurance and under an ugly term propagate a so-called sex education, falsely imagining they can forearm youth against the dangers of sensuality by means purely natural, such as a foolhardy initiation and precautionary instruction for all indiscriminately, even in public; and, worse still, by exposing them at an early age to the occasions, in order to accustom them, so it is argued, and as it were to harden them against such dangers.[13]

The danger is very real, says the Pope, that in taking remedies against sin we expose the child to occasions of and inducements to sin. Consider-ing the faltering weakness of human nature, then, we should be wise to leave instruction to agencies outside the school or, if instruction is neces-sary of inclusion, to handle it with the very greatest of care.

This concern with instruction in sex is indicative of a general repug-

12 A. Manzoni, *Osservazioni sulla Morale Cattolica,* Chapter III, quoted in Pope Pius XI, *op. cit.,* pp. 8–9.
13 *Op. cit.,* p. 25.

nance toward what may generally be labeled "the carnal" in life, and of the demotion of all those human pursuits of a purely physical sort. It has its application, although somewhat indirectly, in the elimination of football from the educational program of the University of Chicago during the regime of Chancellor Hutchins, perhaps the most famous contemporary Lay Neo-Thomist. Hutchins, it is only fair to say, never repudiated football itself. He merely repudiated football as education; it is simply a physical recreation, and, while this is legitimate enough, it is not what education is properly concerned with.[14]

Perhaps an even more relevant example is found again on the Ecclesiastical side:

> False also and harmful to Christian education is the so-called method of "coeducation." This too, by many of its supporters, is founded upon naturalism and the denial of original sin; but by all, upon a deplorable confusion of ideas that mistakes a leveling promiscuity and equality for the legitimate association of the sexes. The Creator has ordained and disposed perfect union of the sexes only in matrimony, and, with varying degrees of contact, in the family and in society. Besides, there is not in nature itself . . . anything to suggest that there can be or ought to be promiscuity, and much less equality, in the training of the two sexes.[15]

In keeping with this papal requirement, most Catholic schools maintain separation of the sexes as much as possible. There is usually a separate door for each sex. Preferably, if the student population is large enough, there are separate schools altogether. This policy is not universally observed, but it is the clear desire of the Church.

In all of these many ways, instructional and administrative, the Neo-Thomist school intends to shape the moral tendencies of the young along preferred lines. By the nature of the case, this moral program is more consistent and unequivocal about its aims than perhaps any other we are here discussing. This constitutes, of course, both a strength and a weakness, for moral certainty is always purchased at the price of a certain moral rigidity, and in modern America there may be some question as to how much of the latter the twentieth century will stand.

The relativity of values and learning through living

This last remark is perhaps most likely to be made by Experimentalists, standing as they do at the opposite end of the axiological spectrum from

---

[14] In expanding on his position concerning football, Chancellor Hutchins is supposed to have once waxed jocularly aphoristic concerning physical endeavors in general. On being asked whether he did not think it wise for the man of thought also to "keep in trim," he is reported to have said: "Whenever I get the feeling that I need some exercise, I lie down till the feeling goes away."   [15] Pope Pius XI, *op. cit.*, p. 26.

the Neo-Thomists. Rigidity is only one of the unfortunate by-products, they say, of the Neo-Thomist value theory. Its fundamental difficulty is not that it is rigid but, rather, that when put to use in the affairs of men it produces dispute and disagreement in the area of moral judgment. For men, even when exercising their reason, do often come to alternative conceptions of what is good, and the Neo-Thomists have no method beyond reason to settle moral disputes.

This phenomenon points to a peculiar difference between science on the one hand and classical philosophy and organized religion on the other. The latter — the philosophies and the religions — magnanimously set out upon the search for a unified conception of Man and a universal and catholic sense of brotherhood among all men. But nothing is more divisive and fractured into small, well-guarded citadels of thought than the systematic philosophies (the schools discussed in this book), unless one considers the even more divisive and warring factions of systematic religion. Organized religions have historically been the vehicles for perhaps more rancor and bloodshed in the world than any other single institution of man. And the reason for this, according to the Experimentalists, is that they are founded on metaphysical, hence, inaccessible, grounds of judgment. One man's metaphysic is another man's nonsense, and when there is dispute among metaphysicians or theologians, particularly on moral concerns, there is no court of appeal to which we may repair to settle the question.

Science, on the contrary, begins its work with no particular pretensions whatsoever about bringing men together into a moral unity or a social brotherhood. It is simply a modest methodological procedure for increasing our knowledge. Ironically, however, science has succeeded, and quite unintentionally, in producing the only true international, intercultural brotherhood — what we sometimes call the "scientific community" — which the world has ever seen. Even the arts cannot match it for finding a truly global language of discourse. Whatever else, then, may be the limitations of science, it certainly is a method which has the capacity to resolve the disparate views that men entertain about their conduct.

If the fact of *agreement* on the matters of life, therefore, has any utility as a criterion of adequacy — that is, if there is some feeling that we are closer to the good in ethics and conduct when we freely join hands and, *without* coercion, agree on something — then science is a method worth trying. It is this possibility of a kind of nonmetaphysical, nontheistic, wholly secular brotherhood which some people feel is most nearly realized in the free, universal, secular public school in America. It is the "melting-pot" idea expanded to include not only language and custom and style of dress but basic beliefs and life values. Since a teeming America could not hope to find any unity in such diversity on purely metaphysical or cultural or religious grounds, it decided to try to find it on practical, empirical grounds. And what has happened is that we have stumbled upon two great moral inventions: the open society and the universal public school, both of which are officially free of dogma and yet capable of forming moral dispositions in the individual person.

In the society at large the forming of moral dispositions is generally accomplished through politics and law, but in the more microcosmic society of the school it is done through a methodology which the Experimentalist considers capable of application to almost all moral questions. This methodology is simply the arrangement of learning situations so that the child learns the morality and the patterns of conduct the society wishes him to follow by actually *living* those patterns while he is in school. This pedagogy is drawn directly from the "theory of consequences" spelled out in Chapters Six and Nine. For it is quite obvious that if a child can be made to experience the consequences of his actions, in as lifelike and direct a way as it is possible to create, then he will learn the rightness or wrongness of those actions far more quickly, efficiently, and permanently than if he is merely offered some remote heroic exemplar to emulate (Idealism) or some naturalistic moral law to be conditioned to (Realism) or some rational principle or catechetical dictum to master (Neo-Thomism).

To the Experimentalist educator, moral instruction is based upon the generalized notion that "we learn what we live." This thesis has perhaps been explained best by one of John Dewey's most faithful disciples and interpreters, William Heard Kilpatrick.

Let us, says Kilpatrick, consider a specific, concrete, and limited instance of a moral value which we wish to be adopted by the young: "taking turns." This, by way of reduction, can be said to be the child's equivalent of the American principle of "equality of opportunity." Now there are four swings on a playground. During recess a class of twenty youngsters comes to the playground; ten want to swing. At this point a problem situation is apparent: How will the allotments of swinging be distributed? Several alternative solutions present themselves. First, an undirected situation may produce the "law-of-the-jungle" alternative, in which the stronger wrest the swings from the weaker pupils. This laissez faire policy would certainly be in the American tradition (more accurately, our nineteenth-century tradition), but it would tend to produce effects and consequences unwanted by the group, namely, acrimony, fighting, conflict, and at the very least lowered morale; it would, that is, produce the very consequences which occasioned the decline of laissez faire morality in American life. Sensing the futility of this solution, the teacher might suggest and execute a second, the "complete-embargo," alternative, in which a fiat is issued under which *no* child shall swing.

This would have the effect of restoring order but also of producing some of the same consequences as the earlier policy, i.e., frustration, rancor, and impaired morale.

The Experimentalist teacher, having deliberately permitted the youngsters to "live," that is, undergo and experience, the consequences of the above possibilities, would at this point suggest — or maybe one of the group would suggest — the possibility of taking turns, so that all the youngsters could swing. This would then be tried, and if the consequences which issued from this trial were seen to be superior to the former sets of consequences, then a moral disposition in favor of turn-taking would be planted in the child's moral self.

The point here is that children do not learn the morality of turn-taking because it is drawn from the Judeo-Christian ethic, or because Jefferson said it is self-evident that all men are created equal, or because reason insists on it. They learn the morality of this item of conduct by using it in their lives, by living through its application in real circumstances formulated at their level of behavior and comprehension — in short, by seeing that *it works.* Kilpatrick has repeated this theme in many of his writings, but his most explicit pronunciamento on the matter appears in his essay on "Philosophy of Education from the Experimentalist Outlook." Here he says:

> . . . we see (1) that each child learns what he lives; (2) that he learns it as he accepts it in his own heart to act on; (3) that he learns it in the degree that it is important to him and in the degree that it has meaningful connections with what he already knows; and, finally, (4) that what he learns he builds at once into character.[16]

Select, then, the moral dispositions you wish the child to have, not only in his thoughts but in his overt conduct. Then contrive real, life-like situations where those dispositions may be tested out at the youngster's level of experience, where he can recognize through the living of a situation that there are alternative solutions to moral problems and that some alternatives are better than others, because they lead to better consequences.

If this procedure cannot be directly rendered in concrete experience — as in the case of sex education — then at least the child should be given an opportunity to examine vicariously and reflectively what different moralities produce in society and what variant recommendations can be made for them in terms of their historical social consequences. If what

16 Chapter II in *Philosophies of Education*, Forty-first Yearbook of the National Society for the Study of Education, ed. N. B. Henry, Part I (Chicago: the Society, 1942), p. 69.

is found to be the most humane morality disagrees with the public morality in force at the moment regarding any sensitive area of social experience, then a larger study should be made of the matter. If disagreement still persists, then it is possible to suggest that the society itself is in need of moral reform, and that the individual should anticipate the acceptance of personal responsibility to help reform it when he grows to maturity.

In the long run, says the Experimentalist, the public standard is the result of this selfsame procedure, i.e., the testing of alternate ways of living to see what consequences ensue. In certain sectors of life — sex and religion in particular — there is a tendency for the public standard *as expressed in professions of belief* to change more slowly and to lag behind adjustments in the public standard *as expressed in concrete behavior;* and it is the latter — the behavioral standard — which is perhaps the more authentic expression of the society's morality, because it is through concrete behavior that real, living consequences are produced. If these consequences continue to be pernicious and mean it is doubtful whether the behavior will continue.

The school, then, says the Experimentalist, has a larger moral duty than merely the inculcation of this or that ethical practice; its function is the intelligent criticism of the public standard, wherever that standard is expressed in the words and deeds of men in day-to-day life.

The baselessness of values and individual choice

It is at this point that the Existentialist notices a flaw in the Experimentalist's moral theory. If the ultimate reference for moral training is to be the thing called "the public standard," we are immediately cast in a pedagogical circumstance of working *from* that standard as our point of departure in the classroom. Whether we embrace or repudiate the standard makes no difference. In either case we are using the Experimentalist's method, *itself committed to the morality of public decision,* the assumed morality of what has earlier been spoken of as "the uncoerced community of persuasion."

Nothing is said in the Experimentalist doctrine about the kind of persuasion that affects the individual when he is viewing the consequences of moral choice. This kind of persuasion must, by the very nature of the case, be individual rather than social. Each individual must speak out on what consequences he prefers. Then the community can establish its public standard in favor of this or that choice.

Hence, says the Existentialist, what we are obligated to do with the child in school is more than to supply him a method of valuing; it encompasses much more than providing him lifelike situations in which he can undergo the consequences of his acts. The school's job pre-eminently is to awaken the child to the ultimate responsibility he must bear for the selections he makes between alternate sets of consequences. And since this is a supremely private enterprise, assisted but never determined by the community, moral instruction can never be merely communal or social in the classroom if it is to produce authentic responsibility in the child as he matures.

It is at this point that we should remind ourselves of a comment earlier in this chapter to the effect that in axiological matters Existentialism may be said to separate itself from the other four philosophies in a sharper and more uncompromising way than in the other branches of philosophy. It shares much, of course, with Experimentalism, in that it agrees that man is the author of his morality and not the compliant creature that the other three positions would make him out to be. Furthermore, Existentialism might be said to applaud Experimentalism's concern with the open and doctrine-free procedure of science in arriving at truths and goods.

But the Existentialist insists that the scientific method itself may be said to be assuming certain doctrinal tendencies; specifically, there is the growing feeling that science is the ultimate method and that scientific propositions and scientifically validated values have some kind of dominion over us. We are turned, that is, into creatures with a new mode of compliance — compliance to a social method. In the school, this proclivity of Experimentalism to consider the scientific method as ultimate leads to group-determined rules in the classroom, to group-validated ethical choices (as exemplified in the playground situation in the previous section), and, indeed, to the socialized character of learning in all its many phases.

But this pedagogy, says the Existentialist, is merely the result of another philosophic *system* replacing an earlier *system*. Experimentalism places the child in the context of the group-working-scientifically instead of the context of the Absolute Self or Nature or Reason or God or what have you. It is a new context, to be sure, and a radical and well-intentioned departure from the older contexts. But it is still context, i.e., it is still an ultimate medium in which the child is presumed to grow. Anything outside this context — the content of the private self or the proclamations of private conscience, for instance — is not considered proper for educators to pay any attention to. Indeed, the private, lone individual is not allowed to exist in an Experimentalist school. He is flushed out from his back-row seat, his reticence and detachment are taken as signs of emotional imbalance, and as soon as possible he is turned into a public, gregarious social product.

To an Existentialist, this is perhaps the greatest fault in so-called

Progressive Education, namely, its loving attention to the sharable in life and its consequent obsession with group dynamics, social development, and public morality in the life of the school.

> Problem-centered methodology the existentialist would consider to be impersonal and unproductive, largely because the problems are usually socially oriented; they are of immediate concern to the individual only in his social obligations.[17]

What we must do, says the Existentialist, is to find a pedagogy which will reawaken the individual child's sense of identity, which will help him rediscover that he is the ultimate base of all valuation and that when the group has completed its project or the committee its investigation he is still on his own to find his way through life. No group's conclusion and no committee's recommendation has final domain over a child's choices. In an Experimentalist school he usually strings along, because he has been taught that scientifically group-processed choices are the best and that he would be a dunce to repudiate them. But when he does this he is merely consenting to a new moral imperium, whether he or his teacher realizes it or not.

So the search for an Existentialist pedagogy may be said to originate in the desire for the release of the individual — his absolute release from all moral doctrines, both *systematic,* as in the case of Idealism, Realism, and Neo-Thomism, and *methodological-social,* as in the case of Experimentalism. The teaching procedure we are looking for must be one which will apply to children in *physical* groups, since that is the way they are found in the school, without treating them simultaneously as *psychological* or *social* groups. That is, it must be a pedagogy which can rise above the physical sociality of the typical classroom to affirm the psychic identity of each of the several human beings located there.

Much can be borrowed from the older pedagogies to satisfy these conditions. It is true, for instance, that despite their doctrinal shortcomings the traditional pedagogies of either the intellectual-discipline or the knowledge-transmission sort do give the child more time to work alone than is provided in modern Experimentalist schools. The private effort of the learner would certainly be given new attention in Existentialist classrooms, especially in ethical concerns, because of the obvious necessity for some old-fashioned soul-searching before being able to make up one's mind on the tougher sort of moral problems. But there is no intimation here that the child is to be left by himself to come by dint of

17 G. F. Kneller, *Existentialism and Education* (New York: Philosophical Library, 1958), p. 135.

306

private effort into harmony with some external moral frame. He is left to do his own moral reflection because he is the author of value! By this tactic alone the teacher imposes responsibility on the child for coming to his own views on the matter in question. And by this tactic the teacher also suggests that genuine self-discovery can be accomplished neither through an external moral system nor through a public exposure to group dynamics in ethical questions but, instead, in the quietude of the self's inner chamber of decision and the attendant responsibility the individual is existentially committed to assume for the decisions he reaches. First of all, then, the Existentialist recommends more time for private reflection and more assignments which call for moral decisions, which in turn call for more privacy of judgment in the child's in-school and out-of-school life. And it goes without saying that the Existentialist teacher will honor the need for privacy wherever and whenever the learner petitions for it.

This approach requires a heavy emphasis on the Socratic method of instruction, which — as it was pointed out in Chapter Seven — is the most prominent type of Existentialist pedagogy; for the kind of knowledge that the Socratic method is pre-eminently successful in producing is self-knowledge, and this kind of knowledge — if, indeed, it be knowledge — is primarily of the moral sort, i.e., feelings, dispositions, attitudes, commitments, beliefs, awarenesses.

The Socratic method, far removed from its Platonic origins in this context, will not be employed to trigger some "reminiscence" in the learner's "soul" but, rather, to awaken him to the moral difficulties that must be encountered in human existence, the alternatives those difficulties suggest, and the real meaning of ultimate responsibility for private choice. The youngster will be asked to think over his own choices — to reflect on what he is going to do with his life, not just in the narrow career sense but in the larger, value sense. What values is he going to live by, and with what purpose? What gods — both theistic and secular — will he worship, and why? What, in short, does he think his life on this planet, his unique self in this cosmos, is *for*?

It is in this vein that Ralph Harper reopens the question of religious values in the school. We must remember, he says, that the *need* for religion, the *need for recognition* by some ultimate agency, is a need every human being experiences. But:

> The religious need is not necessarily a need to which there is a religious answer. It is simply the human need of ultimate recognition. The individual . . . wants above everything, some evidence that at least his need is recognized by others as the most important thing about him. He wants the universe itself to give some evidence, if possible, that it, too, recognizes

this need as legitimate and appeasable. But there is no logical necessity which says that if there is a need for the universe to recognize and appease, the universe will oblige.[18]

No logical necessity, indeed. It is just because man has historically insisted that his universe appease him in this way that he has concocted so many competing religions. And the basic difficulty with the religion-in-education issue, in its customary formulation, lies in the notion that the *need for appeasement* cannot be separated from the variety of *answers* that organized religions have, down through the centuries, given to this need. Operating on this notion, we have felt in America that to confound the school's curriculum with sectarian "answers" to the need would serve only to promote division and contention. And so we have secularized the school by driving sectarianism out of it.

But secularizing the school has unthinkingly been interpreted to mean wholly eliminating consideration of this need we all experience. And if there is one thing that boys and girls desperately require somewhere — if not constantly — in their maturing process, it is a reflective concern for the types of questions that the "need for recognition" provokes — questions concerning who they are, what they are doing around here in existence, and why. This set of questions simply cannot be brought under study outside the scope of the so-called religious need.

But to study the need, the Existentialist reminds us, does not require specifying any answers. Merely to state the religious need of man in the classroom is not the same thing as "appeasing" — to use Harper's word — the child with this or that comfortable religious solution to his need; it is, on the contrary, to awaken him to the problem of ultimate recognition and to what this problem signifies in our lonely search for ourselves.

Existentialists complain that Experimentalists have so thoroughly secularized the school that they have not only eliminated from it all sectarianism, and even any mention of God, but have been guilty of the complete expungement of any ultimate questions whatsoever from the child's experience. But the ultimate questions of life — quite unlike their answers — belong to all men. This is not because they are religious or metaphysical; it is because they are existential. That is, they reside at the very base of our being. Hence, every child in the school has a right to be assisted in viewing these questions and in considering what they mean for a human self. The Existentialist educator can be expected to put these questions back into the school's program.

[18] "Significance of Existence and Recognition for Education," Chapter VII in *Modern Philosophies and Education*, Fifty-fourth Yearbook of the National Society for the Study of Education, ed. N. B. Henry, Part I (Chicago: the Society, 1955), p. 245.

REFINING AESTHETIC TASTE

If the development of right conduct is a puzzling and perplexing educational task, the development of taste is perhaps more so. The field of aesthetics itself is difficult of compass and rational analysis; as a result it is not clearly plotted and mapped. Even well-trained and scholarly philosophers have difficulty taking their readers through it with the same facility they exhibit in other branches of their discipline. The reason for this may be that art, itself a symbol system, resists translation into the more literal, matter-of-fact symbolism of ordinary language. Can we really reduce aesthetic feeling to verbal terms? Can the experience of enjoyment be rendered in subjects and predicates? To raise the question is to imply the possibility of a negative reply. In any event, educational theorists have generally had little to say about instruction in aesthetics in their books on teaching and learning.

It is unnecessary, therefore, to apologize for what may at first appear an altogether too brief treatment of so important a matter as aesthetics in general and the arts in particular as they influence teaching and learning. There is no intention here to diminish or depreciate the importance of the arts in education, only an effort to be realistic about the level and intensity of discourse that can be maintained concerning it.

With this rather hesitant beginning, we may proceed to say a few things about the way educators in the various schools of philosophy go about the business of refining taste.

Masterworks and the idea of beauty

Certainly if an Idealist were cornered on the question he would be likely to repair to his general theory of aesthetics for clues. There, as we have seen, the label of *ideal* can be taken in its common-sense and more or less literal meaning, i.e., the idealization of the world we see about us. If, then, art is to be measured by the degree to which the work of art succeeds in capturing the idealized representation of that which may look commonplace in our day-to-day lives, the Idealist will wish to use such works as the stimulants to aesthetic feelings in the young. Just as the ethical training of a youngster in Idealism is built upon imitation of heroic exemplars of history or contemporary life, so likewise will his aesthetic sense be quickened by exposure to those great works of art — like the "Mona Lisa," the "Emperor Concerto," the *Swan Lake* ballet, *Hamlet* — which have aroused the sensibilities of men down through time. In the Idealistic aesthetic catalogue such works are the true objects of civilized taste; and if we mean to bring children to like and enjoy them, then certainly the very first business of the school is to bring young-sters into direct exposure to them.

What follows is of course not necessarily peculiar to Idealism: These works are exhibited or performed for the child, and it is hoped and expected that there will be an emotional reponse. But the object of the Idealist teacher is never to settle only for such a response but to expect and require *understanding* of the work as well; that is to say, the "ex-posure phase" should be followed by the "understanding phase," in which the child studies the characteristics and symbolic meanings of the work under view, the artist and his life and times, and the cultural origin of the style and mode of what he has done.

This suggests once more the primacy of Mind to the Idealist. His ontology, as we have seen, is of the Infinite Mind; his epistemology sets forth the "approximation" of that Mind through the absorption of knowledge and wisdom. Now again, in aesthetics, the mind becomes the constant companion of "the feelings" in the child's growth toward cul-tivated taste. Indeed, it might even be said by an Idealist that one can never truly develop a taste for anything *until* he understands it. It is possibly for this reason that in most schools and colleges the courses in art appreciation or music appreciation are really nothing more than at-tempts at (1) exposing the learner to great works, and, more importantly, (2) building his *understanding* of those masterworks through a study of them in much the same manner as he would study wars or historical move-ments or natural phenomena — that is, with the aim of objective mastery of information concerning them. Aesthetic feeling and emotional response are the end object of all this; but in order to be truly mature such re-sponses must be built upon thorough comprehension of what has been done in the work of art. Once you understand a work of art you can then proceed to a genuinely cultivated aesthetic enjoyment of it.[19]

Beauty in nature: form, balance, and structure

The Realist certainly would not dismiss the above approach; indeed, he might adopt part or even all of it. But his interest in the *understand-ing* of art works would take a decidedly more mechanistic and structural turn. He would wish the learner to witness masterpieces, of course; his abiding belief in the primacy of sensation would require that we begin here in aesthetic training. But in the study of masterpieces their *con-struction* would assume first pedagogical interest. Beethoven's patterns of

[19] Vincent Price, Hollywood actor and TV quiz expert on art, has published a book with this theme as its title: *I Like What I Know* (Garden City, N.Y.: Doubleday and Company, Inc., 1959).

A-A-B-A in symphonic design, the intricacy of Bach's fugues and mathematically precise polyphonies, Da Vinci's structural symbolism in "The
Last Supper," Shakespeare's genius at exposition-development-climax-
denouement would be singled out for special emphasis.

It is, you will remember, the *design* and *order* of nature which the
Realist wishes to see celebrated in art, and for this reason he wants the
learner in art to attend first of all to these particular qualities. Later on,
of course, the learner can be shown the other things art contains — sym-
bolisms, meanings, an underlying mystique — and perhaps experience the
emotional impact it is presumed to have on others. A grasp of structural
principles in the arts, however, comes first.

There is also, to be sure, a persistent theme in Realism — one which
runs somewhat counter to Idealist tendencies — elevating the physical
and sensuous to first rank in human experience. It is to be presumed,
then, that the Realist would wish his art student to take hold of the
medium itself, even if only briefly, to get the feel, literally, of what the
artist is working with. Studio contact with art media — playing an
instrument, shaping a clay figure, painting a still life, producing a play,
learning a dance — such kinesthetic, tactile experiences must somehow
be included before the learner can be said to have received instruction
in the arts.

When, through this method, the learner begins to see the nature of
technique and the importance of the physical control that the artist must
bring to his medium, he will then begin to develop a mature appreciation
and, following this, a more cultured taste for what constitutes greatness in
aesthetic production.

Beauty through intuition and revelation

By all measures, the most obscure of the several educational theories
in aesthetics is that of the Neo-Thomist. This is due partly to the apparent lack of relationship between the arts generally, which quicken our
feelings and arouse our emotions, and Reason, which, as we have seen, is
the governing principle for most if not all Neo-Thomist thought. However, a more likely reason for the obscurity of Neo-Thomist educational
prescriptions in the arts is that a very specialized and abstruse type of
Reason is involved, namely, intuition.

Intuition is one of those notions on which, unless one is a Maritain,
it is difficult to discourse. And when we are asked to apply such a notion
to the training of boys and girls in aesthetic judgment and artistic taste,
it is not an easy business.

Presumably, as in the case of ethics and morals, the training of the

Reason would be a necessary prerequisite to any successful pedagogy in the arts. Intellectually the child must be brought to a point of clarity and sharpness, via the customary disciplinary subject matters, before he can be expected to achieve anything on the order of genuinely rational taste. Once this point has been reached, it is the purpose of the Neo-Thomist instructor to single out for special cultivation intuitive "perceptions" of great works of art. In ordinary language we usually speak of this as *inspiration,* and when we fix the child's attention on that specific quality of art — that thing we might describe as a "lurch" of the artist into a completely new but essentially private vision of the ultimate nature of things — we recommend that quality to him as the most important thing to look for.

Maritain frequently speaks of the "contemplative tendencies" of the child and suggests that we encourage those tendencies by providing occasions for them to emerge. The child's confrontation of truly great works of art, especially if their theme is Christian, will provide at least the raw materials for such occasions, and if the teacher can somehow infuse the atmosphere of the learning situation with a contemplative mood, then the learner may be drawn to this mode of activity.

It would not be altogether irrelevant to comment also on the more immediate but less spiritual kinds of enjoyment which we find in pure reason. The Neo-Thomist often points out that mathematics has its own aesthetic satisfactions; there is a transport and delight in taking intellectual hold of complicated abstractions in the calculus, or of the beautiful intricacies of conic sections and parabolas in geometry. The utter rationality of mathematics is a pleasure to behold, and it is presumed that the Neo-Thomist would not allow this pleasure to be lost upon his students.

The Neo-Thomist's constant emphasis on the intuitive nature of creative endeavor and his location of aesthetic delight in the pure abstractions of mathematics may help to explain why the *"Ars gratia artis"* point of view in aesthetics, discussed in Chapter Eight (see pages 237–238), has found so ready a champion in this particular school of thought. Art for its own sake is splendidly consistent with a view that holds the intellect aloof from the concerns of life. The intellect is trained to see Truth, not to solve problems; and so the aesthetic powers of the individual are developed to love Beauty-in-abstract, not to render our own experience more lovely. To solve problems and to render the conditions of life more aesthetically satisfying are certainly noble activities, but in Neo-Thomist thought they are essentially secondary to pure intellection and pure creative intuition in and for themselves. The school's task is to make this distinction between the pure and the applied clear to the learner, and to insist that the former is always of higher rank than the latter.

Aesthetic experience as the widening of meanings

Experimentalists, as one may expect, begin to balk rather vigorously at this line of argument. In the first place, intuition has no public dimensions; that is, it cannot become an object of philosophic discussion because it is essentially private and solitary in nature. Since Experimentalists value so highly the socialized approach to life and learning, it is little wonder that they have slight confidence in the "private intuitions" of the Neo-Thomist educator. Furthermore, to set art off in a pure and uncontaminated region of its own is to demolish the very purpose of teaching it in school, namely, to arouse new meanings and new feelings in the child, to suggest to him a new and somewhat keener dimension to life, and, in the end, to bring more beauty to the affairs of men and to equip them to feel it and enjoy it in their daily occupations.

From this platform, the Experimentalist recalls his generalized pedagogy of "learning through living" and simply applies it to the aesthetic field. If we want boys and girls to develop taste we must present to them situations in which certain objects are seen to produce aesthetic effects or consequences of a higher order than what they have hitherto given their attention to. If the school wishes to awaken taste, then the place to begin is in the experience of the learner.

Start with his taste in clothes, or start with rock-'n'-roll, or start with automobile design. Or, better still, start with the school. A project in the beautification of the classroom or the aesthetic improvement of the grounds would be a genuine living situation in which all kinds of aesthetic learnings could take place. Maybe it would be a project in making the cafeteria more pleasant, or a project in piping good music to the lunchroom, or a project in which the students are given responsibility to select paintings for the hallways. Let the consequences of the youngsters' own choices be felt and undergone; let them, that is, take hold of their own experience at the aesthetic level to see what they can make of it.

It would be hopelessly naïve to think that what they would come up with would be altogether lovely — paintings in the hallways or Muzak in the cafeteria. But that is just the point: They are in school to learn. And we shall never get boys and girls to appreciate anything — whether that thing is among the so-called finer things of life or not — simply by exposing them to it or having them study the life and times of its author or having them master the laws of construction the artist followed in composing or painting or writing it, or advising them to find pure delight in the so-called intuitions it reveals. We get boys and girls to appreciate what we want them to appreciate by introducing that thing into their lives and allowing its aesthetic impact to do its own work on their sensibilities. If it does not do its work, that is, if they do not respond to it, there is not much sense in haranguing them or trying to intellectualize the whole business as if it were just another subject in the school.

Taste is a delicate and fragile trait, to be sure, requiring steady cultivation. Most of us spend precious little time trying to develop it. We go through life letting our likes and dislikes stand without criticism. But this is because we permit art to be enclosed and isolated in concert halls, art galleries, and museums. Once we get art back into life — most particularly, into the life of the child in school as he lives it day by day — then we shall be in a position to manage his aesthetic growth effectively.

It is partly for this reason that the Experimentalist educator in art has so energetically championed the child's direct participation in artistic endeavor. Like the Realist, the Experimentalist wants the learner to get his hands on the medium — to try blowing a horn or carving a piece of soap or creating a dramatic character. But he wants this for motives beyond that of merely involving the senses of the child, as the Realist would say. The Experimentalist wants it because he wishes to involve the total child — not only his senses, but his imagination, his feelings, and his need to communicate to others. Hence in Experimentalist schools one is likely to find much more learner participation in art and music classes than in other schools. Through direct and living experience the learner acquires his tastes and an understanding of why he has acquired them.

Art as the statement of the self

We are, at this point, in the general vicinity of the Existentialist view of the matter. Of all that goes on in an Experimentalist school, the art and music departments look like the most likely beachheads for an Existentialist. This is because they, alone among all the departments in the school, are avowedly militant in their concern for the individuality of the child. This individuality, as we have seen, is given room for growth when the Experimentalist involves the learner directly in the artistic enterprise, and it is applauded, both theoretically and practically, in the desire to have the youngster release his feelings and express his sentiments about the world in such a way as to communicate them to his classmates.

So far, so good, says the Existentialist. We will accept this program as the base of our operations. However, we will begin to lose interest in the child's artistic productions in the degree that they are supposed to be socially consumed, i.e., enjoyed and fawned over by other people. If the child is given rein to paint or sing or act in order to arouse a peer interest in what he is doing, then we have begun to compromise the entire pedagogy. Rather should we concern ourselves with his aesthetic production as a statement about his own selfhood and how he conceives his selfhood to be existing in the world. It does not matter whether he will put his water color up on the bulletin board; what matters is that his water color be in some way his very own, *his* particular statement of the world as he sees it.

This theme is, we say, already in the ascendancy in Experimentalist thinking. It needs only a firmer and more aggressive statement to make it acceptable to Existentialism. For it is worth noting that the place in the Experimentalist's school where group dynamics has the least effect is the art room. Here, finally, is a subject matter that does not yield to the "committee approach."

So, once the child is set free from the inherited traditions of study and criticism in the arts and, *more important,* once he is set free from the heavy pressure of the group and from its dominion over him, he can finally set out in the Existentialist mode to make his own artistic statement about life.

It is not possible to set down any particular criteria as to what shall or shall not be acceptable in the way of aesthetic productions — paintings, statues, dramatic skits, music. But the Existentialist teacher will insist on two things. First, the productions must be authentic; that is, they must emanate directly from the existential consciousness of the individual child, without his having the customary feeling that he is to paint this or that or draw in this way or in that way to satisfy some prior condition laid down by the teacher. He must be completely free to portray his situation as he sees it.

Second, and this follows from the insistence on authenticity, the learner must take responsibility for what he has produced. He must not be permitted to escape his personal commitment to what he has created, even if others upon viewing it do not like it. There will always be temptations for the child to do this, to repudiate his artistic products and to try to undo them. But, of course they can never be undone. And the teacher must help the child to see this. If, however, his products are unsatisfactory to him not because they fail to be popular with his classmates but because they have not said what he wanted to say with his painter's brush or his sculptor's knife or his dancer's body, then he should be encouraged to improve upon them, to transcend them, in a similar or perhaps more elaborate assignment. In this way the teacher can help the child to reaffirm his aesthetic selfhood at a continuously higher and higher level.

Continuous involvement is the key. To yearn constantly for expression is to be in rapport with the Existentialist frame of mind in aesthetic instruction. And if the learner is infused with this yearning for expression,

COMPARATIVE PHILOSOPHIES

		Definition	Idealism	Realism	Neo-Thomism	Experi-mentalism	Existen-tialism
ONTOLOGY		The study of reality: What is real?	A world of mind	A world of things	A world of Reason and Being/God	A world of experience	A world of existing
EPISTEMOLOGY		The study of knowing and knowledge: What is true?	Seeing with the "mind's eye"— consistency of ideas	Spectator Theory: sensation and cor-respondence	Intuition, logical reasoning, and revelation	Testing to see what works	Subjective choice, personal appropria-tion
AXIOLOGY	Ethics	The study of valuing and values: What is good?	The imitation of the Absolute Self	The law of nature	The rational act	The public test	The anguish of freedom
	Aesthetics	What is beautiful?	Reflection of the Ideal	Reflection of nature	Creative intuition	The public taste	Revolt from the public norm

EDUCATIONAL IMPLICATIONS

	Idealism	Realism	Neo-Thomism	Experimentalism	Existentialism
Curricular Emphasis	Subject matter of the mind: literature, intellectual history, philosophy, religion	Subject matter of the physical world: mathematics and science	Subject matter of intellect and spirit: disciplinary subjects: mathematics and language and Doctrine	Subject matter of social experience: the social studies	Subject matter of choice: art, ethics, moral philosophy, religion
Preferred Method	Teaching for the handling of ideas: lecture, discussion	Teaching for mastery of factual information: demonstration, recitation	Disciplining the mind: formal drill— readying the spirit: Catechism	Problem-solving: project method	Arousing personal response: Socratic questioning
Character Education	Imitating exemplars, heroes	Training in rules of conduct	Disciplining behavior to reason	Making group decisions in light of consequences	Awakening the self to responsibility
Developing Taste	Studying the masterworks	Studying design in nature	Finding beauty in reason	Participating in art projects	Composing a personal art work

not for its social effect but solely for its private effect on his own personal selfhood, then the Existentialist teacher has truly succeeded in his educational undertaking.

*　　*　　*

With the present chapter, we have completed our analytical tour of the major philosophies; we have examined their theories of reality, knowledge, and value and how they relate to the educative process. A schematic summary of these views is presented on pages 316–317. To the left of this chart are the three primary questions which philosophy attempts to answer: What is real? What is true? What is good? In the left half of the chart are the short answers that each of our five philosophies gives to these questions. In the right half of the chart are the applications of these answers to the educative process.

In Part V we shall have occasion to review these several theories as they are collected in systematic schools of thought, and to look at them as concrete programs of action in the design of American schools.

QUESTIONS

1. One of the underlying moral values of American life is freedom. Suppose you were given the task of preparing five separate lesson plans — one for each of our ethical theories — on teaching this value to a ninth-grade civics class. What would these lesson plans contain?

2. In Chapter Eight there appeared a discussion of the discrepancy between what people say and what they do in the field of morals and conduct. Which of the above theories of pedagogy presented here would be most likely to narrow this gap in the course of the next generation of school children? Explain.

3. The distinctions in axiological theory and practice between Experimentalism and the three traditional philosophies are relatively clear. The distinctions between Experimentalism and Existentialism, however, appear to be still in a state of flux and formulation. What can you add to the preceding analysis by way of specifying more particularly how these positions differ? In doing this, you will certainly wish to consult the earlier segments of the book and some of the reference readings.

4. Visit an art class in session somewhere in your community, at either the elementary or secondary or college level. Then write a report describing, with examples, which educational theory appears to be operative there.

5. One of the ways to test these alternate pedagogies is to single out a field of aesthetics with which you are not very familiar — say, ballet or Elizabethan poetry — and then describe the educational program you think would be pre-

pared for you by an avid disciple of each of the five positions. Try it and see what results.

6. Presumably architecture has something to do with the function and purpose of a building. Suppose that exponents of the five theories discussed in this chapter were each to design a school building for construction in your community. What features would you expect each to emphasize in his design? Illustrate, either graphically or verbally, how these school buildings would be different, if you think they would.

FURTHER READING

Idealism

Berkson, I. B. *The Ideal and the Community.* New York: Harper and Bros., 1958.
Berkson's point of departure is Dewey-Kilpatrick Experimentalism, but the general thesis of the entire volume consists in a revision of this conception of education in the general direction of Idealism. In Chapter 14 he considers the matter of intelligence and character and whether they stem from idea and belief or experience and inquiry. He inclines toward the former source, and in effect restates the case for community ideals as they are found in history, tradition, and conscience.

Horne, Herman Harrell. *This New Education.* New York: Abingdon Press, 1931.
Professor Horne, the "Mr. Idealism" of the educational world, in this book develops a cogent rebuttal to the Progressives. In Chapter X he considers "How Character is Created," presenting in careful progression the steps by which the Idealist teacher would shape the conduct of the child.

Realism

Broudy, Harry S. *Building a Philosophy of Education.* New York: Prentice-Hall, Inc., 1954.
Professor Broudy classifies himself as a Classical Realist. Here, in Chapter 13, he examines how aesthetic values are taught in the school. Then, in Chapter 14, he considers the companion problem of how moral values are introduced into the experience of the young by Realist teachers. He concludes with some moral criteria: self-determination, self-realization, self-integration, and democracy.

Perry, Ralph Barton. *Realms of Value.* Cambridge: Harvard University Press, 1954.
Perry is a Realist with Experimentalist tendencies. In Chapter XXI, on "Education and the Science of Education," he considers the general meaning of education; the curriculum; the explanatory, normative, and technological

methods; indoctrination; moral education; and liberal and humane education. This is not so much a partisan prescription as it is a thematic review of major value questions as they are met in educational practice.

Neo-Thomism

Maritain, Jacques. "Thomist Views on Education," Chapter III in *Modern Philosophies and Education,* Fifty-fourth Yearbook of the National Society for the Study of Education, ed. N. B. Henry, Part I. Chicago: the Society, 1955. Most of Maritain's writings have an axiological flavor even when they deal with other matters, and this one is no exception. Here he treats of the aims of education, the hierarchy of values, moral education and religion, and the teaching of theology. In this essay the Thomist position is put clearly and persuasively.

Pope Pius XI. *Christian Education of Youth.* Washington, D.C.: National Catholic Welfare Conference, 1936.
When Pius XI spoke, it was well to listen, not only because he was as Pope the one authentic voice on doctrinal matters but also because as a man of deep feeling he spoke eloquently and well on the position of the Church. This little pamphlet places you in direct contact with a moral tradition of enormous consequence in the Western world; and it says with beautiful yet simple persuasion what the Catholic educator is obligated to do for the proper training of the child.

Experimentalism

Mason, Robert E. *Moral Values and Secular Education.* New York: Columbia University Press, 1950.
Mason is an Experimentalist, but he prefers to speak of his own moral theory as "evolutionary naturalism," to which two chapters are devoted. This volume also contains an axiological discussion of Essentialism, Traditionalism, and Individualism.

Neff, Frederick C. "How Moral is Secular Education?," *The Christian Century,* LXXIII, No. 46 (November 14, 1956), 1323–1325.
In this concise and pointed statement, aimed partly at the Protestants themselves, Professor Neff separates the moral from the religious and the religious from the theological. Then he develops the idea that the highest morality of all is the recognition of individual human differences — a value proclaimed by theists, intellectualists, empiricists, metaphysicians, humanists, and scientists alike — and that this value is a secular principle and eminently teachable in the secular school.

Existentialism

Morris, V. C. "Conformity, Rebellion, and the Authentic Life," *Teachers College Record,* LXI, No. 3 (October, 1959), 46–50.
In this essay, subtitled "A Look at Contemporary Guidance Theory," an effort

is made to prove whether modern schools, operating perhaps too much on the Experimentalist's "doctrine of the social man," have unwittingly become instruments for the perpetuation of conformist tendencies in today's youth. A prescription is given for the release of the authentic self in the work of the guidance counselor.

————, and De Francesco, I. L. "Modern Art and the Modern School," *The Clearing House*, XXXII, No. 2 (October, 1957), 67–71.

An educationist and an artist combine to speak on the function of art in the contemporary school. The Existentialist thesis is treated only indirectly, in the attempt to show that a release from the expectations of other people is a prerequisite to effective pedagogy in aesthetics and that the child's private expression of his inner feelings and individualistic assessments of the world he lives in can become an exciting focus for instruction in the arts.

Five Philosophies in

American Education

We have now accomplished the first major task of this book, namely, to examine analytically the three questions of the philosopher: What is real? What is true? What is good? We have treated each of these questions separately, and, for each, considered first the nature of the problem it presents, then the respective answers given by our five philosophies, and, finally, the meaning and significance of those answers for the management of the learning process. In a manner of speaking, the first four Parts of this book have been descriptive and analytical; that is, they have examined the "anatomy" of philosophical thinking.

We must now bring the argument directly to bear upon the work of the educational profession. We have seen, of course, in Chapters Four, Seven, and Ten some of the implications of these concepts in the educative process. But, in a more direct way, how can these ideas help us to understand and evaluate what is going on in American schools today? The answer lies in a consideration of the question of American educational policy and of the general question of what the American people want of their schools; and in order to embark upon this discussion we must rearrange the material of Parts II, III, and IV in such a way that it will shed more direct light on how teachers, administrators, school board members, and parents think about education and its problems in contemporary America.

To change the metaphor somewhat, we might say that Parts II, III, and IV represent a giant canvas of conceptual brush strokes which taken together "tell the story" of *educational theory*. Within this giant canvas we have added — in Chapters Four, Seven, and Ten — some detail touching upon *educational practice,* which is particularly relevant to the business of teaching and learning. Now, in the present Part V, we wish to single out the theme of these three "chapters of application" and to expand on this theme by painting an altogether new canvas. The new painting will be of the same subject but will be done from a somewhat different point of vantage, one which will reveal a new dimension to educational concerns.

The point of vantage referred to is that provided by considering the five positions so far studied as *schools of thought,* or coherent *systems,* which in practice are not fractured up into tiny, analyzable bits, as we have treated them in the earlier parts, but which, rather, are working theories of life and learning in America today.

The new dimension thereby revealed is the dimension of *policy. Policy* is a word which describes that point where educational theory and concrete practice come into contact. Or, to change the figure once again, policy is the vehicle by which theory exerts its influence on practice and, conversely, the vehicle by which concrete practice corrects and modifies theory. The great American educational debate is not, after all, an engagement at the purely theoretical level (perhaps it ought to be), nor is it a dispute over methods and techniques (though, of course, such matters now and then work their way into the discussion). Primarily, the American debate is being conducted at the level of policy, that level from which we look at our schools institutionally, i.e., as a group of separate endeavors which, taken together, are working for a cultural end, an end considerably larger in scope than their local and municipal origins would seem to imply. That is, our schools are "owned and operated" by individual communities; but they now serve national ends. And so we must now begin to think of them in larger terms of reference. "Policy," then, is the general region in which our analysis up to this point can get a new grip on the educational situation prevailing in the United States today.

We shall proceed, therefore, in this Part V in somewhat the following fashion. First, we shall try to gather up the disparate elements of each philosophy as they have been presented so far, spending only enough time in review to gain focus for the task ahead. Then we shall examine the policy outcomes of the philosophies as they individually present prescriptions for the design of education in America.

This will require three chapters — Eleven, Twelve, and Thirteen. In Chapter Eleven the traditional outlooks of Idealism, Realism, and Neo-Thomism will be considered. The first two of these will be combined and treated together under the educational rubric of *Essentialism*. As we shall see, Essentialism is an active and viable policy program in contemporary American education and, though it draws its theoretical sustenance from the somewhat incompatible positions of Idealism and Realism, nevertheless its statement concerning what America needs in education is relatively concise and coherent.

The third of the traditional philosophies, Neo-Thomism, will then conclude Chapter Eleven. When Neo-Thomism in either its Lay or Ecclesiastical frame arrives at the level of policy, it has come to be known as Perennialism. *Perennialism* is a label which is applied to educational programs built upon Aristotelian and Thomistic premises. But since the Ecclesiastical Thomistic Wing of Perennialism is confined largely to Roman Catholic parochial schools, Chapter Eleven will turn its major attention instead to the policy formulations of Lay or Aristotelian Perennialism, which is more relevant to the American public school.

Chapter Twelve is given over entirely to the views of Experimentalism and their policy implications for American education. As is well known, the philosophy of Experimentalism (Pragmatism and Instrumentalism are loose but generally adequate synonyms) is usually thought of as the philosophical source of Progressive Education, or *Progressivism*; and it is also the source of a somewhat newer educational development, *Reconstructionism*. As educational (as against philosophical) theories, both Progressivism and Reconstructionism will serve as vehicles for our analysis of Experimentalist educational policy.[1]

---

[1] The terms *Essentialism, Perennialism, Progressivism,* and *Reconstructionism* have been around for a long time, but it was Professor Theodore Brameld, in his *Patterns of Educational Philosophy* and his later *Educational Philosophies in Cultural Perspective,*

Chapter Thirteen will complete the trilogy of "policy" chapters by turning the light on Existentialism. As mentioned earlier, Existentialism as a philosophy has not yet brought concentrated thought to bear upon educational questions; indeed, all social and political phenomena seem to lie, for the moment at least, outside its scope of interest. For this reason Existentialism cannot be said to be the "source" of any educational program; and we shall therefore be on our own in formulating a policy statement for this point of view.

---

who first established them solidly in the dictionary of educational philosophy. Indebtedness to Professor Brameld in the developmental organization of Part V is therefore considerable, and it is hereby acknowledged.

CHAPTER ELEVEN

Traditional Views:

Idealism, Realism,

Neo-Thomism

THE ESSENTIALISTS

In keeping with the admittedly deductive plan of this book, we must now reorder our conceptual materials in a somewhat neater and more systematic way. Having engaged in dissective analysis (in Parts II, III, and IV), we can now engage in systematic synthesis; this will, as we have said in the introductory statement to Part V, facilitate our embarking upon another theoretical excursion — this time in terms of over-all policy — into the more immediate territory of American education.

Idealism

BASIC VIEWS. Your attention is directed to those sections in Chapters Three (pages 47–53), Six (pages 134–140), and Nine (pages 250–255) dealing specifically with the Idealist notions of ontology, epistemology, and axiology. In those sections we have seen that the Idealist frame is constructed on the thesis that Mind is the central element in reality. There are many different ways of conceiving this element, but perhaps the most familiar and uncomplicated is that conception by which the world is seen as the manifestation of a super intelligence at work in the cosmos. It is true, of course, that the common citizen, the much celebrated "man-in-the-street" in America, is a very empirical sort of person; the day-to-day affairs of this world occupy the foreground of his life. But as empirical and scientific as he is made out to be, chances are that he is in some measure an Idealist at heart. For there is in the Western mind today a continuing popularity of the view that there is some kind of intelligence, some deity, working behind the scenes — at the very least, an *intelligent quality* to the world we inhabit.

What the Idealist has done, ever since Plato, is to take this common-sense notion of the ordinary man and build it into a formal doctrine; and he does it by the use of macrocosmic analogy. That is to say, analogically the super intelligence can be thought of as a human mind infinitely extended in macrocosm across the measureless reaches of all creation. In its infinite capacity, this Ultimate Mind is capable of thinking ultimate thoughts and, hence, of authoring final and ultimate truths.

Thus, if we mean to lead an intelligent life we must "tune in" to this Ultimate Mind and situate ourselves in such a way that we can increasingly discern and interpret the insights that the Ultimate Mind seeks to awaken, through our participation, in our microcosmic minds. Epistemologically, this signifies that we come to true knowledge first of all by rendering ourselves receptive to the quality of mind in the universe, by closing the windows of our senses and permitting our so-called mind's eye to focus upon truth. We promote this undertaking by turning from purely sensate experience to what is called symbolic experience, that is, the experience gained with words and numbers. Since symbols are the carriers of ideas and, hence, of the very content of the Universal Mind, it is with symbols that genuine knowledge-seeking is for the most part concerned.

Axiologically, we may say that the Universal Mind can be thought of as the Infinite or Universal Self, the concept of *person* extended to its completely perfected form. Because it is the very author of ultimates in ethics and aesthetics, this Infinite Person is capable of infinite goodness in conduct and infinite love for beauty; and our axiological task is to know the good and feel the beautiful in the way the Ultimate Person does, for it is only through this identification that we can truly justify our conduct and certify our tastes. We must, that is, endeavor to imitate the Absolute Self in our search for right conduct and aesthetic appreciation.

As abstract and poetic as this may sound, it happens to be, as we have noted, a generally recognizable point of view in contemporary American life. Idealism is not just the plaything of a few mystical philosophers; quite the contrary, it is a living system of belief in the United States. To be more specific, we may permit ourselves the generalization that Idealism is the philosophical position which provides the intellectual rationale for modern Protestantism. This is not to say that Idealism's ontology of Ultimate Mind and Absolute Person necessitates a theistic or supernaturalistic interpretation; one can hold these ontological views with no reference whatsoever to a deity. It is to say only that the "Ultimate Person" of Idealism is, for all practical purposes, equivalent to the Protestant's conception of God.

Hence, when Idealism is said to constitute a major division of Essentialism in American education today, we may think of it arriving at the policy conference table somewhat in the role of the unofficial spokesman for lay Protestant thought. Like all generalizations, this one is hazardous; there are many sects in Protestantism and many versions of Idealism. But, generally speaking, there is a rapport and affinity between the two which is important to recognize in modern American life.

EDUCATIONAL THEORY. Out of the basic propositions of Idealism we attempted to construct some working theory of the educative process in Chapters Four (pages 84 and 89–91), Seven (pages 181–185 and 207–208), and Ten (pages 292–293 and 309–310). In these sections reference was made to the emphasis that Idealists place on all those pedagogical situations in which the element of mind is predominant: the subject matters of literature and history, in particular, and generally any subject matter which is essentially symbolic in character.

In pedagogical method, the continuing reliance upon words spoken, as in the lecture method, or words written, as in the reading of books, is to be expected in Idealist schools. When college students speak of so-called reading courses they are referring to subjects given on the principle that the best way to teach is to saturate the student in vicarious, symbolic experience in the world of books. More than anyone else, the Idealist educator is responsible for this.

In moral and aesthetic training the Idealist emphasizes the traditions of the community. Here, he says, is the best working approximation of the Infinite Moral Self. Hence, custom and convention, as specific items of tradition, are singled out in history and civics classes as worthy of our emulation. Sometimes, as we have said, the essence of a specific social tradition is captured by a school or college in what has been called "institutional ethos," a feeling-tone which insinuates itself into the very mood and climate of the learning situation, e.g., serious intellectualism in, say, an eastern prep school or quiet and reverent devotionalism in a church-related college. Whenever a school or college becomes conscious of its own distinctive "ethos," Idealists on the staff may point to that awareness as perhaps the most important educational benefit of the place. The "ethos" is thought to be a refined and idealized interpretation of the moral sense of the community, which, as an approximation of the Infinite Self, it is important to pass on to the young.

Referring again to the affinity between the Idealist and Protestant conceptions of life, we may see that it is no accident that the emergence of a distinctive "ethos" is peculiarly characteristic of many Protestant denominational schools and colleges. In fact, most of them were founded in the nineteenth century with the deliberate intention of *creating* an ethos to which young people could repair in an increasingly mechanistic and hard-boiled age.

However, let it simply be cautioned at this point that the idea of "ethos" is not peculiar to denominational colleges; many, in fact, cannot claim one. And there are many public, secular institutions which may be said to have created one.[1] We cite "ethos" here only for its illustrative use in seeing Idealism in action in today's education.

Realism

BASIC VIEWS. To remind ourselves of what has already been said of Realism's philosophical thesis, we may return to Chapters Three (pages 53–59), Six (pages 140–147), and Nine (pages 255–261). In those sections we discovered that Realism's view of the cosmos is essentially material and even mechanistic, i.e., that the world is built essentially of matter, or, more precisely, of atoms and molecules; that these material constituents of reality arrange themselves into different things; and that *things,* in their many varieties, constitute the real world that our senses take hold of day by day. There is no need to imagine some mysterious intelligence behind it all; we may simply consider the world as capital-*N* Nature. In this light it is an empirically observable world, constantly open for our inspection.

Nature, according to this view, contains laws and principles which help us generalize its movements and processes; and these laws are the ultimate object of our epistemology. Before we get to them, however, we must begin in the root operation of sensation. Since all real knowledge comes

[1] For instance, many midwestern state universities have allegedly created the ethos of "country club," probably the lowest-ranking in the Essentialist scale. On the other hand, some of our urban "streetcar" colleges and "evening divisions" have created an atmosphere of a highly motivated and earnest practicality which far surpasses the level of eagerness and enthusiasm for learning generally exhibited at undergraduate liberal arts colleges.

from the activity of perception, we must not contrive any ideas which are not based in perception. Once apprehended correctly, the perception of the real world will yield true ideas by virtue of their correspondence with the actual facts. Then, through the manipulation and comparison of precise ideas, we can find our way to larger and larger generalizations concerning the operations of Nature, and finally reach those generalizations which are large and imperial enough to be designated laws.

Axiologically, as we have seen, man finds his way to the good in somewhat the same way as to true knowledge, i.e., via close observation of Nature. Nature contains the elements of good and right; if we attend carefully we can discern a moral law at work there. We can also discern the underlying principles of beauty, for Nature abounds in design, in balance, in proportion — that is, in all the attributes of aesthetic content which it is our privilege to reproduce and celebrate in art.

These notions of Realism, like those of Idealism, make a strong appeal to our common sense. In fact, if, as we said in the previous section, all men have "a touch of the Idealist," then they have also "a touch of the Realist," and in somewhat the same sense. For there is a persistent feeling, especially in a technological, gadget-conscious America, that Nature is the ordered home in which we live and that the reason science works is that it proceeds on the assumption that Nature will "answer back" in ways that are not capricious. Hence, there appears to be a stability and dependability to Nature which we feel justified in considering real. The common citizen is drawn to this view and exhibits a serene trust that this is the way things really are.

It is perhaps an isolated instance, but nevertheless worth our note, that Peter Cooper's words on the occasion of the benefaction and founding of Cooper Union in New York City in 1859 were singled out for reutterance at the centennial celebration of that remarkable institution:

> The great object I desire to accomplish by the establishment of an institution devoted to the advancement of science and art, is to open the volume of nature by the light of truth —
> My heart's desire is, that the rising generation may become so thoroughly acquainted with the works of nature, and the great mystery of their own being, that they may see, feel, understand and know that there are immutable laws, designed in infinite wisdom, constantly operating for our good — so governing the destiny of worlds and men that it is our highest wisdom to live in strict conformity to these laws.[2]

Though these words are over a hundred years old, they sum up the common sense of the matter as far as many Americans are concerned. And since policy — our current concern in the present chapter — eventu-

[2] From a personal letter of Peter Cooper accompanying the Deed of Trust conveying the property on which Cooper Union stands.

ally springs from people's views of the world, it is the belief of the Realist that we can do no better than to elaborate this common-sense notion into a working doctrine of life and education.

Modern Realists have attempted just this, and in thinkers like Breed and Montague and Wild they have found increasingly articulate spokesmen for their views. Moreover — and this is the Realist's "clincher" — Realism constitutes a rationale which helps us understand the great contribution of the modern Western mind: science. Science, to the Realist, is at bottom the discovery of — literally, the taking the cover from — a pre-existent physical reality.[3] And as for scientists themselves, though many of them have begun to accept the Experimentalist conception of science as simply a method of knowing, with no attendant ontology, still a great proportion of them remain on the Realist side. As long as a scientist believes that he is *finding* truth, not tentatively *manufacturing* it, he must be listed among the Realists.

When Realists, then, approach the policy conference table they bring with them the traditional, pre-Dewey view of science. They therefore may be said to represent a large segment of the scientific community in the United States today. This is said with the open presumption, as mentioned above, that much of the scientific community remains Realist in orientation. Physical scientists in particular — physicists, chemists, biologists, zoologists, engineers, etc. — have become famous on college and university campuses for their belligerent repudiation of John Dewey. Even those who really understand Dewey's epistemology and logic often continue to hold a Realist position when it comes to philosophical matters.

EDUCATIONAL THEORY. Working from these general doctrines, we have seen, in Chapters Four (pages 84–85 and 91–94), Seven (pages 185–191 and 208), and Ten (pages 293–296 and 310–311), that a Realist pedagogy will tend to emphasize those portions of the learning experience which rely upon sense perception. Books are important, of course, but there is a limit to what one can learn from books. We must at some point get the youngster into the perceptual world of things. This is sometimes done through concrete demonstrations in the classroom, through audio-visual aids, which bring the outside world perceptually into the classroom, or through field trips, which take the "perceptual apparatus" of the child directly out into the real world of things.

[3] Keep in mind that this conception of science is quite at variance with the Experimentalist's conception of science. The Experimentalist has nothing to say ontologically about the "reality" his science helps him know; to him science is merely a method of managing experience. To a Realist science is an epistemological means to an ontological end, but to an Experimentalist science is both epistemological means and ontological end rolled into one. That is, science is the means to more science. It is its own end.

Generally, then, we can say that Realists are inclined to favor that whole section of the curriculum which is concerned with *things:* the physical sciences. Mathematics, of course, also rides high in the curriculum, because as the language of quantity it is the language by which the real, material world is understood.

In terms of more detailed consideration of teaching practice, we may also point to the tendency in Realism to look upon the child's mind as a receptacle for information which can be given knowledge for later application and use. Thus, producing factual mastery of content is a standard method, and since the mastery of content can be facilitated by organization the Realist teacher tries to present content to the learner in an ordered and systematic way, through textbooks and lectures. The method of ascertaining whether the youngster has learned the content or not is to ask him questions about it, customarily questions in the form of what the educator calls "paper-and-pencil" tests. Objective items — multiple-choice, true-false, etc. — are likely to be favored by the Realist, because they are precise, have definite answers, and, if properly constructed, do not permit open interpretation. In this connection, we might note that the Idealist leans in the direction of subjective or "essay" questions on his examinations. He is not so much interested in the precise, factual, encyclopedic character of subject matter as he is in ideas, concepts, interpretations. To the Idealist facts are too cold; they need to be adorned with *significance.* And a youngster's grasp of the significance of facts cannot be measured in a true-false test. So the open-ended essay question is used for the learner to reveal his ideational grasp of the subject matter under study.

But, to return to our review of Realist educational practices, we may also cite the tendency of Realists to try to reduce education to a quantitative system. This is revealed not only in their penchant for objective tests, mentioned above. It is also revealed in the tendencies in modern education to systematize the learning process into schedules, specific periods of instructional time — say, forty-two minutes between bells — and the whole regular routine of the operations of school life. It is revealed in the line-and-staff "chains of command" that characterize large-scale urban education. Some of our big school systems have taken on the organization of heavy industry, with a board of directors (the board of education) directing policy, a corporation president (the superintendent) as over-all manager, a tier of vice-presidents (the assistant superintendent for personnel, the curriculum director, etc.) performing specialized system-wide tasks, a second tier of junior executives (the principals) in charge of the "branch offices" and plant subsidiaries, a labor force of teachers on the production line, and, of course, the "raw material" of boys and girls, toddling in one end tiny, unformed, ignorant, and immature, and marching out the other end at graduation time presumably knowledgeable, mature, and adult.

The thing that keeps this whole industry going, disturbingly enough, is the relatively innocent concept of the "Carnegie Unit." The Carnegie Unit and the college "semester hour" are perhaps the greatest single "invention" of American education. College credits may be likened to coupons which designate that you have spent an allotted amount of time — say, fifty minutes, three times a week, for fifteen weeks — within the reach of an instructor's voice. If you do your work diligently, learn the material systematically, and get your assignments in on time, it is no trick at all to earn three of these little "coupons," and the registrar jots down the number 3 in his book so that no one will forget that you "took" that course.

If you can keep this up for four years, you can collect all of your coupons, maybe 120 of them, take them to the "box office," and turn them in for a much larger and much more imposing coupon, on which there are some Latin and the magic designation of A.B. or B.S. This coupon now certifies that you are an educated person; it becomes your ticket to any number of life's attractions — graduate school, a teaching certificate, or genteel life among the so-called college-bred.

This admittedly Veblenian treatment of the "college-credit syndrome" is not meant to imply that the Realists are wholly to blame for our excesses. We are all to blame. It is only intended to show that we can sometimes be lured into educational practices too confidently based on the Realist premise that all life and all reality can be rendered in *quantitative* terms. Which is perhaps another way of saying that any ontology can perhaps be carried to a ridiculous extreme.

But, for all its possible qualifications, Realism still occupies a dominant place in American thinking; and it is perhaps significant to note that psychological research in the mid-twentieth century appears to be reconfirming some of our older, more mechanistic conceptions of human nature. Reference was made in Chapter Seven to Watsonian Behaviorism, a psychological movement early in the twentieth century whose supporters argued that the human personality is merely the result of the sum total of all experiential stimuli in the individual's past, and that, consequently, the shaping of human character can theoretically be brought within the control of man through control of the individual's experience. As noted in that chapter, this Watsonian conception has suffered some decline in recent decades, largely, perhaps, because we do not like to think of ourselves as mere S–R machines.

Moreover, Gestalt psychology has come along in Watson's wake to modify the mechanistic theory of human behavior by pointing to the fact that we ourselves are in some measure the determiners of the stimuli to which we respond; that is to say, in the "field of forces" we recognize a total situation comprising multiple stimuli. Not all of the stimuli present actually evoke response; only some do. The stimuli which eventually stir us to response are selected by us. Hence, in contemporary psychology we are seen to be partly the authors of our own environment by virtue of the fact that we choose only some portions of our environment to react to.

Psychologists, however, have pressed their recent researches beyond the Gestalt theory, most notably in the study of brainwashing. Brainwashing is, of course, primarily a military and political weapon, but the psychologists are becoming interested in it as a purely experimental problem, i.e., as something to investigate for its own sake.

Returning briefly to the Realist notion that perception stands at the base of all knowledge, we may now refer to a somewhat bizarre question which the brainwashing experimenters are asking: What would happen if all five of our senses were arbitrarily turned off? Suppose we were to cut off the flow of sensations reaching the human perceptual apparatus and, in effect, reduce an individual's perceptions to zero. What would happen? The answer has turned out to be astonishing.

In a spectacular experiment at the National Institutes of Health in Washington, D.C., one study was designed in which the subject removed all his clothing and placed himself floating head downward in a tank of body-temperature water with nothing touching his body except a face mask connected to a tube which delivered fresh air for breathing. All sensations were reduced nearly to zero: complete pitch darkness; absolute silence; no change in water temperature and hence no sense of touch; no tasting of anything; and no smells of any kind. Dr. Robert H. Felix, Director of the National Institutes of Health, reported the results to a Congressional committee:

> Now this is a most comfortable feeling for an hour or two. It is the most relaxing thing. It is like floating in air. It is like going back before you were born.
>
> For the first two or three hours in the water there are no sensations except this mask on his face. He hears nothing. He sees nothing. He feels nothing. He can't tell which is right side up or whether he is right side up, crosswise, or what-not.
>
> The first hour or two of this is rather comfortable. It is the most delicious sensation and the subject very frequently goes to sleep.
>
> In about an hour or two he wakes up and then finds his thoughts are going over and over, sort of like a closed circuit. He will get on some subject and go over and over it.
>
> The reason for this is deprivation of outside stimuli. And part of the reason that you or I do what we call logical thinking is that there are

things that feed in through some source — some reception source — ear, nose, eyes, skin, what-not — so that these things, feeding in, orient us, and tell us where we are thinking, and give us stimuli for additional thinking.

With all these turned off, one is left with this closed circuit. And this begins to go around and around and magnifies, distorts, and completely changes the whole thinking process.

The patient first becomes anxious, then becomes quite anxious, and then begins to hallucinate usually, and finally becomes completely disoriented.

Once you have cut these all off, and have cut them off long enough that the person is completely disoriented and disorganized, then, if you feed back in information you want this individual to have and this is the only feed-in he gets, slowly, or sometimes not so slowly, he begins to incorporate this into his thinking and it becomes like actual logical thinking because this is the only feed-in he gets.

The problem is that this can happen to any person, some sooner than others.

But you can break down anybody with this. I don't care what their background is or how they have been indoctrinated. I am sure you can break down anybody with this.[4]

A similar experiment was conducted at McGill University in Montreal under the direction of Professor Donald Hebb. Here students were paid twenty dollars a day to lie down on a cot in a darkened, air-conditioned room and do absolutely nothing — that is, *absolutely nothing* — for as long as they could stand it. Professor Hebb found that few students could endure this for more than two or three days. Even at a salary of twenty dollars per day, for most of his subjects this was too difficult a "job."[5]

One result of such isolation experiments is an "erasing effect" on the individual's personality; temporarily, that is, the subject's sense of who he is, where he is, and what he is doing is partially wiped away. His personal structure — his substantial "density" as a human self — partially evaporates; his selfhood is seemingly thinned and diluted by the privation of isolation.

The conclusions from these "isolation" experiments are not yet definitive, but they do seem to point to the possibility that we are much more dependent upon our perceptions, upon the continuity of our perceptions, and upon the empirical "problems" they provide than we have hitherto thought. Perhaps Watson's Behaviorism was right all along. At the very least we can say that the Realist's insistence upon a sensate base for all that passes as human experience has more to it than human egotism has been willing to admit. The possibility persists: Maybe we are nothing but "nervous machines" after all.

4 *New York Times,* April 15, 1956, p. 18.
5 For a description of this experiment, see D. O. Hebb, *A Textbook of Psychology* (Philadelphia: W. B. Saunders Co., 1958), pp. 173–174.

The educational implications of this line of investigation are staggering. If it turns out that we can artificially "erase" a human personality and begin anew with new experiences and new stimuli, think what we could do with the mentally ill; think what we could do with delinquents and criminals. Educationally, perhaps we could finally solve the age-old problem of the first-grade teacher in trying to "unlearn" some of the things boys and girls bring to school with them; we could "erase" their previous experience on the first day of school, and next morning they'd be ready to start learning things straight.

Obviously, the opportunities for evil in this realm of possibility are equally staggering in scope. But at least there is some reason to entertain the Realist's notion of "mechanism in nature" — that is, his basic ontology and epistemology — in order to ask the right questions for the psychologists to investigate. The answers we get may not be very happy ones; but we must know them if we can.

Essentialist policy in American education

THE CONSERVATIONIST THESIS. The policy and program that the Essentialists propose for American education obviously grow out of their fundamental views in philosophy and educational theory. But to find concrete expression for this body of theory, the Essentialists frequently refer to what has come to be called the Conservationist conception of the school. If you will refer to Figure 1 in Chapter One (see page 16) you will recall the notion that in considering the function of education in an epoch of social change and cultural transition the Idealists and Realists prefer to place the school at the "trailing edge" of the present.

This means that the school's primary function is to establish for the child an anchorage of reference in the accumulated knowledge and traditions of the race. And in order to do this it must remain at the rear of the human parade, so as to select and choose what is genuinely true and right for the young to learn. It takes time for the frontier scholar's new knowledge to be tested, tried out in social experience, verified, written up in books, taught to teachers at the university, and worked into lesson plans.

In compliance with the "Spectator Theory" of Idealist and Realist epistemology, the Essentialist insists that the reports of the "spectator" must be organized into relatively certain principles before being included in the experience of the young. The growing edge of culture — what might metaphorically be called the "crow's-nest" observations of the scholarly "spectator" — certainly should be fostered and encouraged; we should spend money for research, for new ideas, for pressing back the boundaries of knowledge. But this is not the work of the school. The school's job is to wait until something definite has been located and

337

certified as true about our world. Then, and only then, should it be introduced into the curriculum.

In this particular office, the school obviously cannot and, indeed, should not aspire to a more active and prominent position in modern culture. Its true purposes lie in coming along behind the "entourage" of American civilization, consolidating and organizing new truths into our current knowledge, serving as the curator of the moral and aesthetic traditions of our way of life, and dispensing these through pedagogical means to each new generation.

One of the best expressions of this thesis came from Professor John Ciardi on the occasion of his informal remarks to the incoming freshman class at Rutgers, the State University of New Jersey, in September of 1954. Professor Ciardi, a man of letters and Poetry Editor of *Saturday Review,* said:

Assume, for example, that you want to be a physicist. You pass the great stone halls of, say, M.I.T., and there cut into stone are the names of the master scientists. The chances are that few if any of you will leave your names to be cut into those stones. Yet any one of you who managed to stay awake through part of a high school course in physics, knows more about physics than did many of those great makers of the past. You know more because they left you what they knew. The first course in any science is essentially a history course. You have to begin by learning what the past learned for you. Except as a man has entered the past of the race he has no function in civilization.

And as this is true of the techniques of mankind, so is it true of mankind's spiritual resources. [Here, you see, Professor Ciardi turns from the Realist subject matter of physics to the Idealist subject matter of literature.] Most of these resources, both technical and spiritual, are stored in books. Books, the arts, and the techniques of science, are man's particular accomplishment. When you have read a book, you have added to your human experience. Read Homer and your mind includes a piece of Homer's mind. Through books you can acquire at least fragments of the mind and experience of Virgil, Dante, Shakespeare — the list is endless. For a great book is necessarily a gift: it offers you a life you have not time to live yourself, and it takes you into a world you have not time to travel in literal time. A civilized human mind is, in essence, one that contains many such lives and many such worlds. If you are too much in a hurry, or too arrogantly proud of your own limitations, to accept as a gift to your humanity some pieces of the minds of Sophocles, of Aristotle, of Chaucer — and right down the scale and down the ages to Yeats, Einstein, E. B. White, and Ogden Nash — . . . you are neither a developed human being nor a useful citizen of a democracy. . . .

I speak, I am sure, for the faculty of the liberal arts college and for the faculties of the specialized schools as well, when I say that a university has no real existence and no real purpose except as it succeeds in putting you in touch, both as specialists and as humans, with those human minds *your* human mind needs to include. The faculty, by its very existence, says implicitly: "We have been aided by many people, and by many books, and by the arts, in our attempt to make ourselves some sort of storehouse of human experience. We are here to make available to you, as best we can, that experience.[6]

BASIC EDUCATION. This statement of purpose concerning a university can certainly be generalized to refer to the Essentialist's conception of the purpose of the American school. Essentialism has been championed by many groups in American life, but perhaps the most articulate and persuasive is an organization known as the Council for Basic Education, with headquarters in Washington, D.C. The Council came into existence in the 1950's in response to what some educators felt to be a gradual corruption of American education by the excesses of so-called Progressive Education.

Progressive Education, with or without the capital *P*, was a movement, most influential during the 1920's and 1930's, whose central aim was to lift the heavy hand of traditionalism and rote mastery from the public school and to turn the business of learning into a more lifelike, meaningful activity on the part of both teacher and student. The movement grew out of John Dewey's Experimentalism (which we shall examine in Chapter Twelve) and its main emphasis was given to "problem-solving" in learning, in place of brute mastery of content.

According to the Council for Basic Education, the whole Progressive movement was wrongheaded, in that it failed to recognize the importance of providing the child a secure linkage to a body of truth and to a historical tradition *before* developing his thinking processes and his ability to solve problems. So the Council now publishes a regular *Newsletter* and other publications designed to reaffirm the principle that the school's first task is to teach basic knowledge. A basic knowledge of English, history, mathematics, science, and foreign language should become the common equipment of all American youngsters in high school. Scoffing at so-called life-adjustment education, the Essentialist Council asks for a hard core of fundamental learning as the basis of an educational program for all American youth.[7]

In a less organized but more volatile way individual advocates of the Essentialist position have also sounded the cry for a return to funda-

[6] *Rutgers Alumni Monthly*, XXXIV, No. 2 (November, 1954), 2–3.

[7] See *The Case for Basic Education: A Program of Aims for Public Schools*, a major publication of the Council, in which several distinguished American scholars specify what knowledge and understanding a student in America ought to have at the end of twelve years of schooling. (See FURTHER READING at the end of this chapter.)

mentals. Admiral Rickover, father of the nuclear submarine, has used his eminence in science as a platform from which to warn of what he considers a tragically misdirected American educational policy. The Admiral has proposed that a toughening of all educational procedures is required at once, a return to the hard core of basic educational subjects of the older curriculum is urgently necessary, and an organized segregation and instruction of the gifted must be initiated without delay.[8] On this last point, he has suggested the founding of twenty-five elite public high schools throughout the country to serve the really top group of adolescents.

Perhaps the most vigorous spokesman for Essentialism in recent decades has been Professor Arthur Bestor of the University of Illinois. Speaking with frequent sharpness and occasional venom, Professor Bestor has "blown the whistle" on anything and everything connected with John Dewey, the Experimentalists, and the Progressive "Life-Adjusters" (as he calls them). In his many books and articles[9] he has sounded the call for a massive popular missionary movement to clean out the humbug and foolishness from contemporary educational programs and, if possible, to destroy the influence of the real bad guys in the melodrama, the despised professors of education in teachers' colleges and schools of education across the land.

Although the Essentialist message frequently sounds strident and shrill, it occasionally appears in more reasoned presentations, such as the Rockefeller Brothers Fund policy statement entitled *The Pursuit of Excellence: Education and the Future of America,* published in 1958. In pronunciamentos of this quality, like the earlier Harvard Report,[10] the integrity and persuasion of the Essentialist position are more evident. Here the full panoply of our Western tradition — its factual knowledge, its social institutions, its ultimate moral principles, and, of course, the expression of all these in contemporary civilization — is set before us as the very heart of the education of the young. In terms of educational *policy,* says the Essentialist, here is where all true education begins.

THE PERENNIALISTS

Neo-Thomism

BASIC VIEWS. You might turn to Chapter Three (pages 59–66), Chapter Six (pages 147–155), and Chapter Nine (pages 261–267) to re-

8 See FURTHER READING at the end of this chapter.
9 See FURTHER READING at the end of this chapter.
10 The Harvard Committee, *General Education in a Free Society* (Cambridge: Harvard University Press, 1948).

mind yourself of the Thomist's views on reality, knowledge, and value, in that order. Recall specifically the ultimately logical and intellectual character of the world the Thomist thinks we inhabit.

Ontologically, the basic building blocks of this universe are logical in character, namely, the companion principles of actuality and potentiality. Everything that exists is not only a combination of matter (potentiality) and form (actuality), as Aristotle told us, but also a coming together of some basic "what-ness" (essence, potentiality) with the act of existing (actuality), as St. Thomas told us. Furthermore, the actualizing principle, which finds Aristotelian expression in *Form* and Thomistic expression in *Being*, is at root the principle of *Reason* at work in the world. Hence, the world we wish to comprehend is potentially comprehensible, because our human minds are oriented to its logical requirements; there is a kind of metaphysical rapport between ourselves and the cosmos. This is not to say, of course, that knowing the cosmos is easy; it is only to say that potentially the cosmos can be known.

Knowing, then, in Thomistic epistemology centers largely in the cultivation of the logical powers of the human mind. If this mind, beginning in a state of potentiality, can be brought to the fullest expression of its powers, it will then be able to take hold of truth and to possess it permanently. The cultivation of Reason, consequently, is the paradigmatic channel to genuine knowledge. As we have seen, the Ecclesiastical Thomists have superadded the category of revelatory knowing to the epistemological spectrum; this kind of knowing, while relatively rare, is of course supreme among all methods.

In axiology the principle of Reason persists. Ethically, the good act is that which conforms to the rational nature of man. And since men naturally tend toward Reason, they tend toward the Good as well. Furthermore, in Ecclesiastical doctrine, whenever Reason departs and human behavior comes under the dominion of the will unbridled, there is no sin; sin is committed only when a man, with all of his rational faculties at work and in control of his conduct, persists in doing wrong. In aesthetics, likewise, we have seen the imperium of Reason, for there is no beauty in the world which cannot be reduced to rational terms. It is the intellect which ultimately appreciates and loves the beautiful. While the senses of man grasp beauty in the applied and practical arts, it is the intellect of man which has exclusive privileges of laying hold of beauty in the pure and fine arts.

EDUCATIONAL THEORY. Out of these fundamental propositions we have tried, in Chapter Four (pages 85–86 and 94–97), Chapter Seven (pages 191–197 and 208–209), and Chapter Ten (pages 296–300 and 311–312), to organize an educational doctrine for Neo-Thomism.

In those sections the argument centers principally around the procedures of the school which can take hold of the intellectual and spiritual powers of the child and develop them to their fullest actuality.

In terms of curricular theory, as we have seen, such procedures incline in the direction of subject matters such as mathematics and foreign languages, which have a disciplinary effect on the mind by virtue of their internal "form." Hence, formal discipline refers to those bodies of knowledge which not only tell us about our world but which themselves are characterized by a logic and internal system likely to produce a salutary effect on the intellective faculties of the child. In addition to this, of course, the Ecclesiastical Neo-Thomists include a goodly amount of doctrinal material in their curriculum, to bring the child into direct confrontation with Jesus Christ and, through him, with Almighty God.

In terms of pedagogy the Neo-Thomist prescriptions tend in the direction of disciplinary and catechetical methods. Here the learner is provided exercises in reasoning and memory and by rigorous mental calisthenics is brought to a higher level of thinking ability. The moral tendencies of the young are strengthened and guided by teaching procedures which exercise the will, i.e., assignments the teacher gives the child which he finds distasteful but which he forces himself through to develop his inner strength of character.

Perennialist policy in American education

Throughout the Neo-Thomist sections of the previous three Parts the underlying emphasis has been upon the intellectual and spiritualistic character of the world in which we live and our obligation to adjust ourselves to those features of our world by strengthening and fortifying the intellectual and spiritual tendencies within our own natures: Since our own human nature is, as we have pointed out, already tuned to the ultimate features of reality, our educational program should address itself to human nature as a starting point in the development of a sensible educational policy.

This, indeed, is the crux of the matter as it is developed by the Lay Neo-Thomists. And since they have had more to say about public educational policy in America than have the Roman Catholic educational theorists, we should direct the bulk of our attention to them. However, before we do this, it is necessary to touch briefly on educational policy in the Roman Catholic Church.

ECCLESIASTICAL NEO-THOMIST EDUCATIONAL POLICY. When it comes to public educational policy in America, the Roman Catholic Neo-Thomist position is somewhat ambivalent. On the one hand, Catholics have voluntarily separated themselves from the policy councils of the American public school by establishing their own school systems, and the secular courts in America have protected them in withdrawing their children from the public schools and placing them in parochial schools. This discrete division and separation of the two educational groups — the one secular, the other ecclesiastical — signifies that the Roman Catholic educator has voluntarily withdrawn his moral right to help shape public educational policy.

On the other hand, every parochial school carries on a certain amount of public business; it instructs children in secular subject matters such as reading, writing, arithmetic, history, social studies, and science. Indeed, perhaps the greater part of its total educational energies is still occupied in what may be termed the "secular" areas of education. Hence, there remains the question whether the parochial school is not entitled to certain public moneys to support that portion of its work which is in the public interest, namely, all the things it does for the young which the public school does.

In practical terms, the issue simply reduces to a claim by Roman Catholic educators and parents that they are paying a double tax for education: They continue to pay a public tax for the education of other people's children, and then they pay their church tax for the education of their own children. Hence, in terms of over-all policy, Roman Catholic educators have been building up pressure for their being granted certain amounts of public funds to offset this "double taxation" and to help them finance that portion of their work which is truly public, indeed, even secular in character. After all, the public does benefit from the "free" instruction given to some of its younger members in parochial schools. Why, then, ought not the public treasury help and assist in this, *quid pro quo?*

The answer to this question is admittedly not an easy one. Many secular educators rejoin by saying that the mere fact of separation from the main body of public education in itself constitutes a forfeit of any moral right to public funds. Every private activity, from a laundry to an international airline, can be said to be carrying on "public" business. Are we obligated to subsidize all such activities from the public till?

Perhaps at a more crucial level of judgment is the companion view that separation from the secular body of society in itself constitutes a kind of immorality. Parochial schools tend to introduce a divisive factor in society; they segregate and isolate one body of the community from another. As such, they confound the very value system they mean to argue for, namely, human brotherhood. By artificially segregating children and emphasizing their distinctive difference by special uniforms, holidays, etc., parochial schools actually set up in the minds of children (both their own and the public school's) the unhealthy and fundamentally un-Christian sense of alienation from one's neighbor. John Dewey frequently pointed to this phenomenon, suggesting that an unexpected dividend of public education in America is a "sense of community" which develops in the child throughout his formative years. This "sense of community," Dewey reminds us, was never achieved in Europe; indeed, it is a peculiar and unique feature of American schools, something of a social invention stumbled upon by American educators. It is in this sense, said Dewey, that the American public school is a truly religious institution, in a way which purely ecclesiastical schools by their very existence tend to repudiate.

The basic difficulty of the problem resides, some think, in an ultimate contradiction in Neo-Thomist logic. As we have seen in earlier chapters, the Lay Neo-Thomists have tried to establish a dichotomy of realms — the empirical and scientific, on the one hand, and the rational and intuitive, on the other; the Ecclesiastical Neo-Thomists have added a third realm — the spiritual and revelatory. Each of these realms, we are told, is distinct from the others, containing its own peculiar sort of problems and its peculiar methods of handling those problems. Hence, says the Neo-Thomist, science is helpless when it comes to metaphysical or theological questions and, likewise, metaphysics and theology are helpless in empirical and scientific matters.

When we apply these doctrines to social life, the Thomists insist, we must remember that each realm must be autonomous. In the present case of the Ecclesiastical wing, this usually means that the Church must remain separate from the State and that these two human "environments" can never be permitted to intrude on each other, thus permitting each to govern its own special sphere. In this splendid "division of labor" true harmony is thought to lie.

This is all very well and good, says the secularist, but it contradicts the very spirit and meaning of both metaphysics and theology, namely, their presumed usefulness in helping us to live the civilized life. Men develop their metaphysics and their theologies not just as idle pastimes but to find out what their world is like and what it requires of them. What good is a religion if it does not have something fairly specific to say about how to live? What good is a doctrine if it does not issue somehow into the stream of our experience? What good is a metaphysic if it is claimed to be utterly irrelevant to human affairs?

This, to the secularist, is the box we get into when we try to render our world discontinuous, i.e., constituted of separate divisions each supreme unto itself. When we indulge this tendency to discontinuity we wind up announcing to ourselves that the noblest part of us — our mind and spirit — has nothing whatsoever to do with the way we live our years here on this earth. Certainly no man, not even the Neo-Thomist, can find such a position tenable.

The point is that if we mark off boundary lines between metaphysical and theological problems on the one hand and secular and civil problems on the other and declare each area to be autonomous, then we can permit no intercourse between the two. For we cannot have it both ways; we cannot insist on a separation of powers in one breath and a "mutual assistance" policy in the next. We cannot say that Church and State are separate, for instance, and then turn around and let the Church help make State policy.

What are we to do when specific cases come up — and they often do — when the requirements of Church and State are in conflict: the Quakers and military service, Jehovah's Witnesses and the flag salute, the Roman Catholic Church and birth control (a potential State problem in the not too distant future)? When Church and State disagree on a segment of public behavior, which shall prevail?

The principle at issue here is relatively simple: Either there are two realms — the secular and the ecclesiastical — separate, autonomous, and independently sovereign, with no power to correct and modify each other, OR there is a continuity of realms, according to which all questions must be settled by the open and public method of assessing what is the best thing to do.

As a matter of actual fact, Quakers, Jehovah's Witnesses, and Roman Catholics alike have yielded to the latter principle; they have ultimately submitted to the rule of secular authorities. This is best illustrated by remembering that the Supreme Court of the United States has frequently ruled on questions such as those noted above, and many others like them, with respect to religious groups. It is true, of course, that the Roman Catholic Church (and the other churches too) in its representations before both the Supreme Court and lower courts has been permitted to argue its religious immunity from civil authorities. And many decisions have been reached by the Court on precisely this ground, namely, the privilege of private conscience to establish its own behavioral requirements in American life.

But, says the secularist, what the Catholic Church is actually doing in arguing its immunity is to contradict that argument by the mere act of presenting its case to the Court in the first place. For the Court is a secular institution, and to appear before it signifies that you are willing to submit to a secular adjudication of your complaint. If the Church were wholly consistent in its separation of the ecclesiastical and secular realms, it would not bother making its argument at all. It would merely proclaim its prior allegiance to God and go about its business as it saw fit. The fact that the Catholic Church does not actually do this in contemporary American life signifies that the secular principle has been established as a working doctrine in our time.

Most precisely does it apply to educational policy, for Roman Catholic parochial schools (and those of all other private sects) continue to exist only by sufferance of the public polity, i.e., the American people as they express their public policies through the instrument of secular courts. As such, these parochial schools ultimately fall within the domain of authority of the American people and not of some metaphysical or divine realm.

The separation of Catholic children (and other groups) off into their own school system, while sanctioned by the courts, is an unhappy concession we make to freedom of conscience. In the eyes of the secularist, the price we pay for this freedom is rather steep: a divisive splintering of public conscience between competing value systems. We shall continue to pay this price only so long as the splintering effect does not unduly disturb the quality of public life. When private conscience reaches that point — as it has done in such groups as the Ku Klux Klan, the Columbians of the 1940's, and the White Citizens' Councils of the 1950's — then the privilege of private conscience begins to diminish as a moral right of the individual.[11]

The point is that the "orbiting away" of any group from the idea of an open and secular America is always, if only incipiently, a compromise of that idea. So it is, says the secularist, in the case of Roman Catholic educational policy. But once the separation has been effected — and if the Catholic insists upon maintaining it — then the secularist cannot permit him to find his way back to the educational policy conference table. For the Catholic educator, like his metaphysical and theological brethren, cannot have it both ways.

LAY NEO-THOMIST EDUCATIONAL POLICY. We must turn now to a perhaps more directly relevant body of ideas in Neo-Thomist thought. Unlike the Ecclesiastical wing, the Lay wing of Neo-Thomism has a proposal for adoption by the secular public schools of America. Lay Thomists claim to be committed as much as any other group of educators to the proposition of educating all our citizens in a single school system, and they suggest that an education for all American youth can be found, as we intimated at the opening of this section, in the common nature of man.

The most cogent and spirited development of this theme is found in

11 Even the Quaker conscientious objector to war is not free to run loose but is "drafted" by the federal government and detained in a camp. In principle, the Quaker has yielded to secular authority when he enters a "C.O." camp.

the writings of Robert M. Hutchins, former Chancellor of the University of Chicago, who later became identified with the Fund for the Republic, an autonomous organization established by the Ford Foundation for the study of public questions having to do with liberty and freedom. What Hutchins in his many books has done is to extend the underlying philosophical thesis of Lay Neo-Thomism, which we have already examined in previous chapters.

This thesis begins with the proposition that the very first question to ask in considering educational philosophy is: What is the nature of Man? As Mortimer Adler has shown us, the answer to this question can be put in more or less strictly Aristotelian terms: Man is a rational animal. As it turns out, the Neo-Thomists are not too interested in the animal part of man; they have turned instead to his rational nature for the center of their theory of learning. Our first interest, then, is directed to this feature of our nature which is intellectual in character.

What is essentially important about this feature is, of course, that it is shared by all men; it is a common trait. In considering this common trait, Hutchins has this to say:

> Every man has a function as a man. The function of a citizen or a subject may vary from society to society, and the system of training, or adaptation, or instruction, or meeting immediate needs may vary with it. But the function of a man as man is the same in every age and in every society, since it results from his nature as a man. The aim of an educational system is the same in every age and in every society where such a system can exist: it is to improve man as man.[12]

What this means of course is that the aim of an educational system is "the development of the intellectual powers of men."[13] Hence, Hutchins has been unequivocal in his advocacy of the view that the American educational enterprise should cease the foolishness of trying to adjust the individual to society, or to "meet his needs" in all their multivariety, or to reform the social order. It should, instead, turn its attention specifically to the training of the intellect.

So thoroughgoing is Mr. Hutchins in this commitment that he has asked for the removal from the school of all nonintellectual activities. Among the first to go would be those activities which are perhaps the most remote from the intellect: athletics. As we saw earlier, Chancellor Hutchins made himself famous in American educational circles by successfully removing the intercollegiate football program from the Univer-

12 *The Conflict in Education* (New York: Harper and Bros., 1953), p. 68.
13 *Ibid.*, p. 70.

sity of Chicago during his tenure there. But he also implicitly proposed the removal of all physical education from the school's work. High on the black list too are extracurricular activities of all kinds, social and recreational projects, driver training, basket-weaving, cooking, and dancing.[14] Even art and music will have to go, insofar as they are emotive rather than intellectual in character. And finally Hutchins has annoyed even the Ecclesiastical Thomists, by insisting that moral training must be surrendered by the school because it does not succcessfully yield to intellective criteria.

So, what are we left with? We are left, says Hutchins, with the intellect. The intellect is the only part of man which the school should have anything to do with. Other agencies — home, church, the mass media, Boy Scouts, etc. — may supply other needs, but the school's task is singular: the training of the intellect.

It turns out, as Hutchins sees the problem, that the school can best begin to fulfill its proper function by referring to our common human nature and, as he has often said, "drawing out" this common nature through the application of the student to purely liberal studies. The "liberal studies," he says, are those studies which have always represented "the best education for the best"; that is, from Plato to the present, they have consistently formed the core of that education which is given the ruling groups in all Western societies. This is because they are studies relating to the timeless truths of all mankind; and these truths constitute the base of all human wisdom and all political vision, wherever and whenever men happen to live.

Now, asks Hutchins, if a liberal education — an education in the disciplines of language, mathematics, logic, science, and history leading to the development of the powers of understanding and judgment — if this kind of education has always been thought "the best for the best," is it the best for all? Hutchins answers with a resounding Yes. For in a democracy the "ruling class" consists of common citizens. And if we

---

14 "Think [he says] of the most futile, childish, irrelevant subject you can — think of parlor games, think of self-beautification, think of anything you like — I will undertake to find it for you among the courses offered by American institutions of higher learning.

"I had no sooner written these words than *Life* magazine came along to prove my point by announcing that at an American university it is possible to get college credit for being a clown, something that even I, after decades of disillusionment, could never have thought of." (*Ibid.*, pp. 12–13.) Reference here is to Florida State University, near which the Ringling Brothers Circus once maintained its winter quarters. Since 1947 Florida State has offered a physical education course in circus activities. According to authorities there, this course develops physical fitness through vigorous, large-muscle activities: tumbling, apparatus work, trapeze work, adagio dancing, etc. No clowning, though. But one of the big, spectacular extracurricular activities at F.S.U. is the annual student circus, *Flying High,* in which there is a good deal of clowning. Dr. Hutchins is technically wrong, but perhaps he has made his point.

have elevated the common citizen to be his own governor we must make available to him the education that all governors throughout Western civilization have been required to have.

> Liberal education was the education of rulers. It was the education of those who had leisure. Democracy and industry, far from making liberal education irrelevant, make it indispensable and possible for all the people. Democracy makes every man a ruler, for the heart of democracy is universal suffrage. If liberal education is the education that rulers ought to have, and this I say has never been denied, then every ruler, that is every citizen, should have a liberal education.[15]

Hutchins' educational policy for America, then, is straightforward: Let us return to the liberal tradition and the training of the intellect which has characterized the education of the ruling classes for over 2000 years. Here is where our common nature as men truly lies. What is more, such an education is admirably suited to our own times; it is utilitarian in the highest political sense, for it prepares us for the responsibilities of democratic citizenship.

Hutchins has never spelled out any more specifically than this how such an educational program could be rendered teachable and learnable in the common school in America. Certainly in their customary form the liberal arts and the mathematical and linguistic disciplines have proved to be completely beyond the reach of a sizable segment of the young people who are forced, at the pleasure of our compulsory-attendance laws, to attend school until the age of sixteen. Even average students have difficulty with foreign languages and advanced mathematics which can turn them against the school. Presumably Mr. Hutchins has in mind some as yet unspecified procedure for rendering the "liberal arts" really achievable by all intelligence levels from 70 on up, but present-day educators would like to know what that procedure might be.

Where Mr. Hutchins' views have had more direct bearing is at the college and university level. Here he has assiduously applied his doctrine and developed a theory of higher education — most notably in his famous volume *The Higher Learning in America* — which unambiguously insists upon the liberal subjects and the arts of intellectual discipline as the only suitable ingredients of higher education. Not only has he theorized about this, but he has taken an active role in reorganizing a whole college's curriculum in this direction: In the mid-1930's Mr. Hutchins, together with Carl Van Doren, Stringfellow Barr, Mortimer Adler, and others, helped to establish the famous Great Books Curriculum at St. John's College in Annapolis, Maryland.

15 *Ibid.*, p. 84.

St. John's was and is a small liberal arts college. In 1937 the College adopted a plan whereby its undergraduate curriculum would consist principally of the critical reading of the 100 greatest books of the Western world — books ranging all the way from Homer's *Iliad,* Euclid's *Elements,* St. Thomas' *Summa Theologica,* and Newton's *Principia* to Hegel's *Logic,* Marx's *Capital,* and Maxwell's *Electricity and Magnetism.* The list of Great Books has grown since the original inception of the idea, but the idea is still the same, namely, that a thorough saturation in the greatest thinking of the greatest minds is the way to train the intellect.[16]

The "greatness" of a book lies in its status as a classic, and a classic can be defined simply as a book that is relevant to every age. Since a classic is relevant to every age it may be said to stand above man's lesser works as essentially nobler and higher, and, in that sense, truer. If men can claim to have found truth, certainly the likeliest candidates for truth are those ideas which have stood the test of time and have been found to be applicable to every epoch and every civilization in recorded human time.

Hence, the basic criterion for selection of the Great Books is their individual longevity as great books. For this reason, the more recent the publication date of a candidate for the list, the more difficult it is to judge. There is in this curriculum, therefore, a built-in bias against recency and modernity; and it is this selective factor in favor of the past which troubles many otherwise friendly critics of the St. John's plan, for there can be no denying that a very large segment of intelligent human thought has been generated in just the last thirty or forty years. To disqualify this segment by the criterion of longevity is to risk the possibility of not acquainting today's undergraduate with an understanding of the world in which he is expected to live and make his way.

But this is just the point, says Hutchins. If a young man can master the greatest work of *all* time, then certainly he can find his way in *our* time. These books are, after all, still relevant, still Great. But that is beside the point. What matters is that the development of the intellectual and rational powers — not some present adaptability — become the central objective of higher learning. Once this is accomplished in the liberal college, the practical affairs of life will take care of themselves by reason of the individual's rational control over them.

In addition to the Great Books, the undergraduates at St. John's study several languages, both ancient and modern, to enable them to read

16 Although these books are read and discussed in semiweekly tutorial sessions, they represent only about a third of the curriculum at St. John's. The students also study mathematics, laboratory science, and languages throughout the four years, and music for three semesters, and attend lectures and concerts every week throughout the academic year. Since there are no "majors," every student takes exactly the same course.

some of the works in the original. Furthermore, since linguistic training itself has a disciplinary effect on the intellect, it is not a "tool subject" merely but a central feature of the curriculum.

Then, besides language study, the St. John's people have also added the interesting feature of requiring the students in their science courses to recreate and re-enact the seminal experiments of the great men of science — Galileo, Kepler, Newton, Boyle, Lavoisier, Harvey, *et al.* Here, by actually imitating the greatest intellects of our scientific past, the student begins to sense the inner workings of those intellects, in a sense sharing in their genius for experimental design; and it is presumed that through this method the undergraduate will "absorb" genius by associating with it in so direct a manner. Through association with great intellects we train the undergraduate intellect to think greatly.[17]

Here, then, is the St. John's answer to the confusion of our time: a liberal education built solidly on our intellectual past and on the rigorous discipline of the young mind to pure reason. What Hutchins and his friends have wrought in this particular instance may or may not be their recommendation for other colleges. But something approximating this would appear to stand paradigmatically for the policy they would hope to have adopted by American higher education generally. The great fault, they say, in American education at all levels is its apparent retreat from pure reason and rigorous intellectual discipline. We are lost as a civilization, they believe, until we find our way back to Aristotelian principles and to the training of intellect in all our citizens at every level of their educational experience.

QUESTIONS

1. "Of all the doctrines of education extant the one which most nearly describes how American schools actually operate is Essentialism." What do you think of this generalization? Is it accurate? Prepare a list of examples which would support your position.

2. What is your evaluation of the "Conservationist Theory" of the Essentialist school? In a period of rapid social change, is it better to emphasize the unchanging truths of our heritage or to play these down in favor of an ability to manage change itself?

[17] We might refer to this as a kind of "intellectual osmosis": We rub a sophomore up against a Great Thinker and across the psychic membrane is supposed to pass the power of intellect. As facetious as this may sound, it is a plausible hypothesis because it involves the kind of phenomenon which, theoretically, could be empirically tested. Contemporary psychology would appear to have rejected it, but it still might make an interesting pedagogical experiment.

3. In every college catalogue a number of educational policies are evident, if only by implication. Take a look at the catalogue of your institution. In it can you find concrete illustrations — either in the rules it enumerates or in the courses it offers — of Essentialism in action? Of Perennialism in action?

4. What is your position on the question of public financial aid to Roman Catholic parochial schools? How can your position be defended on rational grounds to opponents from the other side? Develop your thesis in a short essay.

5. Is it possible to teach the liberal arts — the familiar "college prep" curriculum — to all ability levels? Take any one of the subject matters of this curriculum — algebra, trigonometry, French, ancient history, chemistry, physics — and develop a lesson plan by which you would teach this subject to a group of high school students whose IQ's averaged 90.

6. Secure a copy of the current catalogue of St. John's College and review the Great Books listed therein. Are any of these books currently used in your institution as required reading at the undergraduate level? Should they be? What would you say are the main strengths to the Great Books Plan? What are its weaknesses?

FURTHER READING

Essentialism

Bestor, Arthur. *Educational Wastelands.* Urbana, Ill.: University of Illinois Press, 1953.
In a no-holds-barred attack on "professional educationists" and all they stand for, Bestor tears into what he considers the mumbo jumbo of modern educational theory. His first chapter, on "The Vanishing Sense of Purpose in Education," and Chapters 11 and 13, on "The Structure of Liberal Education" and "The Study of Our Own Civilization," will give you a vivid picture of what an Essentialist stands for in America today.

Council for Basic Education. *The Case for Basic Education: A Program of Aims for Public Schools.* Boston: Atlantic-Little, Brown, 1959.
Here a group of scholars, representing all of the major areas of knowledge, pronounce what they feel should be the content of the secondary school in America. The university professor has gradually been squeezed out of educational policy councils in the United States. Here the C.B.E. attempts to find a seat for him at the table.

The Harvard Committee. *General Education in a Free Society.* Cambridge: Harvard University Press, 1948.
This famous "Harvard Report" originally began as a project in redesigning the Harvard College curriculum. To think through this problem President James B. Conant appointed a distinguished group of faculty members to

examine the kinds of preparation Harvard students bring to the College. What they found, and what in consequence they propose for the American high school, is one of the most eloquently written documents in educational literature. The first four chapters, dealing with general theory, the problem of diversity, and the curriculum of the secondary school, are the most directly relevant to the present chapter.

Keats, John. *Schools without Scholars*. Boston: Houghton-Mifflin Co., 1958.
This is not so much a policy statement as it is a sharply satirical attack on contemporary schools. "What Goes on Here?" asks Keats in the title of Chapter 1. He answers it with Chapter 5's title: "Life Adjustment, Anyone?" So it goes. The author of *The Crack in the Picture Window* and *The Insolent Chariots* here gives education a similar going over.

Rickover, Hyman. *Education and Freedom*. New York: E. P. Dutton and Co., Inc., 1959.
Using what a Harvard professor describes as "perception by periscope," the Admiral here attempts to develop his expertise in what is for him an un-familiar region — educational theory. His chapters on the education of talented youth, mass education and merit, and demonstration high schools and national standards provide the most representative examples of his Essentialist predilections.

Perennialism

Hutchins, Robert M. *The Conflict in Education*. New York: Harper and Bros., 1953.
In this volume of lectures you can get the sharp taste of Hutchins' testy con-tempt for those educational policies which propose to adjust the child, meet his needs, reform society, or — lowest man on the totem pole — disclaim the need for any policy whatsoever. When he finishes with these matters, Hutchins proceeds to a discussion of the basis of education, liberal education, and the university.

————. *The Higher Learning in America*. New Haven: Yale University Press, 1936.
This little volume, representing the Storrs Lecture by then President Hutchins of Chicago, is perhaps his most widely known work. He first examines the external condition surrounding higher education in this country which pro-duces a fundamental dilemma for college and university educators, then goes on to state, in the last two chapters, "what a general education is" and "what a university might be." Like all of Hutchins' writing, this is a lively and read-able treatise.

————. *The University of Utopia*. Chicago: University of Chicago Press, 1933.
These, the Walgreen Lectures, represent Mr. Hutchins' considered thought on the nature and purpose of the university in America: ". . . the essence of the Utopian Way of Life is that it is rational." To achieve this realizable Utopia, says he, is to educate the citizen in reason. In developing this theme

Mr. Hutchins examines the phenomena of industrialization and specialization. Then he comes to the heart of the matter in chapters dealing with philosophical diversity and social and political conformity.

Maritain, Jacques. *Education at the Crossroads*. New Haven: Yale University Press, 1943.
Ecclesiastical Neo-Thomists do not often speak directly on public educational policy. This little volume, comprising the Terry Lectures, is an exception. After discussing the aims of education and the dynamics of the learning process, Maritain turns to educational policy for America. In Chapter III he discusses elementary, secondary, and higher education, with understandable emphasis on religion and the spiritual life. Then, in Chapter IV, he examines some of the particular "trials" of present-day education.

CHAPTER TWELVE

The Contemporary Outlook:

Experimentalism

EXPERIMENTALISM AND
AMERICAN EDUCATION

The rationale of a scientific age

Essentialism, as we stated earlier, may still be considered the most widely practiced philosophy in the American school. But there are many who say that its star is falling and that its place is about to be taken by Experimentalism. Certainly in theoretical circles — in teachers' colleges and schools of education — Experimentalists have captured almost all of the major strongholds. Understandably this causes much hand-wringing and brow-wiping among the more conservative elements in the educational community, and they are delaying their retreat as long as possible and leaving the field to the newcomers only with the greatest reluctance.

One of the things which tend to delay full acceptance of Experimentalism is its rather marked novelty as a philosophic system. As noted earlier, when we come to Experimentalism we must recognize a sharp break in continuity — both historical and analytical — with the older views of Idealism, Realism, and Neo-Thomism. One of the things that characterize this break is the somewhat unorthodox way in which Experimentalism was born. The earlier philosophies were, for the most part, products of magnificent theoretical speculation carried on by men of great genius. Some of these philosophies sprang, at least in general outline, from the mind of a single man — which is one reason why they lend themselves more easily to systematic treatment. Experimentalism, however, is an intellectual reaction to a way of life, a methodical putting together of the disparate aspects of what we are already doing into some recognizable and intelligible whole.

The Idealist Horne once said, "We probably live our way into a system of thinking rather than think our way into a pattern of living. This means that living is more influential in determining thinking than thinking is in determining living."[1] He was not talking about Experimentalism, but he could have been. For Experimentalism is the supreme historical example of man living his way into a system of thinking. It is not the product of speculation, even though it has found expression in the thinking of great minds — Chauncey Wright, Charles Peirce, William James, John Dewey. Experimentalism is, rather, a rationalization of the kind of living we have been doing increasingly in the Western world over the last 300 to 400 years.

What kind of living is this? To put it briefly, it is a kind of living which has grown increasingly more empirical and pragmatic, a mode of life in which men try out their ideas before believing them.

This approach has had its most spectacular application, as we all know, in the field of the technological sciences; in their encounter with the physical environment, men test and try before believing anything. It is unfortunate, in a way, that such spectacular success has been achieved in this particular sector of life. Western man has a right to feel bad about having become famous for the wrong thing. He has become famous for his great industries, his technology, his machines! But what he wants "to go down in history" for is not a pile of machinery or the "machine" way of life he has built up around it. Western man wants to be remembered most of all for having invented a new way of knowing — Science.

The thoughtful Westerner is properly annoyed when too much is made of his technology. He is not apologetic about it, certainly, but his machines represent only the first, primitive (albeit spectacular) fruits of his new method. From a larger perspective, they are little more than adult toys which he has reveled in inventing for his own use. This is because, up to now, he has treated science itself as a kind of sophisticated plaything — useful enough in the lower order of material pursuits, but quite incapable of dealing with the larger questions of life.

Enter the Experimentalist. He says technology is but the opening

[1] While this is the way things go, thought Horne, true philosophy is the attempt to reverse the process, i.e., to "think our way" into a nobler and more humane way of living. Idealism he considered the finest example of how this could be done.

round. Our machines, he claims, will some day be regarded as merely the impulsive and somewhat puerile beginning of man in the use of his new method. The childish excitement and obsessive materialism of a mechanized "toy" culture shall mature — when man wills it — in an era in which science is turned to the task of elevating the human condition in all its many sectors, beyond the merely material and technological. Man will find something more strategic and important to spend his science on than finned automobiles, blinking computing machines, sputtering rockets, and earth-quaking explosions. And when he does, he will have realized at last the true significance of his new invention.

But the point is this: We have had to "live our way" through this epoch for over 300 years in order to realize what is happening to us. Now we are beginning to see how science works and how it can be extended beyond our physical world into problems of social relations and moral judgment. Experimentalists are practically unanimous in the belief that science will someday prove its superiority over other methods in every corner of human experience.

The source of Progressivism

What science has done first of all is to give us a sense of control over our physical surroundings. Men down through the ages have always flexed their muscles on their physical world. But the "flexing" never amounted to much until the seventeenth, eighteenth, and nineteenth centuries, when it was brought within the control of a scientific procedure. And when men began to recognize what power they possessed when they used their heads in concert with their hands, it dawned on them that the world might just possibly be improvable.

It is out of this gradual awakening that the idea of "Progress" eventually grew. Increasingly men realized that the world was the way it was not because it simply had to be that way, but, rather, because we persisted in consenting to its imperfections and inadequacies. So *Progress,* a term which today seems so thoroughly familiar to us as to be unarguable, is actually a relatively recent notion; it was not until the eighteenth century that men really understood what it meant.

By now, of course, we in America have turned Progress into a kind of national religion, especially as it relates to our material standard of living. But it was inevitable that this cultural sentiment in favor of deliberately trying to improve the world should "boil over" into other sectors of our experience — into politics, community affairs, human relations, family life, child-rearing, and, in some instances, even religion. For our purposes the most prominent area in which this idea has taken hold is education.

The term *Progressive Education* first came into widespread use in 1919, when a group of educators from all parts of the country founded the Progressive Education Association. Ever since, "Progressive Education" has been the name applied to that general body of educational ideas which is most closely associated with the philosophy of Experimentalism.

Experimentalism and educational theory, as a matter of fact, have always been closely allied. This is partly because John Dewey, the great "empire-builder" of Experimentalism, was the first major academic philosopher to take an active interest in education. While he continued primarily as a philosopher throughout his life, he became a rarity in the philosophic brotherhood — and a considerable annoyance to his academic brethren — by periodically addressing himself to educational problems. Another reason for the affinity, of course, is the obvious fact that Experimentalism, precisely because it grew out of a "pattern of living," is closer to the cultural circumstances in which education operates than any of the abstract, speculative outlooks of earlier philosophic epochs. So close is the affinity, as a matter of fact, that Dewey considered philosophy and education really the same thing, the former merely the generalized version of the specific instance of the latter.

At any rate, we may speak of Experimentalism as the "source" of Progressivism in the sense that its conceptual handling of the problems of life seems to imply a distinctive and recommended way to manage the learning process. As we have tried to show in Chapters Four, Seven, and Ten, this pedagogy is distinguishable on several counts. Experimentalism, as the ultimate rationale for a scientific way of life, is committed to the ideas of change and progress. From this platform it is inclined to favor and support those practical movements — in politics, social affairs, the arts, and elsewhere — which likewise work for change and progress in the daily concerns of men. In Progressive Education Experimentalism finds the best expression of its educational policy.

The source of Reconstructionism

It is now possible, here in Chapter Twelve, finally to bring our light upon an educational point of view which, because of its prominence in theoretical circles, deserves a much earlier and more important place in our presentation than we have been able to give it.

Reconstructionism is not a distinctive philosophy, building upon its own peculiar set of principles in ontology, epistemology, and axiology; in general, it has developed out of the philosophic conceptions of Experimentalism discussed in Chapters Three, Six, and Nine. Nor can it be said that the pedagogical prescriptions it offers are substantially different from those of Experimentalism discussed in Chapters Four, Seven, and Ten.

What Reconstructionism has contributed particularly to educational thinking is a new and militant policy formulation for the American educational enterprise. As policy-maker, Reconstructionism has become the most articulate branch of Experimentalism when it comes to the specifications for an educational design in America. It has had much to say, especially recently, about the urgency of our present situation and about the character that American education should assume in the years ahead.

THE PROGRESSIVISTS

Basic views

The sharp *historical* break in continuity between the older philosophies and Experimentalism has been examined in the previous section. The *analytical* break is quite as noteworthy. The earlier philosophies of Idealism, Realism, and Neo-Thomism all argue from the premise that ontology is the central problem in philosophy; the nature and character of the real world must somehow be specified before we can think straight about knowledge, values, and education. Experimentalism, on the other hand, has turned to other concerns and, by ignoring ontological questions, has reduced ontology itself to a relatively insignificant, merely speculative "armchair" sport of old-fashioned philosophy.

However, when a man says he is not interested in ontology, what he is really doing is revealing another ontology. There is no escape from some view, however simplistic and unassuming, of the ultimate nature of things. And so when the Experimentalist turns from the traditional concerns of ontology and metaphysics to examine ordinary human living and how it can best be managed, we say he has concocted "an ontology of experience." What this means is simply that, for better or worse, we shall take ordinary human experience to be *real* and let it go at that. To say anything more than this is to say too much, because there is no method beyond experience to validate our assertions. But to say anything less than this would render all thinking and philosophizing futile and empty.

So we begin, as we saw in Chapter Three (pages 66–73), with the fundamental Experimentalist concept of Naïve Realism (see Chapter Three, pages 67–68), a view of reality which is splendidly unsophisticated in approach. Reality is just what it seems to be; it is just the way we experience it to be. No need for fancy notions of other worlds of ideas or spirits or Gods or essences. Not even any necessity for an ultimate world of "inner things." All we are obligated to say ontologically is that our *experience* of reality is as close as we can get to reality; why not call experience reality and be done with it?

The kind of reality this ontology presents to us is quite obviously one in which *becoming* and *change* rank above *being* and *fixity*. Movement, process, i.e., the "verb-al" quality of life, is set ahead and in front of the static, substantive, "noun" character of life. The whole foreground of our experience — what we engage in day by day — is taken to be the ground not only of living but of philosophy itself. The hazy background of things-in-themselves, essences, ultimate ideas, and absolutes is dismissed from attention.

Where Experimentalism spends the bulk of its time is in epistemology. A "verb-al" world is a much more exasperating place in which to live; it requires much more of us in deciding what is true and good. Set adrift as we are in this ocean of flux, this flowing medium of occurrences, we must take greater pains with our efforts to steer ourselves straight and right. Hence, epistemology (together with axiology) assumes a more prominent position, simply because it is more crucial in the kind of reality Experimentalism has set for itself to manage.

What this epistemology sets out to do (as we saw in Chapter Six, pages 155–165) is to place all candidates for truth into the stream of human experience to see what consequences will follow when we act on them. That is, what happens when you take an idea and act on it *as if it were true*? What practical effects will it have? From those effects you will be able to tell whether it is true or not. But things are never completely true or untrue, only more or less so. Since truths are derivative from the consequences they produce in our experience, they can have no higher status than the consequences themselves. And since the "consequences" are merely the so-called undergoing phase of our experience, the truths we find there are ultimately contingent upon the specific character of this or that experience as it unfolds in our own particular lives: hence no such thing as absolute truth.

What saves this epistemology from becoming a private, insulated type of solipsism, whereby each man may believe anything he wishes, is the fact that we can share our experiences, we can report to one another our individual estimates of consequences. Through group judgment of consequences we can develop a plural and therefore more reliable estimate of what is warrantably to be asserted about the world. But a "warrantable assertion" is not ultimate truth, only a kind of truth, called "tentative," which will serve until future experience modifies or repeals it.

This is really what we mean by the scientific method; it is a method for controlling and systematizing the flux and flow of experience in limited, analyzable units, so that we can "undergo the consequences" in a confined and concentrated way. When many individuals — either scientists in the laboratory or citizens in a society — place themselves in a position to undergo the consequences of certain actions made upon the environment, and if they accurately report the nature of those consequences, then together they can arrive at what is called a scientific judgment of whatever problem is under view.

It is in the latter instance — of citizens in a society — that we see the beginnings of a scientific axiology. When a situation presents itself in which some question is raised about the better or best course of action to follow, then the scientific thing to do is to consider alternative courses of action to see what they lead to. In the field of politics, this process is undertaken in a more or less deliberate way. Congress studies a problem and passes a law. Law is merely a prescription of social action: "We all agree to behave in such-and-such a way until further notice." But what makes the law stick is the quality of political and social experience it produces. The law can be changed; it can be repealed. But it is changed or repealed or left standing, as the case may be, on the basis of its ultimate consequences.[2]

In the area of personal ethics the same process goes on. In a situation of competing ethical judgments — in, say, the problem of premarital sexual intercourse, or the larger problem of world birth control — that course of action is called *good* which produces the over-all best consequences for all concerned. As we have pointed out earlier, modern man has increasingly shown his willingness to alter his moral judgments on the basis of *what they lead to* in contrast to *where they come from,* e.g., some doctrine, some dogma, some inherited moral code.

It goes without saying that the moral sphere of life, in contrast to the physical and social, is destined to be the last citadel to fall to the scientific way. But eventually, says the Experimentalist, it will fall. If an ethical mandate from somewhere on high continues to produce unwanted results, men will abandon it. If a better way is found, men will take it — perhaps not immediately but eventually, even though it may break with a previously held view. The contemporary revolution in sexual values, prominently reported by Alfred Kinsey, is perhaps the most spectacular case in point. Here men are finding their way to some new morality; they may turn out to be wrong, of course, as men sometimes do. But if so, it will be because they shall have had an encounter with unwanted consequences. When wanted consequences are obtained, then right has been to that degree achieved.

---

2 Political moralists sometimes declare that democracy is the best of all political forms because it is "a government of law instead of men." This is open to question. Men can, after all, change the law; therefore they are superior to it. What makes democracy a preferred political system is that it can readily *change* its law in the light of social experience. Democracy is a blessed method of life because it does not commit us to any prescribed pattern of behavior but leaves the way open for changing the behavior when the situation warrants.

Educational theory

From these basic conceptual materials we have been able to see certain tendencies in Experimentalist educational theory. In Chapter Four (pages 97–100) the point was made that the living experience of the child, because experience itself is ontologically basic, becomes in Experimentalist schools the very medium in which learning takes place. It is in the "present" of the child's life, the situations he finds himself in, the curiosities he has, the problems he confronts, that the raw materials of learning emerge.

These raw materials, we saw in Chapter Seven (pages 197–203), yield what the Experimentalist educator calls "problematic situations." When organized into pedagogical form they become "problems," and when deliberately manipulated in the classroom for educational purposes they take the form of "projects" and "activities" in which the learner meaningfully finds his way to a solution to some felt need. Subject matter in its customary form of something set out to be learned is not to be found in this kind of school. The *logical* presentation of material is seen to yield to the *psychological* arrangement of learning experiences for the young.

The "psychological method" carried to its highest form may be generally described as the pedagogy of "learning through living," and it is this doctrine which has become, for better or for worse, the central thesis of Progressive educational theory. Progressivists have dedicated their careers to elaborating upon it and showing how it can be made to apply to every educational situation on every level of instruction. All learning, they say, starts with felt needs, curiosities, interests, problems. It makes no difference whether we are dealing with a kindergartner or a research scholar; all learners proceed in the same generic way. Whatever is eventually learned — really learned, in contrast to memorized and handed back — originates in some genuinely felt interest or concern in the learner.

We have also seen, in Chapter Ten (pages 300–304 and 313–314), that growth in values, in finding the "goods" of life, likewise originates in what we may speak of as moral and aesthetic "curiosity." How one organizes his own behavior and how one determines his tastes is derived from the questions which arise in ongoing life. So when boys and girls are to be educationally assisted in developing character, they must first find out of their own experience some situation which calls up an active concern for testing certain alternatives in day-to-day living. Boys and girls do not learn the good and the beautiful in the abstract; they learn these qualities in examining their own behavior day by day.

In every branch of Progressivist learning theory there is a heavy emphasis upon working together. Since the basic epistemology of scientific logic depends so much on the sharing of findings, all learning founded on that logic must become thoroughly social in character. Progressivist schools, therefore, are places where boys and girls work together more than they work alone. Especially in character-building is this so; for we find our way to an ethical life primarily by associating with others and by living with them in morally significant situations. The so-called doctrine of "public-ity," so central to all of Experimentalist thinking, finds constant application in Progressivist schools.

Progressivist educational policy

THE "GROWING-EDGE" THEORY. From all of this we may now begin to see the general outlines of a program of education which the Progressivists have increasingly been recommending to the American people. At the outset we might refer once again to our time-line chart in Chapter One (see page 16). At that stage in the presentation we indicated that Experimentalism-Progressivism is to be understood primarily as a dynamic educational philosophy. If it is true that we are at present living through a period of far-reaching social change and cultural transition, what shall be the social policy of the school? The Progressive has a quick and ready answer; he says that the school must cast its cards on the side of change and movement. And so in the time-line chart we placed Experimentalism on the "leading edge" of the present.

It is at the leading edge of social movements that the most genuine living goes on. In one way or another, we are all involved in this frontier area of contemporary experience. The world is full of problems which have not yet been solved and which, moreover, do not seem to refer back to any established precedents. For a number of crucial human affairs — making a living, raising a family, building a civilization, waging a cold war, finding an ultimate meaning to life — the precedents of the past no longer suffice. Cultural changes come at us too fast to enable us to integrate everything neatly.

Therefore, the first rule of our educational policy must be to introduce the young to the fact and utter reality of *change* itself. And how can this be done any better than by making the school an active participant in the changing conditions of modern life? The "growing edge" of American life is where the spirit of Experimentalism is found; it is literally "experiment-al," in the finest sense of the term. Many writers have commented on the fact that there is only one thing we know for certain about the future: It will be different from what we have now. So, if we are going to teach the young intelligent control of the future we must teach them most of all the "management of change" itself.

This is what is embodied in the advice, "Teach them how to think, not what to think." Despite the abuse this epigram has suffered in recent decades, it does provide the "Scripture lesson" for a further elaboration of Progressivist educational policy. And to teach the young *how* to think, we must deliberately place them in the thick of man's affairs. We must never shy away from controversial questions in the classroom merely because they are controversial, but present them for study and analysis as the most vibrant and viable medium for learning.

The school, of course, should not become a partisan ax-grinder for any particular movements presently afoot. But this means also that it should not, by default, become the apologist for the status quo. By avoiding controversy and dispute in the classroom the school tends to side with the prevailing powers; it is, therefore, the furthest thing from being a neutral agent in these changing times. None of the powerful special groups in America today — the National Association of Manufacturers, the American Legion, the Daughters of the American Revolution — has ever been casual about its views on education. One of their most urgent themes is that the school steer clear of anything which might be considered unsettled and controversial in American life. But what they are in fact asking, says the Progressive, is that the school take *their* side in public questions by refusing to deal with such questions in the classroom. This the Progressive cannot do.

Instead, the school must become the place where youngsters can get the feel of the times in which we live, where they can begin to put their hands on the important issues in life. And since the really important issues are those which are not yet completely settled (that is partly why they are important), the young must have a chance to be exposed to them as part of their regular fare in growing up. Growing, as we have seen, is something on the order of an ultimate value to Experimentalists and Progressives. Going to school is not just maturing to some pre-scheduled terminus of adulthood, but, rather, learning how to go on learning; and there is no better material for this enterprise than the unsettled and controversial questions that present-day life holds in such abundance.

It would not be too much to say that the major policy difference between Essentialism and Progressivism is found at this point. The Essentialists wish the school to traffic only in the given, the settled, the agreed-upon — which, after all, is what the Policy of Conservationism really means. The Progressivists, on the other hand, eschew the security of settled truth. If anything, they actively seek out the non-agreed-upon as likely material for a curriculum. The Essentialists want questions to be *closed* before they come into the school; let somebody else, politicians maybe, take care of the open ones. The Progressivists want only *open* questions in the school; let somebody else, mystics and theologians maybe, contemplate the closed ones. To contemplate them is about all one can do with closed questions. Certainly we cannot question them.

THE "MORALITY" OF PROCESS. There is a pertinent corollary to be added here. The Progressivist's keen interest in growth, change, and openness has led him to elevate those qualities of life to moral values in and of themselves. As we have pointed out, growth has consistently been and is a very high-ranking item on the Experimentalist scale of values. So is change. Things that change are generally healthier than things that do not. The same for openness; an "open society" is by definition better than a closed one.

This tendency was examined with exceeding good sense by John A. Kouwenhoven in an article entitled "What's American about America?" in the July, 1956 *Harper's Magazine*. Briefly, Kouwenhoven notes the difficulty Americans have in understanding the central thesis of their own way of life. Perceptive foreign visitors who go home and write books about us often come close, he says, but even they are in disagreement. Taking this tack, he then lists a dozen specific items which are generally thought to be "typically American." Some of them are these: the grid pattern of urban street layout, the modern skyscraper, the New York sky line, the Constitution, jazz, Mark Twain, assembly-line production, and chewing gum.

Kouwenhoven then attempts to find a common element in all of these. He points out first of all that the grid pattern of streets, providing Cartesian coordinates for house numbers, enjoys one great advantage over any other plan, namely, it is *infinitely extendible*. This feature partially accounts for the use of the same system in surveying the vast open territory west of the Ohio River in the eighteenth century, most notably the Northwest Territory. The skyscraper is what we might call, he says, the grid pattern in three dimensions. Architecturally, the minimum "argument" of a skyscraper is the "upward-thrust" motif; skyscraper architecture tries to do little else. After the addition of so many stories the motif has been established; further elaboration of it with more stories is not architecturally necessary. That the building *could* have gone higher is about all the architect wants to convey; so, no towers, no peak roofs, no cornices, no attic friezes to provide a climax. Just a clean stoppage of construction.

The New York sky line is a product of grid-pattern streets and skyscrapers. From a city-planning point of view it is hopelessly unplanned, irregular, and irrational. In short, it is artistically chaotic. But it is beautiful. Somehow the freedom of the American spirit, the infinite extendibility of the American principle, is captured here.

Infinite extendibility happens to be the basic ingredient of the Constitution also, says Kouwenhoven. Its brevity and simplicity provide only the general sketchy outline of a political system. What counts politically is the "living out" of this Constitution to discover its many meanings. And the provisions for its amendment suggest that the Founding Fathers anticipated the kind of life we want to create in this land.

Musically, jazz is an expression of this same thesis. There is no ultimate plan around which jazz is built. Jazz, rather, is simply "on-going sound," continued for sixteen or twenty-four or thirty-two bars, or as long as a needle can fit on two inches of phonograph record. Unlike the symphony or the popular song, jazz succeeds without heavy reliance on over-all structural design — notwithstanding the fact that in its detail it is highly complex and intricate. Like the skyscraper, its main motif is "on-going-ness," and it can be stopped at any place without compromising this basic idea.

Mark Twain is a kind of "jazz in print," says Kouwenhoven. Twain never tried to develop big plots in his writing. He was primarily a story-teller, a yarn-spinner de luxe. The ongoing quality of his stories is the important thing, the tumbling movement of episode upon episode, with nothing particular at stake except the vivid portrayal of ordinary people facing life's little problems. And assembly-line production methods are something like this. Their beauty lies not in what they produce but in how they work. European auto manufacturers can easily produce a better automobile than our companies. But still they come over here to visit Detroit. Why? To see *how* we do it.

We have made a very big thing out of "how" in this country. *What* we do is often shabby, hastily crafted, expected not to last. The "planned obsolescence" of the American automobile is the supreme expression of our technological way of life. But the *methods* we use in manufacture are the object of great admiration throughout the world; to the engineer they are almost beautiful. Engineering, indeed, celebrates this quality of process. Engineering seldom says, "Look what we did." It says, "Look what we're doing!" There is quite a difference.

Finally, says Kouwenhoven, consider chewing gum, an American product which has been spread, in every sense of the word, all over the world. What is chewing gum? It is the perfectly nonconsumable confection. Its sole value lies in the process of chewing it. The infinite-extendibility principle here finds perhaps its grandest, yet simplest, expression. Plastically, we can stretch it all over the place; in chewing it, we can enjoy it forever, world without end. It is Process, pure and simple.

In the end, says Kouwenhoven, what makes America American is our having fallen in love with "process" and out of love with "product"; in love with "method" and out of love with "result"; in love with "means" and out of love with "ends." Or, better yet, we have turned means into ends! We have, therefore, begun to place value upon process and method in and for themselves. Our absorption with these is more than just an interesting new awareness in modern life; it is a fundamental value judgment we place on our experience.

More than anybody else, the Experimentalist is the missionary of this new way of life. And the Progressive educator is his lieutenant and tactician. Schoolteachers are the functionaries of the movement, and they mean to imbue the young with the great glories of *doing,* of *solving,* of *inquiring,* on and on into eternity.[3]

THE UNCOMMITTED SCHOOL.   Among the many practical effects of this policy is the creation of school programs which are noteworthy for their lack of commitment to any particular view of life. This is the way it should be, says the Progressivist. We want no religious materials in our schools, not because they are religious but because they are dogmatic and *closed.* Doctrinal materials tend to shut off thought, instead of provoking it. Intellectually they are tied to products and not to processes. If we must have religion in the schools, let it be some kind of secular thing which is open-ended.

Nor do we want in our schools people who are committed to some particular point of view and who insist on it in the classroom. This is the great danger of Essentialist teachers, says the Progressivist. Committed as they are to a given world and a given tradition, they must, almost by definition, seek to inculcate this tradition in their students. Their whole mood of professional endeavor is to instruct the young in what is settled and true. Hence, they tend to give the child the sense that the world is immutably established a certain way, that it is fixed and secure, and that it is possible to learn some things about the world and then stop thinking about them, because they will forever stand still. The Progressivist understandably objects to this.

The Progressivist's educational program for America is founded on no ultimate principle. The only thing to which a Progressive educator is committed is noncommitment itself. Truths change. Values change. The curriculum will have to be revised from time to time, as the situation warrants. Teaching methods will be tried out, adopted, rejected,

3 In all fairness, it should be said that Dewey and a good many other Experimentalists would find the account given here somewhat objectionable, in that it may appear to be saying that process can be separated from product or that Experimentalism is not interested in achieving results or in reaching ends. Certainly this is not the case. Nevertheless, Dewey's famous phrase, "Growth is its own end," intones a clear preference for the "process" side of life. And in *The Quest for Certainty* (New York: Minton-Balch and Co., 1929) he confirms this view by dropping the remark: "The scientific attitude may almost be defined as that which is capable of enjoying the doubtful. . . . No one gets far intellectually who does not 'love to think,' and no one loves to think who does not have an interest in problems as such." (Page 228.)

revised, remodeled constantly. The flux of life shall find microcosmic expression in the work of the school.

EDUCATION AS SOCIAL. What makes a world of flux tolerable, of course, is the fact that "we are all in this thing together." We act *with* others; we act socially. Indeed, sociality is perhaps the most important characteristic of modern civilization, which is based upon the principle of groups of individuals working in concert. Even if the world is utterly precarious as an unspecified reality, we know that we can find some working solace in sharing with others in this great undertaking of building a free society.

If this be the case, then the work of the school must reflect this basic principle in the policies it lives by. And certainly one of these policies is to make learning itself a thoroughly social enterprise. Not only have we universalized the school and made it available to all youngsters of whatever background or race or creed or national origin, but we have thought so highly of its socializing powers that we have made school a compulsory feature of growing up. Going to school in an Experimentalist America is not just a personal privilege which one may exercise as he will. Going to school is a *public duty!* A democracy does not hesitate to insist on this. Compulsory-attendance laws are now so thoroughly accepted as to be beyond all argument in contemporary educational theory.

But compulsory attendance would be a left-handed thing if we were to provide boys and girls with different kinds of schools depending upon their interests and abilities. If we were to take this course we should soon have the old problem of class divisions building up in our educational system. European countries for centuries have chosen to separate their young people into dual-track educational programs — one for the superior, university-bound group, the other for the average and slower individuals, who prefer a shorter, terminal course; and two school systems are the inevitable result.

Our policy is quite different. We have decided to have all youngsters attend the same school. This is sometimes called the "single-ladder" system, the "single-track" plan. What it means is that the "melting-pot" principle is institutionalized in our school system, in the name of socializing all youngsters to a common outlook. Dewey said it in so many words:

> . . . it is the office of the school environment to balance the various elements in the social environment, and to see to it that each individual gets an opportunity to escape from the limitations of the social group in which he was born, and to come into living contact with a broader environment.[4]

[4] John Dewey, *Democracy and Education* (New York: The Macmillan Co., 1916), p. 24.

To dualize education, to segregate young people in any fashion whatsoever, is in some degree to destroy the socializing power of the school.
Since sharing is a fundamental principle of Experimentalist epistemology
and axiology, then any policy that interferes with sharing must be rejected by the Progressive educator.

It is at this point that we may note some rather marked contrasts with
the Essentialists. While the Essentialists are patriotic enough to advocate
education for all American youth as a matter of policy, they are not so
unmindful as the Progressives sometimes are of the price that must be
paid for throwing all youngsters together into the same educational
hopper, namely, the tendency to neglect the able and gifted in trying to
take care of the more numerous average and slow pupils. With classes
growing to forty, fifty, and sixty pupils, what is a teacher to do with the
20 to 30 per cent who really need his best professional skills to challenge
them? The Essentialists claim that the "socialization" policy has had
the unfortunate result of orienting the American teacher mainly to the
mediocre and slow, at the expense of the gifted and brilliant. Hence we
lose much, they say, simply by defaulting on our pedagogical duty to
challenge the finest minds to the limit of their capacities. Socialization,
yes, by all means. But never at the expense of the talents of the able.

It is from this general line of reasoning that the Essentialists have become much more friendly than the Progressives to the classifying of
youngsters in school according to some kind of ability criterion. If we
cannot have two separate tracks in our educational policy, then let us
have within the single track a clear separation of pupils into ability
groupings. Hence "homogeneous grouping" has become the darling of
the Essentialists, who feel that segregating children into ability sections
salvages at least some of the really top youngsters in the school.

This policy seems to work all right until some Essentialist parent comes
along and discovers that his child is not in the top ability group, at
which point something on the order of hell may break loose. Phones
ring, parents beat on desks, superintendents and principals become de-
fensive, and teachers quiver — all signifying that the Essentialist principle of ability segregation has found only partial acceptance in an otherwise Essentialist-oriented American educational system.

More extreme Essentialist proposals call for the establishment of
special high schools for the gifted. The Bronx High School of Science
in New York City is usually cited as a successful case in point. Admiral
Rickover has suggested that twenty-five such high schools be established
throughout the United States to serve the most able youngsters in our
country. Somewhat more modest, and therefore possibly more likely of
acceptance, is Dr. James B. Conant's proposal that we have no separate
schools or even separate study "tracks" within the school (the academic

course, the general course, the commercial course, the trades course), but that youngsters be homogeneously grouped class by class and subject by subject; for instance, a youngster might be assigned to the top mathematics group for his grade but be in the middle or slow language class. In some subjects, however, such as art, civics, and social studies, the students would be heterogeneously grouped, i.e., without distinction of ability or intelligence.[5]

In any case there is no way of segregating youngsters which does not compromise and weaken the power of the school in socializing the child. Such policies of segregation, even when they are based on the soundest of pedagogical principles, tend to obstruct the sharing proclivities of the individual. Hence they stand against the developmental growth patterns of the young as Progressive educators see them. For this reason most Progressivists have stuck to the policy of heterogeneous grouping from kindergarten straight through the twelfth grade.

JEFFERSONIANISM AND JACKSONIANISM. We may summarize this discussion of the socializing function of the modern school by drawing attention to two major social theories of education: Jeffersonianism and Jacksonianism. Jefferson, as most of us know, was a master of many trades — politician, political scientist, scientist-engineer, and farmer. He also had much to say about education.

Like most of the other Founding Fathers, he was repelled by the caste systems of Europe, which were based on either blood lines or property. Hereditary and landed aristocracies he found ignoble and wholly "un-American." Many people have taken this attitude of his to signify a repugnance for aristocracies in general. But this is not true. Jefferson was as much an aristocrat as any of the other leaders of the new Republic. All Jefferson wanted to do was to change the criteria for membership in the aristocracy — from blood or property to ability. He spoke frequently of the so-called natural elite, "the aristocracy of talent," and it was this group which he thought should inherit the earth, or at least the seats of power in the new nation.

This, as most people can see, is a kind of Platonism brought up to date for an eighteenth-century frontier society. And it has had a peculiar fascination for political scientists ever since Plato first spelled it out in *The Republic*. Under this plan, the educational system of a society becomes one of the chief arms of the state, carrying on the vital function of preparing, generation by generation, a supply of gifted and talented individuals to take over the positions of responsibility.

Jefferson, as a matter of fact, actually tried to incorporate this social

5 Dr. Conant spells out this proposal in his book *The American High School Today* (New York: McGraw-Hill Book Co., Inc., 1959).

philosophy in his *Bill for the General Diffusion of Knowledge,* submitted to the Virginia Legislature in 1779. In brief, he proposed that the State of Virginia educate at public expense those individuals who could exhibit exceptional ability and intellectual potential. The few very best youngsters were to be carried through the College of William and Mary on public funds.

The bill was never passed, but the point is that Jefferson's spirit lives on, most particularly within the company of Essentialists and Lay Neo-Thomists. These groups have always been and are to this day more interested in the abler child than in the slower child. Because support of equality of opportunity is fashionable, they are willing to go along with plans for "Education for All American Youth" and all that that slogan involves. But once at work, Essentialists and Neo-Thomists show a much keener interest in college preparatory curriculums, in the "hard" subject matters, and in all those scholastic pursuits which have for many centuries been thought to be the special hallmark of the "intellectual elite." They are noticeably less interested in auto mechanics, Business English, and the other nonintellective segments of the school program.

Toward the middle of the nineteenth century a new kind of social theory came into being; and, although he apparently did not have any particular thoughts on education, President Andrew Jackson has given his name to this theory of education. Jackson's major contribution to American politics was what we might call the Common Man Theory of social life: What we need is not an intellectual elite to look out for us; we need, rather, to take charge of our politics ourselves. Jeffersonianism is, after all, a rather hesitant policy; basically it distrusts the common man, holding him incapable of ruling himself. Jacksonianism, on the other hand, puts a new faith in the common man. Given access to relevant information, this theory contends, the common man can govern himself, and do so at a higher level of performance than any elite could ever hope to attain.

The fundamental necessity for such a theory to work, however, is obviously a school system which will educate the masses. Since we can no longer depend upon some Platonic cadre of philosopher-kings, we must take special pains to see to it that every citizen is given the intellectual tools necessary to carry on his functions of citizenship. Hence mass education, education for *all,* an education for each citizen according to his special need, has arisen as the new educational objective of the American state. The nineteenth century saw this enormous undertaking begun and completed at the elementary level. The first half of the twentieth century has seen the job pretty well completed at the secondary level. Now we stand on the awesome threshold of bringing Jacksonian universality to the college and university.

For better or worse, the Progressive educator has attached himself to Jacksonianism as a working policy of American education. He has, as a matter of fact, become its most ardent champion, even though he does not usually call it by Jackson's name. Every human talent, no matter where it may be found, is the "religious" object of his pedagogical faith. And since we have wretchedly ignored the lesser talents of the middle and lower groups throughout our Jeffersonian history, is it any wonder that over the past fifty years the Progressive educator has found a kind of spiritual fulfillment in becoming the passionate champion of these more humble needs in the American school?

THE RECONSTRUCTIONISTS

The title of this chapter announces a discussion of the *contemporary* outlook in education, namely, Experimentalism-Progressivism. When we come to that special wing of Experimentalism called Reconstructionism, it is necessary to offer a minor caveat on just how "contemporary" it really is.

Reconstructionism is not widely practiced as an educational policy. Its strength resides in theoretical, academic circles around the country. In these groups, usually found in university departments in the social and philosophical foundations of education, Reconstructionism has taken on the trappings of a "movement," with ardent advocates writing about it with great enthusiasm. There are signs, moreover, to indicate that as a movement it is gathering some momentum in the field of educational theory.

The main point to notice is simply this: Unlike the policies so far studied, Reconstructionism is not at the moment a working program in American schools, not presently "at large" and in operation in the same way as are the others we have examined. It is, rather, a highly sophisticated and delicately articulated frontier position in educational theory, still awaiting its large-scale application to American education.

Basic views

The fundamental position from which Reconstructionism springs is, as we have already seen, Experimentalism. The only proviso one might make here is that Reconstructionism singles out for special emphasis the social and culturological aspects of Experimentalist doctrine. Reconstructionists generally hold, for instance, that the "culture concept" of the anthropologist is perhaps the best place to begin thinking about philosophy. According to this concept, all that man is, all that his human nature presumably is, must be looked for in the patterns of life which ordinary human beings have developed over the course of time. These patterns of life, technically called "cultures" by the social scientist, contain the vital content from which all serious thought about man germinates. We cannot think straight about man and the ultimate nature of his world except from the beginnings provided by actual human cultures actually lived somewhere and somewhen. What man thinks about the ultimate nature of the world and his role in it is born in the life he lives.

In the section concerning Experimentalism we saw this theme in its incipient phases as a rationale for the age of science. Experimentalism, that is, could not have come into existence as a theory of life until we had built a scientific culture. Now Reconstructionism picks up this theme and runs it a little further: All philosophies are culturally based, they are all outgrowths of cultural patterns occurring in some human group living in a given place and at a given moment in history.

This means two things, both of them of great importance. First, in order to think clearly about philosophy and, hence, about education, we must take a good, honest look at the current state of American culture to see what it requires in the way of a philosophic orientation. If culture produces philosophy, then let us examine our culture first. The second grows out of the first: Every philosophy which asks for acceptance must stand the test of *cultural adequacy*. Does it, that is, satisfy the philosophic requirements of its own times?

This latter point deserves special comment. Philosophies, according to the Reconstructionist, are not pretty pictures of ultimate reality (as Idealism, Realism, and Neo-Thomism might hold), nor are they merely attempts to sum up a way of life (as Experimentalism might hold). Philosophies are direct products of their age. And as products they present themselves to men in a much more urgent fashion than we usually think. That is, they are programs of life not just to be admired and thought about but to be acted on. Like all other cultural products, philosophies in their final sense are "tools" for life; they are the ultimate intellectual tools man uses to organize and direct his experience. Competitive philosophies, therefore, must ultimately be tested on their prospective function, i.e., on the quality of life they make possible.

Some philosophies, after all, are better than others. But how are they better? The earlier, traditional outlooks might say that some philosophies are better than others because they are truer. Experimentalism might say that some are better than others because they rationalize experience better. But Reconstructionism says some are better than others because they fulfill more adequately the demands of the culture they propose to serve.

The philosophy one entertains has to stand the test of relevance and adequacy; it has to prove itself as a living program for advancing the cause of civilization. In Experimentalist terms, it has to *work*. But to work, a philosophy has to do more than rationalize experience. It has to point the way to a better life. And since the building of a better life is really the whole business of human culture — what culture ultimately is all about — we must select our philosophic ideas on the basis of how well they lead us on to a desired future.

To sum up, then, when Reconstructionists adopt Experimentalist views they do so with the understanding that the social and cultural features of these views shall be given special emphasis. For instance, the Experimentalist's ontology of "experience" might be adjusted to read "social experience." Epistemologically, the Reconstructionist turns to the "publicity" doctrine and builds an emphatic case for *group* knowing. The *group* at work — doing, knowing, feeling, deciding — this is the epistemological evangelism of Reconstructionism. Axiologically, values are found in the content of the group mind. What the community, qua community, wants from the future are its values. Finally, as we have said, that special temper of Experimentalism which stresses progress and forward movement is singled out and capitalized into a major article of faith in Reconstructionist thinking. It is the prospective dimension of human reality, the forward thrust of man's efforts to build a better world, which most genuinely represents what *Progress*-ive Education basically believes in.

Educational theory

Likewise, there can be little added to what has already been said about Experimentalist notions of learning theory except what might ordinarily follow from the above emphasis on man's ultimate *sociality*. Group endeavor in the school is emphasized even more in Reconstructionism than in Experimentalism. Furthermore, we shall not be engaged in problem-solving merely because it is a way of learning how to think and how to manage an uncertain future. We will be solving problems in order to get them solved!

Experimentalists, the Reconstructionists say, do not take their own philosophy seriously enough. They are content to outline a method for handling life and to let it go at that. As we have seen, Experimentalists often seem enamored of method for its own sake, merely enjoying the processes of inquiry and investigation in and for themselves. In short, they elevate process over product. But what is problem-solving for, if not to solve problems? says the Reconstructionist. Let's get on with the job of building a better life by using this problem-solving method in the serious undertaking of advancing the quality of our civilization. And since the school is the place where people learn how to think about life, it is there that we must teach them to engage in problem-solving with some ultimate purpose in mind, some plan of action for the future society we hope to create. Problem-solving, after all, is more than a pedagogical plaything of teachers or a handy intellectual instrument of the scientists; it is at bottom a tool of vast significance for the shaping of a world more to our desire.

Reconstructionist educational policy

THE PURSUIT OF UTOPIA. From these preliminary remarks we may now see the general theme of Reconstructionism emerging. This theme is perhaps best understood by returning to our time-line chart in Chapter One (see page 16) and noting where Reconstructionism is placed on it. If we live in an age of upheaval and change, then the school's attention, says the Reconstructionist, should be fixed constantly on the future. The future should be the fulcrum around which all of the school's work should be organized. What kind of world do we want? What quality of life do we wish to prevail? What do we want to make of human civilization? These are the questions which shape and define the curriculum of the school.

In an earlier literature all of these aspirations were customarily summed up in the word *Utopia*. And this is precisely the orientation of the Reconstructionist. Let us, he says, launch forth once again in search of a Utopian way of life. We need no longer be confused by the older Utopias. They were illusions, dreams, "pie-in-the-sky" projects of one kind or another. Let them go; let them gather their dust in the library. We shall begin afresh, for we have the power to make *our* plans come true!

For the first time in his history, man has the tools to build a better life. We now see that we have some real power over our own destiny. Science and the free life are the great levers we have been waiting for to lift civilization to a higher level of expression. For the first time we do not have to be embarrassed or apologetic about talking openly of Utopia. It is really possible! The only thing that keeps us from it is our own slothfulness, our timidity, our inertial stupidity in permitting less than Utopia to prevail. Let us, says the Reconstructionist, get on with the job!

THE "MORALITY" OF REFORM. This is, to put it mildly, a vast injunction. Some sense of what it means may be gotten by referring to perhaps the greatest evangelist of reform who ever lived — Karl Marx. Indeed, there is much of the flavor of Marxism in Reconstructionism.

Marx constantly stressed, as does Reconstructionism, the social character of man. He wanted, more than anything else, to be the founder of a "science of society." Failing that, he was willing to settle for something less, namely, a general acceptance of one simple truth. As put by one commentator, it is this:

> . . . man never exists in himself, he never lives as a true hermit. "Man" is the wrong word; we should speak of "men" and we should ground our every speculation about men on the concrete behavior and relations of men as we find them. The most conspicuous feature of men and women is that they must be discussed in the plural; they are social by nature.[6]

From this prime concept, which once again emphasizes the Reconstructionist's affirmation of the "ontology of social experience," Marx moved on to a much more advanced idea, what we may now refer to as the "Activist Principle." In brief, this principle states that *work* is the source and center of all human value.

> Labor is the very touchstone for man's self-realization, the medium of creating the world of his desire; and it is labor which should make him happy. Indeed, the essence of man is in his striving to achieve his desires. He is not provoked into learning and achieving by the pragmatic stimulus of an external threat. He labors to transform his world, to put his own mark on it, to make it his, and to make himself at home in it.[7]

It is something of a very sad and tragic joke, Marx reminds us, that modern Western civilizations have effectively turned man "upside down" on this matter of labor. Labor has been turned into a grinding chore, instead of the medium of human fulfillment. Work has been made an ignoble means to something alien to and outside it, to wit: leisure. It is leisure, we think, which is the real end of life; work is just a degrading necessity. Marx had some rather poignant things to say about this:

> [The worker] first feels he is with himself when he is free from work and apart from himself when he is at work. He is at home when he does not work, and not at home when he does. His working is, therefore, not done willingly but under compulsion. It is forced labor. It is, therefore, not the satisfaction of a need, but only a *means* for the satisfaction of wants outside of it. [In consequence] man, the worker, feels himself acting freely only in his animal functions like eating, drinking, begetting . . . whereas in his human function he is nothing but a [work] animal.[8]

[6] Robert S. Cohen, "On the Marxist Philosophy of Education," Chapter VI in *Modern Philosophies and Education,* Fifty-fourth Yearbook of the National Society for the Study of Education, ed. N. B. Henry, Part I (Chicago: the Society, 1955), pp. 177–178.
[7] *Ibid.,* p. 190.
[8] *Ökonomisch-philosophische Manuskripte,* as translated in Herbert Marcuse, *Reason and Revolution: Hegel and the Rise of Social Theory* (New York: Oxford University Press, 1941), p. 277, as quoted in Cohen, *op. cit.,* p. 191.

Perhaps the most advanced form of this inverted morality is to be found in the United States. So hectic and mechanized has our work become that leisure is sought after with a kind of religious vehemence. Finding meaningful leisure has, as a matter of fact, become an increasingly troublesome problem in our country. Characteristically, we have "solved" the problem by turning leisure itself into a major industry. Above all, there lingers the consummate legitimacy of pleasure, of downright self-indulgent creature comforts and delights. Many Americans feel closest to themselves when they are engaged in recreation, having a "good time," not producing but utterly and splendidly *consuming*. Summed up, this view of life is based on the idea that man's true being is to be found in something other than work; it can be found in work's opposite — play. As Max Lerner has so aptly said, American civilization is built upon "the morality of fun."[9]

The mark of a truly mature civilization would be to turn back to the basic essence of man and find there the natural desire to change things, to reform the present conditions of life, to reconstruct the cosmos more to our hearts' desire. This is what men are for in the world, to fashion the qualities of their own existence, to make the world over into something more nearly what they think it ought to be.

A CULTURE IN CRISIS. If Reconstructionism were to rest its case here, it would have said quite enough. But reawakening man's "reconstructive" impulse can also be argued for on other than moral grounds. It can be argued for on the much more pragmatic ground of social necessity. If the examination of one's culture is, as we have seen, the first order of business in philosophy, we need only look at American civilization to feel the sense of urgency which grips Reconstructionist thinkers.

If we take a close and honest look at American life today, says the Reconstructionist, we can hardly escape the conclusion that we are living in a culture which is in crisis. We are not just moving along through history casually searching for the right philosophy to believe in. On the contrary, we are in a fight for our very lives. We live in an age which is more than one of social change and transition; we are living in an age of outright upheaval, a time when the basic values men live by are in question, a time when survival itself is at stake. The older philosophies — including the original strains of Experimentalism — cannot be expected to offer a truly viable plan of life for those of us living today. They can afford to be more purely theoretical, more bookish and methodological,

9 Too much must not be made of this whole line of argument for fear that Reconstructionism will emerge as a kind of humorless, austere, and unrelenting philosophy of life. It most assuredly is not. But the temper of its message is clearly this: that the hour has arrived when men must begin to take some conscious charge of their own destiny.

about the management of life. This is because the "traditional" philosophers grew up in a different age. Even John Dewey, who died in 1952, is
no longer wholly relevant for the present hour.

When he asked that the method of science be extended to the social
and moral spheres of life, Dewey did not realize how tragically prophetic
he was. He asked this primarily from a sense of duty as a philosopher of
science; he asked it merely to enjoin men to be intelligent. Pointing to
the lag of social institutions and moral systems in keeping up with the
fast-moving age of technology, he summoned men to close the gap by
employing an experimental logic in all human problems. But it was more
a philosophical than a political appeal; it failed of the utter urgency with
which we might make the same appeal today, because the stakes were so
much lower.

But now we see it in another light. The days of intelligence are num-
bered. No more accurate statement of our problem has been given than
in H. G. Wells' famous aphorism: "Human history becomes more and
more a race between education and catastrophe." This dictum has taken
on a new meaning today. For the first time we can see the clear outlines
of the latter alternative, something that earlier men could not do. And
so our educational problem is now a matter of dire urgency. Where
before the educational theorist could afford to spend his time on matters
of curriculum design and teaching method, today he must take on the
vast task of mobilizing men to programs for their own survival.

THE SCIENCES OF MAN. Granted that this vast task is one of enormous magnitude, we really have no choice in the matter. We must begin
the long and arduous enterprise of educating men to take conscious
charge of the future. We are not without precedent, either. For, if science can exploit the technological areas of life so splendidly as to project
a future of economic plenty, of freedom from disease, of voyages to the
planets and the stars beyond, is it at all fantastic to think that science
might also help us map out and eventually achieve a future of peace,
of brotherhood, and of political freedom for every single citizen of this
world?

Science can do it, says the Reconstructionist, if we but turn it free on the
study of man. It is something of a curious irony that the last object for
scientific inquiry has turned out to be man himself. Perhaps we have
always been too close to the "subject" to see it as an "object." At any rate,
psychology has shown us the way; it is perhaps the primary science of
man. And psychology has been followed by social psychology and cultural
anthropology, both of them dedicated to inquiry into the behavior of
man. As a matter of fact, all such fields of study are now spoken of as the

"behavioral sciences." Their province is human conduct; nothing more, nothing less.

But these are only the slightest of probes into what may lie ahead. They are only the beginning of a much wider adventure into the understanding of man. For instance, we have made only the barest beginnings in understanding Freudian psychology — the nature of subconscious factors in motivation and all that region of human experience which lies beneath the empirical surface of things.

Or take neuropsychology. Here is a field of tremendous excitement. The real understanding of the human nervous system and how it works is in its infancy. Neuropsychiatry and neurophysiology now join forces in a new science. Even the chemists and physicists are called in to examine the neurochemical properties of certain substances in the blood stream and the electrical phenomena that occur in the brain. We are undoubtedly on the brink of a whole new breakthrough in the human sciences.

In a somewhat less technical setting, we are asking ourselves anew what precisely the "creative" element in the human being may be. If creativity is a thing to be provoked and unleashed, how are we to recognize it when we see it? What are the conditions that must be present before creativity is emergent? Are these conditions the kinds of things we may artificially organize in the experiences of men? That is, can we teach people to be creative?

If creativity is a personal and somewhat private quality of an individual human being, perhaps it can also be a public and cultural quality of a whole society. Is it possible, that is, to take an entire culture and arouse its creative tendencies in the name of social reconstruction? What does one do to initiate an "Operation Bootstrap" and to keep it fueled for the long haul? Can cultures really make themselves over? In his recent book *The Remaking of a Culture: Life and Education in Puerto Rico*, Professor Theodore Brameld, who has made a special study of these questions, shows how Reconstructionism as a social policy has actually worked in a concrete historical setting.

THE SCHOOL AS "HEADQUARTERS" FOR GOAL-SEEKING. All we need say now is that the total orientation of the Reconstructionist — his group ontology, his "Activist" axiology, his Utopian sense of destiny, his interest in the human sciences, and his passionate concern for creativity, both individual and social — becomes the basis for his educational policy. The school in America must become the organizer for this great enterprise of building a new life. It must become, in a manner of speaking, the "Supreme Headquarters" for the creation of a Utopian society.

This means, of course, that it must be the gathering place for all of our new knowledge about man. We should actively seek to use and test that knowledge in the handling of youngsters, to find really effective ways of educating. But more than this the school must become concerned with *goals,* with the goals of individuals and with the goals of society. We can no longer afford a policy of unconcern when it comes to the ultimate ends of life. Boys and girls must be brought into a direct encounter with personal and social values, with the kind of persons they want to be and the kind of society they want to live in. And they must find in their learning in school the patterns for seeking and reaching those goals as they mature to adulthood.

Schools have always been rather antiseptic when it comes to human aims and social goals. This is partly because most teachers consider such subject matter both difficult and dangerous for the classroom; they don't want to touch it. Also, of course, they have argued that there simply isn't time for it. This is nonsense, says the Reconstructionist. There isn't time for anything else! What higher function can the American school perform than to help youngsters begin to specify the Utopian content of a future world and begin actively to bring that world into existence? The time is short. Our patience is too long. Nothing will come of this world except by deliberate human effort.

QUESTIONS

1. The Progressivists and the Reconstructionists both argue that science can be made to apply to moral and ethical questions. Other philosophies hold that science can tell us what *is* but never what *ought to be.* Do you see any conflict here? If so, how would you resolve it?

2. What do you suppose a Reconstructionist's attitude would be to the relative merits of Jeffersonianism and Jacksonianism as educational policies for America?

3. "Except for the organized church, perhaps the most conservative institution in modern America is the public school." Do you think this is true? Whether or no, do you think the typical public school in America can become a "headquarters" for social change? Explain.

4. What examples can you provide, besides those given, for Kouwenhoven's "process-over-product" theme? Are there any signs that this movement may reverse itself in the years ahead? What further developments might we expect in the next couple of generations?

5. How do you personally feel about Utopia? What is your "body tone" when

you hear that word? Does a feeling well up in you to get to work on it, or are you, rather, inclined to relax and let nature take its course? Does one have to believe in the possibility of Utopia to be a "good man"?

FURTHER READING

Progressivism

Childs, John L. *Education and American Pragmatism*. New York: Henry Holt and Co., Inc., 1956.
After discussing "the pragmatic reconstruction in philosophy and education," Childs examines the educational policy positions of three leading twentieth-century Experimentalists — W. H. Kilpatrick, George S. Counts, and Boyd Bode. Then he summarizes these and in Chapter 12 outlines the policy position for Pragmatism in terms of "the future of American education."

————. *Education and Morals*. New York: Appleton-Century-Crofts, Inc., 1950.
If Dewey was the "empire-builder" of an Experimentalist education, then Professor Childs might be said to be the incumbent prime minister of this great "commonwealth." In one of his most famous books, he lays down in Part Two the major planks of a Progressivist educational policy. The best statement of what Experimentalism stands for in educational policy today.

Educational Policies Commission of the National Education Association. *Education for All American Youth: A Further Look*. Washington, D.C.: the Association, 1952.
Originally published in 1944, this policy statement became the major postwar utterance of the National Education Association. It is perhaps the most explicit development of the Jacksonian thesis anywhere in educational literature. If you want to see what "education for all" is going to demand of us, take a look here.

Reconstructionism

Brameld, Theodore. *Design for America*. New York: Hinds, Hayden and Eldridge, 1945.
Professor Brameld is no mere theoretician; he lives his Reconstructionism. When the movement was taking shape in his mind, back in the 1940's, he tried it out on the junior and senior classes of a small high school in Floodwood, Minnesota. The entire curriculum for an academic year was developed from the single question: What is our design for a better America? Here is a vivid portrayal of Utopian goal-seeking at work in a real school.

————. *Toward a Reconstructed Philosophy of Education*. New York: Dryden Press, 1956.
Perhaps more than any other single document, this book sets forth the major outlines of Reconstructionist educational theory. Here we see the "culture

concept" fully developed, the ontology of cultural history spelled out, the "Group Mind" epistemology delineated, and the Utopian axiology set in place as the central principle. Part Two, on educational theory, develops the social policy by which the school is seen as "social vanguard" and the learner within the school as achieving "social-self-realization."

Counts, George S. *Dare the School Build a New Social Order?*. New York: The John Day Co., 1932.

In the heady excitement of its early years, Counts asks whether Progressive Education is not as aimless as a baby shaking a rattle, "utterly content with action." Implying that it seems to have no theory of social welfare, he proceeds to build the whole case for "imposition" in education, showing that an educational system which does not shape the child toward certain ideological ends is a contradiction in terms.

CHAPTER THIRTEEN

The "Open Question":

Existentialism

PROLOGUE

The default of philosophy

The most remarkable thing about philosophy is its agonizing unsettledness. What is noteworthy about the questions that philosophy raises is that they never seem to get answered. This is probably why philosophy, as a way of life, is scorned by the average man. One explanation may be that philosophy deals with questions of greater over-all complexity than any other field of study. And if today we find ourselves asking the same questions that Socrates asked 2500 years ago, it may be due to the fact that they are very difficult questions.

Of course, some people say that 2500 years is long enough. If a question can't get answered in that period of time it is either meaningless as a question or not worth answering; let's get on with something else, something we can succeed at a little more regularly. Experimentalists often talk like this. They tend to think that the ultimate questions of philosophy are not worth bothering with. If a question has no answer, that is a sign that it is basically meaningless. If a question *can* be answered, but if the answer makes no difference anywhere in life, then it is not worth answering. In either case, says the Experimentalist, such questions should not be worried over too long.

The reaction to this view by the traditional philosophies is what one might expect. The philosophies of Idealism, Realism, and Neo-Thomism all insist that we should raise such ultimate questions — questions like: What is the Cosmic Purpose? What is Man? Who is God? — because they *can* be answered, or, where they cannot be, it is due to the limitations and infirmities of the human mind. That there is *an* answer somewhere is not to be denied.

But the reaction of Existentialism is of quite another order. Existentialism agrees with Experimentalism that such questions cannot be answered, at least not with any finality. But *trying* to answer them is what life is all about. Hence, they do, as questions, make a great deal of difference in the way life is lived, precisely because men's *efforts* to answer them — not the answers themselves — do shape and direct experience. To dismiss such questions as meaningless or inconsequential is a grievous mistake.

To put it another way, Existentialism insists that these ultimate questions, for all their impenetrability, constantly provoke the curiosities of men. They represent perhaps the highest level of curiosity, the highest striving of the human within us to make some sense out of this world. To raise such questions is to address ourselves to the meaning of life, and this can never be ruled out of order merely because the task is so arduous or seemingly so unfruitful. Men simply must go on doing it because, being men, they want to know what the world means. Hence the really meaningless question is to ask whether such ultimate questions should be raised. And to give it the answer "No," as the Experimentalists do, is to announce the final collapse of all serious philosophical endeavor.

From this we can now get an idea of how Existentialism considers its philosophical predecessors. First of all, it allies itself with the older, traditional views of life in scorning the easy path Experimentalism has chosen to take.[1] But it separates itself from all of those views because it cannot, like them, agree to settle for any particular answer to the ultimate questions. These questions are ultimately open. The point is that to *raise* such questions is the important thing, not necessarily to find answers for them. This is the confusion of the older philosophies.

But, says Existentialism, there is confusion also in the more recent predecessor of Experimentalism. Since Experimentalism cannot get

---

[1] There is a sly irony here. William James used to rebuke the older philosophies for "a failure of nerve" in confronting an unfinished, "world-with-the-lid-off" universe. Here Existentialism rebukes Experimentalism for "a failure of nerve" in confronting unfinished (and perhaps unfinishable) philosophical business.

answers, it doesn't even want the questions. This, says the Existentialist, is the final default of the philosophical quest.

The feeling of lost-ness

One of the reasons, perhaps, for this default, suggests the Existentialist, is the condition of modern man. He finds his world so hectic and chaotic, so morally naked, that he feels defeated. He wants to know what his world means, but the more he tries to understand it with science the less he seems to understand it philosophically. He gets the feeling that the cosmos is playing him games, that its essential meaning is retreating from him faster than he can advance toward it. With each problem solved, ten or a hundred new ones take its place. And the total mystery tends to deepen, instead of clearing.

Modern man seems to be responding to this circumstance by retracting his extended probes into the meaning of life. He withdraws and cancels his metaphysical questions and, with Experimentalist sponsorship, agrees to settle for something less, namely, the empirical and secular affairs of life only. These affairs represent a world which can be managed, a world which sustains our efforts to solve our problems, a world which can be meaningfully lived in. So, let's make it ours.

To a certain extent modern man has done just this: He has made the world his. But the great truth is that he still aches to know what it is all about. And he is in agony because he cannot shut that question from his mind. He aches to know and he cannot help himself. This is because he exists.

Man is therefore lost, even though he doesn't know it. When he does realize it, he tries to forget about it by busying himself with his science, his technologies, his tools and playthings. This is his little playroom, where things do seem to work, where they fit together the way they should, where things come out even, where problems get solved. A much more manageable kind of place, really. But man is still lost. And down deep he knows it.

His lost-ness is confounded by the sense of alienation which he also feels. Not only is he lost, but nobody seems to care. He is alienated from the universe; he is a stranger in his own home, and the cosmos is ultimately indifferent to his fate. This is what is so hard to take. It is even harder to take when we realize that to be alienated is one thing, but not to know the object of alienation is even worse. This is the point that Norman Mailer makes in his book *Advertisements for Myself*. Speaking of writers, he says, "I would propose that the artist feels most alienated when he loses the sharp sense of what he is alienated from."

This shrewd observation, says literary critic Granville Hicks, summarizes the modern problem. "In the early years of the century there was an enemy called Puritanism. In the Twenties the enemy was Babbittry. In the Thirties it was capitalism. Always in those years there was a target at which [men] could direct their resentments."[2] No such situation exists today. There is no adversary available. And increasingly we feel that without something to stand for, or battle against, life ceases to have any final meaning.

But the poignancy of our situation today is only a clearer definition of what men have always encountered in this world — a sense of feeling a stranger in their own house. This is what the Existentialist calls "the human predicament." It is a predicament of wanting something more from the world than mere ongoing experience with its interesting problems. If this is a sufficient dimension of the world for the Experimentalist, all right. But it is never sufficient for the Existentialist.

For man in his more private moments finds the medium of "social problem-solving" a rather thin, superficial layer of human life. He wants something more; specifically, he wants to obtain some assurance that he individually counts in the cosmic scheme of things, that he really matters, that when he dies he will not be totally erased from the universe. We all have this longing; even Experimentalists. But since the problem posed by this longing does not seem to yield to experimental logic, Experimentalists will have none of it.

Technically, the general problem just posed is introduced in Existentialist literature as "the awareness of nonbeing." When we become aware of the fact that it is possible that when we die we shall be expunged from all existence, completely annihilated, with no trace left, we begin to take a different attitude toward things. Specifically, we begin to hunt around for some way to assure ourselves that this will not happen. We want, in the words of one Existentialist, some *recognition* from the universe, some sign or clue that it acknowledges our presence here. At the very minimum, we want some sign that at least our *need* for recognition is acknowledged. It is as if we were yearning for the cosmos to say "hello."

Three roads home

According to Existentialism the intellectual history of man, at least Western man, has been a long chronicle of trying to figure out how to make the cosmos say "hello." There are three such attempts that particularly concern the Existentialist. They may be technically referred to as (1) the traditional philosophical solution, (2) the theological solution, and (3) the socio-methodological solution.

2 "The Quest in a Quiet Time," *Saturday Review* (November 28, 1959), 20.

THE TRADITIONAL PHILOSOPHICAL SOLUTION. The first and longest-standing method has been to resolve the human predicament by concocting some kind of philosophy which arranges the world in such a way that man is necessary to it. The best examples of this are Plato and Aristotle. Plato had his two worlds — the world of things and the world of ideas. (See Chapter Three, pages 47–51.) Man resides in both these realities; he is the liaison agent between them; as such, he is a necessary element in this dualized, compound reality.

Aristotle, in his turn, had a complicated structure to the nature of the world. (See Chapter Three, pages 53–57.) The world is built, he said, according to a logical plan. Everything is a union of form and matter, including man. And, like everything else, man has his own place in the hierarchy of things. If you remove man, there is a gaping hole left. It is necessary that the "form" of man occupy a certain spot in the total arrangement of things. Otherwise, the whole logical structure will come tumbling down.

Or, for one more example, take Hegel. Hegel's theory, as we have seen, is a kind of Platonism "on wheels," a realm of ideas in motion. Not a realm of ideas just existing, but an ultimate supermind thinking — thinking big, ultimate thoughts. Which led Hegel, as we have said, to say that "History is God thinking." God uses man to express his thoughts. And the implication is that without man the whole thing would be incredible.

The sum of all these positions — and many others — is an effort to construct some kind of cosmos which requires the presence of man. Once that has been accomplished, it is a short and easy logical step to the demonstration that, in a manner of speaking, the universe is "on our side" (precisely because we are on *its*). And when we reach this point it is but a short hop to the companion position that Man, and individual men, must hold a special and favored place in all existence.

THE THEOLOGICAL SOLUTION. But this cold, antiseptic, rationalistic kind of reality never satisfied the more spiritually inclined. What we really need to resolve our problem, they said, is to concoct a world with a God in it to care for us. Various philosophies have produced very neat little realities, where there is a place for everything and everything is in its place. But man, they said, requires more than a billet in a Table of Organization. He requires a Father to care for him. Plato's and Aristotle's worlds had no warmth in them. They were just *there*, existing in mathematical and logical majesty and ultimately indifferent to the psychic needs of man.

But religion came to the rescue: the Hebrew prophets, then Jesus, then St. Augustine, then St. Thomas, then Calvin, and Luther, and theologians down to our own day. What they all offer is a world with warmth and care in it, a world that is governed by a supernatural Person who is capable of compassion and love. In fact, this is what religion is all about. It is the search for recognition in a supernatural Person. It is an effort to make the cosmos say "hello" by the direct approach, i.e., by knocking on the door to see if anybody is home. Some people think they hear a voice answering. Others are sure they do. But in any case the presumption is that, voice or no, there is a God "at home" to man and that our need for recognition has been either fully or approximately satisfied.

THE SOCIO-METHODOLOGICAL SOLUTION. Modern man has turned from all this — both from traditional philosophy and from systematic religion. In fact, he has pretty much given up on trying to get the cosmos to say "hello." He has decided to settle for something less, namely, the recognition that he can get from *other people*. In other words, society — that is, other people organized in culture groups — is now considered to be able to provide the psychic support for man's existence. If we want recognition, if we want to be assured that we individually count in the total scheme of things, we can find it, in a secular kind of way, in social life. Worth, dignity, value — really counting as a self — are all now to be found, if one wants to find them there, in the social collective.

This point does not need to be argued. We all know it at first hand. Our time is one of "other-direction" and organization. "Other people" now represent the ultimate reality in which we move. The sociologists speak of "socialization patterns." The psychologists talk of "acceptance" and "belonging." The educators talk of "adjustment" and "group dynamics." We live in the age of "the *social* man."

The Existentialists believe that Experimentalism, perhaps inadvertently, is responsible for this. A case could be made, they say, to show that the Deweyan notions of "shared experience" and the "doctrine of public-ity" (see Chapter Nine, pages 268–274) represent the underlying intellectual rationale for the supersocialized life we now seem to be leading. Without stopping to test this thesis, we may simply attend to the fact that men now find the answer to their longing for meaning in life primarily within the context of social experience.

The methodology of science has given this undertaking a certain objective character, and scientific logic has lent it an added air of intelligent purpose. In a kind of shorthand way we might say that Experimentalism ultimately stands for "methodical togetherness," in the very best sense of that term. It is a kind of "social methodism" for handling the affairs of life, and it is offered as a philosophy on the premise that *social experience* represents the sum total of human reality.

The fact remains, says the Existentialist, that men still feel lost in this socio-scientific world: The third road home has evidently stopped short of its goal. We find ourselves no nearer our objective than before, and the world of man cries out in anguish and despair at the realization that science has proved no better than philosophy or religion in resolving the human problem.

THE EXISTENTIALIST APPROACH

Basic views

When we finally turn to Existentialism itself and try to seek there some way out of this difficulty, we are immediately confronted with the utter insolubility of the predicament. It turns out, however, that this is a blessing in disguise. For we really do not want to resolve the predicament. We do not want to have an answer to our longing. To achieve such an answer would be to pass from the stage of becoming to a brute kind of mere being. To be a man is to be in this predicament of wonder, this predicament of not knowing the ultimate meaning of life. To be human is precisely *not* to know for sure what one is, what Man is. To know this would be to discontinue the human enterprise.

That is why all the other philosophies examined in this book are essentially wrongheaded according to Existentialism: They offer an ultimate answer to the question, "What is Man?" Idealism holds he is a microcosmic mind and spirit in tune with an Infinite. Realism holds he is a naturalistic mechanism operating in a physical world. Neo-Thomism holds he is a rational animal logically situated in a logical reality. Experimentalism holds he is a social organism whose highest expression is intelligent problem-solving. But all that any of these definitions succeeds in doing is to limit the meaning of man. That is the very purpose of a definition — to set the boundaries for understanding, to provide the context in which an object can be known.

But this really means that man has set his own limits. To define him is to close him in to some presumed essence, some quiddity, which he is supposed to possess. But this finally destroys man because man's essence is not known. Man is an open question. The answer to the question, "What is Man?" is still coming in, like election returns. We don't know yet how the election will turn out. If the world were to come to an end tomorrow morning, we could theoretically set down what man's essence *had been*. But so long as man remains in existence his essence is not finished.

We saw in Chapter Three (pages 73–78) that the unfinished nature of man is grounded on the proposition that existence precedes essence. Man just turned up on the scene. He existed before he had a "what-ness." It is only after we have become aware of our existence, either as a race or as individuals, that we are capable of addressing ourselves to the problem of our essence. This turns out to be a rather difficult undertaking, of course. Just to confront the fact that we individually are responsible for our own essence — and, therefore, for the developing essence of Man — is to recognize a mountainous responsibility. Many people do not want this responsibility. They want to be told what to do; they want to be told *what to be*! Yet even in wanting to be told they are expressing their own essence: That is what they want to *be*, namely, a creature who needs to be told what to be.

To the Existentialist this is the lowest form of human life. It is to default in the human encounter with the predicament. The three solutions to the predicament discussed in the previous section represent "escape routes" as well as "roads home." They are comforting solutions to the human problem; they are like pills we take for our metaphysical headache, or better, our spirit-ache, i.e., the ache in our spirit. These nostrums provide temporary relief; they make the anguish and nausea go away. But they do not treat anything but the symptoms of our sickness. They do not get to the basic difficulty, namely, the encounter of man with the problem of his own essence.

This encounter is, in a manner of speaking, partly an epistemological problem. We saw in Chapter Six (pages 165–172) that it is rather difficult to specify what may be called an Existentialist epistemology. The primary thing to keep in mind is the subjective character of knowledge. What is true of the world is what I responsibly say about it; better, it is what I *do* with my life in the world. I express with my choices what I think is true. Truth is never forced on me. It is always in some way actively chosen by me. As one Existentialist writer puts it, in discussing Kierkegaard:

> [Existentialist] knowledge requires personal appropriation, inwardness or subjectivity. In fact, the only reality which an existing being can know otherwise than through some abstract knowledge is his own existence. Here it is necessary that the existing subject should plunge itself into its own subjectivity.[3]

There is, therefore, a personal element in all knowing. The ancient dictum "Know thyself" is re-established as the central epistemological task. This kind of knowing, as we have seen, is at the other end of the spectrum from the "Spectator Theory" of Realism and Idealism. It is knowing from the standpoint of the actor, not the spectator.

[3] F. H. Heinemann, *Existentialism and the Modern Predicament* (New York: Harper and Bros., Torchbooks, 1958), p. 40.

The encounter with the open-ended essence of man is, however, primarily an axiological matter. As we saw in Chapter Nine (pages 274–282), Existentialism is principally an axiological view of life. It is saturated through and through with "choice," and since choice is always a value enterprise, then all of life is primarily an exercise in valuing.

The main point to take hold of here is the ultimacy of our valuing. We are all individually supreme judges of the moral dimension of the universe. We choose freely and absolutely; no agency outside ourselves dictates or forces our choices. And what we choose we therefore morally *are*. It goes without saying that this situation produces a certain measure of anguish in people. They do not like to have quite so much responsibility for their moral behavior; they would rather have *some* things forced on them, so they wouldn't have to think about them. That is why, say the Existentialists, they so easily fall into moral systems prepared in advance for their acceptance. But to do so is itself a moral choice, and such individuals must be prepared to take responsibility for making that choice, for saying that is what they think a man truly is.

Here is the final guard against rascality in Existentialist doctrine. If every man is his own supreme judge, then he is free, in a manner of speaking, "to do as he pleases." Quite so. But the phrase *to do as he pleases* suggests acting irresponsibly, and the Existentialist is not saying this. He is saying just the opposite; add the phrase *with responsibility* and a different morality emerges. To think that a world in which men were to choose autonomously *and* responsibly would be an inferior world is to take a rather dim view of man.

Existentialism is much more optimistic. We choose freely, autonomously, on our own. No one forces us to do things. We do them because we truly *want* to do them. If a man wants to be sociable, honest, dutiful, obedient to law, he has to *choose* these things; they are not forced on him. What is sometimes lacking is the willingness to stand up for what we have done and to take responsibility for it. If men can awaken to their existence they will see that they are their own moral supreme court. Once they thus awaken they will act responsibly. And when responsibility takes over, the world will be a much better place.

When we choose — and we constantly must — we are choosing for man. We are casting individual ballots in the metaphysical election to determine what the essence of man is. And if we cast our ballots with a sense of responsibility, with a sense of choosing honestly what we believe to be the *meaning* of man in this world, then rascality becomes an academic question. Certainly no one will call this an irresponsible moral doctrine. It is precisely and magnificently, says the Existentialist, the opposite.

391

Educational theory

It is not the easiest thing, as we have seen, to extract from this view of life a working theory of how learning and teaching should be carried on. In Chapter Four (pages 100–103) we attempted to draw attention to the ontological demands made upon the school to emphasize the private and individual features of child growth and development. This means, among other things, that the Existentialist school would probably start from the "humanities" end of the curriculum to develop its program. That is, it would tend to emphasize those subject matters in which private choice and decision have greater prominence, namely, the arts, philosophy, literature, creative writing, the drama, etc. This follows from the view that the subjective growth of the individual is the most important kind of growth. What the curriculum of the school should do, above all else, is to produce in the child a complete and full awareness of *himself.*

Pedagogically this seems to come out in the ways which were discussed in Chapter Seven (pages 204–207). First of all, whatever method of teaching is selected and emphasized, it must be one which recognizes that the learner learns "from the inside out," so to speak. This means, among other things, that the learner in school must be encouraged to identify with his subject matter, to identify with it emotionally so that he can announce a personal reaction to it. The teacher's function is to arouse the learner, intellectually, spiritually, emotionally. Arousal in the learner will quicken his inner senses to perceive what his learning materials are saying to him; the affective centers of "sensation" will then be in a better condition to react to the materials themselves. For it is in the reaction, and not in the materials, that knowing and learning really take place.

Therefore, in every subject matter (if we retain the subject curriculum) a real effort must be made to involve the learner directly. He must get personally "tangled up" in the subject matter. That is why Kneller has suggested a revival of the well-known Socratic method for Existentialist pedagogy. This method is nothing if it is not to awaken the personal commitments of the learner to what he is trying to learn. As such, it is particularly suited to what the Existentialist wants to have happen in the classroom.

Little can be added concerning that portion of the educative process which is specifically ethical and aesthetic in orientation. In Chapter Ten (pages 304–308 and 314–318) our central theme had to do with the school's function in awakening the sense of the "moral self." This means that the learner must be quickened to the awareness of his moral baselessness: Ultimately he stands alone in making ethical choices. And he ought not be shielded from this difficult awareness by the school's giving him too much in the way of group dynamics and social consensus in the classroom. That is, in the development of character the teacher and his students should play down the dominion of the group over the individual. Certainly in some situations such dominion is necessary (for reasons which are themselves moral choices); but insofar as possible the student should be made to rely on his own subjective ingenuity and his own sense of responsibility in finding an answer to moral situations as they arise in the life of the school.

Similarly, in aesthetic considerations the Existentialist educator would be eager to have the individual child become acquainted with an artistic medium as a prelude to his use of the medium to affirm his own aesthetic feelings. The student should wield a brush, blow a horn, carve a piece of soap, to see what the materials make possible. But then he should enter into aesthetic production with nothing standing between him and the finished product save the materials themselves; that is, he should not be badgered by his art teacher to follow some inherited artistic principles in the completion of his work. He should be left free to involve himself with his materials as he sees fit.

As we mentioned earlier, this practice seems to have gained some currency in modern art programs in the schools. There is some reason to think that the arts represent the most likely initial point of contact for Existentialism if or when it makes its influence felt on educational practice in America.

EXISTENTIALIST EDUCATIONAL POLICY

This leads us directly into the central theme of the present chapter, namely, how an Existentialist might view the educational enterprise in the United States and what specifications he would offer for its reform. As noted earlier, Existentialist writers have not taken up the social questions of life — economic theory, political doctrine, social reform, and educational theory. They have restricted their activities almost entirely to purely philosophical issues.

This has not prevented us, however, from drawing certain inferences from this philosophical position for application to the educative process. But when we now attempt to generalize these pedagogical ingredients of an educational theory so as to formulate a social policy, we are compounding our difficulty by operating almost completely outside what Existentialists have already said. That is, we are trying to relate a pedagogical *theory* with an educational *policy,* neither of which has yet been touched to any great degree by our conceptual suppliers, i.e., the fundamental philosophers themselves.

The social policy of the school

As things stand, there is no conceivable way in which we can find a place for Existentialism on the time-line chart in Chapter One (page 16). The rationale of the chart does not provide an access route for Existentialist theories. About all one can say in this respect is that the school's task is only incidentally social; its primary task is "individual." The school is a social institution, of course, but this means only that it carries on its work by a commission from the body social and the body politic to educate the child.

The commission itself is a general one, merely assigning to a particular class of citizens — the educators — a particular piece of public business. And the content of the "commission papers" themselves, the "fine print," so to speak, of the contract assigning this task to educators, is fortunately loose and vague. We can thank Experimentalism, incidentally, for bringing this about; the Progressive school operates on a much looser contract with the public than the traditional Essentialist schools ever did. This has been achieved principally by the Experimentalists' demonstrating to the public that the educator is professionally capable of being left free to discharge the educational function as he sees fit.

We need only extend our removal from public surveillance one step further, says the Existentialist, and permit the educator to work primarily upon the development of absolute freedom in the child who comes to school. Certainly there is nothing immoral about this; indeed, it can be classified as one of the aims of present-day schools. In fact, paradoxically enough, the educational aim of developing self-determination in American children is one of the *social* functions of our educational industry. To single it out and elevate it to central prominence in our educational policy would not, therefore, violate any precedent. It would, rather, confirm and fortify one of the existing aims of education in the United States.

Beyond this an Existentialist educational policy cannot go very far. We may only resurrect an earlier remark, that in the age-old dispute of whether to improve civilization by improving institutions or individuals, Existentialism quite clearly takes the latter side. Hence, if we do live in an age of upheaval and crisis (and Existentialism would be loath to deny this premise, since it is itself a child of this crisis), then the most likely tack to take would be some effort to awaken individual men to the existential demands that the times require.

We are in trouble today, say the Existentialists, not because the Soviets are threatening the West, not because the international military situation is so precarious, not because this or that political problem remains unsolved. We are in trouble on a much grander scale: We do not know what life is all about. Social reconstruction may assist in resolving the political and social difficulties on the international front; but no amount of social reconstruction is likely to get at the root of our existential problem, the problem of achieving some confirmation and endorsement from the universe on the intrinsic worth of the human enterprise as such.

In this light, reconstruction of the social order is only a superficial palliative for what ails us; it is only a specialized and more forthright expression of the socio-methodological solution discussed in the previous section. The school is at liberty to choose that course, but the chances are that once reconstruction had been successfully completed man would feel quite as lost as he does now.

The best policy for the school on this particular matter, says the Existentialist, is to awaken individual boys and girls to the need to know themselves, to the need not to be steam-rollered into social choices, and, ultimately, to the need to assert their own unique selves in a genuine way. Since no one should claim to be exempt from this obligation to be genuinely himself, all youngsters should go to school. They will have to learn how to read and write and figure; they will have to learn their history and science and mathematics. But the real reason they are there is not to perpetuate some tradition, Western or otherwise; it is not to learn how to think about contemporary problems so as better to solve them; it is not to learn how to reconstruct the social order or reform the human race. Children go to school, ultimately, to find out who they are and what a human life is for. If the school in America — with its subjects, its extracurricular activities, its guidance programs — were to turn more resolutely in the direction of this aim, we could say it had taken on a decidedly Existentialist character.

Responsibility for choice

Perhaps this injunction can be better put in a slightly different way. The Existentialist injunction eventually boils down to taking charge of one's own life. If any of us were seriously to set out on the task to find out, as we say, *who we are,* the only conclusion we could come to would be that the question cannot be answered. We have no "who-ness"; we are "unfinished business." What our life is for, what we as unique individual selves are for in this world, is therefore an open question. But this leads on immediately to the necessity of struggling with the question and taking responsibility for our probing answers to it. For even to disavow the question, even to turn from the quest of what and who we are, is a kind of answer to it. If we know what we're doing when we turn away, that is all right. But Existentialists consider this a puling trick. To turn away whimpering is to cast a rather ugly ballot for the essence of man.

In a kind of metaphorical way, this may be precisely the difficulty of the present age here in America. We have turned from the grander question of Man to the lesser question of things: our rockets, our automobiles, our split-level houses in the suburbs. We have, in short, attempted to avoid responsibility for the ultimate questions of life by trying our best to look the other way, by seeming to be occupied and busy with other, smaller questions. When some crisis comes along we attempt to ignore it, because to do otherwise is to involve ourselves in a lot of seemingly needless argument and controversy. To get tangled up with the world, according to this view, is to disrupt and jar the enjoyments of modern sensate culture.

What we forget of course is that to take this course is to say something about what we think a man is. To avoid entanglement, to escape involvement, is to say that noninvolvement is the proper end of man. To avoid deciding things, therefore, is the ultimate good! But, says the Existentialist, this condition can be purchased only at the price of discontinuing the human enterprise altogether; the only place where such a condition prevails is Heaven. No more deciding. All you have to do is to sit there in a state of being. But you therefore will have passed out of the zone of existing. Existing is where choosing goes on.

There is much criticism of today's youth. They are said to be tranquil and docile; they are said to have lost the radicalism youth has usually had in the past; they have been called a "generation without a cause." Aside from the fact that in the United States today adults are probably worse than youth on these counts, we may still say that the purpose of the school is to awaken the young to their existential function, and this function is nothing more and nothing less than the taking of ultimate responsibility for themselves and, by derivation, ultimate responsibility for the world in which they live. Such an educational policy is simply a call to youth to take charge of their own lives, to feel the responsibility for their own life careers, to be willing to answer for what they choose for Man.

In a sense, the nineteenth century had a better grip on the idea of responsibility than we do. It was a century in which men felt the obligation to *deserve* recognition by getting out into the world and succeeding. It was a century of great energy, of fanatic striving. It was superior to our century in at least this one sense: It had a better sense of the personal responsibility of each man to carve his own way in the world and, in the carving, to stand before it and say, "I did this."

Of course, this nineteenth-century morality finally degenerated into a kind of foolish Horatio Alger-ism. Getting ahead for getting ahead's own sake came to be the ultimate value. Furthermore, it was simply a getting ahead in *social* terms, i.e., getting ahead of *other people*. Finally, it collapsed into the twentieth-century infatuation with *blending with* other people instead of outstripping them. This is where we are today; individualism has pretty well been legislated out of existence. And our schools are themselves accomplices in this movement. They have elevated sharing, group dynamics, and social acceptance to such a high art that only the most rugged and hard-boiled youngsters can rise above it and assert some peculiar uniqueness in their studies. It is not too much to say that "getting along with others" now controls educational policy thinking in practically every corner of this country.

But in order to find our way out of this predicament we ought not retreat to the nineteenth century for our model. This older individualism was a pretty thin article, really. It was a kind of self-assertiveness which was at once irresponsible, unmindful of consequences, crude, and vicious — hence, in Existentialist terms, immoral. But it *was* self-assertiveness; and there is no question that as a nation we have lost it today. What we are looking for is a self-determination and assertiveness which is quite the opposite — responsible, aware of the total effects of action, generous. If a man acts responsibly, if he is willing to stand before the cosmos and say, "This, my life, is what I think a man is," what more can we ask of him? An educational policy founded on this principle is what the Existentialist is asking for. If boys and girls, in twelve to sixteen years of schooling, can be brought to this kind of proposition about themselves, our educational undertaking can call itself truly humane.

The affirmative side of freedom

This whole line of argument points to a facet of Existentialism which too often goes unnoticed and uncelebrated, namely, the exciting "Yesness" of this point of view. It is a great misfortune that philosophy has always treated moral judgment in a negative frame; morals are the things one should not do. Morals are prohibitions more often than exhortations. Throughout the history of philosophy their function has been to restrict and confine, not to free and liberate. No wonder, then, that when we arrive at a doctrine which is essentially a *moral* doctrine we expect to hear further injunctions about what we shouldn't do.

This impression is strengthened by the approach which Existentialism uses, that is, the approach by way of the Human Predicament, the Paradox, the Anguish of Nothingness, Nausea, Homesickness. These all give a decidedly negative cast to our thoughts. Dwelling upon the insolubility of the predicament is perhaps the most depressing of all. And dwell upon it Existentialism does; but only to disabuse us of the enormous backlog of happy optimism that we can solve it and *have solved* it with our philosophies, our organized religions, and our social and cultural systems.

Thus, it is because of the tenacity of what it considers a wrong view that Existentialism expends so much nervous energy in the cancellation of this view. And to cancel is to say "No" in a rather abrupt kind of way.

But once we are able to take this initial step of seeing that the paradox cannot be resolved and the further step that existentially we cannot escape the encounter with it, it then begins to dawn on us that we are individually free to get on with the encounter in our own way. There is an awfulness about freedom, but there is an exhilaration about it too. To realize that I can shape myself, redesign myself, do myself over into any likeness I desire, is to find the beautiful "Yes" in my life. To announce with my life what I think a man is — what assignment can be more affirmative than this? It is an awful responsibility, in the literal sense of a responsibility full of awe, to choose for man. Most of us would probably prefer to have more than one life to work on; there are so many mistakes. If Nathan Hale had been a bit more metaphysical about his heroics, he might have said: "I regret I have but one life to give to Man."

But this is precisely the affirmative theme: Awe is a positive, not a negative, condition. One life is all we are allotted. It is our once-and-for-all chance to say something about the essence of man. And, as such, it opens out before us in a wondrously luminous way. Just think, tomorrow morning after breakfast I can change my life in any direction I think it should take. I am not forced to do anything I do not want to do. I am free. I can choose a different life. I can say with my own *self* what a man truly is. What a glorious thing to be asked to participate in defining the essence of Man! Is there anything higher to a human life than this?

Self-transcendence

This idea leads appropriately into the last major idea we wish to develop. What Existentialism calls for is a positive program in shaping the definition of Man. We have seen that each one of us is personally involved in this undertaking. Whether we like it or not, existing as men means to be a prisoner of this encounter with the question of man's essence; there is no way out except to choose our way out.

But to choose our way out, as we have said, is to solicit some new ideas about what man's essence is. It is to view ourselves from the outside, so to speak, and to come up with suggestions about how to make ourselves over. Man is a continual redesigning project, and we are individually the designers. In this sense, each man is a transcending being; he transcends the circumstance of his present existing. He is, as Sartre has said, a "passing-beyond."

This should not in any way be confused with "transcendent" ideas or "transcendentalism." The participial ending of -ing is used advisedly. Man is a self-transcending existent. He is constantly doing himself over. Here, it is obvious, there is a noticeable contact with Experimentalism and its notions of process and dynamic movement. Indeed, there are many features of Experimentalism which seem in retrospect to be anticipations of Existentialist doctrine. All we are at pains to point out here is that Existentialism is a positive program, a formal summons to men to announce an affirmative statement concerning man. In this way it is a further endorsement of all the affirmative tendencies of Experimentalism, and they are many. Both views are attempts to find, positively, the right way to live, instead of merely specifying how *not* to live, a moral position so thoroughly characteristic of the older philosophies.

In terms of policy, therefore, an Existentialist educational program need not become an overbearing and depressing medium, in which the child would grow up with all the grinding problems of the cosmos on his shoulders. Rather, Existentialism enjoins the child to take increasing charge of his own life and to see his life, as it stretches out in front of him, a potential statement of what he thinks he means in the world. It asks the child to specify what he thinks is best in himself and to present that best, through the vehicle of his life, to the world.

Experimentalism may be said to have shown the way on this matter, especially in its emphasis on trained intelligence in a problem-filled world; but its interest lies particularly with societies, cultures, and human groups. The Experimentalist's "Progress," discussed in Chapter Twelve, might be called "cultural self-transcendence." More aptly, this is the Reconstructionist thesis: doing culture over. In any event, says the Existentialist, we must now apply the same principle in our schools to the *individual*. We may even borrow the militancy of the Reconstructionist and say that the "reconstruction" of the individual self, the awakening of the existential, self-transcending self, is the urgent primary task of the public school in America today.

Involvement and care

We may say finally that when the self awakens to its transcendent nature, when it is aroused to personal responsibility for choice in transcending rightly, it enters the zone of concern and regard for the meaning of man. It becomes *involved*, involved in the human enterprise. What is wrong with America is not that we have grown fat and sassy with our creature comforts; that is only a symptom. Our trouble is that we have forgotten who we are; we have forgotten that the American citizen living today is not only the leading defender of the tradition of freedom in the world. He is a spokeman for Man on this planet.

When he organizes his schools and teaches his young to take up this task, he must see to it that boys and girls in the schools have a curriculum with a little stronger bite to it than is customary. Not just diagraming sentences, calculating quadratic equations, solving social problems, and adjusting to others, but getting involved deeply in the poignant realities of life: suffering, pain, tenderness, cruelty, injustice, kindness, neurosis, warmth, disease, death, love, care.

Care. That's the word. Do boys and girls in today's schools care? It doesn't matter about what. Do they care at all? Do they care about the cold war? Do they care about the Russians, or the Chinese, or the Africans? Do they care about their fellow Americans? In the incessant group dynamics and life-adjusting in the modern school, do they really care about one another? Do they care even about themselves?

The Existentialist stops and wonders. Can we have an education which awakens *care* in the young? The Existentialist asks for this.

QUESTIONS

1. One of the standing aims of American schools is what is usually called "self-realization," meaning that each child should be given the chance to develop all of his talents to the fullest extent possible, whatever they may be. If an Existentialist were asked to react to this, what do you think he would have to say about it? Would he react to it any differently from an Experimentalist? Explain.

2. The implication in the foregoing chapter is that moral questions — that is, questions which require youngsters to take a personal stand on things — should enjoy a larger place in American educational programs. Do you think this is possible in the typical American school? Would parents stand for it? If so, what questions might be the most likely ones to start with?

3. Referring to Chapter Ten, prepare an essay on how the Existentialist would handle the policy question of religion in the school's program. Would any particular Congressional legislation seem to be called for to effect an Existentialist educational policy on this national problem? If so, what would it do?

4. Suggestions seem to be increasing for a centralized federal agency to establish a basic curriculum to be followed by all of the nation's schools, especially now that education has become an instrument of national policy. What would the Existentialist have to say about such a thing? Could his policy for American education be incorporated in such a curriculum statement? Explain.

FURTHER READING

Harper, Ralph. "Significance of Existence and Recognition for Education," Chapter VII in *Modern Philosophies and Education,* Fifty-fourth Yearbook of the National Society for the Study of Education, ed. N. B. Henry, Part I. Chicago: the Society, 1955.
This essay is one of the best and most moving of all the testaments on Existentialism in education. Harper deals with conceptual and pedagogical problems and then, in a brief section entitled "School and Society," takes up the role of Existentialist education in contemporary America. Here also is perhaps the finest analysis of the religion-in-education issue.

Kneller, George. *Existentialism and Education.* New York: Philosophical Library, Inc., 1958.
This book has to do primarily with Existentialist concepts and their application to the educative process as such. But in a brief section in Chapter V entitled "The Challenge of Existentialism" Kneller provides a few clues on the role of Existentialist educational policy in a future America. Although there is a slight confusion concerning Riesman's "inner-directed" concept, this is a minor flaw.

Morris, V. C. "Existentialism and the Education of Twentieth-Century Man," in F. C. Gruber (ed.), *Quality and Quantity in American Education.* Philadelphia: University of Pennsylvania Press, 1960.
Touching somewhat obliquely on the question of educational policy, this essay suggests that the school in America, under Existentialist sponsorship, would probably become "a more metaphysical kind of place." Society would turn to the school to discover its conscience, permitting the young to enjoy occasional moments of privacy in the school program to give them a chance to see what their scurrying about is all for.

Ulich, Robert. *The Human Career: A Philosophy of Self-Transcendence.* New York: Harper and Bros., 1955.
There is a certain oblique mysticism in Ulich's writing. In this work he tries to set forth the Existentialist thesis of self-transcendence and how it manifests itself in the philosophical, intellectual, ethical, religious, and artistic spheres of life. Then, in Chapter 10, he summarizes his statement with an essay on educational policy in America. It is not always easy to follow but it nevertheless sets the frame for understanding how this doctrine would actually work in American life.

Philosophy
in Action

The argument of this book up to this point has been abstract and theoretical. We have been living in the "ivory tower" of the philosopher and the educational theorist. We must remember, however, that ivory towers are, after all, towers. They are heights to peer from, lofty platforms to survey the landscape from, eminences from which men may observe, examine, and criticize what they are doing. As such, they are the most practical of buildings.

Of course it is altogether possible to build an ivory tower so high that you cannot see the ground. If this thought has occurred to you, perhaps it arose in the course of Chapters Three, Six, and Nine, wherein we discussed ontology, epistemology, and axiology from the standpoint of the five philosophies.

But in Chapters Four, Seven, and Ten we tried to come down to a lower floor of the tower to take a somewhat closer look at things in relation to what we had seen higher up. In these chapters we examined the implications of the basic philosophic concepts for the educative process as it is seen by the five philosophies.

Then, in Chapters Eleven, Twelve, and Thirteen, we descended a few more floors to look around and see what the individual philosophies, taken as systems, would be likely to lead to if they were officially adopted as American educational policy.

Now, with all this done, one further step remains. We must come down to the ground floor and relate all that has been said to the very concrete situation that prevails in an ordinary American school with real, three-dimensional children in it and real, live adults working with them trying to make learning happen.

If we take a close look at the way today's teachers teach we may discover signs of what they believe about how the educative process should be carried on. And from this we may discern clues as to what they believe about the world, about knowledge, and about human values. We are not about to say that such-and-such a teaching practice is good and another one is bad. Such judgments will depend upon your own philosophic point of view. All we shall do is to indicate that the things you do tomorrow morning, or will do some tomorrow morning, have their origin in your beliefs. This is what Chapter Fourteen coming up will set out to show.

But schools are not just collections of classrooms; they are social organizations. As such, they require managers and directors, the people we call administrators. Sometimes schools resemble big businesses; at other times they resemble miniature communities. But the shape and direction they take are largely the result of the decisions a single individual makes in the head office. Perhaps you aspire to be one of those individuals; maybe you already are one. At any rate, it is time to say that administrative and managerial decisions in school affairs have quite as much to do with the philosophy of education as anything that the teacher does in his own classroom. In Chapter Fifteen we shall examine this thesis to see how supervisors, principals, and superintendents do the kinds of things they do by virtue of the educational theories they hold.

Finally, what about you? Regardless of who you are and what you are reading this book for, perhaps you are just about ready to formulate your own philosophy of education. This is really the whole purpose of this book: to bring you to a point where you can set down your own creed in a reasoned and intelligent fashion. Insofar as any individual can help another individual organize his thoughts, we mean to attempt it here. Chapter Sixteen, therefore, brings our story back home to the individual doing his own philosophizing — which is where philosophy always starts and ends.

So now let us see if theory does relate to practice in a concrete, day-to-day kind of way — in the classroom, in the principal's office, in the quiet consciousness of one's own professional and personal life.

CHAPTER FOURTEEN

The Classroom Teacher's

Philosophy

THE USES OF PHILOSOPHY

The classic joke about a teacher's philosophical attitudes concerns the teacher who worried over a particular teaching problem to the point of discussing it with several of her colleagues. She even spent some time with the principal trying to solve it, but to no avail. Finally she came in one morning and said, "I've decided to be philosophical about it. I'm just not going to think about it any more."

The teacher who says a thing like this unwittingly expresses a kind of popular sentiment about the functions of philosophy. According to this popular view "philosophy is calm and endurance in the face of difficulty and loss; it is even supposed to be a power to bear pain without complaint."[1] But this attitude and the remark above are merely tributes to the enormous influence of one particular philosophy — Stoicism — which flourished over 2000 years ago. The Stoics made much, as Will Durant has put it, of "the apathetic acceptance of defeat." And the fact that the teacher's remark above is not totally fantastic in our own time is proof enough that the Stoic sentiment still persists.

1 John Dewey, *Democracy and Education* (New York: The Macmillan Co., 1916), p. 380.

The wrongheadedness of this attitude, indeed what makes it a joke (at least to philosophers), is the confusion it reveals. Philosophy is a stepping back from the canvas of life to see it in its larger dimensions. But stepping back is not the same as turning away. This is the great error of the above position, that it confuses a more generalized view of things with not seeing or even trying to see anything at all. If that is what philosophy means, then no amount of analysis or discussion is likely to accomplish much in the way of making our teaching or our living any better.

The opposite position is the only one acceptable: that philosophy eventually controls the quality of our conduct, and that it is the quality of our conduct which in the long run adds up to the quality of human living. And since philosophy is nothing if it is not a continued *thinking about* things, it is our fate to be entangled in the difficult business of trying to make some ultimate sense out of our work. There is every temptation to turn away from our problems; but to turn away from them is implicitly to say that we have lost our heads, almost literally. It is to say that we have legislated intelligence out of bounds in discussions of teaching and learning. This chapter proceeds from the assumption that no teacher can or should base his professional life on such a proposition.

In order to establish the utter insanity of the "no-think" position, we have only to direct our attention to some of the practical problems that emerge in the classroom and to show that thought about them can profitably be taken. Once again we must announce the caveat that the following discussion is not intended to pass judgment on this or that way of handling teaching problems. Even less is it designed to show that such-and-such a method of teaching is good or bad because it is generally associated with one or another philosophy.

All we mean to show here is that (1) teachers face practical situations in the classroom, (2) those situations occasionally become problematic, (3) as problematic situations they can be thought about, and (4) how they are thought about will make a difference in how they are handled. This, quite simply, is the argument of this chapter.

CLASSROOM MANAGEMENT

The opening of school

The teacher walks into school on the Wednesday after Labor Day and encounters a group of youngsters. One of the first things she[2] wants to

---

[2] The matter of gender in pronouns referring to teachers is always a little troublesome. The generic *he* sometimes destroys the intended tone and meaning of the discussion; but the more specific designation of *she* at this point and *he* at another tends to be confusing. At the risk of being somewhat cryptic, this chapter employs the pro-

do is to get acquainted. Of course, some teachers are more interested in this than others. If the teacher has Idealist-Essentialist or Experimentalist-Progressivist leanings, chances are that she will go to a good deal of trouble to get acquainted as quickly as possible. For an Idealist, personal rapport with a new group of students is the foundation of the so-called "communion of selves" which we met earlier. Experimentalist-Progressivist teachers might not have so mystical a base for their views; they would be likely to say that social psychology has demonstrated that people learn best when they are *en rapport* and when they feel acceptance and belonging in a group. But in either case the teacher starts out by learning the names of the youngsters, finding out their interests, letting them get the feel of the group and of the classroom, and generally orienting them to what lies ahead.

Seating arrangements

One of the ways to learn names quickly is to seat youngsters according to a certain pattern, usually alphabetically. When this is done the seating chart is meant to be only a means to an end. But it may also be indicative of a deeper sentiment on the part of the teacher. That is, to seat children according to some arrangement — either alphabetically or some other way — is to treat them as things instead of persons. This is not lost on youngsters, either. In this initial act a certain atmosphere is set in the classroom which becomes part of the total learning environment.

No apology is made for such a practice as this among teachers who have Realist-Essentialist or Neo-Thomist-Perennialist leanings. Children are seated according to plan to make roll-taking easier, to regularize and order the situation as much as possible, to "rationalize" and quantify human relations quickly so as to get on with the real business at hand. Not that children are things; but when they are in school they must not be coddled and fawned over too much lest they lose the sense of why they are there, i.e., to learn some objective knowledge and to train their minds.

We may generalize this by saying that Realists and Lay Neo-Thomists tend to be more impersonal and systematic in their procedures. Some such teachers never do get to know their students, not even their names. And they don't feel particularly bad about it, either. The teacher, they insist, should stay aloof. Familiarity leads to egalitarianism, and, while egalitarianism is all right for social contacts, it is out of place in the classroom. In the classroom there is a mature adult leading the immature

noun *she* when referring to elementary teachers and the pronoun *he* when referring to secondary teachers. If you will keep this code in mind as we go along, the discussions will make more particular sense.

toward truth. Getting to know one another is neither good nor bad; it is merely irrelevant to the learning situation. Of course, it wastes time; in that sense it would be bad. But teachers with Realist and Neo-Thomist tendencies would not make a big argument over it. They would simply say that getting to know one's students may be pleasant and interesting, but it is not vital to effective teaching. It is a "fringe benefit" which teacher and pupil can gain after school or in extracurricular activities.

Hence, say Realists and Thomists, how youngsters are physically situated in the classroom has nothing to do with teaching and learning as such, especially in high school; it has to do merely with the conditions that are thought to be necessary *before* teaching and learning can take place. A "seating-chart" teacher, therefore, is not interested, when he glances up from his roll book, in seeing Johnny Jones; he is interested in seeing a human body occupying a designated cubic footage in the classroom. "A place for everything, and everything in its place." When the buzzer sounds, is everybody in place? Very well. We can begin the lesson.

Movable furniture

There is a kind of corollary to this that may bear some attention. When the teacher considers the physical locations which she wants her pupils to occupy, she may have in mind something other than getting to know their names or simplifying her roll-taking. She may be interested in how much contact the pupils are to have with one another. Generally speaking, the traditional philosophies encompassed in Essentialism (Idealism and Realism) and Perennialism (Lay and Ecclesiastical Neo-Thomism) have held to the "auditorium" model for the classroom. The classroom is literally an audit-orium, a place where boys and girls are supposed to sit still and listen. They are being told about the world by a special agent of that world — the teacher — or they are being directed by a mental calisthenicist. In either case, there is nothing much that they can learn from one another; what it is they are trying to learn is something they don't know. Hence there is no need to have the classroom seating arrangement such that they can physically face one another. No, they should face the teacher. And since the teacher's station is at the front of the room, the desks can be permanently arranged in rows and screwed down to the floor.

Like the seating chart which derives from it, this arrangement renders orderly what would otherwise be chaotic. It represents an attempt to regularize the microcosmic "reality" of the classroom and to give it an air of permanence and fixity. When the child comes to school he is expected to learn that "reality" and to adjust to it as a prior requirement of the world. Screwed-down desks, therefore, are not just accidental products of school-furniture designers; they are physical expressions of what the teacher wants to have the child experience in the classroom.

Movable furniture, on the other hand, expresses quite a different feeling. That which can be moved is that which can change; chairs that can be arranged and rearranged in an infinity of patterns suggest a fluidity in the "reality" of the classroom. They present to the child the sense of impermanence and flux which the Experimentalist-Progressivist teacher wishes to draw to the attention of her pupils. Furthermore, movable furniture has the added advantage of facilitating application of the "sociality" principle of Experimentalism. Boys and girls learn much from one another; they learn in group problem-solving situations; they learn in cooperative enterprises carried on independently of the teacher. Hence, they need seats which will turn toward one another so that they can be physically in a position to transact business in the classroom.

Movable furniture, then, is not merely an attempt by Grand Rapids to make the screwed-down desk obsolete and replaceable. Fundamentally it reflects a basic change in educational theory. The attitude you take on school furniture therefore reflects a much deeper sentiment on your part concerning your philosophic disposition.

Hetero- versus homogeneous grouping

Certainly one of the most persistent arguments in contemporary education has to do with the problem of grouping. This problem, unlike so many others, has a way of arousing the emotional instincts of teachers and parents, often to a point of heated dispute. Of course technically it is not a teaching problem so much as an administrative problem. Perhaps it properly belongs in the next chapter. But teachers usually have definite ideas about it, and those ideas in general reflect their philosophic attitudes toward education.

We touched this matter briefly in Chapter Twelve, in discussing contrasts in policy between the Essentialists and the Progressivists.[3] There the point was made that according to Essentialist thinking the really able youngster needs special attention and challenge, and he is unlikely to get it unless he is segregated into his own special classes. This sentiment does not mean that the Essentialists (and Perennialists) are not interested in the average and slower child; but it cannot be denied that the partisans of homogeneous grouping almost never include individuals who champion the cause of the weak student. The argument for homogeneous grouping is hardly ever made on grounds of a presumed advantage for the slower and weaker learner.

3 Usually the Perennialists stick with the Essentialists on this policy question.

As we also saw in Chapter Twelve, homogeneous grouping usually sounds like a pretty good idea until some parent with Essentialist or Perennialist tendencies learns that his or her child has not been selected for the top group. It works the same way with teachers. Teachers often think well of homogeneous grouping; it reduces the range of abilities in a given class, making the total group more manageable. But if a teacher year after year is invariably assigned the slowest group, chances are his enthusiasm for grouping will taper off somewhat. Generally speaking, most teachers prefer to teach brighter children. Only a small proportion of teachers — but thank Heaven for them — find really creative excitement and challenge in teaching the slow and the dull.

A good many of those teachers who enjoy teaching youngsters with limited ability may be classified within the Experimentalist-Progressivist camp. They have found the old-style book learning inappropriate for their charges, and so they have turned to problem-solving techniques, to projects in the classroom, and to the learner himself as the starting point for learning. They do not try to accomplish too much; they are not expected to. But they know that teaching weak students by the "conveyer-belt" method of the Essentialist or the "train-the-mind-like-a-muscle" method of the Perennialist simply does not work. By practical necessity, then, they usually begin to see some virtue in Experimentalist educational theory.

When it comes to the problem of grouping, however, teachers of the slow and dull often point to the fact that segregating the dull off into their own group tends to make them even duller and slower; they do not have the stimulation of brighter youngsters around them. Since another feature of Experimentalist-Progressivist theory concerns the doctrine of "public-ity" and the principle of "sharing," it is seen that no segregationist policy of any kind is compatible with Experimentalist thinking. Insofar as we segregate people one from another, to that degree do we interfere with their development as persons.

Furthermore, the argument of democracy is usually invoked by the Experimentalist-Progressivist educator at this point. Homogeneous grouping not only segregates but, by implication, creates a class distinction among individuals, some higher, some lower. Try as much as you will to avoid this in homogeneous grouping, it seems an almost inevitable result of this policy. Hence, to separate into different classes is to compromise the principle of equality in the American political heritage. Just as "separate but equal" is now seen to be a contradiction in terms with respect to racial segregation, so also is it a contradiction when any other arbitrary criterion is used for drawing distinctions — religion, national origin, social class, sex *or* intelligence or ability.

The Essentialists and Perennialists usually look upon this "democracy" argument as a purely factitious invention. First, they claim, the school is not a democracy; and to consider it one is to misrepresent its whole character. Furthermore, even if it were to serve the wider society so directly in this matter of democratic procedures, it should not confuse artificial criteria concerning human equality — race, religion, national origin, social class — with other criteria which are most decidedly not artificial and arbitrary, chief among these being ability. Our national tradition of the equality of man has never meant the equality of talents; certainly Jefferson knew that some men are smarter than others. Hence, to permit the "equality of talents" idea to direct educational thinking is to make a hodgepodge mediocrity of the whole business; it is to level everybody down to a kind of average by refusing to recognize that some youngsters can learn faster and learn more than others. There is nothing undemocratic, say the "homogeneous" people, in recognizing ability, either in school or out.

To all of this the Experimentalist-Progressive teacher usually presents the counterargument that although homogeneous grouping is customarily adopted as policy for the highest of motives, including the argument given above, it still yields the ugly, undemocratic by-products of snobbery and condescension by the upper groups toward the lower, by the "8Z's" of the "8Y's." The school must fight against these tendencies and protect the educational dignity of those who are not going on to greatness.[4] Heterogeneous grouping is one way, says the Progressivist, of assuring each child an equal chance.

At any rate, the issue of homogeneous versus heterogeneous grouping does seem to produce in educational circles a fairly clear-cut division along "party" lines. You can often get a good clue to a teacher's basic position by asking his views on this single question.

TEACHING METHODS

Teaching specialty as clue

We have already seen, in Chapters Four, Seven, and Ten, some of the practical implications of philosophic theory in educational practice. Oc-

[4] The Experimentalists might be said to have history on their side in this matter. The nineteenth century was the century of "the strong"; it was *good* to be better than one's fellows, to win out over them, to succeed. There was a moral value attached to power. Today the situation seems to be shifting. The twentieth century is the century of "the weak." The "Common Man" thesis is in the ascendancy. It is *good* to be weak, to need help, to require attention. From the New Deal to psychiatry to remedial reading, the weak seem to be gradually inheriting the earth. To be strong is to arouse suspicion; to flourish authority is threatening and menacing. Power is immoral. What is good for General Motors is, almost by definition, *not* good for the country! If heterogeneous grouping is a way to balance the power between the weak and the strong, then the modern school seems morally obligated to adopt it.

casionally it was possible in those chapters to point to specific pedagogic methods which teachers of different points of view find especially important in their teaching.

We also noted that certain subject matters are not inappropriately identified with particular philosophic positions. The Idealist is identified with the symbolic and ideational subject matters; the Realist with the mathematical and scientific; the Neo-Thomist with the intellectual and disciplinary; the Experimentalist with the social and problematic; the Reconstructionist with the cultural and Utopian; and the Existentialist with the normative and aesthetic.

The first thing to know about a teacher's philosophy in the classroom, then, is his teaching specialty. Other things being equal (and of course they never are), the predilections of a teacher for this or that branch of knowledge will provide some clue as to what his underlying educational and philosophic point of view may be. Certainly in most high schools and colleges the mathematics instructors take a different attitude toward education from that of the social science instructors. Not only do their special fields induce such differential attitudes in teachers, but their attitudes quite probably induced them to select those fields in the first place as their particular and special interest.

The direct object of "teach"

There is always, of course, the old cliché: "I don't teach subject matter; I teach children." This peculiar argument, made possible by the purely accidental feature of the transitive verb *teach* by which it is capable of receiving two distinct kinds of direct objects, may be largely linguistic and perhaps trivial, but nonetheless it is a good vehicle for exhibiting a teacher's point of view.

The teachers who usually assign a subject matter as the direct object of *teach* — e.g., "I teach algebra" — are likely to be Essentialists or Perennialists. Their primary orientation is to the knowledge they are purveying to the young in the classroom. This is because their primary allegiance is to the objective world outside rather than to the child inside, to the world "out there" rather than to the child "in here."

The statement, "I teach children, not mathematics," is more likely to come from an Experimentalist-Progressivist. This is because he holds to the learner-centered concept of education, according to which all learning begins with the interests of the child and not with some prearranged subject matter set out before the child to be mastered. This view, as we have seen, stems from his "ontology of experience" and his experimental, problem-solving epistemology.

An Existentialist might possibly agree with the Experimentalist on the

"I-teach-children" emphasis to pedagogy, especially if he means by this that he is trying to teach the *individual* child to come to an existential awareness of himself. Most certainly the Existentialist would be the last of all our philosophers to be caught saying "I teach history" or " I teach chemistry." He is too committed to the *subject* of the existential child (man as subject, not object) to have too much concern for the *subject matter* of some presumed objective existential world outside. We may note here, as we have done earlier, that subject matter to an Existentialist is really *object* matter, i.e., it represents the objective world. Precisely because of its status as "object matter" it is always subordinate to the true "subject matter," the subjectivity of the child.

As a footnote to this distinction in direct objects we might call to mind the familiar reference made by teachers to "covering the material." Often teachers will object to the interruptions in their work brought about by irregularities in class scheduling due to special assemblies, testing programs, and the thousand other things school authorities can think of to take the child from the classroom. The Essentialist teacher is more likely to make these objections because such activities impede progress in "covering ground." As long as subject matter is descriptive of a pre-existent and given reality there will always be a quantitative relationship between how much time a youngster spends on the material and how much material he can master.

An Experimentalist-Progressivist teacher, on the other hand, is somewhat less frustrated by interruptions; this is because he does not look at his subject matter in a quantitative way, but, rather, in an experiential, open-ended way. Any experience is potentially educative, and if interruptions take the child from the room perhaps the experience he is headed for is destined to be of greater ultimate value to him than what has been prepared for him in the classroom. It is out of this background that Progressivist teachers usually concern themselves with the *growth* of the child, and, it might be added, the whole child — the social, physical, and emotional, as well as intellectual, child. Not "How much ground did we cover today?" but "How much growth occurred today?" There is a world of epistemological difference in these two sentiments.

Techniques of teaching

It should not be difficult now to press the argument a little further to see how different practical devices of instruction relate generally to different philosophical positions.

LECTURE. Certainly the oldest teaching method is outright *telling*. The only possible predecessor to it in primitive prehistory might be actual *showing* (see DEMONSTRATION below). Pre-speaking man probably did educate his fellows by actual exhibits of recommended behavior. But it is precisely because pre-speech man could not verbalize that he never got very far. That is why the lecture is so important in education; it is capable of rendering symbolic that which cannot be brought directly into the classroom. Hence, in its vicarious function, lecturing is supremely flexible in the kinds of things it can do: describing, defining, explaining, analyzing, inquiring, provoking, arousing, exciting. It is perhaps the only teaching method which is easily adaptable to every subject matter in the school. (A possible exception might be the arts.)

On the other hand, since the lecture is founded upon symbols, its use signifies a belief on the part of the teacher that mere noises made with his throat and tongue will suitably represent the world he is trying to get his students to learn. We have seen that English teachers, for instance, may rely on the lecture more than other teachers because of the symbolic nature of their subject matter. Grammar and literature are not found in nature; they are found only in the symbolic artifacts of man. Hence lecturing is an extension of the subject matter itself. But to rely heavily on symbolic communication — in English or in any other subject — is to place one's confidence in *ideas* as the medium through which the child comes to learn his world. Consequently we may say that use of the lecture method shows at least incipient tendencies in the direction of Idealism. This is true particularly when the lecture is intended to convey an understanding of some ideational (as against physical) feature of the world outside the classroom. Since this is almost always the case, we may say that the systematic lecture is primarily an Idealist device.

RECITATION. A customary companion of the lecture is the recitation. This, in microcosm, is the same principle applied to the student: He "lectures" back to the teacher. What this method implies is, again, the belief that symbolic behavior, i.e., talking, is a suitable and sufficient medium for carrying on the learning process. The recitation has a superficial resemblance to Socratic dialectic, which Plato, the father of Idealism, made famous in the *Meno* and *Theaetetus,* and many teachers have thought it a respectable method on that account. It may be respectable, but not by reason of its classic origins; for the recitation is really a test of mastery of a prior body of knowledge, rather than a "recall" or "remembering" of inner, spiritual knowledge, as Plato claimed. For this reason the recitation is perhaps more nearly associated with Realism.

Specifically, the recitation has more genuine resemblance to the Realist's stimulus-response model of the nature of knowing. Here, in this epistemology, man is considered a responding mechanism. Questions and answers are a kind of intellectual analogue of stimulus (pin-prick) and

416

response (retraction). It is felt that a conditioning to certain answers for given questions will result in learning.

CATECHISM. It is this mechanistic conception of mind which, perhaps more than any other, is responsible for the catechism as a teaching device. The catechetical method is simply a refined version of the recitation method: All of the questions relevant to the subject matter are ordered and organized in a published list; each question has one and only one answer; the questions and answers are to be committed to memory; and the catechetical recitation is primarily a testing device to see if the student has memorized his lesson.

In the catechism, incidentally, we can witness an interesting confirmation of a theoretical kinship noted earlier between Realism and Neo-Thomism. In Chapters Three and Six it was found that these positions share certain concepts about the ontological and epistemological characteristics of man. Now here in practical teaching techniques their views converge again. The catechism is an Ecclesiastical Neo-Thomist technique used principally in parochial schools. It was "invented" long before the age of experimental psychology. But now it is seen to be in general harmony with all those mechanistic conceptions of man, most notably the Realist's stimulus-response psychology. Indeed, many contemporary Catholic educators sound like modern apostles of Watsonian Behaviorism; they say, "Give me the child until he is six; you can have him after that."

It goes without saying that Experimentalism-Progressivism and Existentialism are repelled by the recitation-catechetical method. It is the very denial of the problem-solving procedure to think that the child should learn prescribed answers to questions; even more it is a rebuke of his unique selfhood in Existentialism and his power to choose his own answers. In Chapter Seven Socratic dialectic was suggested as an Existentialist method, but only on the proviso that the answers to the Socratic questions are *not* given beforehand. If they *are* given and therefore control the child in the directions of his learning, then we are back in the Realist-Neo-Thomist camp.

There is only one possible qualification to this. Certainly neither an Existentialist nor an Experimentalist-Progressivist would deny the value of learning the multiplication tables. Yet what is this if it is not the catechetical method applied to secular materials? Flipping flash cards in front of second-graders and getting them to blurt out the answers as quickly as possible is perhaps the best example of "mechanical man" pedagogical theories at work in today's schools. In some of the basic subject matters — the tool subjects, as we call them — probably no other educational device would work.

DRILL. This brings us, rather conveniently, to the problem of drill and practice in teaching technique. When a teacher uses drill he presumes that the mind is built somewhat like the body, i.e., it develops through exercise. As such, drill has always been a teaching device closely associated with Perennialism. There is a manner, say both the Lay and the Ecclesiastical Neo-Thomists, in which the mind can be strengthened by giving it "mental calisthenics." Putting mathematical problems on the board and having the pupils work a couple of them every day at the start of the period is a way, it is thought, to develop their "thinking muscles."

In a slightly different interpretation, drill is a kind of "stamping-in" method. Hammering in the connections between stimuli and response by exhaustive exercise is thought to wear a path across the synapses and thus facilitate desirable learning traits. Hence, Realist-Essentialists find this method compatible with their views. What is more, it is particularly suitable for their favorite subject matter of mathematics. But even a teacher of English could use it — in spelling lessons, in sentence-diagraming practice sessions, in punctuation exercises. To the extent that a teacher turns to drill he reveals Realist inclinations. He thinks that the human mind is best thought of as a mechanism of some sort.

Quite obviously, the mechanism principle has always worked splendidly in the teaching of motor activities. Teaching a youngster typewriting, penmanship, sight reading of music, tennis, bicycling, or any other motor skill consists principally in conditioning his body mechanisms to automatic responses so swiftly made that the individual actually does no thinking whatsoever. The most spectacular example of this certainly is in the teaching of typewriting; the human organism can be so efficiently "mechanized" and the response of finger muscles to black marks on paper made so lightning quick that a typist frequently can type an entire theme or term paper without having the faintest idea of what it says. That is because she never really reads it while typing it.

DEMONSTRATION. It is quite obvious that methods of demonstration likewise would find the greatest favor in Realist circles. Here is a technique for presenting the world to the student through his senses. It is usually a common feature of courses in science — biology, chemistry, physics — in which the physical world is under study. Here, the lecture can go just so far; it must be supplemented with direct, concrete sense experience.

In the degree to which we thus supplement vicarious experience with direct experience, we move that much closer to Experimentalist-Progressivist notions of the educative process. One of the things that Progressive educators have railed at most consistently is purely vicarious symbolic learning removed from the living experience of the learner. Ancient history, quadratic equations, the binomial theorem, the pluperfect subjunctive — all these mean nothing to the child. They represent the *end* of learning, not the beginning. If there were some way of demonstrating their function in life, of showing the child, literally or figuratively, how they connect with his own experience, then we would have a better ground for problem-solving activities.

This is really what the biology teacher is doing when he cuts open a frog, or what the physics teacher is doing in his demonstrations of Boyle's law of gases with balloons and diaphragms, or what the civics teacher is doing when he turns his class into a parliament. By such techniques the teacher is visualizing, and thereby extending the learners' comprehension of, those features of experience which they already know but only partially and dimly understand, e.g., the processes of digestion, the mechanics of breathing, and the functions of Congress sitting this very day in Washington, D.C., planning out our destiny.

As long as the demonstration serves only to exhibit a pre-existent reality beyond the classroom, the motivation is primarily Realist. If there is more than this, if the demonstration leads on to curiosities, questions, problems, and eventual investigations by the students themselves, then we pass into Experimentalist-Progressivist ideas of teaching.

PROJECTS. Which brings us conveniently to a teaching technique which has become so thoroughly associated with Experimentalism as to need no particular argument here, namely, the project method. Is there a sand table in the first-grade room and do the children do something more there than run the sand through their fingers and build castles; do they learn cartography by making a model of the schoolyard or of the topography of the town in which they live? Does a unit on Shakespeare in the eleventh-grade English course provoke a class into writing their own play and producing it? If so, then we have the beginnings of the problem-solving, project method of instruction. We have passed from the portrayal of an antecedent reality by word (lecture or reading assignment) or deed (demonstration) to the direct involvement of the individual pupil in the world of real experience. Here, in the direct *use* of his knowledge, says the Progressive teacher, the pupil really begins to learn it.

Essentialism and Perennialism disagree with this: You can learn something before you use it. Using it helps, but it is not absolutely necessary. For this reason teachers with Essentialist and Perennialist leanings usually think that class projects are a fantastic waste of time. So much precious time is put into the incessant planning that Progressive teachers lovingly emphasize. By the time three or four or a dozen class periods have gone by there is nothing to show for it except the completed project of the class. No solid knowledge that the pupil can be tested on; no new or deeper awareness of the subject matter under study.

Of course the Progressive teacher would deny this. Maybe no "solid" knowledge that can be measured in a paper-and-pencil test in the usual stock way. But a living awareness of the meaning of the subject matter in life! Try writing a play yourself; you'll discover why Shakespeare is such a giant among dramatists. Try laying out the ideal town on a sand table; you'll soon see what city planners, architects, housing experts, and traffic consultants are up against in modern urban life. Try getting your students to put their hands and minds directly to some real situation as it exists in today's world by means of a project, and you will awaken more genuine learning than in ten miles of lecture notes laid end to end.

Aids to teaching

BOOKS. By all odds the greatest invention of all time as far as education is concerned was the printing press. Educationally, a book is the most utilitarian of devices. It is cheap, it is portable, and if used properly it can open up almost the entire world to the learner. Furthermore, it is permanent; the student can go over and over it, something that he cannot do with a lecture. Some educational historians have mused over this. Why, they ask, does the lecture persist in educational institutions when it would be far simpler to commit the lecture to the printed page and let the student study it on his own? Why does he need to sit in class looking at a human being and listening to noises? Isn't the teacher, in this case, really the audio-visual aid and the book the true teacher?

However one looks at it, books are a vital instrument in all learning. How they are used, and how much, is perhaps the more vital question to ask. As we have previously noted, Idealists tend to use books a good deal. Mountains of reading assignments usually characterize Idealist-oriented college history courses. And the same is true of Perennialist education. Books are the avenue to the past. They are the summations of articulate people thinking important thoughts. Great books are the highest and noblest products of mankind; they contain the results of great minds thinking ultimate thoughts. These are what the student should read.

The Experimentalist-Progressivist teacher also employs books, but he is more likely to wait to assign them until they are needed. Books are more in the nature of reference works to a Progressivist. Hence they are not used as the foundation of the learning program, but as auxiliary tools to widen the experience of the learner once the learner has established the general lines of his own inquiry. Books used in this way usually mean much more to learners; they see the relevance of what they are reading.

Their interest in reading is intrinsic, that is, "built in" to the learning situation. They usually do not have to be cudgeled into doing their homework assignments quite so much as when books are assigned to be read in and for themselves.

It is for this reason that Experimentalist-Progressivist teachers usually scorn textbooks. Originally, textbooks were literally that — books containing various texts. Nowadays, however, they are (like the present book) written from scratch by specialists using original texts only incidentally throughout. But all they do is to organize and re-explain material in a systematic way so that it can be more easily pumped into the learner's head. Hence, says the Progressive educator, they are based on a faulty pedagogy, namely, that the specialist — rather than the learner — is the starting point for learning. Textbooks therefore continue to violate what we know about human psychology. They continue to be based on the Essentialist notion that knowledge is something to be organized in advance and set out to be mastered. No matter what they say or how they say it, all textbooks pretend to be expository descriptions of the objective world (either of ideas or of things) beyond the classroom and to bring the world by word of page into the mind of the student. Hence all textbooks are built upon a wrongheaded view of how human beings learn.

Better to steer clear of prearranged bodies of subject matter, maintains the Progressive, and let the learners themselves, through their problematic curiosities and interests, dictate the reading materials that will be assigned in any given class.

AUDIO-VISUAL AIDS. The term *teaching aids* usually calls to mind some machine that emits light or makes noises; but, as we have seen, a book is perhaps the basic aid to teaching, even though in the teacher's lexicon it is rarely referred to in this way.

Neither is the blackboard; but the blackboard stands next to the book as the greatest visual aid of all. It is a ready helper in presenting in sensory fashion what had been only symbolic before. Are you explaining the three branches of government in civics class? Are you drawing a distinction between transitive and intransitive verbs or showing how "helping verbs" really help in an English lesson? Are you showing how World War I shifted the balance of power in Europe? What better place to go than to the board with a piece of chalk in your hand?

Some teachers even use the board for emotive purposes. What student has not had a professor who in a state of great emphasis slashed a diagonal chalk mark on the board solely to draw attention to a point he was trying to make? No visual representation; just a bold flourish of white on black to arrest attention!

The same could be said of all the other audio-visual aids. Precisely because they *are* audio-visual they are especially adaptable for sensory learning. Furthermore, such aids provide a happy compromise between those Idealist partisans of purely *symbolic* learning (through books, lectures, recitations, themes, term papers, oral reports, etc.) and those Realist partisans of strictly *sensory* learning (through demonstrations, object lessons, field trips, and laboratory exercises). That is, audio-visual aids such as motion pictures, tape recordings, filmstrips, phonograph records, bulletin board displays, charts, and posters are not merely symbolic experiences for the child; they take on the aspects of reality. But, on the other hand, they are always edited versions of the real, sensory world; hence they are not completely sensory experiences for the child. They stand, rather, somewhere in between. Furthermore, they can be utilized on school property. The Idealist-Essentialist and Perennialist are happy because the student does not get too far away, geographically speaking, from the headquarters of learning, i.e., the library and the classroom. And the Realist-Essentialist is happy because he mechanically transports his students outside the classroom into the world beyond, where, it is thought, a more vital kind of learning goes on.

LABORATORY. Even before the invention of mechanical audio-visual aids, the laboratory had found its way into widespread use in American schools as a vital aid to learning, especially in those subject matters where physical phenomena are studied and examined. The laboratory is a natural extension of the demonstration, in which the learner begins to handle things on his own — test tubes, frogs, levers. In this way he uses the senses other than sight and hearing — namely, touch, smell, and taste. Insofar as all of these sensory receptors can be involved in the laboratory exercise, we reach a kind of learning which finds ready acceptance among Realist educators.

The laboratory at one time in American education was somewhat suspect. Can a student learn anything, they wondered in the latter nineteenth century, by standing at a table and handling some object or some equipment? Is this education? The student is so clumsy; what business has he dabbling in things which the teacher can tell him about so much more quickly? This view gradually yielded to quite an opposite position in today's high schools and colleges. Most science teachers will not even consider granting credit for certain courses unless they are so-called lab courses. Here the Realist is very much in evidence.

The laboratory should not be confused with the so-called project method discussed earlier. It could become the physical site for project work; but in its usual use in today's schools the laboratory is a place where prescribed and prearranged lab problems are worked out by the student. This is not problem-solving in an Experimentalist sense. It is, rather, what is sometimes facetiously called "cookbook" problem-solving: merely a matter of following the "recipes" given in the workbook and having a predicted result ensue. As such, it is Realist, not Experimentalist, in motivation. If a real problem comes up, a problem which must be solved by hypothesizing and testing, then we move along into the zone of Experimentalist-Progressivist laboratory learning theory. Here the learner-motivated project becomes the prime vehicle for learning.

FIELD TRIP. One step removed from the laboratory is the whole world of sensory experience outside the classroom. This kind of experience also can have two general motivations. If it is undertaken primarily as a "spectator" enterprise, in which the students simply look upon certain operations in the outside world — fourth-graders at the firehouse, tenth-graders at the United Nations, college juniors on a summer jaunt to Europe — then it is really Realist in origin and motivation. If, however, there is some occasion for inquiry to arise, if some curiosity is aroused which is investigated and reported upon, then the Experimentalist-Progressivist is seen to be behind it all.

Some field trips have this latter objective, that is, to trigger new questions in the learner's mind. The Realist would not object to this, certainly; but it is not uppermost in his mind. He wants first of all to explain the world to the learner. Questions and curiosities beyond the explanations can usually wait. The Experimentalist, on the other hand, considers field trips only as means to this end, namely, new questions. He wants to initiate some problem-solving activity in the learner. Taking the youngster beyond the walls of the classroom is one way to get this kind of thing started.

There are certainly many other teaching aids and devices which might be included here. But this present discussion is not meant to be an exhaustive catalogue of all the things that teachers do. You can go on from here to identify other techniques that are employed in schoolrooms and how they are to be understood in a philosophical and theoretical setting.

DISCIPLINE

Perhaps the topic of discipline properly belongs in the section on "Classroom Management" already treated. Certainly the behavioral, as against the intellectual, meaning of the word *discipline* has a great deal to do with the teacher's success in managing classroom procedures. But we have decided to treat the matter separately here because there is a sense in which it goes beyond mere routines established in the classroom for the management of learning. Specifically, the matter of discipline has a more particular *moral* significance.

Discipline consists fundamentally in answering two questions: How should the child be controlled? and, How should the child be taught to control himself? Quite briefly, this is our problem. The latter question is obviously of much greater importance; it is the question on which every educational philosophy ought to have something to say. Everybody knows there are various ways to control boys and girls; and those ways can readily be tested one after another in the classroom to see which one brings immediate results. But it is rather more difficult to know which of those methods leads to the greatest learning by the child in developing self-control, the end object, after all, of all discipline.

To put the matter a bit too bluntly, and certainly too simply, we may say that the traditional educational outlooks (Essentialism and Perennialism) hold that the child is taught how to control himself by being controlled by the teacher, that self-discipline comes from being disciplined. The contemporary educational doctrines (Progressivism and Existentialism) hold that the child is taught to control himself by controlling himself, that self-discipline comes from practice in disciplining oneself.

The traditional philosophies rebuke the modern philosophies (Progressivism in particular) for being soft and sentimental toward the misbehaving child. They claim that the only way a youngster will develop moral fiber, a real sense of right and wrong, and, hence, a mature level of self-restraint, is by adults' inducting him into rules of conduct which are already set for him when he comes to school. Anything else — call it democracy or self-discipline or whatever — is mere sentimentalism. Children have to be restrained; they are little animals, many of them. And by constant restraint they eventually learn to restrain themselves.

Progressives understandably tend to reject this. It is precisely because boys and girls *are* restrained and controlled by adults that they feel no need to learn self-restraint. They are conditioned to expect somebody else to oversee their behavior. Hence the sure way *not* to develop self-discipline in a child is to make the teacher, rather than the child himself, the chief moral supervisor of the child's conduct.

Some practical examples may help to illustrate this.

Rules and penalties

Everybody knows that schools, like other institutions, have to have rules. A certain amount of social business is transacted there, and boys and girls must be brought into conformity with a minimum level of ordered conduct in order for that business to be carried on. There is, therefore, no dispute about the need for general rules.[5] What is crucial is where the rules come from: from an authority *beyond* and *outside* the life of the child — i.e., the teacher, the principal, the board of education, parents, society at large — or from an authority *within* and *intrinsic to* the life of the child — i.e., the child himself, his peers in the classroom, the student body of the school. Which one of these shall be the source of good conduct and good behavior in the classroom? If you are an Essentialist or a Perennialist you lean toward the outside authority; if you are a Progressivist or an Existentialist you lean toward the intrinsic authority.

THE TRADITIONALISTS.   The former position holds to some form of the authoritarian concept of discipline. That is, the rules of behavior to which the teacher is bringing the child have already been specified. They represent antecedent conceptions of right and wrong worked out beforehand by an adult society for children to adjust to. Like the subject matter itself, they are *prior to* the child, since they originate in a real world of mind or nature or logical "being" which was in place before the child came into it. Hence the child is expected to conform to those rules; and it is not undemocratic to disregard his views concerning them. His views are not wanted, because they are not relevant. His job is to conform to the rules as they are laid down by the teacher.

Failure to adjust to them is customarily punishable by penalties either announced beforehand or, as is customary, arranged on the spot so as to "fit the crime" — a mild rebuke, isolation from the others in the back of the room, exile to the hallway for ten minutes, denial of privileges (no recess today, for instance), a trip to the principal's office, keeping the pupil in after school,[6] corporal punishment, ridicule, suspension or expulsion from school.

This list obviously does not contain all the measures a teacher can use; rather, it merely suggests a kind of hierarchy of penalties which are at the disposal of the teacher. He or she uses these as the situation warrants, not only to exact tribute along the lines of the Old Testament's "eye-for-an-eye" morality but also to deter others from similar misbehavior: When a youngster sees a classmate dragged into the hall by the collar, this theory says, he will think twice about pulling his next prank.[7]

[5] An Existentialist might possibly demur from this view.

[6] Here is a puzzling irony. From their earliest years boys and girls are taught the value of education; teachers, more than any other adults, want children to *want* to learn, to desire schooling, to see the great values in more and more education as they grow older. But the standard way to punish children has been to give them more of it — i.e., keeping them after school. What more effective policy could we have thought of to turn boys and girls against schooling?

[7] There is considerable doubt in social psychology, and particularly in the field of criminology, whether punishments have any deterrent effect whatsoever. In adult society, for example, the crime rate does not appear to be much affected by public

We may see in this list a few other interesting features of basic philosophical position. It is not entirely irrelevant, for instance, to suggest that corporal punishment has a connection, however tenuous, with the philosophy of Realism. Why might a teacher slap a child's cheek for talking back to her or being "saucy"; why might she drag a child to the hallway by the hair for throwing an eraser across the room; why might a high school teacher give one of his students a good cuff on the ear for trying to be the "wise guy"? Is it not based upon an underlying belief that the physical body is in some way associated with the learning of right and wrong? If physical pain can be brought to the child's body for some bit of mischief, it is thought that that pain will eventually influence the child's conduct for the better.

As time has gone on, corporal punishment has yielded to what we might call social punishment. The above list of penalties, you will notice, includes several which involve the isolation of the culprit from his peers. Traditional teachers, especially during the nineteenth century, made liberal use of one of the most vicious forms of social isolation, namely, ridicule. Perhaps the climax of this technique came with the well-known "dunce cap" tactic or, more recently, with the device of having the child stand in the corner facing the wall for a specified number of minutes. Ridicule was and still is perhaps the most powerful of disciplinary weapons; indeed, because it is so powerful and in some cases psychologically damaging to the child, it has been ruled out as a legitimate form of discipline.

But now we see that ridicule is not necessary; milder forms of social isolation are sufficient. Now that we have come to see the thoroughgoing sociality of man, his gregarious tendencies, and his constant hunger for the approval of others, we have discovered for education a new arsenal of disciplinary devices. Banishing a child from the room, separating him from his classmates, segregating him in some way or other from the other youngsters, is now one of the standard devices for bringing him into line.

Educational historians have been mildly startled by the great success of compulsory-attendance laws in this country. How come they no longer have to be enforced as they used to be? How come the "truant officer" no longer exists in our towns and cities? The answer lies simply in the social tendencies of the child. He goes to school because he *wants* to go, not so much to learn as to be with his friends. One of the most significant phenomena in school dropouts, according to educational sociologists, is the great build-up of pressure for the dropout to return to school after he has been out for a few days or weeks. But this pressure is not brought by the

_____

policy on such a thing as capital punishment. Likewise, there is some clinical doubt in educational psychology whether punishments really influence the behavior of other youngsters.

usual arguments of the principal or the teacher, namely, that learning is important, that the student should develop a skill in order to get a good job, or that he will get further in the world with a high school diploma. The pressure is brought by the plain hunger of the adolescent for the company of his own kind. Usually he returns, and usually for this reason.

But (to return to the central problem of discipline), notwithstanding these social controls on the young, the traditionalist is still of the view that the teacher stands *in loco parentis* and *in loco* society in inducting the child into an already prepared and accepted code of proper behavior. While the child may be permitted a certain amount of latitude within the boundaries set by this code, he has nothing to say about the code itself. This is because adults, not he, are the authors of it.

THE PROGRESSIVISTS. When it comes to discipline, the Progressivists heartily agree that the classroom must have rules. But, as previously indicated, such rules should grow out of the classroom situation if the child is to learn the reason for having rules and for obeying them. What is morally confounding to a child — or to an adult, for that matter — is to be forced into certain channels of propriety without really understanding why. Granted that a child cannot easily see why throwing spitballs or talking boisterously or punching his neighbor in the next seat is an unacceptable form of behavior; the point is, says the Progressivist, that he will never be brought to see such behavior as unacceptable merely by being forced to refrain from it. All that force does is to duplicate police action in the classroom. But one thing which police action does *not* do is to invite the culprit to consider the consequences of his behavior.

This is basically why traditional disciplinary policy is so ineffective, says the Progressivist. It apprehends and punishes the guilty, but it does not bring any sense of self-discipline precisely because it does not involve the individual in considering the moral dimension of his act. Involvement in the moral dimension of the classroom is the key to Progressivist disciplinary theory, and one way to produce this involvement is to have the boys and girls themselves engage in making up the rules by which their classroom behavior shall be ordered.

This strikes the traditionalist as an open invitation to anarchy. There are risks, no question, replies the Progressivist; but the long-run educative impact of this procedure will easily be greater than that of a more authoritarian policy. Hence, this procedure is not argued for because it is more democratic or humane or altruistic (though it is probably all of these); rather, it is defended on grounds of being educationally sound. Boys and girls learn good behavior by learning how to control themselves in real situations in the classroom. And when they can be given greater and greater responsibility in managing their own affairs, to that degree they grow in self-discipline.

It is not altogether impossible or improbable that a group of youngsters might come up with somewhat the same rules a teacher would prescribe for their adoption in a traditional setting. And, likewise, the penalties levied might be approximately the same, if not identical. It is a known fact that youngsters are usually harder on classroom culprits than adult teachers would be; often they have to be restrained from an excess use of their new-found power. But the similarity of child-centered vis-à-vis teacher-centered rules and penalties is not the issue; the issue is the "seat of authority" for such rules and penalties. And it is felt that youngsters come to genuine self-discipline more readily and quickly when they are in genuine control of their own affairs.

Here, perhaps, we come to the center of the discipline problem in education. The Essentialist and the Perennialist do not look upon discipline as a learning experience; "classroom penology" is merely a means of control to facilitate learning. Experimentalist-Progressivists, however, regard the microcosm of the classroom as a living medium of human relations. The treatment and handling of misbehavior — what we here call "classroom penology" — is therefore of real concern to youngsters. By living through and witnessing how the teacher handles obstreperous Jack Jones, boys and girls will learn certain dispositions about justice and law. It is felt, therefore, that involving the students themselves in "classroom penology" will better educate them in the handling of offenses and punishment later on in adult society: once again, a clear example of the "learn-by-living" theory of the Progressivist educator.

Misbehavior as symptom

This leads conveniently to a more sensitive area of interpretation. Disruptive behavior in the classroom can be looked at as merely the willful product of an untamed and uncivilized child. The teacher's task here is to tame the wild beast and bring him into the community of men. (In older times, they even talked about "breaking the will" and then remolding it along more socially acceptable lines.) In this view of classroom conduct, the child is wrong; he is bad; he can be spoken of as a *bad child*, and when his parents complain about the poor treatment he is getting, the teacher can insist that as long as he is bad in the classroom he will be punished.

But, according to another interpretation, disruptive behavior can be looked upon as a symptomatic effect of underlying causes. These causes are of two general kinds: Either (1) there is something disturbing the child or (2) the teaching is inferior. In the former instance misbehavior is a phenomenon which is *caused* by some prior experience — home background, childhood training, perhaps neurosis. The teacher's task is to go in search of that "cause" and thus to understand the child better. Perhaps by knowing the cause the teacher can apply something other than a penalty and produce a much better change in behavior than otherwise would be the case. For example, many children, it is well known, "act up" in class because they need attention, sometimes because they are denied attention at home. If this is the case, then the teacher can improve the child's conduct not by punishment but by its opposite, love and attention. In any case, we can no longer speak of a "bad child"; since "all behavior is caused," there is no such thing as a "bad child."

In the case of the other underlying cause — poor teaching — there is a feeling that misbehavior in the class is due to lack of motivation in the child. Since motivation is the first business of teaching, misbehavior is then seen to be the fault of the teacher, not the child's background. Hence if a teacher consistently has difficulty maintaining order, this view would hold that some inspection be made of the teaching procedures used.

In looking upon misconduct as symptomatic of an underlying cause we come upon another point of educational practice which tends to divide our philosophies into opposing camps. In general, Essentialists and Perennialists have never taken heartily to the view that "there is no such thing as a bad child." To them this is merely soft sentimentalism. If we can no longer call certain behavior bad and say further that it has originated in a bad individual, then we are educationally paralyzed in bringing a child to his moral senses.

The Existentialists, strangely enough, tend to line up with the Essentialists and Perennialists on this score. If all behavior is "caused," they say, then no one is responsible for what he does. And a child in the classroom who is no longer personally responsible for his conduct can never be approached directly to improve on that conduct. All the teacher can do is create certain conditions — such as love, kindness, rebuke, or penalty — to redirect behavior; but the child can never take personal charge of his own mode of living. This, to Existentialists, is essentially the fault of modern Freudian psychology and of all those Freudian conceptions that have worked their way into the school: What they eventually do is to legislate the existential man out of existence by relieving him of the responsibility for his own actions. If you are neurotic, it is due to something outside yourself over which you have no control; therefore you cannot be held responsible for your neurotic behavior. If a child misbehaves in the classroom it is due to some empirical cause further back in his experience. The child, according to this logic, is exonerated; we must now go in search of the empirical causes. When delinquency stirs up the community, for instance, someone is sure to say that "the parents are the ones who are really to blame." Existentialism finds this the most incomprehensible of moral logic.

Those who have made the most of the Freudian, "all-behavior-is-caused" theories of child conduct are the Progressivists. They usually have studied more psychology than the traditional educators and the Existentialists. Moreover, unlike Essentialists, Perennialists, and Existentialists, they are willing to accept the findings of the scientific study of human behavior in the field of psychology. We are obligated, they say, to be scientific in our understanding of the young and to teach them accordingly.

EVALUATING THE LEARNER

Testing

Sooner or later in every teaching program some account must be taken of what has been accomplished. Has there been a transfer of encyclopedic information from one individual, the teacher, to another, the learner? Has an immature mind been trained to think? Has the ability to solve problems been developed? Has a moral sense been awakened? In asking such questions we are really asking whether the purposes of an educational program have been achieved. But, since the purposes of education vary from one philosophy to another, we really have to ask a different kind of question for each kind of educational program. And this, in turn, means that our testing for results will take a different complexion depending upon the philosophy we work under.

For instance, a Realist may be expected to consider the transfer of factual information from teacher to pupil to constitute the primary business of his educational program. On this basis, it is easy enough to measure this transfer by giving the child a paper-and-pencil short-answer test. True-false items, a multiple choice, or any other kind of objective examination would seem to be appropriate to the purposes. What such tests as these succeed in doing is to quantify the whole learning experience, that is, to render quantitative and numerical whatever it is that has happened to the learner. Objective tests can be constructed in such a way as to yield a number, usually some proportion of 100, which serves as a ready index of the extent of learning.

The intelligence-testing movement of the last fifty years has sprung primarily from Realist sources. Thorndike announced that "Whatever exists, exists in some amount." Thus, if intelligence exists it possesses quantity and therefore can be measured. As we all know, it *has* been measured, and with a vengeance! There are now on the market hundreds of different tests[8] which purport to quantify whatever man consists of over and above his physiological nature, and to render this thing — called intelligence or mental maturity or scholastic aptitude — in numerical form. The validity and reliability of such tests is an experimental concern of the psychologist, the psychometrist, and the statistician. The underlying rationale of such tests, however, is a *philosophical* matter, and this rationale is plainly Realist.

The Idealists have influenced the testing movement too, of course. Most IQ tests, for instance, are usually divided into a mathematical or quantitative section and a language or verbal section. The former is, obviously, of special interest to Realists; and insofar as the latter involves a technical skill like reading comprehension or punctuation know-how, it is also Realist. But occasionally these tests include sections on literary interpretation. Some even include a writing exercise in which the examinee is to compose some theme. Clearly, in this vein the motivation is Idealist.

Generally speaking, Idealists prefer essay examinations to objective examinations. What can you learn about a growing mind from a bunch of X's on an answer sheet, especially if it is fed into a machine for scoring purposes? Nothing, really. The way to gain access to a student's mind is to have the student write his ideas on a certain topic, analyze a complicated issue, interpret a story. This is more nearly what we would consider to be intelligence, says the Idealist.

Perennialists are likely to combine both of these testing theories in discovering if their students' minds have been disciplined to clear thinking. Sometimes complicated word problems are used, problems which combine mathematical skill with verbal logic. Take, for instance, this, which is claimed to be a standard testing exercise for fifth(!)-grade children in Switzerland:

> A stock of pamphlets is in three piles: the first pile contains 1/6 of them; the second pile contains several fifths [*sic*] of them; the third pile has 6 pamphlets. What is the total number of pamphlets?[9]

The Progressivists would find all these testing devices quite irrelevant to the central business of education, namely, the training of an active intelligence capable of solving problems. It is not unfair to say that Progressive educators have been slow in coming to a clear theory of testing and evaluating learning. The other philosophies have held an advantage in

[8] See, for instance, O. K. Buros (ed.), *Fifth Mental Measurements Yearbook* (Highland Park, N.J.: Gryphon Press, 1959), which lists and annotates 957 different tests currently available for the measurement of mental abilities.

[9] Reported by Professor Harold Clapp in an article, "Some Lessons from Swiss Education," *Modern Age*, II, No. 1 (Winter, 1957–8), 10–17.

testing theory. Factual mastery in Realism is easy to measure; just specify the facts wanted and ask for them. In Idealism verbal facility and the ability to manipulate ideas can be evaluated, perhaps not so precisely, but to a considerable degree. And the answers to logico-mathematical problems like the above from a leading Perennialist are either right or wrong.

But when we come to problem-solving we move into a no man's land so far as precise measurements are concerned. We are thrown back upon the quality of the learning experience itself: Did the sand-table project awaken new insights in the learner? Did the participants in the lunch-room-improvement project come to know one another better or more deeply? Did they study and learn things other than what they started out studying? Was there in putting on a class play a progressive growth in confronting and resolving difficulties along the way? All these, and a thousand other, questions might be relevant to an evaluation of Progres-sivist learning. And it is plain that the answers are not definitive, as they are in the other theories.

The main point is that paper-and-pencil tests of any kind are inade-quate to the testing of problem-solving skill. Rather, the learner must be placed in a situation in which he must use what he has learned. There he will reveal, by the quality of his behavior, whether he has learned well or not. Since this is usually difficult to do on anything but a token scale, most Progressivists are confined to the old standard methods of testing. But since they have no interest in what these devices measure, they often wind up by not evaluating at all. There is some truth in the charge that Progressive educators are weakest in the field of testing. They have yet to develop a clear and workable theory of measuring problem-solving ability.

The Existentialists, quite understandably, have not thought much about testing. Testing always refers to some standard outside the learner. But since right and wrong, true and false, good and bad, real and unreal all have their ultimate and final locus within the child, it is impossible to think of measuring his answers to questions against some other answers and making red checks beside those which do not agree. If a youngster has been brought to question the meaning of life; if he thinks for the first time of what the world is all for and what man is in it for; and if, especi-ally, he has become seriously interested in what he is to make of his own life above and beyond his prospective career — then we might say that the Existentialist student has learned well.

Grades and report cards

Perhaps by now we are getting too far afield; perhaps we have left philosophy so far behind as to be making labored connections between this practice and that philosophy. Teachers have different attitudes toward grading their pupils at the end of the term and reporting those grades to the parents. Whether these differences have philosophic meaning is perhaps a moot point.

It seems on the face of it that a teacher who likes to "grade on the curve," as we say, reveals tendencies toward Realism, in that he is attempting to quantify and render mathematical the comparative achievement of his students. It is probably not inaccurate to say that in the quantitative subject matters of mathematics and science one is most likely to find "grading on the curve."

In any event, when a teacher says he is "maintaining standards" it is probable that he is speaking from an Essentialist or Perennialist background. Standards, to him, are by definition descriptions of an external criterion of achievement; to maintain standards is to measure students' performances inexorably against them.

A Progressivist is usually a little dubious of "standards." Being a relativist and believing that the world of experience is where standards are manufactured in the first place, he is not impressed by exhortations to stick to standards. What he tries to do instead is to measure the performance of each student, not against an external standard, but against the youngster's own potential for learning. This usually turns out to be a vastly complex exercise in psychological measurement, since for the Progressive the whole concept of learning potential is on somewhat dubious logical ground;[10] but the theory is that, since standards themselve shift and change, the fairest measure against which to reckon a youngster's actual classroom performance is himself. If, therefore, you encounter a teacher who attempts to make his report card show how well the student is doing in terms of what he *could* be doing, given his ability, chances are he has Experimentalist-Progressivist tendencies.[11]

On the report card itself there are the usual places for some kind of symbol indicating academic achievement — from reading in the first grade to calculus in the twelfth. But then, in varying degrees on different report cards, there is an effort made to report home to the parents the growth the child has achieved in areas other than the intellectual. Social development, emotional poise, getting along well with

[10] By this is meant that the word *potential* carries the ring of Aristotelian Neo-Thomism, i.e., a potential toward which the human mind naturally tends. Progressives do not believe in this. Furthermore, the word *potential* also has a Realist ring to it standing for capacity. Progressives do not believe in this, either. They are not sure *what* they mean by potential, but they continue to use the term.

[11] Perhaps all he is measuring is industry and effort, in which case there appears a rather ironic bedfellowship with nineteenth-century Puritanism. "Work hard. Do your best. That's all I ask of you. No one will flunk the course who makes an honest effort."

others — all these are nonintellective factors of human development. Essentialists and Perennialists are, generally speaking, not too concerned with them; these educators are interested in the intellective features of the young. But Progressivists pay as much attention to these sections of the report card as to any other. Being committed to the "whole child" concept, they want to measure child growth in every dimension where growth is important.

Report cards have been getting increasingly more complicated in recent years, so much so that parents can hardly read them without trained interpretation. It is not too much to say that Progressive educators have been largely responsible for this trend. Reporting to parents has, indeed, become a major area of study in teacher-community relations. Home visits are made, conferences at the school are scheduled, the teacher-parent relationship is examined and thought about by principals and superintendents; and it is all to be traced to the concern which Progressive Education has given the nonacademic, nonintellective growing patterns of the child.

THE TEACHER
AND THE COMMUNITY

We may wind up this tour through classroom philosophy by expanding upon the last point: the teacher in his relations with parents and with the wider community. Admittedly, the teacher's social role is a rather ambiguous one. Traditionally he has been thought of as someone too timid or too ineffective to make his way in the wider society. "Those who can, do," you know! This embittered, vicious, but in some cases justified attitude seems to be waning, if only slightly. There seems to be a greater acceptance of the idea that teaching is a science, that it requires study of human behavior and learning theory, and that it sometimes approaches the stature of an art when a pupil reacts deeply to a teacher.

At any rate, whatever recognition the teacher may have achieved above the low public estimate of an earlier time is probably independent of any philosophical position. It is true that Progressive Education has carried the work of the school into the community far more than have the traditional philosophies; in the community itself Progressivists have found a segment of their curriculum. They have therefore awakened public interest in public schools and in themselves as apostles of a scientific education built upon problem-solving.

But just as they have attracted much attention, so they have also become the target for hard and often vitriolic criticism; in their well-meaning efforts to win friends they have turned a goodly number of citizens away from the public schools. If one were to strike a balance sheet, therefore, on the state of school-community relations at the present hour, it would not all be credit.

The groups that the Experimentalist-Progressivist has alienated most, as we have intimated, are the intellectually more gifted and talented citizens in our American communities. Parents who, according to the criteria developed in this book, might be classified as Essentialist or Perennialist have taken up the cudgels against the public school. They claim that youngsters are not being worked to capacity (while they themselves perhaps enjoy more and more coffee breaks and fewer and fewer hours in the work week). They claim that intellectual discipline is on the wane and that science and mathematics are being neglected. And all of these charges are based on the presumption that the public school has been captured by the Progressivists.

As a matter of actual fact, however, this presumption turns out to be wrong. The subject-matter curriculum remains in force in most of our schools, and the majority of our teachers, especially at the secondary level, are graduates of liberal arts rather than teachers' colleges. A close inspection of many secondary schools, perhaps most of them, will reveal that Essentialist and Lay Neo-Thomist-Perennialist educators are still in control. Certainly they hold the balance of power in most American high schools. Hence if there is something wrong with contemporary American education all parties will have to answer for it.

Nevertheless, the contemporary teacher — of whatever persuasion — finds himself or herself confronted with a baffling cacophony of public noise concerning the school. This comment should never stop; indeed, there is little likelihood that it ever will. Citizens have been arguing about the purposes of education since Aristotle. But one may hope that public education will some day come to mean *the education of the public* to the point where a greater measure of intelligence will find its way into the public arguments concerning American education.

The school program itself might serve as the vehicle for greater public understanding. Education should become one of the topics of study in the social studies curriculum, along with government, economics, and civics. But beyond subject matter the teacher himself has many avenues of contact with the public. Certainly in parent-teacher associations, where his influence is direct, he can help to turn some of the often trifling program content toward the consideration of educational issues.

Finally, there is an appalling ignorance on the part of the general public as to what is actually going on inside our schools. If we could only bring the citizen to the classroom he would soon realize that there are different ways to educate the young, and that those different ways are not accidental variations or mere expediencies of the moment but

435

living expressions of the differing philosophies of education which American teachers hold.

QUESTIONS

1. If you are interested in psychology, make a study of some of the nonintellective psychological tests currently in use in education (for instance, the Bernreuter Personality Test, the Kuder Preference Record, the Strong Interest Blank) to determine which philosophy of education the authors of such tests reveal. Explain your general thesis with examples.

2. One of the professional duties of the teacher in the modern school is to participate in extracurricular activities. Would our several philosophies view this duty in different ways or not? Explain.

3. Make a study of one of the teachers in your school — his general attitudes toward the topics in this chapter, the way he teaches, the way he treats his pupils. Where would you place him philosophically? No need to name names or places, but you should document your findings with anecdotal materials and illustrations.

4. Make a similar analysis of your teaching (or, if you have not yet taught, of the way you think you would teach).

5. Make a similar analysis of the instructor of the course you are taking in connection with this text. How does this square with the philosophical position he seems partial to?

FURTHER READING

Alexander, William M., and Saylor, J. Galen. *Modern Secondary Education.* New York: Rinehart & Company, Inc., 1959.
In this textbook on basic principles and practices, the authors devote a full chapter to "guiding classroom learning experiences." Here they examine various theories of the teaching-learning process: absorption and telling, memorizing and drilling, experience and guidance, and directing problem-solving activities. With the present chapter, you should have no difficulty locating these in the philosophical spectrum.

Barzun, Jacques. *Teacher in America.* Garden City, N.Y.: Doubleday and Company, Inc., Anchor Books, 1955.
In this highly readable account of the American teacher at work, the irrepressible Barzun contributes his own pithy language to the philosophy of teaching. Barzun belongs to the Idealist-Thomist axis, but in this little volume he ranges across the map. Periodically touching his home base for general effect, he

nevertheless gives warm credit where credit is due to other pedagogical theories extant in today's schools.

Brackenbury, Robert L. *Getting Down to Cases.* New York: G. P. Putnam's Sons, 1959.
In this readable little volume Professor Brackenbury provides, as his subtitle puts it, "a problems approach to educational philosophizing." Concrete classroom problems are taken up: discipline, the gifted child, promotion and reporting, teaching moral and spiritual values, controversial issues, etc. For each of these Brackenbury reports anecdotally how different teachers handle them. Then he shows how the teachers' behavior grows out of their philosophic views of education.

Highet, Gilbert. *The Art of Teaching.* New York: Vintage Books, 1957.
Highet does not treat teaching from the philosophical standpoint as such. But his analysis of the art of teaching will reveal many inclinations in the direction of Idealism. His review of methods, for instance, covers only the basic three procedures of lecturing, tutoring, and recitation; these are, as we have seen, most appropriate to literary and humanistic subject matters.

Hymes, James L., Jr. *Behavior and Misbehavior.* New York: Prentice-Hall, Inc., 1955.
In this "Teacher's Guide to Action," we find a warm and understanding treatment of a prickly problem. Hymes provides an essentially Freudian interpretation of discipline, recommending the consideration of the whole child, emotions and all, in redirecting the youngster's behavior. This more often calls for love than for punishment. And his message would be most appropriate for those of Idealist and Experimentalist persuasions.

Lieberman, Myron. *Education as a Profession.* Englewood Cliffs, N.J.: Prentice-Hall, Inc., 1956.
Lieberman is technically not an educational philosopher, but he has written perceptively and provocatively on the philosophical dimension of teaching as a profession. In Chapter 2 he examines the problem of "professional function," using categories not unlike those employed in the present chapter. Then in Chapter 3 he takes up the whole matter of "authority" in education. In these two chapters you will be able to get a direct glimpse of the connections between educational philosophies and the teacher's professional conception of his job.

Zapf, Rosalind M. *Democratic Processes in the Secondary Classroom.* Englewood Cliffs, N.J.: Prentice-Hall, Inc., 1959.
If you want to see how a thoroughgoing, dyed-in-the-wool Experimentalist would design the dynamics for a classroom, take a look here. Even the chapter headings are revealing: "Getting Under Way," "Working in Small Groups," "Pupil-Teacher Planning," "A Problem to Work on," "Solving a Problem," "Reporting to the Class."

The School Administrator's

Philosophy

PHILOSOPHY AND
THE ADMINISTRATOR

G. B. Shaw's famous maxim, "Those who can, do; those who can't, teach," usually tempts some wag to complete it with: "Those who can't teach become administrators!"[1]

In the "pecking order" of social psychology, it is thought that those lower on the social ladder receive most of the abuse; the reverse seems to be the case in education. Usually it is the administrator who is the target for most of the slings and arrows of criticism. Certainly as far as teachers are concerned, he is the source of all the trouble.[2] And of course he gets a good deal of argument from parents, from his board of education, and from the local self-appointed watchdogs of school affairs who write Letters to the Editor.

He is, one might say, the "storm center" for all educational concerns in the community, the "eye" of the hurricanes which can originate in almost

[1] There is an "inside joke" variant of this in schools of education, to wit: "Those who can't teach teach others how to teach."

[2] Prompting the remark: "It's not the school; it's the principal of the thing!"

any latitude of a volatile community and at the most unexpected times. Because of this, it is difficult to rationalize his task, to order it and place it in a philosophic setting. The chaotic, moment-by-moment, telephone-answering character of his work almost defies comprehensive analysis and rational explanation.

We know, of course, that his work is primarily concerned with human relations; but not entirely. And, anyway, what if it is? Does a philosophic disposition insinuate itself into the areas in which one relates to other humans? The argument of this chapter is that it does; but we are not so bold here, as we may have been in previous excursions into the practical life of the school, in drawing connections between philosophies on the one hand and practical procedures on the other. Rather, we find the administrator at the far end of the philosophic tether, trying with his moment-by-moment decisions to turn the institution this way or that. But, while his efforts are in earnest, the effect of his decisions is often diluted and played out by the time they find execution in the classroom with real boys and girls doing some learning.

Nevertheless, to change the metaphor, the administrator does exert more power on the educational rudder than any other single individual; therefore we are entitled to examine how his philosophic leanings may influence the way he steers.

Before getting started on this, we may be permitted the rather important observation that the phenomenon of administration is the product of Realist tendencies. Administration — whether in business, education, or anywhere else — is principally an attempt to order and regulate some process. So long as schools were small, teachers and pupils few in number, and curriculums constant and uncomplicated, there was no need for administration. But now that everybody goes to school, and a teacher is needed for every twenty-five or thirty youngsters, and now that the curriculum reads like the Yellow Pages of the telephone directory, we see that some cadre must be assigned to take charge of it all. And, as we have said, their job is essentially to order and regulate an otherwise chaotic business.

This urge to regulate and systematize is, we insist, more nearly associated with Realism than with any other philosophy. If education were only Mark Hopkins and a pupil sitting on respective ends of a log — an Idealist image, as we have noted — then administrators would be supernumeraries, supreme examples of Parkinson's Law.[3] Many educators

---

[3] "Work expands to fill the time available for its completion." This, a not wholly satirical "discovery" of one C. Northcote Parkinson, for several years Raffles Professor of History, University of Malaya, Singapore, explains why it is that labor-saving devices do not really save labor but generate *new* labor, why bureaucracies multiply, and why "organization" in modern life has grown beyond mere means to become an end in itself. See *Parkinson's Law* (Boston: Houghton Mifflin Co., 1957). Parkinson has discovered a second law, by the way, which also bears some scrutiny: "Expenditure rises to

today consider them to be just that — people who create their own work!

At any rate, since education is now something to be managed, since lights have to light, since rooms have to be warm in the morning, since books and chairs and motion-picture projectors must be in the right place at the right time and in working order, since the telephone has to be answered, since letters have to be dictated and signed, since new staff must be selected and incompetents released, since curriculums have to be planned and manned — in short, since the school as an institution is required to function — then somebody has to do these things. And when these tasks take up so much of a person's time as to draw him completely away from the teaching process itself, we call that person an administrator. How does philosophy relate to his work?

INSTITUTIONAL MANAGEMENT

Buildings and grounds

One of the most obvious functions of the administrator, as distinct from the teacher, is care and supervision of the physical plant. Some educators make a rather large display of their indifference about physical facilities. These people are, in one way or another, expressing the "Mark Hopkins' log" theory of education: The physical situation isn't the important thing; the important thing is the *human* situation, the quality of the teacher teaching. Hence they are inclined to concentrate their budgets on salaries rather than on paint or grass seed; and they would be expressing, even if in a very rudimentary way, a disposition toward the general theory or philosophy of education which we have ascribed to Idealism.[4]

This sentiment may possibly be illustrated by the physical-plant policies of the older eastern universities. In many of these — Harvard, Columbia, Rutgers, for example — a common practice is to purchase private dwellings on the fringe of the campus to house university offices. Everybody knows that this practice is perhaps the most expensive way to acquire cubic footage; the buildings are old, made of wood, usually firetraps, designed for domestic living rather than teaching and learning, and atrociously expensive to heat and keep in repair. But the Idealist-oriented eastern schools do not claim to be efficient and fiscally prudent; they wish to carry on the humanistic tradition, and almost any kind of

meet (and surpass) income." See *The Law and the Profits* (Boston: Houghton Mifflin Co., 1960).

4 Idealist administrators usually have quite a hard time of it in the typical American community. Well-kept buildings and grounds are much more "visible" to the general public than good, first-class teachers. A principal, therefore, is more easily judged by the building he keeps than the company he keeps.

cubic footage will do. In the somewhat younger midwestern and western universities, when more cubic footage is required, a massive drive is undertaken with the legislature, with the alumni, or with private benefactors to build a new building. These institutions cannot so easily ignore the economics of higher education; they must be business-like in their building policies.

Administrators differ also on other counts. Some superintendents and principals want their buildings to be adaptable to allow for unexpected changes in program. Movable walls are perhaps to the Experimentalist‑Progressivist administrator what movable chairs are to the Progressivist teacher; they permit him to rearrange the interior of his building as occasion demands. His curriculum is undergoing continual change and revision, and if a curriculum change requires some special facility — a music practice room, an auto shop, a listening room for learning French from phonograph records, an office for the school psychiatrist — then he doesn't want to have to build a whole new addition just to provide for it. Movable walls, modular construction, and, indeed, the whole concept of flexibility in the use of space are just now finding their way into school architecture. Dictated partly by shortage of funds, of course, this development is nevertheless expressive of the dynamic, changing mood of Progressivist educational theory.

Neo-Thomists usually stick to the older concept of a fixed interior pattern to their buildings. This is because their curriculum, by definition, does not need to change from year to year; it is always constant. Therefore the cubic space for carrying on this curriculum can be built the way the teachers and administrators want it and then left that way for the life of the building. Neo-Thomists also share with Idealists a general feeling that buildings are not the most important thing about an educational institution. The life of the intellect can be carried on in any reasonably well-ventilated attic or cellar just about as well as in a glass-walled, air-conditioned palace — maybe even a little better!

When it comes to the question of architecture itself, we may be stretching our story a little too far. Certainly no group is immune to the attractions of modern design and the functional benefits which it yields. But we may still think that modern architecture is more unexpected in some quarters than in others. Moreover, even if modern design were employed, what general feeling would the various groups wish it to express in their particular theories of education?

The Realist might be said to lean in the direction of the "factory" concept of school architecture. This sounds unkind; maybe it is. Perhaps "office building" would be better, but this does not convey the sense of efficient functioning as does the former term. The Realist wants his school to be an efficiently planned, systematized, and rational structure.

No gimcracks, no flying buttresses, no filigrees or vaulted towers. Just build it simply and functionally, so that a passer-by glancing at it would sense a business-like and earnest activity going on inside.

It might be well, also, to use the same design for several buildings. Learning is the same in every part of town; why not use the same blueprint? Contracting is cheaper and, furthermore, a sense of uniformity and order to the school system is presented to the public this way. Also, we can name these schools with numbers, starting with P.S. No. 1. This saves a lot of argument over whose dead hero deserves recognition. Furthermore, it saves bookkeeping time and also it is neater to refer to P.S. 138 than to Emanuel Dickinson McKnight School.

Idealists, of course, lean in the other direction. As we have noted, they are not famous for efficiency and parsimony. Better to have a school building suggest an idea of some kind; what if it does cost a little more? The physical school building to the Idealist is a "monument," a remembrance of some age, an expression of some value. Columns with Doric tops suggest ancient Greece; castles and turrets and massive stone walls and buttresses suggest the strength of the medieval period; in the East, colonial architecture recalls a new nation declaring its independence. This, to an Idealist, is what a building is for, to convey a tone, a mood, a feeling of some kind.

Furthermore, let's name our buildings with the names of men who stood for ideas: Jefferson High School, Lincoln Elementary School, Woodrow Wilson Hall. How cold it is to say "P.S. 138"; how cold it is to say "Central High." Certainly a building ought to have more to say to youngsters than that it is geographically near the center of town.

The Neo-Thomist perhaps has no distinctive preference in architecture. Of course, the "Academy" motif of the Greek-columned façade might be associated enough with Plato and Aristotle to be suitable for a Lay Neo-Thomist. But, as we have said, the building is not really important enough for us to be greatly concerned over what architecture it should follow. It should be simple and unadorned, suggesting the preeminence of mind over matter, intellect over material things. For the Ecclesiastical Neo-Thomist the cathedral would be a more likely paradigm: Gothic arches lifting tall ceilings in a library reading room, spires and steeples pointing to the heavens to show the insignificance of this life "here below." A leaded colored-glass window might also be strategically placed to portray some symbol of Christ's message.

An Experimentalist turns from all of this, as might be expected, in designing his buildings. He finds no great fascination in the past or in some godly message. Like the Realist, he wants his schools to be functional and efficient. He has taken to building them ranch-style, all on one floor, to make traffic more convenient; but he is not interested in making them look like factories, with the suggestion of programed labor going on inside. Instead, he wants his school buildings to suggest that something exciting is going on. Learning is not grinding labor; it is fun, challenging, exciting; it leads out to new experiences, new growth, new ideas. Let the building sprawl about the site; let it suggest many different things going on — an auditorium rising here, a music room at one end to keep the noise mercifully segregated, biology and science classrooms with laboratories, greenhouses, and garden plots immediately attached. Let the whole thing look like a workshop-clubhouse where the people inside follow their interests and work together on projects. And let it be artistic and tastefully appointed; boys and girls learn taste not by attending school in a factory or a medieval castle but by being surrounded with loveliness day after day. Landscaping is important; light and illumination inside are important; and the general décor will infect the learner with either a positive or a negative attitude about going to school.

What can be said for the Existentialists? Maybe they are on their way back to Mark Hopkins and his log in the literal sense. They perhaps lie closest to the Idealists, but they would probably retreat much further. If the Existentialist, as we have suggested, would resurrect the Socratic method of teaching, then he could have his teacher stroll peripatetically about in an olive grove . We would all have to move to warmer climates for this; so perhaps we could devise some structure that would provide the same kind of individual freedom, individual searching, individual questioning. Maybe an enormous, sound-dampened "lobby" might be the best physical setting for learning. A playhouse, or maybe several, would have to be attached nearby so that the learner-as-actor could react to his learning. At any rate, the individual would be liberated at last from institutional architecture as we have come to know it.

Schedule-planning

By the time an administrator has his building designed and built, the next major problem involves moving human beings around in it for maximum educational effect. As one can see at the outset, the concern with this problem is in itself of Realist origin. (Now that the factory is in place, let's get the production line going.) First, divide the school day into certain definite and prescribed time blocks, forty-two or forty-seven or some such number of minutes. Schedule bells to ring at the appointed times; install a clock which will ring the bells automatically!

Part of the routine will be a ten-minute home-room period sometime during the day, probably first thing in the morning. At this time there will be announcements for the entire school. The most efficient way to do this is to install a public-address system with speakers in every room;

443

then the administrator can communicate with everybody at once. A mimeograph machine will stand ready for "mass media" communications which have to be rendered on paper.

Classes will meet at prescribed times and in prescribed sequences. Every teacher's or youngster's whereabouts should be known by the office at all times; the lesson being given at a given hour should be known at all times. Order, regularity, system — these are the watchwords of a Realist. Efficiency is also. The school must make full use of its resources. It is a tragedy to many Realists that school buildings stand idle for three months out of the year. It is also a source of great annoyance that colleges use their physical facilities even less efficiently than the public schools. To boards of trustees, most of whose members come from the business and industrial community, there is no excuse for a classroom building to be constructed when the existing classrooms are vacant 50 per cent of the time.

In an eastern university some years ago the administration found the legislature balky about new building funds until the university stopped a wasteful class-schedule policy. Most of the classes were meeting Monday, Wednesday, and Friday mornings. During the afternoons and on Tuesdays, Thursdays, and Saturdays the campus took on a "ghost-town" appearance. So the administrator in charge of such things concocted a new class schedule, which provided for instructors to meet their classes in different patterns, at different hours each day, and for longer stretches of time per class meeting. Educational considerations — of teaching effectiveness and student-faculty morale — were subordinated to practical efficiency. Because it improved the "utilization rate" the new schedule was decreed. You might know the administrator in question was a mathematician by training and background. With his administrator's hat on he was unquestionably a Realist.

Record-keeping

In Chapter Eleven (see page 334) we commented upon the phenomenon of credits in American education and the "credit-chopping" that has now become the principal occupation of clerks, vice-principals, and college registrars. There is no other way to interpret this astonishing development in American education except in Realist terms.

There is presumed to be, as we have pointed out, some kind of quantitative relationship between the number of minutes or hours an individual spends sitting in a classroom before an instructor and the extent of his learning in the course. A certain number of courses make up a major, a minor, or an elective bloc in his total educational program. And a given number of majors, minors, and electives add up arithmetically to diplomas and degrees.

Fortunately for the Realist, we are now getting I.B.M. machines to facilitate this work. Every time a student enrolls in a course he receives an I.B.M. card with the appropriate holes punched therein. This is his ticket to the course. At the close of the course his grade is included by punching another hole or two in the card; the card is then processed, in an amazing labyrinth of wheels, levers, and electrical impulses, to produce some similar designation on another sheet of paper, which has come to be known as the transcript. The I.B.M. card is perhaps the supreme expression of modern academic irony, namely, that an individual's finest product, the work of his mind, can be represented by a hole![5]

Budget policy

The single most potent weapon in the administrator's arsenal is the budget. The discretionary allocation of funds is the medium through which he makes his ideas felt in the educational enterprise. It is here, then, that the administrator's philosophy of education becomes most clearly evident. Here we may back away a bit from our general thesis that administration is primarily a Realist art. For money is everybody's business, and dollars, though they represent quantities, can be exchanged for qualities that an administrator wants his schools to possess. Every philosophy will therefore take to budget-making with the understanding that in the long run institutional aims can be achieved by the way an institution chooses to expend its fiscal resources.

Budget-reading, like map-reading, is a technical art in itself, but it does not require the services of a Certified Public Accountant to tell when an administrator is expressing an educational point of view by the way he spends his money. Let us say that a superintendent entertains competing demands for (1) a French teacher to set up an elementary-school foreign-language program, (2) an I.B.M. installation in the central office, (3) a specialist in mathematics to serve as mathematics supervisor for the entire system and strengthen the mathematics curriculum from the first through the twelfth grade, (4) a publicist to assist the superintendent in charge of public relations to interpret school policies to the community — each of these proposals calling for the expenditure of, say, $7000. Which will he choose?

It is certainly too much to say that a single decision of this kind would reveal a man's entire educational point of view. But would it be too much to suggest that how he chose on this budgetary question would re-

[5] Outwitting a system like this is nigh impossible, but some geniuses have succeeded in doing it. A few years ago a subscriber to a record-a-month club decided to cancel membership. He wrote several letters requesting removal of his name from their mailing lists, but the records kept coming. Finally he took the I.B.M. card which accompanied his monthly record, punched a few random holes in it, and sent it back. He never heard from them again!

veal an inclination for, respectively, each of the first four philosophies we have studied in this book?[6]

It is always hazardous to specify a man's motives; all that is empirically observable are his behavior patterns. But if a hundred such budgetary decisions were made there would be some reason to think that the analysis of them taken together would say something about the educational point of view held by that administrator. There is certainly a difference in mood and point of view between a school system in an established upper-middle-class suburb like Winnetka north of Chicago and a newer upper-middle-class suburb like Park Forest south of Chicago. Winnetka probably has more wealth, and there is undeniably a social class distinction between the two communities; but that is not all. Winnetka's New Trier Township High School is one of the country's leading Essentialist institutions; it can afford to be, since almost all of its graduates are preparing for college. Its principal, William H. Cornog, is periodically applauded by the Council for Basic Education in its monthly *Newsletter,* and he is a featured speaker at Essentialist-oriented educational conferences frequently held about the nation.

But Park Forest's schools, which have been analyzed in William Whyte's *The Organization Man,* are another matter. Whyte reports that they have taken on the mood and feeling of a community which is itself in transition, growing, finding its way. The educational program is strong on social relations and group enterprises, somewhat less concerned than Winnetka with hard-core mathematics, foreign languages, and basic science. Knowledge is to be used in the world, not mastered for its own sake. And the schools are expected to respond to the community's needs whenever budget-making is in progress.

In these two instances — and in thousands more — the distinctions in outlook in educational theory are reflected in budget policy. This suggests a somewhat larger idea, namely, that if there are four or five (and possibly many more) educational philosophies at work in the schools of America, there are at least that many life philosophies at work in the communities of America. The adult citizens of our nation express different patterns of belief by the kinds of lives they lead, the organizations they join, the things they spend their money on, how they raise their children. These differential dispositions on the personal meaning of life are certain to be reflected in the school board's discussion of the budget, in the Taxpayers' League's attack upon increasing school expenditures, by the Citizens' Committee for the Public School in its drive to pass a local bond issue.

Consider these three groups: school board, Taxpayers' League, Citizens' Committee. Boards of education are made up, usually, of professional

[6] It is rather difficult picturing an Existentialist as a superintendent of schools.

men or business executives. They have usually had advanced education themselves and they value it as a way of getting ahead in the world. They tend, in general, to be drawn from the Essentialist sources in American life, but they are pressed both by the lay community and by professional educators to yield to Progressivist demands to broaden the curriculum and make it more nearly meet the needs of average and slower learners.

Taxpayers' leagues are not just opposed to taxes. They are opposed to education! Or at least to that portion of it which to them seems beyond the basic needs of the young. They do not value education so much as do the school boards; they value their own money, especially when it is to be spent, they think, on "frills" and games in the school. Taxpayers' leagues usually draw heavily from the Essentialist and Perennialist elements in the community. If schools would get back to the basic materials of learning, they maintain, school budgets wouldn't be so fantastically high.

Citizens' committees are a recent development in the United States, dating generally from the end of World War II. Usually they stand at the other end of the spectrum; they value education *more* than do the school boards, and they are prepared to accept higher taxes to get it. They see, for instance, that the education of all youngsters, at whatever level of attainment, is a community good, and that good schools, in a very literal sense of the slogan, do make good communities! These committees are likely to be found supporting an expanded school budget, pressing for school bond issues, and generally working for more and more educational services. This puts them in the vicinity of Progressivist policies, and it is the Progressivist mood which they often reflect. On the other hand, many such citizens' groups have organized to lobby for the more standardized fundamentals of basic education. While they value education highly (they are usually led by parents of bright children) and are willing to pay for it, they want their schools to stay loyal to the basic academic-subject-matter orientation traditionally espoused. In this event, we should have to assign such groups to the Essentialist category.

PERSONNEL MANAGEMENT

As we said earlier, the administrator's work is largely that of managing people, or, in the cliché of the times, human relations. Schools are primarily human enterprises, and the success of an administrator's work is more nearly tied to the effectiveness of "people working" rather than "bricks enclosing" or "money buying." It is presumed, therefore, that the ways in which a superintendent or principal deals with the human factors present in his particular situation will have much to do with his professional skill; and it will also be reflective of the kind of educational theory he believes in.

Staff relations

One of the best examples of how an administrator expresses his educational point of view is the image he holds of himself in the institutional structure. Some educational administrators see themselves as the general of an army or the captain of a ship; that is, the principal considers the "line-and-staff" organization an appropriate model. He hands down orders to those in the lower echelons of the organization and receives orders from the "commander in chief," the superintendent. He and his teachers are the "line" officers in an educational enterprise.

Assisting him as "staff" functionaries are the various curriculum coordinators, guidance counselors, research directors, doctors, nurses, psychiatrists, secretaries, clerks, and janitors. With all of these individuals, as well as with his "line" subordinates, he maintains rather impersonal relations. His really close friends are found outside the hierarchy.

In some of the larger school systems, this approach — which we may tentatively attach to a Realistic outlook — sometimes takes on the appearance of considering the teachers and staff assistants as replaceable parts in a giant machine. Substitute teachers are called up and asked to "teach" a certain class for a day; if they are knowledgeable about the subject matter and adept enough, the children will learn just as much as with the regular teacher. Replacements (the very word is suggestive) are hired as needed and the entire staff organization takes on the image of an army brigade's "table of organization." Efficiency and economy in human relations is the central theme; and there are many administrators who become quite successful at this kind of personnel policy.

The Idealist is somewhat warmer in staff relations. He looks on the people around him as unique personalities, whose impact on youngsters cannot easily be measured in quantitative terms. He may find a Mr. Chips on his staff and attempt to expand the influence that such an individual has on youngsters. That individual can never, in a sense, be replaced, and the administrator knows it. If a substitute teacher is required, it is merely going to be a matter of "keeping school" until the regular teacher returns.

What the Idealist is interested in doing is creating a special kind of human climate for the youngsters in his school. The manner in which he gets the most from his teachers, the way in which he provokes them to perform at increasingly higher levels, is the measure of his quality as an administrator. Under the canopy of Idealism, therefore, the administrator will be closer to his teachers, will not avoid personal and social contacts with them, will ask their private advice on school affairs.

A Neo-Thomist would probably share with the Realist a desire to remain somewhat aloof from his teachers. In his mind, an institutional structure like a school ought to be a logical organization, a rationalized human enterprise where emotion, feeling, and "politics" are kept out of the running work. Insofar as he can make his relations with his staff rational and purely intellectual he will consider himself successful.

The Experimentalist-Progressive administrator deserves special comment. Although he shares with the Realist a fundamental interest in administration which grows naturally out of his point of view, his interest is of a slightly different sort. Whereas the Realist is interested in order and system for its own sake, an Experimentalist-Progressive is interested in Process for its own sake. And since administration is principally the business of manipulating processes in a human enterprise, it comes to the Experimentalist quite easily.

With this in mind, we may also say that the Experimentalist does not reject the system and order of the Realist; rather, he uses them as platforms from which to deviate. An Experimentalist's administrative structure is founded not upon the Realist's "line-and-staff" model but upon the democratic-committee model. "Administration by committee" is perhaps not too strong a rubric to apply to Experimentalist schools. And when new ideas come to the fore in group deliberations an Experimentalist is inclined to deviate from previous patterns and precedents if he feels that the new idea is worth trying. Hence under an Experimentalist principal or superintendent there is a great deal of flexibility in staff relations; he usually permits greater latitude of discretion, encourages experimentation on the part of subordinates, and when a policy must be decided turns to the committee apparatus of his institution.[7]

The Experimentalist may be said to be more interested in people than the Realist; but he is perhaps less interested in individual personalities than the Idealist. This is because his primary human reference point is

[7] There is a tangential argument in administrative-philosophical theory as to whether Realists (and Idealists and Neo-Thomists) are not temperamentally more inclined to authoritarian procedures in their administrative work and Experimentalists more inclined to democratic procedures. This argument is sometimes avoided by noting that policy execution is distinct from policy formulation. Whereas the former is properly authoritarian, the latter is properly — in our society, at least — democratic. But putting the issue this way does not clear up the problem; for it is well known that executive influence can be exerted on policy-making procedures and, contrariwise, that the policy formulation can be so specific as to call for no executive discretion, reducing the administrator to the status of a clerk.

Hence we must still ask the question concerning authoritarian as opposed to democratic administrative procedures. If by democracy we have reference to the scope of decision-making enjoyed by subordinate individuals and groups, it seems appropriate to hand the palm to the Experimentalists.

the group, not the individual. It is the "committee deliberating" on a problem which produces answers valuable to an Experimentalist administrator, not an "individual analyzing" and coming up with a particular solution. This difference, subtle perhaps, is nevertheless indicative of the middle ground between Realism and Idealism on which Experimentalist-Progressivist administrators are usually to be found.

Appointment policies

The distinctions drawn here may become more vivid when we consider perhaps the most important task of every administrator — staffing his schools with new individuals. If the human element of a school is its primary ingredient, if it is the people, more than any other feature of an educational institution, which make it or break it, then the administrator's long-run reputation will depend finally on the quality of the people he hires.

We need refer only to the general traits examined in the previous section to get a clue to our problem here. As the Realist looks over the confidential files of candidates for teaching jobs and as he goes to teacher-training institutions to engage them in interviews, he will be looking for clarity and orderliness of mind before anything else. What he wants for the pupils in his school is a teacher-technician who can "get the subject matter across," who can "cover the material" in a systematic and efficient way. He is also interested in people who will "fit in" in the line-staff hierarchy, who will follow instructions and perform assigned tasks willingly and expeditiously.

The Idealist may want some of these qualities also, but he will more likely pay greater attention to the personality of the candidate. He will, for instance, find the paper credentials quite incapable of telling him about a potential member of his staff; he will want to meet that individual face to face. The warmth of that person, the depth of his personhood, the clarity of his expression, the values he holds, the feelings he reveals, and, indeed, the intensity of his feelings — all these will be uppermost in his mind as the candidate sits before him. What kind of an impact will this individual make on my students, not only as a conveyer of knowledge but as a human being with a unique interpretation of his subject matter? This is hard to assess, no doubt, but to the Idealist it is the core of the teacher's qualifications.

The Neo-Thomist is somewhat harder to locate. He will be interested, of course, in many of the above qualities. He will probably be closer to the Realist than to the Idealist. He wants logic more than sentiment. So, before he assays a candidate's feelings, values, and personal outlooks on life, he wants proof of sheer intellect.

The Experimentalist-Progressivist once again represents a significant break in continuity. He will be less interested in a candidate's purely academic credentials for a teaching job in his school, less interested in mastery of the content of the teaching field for mastery's own sake, less interested in the scholarly traits that the individual exhibits. He will be more interested in the gregariousness of the individual, in the novelty or potential novelty of the ideas he expresses, in his orientation to group decision-making and over-all prospects for getting along with his colleagues. Is he shy and retiring? Forward and aggressive? If so, he will not do. Does he have ideas, does he want to experiment with things, does he look to Change rather than Stability as the central principle of his life, does he give evidence of being congenial and socially mature? If so, let's sign him up.

Certainly there is much more to the evaluation of candidates for teaching positions than what is suggested here. But it nevertheless holds true that the differential qualities will find differential emphasis, as we have indicated, in the hiring and firing policies of public elementary and secondary schools.

At the college level the issue becomes somewhat more complicated. Here the credential of scholarship takes on more importance. Teaching ability, as such, is reduced in relative value. In this context the Idealist's interest in the teacher's warmth and personality and the Experimentalist's interest in human relations, social maturity, and gregarious group orientation do not exert the same force on employment policies. Instead, the Realist's concern with factual mastery of content, the Idealist's concern with mastery of the literary tradition, and the Neo-Thomist's interest in intellectual power come into the foreground of consideration.

"Publish or perish," they say. And they say it advisedly. For in those institutions whose interest in scholarship lies ahead of interest in students, the policy of "up or out" eventually takes hold of employment and promotion procedures and rules the administrator's hand at contract-signing time. Knowledge rules the academic world. He who can create new knowledge through research and scholarly activity is admired, appointed, promoted. He who can merely communicate knowledge to others, albeit well and brilliantly, is necessarily of lower prestige and rank.

Supervision of instruction

One of the important but usually slighted functions of principals in modern schools is the supervision of classroom instruction. This is particularly relevant for the new teacher, the emergency-assignment teacher, and those teachers who wish to experiment with different teaching procedures. To include the experimenters in this group is to indicate at the outset that principals with an Experimentalist inclination will wish to identify themselves with such teachers. Their supervision will tend to be a cooperative, "fellow-experimenter" sort of thing. Suggestions will be offered, counsel given, criticisms made, not as a chief might speak to a subordinate but, rather, as a research director might speak to a fellow scientist. In such circumstances *supervision* is perhaps not precisely the best word, but it has come to be used in this connection as denoting the relationship between a "line" or "staff" officer in the school and the teacher in the classroom.

Of course the facetious synonym for this word is "snooper-vision" — which indicates that many teachers feel they should be left completely alone to develop their own teaching "style" as individual professionals. Generally speaking, the custom of leaving the teacher completely alone without advice or criticism tends to be stronger in the traditional philosophic positions and their attendant educational theories. Historically, these philosophies ruled in the day when teachers were fewer in number, more select as a group, and, hence, less in need of — or at least undesiring of — criticism and counsel on what they were doing.

Nowadays, in the effulgence of Experimentalism and Progressivism, not only have teachers become a vast army of functionaries holding a more equivocal professional position, but the work they do has become the object of intense scientific study. Hence, whether they want advice or not, they are bound to get some, if for no other reason than that the behavioral sciences keep coming up with new insights into human psychology, developmental behavior, and learning theory which bear directly on what teachers are doing. Increasingly, it has come to be the function of the supervisor or principal-as-supervisor to make these new insights available to the teachers within his bailiwick. This work can be done badly or well, of course, but the very advent of this type of professional activity testifies to the strong impact that Experimentalism — with its emphasis on scientific experimentation, public reporting of new ideas, and socialized sharing of those ideas as they are put to work in the classroom — has made on the teaching and the administrative professions.

Program development

We come finally to a much neglected but nevertheless central task of the administrator: the planning of new courses and curricular programs. In an earlier era, when the school was not expected to respond to community needs and when the curriculum stayed fixed from year to year and, hopefully, on into eternity, there was no need for a principal or superintendent to concern himself with this. But increasingly in modern schools there is an eagerness to match the program of the school to the needs of the times and to make education meaningful and relevant to the interests and capacities of youngsters.

This inclination is, as we have intimated, of Experimentalist-Progressivist origin. We live in a day when new needs *do* develop — cultural needs, social needs, vocational needs, psychological needs. A contemporary administrator with the slightest commitment to the "needs" theory of educational policy must be constantly alert to see that his curriculum is doing what the community wants it to do. Thus there is a constant obligation for curriculum revision, for the designing of new curriculums, and for preparing and outlining new instructional units.

On these occasions the principal must take his mind from buildings, budgets, schedules, record-keeping, and interviews with job-seekers and turn his attention to the mobilization of staff energies on the instructional program itself, a concern which is ultimately institution-wide in scope and of interest to everyone in the school. The *strategy* of his staff relations is suggested in the sections above; how he approaches this work will reveal, in part, the educational theory he holds. But in terms of *tactics* curriculum-planning is a little different from the other things he does. Specifically, it is full of trouble, a kind of trouble which stems from basic resistances the principal encounters in this part of his job. These resistances may bear some philosophic comment.

First, of course, is the general resistance to change on the part of some of his colleagues. Some teachers are not interested in program development because they are fundamentally, temperamentally opposed to change in general. They may share the desire to meet the needs of community and student, but they interpret those needs on a more general level of application, viewing them on a relatively long-run, slowly evolutionary basis. The most reactionary of such individuals hold to the "What-was-good-enough-for-Grandpa-is-good-enough-for-me" outlook; the less reactionary but still conservative elements of the faculty feel that any changes of program and curriculum should wait upon experimental changes in other schools and other school systems to see how they turn out; the most liberal of this group may welcome change but only after exhaustive and meticulous study of the situation. There are, of course, all kinds in every faculty; but in general those who find program-planning least comfortable teach the standard subject matters, for which community and student needs tend to be relatively constant — English, history, mathematics, and the organized sciences.

Teachers of these so-called hard-core subjects are more likely to be identified with the traditional philosophic positions discussed in this book. If the administrator agrees with their philosophic orientation, he will be as reluctant as they to revise, modify, or redesign program elements. But, since he is usually closer to the community than his teachers and, in a manner of speaking, closer to the needs of students themselves on that account, his propensities for curriculum development are usually stronger than theirs, and all of his skills at human management must come into play.

There is a second resistance which may be equally difficult to surmount. There is in every faculty a spectrum of attitude toward the *institutional* obligations of the teacher's job. Some teachers find reward in participating in the total work of the school, in improving it as an institution; others find greater reward in sticking to their own specialty, trying to do it better, and concentrating their energies on their own *individual* competence rather than on that of the school as a whole. Then there are, of course, all shadings of feeling in between, including, it is regrettable to say, those who do not seem to care about competence in any sphere, who teach for the pay check, who make a public show of the "T.G.I.F."[8] attitude, and who beat the kids out the school door at 3:15.

It is probable that no administrator will have much success in program development with this last group, but there is a defense to be made for those others who are earnest and professional in their work but who are not "institutionally oriented." These people eschew institutional interests in favor of individual-performance interests. They cannot endure the wasted hours in the committee meetings and policy conferences necessitated by program development. It is difficult to locate these people within any particular philosophic outlook, although it appears on the face of it that they are likely to be found in Idealism, Neo-Thomism, and Existentialism, where the personal effort of the individual instructor is considered central to the entire educational undertaking. Certainly an Existentialist teacher, hoping to awaken in his students an awareness of the ultimate meanings of life, would find the typical curriculum-revision committee meeting far beyond his patience. He is, as we have seen, constitutionally suspicious of institutions as such, and it is likely that his greatest fulfillment comes in the face-to-face encounter with individual youngsters in the classroom; a face-to-face encounter with his colleagues in a committee meeting after school to discuss changes in the social studies offerings for the coming year would probably leave him cold.

Realists are likely to offer little resistance to the program-planning administrator. Their propensity for order inclines them to study curriculum proposals in terms of the whole institution; if new needs arise, then a fresh and systematic look must be taken at the entire institution's purposes. If the new program — say a foreign-language program for the elementary school or a course in nuclear physics for the high school —

8 "Thank God it's Friday!"

can be rationally and efficiently integrated into the existing work schedule of the school, then it should be undertaken.

Experimentalists may not be so interested in institutional order and rationale, but they are more hospitable to change as such. Furthermore, on account of their "group" orientation, *institutional* concerns come to them naturally; they are mildly suspicious of people who always want to work by themselves. Hence in Progressivist schools program-planning has been developed into a kind of permanent feature of professional activity. Indeed, a curriculum committee is customarily one of the first standing committees a Progressive faculty will establish. A *standing* committee to oversee *change!* The very combination is, again, illustrative of the victory of Process over Product in Experimentalist thinking.

COMMUNITY RELATIONS

When we arrive at program development in the administrator's work we are nearing the outer orbit of his influence on the community. The greatest impact exerted by an administrator upon his community is to be found in the quality of the school program he supplies to its youngsters. But everybody knows that this quality is always equivocal, always in question, always short of some ideal; and the administrator knows this too. Dealing with imperfect human beings and with insufficient resources, the administrator finds he must preside over an enterprise which is inevitably less than what he thinks it ought to be.

Knowing this, he of course constantly strives to bring his ideal to actuality. But since his means are limited, he must learn to sacrifice some of his ideals in order to realize others. Thus by the very nature of his job the administrator is required to learn the political craft of compromise, what the politician and the statesman refer to as "the art of the possible."

How he handles the art of achieving the possible may or may not show symptoms of the educational philosophy he holds, but there are several things about this aspect of his work that deserve special mention here.

Filling the vacuum

Every public school administrator knows that the last fifty years of educational history in our country have seen the gradual shift of more and more teaching functions into the school. If there is something wrong with today's youth, it is usually laid at the doorstep of the school.

If the parents fail to teach the youngster health habits, the school should do it. If the religious agencies of the community fail to awaken a reverence for human values in the child, the school should assume that responsibility. If moral training is lacking in the home and/or church, the secular public school should develop character. If the parents do not teach the youngster about sexual reproduction, about boy-girl relations, about sex mores and sex morals in the difficult years of adolescence, then the school must do it. If such an extraneous thing as teaching a young person how to drive an automobile is neglected in the community, then the school must do it. Perhaps the most ironic of all is home economics. Cooking, sewing, baby care, budgeting — all these are constantly on view before girls as they grow up. What more obvious place to learn them than at home? But no. We send girls to public school to learn home economics.

In short, wherever a vacuum appears in the community the school has been asked to fill it. What is the administrator's response supposed to be to this constantly increasing demand for school services? If he belongs to the more traditional philosophic positions he will see in vacuum-filling activity a futile diversion of attention from the genuine educational objective of the community, namely, an emphasis on the basic subjects and mental discipline. If he belongs to the Experimentalists and Progressives he probably will not view it with such alarm: Any aspect of life, if it is important enough to teach youngsters at all, is important enough to take charge of in the school. For the school is continuous with life, not separate and removed from it. Therefore the Progressivist administrator may even welcome new opportunities to help youngsters grow to maturity; if home or community defaults in supplying the needs of youth, then the school's moral obligation is to enter the breach.

Certainly it should be clear that this latter position has accounted for the vast expansion of the school's services to the community in recent years. And it has become quite as noticeable at the university level — in our state and large private universities, with their service courses, institutes, and extension divisions — as anywhere else in the educational industry. Of course there is a lot of "empire-building" motivation behind such expansion. Many administrators welcome new opportunities not on moral grounds but merely because the expansion of their operations means more power and influence. Barring this, there is an important residual motivation, springing from basic educational theory, which is not unrelated to the philosophies studied in this book.

Religion in the school

Comment was made above concerning the development of moral and spiritual values as one of the functions currently being neglected in some communities. What should an administrator do about this? We are prevented, of course, by virtue of a long tradition, from introducing sectarian doctrinal materials into the school program. But there is some truth in the charge that in driving narrow sectarianism out of the schools we have summarily driven all religious attitudes out of the schools. The claim, then, is that we should consider the religious *need* of young people, even if we are unwilling to teach them the multiple sectarian answers to this need, that is, all the various religious doctrines in the world. (See Chapter Ten, pages 307–308.)

But how walk this tightrope? How consider a need without giving any answers? In the first place, the degree of urgency which a principal or superintendent ascribes to this problem will in itself provide a clue to his underlying educational philosophy. But, beyond this, the way he handles it may reveal still more. The Idealists, as we have noted, are likely to be found the most active "lobby" for answering the need with nonsectarian yet essentially Judeo-Christian materials and activities in the school: Bible readings, devotional readings, inspirational messages over the public-address system or in assembly. (Of course the Ecclesiastical Thomists are the most vigorous on this question, but since they have their own schools they are not directly relevant to this discussion.)

At the other end of the spectrum are the Experimentalists. They are inclined to stand guard in defense of the complete secular integrity of the modern public school, refusing to introduce into the curriculum any mystical or dogmatic or spiritual materials whatsoever. They hold that moral values are to be found in ordinary day-to-day experience, not in any transcendental realm. But between the Idealists and the Experimentalists there are many other kinds of administrative approach to the problem. Some believe that it is possible to teach *about* religion without teaching religion per se. This somewhat equivocal position would call for a unit in the social studies program, say, on "comparative religions of the world." The main difficulty with this technique is, of course, that religions cannot even be taught *about* without considering doctrine and dogma. And whenever we entangle the school in dogma we encounter animosities and hatreds in the community which the secular public school has succeeded in avoiding.

Then there is the more decisive and somewhat more drastic administrative device of "released time." Under this plan youngsters are dismissed from school for an hour a week to go to their individual churches for religious instruction. There is a kind of curious irony to this practice as it has developed in the United States. Here are the various religions taking advantage of secular legislation — the compulsory-attendance laws — in the name of propagating sectarian and parochial faiths. Irony aside, the practice is in greater question because it tends to be a divisive influence in the school, separating youngsters into "camps" and giving them the impression that to be religious means to belong to some organized group. Furthermore, there is the rejoinder that if the organized religions wish to propagate their beliefs they should be expected to do it on *their* time and not use the school as a crutch.

At any rate, a hornets' nest of difficulty surrounds this particular aspect of community relations in the administrator's job. And it is likely that the question of religion in education will persist for a long time as one of the most troublesome issues of administrative policy in the public schools of a secular and scientific America.

At a somewhat more generalized level, the administrator may become embroiled in the question of public funds for Catholic parochial schools. (We have already considered some aspects of this question, in Chapter Eleven [pages 342–346].) Nowadays the administrator encounters the problem in concrete situations. For instance, should the superintendent of schools order bus drivers to pick up and deliver parochial-school children to the local Catholic school? Should the state board of education approve free-lunch programs and free textbooks for parochial schools?

Questions like these have been wrangled through the courts on and off over the last twenty-five years. Finally, in the famous "Louisiana Textbook Case,"[9] the Supreme Court of the United States affirmed the decisive "Child Benefit Theory," by which it held that any public measure serving to benefit the *child* — as opposed to the private or religious *institution* — shall be considered constitutional and therefore legally proper. Whatever serves to go beyond child benefit to outright assistance to the institution itself was thereby ruled unconstitutional and improper.

It goes without saying that this line is exceedingly difficult to draw. A policeman escorting parochial-school children across the street is performing a public service to which all are entitled; he is only indirectly benefiting the institution. But transporting students to such schools on public buses is perhaps another matter; it releases funds of parents or the institution to be spent on the institution itself, hence representing a much more direct kind of aid. Finally, we encounter the problem of outright institutional aid, the proponents of which argue on grounds (cited in Chapter Eleven) that the parochial school is doing public business and relieving the public school system of a certain burden. According to these arguments "child benefit" and "institutional benefit" cannot be separated. If the public wants its children to learn "public" knowledge it should be willing to support instruction of such knowledge in whatever kind of school the child prefers to attend. How can it be possible, runs this line of argument, to benefit the child without benefiting the institution? So, the argument concludes, public aid should be extended to Catholic parochial schools, and to all other private and denominational schools,

9 Cochran v. Louisiana State Board of Education, 281 U.S. 370 (1930).

Building

A Personal Philosophy

of Education

WHAT LIES AHEAD?

Philosophy's business is all of life. And if philosophy has any central, guiding purpose, that purpose is to bring thought to bear upon the task of living well. In education, its mission is the same: to bring criticism to the task of educating well. Therefore, if a study of the philosophy of education is to have any genuine effect, it must terminate in a recognition of how philosophical ideas come to live within us and how they serve to move and shape our experience.

Therefore, if you are asking, after these many pages, what remains to be done, the answer is just this: to identify some personal set of commitments which you can lay claim to as your own; to extend and enlarge those commitments into a cluster of notions, about the world and about the job of teaching, which fit together and which you can defend; finally, to arrange those notions into an organic whole, so that they may begin to operate in your life and work.

This book has sought to provide you with the philosopher's basic working tools. This final chapter seeks to show you how to use those tools in developing a personal philosophy of education.

SCHEMATIC SUMMARY
OF VIEWS

On pages 466–467 is a schematic summary of the contents of this book. You will note that the chart is divided into two major sections: philosophic concepts and educational views. On the left, the ontological, epistemological, and axiological ingredients of our five philosophies; on the right, the educational ideas these philosophies imply or are associated with. The five philosophies are indicated on the left margin, their educational counterparts (Essentialism, Perennialism, etc.) inserted preceding the "educational views" section.

In each of the boxes of the chart is a short suggestive phrase indicating, in cryptic shorthand form, the central idea involved. Other entries might have been made, but these will do. The point is that if you wish to be really thorough and rigorous in your review of the material in this book you should prepare a full-page expansion for each of the boxes in the chart. Take one box at a time, jot down the indicated idea at the top of a piece of paper, and then flesh out the meaning of the idea as you can reconstruct it from all that we have studied in this book. When you get done you will have something like forty-five pages of review outline of what might be called your "conceptual tools" for active philosophizing.

You can go further than this, if you have time, and prepare a more thorough essay analysis of each page of the review outline, laying particular stress on *lateral* relationships within the philosophy in question and *vertical* relationships with other philosophies. In such analytic essays you should provide as many examples and illustrations as possible, not only those cited in the present book but ones which you can cite on your own. It is often through examples that real understanding of difficult ideas is finally achieved.

But now, with this in hand, how get to the business of philosophy-building?

THE "INSIDE–OUT"
(INDUCTIVE) METHOD

One way to develop a systematic point of view is to start with your own experience, with your own personal situation. Specifically, since it is an educational philosophy we are setting out to identify, the best place to begin, of course, would be with your own teaching behavior.

How do you teach school? Take a typical day in your teaching schedule. (We all know there is no such thing as a "typical day," so take yesterday.) Prepare a general description, without evaluation, of how that day went, how you taught, the methods you used, the ends you tried to achieve, the ways you measured your students' learning. Then, in the second section of your analysis, single out those moments during the day when you felt you were teaching best, when you felt good about what you were doing, when you had the distinct impression that genuine learning was going on in your classroom. Together, these two sections should provide some kind of working base for the inductive approach to developing an educational philosophy.

Now, in the third section, go one step further and attempt to specify the educational theory this kind of teaching would seem to indicate. Remember at this point that you are not to concoct some kind of theory which you *profess* to believe in, but, rather, a theory which would seem to be directing the kinds of things that went on in the day's proceedings (discussed in the foregoing two sections). Now take this projection of an inferred educational theory operating below your level of awareness and, in a fourth section, sketch out the general outlines of what kinds of ontological, epistemological, and axiological views appear to be operating there. Do not go beyond your data, i.e., the descriptions and projections you have made up to this point. Simply try to see if you can organize some basic philosophical propositions that you think may be *inferred from* the procedures you used and the educational theory those procedures point to.

Once you have put these four sections together into some kind of comprehensive running "argument," you are ready for the fifth step: comparison and contrast with the theories set forth in this book. Where, generally speaking, do you think you most probably belong? Explain in your analysis just why you think so, why one set of ideas rather than another hooks up with your own (and yours with it). You will want to make contact with the other philosophies at every step of your argument, indicating these cross references in the margin of your work or perhaps on a separate paper. If these contacts are relatively minor you will want to show how they are merely tangential and peripheral to the main body of your point of view.

Then comes the final step of your analysis: comparison of all that you have said so far with what you started with, namely, the way you teach. Are there any corrections needed? Do you teach the way your point of view ultimately suggests? If not, then alterations are needed here. Or perhaps your teaching is adequate but the statement needs changing. In

PHILOSOPHIC CONCEPTS

| | ONTOLOGY | EPISTE-MOLOGY | AXIOLOGY | |
			Ethics	Aesthetics
IDEALISM	A world of mind	Truth as idea	The imitation of the Absolute Self	The reflection of the Ideal
REALISM	A world of things	Truth as observable fact	The law of nature	The reflection of nature
NEO-THOMISM *LAY* / *ECCL.*	A world of reason ------and------ Being/God	Truth as reason ------and------ intuition	The rational act	Creative intuition
EXPERIMENTALISM	A world of experience	Truth as what works	The public test	The public taste
EXISTENTIALISM	A world of existing	Truth as existential choice	The anguish of freedom	The revolt from the public norm

E D U C A T I O N A L   V I E W S

	The Learner	The Teacher	The Curriculum	The Method	Social Policy
Essentialism	Learner as microcosmic mind	Teacher as paradigmatic self	Subject matter of symbol and idea (literature, history, etc.)	Absorbing ideas	The "trailing edge": Conserve the heritage
	Learner as sense mechanism	Teacher as demonstrator	Subject matter of the physical world (mathematics, the sciences, etc.)	Mastering facts and information	The "trailing edge": Transmit settled knowledge
Perennialism	Learner as rational ------and------ spiritual being	Teacher as mental disciplinarian ------and------ spiritual leader	Subject matter of the intellect and spirit (mathematics, languages, logic, Great Books, Dogma, Doctrine)	Training the intellect	— ----------------- —
Progressivism	Learner as experiencing organism	Teacher as research-project director	Subject matter of social experience (social studies, projects, problems, etc.)	Problem-solving	The "growing edge": Teach how to manage change
					Reconstructionism: The "Utopian Future"— Teach to reconstruct the social order
Existentialism	Learner as ultimate chooser	Teacher as *provocateur* of the self	Subject matter of choice (the arts, moral philosophy, ethics)	Finding the self	?

this case a review of your analysis is in order. At the very least, some coherence must exist between what you have put down on paper in analytical form and the way you actually perform the professional art of teaching.

It is altogether possible, indeed probable, that you will find in your own "inside-out" analysis various points of contact with several if not all of the philosophies studied here. Perhaps these contacts will appear more than merely tangential or peripheral, possibly even crucial and basic in your thinking. If this turns out to be the case, you may get the feeling that, while you fall primarily into one of the philosophies, when you get into the classroom you really borrow something from *all* of them.

This kind of person we call an *eclectic,* one who draws his basic ideas from several different points of view. There is nothing wrong in being an eclectic; most of us are. But the obligation now confronting you is to harmonize your selections from the different philosophies and to put them together into some kind of compatible whole. This is perhaps the most difficult and at the same time the most decisive stage in building a personal philosophy of education. But in the degree that you can organize your ideas so that they "hang together," so that they do not get in one another's way and cancel one another out but are clear of inconsistencies and incompatibilities, in that degree you will have put together something that can be called a philosophy of education.

THE "OUTSIDE–IN"
(DEDUCTIVE) METHOD

Another way to approach this task is to start at the other end, the left end, of the chart. Your first job is to set down as comprehensibly and comprehensively as you can your personal views on ontology, epistemology, and axiology. The thoroughness with which you can manage this will determine how successful you will be later on, so spell out these three positions cautiously and rigorously. Of course you must stick closely to a logical development of your ideas, and, since, as we have seen, there is an intimate, mutual interconnection between ontology, epistemology, and axiology, you will want to take special care in seeing that incompatibilities do not creep in at this early point.

But once having done this you may then proceed to the second stage and spell out the kind of educational theory which would seem to follow from these fundamental propositions. You may or may not wish to use the general schema provided in the chart, but at any rate you will wish once again to be careful and rigorous about the kinds of educational theory you consider implicit in the philosophy you hold.

Then, in the third section of your analysis, you should go one step further and show how your educational theory would produce certain concrete behavior patterns in a teacher: the kinds of things he would do in the classroom, the purposes he would have in his instruction, the methods he would use, the ways he would test his pupils to see if they had learned anything or not. Here the obligation to be careful about connections is just as important as before. For, as we noted in an earlier chapter, the "problem of application" always confronts us in drawing concrete teaching behaviors from educational theories and philosophic propositions. But if you stick closely to just those kinds of conduct that would appear to follow from your views, you will have laid the groundwork for the more important work to follow.

This work consists simply in comparing what you have done with the several theories discussed in this book. This, your fourth section, will require the same kind of rigor in criticism and analysis that was involved in the inductive method. Again, you will want to try to find where you probably belong among the five theories we have examined, making clear just why you feel your own views are harmonious and compatible with the position selected. But then you should also make clear those points of contact which you can see with the other philosophies and how they relate to your own position.

If these points of reference to the other positions turn out to be rather substantial, you will be under the same obligation of clarification and harmonization as with the inductive method of analysis. It is perhaps just as easy to turn out to be an eclectic in this pattern of analysis as in the previous one. The only advantage here lies in the possibly closer linkages that can be shown to exist between a general theory and specific items of conduct. But you should not take this advantage too seriously, for even trained philosophers are cautious in this enterprise of deduction, and they know perhaps better than the rest of us how difficult it is — some say impossible — to draw items of behavior from vast systems of ontology, epistemology, and axiology and their attendant educational theories.

At any rate, in the degree to which you can draw a deductive argument *from* your philosophic position *to* your educational theoretical position *to* the kinds of specific behavior patterns you feel a teacher would follow according to such a view, in that degree you will have put down a complete "work paper" for the next stage.

This stage consists simply in comparing the kinds of teaching behavior you have specified with your own teaching yesterday, the day before, or some such "typical" day which you can recall well enough to describe. Can you, that is, find some connections between your deduced pedagogical prescriptions and the way you actually teach? When you feel you are teaching well, when genuine learning is going on in your classroom, how close are you to the kind of teaching which the final section of your verbal analysis has set forth? This is the final test, you might say; and by the time you have criticized your statement and revised it to meet the criticisms, or, contrariwise, criticized your teaching behavior and revised it to meet the criticisms, you will have put forth a philosophy of education.

Which of the above approaches — deductive or inductive — you find more compatible with your own techniques of study will in all likelihood be a matter of personal taste. If you have not yet entered the teaching profession you will have to omit that portion of each procedure calling for comparisons with actual teaching behavior. Of course, all of us have been *consumers* of education for some sixteen years. Presumably after this length of time spent on the receiving end, we can single out moments when we thought that we were learning well, that the instructor was really teaching, and that whatever the educational process is supposed to consist in was actually taking place. If you can locate such moments in your educational career and project them into the analyses suggested above, chances are that even without teaching experience you will not suffer too much of a disadvantage in this undertaking.

THE CULTURAL METHOD

There is a third alternative which may possibly have some merit, especially for those students who have not yet had teaching experience in the classroom and who have studied education in a more general, "institutional" way. This method of philosophy-building would begin with the last column in the chart: Social Policy.

You will recall that in Chapter One (page 16) a time-line chart served to indicate the varying positions that our philosophies would take on the question: What is the role of the school in an age of cultural change and transition? These positions were not developed on the chart but were presented merely as examples of the kinds of questions which philosophers of education take up. It was left to Chapters Eleven, Twelve, and Thirteen to make a more thorough analysis of these points of view; and, as you have seen, they have been cryptically summarized in the "social policy" column of the chart.

Now suppose you were to address yourself to this question of social policy. What kind of answer would you personally give to it? If you have specialized in one of the social sciences you will probably have a good deal to go on in developing a critical essay on this question. But even if your primary interest lies in other fields, you should be prepared to say some things about how you view the educative process in its socio-politico-historical setting. You might start with the school in your own community and examine the relationship between it and the immediate environment it serves. If the kinds of things that people do there, the jobs they work at, the ideas they hold, the things they are striving for, are likely to change over the course of your lifetime, what should the school's function be?

Or on a larger, national scale, if the whole of American society appears to you to be headed for a new kind of civilization, a newer and, it is hoped, higher expression of the democratic way of life, just what changes in attitude and outlook may we expect in the years and decades ahead? And what would the school's function be in helping to bring about this new way of life? Would it leave the crucial changes to other agencies or would it participate in bringing them forth? All of these questions and others would be relevant to this phase of your analysis.

Then, with this in hand, you should proceed to the next two stages. Working first in the direction of philosophic beliefs, you would specify what you believe to be the ontological, epistemological, and axiological underpinnings of such a social policy for the school in America. Then, working in the other direction, you would spell out the kinds of curriculums and teaching methods which would seem to satisfy the image you have of the school in a period of change.

In your development in the first of these directions, the philosophical, you should be on guard, as usual, to work from your original statement and not from anything you have read, either in this book or elsewhere. It is your own philosophy of education, remember, that is at stake. And, likewise, in your development in the second direction, educational theory and practice, you should remain consistent and faithful to your original statement, indicating only those educational prescriptions that appear to follow from the propositions you have already set down.

Of course, you could just as well reverse the order and head for the area of educational ideas first and then strike out into the perhaps more difficult territory of underlying philosophic dispositions. But the point is to work within your own frame of reference for the initial phases of your analysis. Once you have completed this you will be ready for the more critical stages ahead.

These stages consist, as before, in comparing what you have done with the philosophies and theories presented in this book. And, as before, you will want to see generally where you fall, what connections can be found between your stated views and the views systematically presented here, and whether the connections are minor and tangential or major and substantive. If they are the latter, of course, then you will have to organize an integration for your espoused eclecticism so that you can use your essay in the final stage of criticism, namely, applying it to your own life and work.

This application, also as before, can be made by comparing your views directly with the way you teach and the way you live. And, once again, you are asked either to bring these two into harmony with what you have said or to reorganize what you have said to make it compatible with the way you teach and live. You must do this before a genuine philosophy of education can be said to emerge.

This is the most difficult but, of course, the most rewarding step in all three of our approaches to philosophy-building, namely, the bringing together of *belief* and *behavior,* the harmonizing of what we *profess* with what we actually *do.* It is difficult, to be sure; cherished beliefs or comfortable patterns of living sometimes have to go. And this is never easy. But, then, the enterprise of criticism would still seem to be worth the trouble. The stakes are high and the profits great. Effort here, if seriously undertaken, is the most important investment one can make. It is at this point that this book, the course you may be taking, and, indeed, all reflective thought about what we are doing eventually yield their reward.

THE EDUCATOR'S
PHILOSOPHIC POSTURE

Perhaps the final word should be something like this: Do not feel frustrated, or cheated, or simply unfulfilled if the reward never comes, i.e., if you never succeed in arriving at a definitive personal philosophy of education, one that you can hang on the wall and say of, "There, that's mine. That's what I believe!" Some people insist on something like this; they want to hang out their intellectual shingle; they want to be known under some category or other.

But there is nothing very noble about this; indeed, there is a tendency to stop thinking about things once you have found your own little "-ism." But even short of this, there is no necessary obligation on your part to commit yourself to something and to come to rest in some system of beliefs. Certainly there is no obligation to accept any one of the five positions examined in this book, to become a member of this or that philosophical "fan club." There is no obligation to believe in any one of them, in any combination of them, not even in a wholesome eclecticism that makes room for all of them. In studying philosophy there is only one necessary commitment: to take one's life seriously enough to believe that thought and criticism can be applied to it to make it better, more intelligent, and more civilized.

You should not be intimidated by this chapter, therefore, into thinking that if you do not actually build a "dream house" of a philosophy you have hammered away in vain. Just remember, we have been working away at this task for more than 2000 years.

Furthermore, there is a vibrancy to the continuously inquiring mind, a vibrancy which exactly fits the requirements of teaching. In philosophy, as in education, the *quest* is the important thing: a constant quest in search of the meaning of life and the way to awaken that meaning in the lives of our young.

DI62

Index of Names

Index of Subjects

A priori (term), 65

Ability grouping, 368–372, 411–413

Absolute Mind: *See* Mind, Absolute

Actuality, Principle of, 55, 59–60, 61–64, 148, 261, 341

Administrator: and philosophy, 438–440; and buildings and grounds, 440–443; and scheduling, 443–444; and records, 444–445; and budget, 445–448; and staff, 448–451; and supervision, 451–452; and curriculum development, 452–455; and community relations, 455–460

Aesthetics: and axiology, 21, 234–240; and taste, 234–235, 239–240, 242–243; and aesthetic experience, 235–237; and art, 237–239, 254–255, 259–261, 265–267, 272–274, 280–282; Idealist, 254–255, 466; Realist, 259–261, 466; Neo-Thomist, 265–267, 466; Experimentalist, 272–274, 466; Existentialist, 280–282, 466; and development of taste, 309–318

Allegory of the Cave: *See* Plato's Cave

Aristotle's Form-Matter Hypothesis, 53–56

Art and aesthetics, 254–255, 259–261, 265–267, 272–274, 280–282, 309–318

Arts: cooperative, 3–5, 65, 144*n*, 209; operative, 3–5

Atom, 28–29, 36, 134

Audio-visual aids, 421–422

Axiology: defined, 21; ethics, 225–234; aesthetics, 234–240; and changing patterns, 240–243; of Idealism, 250–255; of Realism, 255–261; of Neo-Thomism, 261–267; of Experimentalism, 267–274; of Existentialism, 274–282; and education, 285–290; schematic summary, 466–467

Behavior: nature of, 36–37; and Theory of Correspondence, 146; as operative value, 221; and morality, 256–257, 264–265. *See also* Conditioning

Behavioral sciences, 36–37, 378–379, 452

Behaviorism, 188–189, 334–335, 336, 417

Being: and metaphysics, 20; and the infinitive *to be,* 30–31; and non-being, 40–41; and Potentiality-Actuality Principle, 59–60, 61–64, 148; and Neo-Thomism, 59–66, 85, 341; Sartre's modes of, 167–170; hierarchy of, 261, 265. *See also* Existence

Books as aids to teaching, 420–421

Brainwashing, 335

Carnegie Unit, 334

Catechism, as method of teaching, 195, 298, 417–418

Progressive Education, 306, 339; based in Experimentalism, 358. *See also* Progressivism

Progressivism, 357–358, 359–361, 467; educational theory of, 362–363; educational policy of, 363–370; and ability grouping, 368–372, 411–413; and Jacksonianism, 370–372; and Jeffersonianism, 370–372; subject matter, 414–415; and catechism, 417–418; projects, 419–420; books, 420–421; laboratory, 423; field trips, 423; discipline, 424, 425, 427–428, 430; tests and testing, 432; grading, 433–434; teacher-community relationships, 434–435; school management, 441; administrator-staff relations, 449–450, 451–452; curriculum development, 453, 455, 467

Project method of teaching, 100, 203, 209–210, 313, 412, 419–420

Puritanism, 251, 256, 386

Purpose: vs. purposelessness in ontology, 37–39

Realism, application: seating arrangements, 409–410; recitation method, 416; demonstration, 418–419; books, 420; audio-visual aids, 422; laboratory, 422–423; field trips, 423; discipline, 426; tests and testing, 430–432; school management, 444–445; administrator-staff relations, 448, 449–450; curriculum development, 454

Realism, philosophy: function of school, 13, 15; ontology of, 53–58, 466; Aristotle's Form-Matter Hypothesis, 53–56; science, 57–59; Naïve, 67–68; learner, 84–85, 467; closed system, 89n; curriculum of, 91–94, 333, 467; Paradigmatic Man, 104; epistemology of, 140–147, 466; Principle of Objectivity, 143; Spectator Theory, 142–144, 190, 196, 337; Pure Theory, 144–145; Theory of Correspondence, 145–147; learning methods, 185–191, 194, 196, 467; teacher, 208, 467; axiology of, 255–261, 466; ethics, 256–259, 466; aesthetics, 259–261, 466; moral education, 293–296; development of taste, 310–311; as Essentialism, 330–338; educational theory of, 332–337, 467

Reality: in ontology, 20, 27–39, 246–247; differing views, 30; and appearance, 31–33; and symbols, 33–36; and thing, 36–37; and process, 36–37; in Plato's "two-world" concept, 47–50; in Hegel's dialectic, 52–53; and Experimentalist ontology, 67–73, 86–87, 332n; as self-choosing, 76–77; and epistemology, 113–114, 246–247; and Natural Law, 141, 331–332; experience as, 157–158; and values, 246–249

Reason: and Neo-Thomism, 85–86, 261–265, 296–300, 311–312, 341; as intelligence, 164; and formal discipline, 193, 298

Receptacle Theory of Learning, 190–191

Recitation, as method of teaching, 416–417

Recognition, 138–139

Reconstructionism: and function of school, 14, 15; and Experimentalism, 358–359, 372–375; educational theory of, 374–375; educational policy of, 375–380

Reinforcement theory of learning, 190

Religion, 232–233, 279, 307–308, 456–459

In this authoritative volume the leading spokesmen for Realism, Thomism, Idealism, Experimentalism, Marxism, Existentialism, and other viewpoints discuss their philosophies of education. Section 4 in each essay presents an analysis of "School and Society," an aspect of education which has most intimately to do with the administrator's work. Here you can get a glimpse of the different kinds of schools and societies in which administrators would like to work.

Lieberman, Myron. *The Future of Public Education.* Chicago: University of Chicago Press, 1960.
Lieberman's main thesis in this book centers on a rebuke of what he calls the "anachronistic and dysfunctional power structure" of American education. His contention is that educational administration is degenerating because "school administrators *ask* instead of *tell* the public what should be taught in the schools." It would be an interesting and profitable exercise to see if, after reading this book, you can locate Lieberman in our philosophical spectrum.

Phenix, Philip H. *Philosophy of Education.* New York: Henry Holt and Co., Inc., 1958.
In Part 1 Phenix treats the topic "Education in the School," and in Chapters 6 and 7 he addresses himself to "School Administration" and "The Control and Support of Schools." He does not relate his remarks to any specific philosophic position, but his analysis of the administrator's role is illuminating and instructive.

beliefs. Not based on what you think, but on how you behave on the job! Illustrate with examples of how you handle buildings, money, and people.

4. Every administrator is a kind of "public utility"; he has to appear publicly and give speeches to Boy Scout troops, P.T.A.'s, service clubs, and child-study groups. Would our philosophies differ in any respect on how this part of the administrator's life should be managed? Explain.

5. In recent years college and university presidents have been appointed from the ranks of politicians, military generals, and corporation executives. Do you think these groups differ in educational philosophy in any significant way? If so, how would these differences be revealed in the way such individuals would carry on the administrative function? Can you give specific examples to illustrate your argument?

FURTHER READING

Brameld, Theodore. *Philosophies of Education in Cultural Perspective.* New York: Dryden Press, 1955.
This comprehensive volume examines Progressivism, Essentialism, and Perennialism as alternate educational philosophies. In the "Educational Beliefs" chapter for each philosophy (Chapters 5, 8, and 11) the final section considers the problem of educational control, social function, and administrative practice. Brameld discusses these topics in somewhat more general terms than the present book, but he nevertheless makes clear distinctions among the different positions.

————. *Toward a Reconstructed Philosophy of Education.* New York: Dryden Press, 1956.
A whole chapter in this Reconstructionist manifesto (Chapter 10) is given over to the administration of schools and how they can be used to bring about a Utopian order. Administration and control are, it goes without saying, centrally important in Reconstructionist theory. Here is its leading spokesman explaining how it works.

Culbertson, J. A., Jacobson, P. B., and Reller, T. L. *Administrative Relationships, A Casebook.* Englewood Cliffs, N.J.: Prentice-Hall, Inc., 1960.
Here is a fascinating interdisciplinary treatment of administrative problems presented in actual case studies. If you want to see an administrator's community relations and leadership skills laid bare and exposed to full view, take a look at Case 1, "The Valley City Consolidation Issue." Also of special relevance to this chapter are Case 8, "The Gifted Child Committee," and Case 17, "Changing the Curriculum at Southside."

Henry, N. B. (ed.). *Modern Philosophies and Education,* The Fifty-fourth Yearbook of the National Society for the Study of Education. Chicago: the Society, 1955.

because they provide a public service. If federal aid to education is legislated by Congress, let a fair proportion of it be extended to non-public schools.

Educational leadership

It would hardly be fitting to consider the work of the administrator in his community relations without saying something about his leadership function. The role of leader may or may not differ from one philosophy to another; but we do know that historically there has been a shift in emphasis in the leader's role, and, without trying to connect this shift to any particular philosophical point of view, we are nevertheless obligated to take note of it.

In an earlier day, when education was less a social and community function and more an activity of scholarship removed into its own "ivory tower," the school's response to community needs was not considered important. Hence the whole concept of "leadership" was unknown; there was nothing to lead or to be led. Our schoolmasters, academy directors, and college presidents were not looked upon as public leaders in the modern sense. They were overseers of a fairly well-understood enterprise — and an enterprise, furthermore, which remained more or less constant in function from one generation to the next.

In our day, however, we see that leadership is a real administrative task because of the inevitable linkages which have been built between community needs and educational programs. Some individuals insist that the community does not recognize its real needs, that it is driven by whim and passion to demand this and that educational service to the detriment of the basic purpose of the school, i.e., to train the mind. Robert Hutchins often talks like this, and his major complaint of educational leadership in our times is that it has become beholden to community pressures. Principals quiver, superintendents cower, and college presidents quietly wring their hands when the public rises against them. Instead of telling the people what kind of education they ought to have, the modern administrator, according to Hutchins, asks them what they want.

Much the same argument is developed by Myron Lieberman in his books *Education as a Profession*[10] and *The Future of Public Education*,[11] even though he speaks from quite a different orientation. It is Lieberman's point that educational leadership, by both teachers and administrators, has fallen into thralldom to public opinion. We teach only those things that are safe; we supply only those educational needs that

[10] Englewood Cliffs, N.J.: Prentice-Hall, Inc., 1956.
[11] Chicago: University of Chicago Press, 1960.

are most immediate; we yield to public pressures in failing to maintain proper scholastic standards. "What the traffic will bear" in the way of the scope of the curriculum and the demands made on students has become the working rule of most educational institutions in the United States today.

There is a good deal of truth in this charge. But there is the counter-argument that an administrator would get nowhere if he were to persist in telling the people what they *ought* to want for their schools and denying them what they in fact *do* want. Herein lies the kernel of our problem. Leadership is a kind of art, a political art, as we have said, of "achieving the possible." But it is also perhaps the more mature and sophisticated art of "identifying the potentially achievable." An administrator cannot morally settle for simply achieving the possible and supplying to the community that which it has indicated it wants. He cannot settle for that because to do so is to reduce himself to the status of a mere clerk in the public employ. An administrator must argue for what he thinks the community *ought* to want, educate them to the point of really wanting it, and then supply it to them.

An educational leader is much like a statesman-like journalist or politician. The editor of a newspaper is not content to place on his editorial page day after day only what he thinks his readers want to read. What he has to do is to educate his readers to what he thinks they ought to want in the world of public affairs, what they ought to prefer in the way of public policy on the questions of the day.

And this too is the meaning of leadership in education. To be a statesman is to consider the needs of the "state." To be statesman-like in education is to consider the wider needs of the community which the educational system serves, and to present those needs to the community in such a way as to educate the public to what it ought to want in the education of its young.

QUESTIONS

1. Arrange to attend the next meeting of the board of education in your town. Can you determine, by the turns of discussion and debate, how different educational philosophies and points of view are expressed? Explain.

2. If you are a teacher, make a philosophic analysis of the educational outlook of your principal. No need to name names or places, but illustrate with anecdotal materials, behavior patterns observed, and ideas expressed by the individual in question.

3. If you are an administrator, make a self-analysis of your own philosophic